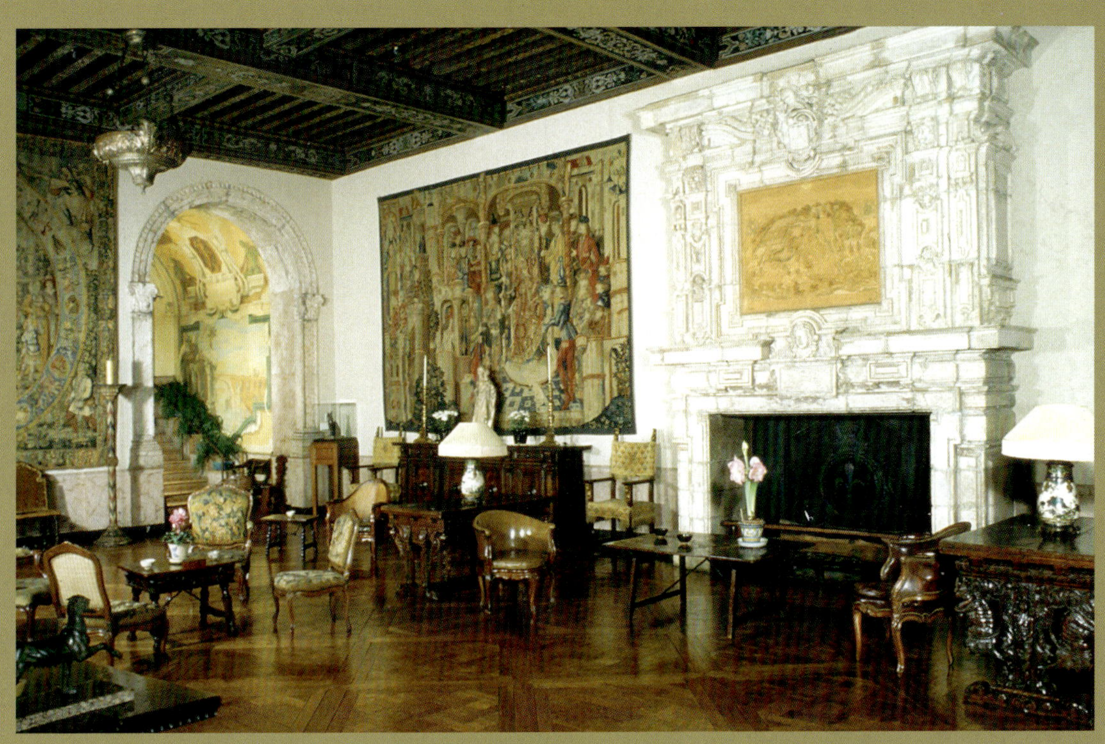

Sacred Art,
Secular Context

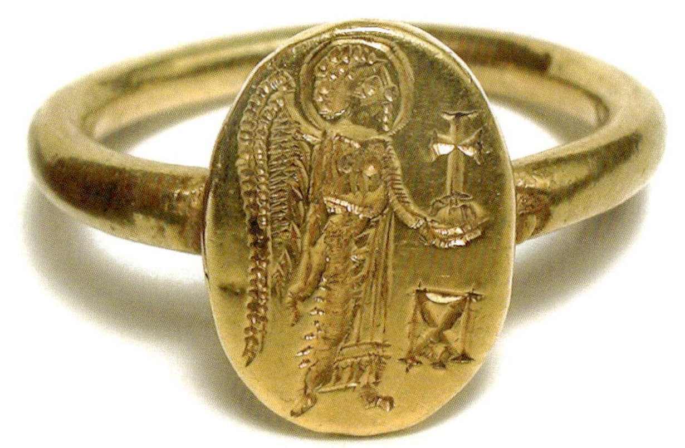

Sacred Art, Secular Context

Objects of Art
From the Byzantine Collection of Dumbarton Oaks, Washington, D.C.

Accompanied by American Paintings from the Collection of Mildred and Robert Woods Bliss

Asen Kirin, General Editor
With Contributions by James N. Carder and Robert S. Nelson

GEORGIA MUSEUM OF ART ◆ ATHENS, GEORGIA

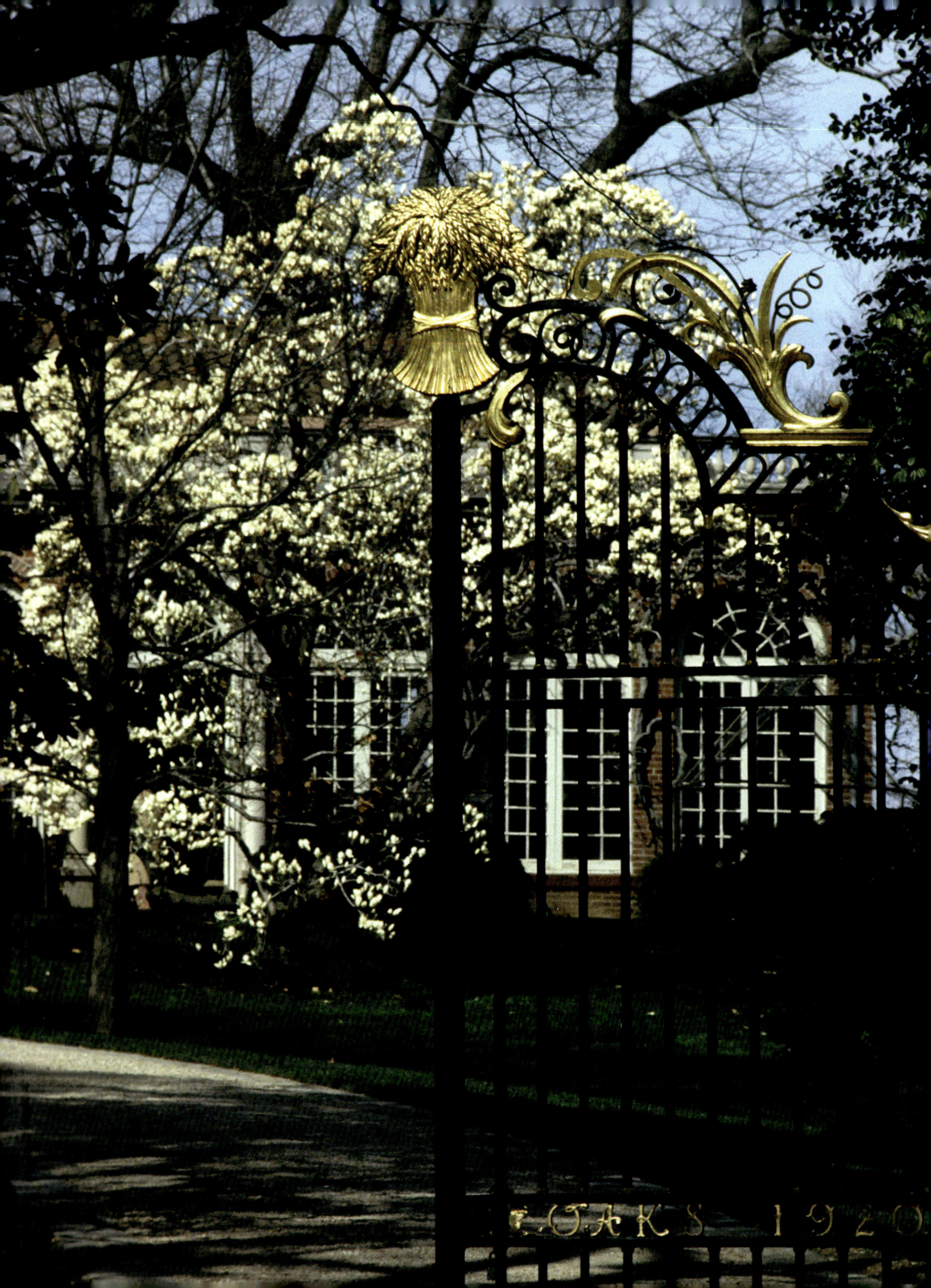
OAKS 1920

Dumbarton Oaks has been conceived in a new pattern, where quality and not quantity shall determine the choice of its scholars; that it is the home of the Humanities, not a mere aggregation of books and objects of art; that the house itself and the gardens have their educational importance and that all are of humanistic value.

Those responsible for scholarship should remember that the Humanities cannot be fostered by confusing instruction and education; that it was my husband's as well as is my wish that the Mediterranean interpretation of the humanist disciplines shall predominate; that gardens have their place in the humanist order of life and that trees are noble elements to be protected by successive generations and are not to be neglected or lightly destroyed.

The fulfillment of this vision of high intellectual adventure seen through the open gates of Dumbarton Oaks will add lustre to Harvard, to the academic tone of our country and to scholarship throughout the world.

—PREAMBLE OF THE LAST WILL AND TESTAMENT
OF MILDRED B. BLISS, AUGUST 31, 1966

An excerpt of the Preamble is engraved on the wall of Dumbarton Oaks' Garden Library.

©2005 Georgia Museum of Art, University of Georgia

Published by the Georgia Museum of Art, University of Georgia.
All rights reserved. No part of this book may be reproduced
without the written consent of the publishers.

Design: Kimberly Adis

Department of Publications: Bonnie Ramsey and Rebecca Yates

Printed in an edition of 1000 by Friesens

Printed in Canada

Partial support for the exhibitions and programs at the Georgia
Museum of Art is provided by the W. Newton Morris Charitable
Foundation and the Georgia Council for the Arts through the
appropriations of the Georgia General Assembly. The Council is
a partner agency of the National Endowment for the Arts.
Individuals, foundations, and corporations provide additional
support through their gifts to the Arch Foundation.

Library of Congress Cataloging-in-Publication Data

Sacred art, secular context : objects of art from the Byzantine
Collection of Dumbarton Oaks, Washington, D.C., accompanied
by American paintings from the collection of Mildred and Robert Woods Bliss / Asen Kirin, general editor ; with contributions
by James N. Carder and Robert S. Nelson.

    p. cm.
Includes bibliographical references.
    ISBN 0-915977-57-5
1. Art objects, Byzantine--Exhibitions. 2. Painting, American--
20th century—Exhibitions.
3. Art—Washington (D.C.)—Exhibitions. 4. Byzantine Collection (Dumbarton Oaks)—Exhibitions. I. Bliss, Robert Woods,
1875-1962. II. Bliss, Mildred, 1879-1969. III. Kirin, Asen,
1960-. IV. Carder, James Nelson, 1948- . V. Nelson, Robert
S., 1947- .
VI. Byzantine Collection (Dumbarton Oaks)
    NK715.S23 2005
    709'.495'074753--dc22

2005023493

SPONSORS

**SAMUEL H. KRESS FOUNDATION THROUGH ITS
"OLD MASTERS IN CONTEXT" PROGRAM**

FRANCES WOOD WILSON FOUNDATION

ALFRED HEBER HOLBROOK SOCIETY MEMBERS

Mr. and Mrs. Harry L. Gilham, Jr.

Mrs. M. Smith Griffith

George-Ann and Boone Knox

Mr. C. L. Morehead, Jr.

BENEFACTORS

Mrs. W. Tapley Bennett, Jr.

Mr. and Mrs. H. Daniels Minor

Mrs. Patsy Dudley Pate

W. NEWTON MORRIS CHARITABLE FOUNDATION

FRIENDS OF THE MUSEUM

Contents

FOREWORD BY THE DIRECTOR OF DUMBARTON OAKS

I KNOW I SPEAK FOR MY COLLEAGUES AT DUMBARTON OAKS IN EXPRESSING gratitude and delight that so many of our objects found a temporary new home in Athens during the exhibition *Sacred Art, Secular Context: Objects of Art from the Byzantine Collection of Dumbarton Oaks, Washington, D.C. Accompanied by American Paintings from the Collection of Mildred and Robert Woods Bliss*, which was on view during the summer and fall of 2005.

Gratitude, because, while we are engaged in our current building and renovation project, we have very practical reasons for wishing our collections to remain accessible to viewers; delight, because Robert and Mildred Bliss always dedicated their efforts as collectors to presenting the best of what could be obtained to the broadest possible American public.

The present exhibition is also a memorable material demonstration that the map of Byzantine studies in the United States is expanding constantly and, more specifically, moving beyond the traditional, essentially Victorian, notions of Byzantium as a confessional and ethnic monolith—a view that the Blisses themselves rejected in their collecting, as the essays by James N. Carder, Robert S. Nelson, and Asen Kirin demonstrate.

It is particularly gratifying that the American paintings collected by the Blisses, which have never before been seen together—and half of which are published here for the first time—will prompt visitors to place Dumbarton Oaks within the context of American collecting of the early twentieth century and to ponder the Blisses' sophisticated vision of American cultural identity.

—EDWARD L. KEENAN
Director, Dumbarton Oaks

Foreword by the Director of the Georgia Museum of Art

When Edith Wharton recommended the Blisses as new friends to Matilda and Walter Gay, she said that the Gays would find Mildred "Pure Bliss." Thus began years of friendship and collaboration in which both parties benefited and through which both contributed to the history of American culture and the humanities.

University museums thrive on similar collaborations, and the Georgia Museum of Art is no exception. This publication is the result of a cooperative venture between the museum and Dumbarton Oaks with the assistance of the Lamar Dodd School of Art and the Samuel H. Kress Foundation. Certainly, all of us involved in this project hope to contribute to a broader understanding not only of Byzantine art, culture, and history, but also of traditions of collecting by Americans. The Georgia Museum of Art is pleased to display and to publish, in some instances for the first time, the Byzantine and related objects that make up the exhibition; given our mission and our focus on American art in particular, we are happy to have developed the concurrent show of paintings by Childe Hassam, Henry Golden Dearth, and Walter Gay, primarily from Dumbarton Oaks' collections. In celebration of this collaboration between two institutions devoted to research, a symposium and a conference are but two of the educational programs for the scholarly and lay communities provoked by the exhibition.

The Georgia Museum of Art fosters scholarship and teaching, a mission that is in sympathy with Dumbarton Oaks' goal of fulfilling the vision of Mildred B. Bliss to "add lustre" to the study of the humanities as well as "to the academic tone of our country and to scholarship throughout the world." Toward that end we are indebted to our sponsors: the Samuel H. Kress Foundation through its "Old Masters in Context" program; the Frances Wood Wilson Foundation; the W. Newton Morris Charitable Foundation; the Friends of the Museum; and the museum's patrons Mr. and Mrs. Harry L. Gilham, Jr., Mrs. M. Smith Griffith, George-Ann and Boone Knox, Mr. C. L. Morehead, Jr., Mrs. W. Tapley Bennett, Jr., Mr. and Mrs. H. Daniels Minor, and Mrs. Patsy Dudley Pate.

Professor Asen Kirin, the catalyst and curator for this project, deserves special commendation and thanks, certainly for his work, but equally for his guidance as the intellectual conduit through whom this collaboration has flowed.

—WILLIAM UNDERWOOD EILAND
Director, Georgia Museum of Art

Acknowledgments

This exhibition is the result of the collaboration between the Dumbarton Oaks Research Library and Collection, the Georgia Museum of Art, and the Lamar Dodd School of Art at the University of Georgia in Athens. I wish to express my deepest gratitude to the individuals whose continuous support over the last three and a half years helped bring this project to fruition: at Dumbarton Oaks—Edward L. Keenan, director; Alice-Mary Talbot, director of Byzantine studies; Susan Boyd, curator, Byzantine Collection; Stephen Zwirn, assistant curator, Byzantine Collection; Cécile Morrisson, Dumbarton Oaks advisor for numismatics; John Nesbitt, research associate for Byzantine sigillography; James N. Carder, archivist and House Collection manager; and Sheila Klos, director of the library; at the Georgia Museum of Art—William U. Eiland, director; Annelies Mondi, deputy director; Romita Ray, curator of the Mark and Debra Callaway Department of Prints and Drawings and the in-house curator for *Sacred Art, Secular Context*; and Betty Alice Fowler, grants coordinator; at the Lamar Dodd School of Art—Carmon Colangelo, director, and Shelley E. Zuraw, area chair for art history and associate director.

Special appreciation is due to those whose efforts contributed to the exhibition and the catalogue: at Dumbarton Oaks—Deborah Brown, librarian, Byzantine studies; Joseph Mills, photographer; Marta Zlotnik, curatorial assistant, Byzantine Collection; Caitlin McGurk, assistant to the director of Byzantine studies; at Princeton University—Shari Kenfield, curator, Research Photographs, Department of Art and Archaeology; Lois Drewer, research scholar, Princeton Index of Christian Art; and Janice J. Powell, librarian, Marquand Library of Art and Archaeology; at the Georgia Museum of Art—Dennis Harper, curator of exhibitions; Paul Manoguerra, curator of American art; Tricia Miller, head registrar; and Larry Forte, art handler; at the Lamar Dodd School of Art—Joseph C. Willey, information analyst, and Brandon Williams, computer services specialist.

I would like to thank Nancy Ševčenko, whose comments and suggestions helped improve the loan-request essay. Special gratitude is due to William Silas Talbot, who generously shared his rich experience and insight on all matters involving museum exhibitions.

I wish to express my appreciation for the advice and counsel of Peter Brown, Slobodan Ćurčić, Helen Evans, Evan Firestone, Sharon E. J. Gerstel, Erica Hermanowitz, Deborah Kahn, Andrew Ladis, Alisa Luxenberg, Hugo Meyer, Robert S. Nelson, Naomi Norman, Thomas Polk, Janice Simon, Frances Van Keuren, and Isabelle Wallace.

I would like to thank Dr. Michael F. Adams, president of the University of Georgia, for his support and for the two grants from the President's Venture Fund through the generous gifts of the Univerity of Georgia Partners.

I am grateful for the grant of a Summer Fellowship in Byzantine Studies at Dumbarton Oaks. During the summer of 2004, it provided me with the opportunity to conduct research on topics related to this exhibition.

The contributing authors to this exhibition catalogue, who are listed separately at the beginning of this volume, deserve a special acknowledgment. In spite of their rigorous schedules, they found the time to compose essays and numerous entries.

Special appreciation is due to Frances Kianka for thorough and thoughtful work on the copyediting of the manuscript and to Dr. Diana L. Ranson, Ms. Federica Goldoni, and Mr. Boris Jetelina for proofreading the bibliography. Kimberly Adis, the graphic designer of this book, has also earned particular praise for her sensitive and creative approach to this project.

I owe a depth of gratitude to Stuart Lee Brown, whose support sustained me, whose efforts improved the manuscript of the catalogue, and whose generosity contributed toward enriching the display.

—Asen Kirin
Assistant Professor, Lamar Dodd School of Art,
University of Georgia, Athens, Georgia

Contributors of Entries to the Catalogue

GB   **Gudrun Buehl**
Curator and Museum Director
Dumbarton Oaks

JNC   **James N. Carder**
Archivist and House Collection Manager
Dumbarton Oaks

SEJG   **Sharon E. J. Gerstel**
Associate Professor of Art History
University of California, Los Angeles

IK   **Ioli Kalavrezou**
Dumbarton Oaks Professor of Byzantine Art
Department of Art and Archaeology
Harvard University

AK   **Asen Kirin**
Assistant Professor
Lamar Dodd School of Art
University of Georgia

GK   **Genevra Kornbluth**
Assistant Professor
University of Maryland

EDM   **Eunice D. Maguire**
Curator of the Hopkins Collection
and Senior Lecturer
Department of Art History
Johns Hopkins University

PM   **Paul A. Manoguerra**
Curator of American Art
Georgia Museum of Art

CM   **Cécile Morrisson**
Dumbarton Oaks Advisor for Numismatics
Directeur de recherches au Centre d'histoire
et civilisation de Byzance
Collège de France

JN   **John Nesbitt**
Research Associate for Byzantine Sigillography
Dumbarton Oaks

MGP   **Maria G. Parani**
Assistant Professor
University of Cyprus

BP   **Brigitte Pitarakis**
Centre d'histoire et civilisation de Byzance
Collège de France

AW   **Alicia Walker**
Post-Doctoral Fellow
Department of Art History
Columbia University

SRZ   **Stephen R. Zwirn**
Assistant Curator
Byzantine Collection
Dumbarton Oaks

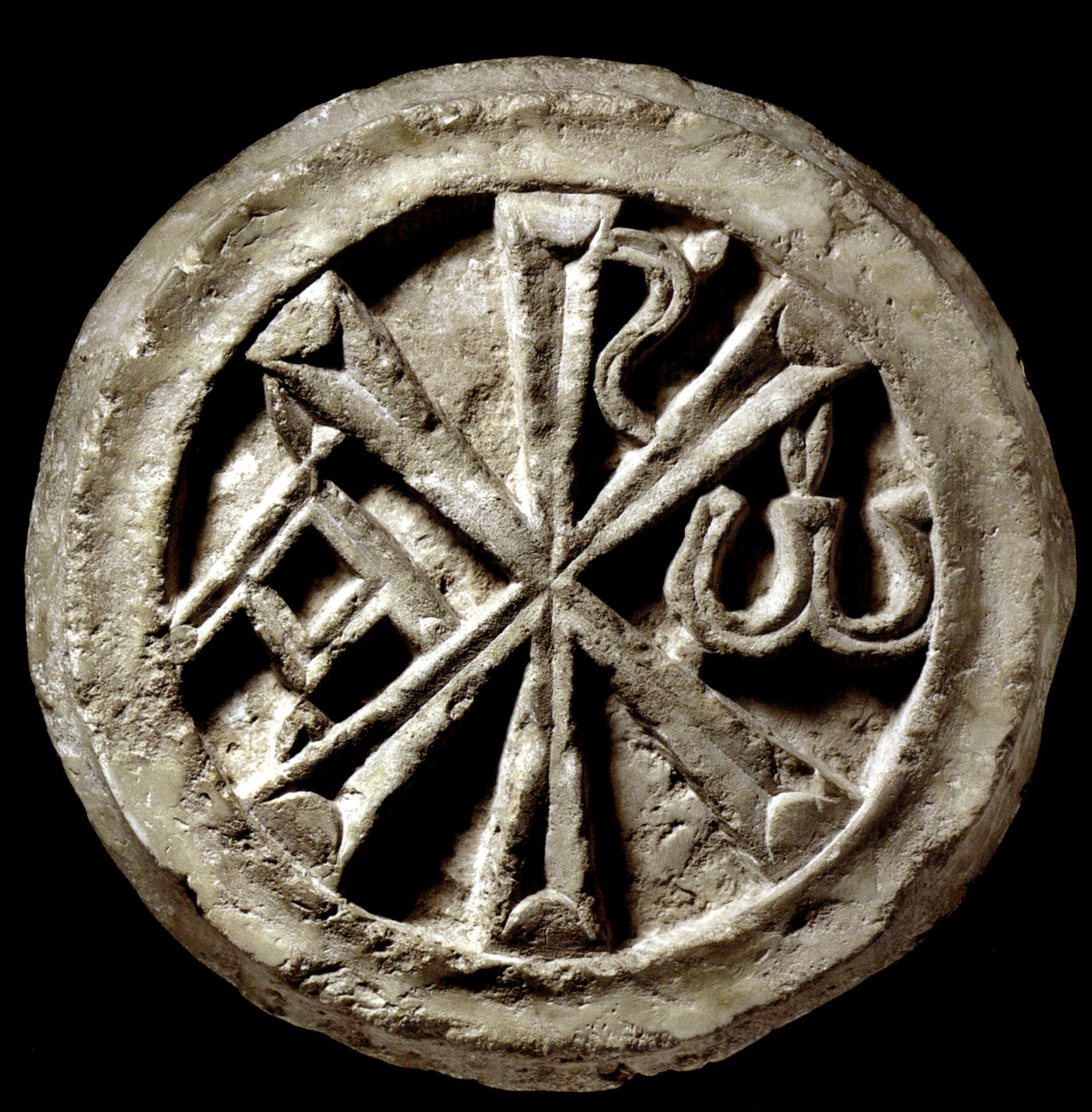

Sacred Art, Secular Context

BY ASEN KIRIN

ACRED ART, SECULAR CONTEXT DISPLAYS SEVenty-one objects from the Byzantine Collection of Dumbarton Oaks. The selection includes carved gems, jewelry, gold and silver coins, bronze steelyards with weights, silverware, ceramic vessels, and sculpture. Only three of these objects, an intaglio, a cameo, and a bronze weight (cat. nos. 1, 3, 51), have been on display in the permanent exhibit of Dumbarton Oaks; the remaining pieces have rarely or never before been shown. Furthermore, three of the Byzantine objects are published here for the first time: the gold ring with a representation of the Virgin and Child (cat. no. 15) and two weights (cat. nos. 50, 52) acquired in 1960, along with the coin collection of the distinguished Italian diplomat and scholar Tommaso Bertelè (1892-1971).

Sacred images and/or inscriptions adorn most of the objects on display, even though they functioned in the realm of life outside ecclesiastical rituals in the secular context of personal adornment, dining, and dealings in the marketplace. The selection includes examples of principal subjects in Byzantine religious art, among them Christ (cat. nos. 1-3, 58, 59), the Mother of God (cat. nos. 4-8, 14, 15), St. John the Baptist (cat. no. 38), St. Demetrios (cat. no. 32), and the archangels (cat. nos. 10, 11, 16). Ultimately, this exhibition's main theme is the fusion of the worldly and the spiritual in Byzantine culture, and it is in this regard that sacred images played the key role by providing a link between everyday material existence and the supernatural.

In terms of chronology, the exhibition spans a period from the fourth to the fourteenth century, including examples from both before and after the era of Iconoclasm, which lasted throughout most of the eighth and early ninth centuries (726-787, 814-843). The objects dating to the pre-Iconoclastic period come from Constantinople, Rome, Palestine, Syria, Egypt, and Persia, emphasizing the unity of Late Antique culture in the Mediterranean region. In contrast, most of the post-Iconoclastic works have been attributed to the city of Constantinople. That being the case, their provenance highlights the dominant role that the imperial capital played in the artistic life of Byzantium after the end of Iconoclasm. These objects are also a reflection of an essential characteristic of those centuries, when "ecclesiastical authorities could monitor lay access to supernatural power more effectively, both through the theology of the icon and through the forms of the icons themselves."[1]

A watershed in the history of Byzantium and its arts, Iconoclasm—lit. "image-destruction"—was a religious movement that renounced the holiness of icons.[2] While expanding on ancient arguments against art, iconoclasts rejected the veneration of icons because they viewed it as a form of idolatry. In doing so they followed the words of Deuteronomy 5:8, "thou shall not make thee any graven image, or any likeness of any thing that is in heaven above." Accordingly, they forbade figural religious art and promoted as proper representations of God only the sign of the cross and the transformed eucharistic gifts, which they understood as an image of Christ "not-made-by-human-hand" (ἀχειροποίητος).[3] For them, any other corporeal likeness of Christ presented the threat of confusing his divine and human natures and obscuring the distinction between material image and spiritual prototype. Such an occurrence could erase the fundamental division between sacred and profane. In order to prevent this split from happening, the iconoclasts also banned any Christian images from private dwellings.[4] Indeed, because religious images from the domestic realm had been a contested issue, their character and their proliferation underwent substantial changes.

These changes constitute the focal point of the present exhibition.

In response to the argument of the iconoclasts, the defenders of icons—the iconophiles (lit. "image-lovers") or iconodules (lit. "image-servants")—asserted that the ultimate justification of their practices was nothing less than the miracle of the Incarnation. The Pauline idea that Christ himself was an image (*eikon*) of God played a crucial role in this line of argument.[5] Not only did the Incarnation redeem the original sin but it made the uncircumscribable God accessible to human senses, thus enabling the creation of his truthful material likeness. By refusing to venerate icons, one would be denying the ultimate source of human salvation—the Holy Spirit's sanctification of human flesh. Conceived in this way, icon veneration constituted an indispensable part of the correct way to pursue religious worship. For the iconophiles, the existence of miraculously occurring images "not-made-by-human-hand"—*acheiropoieta*—was a manifestation of the divine endorsement of icon veneration. Christ himself created the best-known *acheiropoietos*, the Holy Mandylion, a piece of cloth with an imprint of his face.[6]

The period of Iconoclasm ended in 843 when the iconodules restored the veneration of holy images. Tellingly, they chose to call the feast celebrating their victory the Triumph of Orthodoxy.[7] The most prominent proponents of icon veneration were St. John of Damascus (c. 675-749) and St. Theodore of Studios (759-826).[8] On the whole, the arguments in defense of holy images had a profound impact on the visual culture of Byzantium because they elevated the status of the work of art to the realm of theology and effectively cast the artist in the role of theologian.[9]

WITHIN THIS EXHIBITION, THE EPOCHAL change from Iconoclasm back to the official veneration of icons is represented by a pair of coins (cat. nos. 69 and 70) featuring images of two successive emperors. The iconography of both coins involves the juxtaposition of an imperial portrait with a sacred image, thus making the same general statement about imperial authority emanating from God. The notable difference concerns the choices for representing the Divinity on the reverse side of these coins. While the iconoclast Theophilos (829-842) is matched with an image of the cross, the later portrayal of the iconodule Michael III (843-856) is paired with the bust of Christ. Byzantine coins brought sacred images into the realm of everyday life, and, by doing so, they served the purpose of imperial political and religious propaganda. Apart from their primary role as official currency, coins were also used as amulets or portable icons. An example is the coin of Emperor Theophilos, which was pierced above the cross on the reverse so it could be worn as a pendant. (For further discussion, see in this catalogue the essay "Sacred Art on Coins and Their Secular Context" by Cécile Morrisson.)

During the period between the fourth and the seventh century, sacred Christian symbols appeared commonly on everyday objects. For instance, a small bronze bath bucket (cat. no. 42) and a relief for a house (cat. no. 55) feature the Chrismon, Christ's monogram. A cross serves as a finial on the lid of an oil lamp (cat. no. 40). Another intriguing example is the incense burner in the form of the Tomb of Christ, adorned with the sign of the cross and the letters *Alpha* and *Omega* (cat. no. 41). Sacred symbols notwithstanding, this incense burner could have been used either in a church or in a private house. In addition, one of the seventh-century silver dinner plates features a cross monogram. The cross monogram may represent the name of the owner or the name of the owner's patron saint or perhaps a conflation of both (cat. no. 37).

In the pre-Iconoclastic era, the proliferation of Christian imagery in the decoration of everyday objects demonstrates how Christianity permeated all spheres of people's existence and added an additional layer of spiritual meaning to everyday life.[10] Furthermore, as discussed in the essay "Silver Plate" by Maria G. Parani, Christian imagery found on luxurious dining vessels is indicative of how the affluent classes not only embraced the new religion but asserted their Christian identity, a need felt acutely within this social class where Christians and pagans shared the same classical education and a common style of life. Familiarity with classical pagan culture continued to be a measure of sophistication and social prominence among the wellborn far into the medieval period. Two of the finger rings in this show (cat. nos. 17 and 18), dating respectively to the eleventh and the ninth century, represent this phenomenon. Other objects featuring classical subjects provide a glimpse into the custom of attaching Christian interpretations to original works of pagan art (cat. nos. 9 and 12).

In the wake of the victory of the iconodules, the use of Christian images in everyday contexts and on household items was greatly reduced; holy icons could no longer adorn mundane objects. An example may be found in the ceramic bowls (cat. nos. 60-63), whose decoration has a strictly secular character. Nevertheless, after Iconoclasm, a sphere of everyday material existence remained where holy images were present. Certainly, they continued to grace works of jewelry (cat. nos. 3-6, 14, 22). These objects yield an insight into the complex ways in which the ancient custom of relying on the supernatural protection of talismans and amulets merged with the devotional practices reflecting the iconodules' theology of the icon.

In general, the distinction between a talisman and a personal devotional icon corresponds to the different notions about the nature of holy images from before and after Iconoclasm. Before Iconoclasm, images operated directly as potent signs in their own right or as powerful substances, akin to medicine or drugs.[11] The theology of the icon after Iconoclasm, however, dictated that a saint's material likeness was only the mediator between the faithful Christian and a holy person. The recipient of the veneration paid to an icon was not the object bearing the likeness, but this likeness's sacred prototype. The faithful venerated not pieces of wood, stone, or any other, albeit precious, substance, but a saintly figure.[12] It was only the saint's heavenly intercession that could produce beneficial results in response to a supplicant's prayers.[13] Since the choice of intercessor was of crucial importance for the success of the supplication, the visual language of icons had to secure the unambiguous identification of each and every saintly figure. As St. Theodore of Studios asserted, holy images related to their sacred prototype by means of individual features.[14] The repetition of these features provided for the verisimilitude and authenticity of icons. Accordingly, the costumes, attributes, and portrait features of saints became both individualized and standardized. In addition, identifying inscriptions became an obligatory element in the depictions of holy figures.[15]

AN EXPLANATION FOR THE SIGNIFICANCE OF THE identifying inscriptions is articulated succinctly in a lesser-known late ninth-century source, the Old Slavonic *vita* of St. Cyril the Philosopher (826/7-869), very likely composed by his older brother St. Methodius (815-885). As missionaries to the Slavs, the brothers invented the first Slavonic alphabet and made translations from Greek into a new literary language, Old Slavonic. Chapter five of the *vita* contains an account of a dispute between the young St. Cyril and the former iconoclastic patriarch John VII Grammaticus (837-843), who was deposed at the time of the restoration of icon veneration. "Why is it that you venerate the cross without an inscription, and there exist many crosses, while you would not venerate an image that does not bear the name of the depicted [saint]?" asked the former patriarch. To this question, St. Cyril replied: "Every cross has a form similar to that of the cross of Christ, while the depictions [of saints] are not the same."[16]

Among the objects on display in this exhibition are examples of similar iconography rendered without identifying inscriptions before Iconoclasm and examples with inscriptions from the following period. In post-Iconoclastic times, the inscriptions had become an obligatory iconographic element even when they were made virtually redundant by the explicit nature of the image and its popularity. For instance, the figure of the Virgin is flanked by two crosses and has no accompanying inscription on an early seventh-century gold ring (cat. no. 15), while her post-Iconoclastic representations are accompanied by the inscription identifying her as the "Mother of God" (cat. nos. 4-6). Even the smallest images had to be inscribed, no matter how difficult this task was made by their size, as in the gold and enamel plaquette of St. Demetrios (cat. no. 32). Furthermore, the inscription had to accompany the image, and not be separated from it, as could happen on a pre-Iconoclastic hematite intaglio of Archangel Michael (cat. no. 10), with the figure on one side and the engraved name on the other.

Another group of objects, related in terms of iconography and medium, provides evidence for the different types of inscriptions that could accompany sacred images. The post-Iconoclastic sapphire cameo of Christ (cat. no. 3) features the standard abbreviation IC XC ("Jesus Christ"). In contrast, the pre-Iconoclastic amethyst intaglio of Christ (cat. no. 1) does not have his name written or abbreviated, although it uses Christ's monogram—the Chrismon—inscribed in his halo. In addition, this intaglio has the names of seven archangels whose powers were often invoked for healing and protection from all forms of evil. These prophylactic inscriptions are a manifestation of the intaglio's amuletic function. Combining such inscriptions with the image of Christ would have been unacceptable in post-Iconoclastic times because of the discord between image and inscription; it would have compromised the iconic character of the gem, which was meant explicitly as an intercession to Christ. Conspicuously, apart from writing the names of the depicted saints, a common type of inscription added to post-Iconoclastic images contained the verbal formula, "Supplication of the servant of God," followed by the name of either a donor or an artist. Clearly, this formula reveals that the acts of both commissioning and manufacturing an icon were perceived at

that time as gestures of supplication.[17] (For a discussion of related issues, see in this catalogue the essay "Inscriptions as 'Decoration' on Byzantine Jewelry" by Brigitte Pitarakis.)

Within this exhibition, the most evident manifestation of the intercessory nature of post-Iconoclastic devotional pieces involves a group of three objects displayed together. These are the sapphire cameo with a bust of Christ (cat. no. 3), flanked by the quartz cameo of the Virgin Hagiosoritissa (cat. no. 5) and the bronze plaquette of St. John the Baptist (cat. no. 38). As arranged, these three figures form the composition known as the Deesis—lit. "entreaty"—featuring Christ blessing in the center, and the Virgin and St. John turning toward him, with arms raised in a gesture of supplication. Since the ninth century, this composition was closely associated with the idea of intercession and appeared commonly on works intended for private devotion. Also, it was rendered on templon beams in churches, thus alluding to the liturgical prayers of intercession, where it could also include the figures of apostles, angels, and saints. The Deesis composition was the focal point of the elaborate scene of the Last Judgment where the Virgin and St. John the Baptist—witnesses of Christ's divinity—intercede on behalf of all mankind.[18]

Cat. nos. 3, 5, and 38 were not created with the intention of being displayed together, as is apparent from their different materials and dimensions. Nevertheless, their combination here illustrates a phenomenon resulting from the relative constancy of Byzantine iconography. Even a single figure could be sufficient to allude to well-established and easily recognizable examples of intricate multi-figural compositions. Individual images could evoke meaningful associations, thus referring to larger religious themes far transcending the initial direct visual statement.

While the amuletic role of the pre-Iconoclastic amethyst intaglio (cat. no. 1) is manifested in its prophylactic inscription, the function of the three post-Iconoclastic devotional pieces forming a Deesis is alluded to by means of their iconography and the intentional associations that it evokes. After all, the act of wearing a pendant or any other miniature icon involves the notion of entreaty; an act of supplication to the saintly figure is manifested by the worn image. That being the case, the gestures of the Virgin and St. John are visual statements about prayer that reflect the function of these pieces. Notably, image and written word together clarify the intercessory function of a devotional piece, justify it, and even contribute to its success.

Even though theologians sought to ensure the intercessory role of icons by defining the distinction between image and prototype, the confusion of the two surely must have persisted, for when it comes to the tendencies of human thought and the compelling nature of the visual experience, "the philosophy of images is perhaps less important than their magic."[19] Images possessed great power over the faithful because they provided an opportunity to contemplate the limitless and the eternal in a finite material object. The palpability of the saints' presence embodied in their corporeal portrayals overwhelmed the elaborate rhetoric about the difference between depicted and the depiction. As David Freedberg argues, the ontological heart of the problem is whether the effectiveness of images may not depend most of all on the possibility of this kind of fusion; a holy icon performs as if its sacred prototype were present, "but the difficulty lies in cognitively grasping that 'as if.'"[20]

It stands to reason that the fusion between a saint and that saint's depiction would be less likely to occur when the material used for the portrayal of a holy figure is just a humble piece of wood or stone. Yet numerous devotional pieces, such as the majority of the objects included in this exhibition, crafted from precious or rare substances, by their nature, must have encouraged this conflation. As discussed in the individual catalogue entries, these materials did have their own symbolic meanings, and, even more important, some of these substances were believed to exert supernatural powers. The very notion that the substance used for the creation of a work of art can, in its own right, possess meaning, let alone power, appears to undermine the intercessory nature of post-Iconoclastic images. The awareness of the powers that precious stones possessed was manifested in the imperial monopoly on certain gems, concerned with both monetary matters and efforts to limit the use of these stones as amulets.[21]

I N THE ESSAY ENTITLED "INTAGLIOS AND CAMEOS," Genevra Kornbluth explains that, in general, gemstone materials were viewed as supplementing the function of images and inscriptions. It is evident that gemstones were used as medical and protective amulets; thus, most people must not have viewed this use as opposing their Christian beliefs. Certainly, there were persistent objections, but the tradition of using precious substances was firmly established. Their potency was due to a host of reasons, the most apparent of which involved the sheer visual thrill and the pleasure of the tactile experience. Then there were the intangible aspects of their appeal: the presumed magical properties of these materials, the statement that these precious items made about one's social prominence, and the attractive opportunity to mix ostentation and piety by carrying a miniature object opulent in substance and devout in function.

The awareness of the inherent danger of conflating image and substance in devotional objects made of precious materials appears to have stimulated a thoughtful response, one that did not ignore the problem, but instead directly addressed the issue that made the shadow of idolatry loom large over Byzantine devotional practices. A deliberate synthesis between iconography and material distinguishes certain Byzantine gemstones, which apparently were the product of very cerebral artistic creativity. Cat. nos. 3 and 6 represent two different manifestations of this phenomenon.

The large sapphire cameo (cat. no. 3) belongs to a class of cameos carved on monochromatic and translucent stones that became common only in the post-Iconoclastic era. In purely visual terms, these cameos possess a subtlety in the modeling of forms strikingly different from the clear delineation of figures carved on stones having layers of different colors, such as those made in sardonyx and agate (cf. cat. nos. 11-13). Although both types of gems required exceptional skills from the carver, the artist's treatment of the medium is mani-

fested somewhat less obviously on translucent and monochromatic gems. It is tempting to see these cameos' popularity after Iconoclasm as a reflection of their visual characteristics, which seem to suggest that rather than being the outcome of artistic intervention the image has occurred in the stone itself. This visual effect of a fusion between a manmade image and a God-made substance took a human creation as close as it could be to the *acheiropoieta*, the images of saintly figures that came into existence miraculously. Indeed, as noted above, the *acheiropoieta* occupied a prominent position in the iconodules' defense of image veneration.

A NOTHER EXAMPLE OF PURPOSEFUL FUSION BETWEEN image and substance is the bloodstone cameo of the Virgin (cat. no. 6). Most often, when creating bloodstone cameos, Byzantine carvers would set the vertical axis of the composition so that it allowed for the stripes of color to meet the carved figure diagonally without coinciding with the gestures or the directions of the gaze of the figures. In this manner, the carved composition and natural coloring received equal prominence without obscuring each other. This cameo shows a pronounced departure from the common practice. The presence of the blessing hand of God appearing from a heavenly segment in the upper right defines the Virgin's gesture of supplication. An additional reason for depicting her arms raised in a sharp angle is the prominent red stripe that appears along the same diagonal axis. This striking red diagonal compels the gaze of the beholder to the gesture of entreaty and also visually connects the Virgin and Christ in heaven. As if spilling down from the heavenly segment, the stripes of red color emerge as the embodiment of Christ's blessing. The conflation of the visual manifestations of this blessing and his blood becomes the sign of the redemptive role of his self-sacrifice. Its design, at once thoughtful and strikingly simple, creates a strong and lasting visual impact, making this cameo a true masterpiece of medieval gem carving.

In this exhibition, further evidence for the fusion of the realms of everyday existence and the divine is provided by the jewelry related to the ceremonies of betrothal. The gold marriage ring (cat. no. 26) displays an image that represents an essential aspect of the ecclesiastic ritual of matrimony. The composition representing Christ joining the right hands of the standing bride and groom is the visual manifestation of the blessing bestowed on the couple by the Church. In addition, a gold bezel for a marriage ring dating to the late fourth or early fifth century (cat. no. 25) offers an example of the specific manner in which such pieces were manufactured, in some instances involving premade bezels. (For more on marriage rings, see the essay "Early Byzantine Marriage Rings" by Alicia Walker.)

Transactions occurring in the marketplace are represented by a separate group of objects, including two steelyards (cat. nos. 43, 46), weights (cat. nos. 45, 48-54), and coins (cat. nos. 64-71). Apart from the coins on display, imperial images appear also on four of the weights (cat. nos. 48-51). The iconography of these pieces and of the coins functioned as a visual statement about the control and supervision of the state in the realm of commerce. Even on such a mundane level of life, the Byzantines used images reflecting their notion about the organization of the universal Christian empire. Another demonstration of the importance of imperial representations in the sphere of commerce and craft is seen in Byzantine silver hallmarks, such as the ones that appear on the seventh-century silver dishes from Constantinople (cat. nos. 36 and 37).

Sacred Art, Secular Context includes five examples of relief sculpture (cat. nos. 55-59). As dissimilar as they might be in terms of dates, origins, and intended functions, these pieces fulfill a very significant role in this exhibition. They allude to the associations between Byzantium and the Holy Land, as well as Late Antique and medieval Italy. Furthermore, these sculptural reliefs complement the majority of the objects, which are, in a very real sense, miniature reliefs. By exhibiting together works executed in radically different sizes, the aim is to stimulate the beholder to contemplate the symbolic implications of a miniature format. Aside from the preciousness of the substances used, this small scale also distinguishes an object conveying an important message and possessing "condensed meaning." One might say that the minuscule scale of a work of art is the artistic equivalent of rhetorical understatement.

Exhibiting together large and small reliefs emphasizes the relevant visual characteristics of the miniature pieces—the cameos, coins, and weights. These visual features were the function not only of the particular dimensions but also of the different substances used in creating the individual objects.

✦ ✦ ✦

T HE IDEA OF CONSIDERING THE MATERIAL INvolved as an integral component of the visual language of a work of art was of great importance for artists, art critics, and connoisseurs when the founders of Dumbarton Oaks, Mildred and Robert Woods Bliss, were building their collection.[22] The persons and events that shaped the history of the Bliss Collection are discussed in the essays by James N. Carder and Robert S. Nelson. These two essays show clearly that the Blisses' most important advisor in collecting was Royall Tyler, who also was their lifelong friend. In 1926, Tyler and Hayford Peirce published a book on Byzantine art. The Blisses' personal copy of this book inscribed by Tyler is on display in this exhibition. In the foreword, Tyler and Peirce emphasized a "Byzantine characteristic of letting the medium determine the plastic treatment" of a work of art. In the following passage the authors explain the significance of this issue:

> The earth yields purple porphyry, green serpentine, black diorite, marble white and coloured, precious and curious stones and metals in endless variety. From the animal and vegetable kingdoms are derived such things as pearls, amber, ivory, wood, silk, wool, linen and dyes. The ancient Greeks and Romans schooled the objects of art which they made out of these elements into plastic uniformity, imposing upon them standardised types of humanity and of ornament whatever the medium and whatever the dimensions. The Byzantines, moved by the reviving spirit of Egypt, Syria and Mesopotamia, were more alive to the quality of the medium and perhaps weary of Hellenistic facility of technique. They treated hard stone with a sense of its texture and Proconnesian marble in a new manner, produced an art of coinage based on a true appreciation of gold, brought out the essential character of ivory, [and] conceived an imperial use of plate, gems and jewellery.[23]

This issue brings us to the next theme of this exhibition: the appreciation of Late Antique and medieval everyday objects as works of art. The artistic excellence that they represent was of essential importance to the Blisses. As Robert Nelson demonstrates, the Blisses, who were highly sophisticated, cosmopolitan, and distinctly secular-minded, collected Byzantine art not for its religious and spiritual content but, instead, for its artistic qualities.

This exhibition calls attention to an essential characteristic of the Byzantine Collection at Dumbarton Oaks, namely that it contains mostly works of decorative or minor arts. In a review published in the first issue of *The Art Bulletin* in 1941, and written on the occasion of Dumbarton Oaks opening its doors to the public, Hanns Swarzenski of the Institute for Advanced Study, Princeton, New Jersey, asserted that

> ... [w]ith the single exception of the Cabinet des Médailles in Paris, this is the first museum in the history of collecting to emphasize in its presentation the purely artistic importance of material which the old historic museums arranged so unattractively in dusty, overcrowded cases that it would tend to frighten and bore any visitor except the scientific specialist.[24]

In 1913, almost thirty years before the publication of Swarzenski's piece, the Cabinet des Médailles was the subject of discussion in a private letter written to the Blisses by Royall Tyler; an excerpt of this letter is published in James Carder's first essay included in this catalogue. Tyler suggested "that it would be a happiness for life" if eventually he and the Blisses together donated certain important pieces of their collections so that they might "live happily thereafter at the Cabinet des Médailles." For Tyler, the appeal of this museum was its resemblance to a private house where the objects live and "glow sleek and glossy and are patently happy." It was the appreciation of these pieces' aesthetic quality that made both the objects and their collector glow with happiness. One finds a confirmation of this notion in the foreword to Tyler and Peirce's book from 1926:

We owe the preservation of what we have to the precious character of the objects that originally caused them to be looted and the sacred associations for the sake of which they have been preserved through ages of indifference to their aesthetic claims.[25]

THE BLISSES' CONSCIOUS AND SUSTAINED FOCUS on works of decorative art earned them a graceful jest from an acquaintance. Charles Henry Coster attended the events marking the transfer of Dumbarton Oaks to Harvard University, which took place in November 1940. He wrote: "The Byzantine and Roman jewelry and bibelots must have been pleased to have found themselves, after a lapse of centuries, in a crowd of gay, fashionable, chattering people."[26] Coster's humor shows that what the Blisses were doing was unusual and also that they were successfully conveying a sense of the significance of their collection. In a distinctly different tone, Swarzenski made a comment reflecting the same two issues:

> [T]he attentive visitor at the more important art exhibitions of the last fifteen years has always been attracted by the unusual objects loaned by Mr. and Mrs. Bliss—objects, which evidenced a peculiar personal certitude of artistic taste and judgment.[27]

It is significant that it was the Blisses' judgment to avoid buying Byzantine paintings, the works of art that at the time had already achieved the status of high art and were deemed worthy for display at the major fine arts museums. In 1906, in a piece entitled "Ideals for a Picture Gallery" published in the *Bulletin of the Metropolitan Museum of Art*, Roger Fry, a well-known British art critic of the time, included Byzantine painting in the great sequence of European creative thought at the beginning of a line that included Giotto, Mantegna, and Botticelli.[28]

There were scholars who considered the absence of icons to be the great lacuna of the Byzantine Collection of Dumbarton Oaks. One of them was Kurt Weitzmann, who attributed this to the Blisses' close association with Tyler, who was, in Weitzmann's estimation, not a professional art historian and, therefore, neglected icons and favored minor arts such as goldsmiths' work and ivories.[29] It appears that avoiding icons was a consciously made choice, which by no means reflects a lack of knowledge or inability to appreciate their artistic value. Confirming this choice is a very revealing passage found in a letter written by Tyler to Mrs. Bliss on August 1, 1935. Tyler was traveling in Soviet Russia visiting museums and examining works of Byzantine art:

> [In Kiev] The Laura contains a lot of icons (I never wish to see another Russian icon again, not even of the best, early ones), and a very few Byz. objects, including 3 Coptic paintings on wood (fr. Sinai).
>
> <u>Moscow</u>. What I chiefly wanted to see was the Chloudoff Psalter, and I saw it to my heart's content, and several other superb Byz. MSS as well, all in the Library of the Historical Museum. There, there are the icons in the Tretiakoff Gallery, beginning with the celebrated Vladimirskaya Madonna, which is said to have been a present from Constantine Monomachos (1046). Much more likely XII-XIII, I think. It's a ruin and a palimpsest, with a vestige of beauty. Then the late XIV paintings of Theophanes the Greek, pretty good, and well preserved (cleverly cleaned from repaints), and the few

greatly vaunted icons by Roubleff, early XV, who followed Theophanes.

> The great work by Roubleff is the Troitskaya Troitza, three angels representing the Trinity, and it is a very lovely thing, of indefinable shimmering colours. I went and gazed at it every day while I was in Moscow, and came to the conclusion that its charm is mainly of the nature of the charm of an iridesced glass or Persian pot—fortuitous. As one sees it now, the colours bear no relation to what Roubleff intended, and are commanded by a most lovely egg-shell white, which is really the sub-preparation of the panel and was not intended to show anywhere.... The effect is perfectly lovely, and Roubleff designed well, but where his colour is well preserved it is heavy and murky, and I'd be prepared to bet heavily that if we could see the panel in anything like its original condition we'd get a bad shock.
>
> Then, in the Kremlin Museum, there are the treasures of the Czars.... Perhaps the loveliest thing there is Catherine the Great's Wedding dress (she was 14), in cloth of silver, with silver embroideries on it. No colour, made in Paris. It's like a white lily seen in moonlight, and it took my breath away—a marvel of marvels.[30]

Tyler, who was an extraordinary connoisseur, made observations, both discerning and well informed, that stand on a par with some of the best art history writing about the famous icons he saw. Yet, most striking of all is the last thought in the paragraph above, where he expresses his uninhibited admiration for a dress that he described as a work of art. This eloquent statement of Tyler's reveals a disregard for the hierarchy of the arts that stipulates the supremacy of painting and sculpture over decorative arts. For Tyler and the Blisses their focus on collecting works of decorative art by no means diminished the overall reputation of Byzantine art. On the contrary, they intended to show the significance of Byzantium within the Western visual tradition through examples of artistic excellence outside religious painting, very much in the spirit of the formalist Roger Fry, who wrote in 1908:

> It is probably a mistake to suppose, as is usually done, that Byzantinism was due to a loss of technical ability to be realistic, consequent upon barbarian invasions. In the Eastern Empire there was never any loss of technical skills; indeed, nothing could surpass the perfection of some Byzantine craftsmanship.[31]

Future research will establish the degree to which Tyler is indebted to the ideas of Roger Fry. A lot of what they shared was described by Fry himself as something characteristic of his generation. Among these ideas is the conviction that objects used in daily life can express the joy of their creator and convey a corresponding delight to the user.[32] They favored Italian primitives over High Renaissance works and shared a fascination for the art of El Greco. As Fry asserted, "was it not rather El Greco's earliest training in the lingering Byzantine tradition that suggested to him his mode of escape into an art of direct expression [instead of emulating nature]."[33]

This brings us to an important distinction in the attitudes of Fry and Tyler. Fry's enthusiasm about Byzantine art had to do with the notion that it anticipated modernist and avant-garde art. Consistently Fry, just like the French painter and theorist Maurice Denis before him, referred to the Byzantine sources of the post-Impressionist art of Paul Cézanne and Henri Matisse:

> Byzantine art fixes for centuries the compromise between the vision and the *objet d'art* so strongly on the side of the latter that we may perhaps be allowed

to use Byzantine as a term generally expressive of the recovery of the *objet d'art* from the predominance of the representative side of pictorial art.[34]

In contrast, for Tyler and for the Blisses the importance of Byzantine art came mostly from their conviction that it implanted non-Christian and non-Western sources into the Western tradition of art:

> Byzantine art is often confounded in its inception with early Christian art. We begin [the discussion in this book] with pagan Diocletian and his pagan associates and successors, for the purpose of showing that the new plastic order came in spite of rather than because of the new religion. [This comes with the belief that the Byzantines were] moved by the reviving spirit of Egypt, Syria and Mesopotamia.[35]

Ultimately, within the Byzantine Collection of Dumbarton Oaks, this point of view is manifested by the presence of objects of art coming from Palestine, Syria, Persia, Egypt, the Balkans, and Italy—a veritable embodiment of the intellectual and artistic continuity of Mediterranean culture. In 1966, in the Preamble of her Last Will and Testament, Mrs. Bliss explained that her and her late husband's goal was to contribute toward perpetuating the "Mediterranean interpretation of the humanist disciplines."[36]

Furthermore, the notion that non-classical and non-Christian sources contributed to the Western visual tradition was of great importance for Tyler and the Blisses because of their shared interest in pre-Columbian art. As discussed by Carder and Nelson, the first object that Mr. Bliss bought was an Olmec jadeite figurine (Nelson, fig. 3). In its final form the museum at Dumbarton Oaks came to display antiquities of both Old World Europe and the Americas. Clearly, more recent history also mattered, as evidenced by the simple fact that this display was set in the heart of historic Georgetown, the oldest part of the capital of the United States. And it is no accident that the balance between the Old World and the distinctly American objects on display within the museum finds itself echoed in the gardens of Dumbarton Oaks, where the features of rustic American landscape were made to coexist perfectly with forms of historic European garden design.[37]

American Paintings from the Collection of Mildred and Robert Woods Bliss

The second component of this exhibition's title, "Secular Context," refers not only to the sphere of everyday life in Byzantium, but also to the environment within which Mr. and Mrs. Bliss collected art in the early twentieth century. Highlighting this focus is the display of ten works of modern American art from the House Collection of Dumbarton Oaks, including paintings by Childe Hassam (cat. nos. 72-74), Walter Gay (cat. nos. 75-80), and Henry Golden Dearth (cat. no. 81). The Blisses acquired these paintings as they were building their Byzantine collection. The American paintings from the House Collection have never been exhibited together and rarely, and in some cases never, have

they been seen outside of Dumbarton Oaks. Notably, five of them (cat. nos. 74-76, 80-81) have remained unpublished until now.

In his essay on the opening of Dumbarton Oaks, Swarzenski emphasized that the Blisses owned several paintings that complemented Harvard's academic resources. Along with the gardens and the Federal mansion, the paintings contributed to creating a most refined environment that, by its very nature, would stimulate excellent scholarly work. While listing all the works of European art owned by the Blisses and donated to Dumbarton Oaks, Swarzenski's review does not acknowledge the fact that the collection included several American paintings.[38] As Carder's second essay in this catalogue demonstrates, these works must have been of great personal relevance to the Blisses, who had long-lasting friendships with some of the artists with whom they shared strong Francophile sentiments.

This auxiliary exhibition underlines two relevant issues. The first one involves the intentional bringing together of old and new art from Europe and America, aspects of which have been discussed earlier in this essay. The second issue is the underappreciated contribution of the Blisses to twentieth-century art in America. As James Carder remarks in his essay, Mildred Bliss served on the board of

trustees of the Museum of Modern Art in New York, while Robert Woods Bliss was the president of the American Federation of Arts, vice president of the Smithsonian Art Commission, vice president of the board of the National Trust for Historic Preservation, and a trustee of the Santa Barbara Museum of Art.

The ceremony marking the opening of Dumbarton Oaks took place on November 2, 1940, the same winter season when Washington saw yet another illustrious art museum event: the opening of the National Gallery of Art on March 17. An editorial entitled "The Benefits of Great Art" by Forbes Watson, published in the March issue of *Magazine of Art*, discusses the inauguration of Andrew W. Mellon's donation. While proving the point stated in the title of his editorial, Watson does not hesitate to discuss "the heathenish idolatry of wealth," yet asserts that one should not "treat with ingratitude the generosity which [the donors'] excess profits have made so fortunately possible." Furthermore, Watson states that

> [t]he surest road on which to proceed in quest of immortality is the road of art. First on the list of beneficiaries are the artists themselves who create great art. Then, I suppose, would come those men and women for whom art is a living, vital force. These react to the great art of all periods including their own. They encourage the artists of their day, buy and collect their work. Art for them is a going concern, not merely a portion of the burden of the past. These are the immortal collectors. They are necessarily deeper and warmer in their response to art than those collectors who rely upon the test of time and hold themselves aloof from the art of their contemporaries.[39]

THROUGHOUT THEIR LIVES THE BLISSES
believed that strong personal affections and attachments were
an essential component in their efforts as American collectors.

OVER THE THIRTY YEARS PRECEDING THE publication of this editorial, the Blisses, to use Watson's own words, had not been living the life of "collectors who have concentrated on the past and ignored the present." For them art did not "belong to bygone centuries exclusively."[40] The Blisses could not attend the festivities surrounding the opening of the National Gallery of Art because they were in Santa Barbara where Mr. Bliss was recovering from an illness. Still, they made their contribution by offering residence at Dumbarton Oaks to distinguished visitors who came to Washington for the opening. After reading Watson's editorial, Mrs. Bliss wrote a letter on May 27, 1941, to Edward Forbes, director of the Fogg Museum of Art at Harvard University. In this letter, she graciously overlooked the harsh assessment of American collectors and instead noted simply that Watson's essay "on the great Mellon Collection" showed "an unfortunate obliviousness to the affection that collectors feel for the objects they assemble."[41]

Throughout their lives the Blisses believed that strong personal affections and attachments were an essential component in their efforts as American collectors. Indeed, concurrent with their development of Dumbarton Oaks there seems to have been a growing trend in America to embrace its past in a variety of individual ways. As Michael Kammen remarks in analyzing the push to bring about the Mount Rushmore project: "We must recognize the increasing number of people in public life at this time who felt a genuine enthusiasm for American history and traditions."[42] He points out that this project "from its inception in 1924 until its completion in 1939" had a singularly devoted proponent in William Williamson, a congressman from South Dakota, "whose Americanism had roots in a highly personalized past"—that is, his own sense of what each monumental president symbolized for him.[43]

This general trend finds a different expression in the case of the National Gallery. The great American collectors Andrew W. Mellon and Samuel H. Kress reflected in their extensive purchasing of major works by old masters a vision of the American past mostly in terms of its European cultural inheritance. Any truly personal aspect to their achievements is overwhelmed by the sheer scale of these once private collections and by the prominent place they have come to assume as part of a public national institution.

By contrast, Dumbarton Oaks, once an actual private residence, as well as a private collection, was made public by the Blisses and retained the stamp of their personal ideas and individual characters. Thus, Dumbarton Oaks enriches the lives of Americans who come through its doors and enables these visitors to relate to the past, both the specifically American/pre-Columbian inheritance and the European/Byzantine tradition. Robert and Mildred Bliss managed to pull together these elements, and, in so doing, they showed how the arts of these two different traditions anticipated modernity in terms of form and use of materials. This notion was particularly attractive to the Blisses as modern American collectors who always strove to marry the best of the past and the twentieth century. In their sophistication, the Blisses broadened, over the years, their view of American cultural identity; the institution they left behind continues to affect that broadening of perspective in the lives of generations of new seekers of knowledge. ◆

1.   Maguire 1996, 145.

2.   *ODB* 2, 975-977. Also, see Bezançon 2000 and Brubaker and Haldon 2001.

3.   *ODB* 2, 975-977; cf. also Barber 2002, 138-139.

4.   Maguire 1996, 140.

5.   II Corinthians 4:4, "Christ, who is the image of God," and Colossians 1:15, "He is the image of the invisible God."

6.   *ODB* 2, 1282-1283.

7.   The feast is celebrated on the first Sunday of Lent; cf. *ODB* 3, 2122-2123.

8.   Anderson 2000 and Roth 1981.

9.   Barber 2002, 138.

10.   Urbana-Champaign, *Art and Holy Powers* 1989, 1-2.

11.   This argument is eloquently developed in Maguire 1996, esp. 138 and 144.

12.   St. John of Damascus composed the treatise that articulated the Orthodox theory of images; see Anderson 2000. Yet, even well before him, St. Basil the Great (d. 379) stated that "the honor paid to an image passes to its prototype," (*On the Holy Spirit* 18:45). Cf. Roth 1981, 57-58 and Maguire 1996, 137-138.

13.   Ultimately, a substantial gap remained between the theory and the practice of icon veneration. The crucial question that did not find a resolution and that made the shadow of idolatry loom large was "the issue of divine inhabitation of images," to use the expression of Cyril Mango. Cf. Mango 2001, 29.

14.   Roth 1981, 51-59, 78-102.

15.   Maguire 1996, 198.

16.   Translation mine based on Dvornik 1969, 354. Dvornik 1970, 61-62, interprets the debate episode without mentioning the question about inscriptions on icons.

17.   Kirin 1989, 91-92.

18.   Cutler 1987; *ODB* 1, 599-600.

19.   Mango 2001, 29.

20.   Freedberg 1989, 402.

21.   Gemstones, as was the case with other valuable substances such as gold and ivory, became the subject of imperial policy and legislation. Furthermore, there existed regulations according to which private individuals were prohibited from using pearls, emeralds, and sapphires on harness trappings. This was less unjust than it might seem, for those Byzantines who so desired were allowed to use other gemstones on their horse fittings. See *ODB* 2, 828.

22.   Not surprisingly, for the Blisses this concern extended even to the very buildings housing their collection. In his foreword to Tamulevich's book on the gardens of Dumbarton Oaks, the architect Philip Johnson describes what a pleasure it was to work so closely with Mildred Bliss on designing the museum pavilion for her husband's collection of pre-Columbian art. The architect received the commission in 1958. He sums up Mrs. Bliss's positive response to his essentially post-modern building in terms of her visual sensibilities: "She liked materials: the bronze, the marble, the up-ended slate. It was the combination of daring design with the use of conventional, beautiful materials that made it all palatable to her. I guess she didn't even think of the building as modern, just as materials and shapes." Cf. Tamulevich 2001, 20.

23.   Peirce and Tyler 1926, 5.

24. Swarzenski 1941, 77.

25. Peirce and Tyler 1926, 7.

26. Letter to BB of November 30, 1940, Constable 1993, 144.

27. Swarzenski 1941, 77.

28. Reed 1996, 262.

29. Weitzmann 1994, 144-145, 487-488. Between 1946 and 1958, the Blisses and some of their friends donated icons to the Byzantine Collection of Dumbarton Oaks. Cf. *DOCat* 1, nos. 124, 125, 129, 130, 131, as well as Nelson's essay in this catalogue.

30. RT to MBB, August 1, 1935, Tallinn, Estonia, HUA. I would like to thank Dr. Edward L. Keenan for informing me in early 1999 about this trip to Soviet Russia and giving me access to Tyler's letter to Mrs. Bliss.

31. Reed 1996, 73.

32. Ibid., 198.

33. Ibid., 49.

34. Ibid., 401-402.

35. Peirce and Tyler 1926, 5. Notably, Peirce and Tyler's book was a part of *Kai Khosru Monographs on Eastern Art*, which also included volumes on Scythian and Babylonian art.

36. See the epigraph of this catalogue.

37. See the comments on the symbolic significance of the gardens by Michel Conan, director of Landscape Studies at Dumbarton Oaks, cited in Tamulevich 2001, 86-87.

38. Swarzenski 1941, 77-78.

39. Watson 1941, 113.

40. Ibid.

41. See Carder's first essay in this catalogue, note 4.

42. Kammen 1991, 452.

43. Ibid., 453-454.

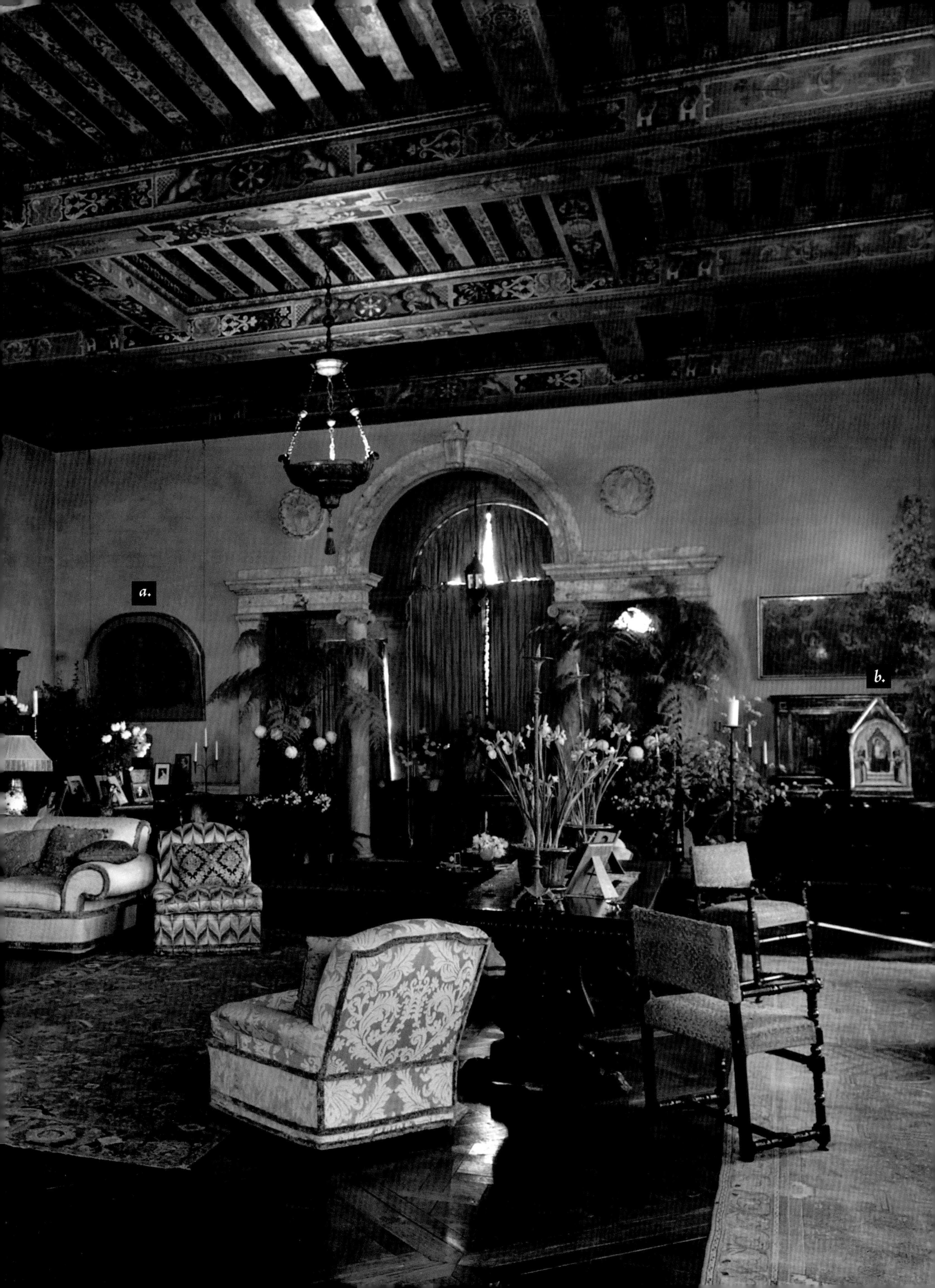
a.
b.

Mildred and Robert Woods Bliss and the Dumbarton Oaks Research Library and Collection

BY JAMES N. CARDER

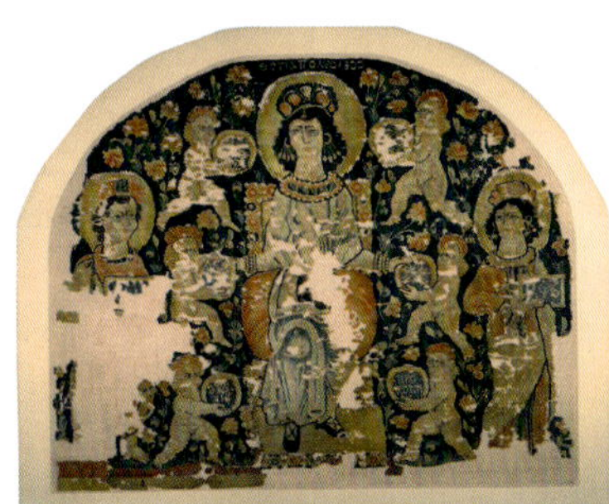

a. (see left)
Hestia Polyolbos
("Hestia—Goddess
of the Hearth—
Rich in Blessings").
Wool tapestry.
Egypt, 6th century,
113 x 137 cm,
Dumbarton Oaks,
acc. no. BZ.1929.1

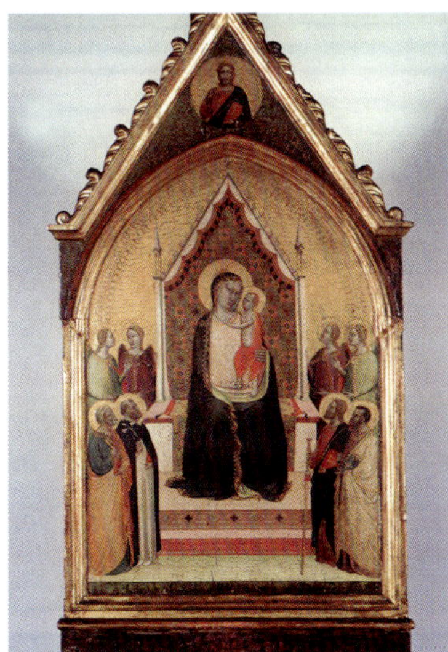

b. (see left)
Bernado Daddi
(active 1320-1348),
Madonna and Child
with Saints and
Angels, 1337,
tempera and
gilding on poplar
panel, Dumbarton
Oaks, acc. no.
HC.P.1936.57.(T)

At Dumbarton Oaks you have created something very beautiful, very special both in the garden and inside the house. It will remain a monument to your taste, knowledge and understanding—a delight to all who visit it and a great resource to those who are fortunate enough to work there. And it is all due to you—to your inspiration, insight and foresight and may you reap the satisfaction and comfort you deserve.[1]

ROBERT WOODS BLISS WROTE THIS TESTIMONY to his wife Mildred on December 3, 1940, four days after their gift of the Dumbarton Oaks Research Library and Collection[2] had legally transferred to Harvard University, Robert Bliss's alma mater.[3] The Blisses had, in fact, created this remarkable property as a joint effort over a twenty-year period, guiding and overseeing the renovation and enlargement of their house, the design of their world-famous gardens, the formation of a museum-quality art collection, and the accumulation of scholarly resources— books and photographs—that would enable the academic community to understand better their art collection and the cultures that it represented. Rather than waiting until their deaths for this gift to be realized, the Blisses had chosen to witness their dream during their lifetimes, and they would continue to support and develop this unique institution until Robert Bliss's death at the age of eighty-six in 1962 and Mildred Bliss's death at the age of eighty-nine in 1969. Robert Bliss articulated their purpose at the dedication ceremony on November 1, 1940: "There was a need in this country, we thought, of a quiet place where the advanced students and scholars could withdraw, the one to mellow and develop, the other to write the result of a life's study."[4]

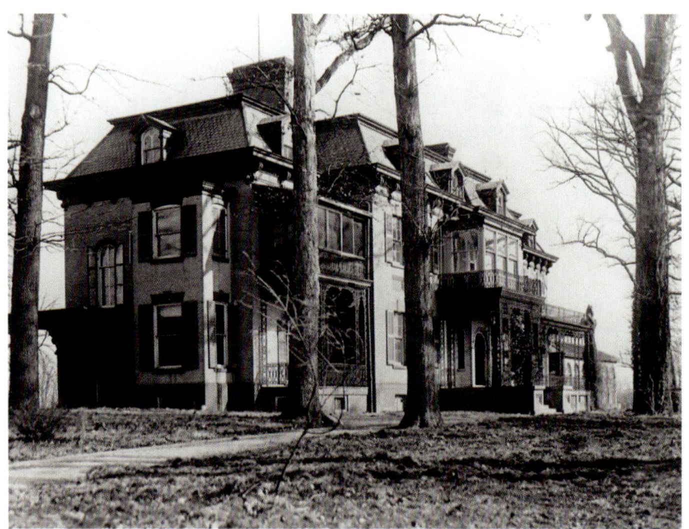

Figure 1. The Oaks viewed from the southwest, c. 1920.

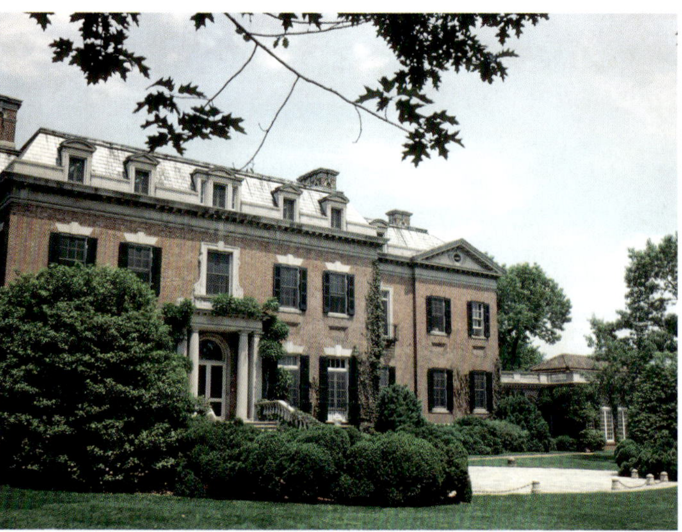

Figure 2. Dumbarton Oaks, Main House, as redesigned, c. 1921-1923, by Frederick H. Brooke, Washington, D.C.

DUMBARTON OAKS, THE RESIDENCE

MILDRED AND ROBERT WOODS BLISS purchased the property they would later name Dumbarton Oaks on June 30, 1920, for $180,000.[5] Having married in 1908, the Blisses had come to Washington, D.C., in 1919, following a succession of Robert Bliss's overseas postings in the Foreign Service. With his assignment to the Department of State in Washington in 1920, the Blisses were in a position to realize their shared goal of having a permanent residence in the United States or, more particularly, as Robert Bliss later reminisced, to fulfill a dream "during the years of professional nomadism" of having "a country house in the city."[6] Dumbarton Oaks was to be the realization of this dream.

The house that the Blisses purchased in 1920 was much altered from its initial 1801 construction. The original Federal house, built by William Hammond Dorsey, had been a two-story brick structure with a center stair hall that separated a parlor and dining room on the ground floor and two bedrooms on the upper floor. In the third quarter of the nineteenth century, a wealthy owner, Edward Magruder Linthicum, considerably enlarged the central block by adding at the back an enclosed double-staircase gallery with a polygonal tower—essentially a long cross hall that eliminated the need for a staircase in the entrance hall. He also had built an L-shaped kitchen and dining wing on the east side of the house, an addition with *porte-cochère* at the west, and a full attic enclosed within a mansard roofline. Magruder annexed to the house the formerly freestanding greenhouse (or orangery) of early nineteenth-century date, creating through these additions a mansion of impressive dimensions, having a front range of over 216 feet (fig. 1).[7] The enlarged dwelling, which he named The Oaks, fronted what is now R Street in the Georgetown section of Washington, D.C., and sat at the height of ungraded pastures and woodlands that dropped steeply away from the house to the north and east. This land had once been part of 795 acres that Queen Anne had granted in 1703 to Ninian Beall, who gave it its first name, the Rock of Dumbarton, after the landmark in his native Scotland and its supposed resemblance to the Beall grant. The Blisses, who would as early as 1933 rename the property Dumbarton Oaks by combining its two historic names,[8] would also augment their initial six-acre purchase by acquiring, between 1921 and 1932, considerable parcels of the surrounding land, spending an additional $975,000 to increase their holdings to more than 53 acres.[9] In a letter dated August 13, 1925, Robert Bliss was able to write his wife: "Dumbarton is heavenly … and now that we have the hillside and need no longer worry lest that become covered with 'homes' we have an outlook which is unique for a city house and we can look forward to the realization of our dream in a garden of enchantment."

In 1921, the Blisses embarked on a three-year renovation of the "old-fashioned house standing in rather neglected grounds, encumbered with farm buildings," under the direction of the Washington, D.C., architect Frederick H. Brooke. Their aim was to strip the house of its nineteenth-century accretions while at the same time retaining its size and grandeur. To this end, Brooke removed the various bays and cast-iron-covered verandas that supported second-floor balconies and sleeping porches. He erected a west wing symmetrical in design to the east wing, thereby creating in effect pavilions connected to the main block by recessed extension bays. He also added a classical, colonnaded front porch, redesigned the rear polygonal tower as an elliptical exedra, and removed the gray paint that covered the exterior brickwork. The result was the creation of a unified Georgian-style mansion (fig. 2). Brooke further removed the farm dependency

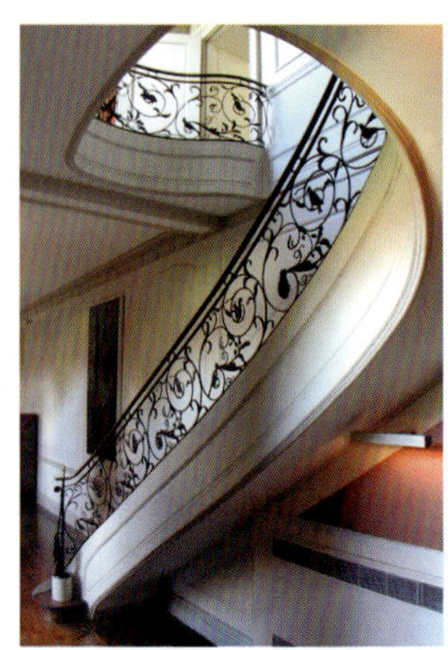

Figure 3. West staircase, first floor gallery, Dumbarton Oaks, designed and fabricated by Samuel Yellin (1885-1940), Philadelphia, PA, c. 1923.

buildings, substituting, in part, a swimming pool, changing pavilion, and tennis court. Similarly, Brooke extensively renovated the interior of the house, installing in most rooms random-width floorboards, pediments over doors and windows, and raised paneling on the walls. These last were capped by classically inspired entablature moldings and, in the principal rooms, molded plaster ceiling medallion frames. Among the more unusual additions were two matching iron staircase railings, placed on the inner walls at either end of the long back gallery, that comprised openwork twining oak branches populated with birds and animals (fig. 3). The Philadelphia ironsmith Samuel Yellin designed and fabricated these railings on commission. Yellin also supplied the exterior first-floor balcony railings and grills, as well as the sculpted downspout scuppers, each of a unique design and each in its imagery relevant to either Dumbarton Oaks or the Blisses.

I N THE SAME YEAR THAT RENOVATION COMMENCED, Mildred Bliss began planning for the transformation of the farmlands surrounding the house into terraced gardens and vistas; she envisioned an estate that progressed from formal and elegant stepped terraces, in the near vicinity of the house, to a more recreational and practical middle zone of pools, tennis court, orchards, vegetable beds, and cutting gardens, and concluding at the far reaches of the property with a rustic wilderness of meadows and streams. She was assisted and inspired in this transformation by the landscape designer Beatrix Jones Farrand, with whom she first met at Dumbarton Oaks on January 25, 1921, and with whom she would closely collaborate as her "gardening twin" until Farrand's gradual retirement from the project in the late 1940s and early 1950s. Mildred Bliss also involved herself in the renovation of the house and its interiors and attempted a similar collaboration with Frederick Brooke. To this end, she wrote Frank Alvah Parsons, founder and director of the New York School of Fine and Applied Art (now the Parsons School of Design), of which she was a benefactor, inquiring whether he could recommend a young design student who could facilitate her "cooperation with the architect's office," as she put it. "It would be of great help if some one of your students could spend several weeks in Washington, expressing on paper the ideas of which my head is full, but which I cannot, unfortunately, draw." She dispatched this student almost immediately to Charleston, South Carolina, to make measured drawings of details of exterior and interior trim that she wanted to implement at Dumbarton Oaks.

Despite this involvement and seeming enthusiasm, Mildred Bliss had been initially reluctant to commit to the purchase and renovation of Dumbarton Oaks, and she seems to have been somewhat mistrustful of Brooke's design decisions once the work began.[10] Robert Bliss attempted to reassure her of the importance of their decision, writing her in Paris on August 19, 1921: "Altho' Fred may not be as resourceful as Pope or White, I think it would have been impossible to have worked satisfactorily on such a problem as altering the Oaks with an architect from another city. I too, dear heart, have my days of wishing that I had never bought the Oaks, and that we might be care free without the responsibility which that place will bring to us, and yet I know that it was a sensible step to take and that in the years to come we will be happy in possessing it and living there. It is all very well to be care free and loose, but we must have roots, and these roots

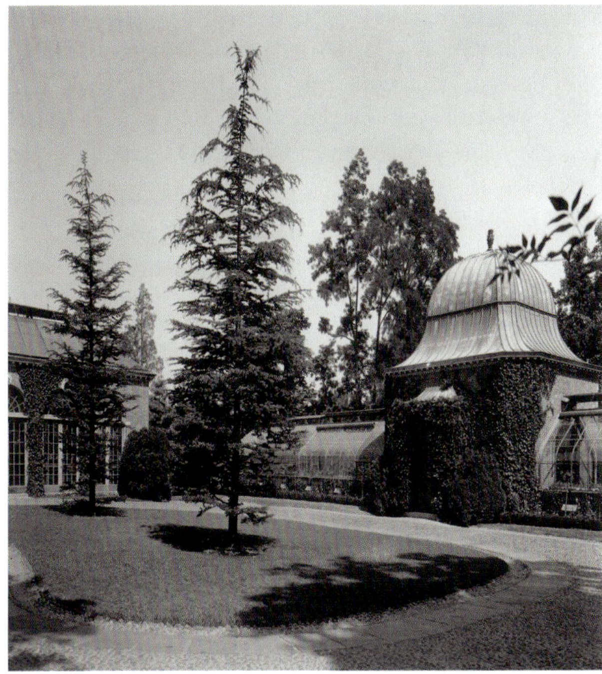

Figure 4. *Service Court, Green House, and Orangery (Cool House), c. 1932, as designed by Lawrence Grant White.*

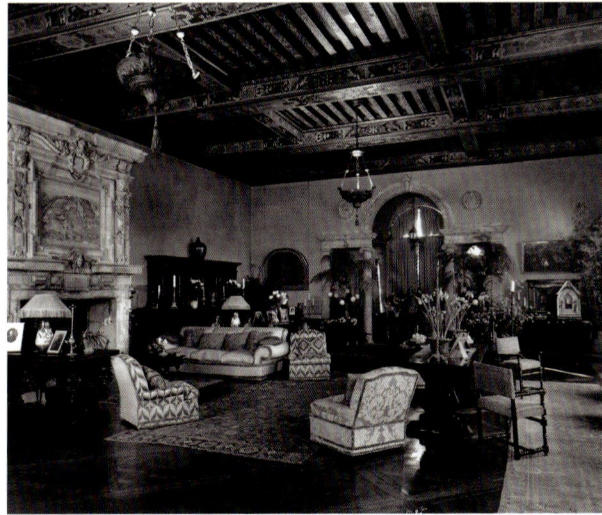

Figure 5. *Music Room, Dumbarton Oaks, c. 1940, as designed and built by Lawrence Grant White with ceiling and floor designed and fabricated by Armand Albert Rateau, Paris.*

to flourish and nourish themselves must be deep in native soil."

As the first phase of renovation neared completion in 1923, Robert Bliss was named U.S. Minister to Sweden, and the Blisses decided that work would continue at Dumbarton Oaks in their absence.[11] This phase, however, would involve the collaboration of a new architect, Lawrence Grant White of the New York architectural firm of McKim, Mead and White, with Beatrix Farrand, who also maintained an office in New York. Beginning in 1923, White designed four Georgian-style dependency buildings known as the Service Court, which lay to the northwest of the house: the Gardener's Cottage, a duplex for the head gardener and butler; a small Orangery (later called the Cool House); a double-winged greenhouse attached to a central brick potting shed; and a garage and dormitory for male staff (fig. 4). This complex was finished in 1929.

The most important alteration to the property in this period, however, was the construction of a large Music Room attached to the west wing of the house, which White designed and built between 1926 and 1929 (fig. 5).[12] This room more than any other in the house would come to embody both the Blisses' taste as collectors and connoisseurs and their vision for the recreated Dumbarton Oaks. Provisioned with magnificent works of art and furnishings, this room would convey to Harvard University—purposely unaltered—as a space suitable for both refined musical programs, scholarly lectures, and intellectual discourse.

As EARLY AS 1924, THE BLISSES HAD BEGUN PLANning for the Music Room addition. They wanted the room to be essentially Renaissance in character (or, rather, "Mediterranean," as White called it in his correspondence of December 4, 1924, to Mildred Bliss), but they also wanted the addition to harmonize with the Georgian style of the main house. Robert Bliss had already envisioned the character of the room by August 25, 1926, when he wrote White: "We see marbré-stucco wainscot in music room; rough plaster walls; a very good polychromed ceiling (shall it be old or copied?); the best big mantle we can find, and we want a fine floor."[13] On December 29, Bliss again wrote White: "All things being equal, we do not want modern mechanical and structural details to intrude themselves on the impression of the whole, which we hope to make mellow and old-fashioned." The Blisses considered adding a double- or triple-arched window on the south wall to the right of the fireplace. Robert Bliss wrote White on January 20, 1927: "This was very successfully done in Italy and Spain and we do not think it would be inharmonious with the rest of the music-room, which, after all, is a delightful medley of Italian renaissance, French eighteenth century, Georgian and American!" After seeing White's model for the Music Room, Bliss wrote in the same correspondence: "It shows that you sense just what we want—simplicity, broad lines, large space…. It is all bearing fruit."

Late in 1926, the Blisses had found two Italian Renaissance, sixteenth-century marble arches, said to be from Ravenna, which they purchased for the equivalent of $6,700 from Bacri Frères, a Parisian antiques dealer, in early 1927. The acquisition of the arches for the Music Room firmly established the room's aesthetic quality. Soon after, it prompted the inclusion of similar marble for the floor edging

and, at the west end of the room, for the large Palladian arch surround and columns that were commissioned from the Standard Art Marble and Tile Company, Washington, D.C., for $16,260.[14]

The Blisses wanted an antique Renaissance ceiling and flooring for the Music Room, and, on October 13, 1926, Robert Bliss wrote White: "We are starting people to hunt for old ceilings and old floors for the music room and will let you know what success we have in this quest." Although they did locate an antique ceiling, which later proved to be of inadequate size for adaptation, in 1927 the Blisses commissioned a reproduction sixteenth-century painted French ceiling and reproduction seventeenth-century "Versailles-pattern" parquet flooring. These were inspired by examples at the guardroom of the Château de Cheverny near Paris, and the Blisses commissioned the Parisian designer Armand Albert Rateau to fabricate both. On August 6, 1928, Rateau wrote White that he was shipping the ceiling immediately: "It is the first time that an ensemble of such importance has been executed with so much regard for exactitude and I shall be very happy to have your opinion as soon as possible [McKim, Mead and White office translation]." By November 12, the ceiling was installed, having cost $32,000. When Robert Bliss returned on March 1, 1929, for a first visit to Dumbarton Oaks since his ambassadorial posting in Buenos Aires, he cabled White: "Just arrived and thoroughly delighted [with] our Music Room."

It was probably Lawrence Grant White who suggested that the Blisses engage the American artist Allyn Cox to paint murals for the

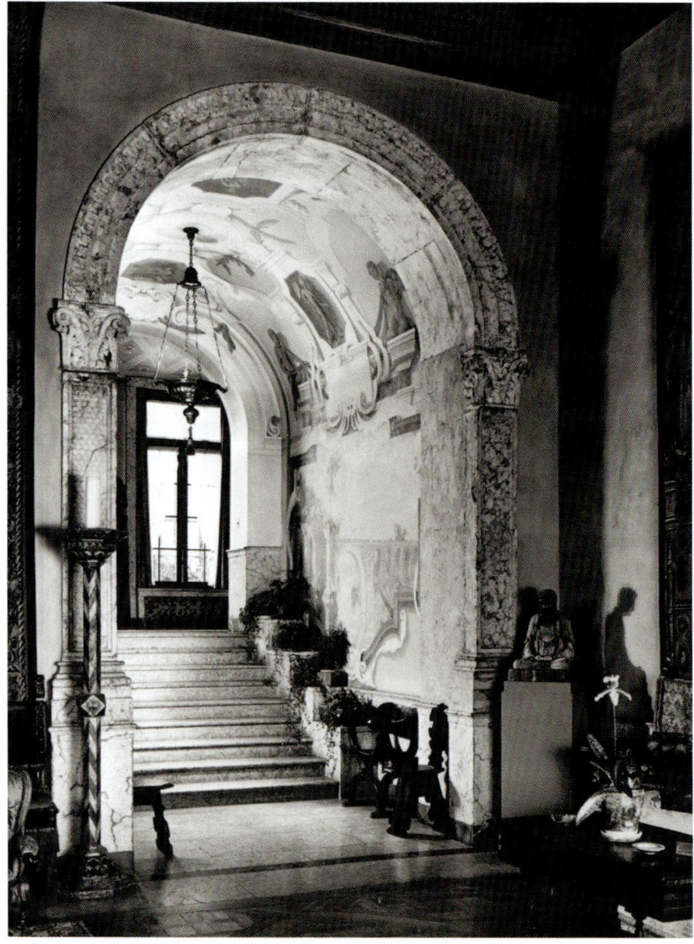

Figure 6. Entrance staircase, Music Room, Dumbarton Oaks, c. 1940, with canvas murals by Allyn Cox (1896-1982) and Italian Renaissance sixteenth-century marble arch.

walls of the Music Room corridor and entrance staircase (as well as the swimming pool loggia). On January 9, 1927, Cox delivered sketches for this project with estimates of $4,000 for the corridor and $5,000 for the staircase. The staircase murals—the more ambitious of the two Music Room projects—had a vault compartmentalized by *trompe-l'oeil* Baroque-style architectural frames of simulated white and variegated red and green marble stonework. Within the principal frames to the left and right of the staircase were depictions of classical architectural ruins and various Italian Renaissance-style buildings, as well as humans resting or engaged in work activities, much in the manner of eighteenth-century paintings of classical ruins (fig. 6). Indeed, the nature and style of the Cox paintings may relate directly to four late eighteenth-century pendant canvases of classical ruins attributed to Hubert Robert that the Blisses owned and that White envisioned installed in the Music Room corridor.[15]

The last architectural feature to be acquired for the Music Room was a French Renaissance, sixteenth-century stone (*pierre de Dordogne*) mantelpiece that the Blisses purchased for $15,000 on May 4, 1929, from Arnold Seligmann, Rey and Company, Inc., a New York antiques dealer. The mantel originally came from the Château de Théobon, Loubès-Bernac, France, but had been found lying in pieces on a farm in southern France. In 1935, the Blisses commissioned a watercolor and ink topographical plan of the Dumbarton Oaks house and gardens from the American cartographer Ernest Clegg, and they installed the watercolor rendering in the empty overmantel frame at the center of the upper section.

The Music Room was fully appointed by the time of Robert Bliss's retirement in 1933. On June 28, 1929, the Blisses had purchased Italian Renaissance furniture from the Brambilla collection at the Villa Farnese, Caprarola (near Rome). The acquired pieces included an important late fifteenth-century intarsia-decorated book cabinet whose inlaid inscription, *Quiescit Anima Libris* ("The soul finds respite in books"), came to serve as one of the mottos of the research institution.[16] Originally, the room employed important antique rugs, the most significant of which were an early fifteenth-century Spanish armorial rug and a sixteenth-century Ottoman rug from Cairo, both purchased in 1933 and both now in the collection of the Textile Museum, Washington, D.C. Other rugs displayed in the room included three rare sixteenth-century Persian Isfahans and a seventeenth-century Mogul Seven Mihrab (Saf) prayer rug.

The Blisses as Collectors and Royall Tyler

Mildred Bliss had developed early the interests and tastes of a collector,[17] and, with their marriage, Robert Bliss quickly came to equal his wife's passion to collect. He later recounted that on the day in 1912 when the Blisses' close friend Royall Tyler first brought him to the Parisian dealer Joseph Brummer to see pre-Columbian objects, "the collector's microbe took root in … very fertile soil."[18] It is eminently possible, in fact, that the Blisses would not have sought out or formed the collections that eventually became their legacy had they not been close friends with Royall "Peter" Tyler, whom Mildred Bliss had known since childhood. It is evident from their correspondence that Tyler's enthusiasm, connoisseurship, and, especially, his "phenomenal acquaintance with works of art of great diversity"[19]—as evidenced in his impassioned descriptions of art and his admonishments for or against certain objects or artists—both piqued the Blisses' interest as collectors and propelled them in like-minded directions. During the years of Robert Bliss's diplomatic posting in Paris as secretary of the embassy (1912-1916) and counselor of the embassy (1916-1919), Royall Tyler's ability to direct the Blisses to important Byzantine and pre-Columbian dealers and objects proved inestimable to their ultimate success as collectors. Tyler's similar enthusiasm for such things as Gothic art, the Italian "primitives," tapestries and textiles, ceramics, the Spanish Baroque, and especially the artist El Greco would also equally influence the Blisses' tastes and their ultimate art collection. What has come to be called their House Collection—the art and objects that filled the interiors of Dumbarton Oaks—should be credited in large part to Royall Tyler's remarkable perceptions and influence. Between approximately 1912 and 1953, when he died, Tyler would seek out and recommend art objects that he believed were of the kind and quality that the Blisses should collect. On occasion he would even purchase art for them on his own initiative, using reserve funds provided by the Blisses to ensure that important finds were not lost to other collectors or dealers.

Above all else, the Blisses responded sympathetically to Royall Tyler's passion for art of the highest aesthetic quality and his championship of the arcane and the underappreciated in the art world. In 1904, at the age of twenty, Tyler wrote Mildred Bliss from New College, Oxford, where he was enrolled: "I wish you could see my picture [an Italian primitive]. I am devoted to it, all the more so that there are very few people who really care a scrap for an old picture." Similarly, in 1906, he wrote her: "I have been horribly worried by Americans in the last months. I fear I have made a few enemies, but that is always better than making a lot of suffocating friends, which is the fate of every American I know who lives here. They see no one but other Americans and an occasional foreigner who wants meals, and they occupy themselves with—art. The horrible stagnation of it! They have their people they admire, their modern and ancient painters, and they all conform." After a visit to Greece, he confessed to Mildred Bliss that the art of the age of Phidias moved him little and that he much preferred the sixth-century BCE fragments in the Acropolis museum and the metopes at Delphi. He expressed delight on learning that Phidias left Mildred Bliss "cold" as well.[20] On August 23, 1929, Mildred Bliss would recommend Tyler to her friend Geoffrey Dodge: "If you want to learn some very useful and fundamental facts about art, see as much of Royall as you can. His learning is thorough and uncommonly wide, and as he follows all the sales of interest, and has a standard of measurement from his unusual familiarity with all the museums and most of the private collections of Europe, he is by way of having much to contribute."[21]

Occasionally, Royall Tyler and the Blisses differed in their opinions on art, but in such cases Tyler would neither back down nor give up on his efforts to educate and convert them. His love of the Spanish Baroque, which he first encountered during his studies at the University of Salamanca, is a case in point. In 1906 he wrote Mildred Bliss: "I am starting for Spain in a few days. I will try to

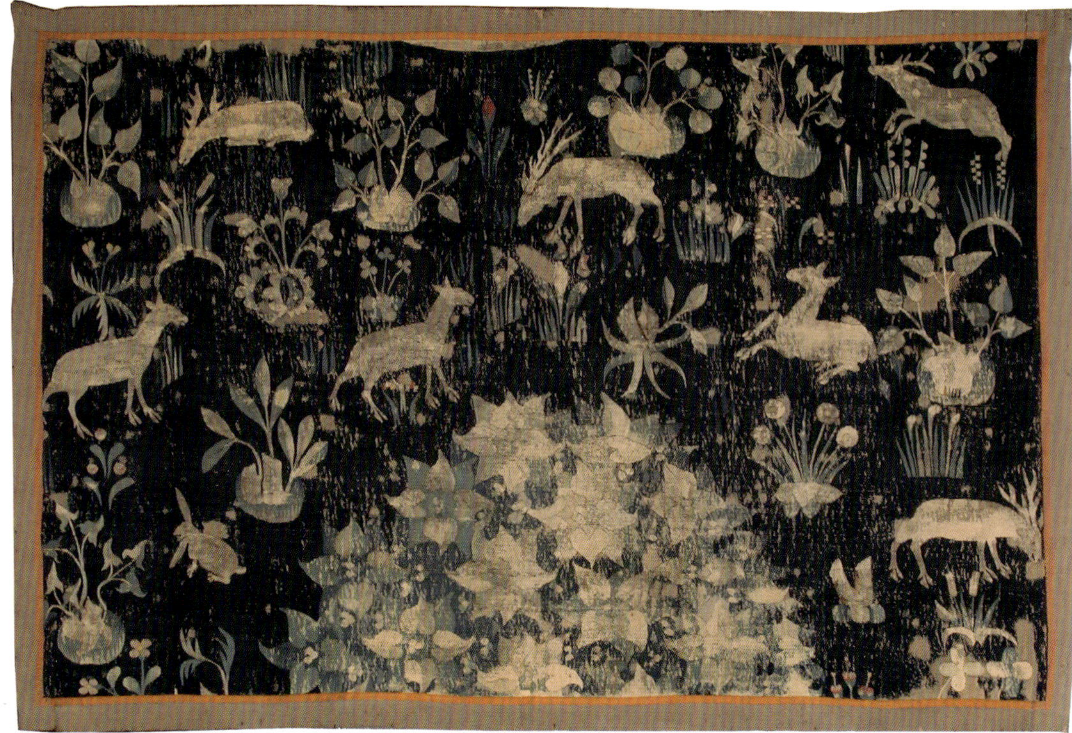

follow your advice as nearly as possible, but I cannot promise to beware of Baroque. Oysters I will forego. In fact I intend to look mostly for Baroque. I rather think it is the most individual of the Spanish styles." Later, in an undated correspondence of 1907, he admitted: "I am now an open and shameless devotee of the base Baroque, not the whole Baroque, only the Spanish. But won't you join with me about the Spanish Baroque? I did it all myself. I don't know a human being with any capability of passion in such matters who agrees with me." In 1913, the Blisses requested his opinion on two expensive tapestries that they liked and on which they had options to purchase with the Parisian dealers Bacri Frères and Van Straaten. Tyler wrote Robert Bliss:

> I have been to Bacri Freres [*sic*] since I saw you last, and have seen the tapestry…. In brief, the piece is interesting and in parts beautiful, but to my taste not a supremely fine thing. What I do wholeheartedly admire at Bacri's is a much smaller and earlier square of tapestry, simply plants and animals—stags, horses, a rabbit, etc. Besides being of a period that produced the most beautiful tapestry we know, it is in itself exceedingly sensitive and distinguished in drawing…. I think it is one of the most beautiful bits of the art of tapestry I have ever seen…. Make Mildred see the small piece.

Two weeks later he saw the other tapestry at Van Straaten's:

> What, to sum up, prevents me from liking the thing is that it is the work of a vulgar designer full of nothing but the desire to make people say that his tapestry looked like painting, and who had entirely lost sight of the lines tapestry must follow. There's no choice. In spite of its sumptuousness, its wonderful state of preservation, its lovely colour, the thing has no more art in it than—prepare yourself—a Chinese lacquer screen. I believe we shall live to see the day when the little piece Bacri has will be worth more money. It certainly is immeasurably finer in every respect…. Once you have a piece like that in your house, and it sinks into your eyes, you would be unable to put up with the other, except as part of

a general scheme of decoration, and if you want that, Van Straaten himself has 17th cent. Brussels tapestries at about ¹⁄₂₀ the price of the other, and much better as tapestry: much more within tapestry possibilities. Not that I care so very much for them. But when one considers that at the present day, owing to the prevalent vulgarity among rich people, the worst among the great classes of tapestry are far more expensive than the best, one stops and wonders what is the reason. Is it because people insist on thinking that tapestry is fine in proportion as it apes painting? Is it because the metal thread enmeshes them?—Metal thread! Unless used with exceeding discretion and a most sparing hand, metal thread always indicates perversion in tapestry; and the needle veers 'round in the direction of Morgan.

The Blisses would acquire for 28,000 francs ($4,875) "the little piece" from Bacri but neither of the other two tapestries. The Bacri tapestry remains in the Dumbarton Oaks House Collection (fig. 7).[22]

Royall Tyler's first experience of Byzantine art, which he would research and champion for the remainder of his life, was in the summer of 1900 while on a vacation in Venice with his mother.[23] His acquisition in 1913 of an important Byzantine silver chalice (see Nelson, fig. 5), perhaps more than any other event, ignited the spark of collecting excitement that would consume both the Blisses and Tyler.[24] Tyler recounted to the Blisses the details of the chalice purchase and how he had waited in the wings while the dealer Brummer refused three offers from the wealthy Belgian collector Adolphe Stoclet for a group of objects including the chalice: "Brummer said he must decide at once or he would not undertake not to sell in the meantime. Stoclet thought it prudent to disregard this, and five minutes after he'd turned his back, I was running home, *toreando los automobiles por la calle* [fighting traffic] with *la santissima* under my arm." The euphoria of this event was repeated some eleven years later when Tyler recommended that the Blisses purchase the now-famous Riha paten (see Nelson, fig. 6), which was from the same silver treasure hoard as the chalice. He concluded his impassioned appraisal by writing:

Eventually, give it [the paten] to the Cabinet des Médailles, the only place in the world I know of that's fit to receive it. I hope some day to give my chalice to the Cabinet des Médailles, but have said no word about it to anyone and will ask you to say none…. The Cabinet des Médailles [is] the one museum that has an atmosphere in which works of art live, glow sleek and glossy and are patently as happy as they would be in any well-appointed private house…. You may imagine how excited I am. The thought of your having it intoxicates me, and it would be a happiness for life to think that the two pieces would one day be joined together and live happily ever after at the C. des M.[25]

The Bliss paten and the Tyler chalice now reside together in the Dumbarton Oaks Byzantine Collection in the Blisses' former "well-appointed private house."

Royall Tyler was also instrumental in increasing Robert Bliss's pre-Columbian collection, and Bliss would at one point cable him: "Although Aztec is not Byzantine [I] have complete confidence as always [in] your judgment."[26] Tyler was able occasionally to secure large numbers of objects for the Blisses as in 1929, when he commissioned the dealer Kalebdjian to bid for various objects at the Rosenberg sale in Berlin. On November 8, with the conclusion of the sale, Tyler wrote Bliss recounting how one transaction had been advantageously realized:

Prices at the Rosenberg sale went high…. However, I did get for you three lots of Pre-Columbian gold objects, some of which look superb in the catalogue, and Kaleb. says they are much better than they look in reproduction. These—there are some 30 odd pieces, all gold and some fairly large, I got, all together, for 181, which is very cheap. Kaleb. had recourse to a little device to get them. I think you'll laugh. They were right at the end of the second day of the sale. Kaleb. saw some people, at the exhibition before the sale started, examining them, and overheard them saying that as they weren't interested in anything but the American objects, they would come in late on the second day. So, early in the proceedings on the second day, Kaleb. went up to the auctioneer, told him that he had got to catch a train, and induced him to put up the Am. things at once, out of the numerical order, with the result that Kaleb. bought them without the competition of the amateurs, who when they arrived found the bird had flown. You'll like those objects, there are birds, frogs, little people, all sorts of things, all in gold.[27]

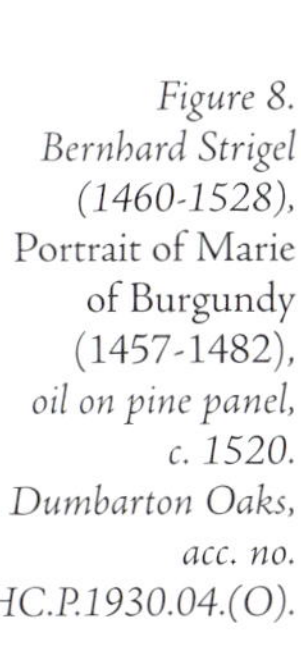

DURING THE YEARS OF ROBERT BLISS'S DIPLOmatic postings, the couple also acquired significant works of art outside the Byzantine and pre-Columbian fields. In these acquisitions, as with those of their primary areas of interest, aesthetic quality and visual interest rather than fashion were primary motivating factors. Their first major acquisition after purchasing Dumbarton Oaks in 1920 was an early Rembrandt portrait of his father as St. Bartholomew. As was true of many of their purchases made before Robert Bliss's retirement in 1933, their inability to see firsthand important pieces offered on the market required that they rely on the judgment of trusted friends. While Royall Tyler was chief among those, this group also included the expatriate American artist and close friend Walter Gay and the designer Geoffrey Dodge, who, like Gay, lived in France and who was instrumental in the renovation of the Blisses' Parisian apartment on the rue Henri-Moisson. Concerning the Rembrandt, which Dodge

had learned was for sale from the collection of the Comte de Leusse and which he recommended for purchase, Mildred Bliss wrote him on December 2, 1920: "I hope Robert's telegram about the Rembrandt reached you promptly. Only the unusual combination of your, Walter Gay's and [Abraham] Bredius's three verdicts would warrant our going ahead without having seen the picture ourselves, but I feel sure about it and more eager than I can say to have it come here. Do have it shipped promptly." Similarly, in 1927, the Blisses purchased a Guardi canal scene from the Société Anonyme Ffoulkes [Abdy and Company, Paris], and on December 5, Robert Bliss wrote the dealer, Sir Robert Abdy: "As it is contrary to our custom and principles to make purchases of art objects from photographs, we broke a family rule in succumbing to that picture, but we were glad to follow your suggestion of having someone pass judgment on it, for the photograph indicated it to be a very fine canvas. Our advices were enthusiastic—and the rule was broken!"[28]

On September 29 and 30, 1930, art assembled by the Viennese collector Albert Figdor was auctioned in Berlin. On Royall Tyler's recommendation, the Blisses were interested in two German paintings: a Hieronymus Bosch and a Bernhard Strigel portrait of Marie of Burgundy (fig. 8). Although Mildred Bliss's fortune was conservatively invested in a trust, mainly in government vehicles, the Blisses were hesitant to spend large amounts in the early years of the Depression, and Mildred Bliss would write Royall Tyler in October 1930: "Our bank accnt. is low. Although we've come through the crash unscathed there is a temporary shrinkage. We're not worried but don't feel like drawing on capital." Nevertheless, the Blisses authorized limits to attempt to acquire the Bosch and Strigel, the latter of which Tyler was able to win at 67,800 DM [$20,550]. The day of the sale,

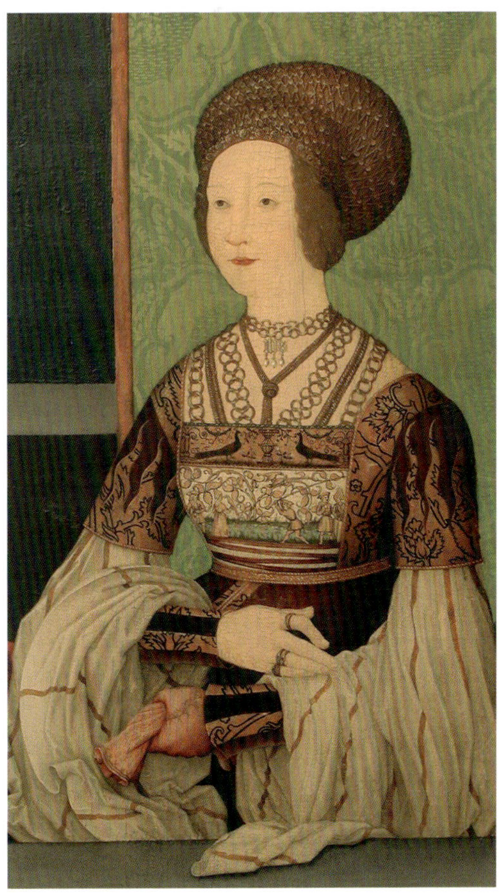

Figure 8. Bernhard Strigel (1460-1528), Portrait of Marie of Burgundy (1457-1482), oil on pine panel, c. 1520. Dumbarton Oaks, acc. no. HC.P.1930.04.(O).

he wrote Mildred Bliss: "You'll like Marie de Bourgogne. She is fresh and very pretty indeed, and in excellent state. The only picture in the sale except the Bosch—and now you've got her I don't think you'll need another German picture…. It came at a moment when everyone in the sale was at a low ebb, and many had already gone off to lunch, or Marie might have gone much higher, I should think."[29]

Royall Tyler's interests in and prejudices against certain art undeniably and greatly influenced the Blisses in their collecting. Already on October 10, 1905, at age twenty-one, Tyler had written Mildred Bliss: "People are finally waking up to the fact that El Greco is one of the greatest painters of all time…. Also I like Dutch pictures more and more—de Hoogh and Jan Steen and a certain I. Ver Meer, and of course the really big ones, Rembrandt and Hals. Also I like less and less the Florentines, and more and more the Venetians, Milanese, etc. I have always nourished a dislike for Botticelli, and the gang, including Perugino, and Raphael, except some splendid portraits." It is not mere coincidence then that among the Blisses' subsequent major art purchases were paintings by El Greco, Rembrandt, Hals, the minor Dutch painter Carel Fabritius, Italian "primitives" by Bernardo Daddi, Gentile da Fabriano, the Venetian Jacobello del Fiore and a fifteenth-century *desco da parto* from the Ferrara School, and none by those artists denigrated on Tyler's list. It was the art styles of "primitive" visual expressiveness and visual power as well as the qualities of the unaccustomed and unknown found in "archaeological" art that excited Royall Tyler, and his enthusiasm for this non-classical canon also excited the Blisses in their collecting. On November 9, 1911, Tyler wrote Mildred Bliss: "I would give anything to know primitive painting in and out; it is always the art that most delights me, and seems ever deeper. What I respect in it above all is the enamel like quality of the paint, that hardens with time into the consistency of precious stones and takes all their brilliancy. Among the painters of the Renaissance only one man knew how to make pigment with these properties, and he was El Greco. His pictures will be as clear as when painted when all but a few Titians will be like mud." By February 5, 1931, the Blisses' adoption of Tyler's particular passions would enable Mildred Bliss to summarize enthusiastically for Geoffrey Dodge the pace and scope of their collecting: "Last year we made one or two good bags—a German primitive painting, an Assyrian bas-relief, a white [archaic Chinese] jade blade and an entrancing Coptic Jewel. If you want to know what is going on in the world of archaeological art, you had better dine with Royall."

DUMBARTON OAKS, THE INSTITUTION

As early as 1932, the Blisses began to set in motion a plan to leave Dumbarton Oaks and their collection to Harvard University at the time of the death of the surviving spouse. In making this decision and in the early stages of their planning, the Blisses increasingly relied on the collaboration and endorsement of Paul Sachs, Harvard professor and associate director of the Fogg Museum of Art (as the Fogg Art Museum was then called).[30] In a lengthy letter of July 19, 1932, to the lawyer Alfred Gregory, Sachs attempted to articulate the rationale behind the Blisses' intention—as well as his own philosophy on the importance of the fine arts in the life of a nation—in order to enable the lawyer "to draw up a legal document which might someday indicate clearly to the President and Fellows of Harvard College and to the Directors of the Fogg Museum of Art the grandiose scheme that Mr. and Mrs. Robert Bliss have thought about so much." As Sachs envisioned Dumbarton Oaks at this early stage, he saw it as the logical development of the "Fogg idea." As he explained:

> [I]t is perfectly clear to all of us that the older generation of teachers would be immensely benefited if, now and again, they could be set free to finish a book or to carry on a further investigation under the sheltering arm of the Bliss Institute…. So you see the thought that underlies the Bliss Foundation has, ever since 1916, been put into practice right here [at the Fogg] in a very limited fashion, because, as I say, we have only one such fellowship <u>but</u> the benefits that have accrued to the country from the existence of this one single fellowship have convinced [Edward] Forbes and me that what Mr. and Mrs. Bliss propose on such a grandiose scale is bound to lead to highly satisfactory results, and particularly if under the guidance of the Fogg Museum, young and older scholars of trained ability may be drawn to the Bliss Institute, not only from Harvard, but from other institutions like Princeton, Yale, University of Chicago, etc.

On August 4, 1935, only two years after the Blisses had begun permanent residency at Dumbarton Oaks, their lawyers drafted three "instruments which might be available for use should you decide to make immediately effective the plan for the disposition of Dumbarton Oaks set forth in your wills": (1) a Deed to the United States of America [for the gift of Dumbarton Oaks Park to the National Park Service]; (2) an Instrument of Conveyance and Assignment, conveying the house and its contents at Dumbarton Oaks to Harvard University; and (3) an Assignment of a maintenance fund to Harvard University.[31] In 1936, the Blisses began negotiations to establish a formal affiliation between Dumbarton Oaks and the Fogg with the express intention of giving Dumbarton Oaks and their collection to Harvard during their lifetimes, thereby creating the Dumbarton Oaks Research Library and Collection.[32] On March 4, 1937, Paul Sachs received "authority from the President to proceed in all matters that pertain to our 'affiliation' in any direction that may seem wise." This authority included appointing Marvin Ross, then at the Walters Art Museum, to catalogue the Byzantine Collection and hiring Barbara Sessions, who had worked with Bernard Berenson at I Tatti, to build and catalogue the research library. Sachs also succeeded in affiliating Dumbarton Oaks with the *Princeton Index of Christian Art*, launching the *Census of Early Christian and Byzantine Objects*, and establishing the format of the *Dumbarton Oaks Papers*. The announcement of the affiliation was drafted in 1937:

> It is a great pleasure to announce that the Dumbarton Oaks Collection in Washington owned by the Honorable Robert Woods Bliss, Class of 1900, and Mrs. Bliss, has become affiliated with the Fogg Museum of Art. The collection includes important objects of Byzantine and Early Medieval art (textiles, liturgical objects, sculpture, ivories, enamels), as well as examples of painting and sculpture from other periods in the history of European and Far Eastern Art. The Fogg Museum is cooperating in building up at Dumbarton Oaks a distinguished collection of books, photographs, and other material for the study of Early Christian and Byzantine Art.[33]

The Blisses' conception for the Dumbarton Oaks Collection—modeled in large part on the Fogg Museum of Art and its relationship to Harvard University and, perhaps more important, as guided by Paul Sachs—was based on the belief that the objects of their collection were paramount to the Blisses' interest in furthering humanistic research. This object-centered or "material culture" approach to scholarship was not uncommon during the first half of the twentieth century. It was undertaken not only by art historians, but also by historians and philologists and was often the primary focus of archaeological research. As George Stocking has observed: "To a much greater extent than today, knowledge itself was thought of as embodied in objects."[34] The early Dumbarton Oaks affiliation with the *Princeton Index of Christian Art* and the establishment of the *Census of Early Christian and Byzantine Objects* are best understood in this object-centric context. Similarly, the original scheme for fellowship research at Dumbarton Oaks, as conceived and directed by Wilhelm Koehler, furthered not only interest in the Bliss Collection but also sought to ensure that art objects would be contextualized through literary and archaeological references. Young scholars received two- or three-year postdoctoral fellowships in order to divide their time equally between their own research interests and collective research projects as organized by Koehler. David Wright summarized the scheme as follows: "The historians and philologists were to search original sources for passages relevant to art while the archaeologists and art historians were to review existing literature of Late Antique sites, to review problems revealed by the literature and compile critical dossiers with copies of published illustrations.... The long-term goal was the publication of an anthology of sources and the preparation of a 'Research Archive' to be made available to all studying at Dumbarton Oaks and to prepare for future field work."[35] The institutional *modus operandi* was, in short, to identify the art objects and to contextualize them through a corpus of literary and field report records.[36]

On July 2, 1940, the Blisses formally wrote the president and Fellows of Harvard College a letter of intent to give their property and collections to Harvard and to create the Dumbarton Oaks General Endowment Fund. In this letter, they expressed their specific wishes:

Shortly after Dr. Conant became President of Harvard University, we informed him that provisions had been made in our wills to leave to Harvard University our dwelling house and other buildings and improvements erected on a parcel of land in Georgetown, District of Columbia, known as Dumbarton Oaks, together with the library, art collection and other contents therein.... [W]e have heretofore explained our plan and desire to have Dumbarton Oaks eventually become a center for study and research in the Humanities, and especially in the field of Mediaeval Art.... We believe that our project has now been carried to a point where Dumbarton Oaks can be turned over with profit to the University. Moreover, we should be glad to see our hopes definitely realized in our lifetime rather than letting them come to fruition after our deaths. We, therefore, offer to the President and Fellows of Harvard College, as a gift to the University, Dumbarton Oaks, its grounds, its buildings, its library, its art collections and other contents therein.... From the above, it will be realized that we envision Dumbarton Oaks as a vital center of distinguished and productive scholarship, a useful ornament to Harvard University, and a continuing haven for seekers after Truth. It is our expectation and desire that this gift shall be used for the study and research in the Humanities and Fine Arts, with especial emphasis upon

Byzantine art and the history and culture of the Eastern Empire in all its aspects.

Later, in 1945, Robert Bliss explained another reason for this change in plans:

As the depression increased and Nazism gained control of Germany we knew war was a certainty and that inevitably this country would be sucked into the cataclysm. So we faced the future squarely and decided to transfer Dumbarton Oaks to the University in 1940. To ease the wrench, we assured each other that freedom of choice is a privilege not often granted by Fate and that to give up our home at our own time to assure the long range realization of our plan was the way of wisdom. Thus we are enjoying the transformation of Dumbarton Oaks into an institution—the only one of its particular sort in existence.[37]

In making this decision, it is certain that the Blisses were increasingly worried about the inevitability of war and the possibility of German occupation and destruction in America. Both Blisses had witnessed firsthand in Paris the German invasion of France during World War I when Robert Bliss was posted as secretary and counselor to the United States Embassy between 1912 and 1919. They grew increasingly pessimistic during the second half of the 1930s as the inevitability of World War II became evident. On September 13, 1938, Robert Bliss wrote Royall Tyler: "We are very low in our minds over the situation in Europe and see little hope for a peaceful outcome. It is monstrous." With the declaration of war in Europe, Mildred Bliss wrote despondently to Geoffrey Dodge on September 9, 1939:

Well, Geoffrey dear, the nightmare is upon us again. I know your thoughts are harking backward to 1914 when you arrived that Christmas and took up the work which gave us all satisfaction in doing some good during those nightmare years, but this time some of us cannot be in France, at least for the present.... The institutional part of Dumbarton Oaks must be wound up and the drain on one's resources in time, vitality and money are very great. One man's guess is as good as another's and who am I to have an opinion about the endurance of time of the Four Horsemen of the Apocalypse, but if I dare look ahead beyond the immediate conflict, I should think it would take a long time to fight this out to a finish.[38]

When America entered the war, the Blisses held fast to their decisions regarding Dumbarton Oaks and vowed to ensure the institution's survival. On May 9, 1942, Mildred Bliss explained to Paul Sachs, who had become chairman of the Administrative Committee at Dumbarton Oaks: "We understand, of course, the financial uncertainties of the times—who better?!!.... If ever the Humanities were necessary, if ever they should be recognized as inherently realistic essentials of life, it is in this epoch of disintegration and dislocation. We feel very strongly that whatever can be done—within reason—for living scholarship should be done by Dumbarton Oaks." These sentiments had found published expression earlier in a 1941 first-anniversary piece on Dumbarton Oaks in the *Washington Post*:

With the present cultural blackout in Europe, the destruction of whole libraries, the suppression of research and production at a standstill, a heavy weight of responsibility rests upon scholars and all others who esteem culture and would uphold civilization.... How proud we should be that this work is going on here in our midst![39]

The Blisses also agonized over the plight of Jewish friends and scholars as well as over private art collections. In a telling cable to Royall Tyler in Geneva on November 15, 1938, the Blisses set in motion a successful scheme to bring the art historian Doro Levi to the United States and encouraged a scheme to ensure the survival of Bernard Berenson's Tuscan property, I Tatti, and its collection and library, a scheme that was similar to the one they were pursuing for Dumbarton Oaks.[40] The Blisses cabled Tyler: "What news Gogo. What status Volbach. Avoiding post and telegraph. Convey Doro six months invitation lecture universities bringing wife for work Dumbarton. If without funds advance necessary for journey. If affidavit or university papers required cable me naming consulate having jurisdiction. Also convey BeeBee [Bernard Berenson] suggestion he transfer Tatti to University now making financial arrangements later. Both foregoing messages have Sachs full collaboration."

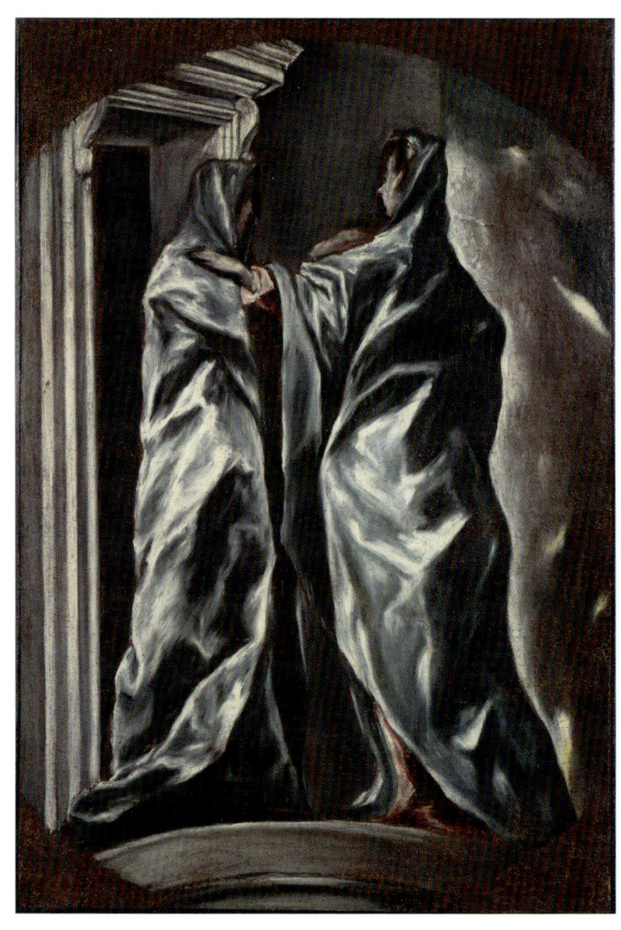

Figure 9.
Domenikos Theotokopoulos
a.k.a. El Greco
(c. 1541-1614),
Visitation, *oil on canvas,*
c. 1610-1614.
Dumbarton Oaks, acc. no.
HC.P.1936.18.(O).

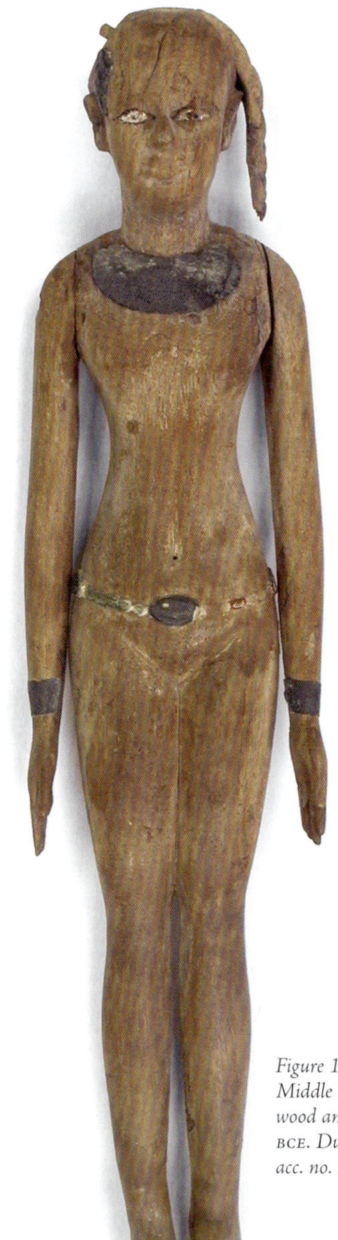

Figure 10. Ancient Egyptian,
Middle Kingdom, Concubine,
wood and silver, c. 1938-1759
BCE. *Dumbarton Oaks,*
acc. no. HC.S.1937.011.(W).

THE BLISSES, IMPROVING THE COLLECTION AND INSTITUTION

A S THE BLISSES FIRMED UP THEIR PLANS TO CREATE the Dumbarton Oaks Research Library and Collection, they realized the need to ensure that their collection was not only of the highest artistic quality, but also as comprehensive as it could be. It is possible that they at least subconsciously compared their plan with Andrew Mellon's nearly simultaneous plan to give his art collection—and a building to house it—to the United States; at the very least, their correspondence of this period frequently refers to Mellon's plans for the National Gallery of Art.[41] They may also have believed that their collection was not yet adequate for public scrutiny. When the E. and A. Silberman Galleries of New York proposed on September 12, 1938, that the Blisses allow two visiting European aristocrats to visit Dumbarton Oaks, Robert Bliss wrote: "I request that you warn Baron Hatvany and Baroness Beck that they should not be expecting to see a great collection of art at Dumbarton Oaks, but I shall of course be glad to show them such things as we have here." Five days later he wrote to the Baron and Baroness, "but I hope that you have not an exaggerated idea of the things that my wife and I have collected, as they are rather special and not arranged for public display."[42] The subsequent accelerated pace of the Blisses' collecting of Byzantine art, other antiquities, and old master paintings and sculptures is testimony to their desire to give Harvard an "A-1" collection, as they called it. During this period of increased collecting, which was considerably accelerated in 1936 and 1937 and reached its peak between the years 1938 and 1940, the Blisses acquired some 333 Byzantine objects, 43 pre-Columbian objects, and 47 objects that became part of the House Collection.[43] However, during this increased period of collecting, they remained true to their collection philosophy, which Robert Bliss would later state in his residual bequest to Harvard University: "[M]y desire is for the acquisition only of objects of great rarity and artistic appeal … and, furthermore … I do not want the character of the Collection altered or changed."[44]

Although the Blisses continued to rely on expert advice, during this period they became increasingly sure of their decisions from an aesthetic standpoint, often informing Royall Tyler of purchases only after the fact. On February 1, 1936, for example, Tyler would write the Blisses: "I'm much excited about your recent acquisitions. Hurrah for the Drey cross! And for the Rhipidion (fan). And I'm prepared to enthuse about the pyx, when I see it or a photo." He was similarly delighted to hear of their purchase of El Greco's *Visitation* (fig. 9), which the Blisses negotiated directly with the Spanish dealer Mildred Byne that same year. His expressed support notwithstanding, the Blisses' accelerated collecting during this period also worried Tyler, who admonished the couple to concentrate only on strengthening the Byzantine Collection, as it was the nucleus around which the research institution would be formed. This sentiment had earlier been endorsed by Edward Forbes, who, on November 8, 1935, had written to Robert Bliss: "In general, the wiser principle would be to stick more or less to Byzantine art, great paintings, and sculpture." Forbes advised against continuing to collect in areas already represented in Washington, D.C., public collections, as was the case with the Blisses' extensive and important collection of ancient Chinese art and their paintings and prints by Whistler, both of which were well represented in the Freer Gallery. Similarly, on September 24, 1937, Tyler wrote somewhat disingenuously to Mildred Bliss: "Precious Mildred, I'm appalled by your list of things to be acquired. A bit reassured when you told me you didn't want to scatter too much, and that Byz. remains the main thing…. I do implore you to go easy on Greek and pre-Greek, on Germanic and on Ital. primitives. Such a racket, both the latter. And not to aim at forming an all round representative collection." Three months later, Robert Bliss wrote Tyler: "In truth, as you know full well, both Mildred and I are entirely of your opinion that we should keep to our Byzantine field and its allied arts, but, also agreeing with you, there are occasions when one falls from grace! We have been tempted by a … bronze horse, unlike anything I have ever seen before…. We are trying to resist it, and hope we shall succeed, but I do not know." The Blisses purchased the South Arabian/ancient Roman bronze horse in February 1938.[45]

On November 18, 1938, Mildred Bliss wrote Royall Tyler about the purchase of a Degas drawing and a Middle Kingdom Egyptian statuette (fig. 10) and informed him that they had not yet decided on his recommendation to acquire an ivory of the Virgin and Child between John the Baptist and Saint Basil.[46] Tyler wrote back: "I grieve that you should be lured by the old Egypt. thing…. Only I'll go into decline if you don't get that ivory." Tyler also unsuccessfully recommended against the acquisition of an important early Fauve watercolor by Georges Rouault,[47] later writing Mildred Bliss on June 24, 1938, that the dealer "Kelek[ian] is disgusted with me for having crabbed his Rouault to you." The Blisses' eventual acquisition of "the old Egypt. thing," as Royall Tyler disparagingly called it, illustrates well their passion for collecting in this period as well as their interest to assure authenticity and favorable terms of purchase.[48] Already on March 22, 1937, Robert Bliss had written to Paul Sachs:

Kelek[ian] is, as usual, asking a high price, but I think that he may be more reasonable when it comes to a definite showdown…. The … object is an enchanting wooden Egyptian figure either of a doll or a statuette portrait. It is a charming object. I have known of it for some time, Kelek having taken me to the vaults of the bank and shown it to me in 1933. He has now brought it to America, and has shown it to no one (so he says) except Winlock of which I shall take the first opportunity to ask about it. Kelek claims that it is a unique piece. We both would like to acquire it, but think we ought to go a little slowly and also ask your advice. Perhaps you would show the photograph to the Egyptologist of the Boston Museum…. I may add that the photograph of the Egyptian statuette gives but a poor conception of its beauty and grace of line.

Sachs wrote Robert Bliss back on March 29, agreeing that the Egyptian figure was "an enchanting statuette" and informing Bliss that he had sought the advice of Dows Donham of the Boston Museum of Fine Arts who had found the figure "distinguished."

THE BLISSES' NEW CONFIDENCE IN THEIR ABILITY to purchase art of high aesthetic interest on their own initiative did not blind them to the possibility of purchasing misattributed works or fakes and of the need for technical expertise. This concern for authenticity and the Blisses' awakening to connoisseurship were likely due to a number of previous misguided acquisitions: a "Rembrandt" in 1926, now attributed to Solomon Koninck; a "Watteau" in 1926, which is now seen as a nineteenth-century copy; and two pendant "Chardin" still lifes in early 1936, now viewed as near-contemporary copies of Chardin originals. On June 22, 1937, Robert Bliss confessed to Tyler that a Medieval mortar that the Blisses had purchased was not right: "You never liked it and I think there is no doubt that it is a dud." The year before, Robert Bliss also had become suspicious of a Renoir that the Blisses had purchased on the recommendation of Geoffrey Dodge and Walter Gay. He wrote Dodge on October 31, 1936: "We did not see the Renoir until our return to Dumbarton Oaks a few nights ago, and find it a really charming little picture. I am curious to know, however, something regarding its history for I do not feel entirely sure that it is by Renoir. Far be it for me to set myself up as an authority against the opinion of dear Walter Gay, for I trust his opinion and sureness of eye…. But to return to the Renoir and the photographs of the two little pictures you sent in your last letter, I really have some questions as to the justification for the attributions given, and I think you ought to investigate pretty thoroughly the whole background."

In late 1936, the Blisses spent "three delightful days in Cambridge, learning the technique of examination and care of paintings and bronze at the Fogg Museum and having long uninterrupted talks with that remarkable young man, President Conant," as Mildred Bliss wrote Geoffrey Dodge on December 7. This tutelage appears to have taken hold, for in the following year, Robert Bliss became increasingly

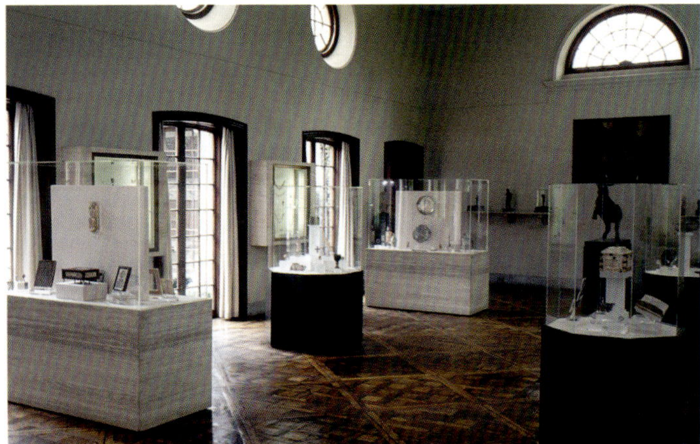

Figure 11. Byzantine Collection, Dumbarton Oaks, 1968.

more mistrustful of accepting attributions as well as more opinionated in his suspicions, requiring professional vetting by established scholars and technical examination before making a purchase. His unease is amusingly apparent in a letter written to Paul Sachs on November 11, 1937, where he states: "I have myself no doubts about the Byzantine bronze, but not having full confidence in my own judgment, I am waiting to hear what [Charles Rufus] Morey thinks of it." The Blisses' wariness was not lost on Dodge, who redeemed himself by finding the ivory of the Virgin and Child discussed above. On April 16, 1938, Dodge wrote Robert Bliss: "I am enclosing a photograph of a Byzantine ivory plaque which I have known about for some time, but did not wish to speak about until I showed it to Royall Tyler. He has just come to Paris and this afternoon spent an hour and a half examining it, and he is writing you his opinion. I am glad to say my opinion was justified and he is very impressed…. I will leave the description, etc., to the more capable hands of Royall." Despite Tyler's enthusiasm, the Blisses wanted the ivory examined by Marquet de Vasselot, who pronounced it a fake. Robert Bliss wrote Dodge on June 14: "Royall and I have discussed the ivory at some length. He still is quite sure that the ivory is genuine but I should like to put it through the acid test (figuratively speaking) before making an offer for it, and to do this will take some time. When a man like M[arquet] de V[asselot] pronounces it a fake, one has to give careful consideration to it." Dodge wrote back on June 24: "I was pretty pleased at his [Royall Tyler's] reaction and I think he probably wrote to you as enthusiastically as he spoke to me, and he also agreed with me that Mr. Marquet de Vasselot's opinion could not be taken seriously, as he only gave two minutes to look at the object." The Blisses finally acquired the ivory in 1939.[49]

With their decision made to convey Dumbarton Oaks to Harvard, in 1937 the Blisses began planning to house properly their Byzantine Collection and to provide a facility for their library of approximately fourteen thousand volumes[50] and space for the anticipated research activity that would revolve around it and the collection. After considerable study, they abandoned Paul Sachs's recommendation of February 5, 1937, to build a second-story library above the Music Room, "thus providing an area which would have the added merit of being in close proximity to the objects themselves which are to be studied." In 1938, the Blisses engaged the Washington, D.C., architect Thomas T. Waterman to construct two pavilions for the library and collection (fig. 11) to be located west of the Music Room.[51] These pavilions flanked an

open-air courtyard, which later became the exhibition space for an octagonal Late Antique mosaic from Antioch, and were connected by an enclosed walkway at the south side and communicated as well directly to the Music Room at the north, providing a complete circuit within the research and public area of the property. The one-story collection pavilion also had a small subterranean sculpture hall, and the library pavilion had administrative offices on the ground floor and stack and research space on the floor above.

The Blisses' initial gift to Harvard, which, in essence, established the Byzantine Collection and the Studies Program, as well as conveyed the House Collection, was followed by additional bequests that increased endowments and provided for acquisitions. In particular, it endowed what would become the Garden Library and Rare Book Room, the Landscape Architecture Studies Program, and the Pre-Columbian Collection and Studies Program. In 1951, the Blisses specifically established the Dumbarton Oaks Garden Endowment Fund:

> [It is] our intention that the Dumbarton Oaks Gardens shall serve constructively to advance garden design and ornament through example in design and ornament, through the use of media not always emphasized and through the dissemination of historical, cultural and technical information…. [And it] is our hope and expectation that the Dumbarton Oaks Gardens may in time attain as high a standing in the study of, and for its publications on, Garden Design and Ornament as the Dumbarton Oaks Research Library and Collection has already attained for its scholarly work and research. Thus will the unusual potentialities of its Gardens be fully realized.

In late 1957, the Blisses began planning additions to Dumbarton Oaks that would allow for the proper housing of Mildred Bliss's collection of rare books on landscape architecture and its attendant library of secondary sources. On December 20, Robert Bliss wrote the president and Fellows of Harvard College:

> For some time past it has been evident that additional space must be provided at Dumbarton Oaks for the exhibition of objects in the Collection, not now on display, as well as to provide suitable rooms for the use and study of a library of books on gardens (their design and ornament) and related subjects, which Mrs. Bliss has been collecting in recent years and which it is her hope eventually to convey to Dumbarton Oaks. Also, adequate space should be prepared where the collection of Byzantine coins and seals at Dumbarton Oaks can be exhibited and studied. In addition, it will be necessary to make provision for increased stack room.

Similarly, on September 6, 1960, Robert Bliss wrote again to President Nathan M. Pusey:

> I now write to ask if you will be so kind as to inform the members of the Corporation that I am desirous of giving to Harvard my collection of Pre-Columbian Art, now on loan exhibition at the National Gallery of Art in Washington, together with my Library of Pre-Columbian Art and Archaeology, for permanent exhibition and study at Dumbarton Oaks. In order to display the Collection to advantage, it will be necessary to erect a special building for that purpose and this Mrs. Bliss and I are prepared to do at our expense.

To this end, the Blisses commissioned Frederick Rheinlander King of the New York architectural firm Wyeth and King to design and build a Georgian-style Garden Library wing with an interior reading room of French eighteenth-century inspiration. They also commissioned the New York architect Philip Johnson to design and build a minimalist, glass Pre-Columbian wing with subterranean office and library facilities. The financial stability of these additions—and particularly their collections and study programs—was eventually ensured by the Blisses' residual bequests, that of Mildred Bliss containing a separate provision for the Dumbarton Oaks Garden Endowment as well.

I T WAS ALREADY CLEAR BY 1941 THAT THE RESEARCH library and collection pavilions at Dumbarton Oaks were insufficient to accommodate the growing institution, and the first director, John S. Thacher, had hopes for a new separate library wing to be built on Thirty-second Street, adjacent to the museum. The cost for such an addition, however, was prohibitive. After consultation with the Blisses and the administrative committee, he proposed altering the second floor of the house to accommodate the Byzantine Library and Studies Program. On May 27, 1941, he wrote Paul Sachs: "The important thing at this time to decide is whether, in principle, you and the Committee would be sympathetic with the idea of visualizing the main part of the house as the Library.... I hasten to say, however, that as I see it, the music room, the oval room, the present library [Study] and the drawing room [Founders' Room] would remain unchanged, but it would mean that the service end of the house, as well as the second floor bedrooms, would be completely altered. Therefore, the house would cease to exist as a domicile.... As I have dreamt about the possibilities resulting from such a change, I can see both a permanent solution to our Library and Museum problems, as well as giving to the whole institution added dignity and seriousness of purpose."

In that same year, Dumbarton Oaks commissioned Thomas Waterman to retrofit the upstairs bedrooms and service rooms as library facilities, a design task that included the creation of the elegant Byzantine Reading Room from two guest bedrooms and the employment of one room's English eighteenth-century pine mantel and trim as the design conceit for the larger Reading Room decoration (fig. 12). During this period, Waterman also retrofitted the garage and staff dormitory as a residence for the director and redesigned the Superintendent's Dwelling—designed by Beatrix Farrand in 1933—as the Students Quarters (or Fellows Building as it later came to be known). With Waterman's construction in 1946 of a marble hallway between the Byzantine Collection office pavilion and the main house, the realization of Thacher's dream was complete.

Paul Sachs, having visited Dumbarton Oaks in 1942 to see the results of the architectural adaptations, wrote Robert Bliss on March 12:

> And this brings me to my impressions during my visit to Dumbarton Oaks. I have no hesitation in saying that I came away after ten fascinating days more encouraged than ever before that we are really building along lines that are worthy of you and of the University and that carry out the spirit which all of us cherish. The grounds are in beautiful shape; on entering the house there is an unchanged scene on the ground floor due to Jack's [John Thacher's] care and skill; and then on the second floor there is a dignity in the beautiful library and the excellent offices.

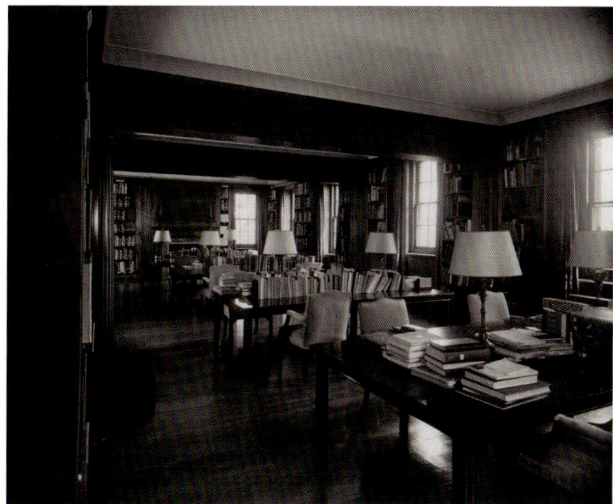

Figure 12. Byzantine Reading Room, Dumbarton Oaks, 1950. Designed by Thomas T. Waterman, 1941.

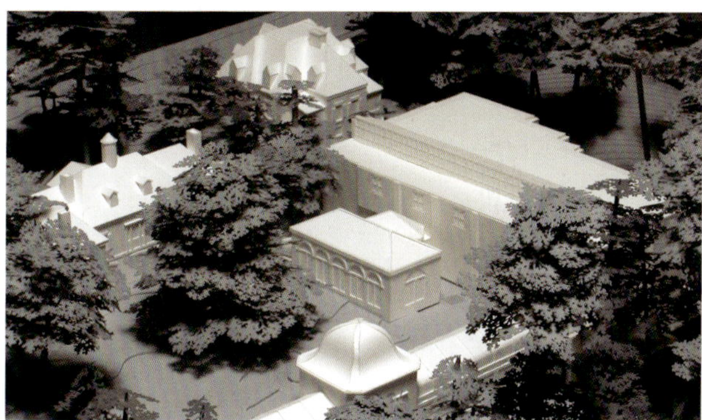

Figure 13. Model of Service Court with new library (upper right) designed by Robert Venturi (Venturi, Scott Brown and Associates), Dumbarton Oaks, 2002.

The enlargement of the library facilities in the 1940s quickly proved inadequate for the needs of the growing institution. By the 1970s, the attic floor had come to house book stacks, and book shelving was introduced into many of the principal rooms that John Thacher earlier had wanted to preserve in their original state. Shelving increasingly lined many corridors and even closet interiors. A solution to this overcrowding—a proposed underground addition to the library to be located beneath the North Vista of the gardens—was abandoned after its escalating cost and public mistrust of the plan became seemingly insurmountable obstacles. In 1999, the present director, Edward L. Keenan, addressed the acutely critical need for increased library and research space, finding a suitable building site away from the gardens and to the side of the Service Court where obsolete storage sheds were located. Keenan commissioned Robert Venturi of the Philadelphia architectural firm of Venturi, Scott Brown and Associates to design and build a 44,500-square-foot, freestanding library that would integrate the institution's diverse library holdings and become the centralized intellectual center of Dumbarton Oaks (fig. 13). Robert Venturi also designed and built a Gardeners' Lodge behind the Fellows Building, renovated the original Director's House as a Refectory and the Gardener's Cottage as a Facilities Office, and, by 2007, the

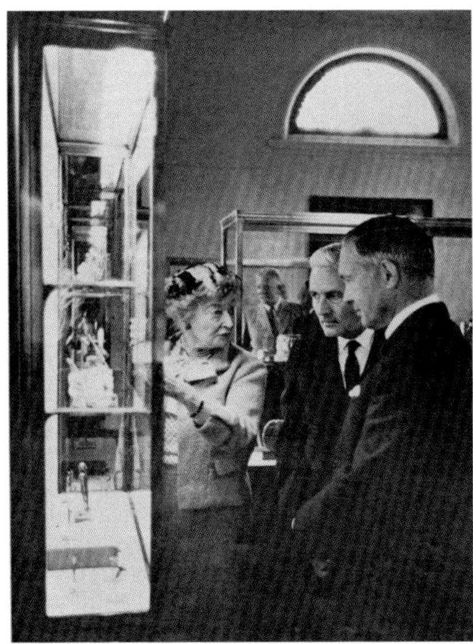

Figure 14. Mildred Bliss with L. Gard Wiggins, administrative vice-president of Harvard University, and Francis H. Burr, Fellow of Harvard College, 1963, from Harvard Alumni Bulletin, *June 8, 1963.*

firm will have completed renovations of the Main House and Museum Wing and the Fellows Building.

Despite these necessary increases to the physical plant and the additions and refinements to the library holdings and art collections since the Blisses' deaths, the Dumbarton Oaks Research Library and Collection remains remarkably true to their vision and design, a vision that Mildred Bliss so eloquently stated in the preamble to her last will and testament.[52] It is most probably certain that the many scholars who have benefited from its collections and library resources and the visitors who have delighted in those collections and the gardens would concur with Paul Sachs's testimony to the Blisses on June 26, 1940, after Harvard University's formal acceptance of their "magnificent gift" (fig. 14):

> Your gift is so tremendous; the responsibility is so great; the opportunity is so unlimited—that adequate words fail me…. Your gracious presence; your vision; your energy, your knowledge, your taste; and above all your creative imagination have made the place and the undertaking quite unique in the world…. We shall aim to make Dumbarton Oaks worthy of you and your unique, constructive vision; worthy of the University and of its finest traditions; worthy of the Fine Arts Department and the Fogg Museum; worthy of scholarship and of the best humanistic tradition—a tradition more sorely needed in this hour of trial and tragedy than ever before. ◆

1. Unless otherwise indicated, all quoted material is from the Papers of Robert Woods Bliss and Mildred Barnes Bliss: an Inventory, organized by correspondent and date, at the Harvard University Archives (HUA), Pusey Library, Cambridge, MA, call no. HUGFP 76.xx.

2. The term "Collection," in the singular, has been used consistently at Dumbarton Oaks since 1940, although there have been occasional attempts to adopt the plural "Collections." In *Dumbarton Oaks Bulletin* 1950, 31, Elizabeth Bland (attributed) explained: "In a consideration of the objects of art assembled at Dumbarton Oaks, the word 'Collection' should be interpreted in its broadest sense. Otherwise the full meaning of the term as it is truly applicable to Dumbarton Oaks cannot be grasped. One is grateful for the catholic taste and diverse interests of the founders, who assembled objects of various periods, representing many cultures, all of which have a definite meaning and place in a foundation which in its broadest aspect is dedicated to the humanities."

3. The Blisses gave approximately sixteen acres, including all principal buildings and their contents, to Harvard University; the dedication ceremony was held on November 1, 1940, and the legal transfer occurred on November 29 (Deed recorded in Liber 7551 at Folio 427-429, Washington, D.C.); the Blisses deeded a substantial portion of their remaining property, some twenty-seven acres now known as Dumbarton Oaks Park, to the National Capital Parks and Planning Commission [now National Park Service] on November 29, 1940 (Deed recorded in Liber 7551 at Folio 422-424, Washington, D.C.). Because Harvard University was not incorporated in Washington, D.C., the president and fellows of Harvard College legally transferred Dumbarton Oaks to the Trustees for Harvard University, Inc., a District of Columbia corporation, on June 9, 1941 [recorded in Liber 7629 at Folio 459-460, Washington, D.C., and designated as Lot numbered 812 in Square numbered 2155].

4. *Fogg Bulletin* 1941, 63.

5. The actual price recorded in the agreement of sale dated June 30, 1920, between Lucia E. Blount and Robert Woods Bliss was $163,000. The seller, however, had desired that the public record of the sale show a price less than was actually realized. To that end, Robert Bliss agreed to pay Lucia Blount $12,000 "to give him or his wife, Mildred Bliss, the benefit of her professional advice and counsel as landscape gardener whenever during her lifetime they ask it as regards the care and planting of trees, shrubs and plants, and as regards gardening or care of the grounds, on and in the property known as The Oaks situated at 3101 R Street, Washington D.C." Letter of agreement dated June 25, 1920, and signed by Lucia E. Blount, Dumbarton Oaks Archives (DOA), Dumbarton Oaks History, Blount correspondence.

6. *Fogg Bulletin*, 1941, 63.

7. For published histories of Dumbarton Oaks, see Whitehill 1967; Sutton 1984; Joseph, Fanning, and Davison 2000; and Tamulevich 2001.

8. The Blisses begin referring to the property as "Dumbarton" as early as 1925 (used in letter dated July 28, 1925, DOA, Bliss correspondence); the name "Dumbarton Oaks" is used in correspondence and for the letterhead as early as April 12, 1933.

9. The remaining portion of the Blount estate was purchased in 1921 for $60,000; the "Home for the Incurables parcel" was purchased in 1923 for $75,000; the "Clifton property," which later became the majority portion of Dumbarton Oaks Park, was purchased in 1925 for $700,000; parcels on S Street were purchased in 1926 for $70,000; and the "Woodward and Lothrop parcel" was purchased in 1932 for $69,297. Deeds and titles in DOA, Dumbarton Oaks History, legal documents.

10. For later changes to the Brooke interior design, see in this volume, Carder's second essay.

11. On August 31, 1922, Mildred Bliss wrote to a friend, Joseph E. Stevens: "The house is now in the most distressing stage of apparently arrested motion: Did anyone ever get into a new house on time?" And on May 2, 1923, she wrote another friend, Clarence Hoblitzelle: "The house is nearly done, but just not nearly enough for us to get into, so we stay here until we leave." Bliss Papers, HUA. The Blisses were living in an apartment at 1786 Massachusetts Avenue, Washington, D.C., in the building that presently houses the offices of the National Trust for Historic Preservation.

12. Many important musical events came to be held in the Music Room, including the 1938 world premiere of Igor Stravinsky's *Concerto in E flat (Dumbarton Oaks Concerto)*, which the Blisses had commissioned to commemorate their thirtieth wedding anniversary. In 1946, the organization known as The Friends of Music at Dumbarton Oaks was formed in order to offer a yearly chamber music series in the Music Room. In 1944, the Music Room served as the site of the Dumbarton Oaks Conversations, informal discussions on the general question of an international organization for the maintenance of peace and security, which led to the formation of the United Nations the following year.

13. Unless otherwise indicated, quoted correspondence between the Blisses and Lawrence White is from the McKim, Mead and White Archives, New-York Historical Society, New York, call no. 396.

14. Correspondence of November 28, 1927. The same company may have provided eleven "round marble discs, all 3" thick," for the exterior walls of the Music Room (contract in the amount of $560, September 15, 1927).

15. Correspondence of September 17, 1926. White questioned the advisability of decorating the niches and overdoors in the corridor, adding: "The Hubert Roberts are so magnificent that I do not think they should have any competition in paint. Why not put sculpture in the niches?" The Blisses installed a Swiss Neo-classical stove in one niche of the final design of the corridor. The Hubert Robert canvases were installed, however, in the living room (Founders' Room).

16. This motto is inscribed on the frame of the stone plaque set into the exterior wall of the Garden Library pavilion.

17. Whitehill 1967, 60, recounts: "While still in her teens in New York she had seen, coveted, and bought a piece of *opus Anglicanum* at a time when such medieval embroideries were little studied or known. As a girl fresh out of school, she was in correspondence with booksellers in Paris, Tours, Clermont-Ferrand, and Rome, seeking precise literary, biblio-

graphical, and artistic information—a habit that remained with her." The *opus Anglicanum* piece remains in the Dumbarton Oaks House Collection, HC.T.X.xxxx.21.(E).

18. Lothrop 1957, 7.

19. Walter Muir Whitehill, unpublished introduction to the correspondence between the Blisses and Royall Tyler, p. 1. Bliss Papers, HUA. Unless otherwise indicated, all quoted correspondence between the Blisses and Royall Tyler is from the Bliss Papers, organized by date, at the HUA, call no. HUGFP 38.6.

20. Correspondence of September 25, 1927, and May 10, 1928.

21. Unless otherwise indicated, all quoted correspondence between the Blisses and Geoffrey Dodge is from the DOA, House Collection, Geoffrey Dodge correspondence, organized by date.

22. HC.T.1913.04.(T). Another fragment from this tapestry or a fragment from another tapestry in this series is in the Victoria and Albert Museum, London (acc. no. T.37-1914); cf. George Wingfield Digby assisted by Hefford 1980, 21, cat. no. 9, pl. 17; the tapestry is Flemish (probably Arras), c. 1425-1450, made from a cartoon possibly based on Gaston Phoebus, *Livre de Chasse* (one example is in the Bibliothèque Nationale, Paris, MS fr.616, dated 1405-1410); cf. Panofsky, 1953, pl. 50.

23. Royall Tyler and Hayford Peirce would publish *Byzantine Art* (Peirce and Tyler 1926); organize an exhibition of Byzantine art at the Musée des Arts Décoratifs, Paris, in 1931, to which the Blisses would lend (see in this volume, Nelson's essay); and publish *L'Art byzantin* (Peirce and Tyler 1932).

24. This chalice (acc. no. BZ.1955.18) was given to the Dumbarton Oaks Byzantine Collection in 1955 by Tyler's widow, Elisina, and their son, William.

25. On January 2, 1924, Tyler wrote Mildred Bliss: "I don't know where Bréhier heard that the chalice and paten were found together. I rather think I told you that Col. Lawrence, of Arabian fame, told me he was at Riha when both objects were discovered, and that he bought the chalice, which was soon after stolen from him…. That paten is a most snorting, magnificent object. Remember that when the dealers and their jackals are loud in praise of an object, it's because they want to work it off on an amateur. When they are silent about it it may be because one of them wants it for himself."

26. Cable of June 4, 1937; Tyler would both collect and enthusiastically write Robert Bliss about pre-Columbian art throughout his life, as on February 7, 1913: "And I was absolutely swept off my feet by the Aztec masks in the British Museum, the most marvelous things [that] ever existed; there is a limestone one which might just as well come from S. Denis c. 1150. See also Elizabeth P. Benson, "The Robert Woods Bliss Collection of Pre-Columbian Art: A Memoir," in Boone 1993, 15-34.

27. Similarly, Tyler sent a radiogram to Bliss on June 4, 1937: "Sale Sothebys June ninth magnificent Mexican gold silver obsidian jadite crystal etc. Perhaps great opportunities. Shall I buy for you to total say two thousand pounds? Tyler," followed by a radiogram on June 6, 1937: "Secured for you gold necklace and numerous jade obsidian etc. objects total 567 pounds."

28. DOA, House Collection, Robert Abdy correspondence.

29. Dumbarton Oaks House Collection HC.P.1930.04.(O). The sitter of this painting frequently has been identified as Marie of Burgundy (1457-1482), first wife of the Archduke Maximilian of Austria, later Kaiser Maximilian I, although Maximilian's second wife, Bianca Maria Sforza, has also been suggested; Strigel painted at least one other posthumous portrait of Marie of Burgundy (Kunsthistorisches Museum, Vienna, inv. no. 832, dated 1516). Another version of the Dumbarton Oaks painting exists with a landscape seen through the window (Tiroler Landesmuseum Ferdinandeum, Innsbruck, inv. no. 100). A pendant portrait of Maximilian I was also in the Figdor Collection, Austria.

30. Sachs presented the Bliss plan for Dumbarton Oaks to Harvard University president Lowell on March 10, 1932, and reported that the president was "deeply appreciative [and] in thorough accord." The next year the plan was explained to Harvard's new president, James B. Conant, who wrote Robert Bliss on October 19, 1933: "Mr. Sachs and Mr. Forbes have just told me in strict confidence of your intention to bequeath your home and library to this University to the end that scholarly work in Fine Arts may be encouraged and strengthened. I hope you will permit me to express my great satisfaction on hearing this news. I am so pleased that you have confidence in us." Unless otherwise indicated, all quoted correspondence between or about the Blisses and Paul Sachs and/or Edward Forbes is from the Bliss Papers, organized by correspondent and date, at the HUA, call no. HUGFP 76.xx.

31. Unless otherwise indicated, all documents pertaining to the Blisses' gift of Dumbarton Oaks to Harvard University are from the DOA, Dumbarton Oaks History, Legal Documents.

32. In a letter of November 4, 1936, to Robert Bliss, the Blisses' lawyer from the firm of Hawkins, Delafield & Longfellow discussed Mildred Bliss's intention to employ slight-

ly less than one half her fortune to endow the Dumbarton Oaks maintenance fund, stating that "the Donor (I advisedly omit names) is now definitely committed to a gift … to be made in her lifetime, but that the time of making the gift remains indefinite." He concluded his letter by stating: "As you know, I have not been persuaded that the making of so large a gift in the Donor's lifetime is desirable in her interest, but as that matter has now been decided, I mention it only for the purpose of a record on my own letter files."

33. The Dumbarton Oaks-Fogg Museum affiliation was voided and superseded by the Blisses' subsequent outright gift of Dumbarton Oaks to Harvard University in 1940.

34. Stocking 1985, 114. I am grateful to Jeffrey Quilter and Jennifer Younger for providing this citation from their unpublished paper, "Archaeology and Dumbarton Oaks," delivered at the 2001 meeting of the American Anthropological Association in Washington, D.C.

35. Wright 2002, 150-151.

36. That this scheme had changed by 1965 to include more traditional historical and cultural research is evident from Kitzinger 1965.

37. Whitehill 1967, 78.

38. Mildred Bliss had led a group of Americans in instituting a "Distributing Service" in France called the "Service de Distribution Américaine," which was established in December 1914, growing out of personal work she had done since the beginning of the war; ultimately, the purpose of the service was to supply hospitals throughout France with whatever they needed. Mildred Bliss and her friends also conducted a work project for "frontier children" beginning in August 1914, which cared for 1,500 French, Belgian, and Alsatian children (cf. Gleason 1917, section IV, chapter XII, as retrieved from URL http://www.ku.edu/carrie/specoll/AFS/library/Gleason/ourpart7.html#ch12).

39. Leila Mechlin, "Dumbarton Oaks passes its first anniversary," *Washington Post*, November 9, 1941, E6.

40. When presented to President Conant, however, this plan was thwarted as Conant, "under present changed and uncertain conditions…, was emphatic in his view that he could not possibly recommend to the Corporation the owning of property by the University in Italy." Correspondence of Sachs to Robert Bliss, November 16, 1938.

41. The Blisses were unable to attend the opening of the National Gallery due to Robert Bliss's serious illness and convalescence in California. On May 27, 1941, Mildred Bliss wrote Edward Forbes at Dumbarton Oaks: "How pleasant and fortunate to all that Dumbarton Oaks was a going concern before the National Gallery was opened, so that you were all able to participate in offering hospitality to the distinguished guests from all over the country…. When you next write me, do tell me what you thought of Forbes Watson's editorial in the *Magazine of Art* on the great Mellon Collection. It had, to me, an unfortunate obliviousness to the affection that collectors feel for the objects they assemble."

42. DOA, House Collection, S correspondence.

43. Included in the House Collection acquisitions of this period were drawings attributed to Hugo van der Goes, Alessandro Magnasco, and Claude Lorrain; watercolors by Degas and Rouault; paintings attributed to Bernardo Daddi, Gentile da Fabriano, Hieronymus Bosch, El Greco, and Vuillard; a sculpture by Tilman Riemenschneider; and an ancient Egyptian statuette.

44. In discussing with Edward Forbes the possible purchase of a Coptic textile from the Thomas Whittemore collection, Robert Bliss wrote on August 5, 1942: "As far as the textiles in the collection [are] concerned, I think we have reached a stage when we can pick and choose, and that we should get nothing now that is not essential in filling out the pieces already on hand. This theory does not apply, of course, to a piece of very great beauty and importance, even though it might duplicate as to period and weave what is already at Dumbarton Oaks."

45. Dumbarton Oaks Byzantine Collection BZ.1938.12.

46. Dumbarton Oaks Byzantine Collection BZ.1939.8.

47. Dumbarton Oaks House Collection HC.1938.94.(WC).

48. Cf. Carder 2000, 101.

49. Their wariness notwithstanding, the Blisses continued unknowingly to acquire forgeries in the late 1930s. Of note, they purchased on August 26, 1939, from the Parisian dealer Kalebdjian, twenty-nine objects reportedly found in Egypt in the ruins of a church at Kom-El-Ahmar, all of which are now considered forgeries.

50. Whitehill 1967, 79.

51. It is of interest that the numerous plans for the Byzantine Collection wing produced by Waterman's office cite Mildred and Robert Woods Bliss as the designers rather than Waterman as the architect.

52. See the epigraph of this catalogue.

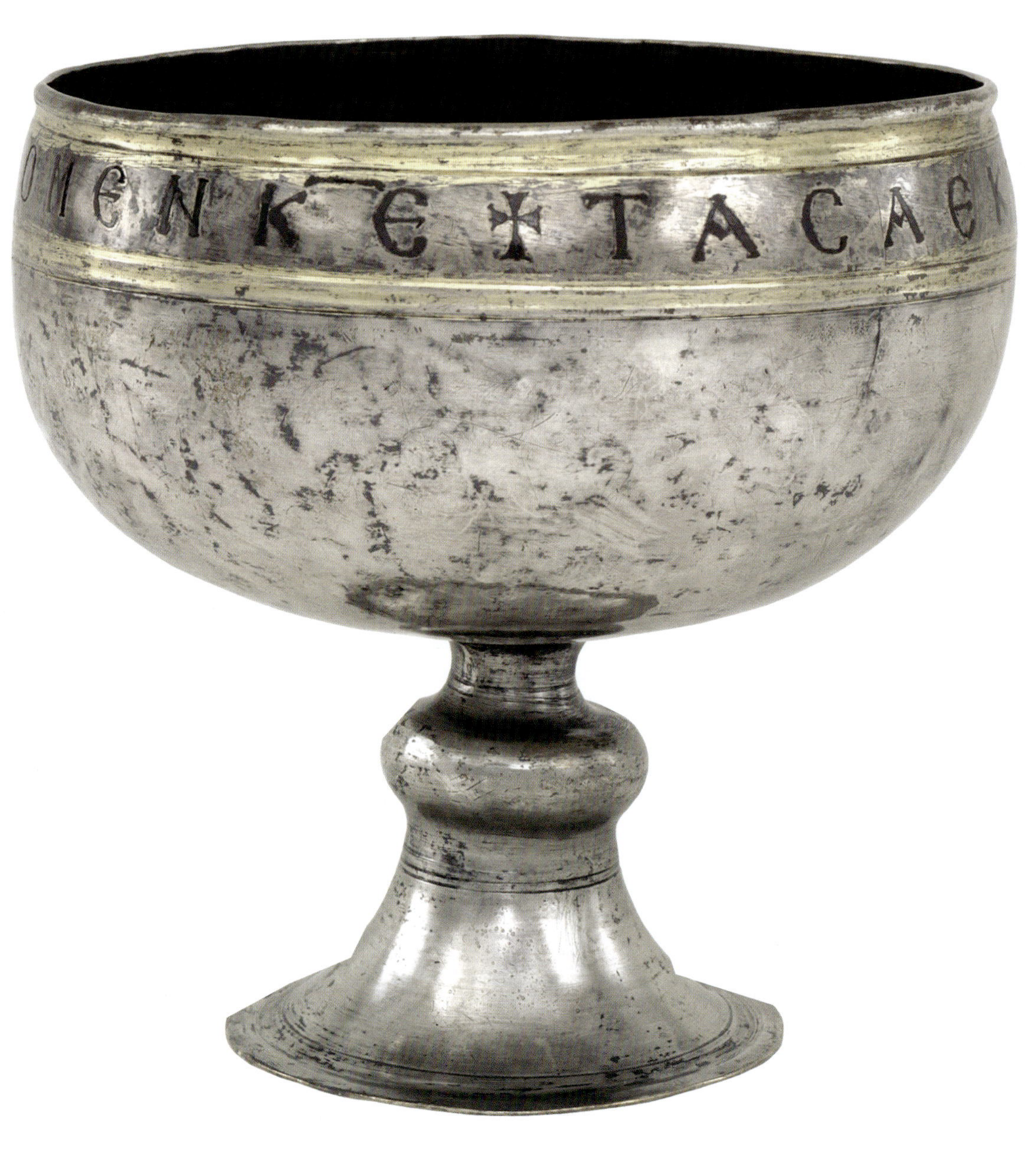
OIϹΝΚΕ✝ΤΑϹΛΕΥ

Private Passions Made Public:

The Beginnings of the Bliss Collection

BY ROBERT S. NELSON

O N FEBRUARY 2, 1945, BERNARD BERENSON, the famed American connoisseur of Renaissance painting, wrote from I Tatti, his villa in Florence, to Robert Woods Bliss, the former owner of Dumbarton Oaks in Washington D.C. The subject was a corpus of early Christian ivories that Berenson and Fritz Volbach were promoting.[1] From the 1920s, Bliss and his wife, Mildred Barnes Bliss, had compiled an outstanding art collection, especially of Byzantine art, and had given it, together with a library of fourteen thousand books on Byzantine studies, to Harvard University in 1940. Dumbarton Oaks would grow into one of the finest research institutes for Byzantine studies in the world and would become the single most important factor in the growth of the history of Byzantine art as a scholarly discipline in America. Berenson himself created a similar research center when he also donated his home, library, and art collection to Harvard some years later—a dream that the inauguration of Dumbarton Oaks had reinforced. His friend Charles Henry Coster wrote to Berenson in November 1940 about the inaugural ceremonies at Dumbarton Oaks: "We thought of you constantly, not only because we saw so many of your friends, but because what the Blisses are doing at Dumbarton Oaks is so nearly what you want to do at I Tatti."[2]

Although Dumbarton Oaks belonged to Harvard in 1945, the Blisses still controlled it behind the scenes and made major contributions to it until their deaths. Berenson, always well-informed about power and wealth, thus knew to write to Robert Bliss, his friend, not to the current director of Dumbarton Oaks. Receptive to the proposal, Robert Bliss responded that "Dumbarton Oaks is definitely interested" in publishing the project, which, however, was never realized on this basis.[3] The exchange between Berenson and Robert

Bliss, though minor, may stand for an often discreet, if not invisible, network that assembled art collections and supported scholarship on medieval art well into the twentieth century. With today's peer-reviewed grant applications, university promotions and tenure committees, and the complex bureaucracies of major museums, it is difficult to imagine that earlier system, so informal, even casual, and subject to the whims and passions of amateur donors, but also nourished by extraordinary financial support that could dwarf what is available today. As my contribution to this publication, I will look more closely at those interests and friendships that inspired the Blisses to begin collecting during the 1910s. I will then follow that collection as it focuses on certain aspects of Byzantine art during the 1920s and conclude with the first public display of the Bliss Collection at the international exhibition of Byzantine art held in Paris in 1931. My account is based substantially upon personal correspondence preserved at Harvard University and to a lesser extent at I Tatti in Florence and the Isabella Stewart Gardner Museum in Boston.

At the end of Berenson's letter there is a postscript: "What has become of the Royall Tylers, father and son?" Robert Bliss later replies, "Royall's boy, Bill, has just returned from Europe and is now filling an interesting position, at least for the time being, with the Department of State."[4] The "Bill" mentioned was William Royall Tyler (1910-2003), career American diplomat, who became the director of Dumbarton Oaks from 1969 to 1977. Ultimately more important for Byzantine studies and Dumbarton Oaks was William's father, Royall Tyler (1884-1953), because he encouraged the Blisses to begin collecting pre-Columbian and Byzantine art while they lived in Paris between 1912 and 1919. Later he served as an informal advisor for their purchases of Byzantine art. But how did Royall Tyler become interested in Byzantine art, and why was Byzantine art of

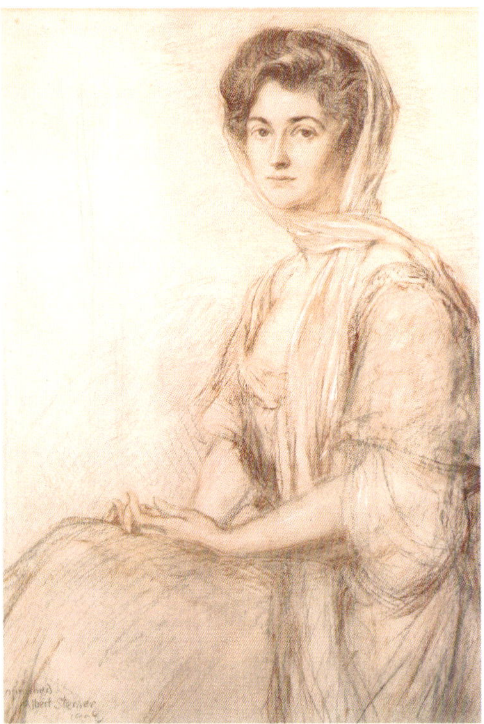

Figure 1. Albert Sterner (1863-1946), Mildred Barnes Bliss. *Crayon portrait. Dumbarton Oaks, acc. no. HC.D.1908.03. (Gr).*

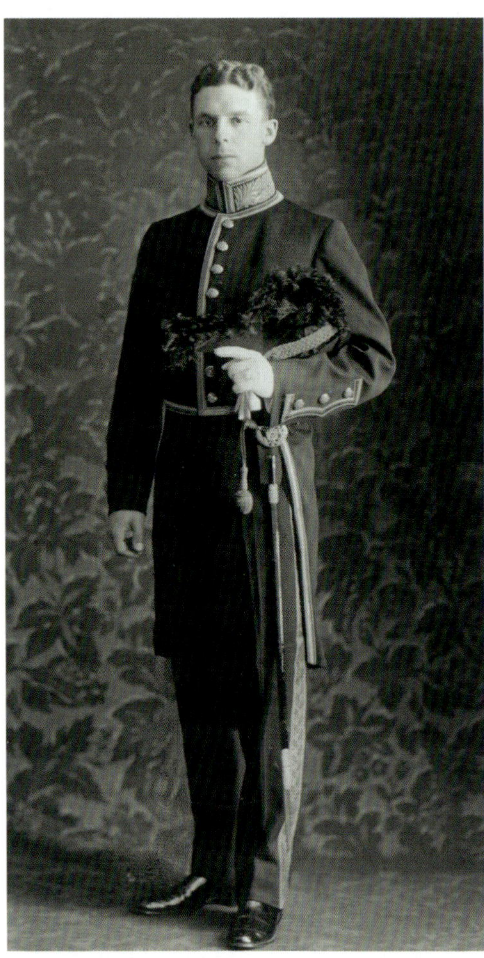

Figure. 2. Robert Woods Bliss, *St. Petersburg, c. 1905. Bliss Papers, Harvard University Archives.*

such interest to these wellborn Americans at the beginning of the twentieth century?

Royall Tyler was a descendant of a prominent New England family who was proud of its male lineage. By custom, family names skipped one generation, so Royall's father and son were William Royall Tyler; his grandson Royall Tyler. A more distant Royall Tyler (1757-1826) was a lawyer, jurist, and the author of the first American comedy. The father of the Royall Tyler of interest here was a Harvard graduate, class of 1874, and later the principal of Adams Academy in Quincy, Massachusetts. He died in 1897, when Royall Tyler was thirteen. Three years later, Tyler's mother married Josiah Quincy, the former mayor of Boston. The family spent considerable time in Europe, and in 1900 they visited Venice.[5] It was an epiphanic moment for the teenager, as he described:

> Domes, pendentives, marble wainscoting, porphyry columns, carved capitals, mosaic pavements and the light in which they bathed suddenly made me feel that these things were for me…. My experience in Venice opened the door leading to Byzantine art, the central point from which I approached other domains. For the time being, the Byzantine vision alone held me.[6]

His interest in Byzantine art, he later wrote, began in this period.[7] Four years later, Tyler's mother died, leaving him financially secure and established in Europe, where he would remain for the rest of his life.

A FTER HARROW SCHOOL, ROYALL TYLER ATTENDED New College, Oxford, and the University of Salamanca. Intending to be a diplomat, he studied a number of European languages but then pursued several careers, often simultaneously. At age twenty-five, he was an independent scholar and the author of a well-informed book about Spanish art, *Spain: A Study of Her Life and Arts* (London: G. Richards, 1909), as well as many translations from Spanish. In 1911, he became the editor for the British Record Office of the Spanish Calendar of State Papers, which ultimately resulted in five volumes. During the 1920s, he was an expert in international finance for the League of Nations and later the World Bank. Throughout his life, Tyler was also a collector and historian of Byzantine art and with his fellow American Hayford Peirce, of Bangor, Maine, wrote three books on Byzantine art beginning in 1926.[8]

Because their mothers were friends, Royall Tyler had known Mildred Barnes since childhood. However, in 1902, their relationship grew more serious. The two saw each other in Europe and corresponded frequently. Having fallen in love, they were planning to tour Europe together in 1908, when Mildred Barnes, then twenty-eight (fig. 1) suddenly broke off the relationship and one month later married Robert Bliss (fig. 2), a rising young diplomat, who was four years older. While Mildred and Robert Bliss would remain married for fifty-four years, the actual ceremony caused comment at the time, for Robert Bliss and Mildred Barnes were stepsiblings. Robert Bliss's father had married Mildred Barnes's mother when both children were nearly adults. Marrying, among other things, kept the family fortune intact. The source of the wealth was oil, but not of the usual sort. Mildred Barnes's father was a major investor in Fletcher's Castoria. Patent medicine ultimately paid for Dumbarton Oaks and everything else.[9]

After Mildred Bliss married, her correspondence with Royall Tyler cooled for a bit, but then resumed. In 1910, Tyler wrote Mildred Bliss about his work on the aforementioned book on Spanish art and about the love of his life, Elisina Richards, who it so happened was the wife of his publisher and the mother of four children.[10] The ever-gracious Mildred Bliss promptly wrote to congratulate Elisina Richards,[11] and the two women began a friendship that lasted for decades. Mildred Bliss soon came to the aid of the couple. It seems that Elisina Richards's husband would not grant a divorce, and the

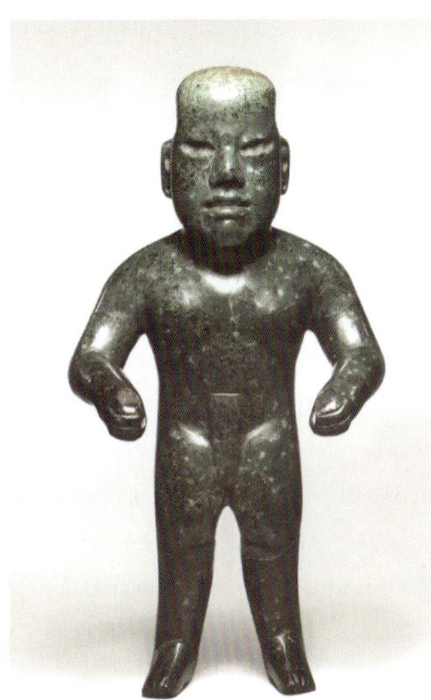

Figure 3. Diopside-jadeite figure, Olmec period (Middle Formative phase—c. 900-400 BCE). Dumbarton Oaks, acc. no. PC.B.014.

problems multiplied when Tyler wrote several months later that Elisina was pregnant. He invited Mildred Bliss to be the godmother, to which she readily agreed and proceeded to do even more.[12] The correspondence indicates that the Blisses invested one thousand pounds in Richards's husband's publishing firm shortly before he agreed to a divorce.[13] Soon Mildred Bliss was paying the school tuition for Elisina Richards's children.[14]

In 1912, the two couples became closer still, when Robert Bliss was posted to the American embassy in Paris, where the Tylers had been living for some years. Immediately the two couples were dining together, and Royall Tyler was taking Robert Bliss to art galleries, something that he did regularly, especially if he could see "Gothic sculpture or Persian pottery, or … early Chinese things," as he wrote a few months before their arrival.[15] Robert Bliss long remembered those outings and the purchases that resulted, later describing them in the introductions to two catalogues of his pre-Columbian collection:

> Soon after reaching Paris in the spring of 1912, my friend Royall Tyler took me to a small shop in the Boulevard Raspail to see a group of pre-Columbian objects from Peru. I had just come from the Argentine Republic, where I had never seen anything like these objects, the temptations offered there having been in the form of colonial silver. Within a year, the antiquaire of the Boulevard Raspail, Joseph Brummer, showed me an Olmec jadeite figure [fig. 3]. That day the collector's microbe took root in—it must be confessed—very fertile soil. Thus, in 1912, were sown the seeds of an incurable malady![16]

When he wrote this, Robert Bliss was actively engrossed in that passion (fig. 4). In the decade before, he had written of the larger context and motivation for his enthusiasm:

> In the Edwardian world of spacious living when the accumulating of possessions was regarded in Europe as an innocuous but "distinguished" pastime, I became aware of Pre-Columbian stone and gold work. The first few objects acquired in

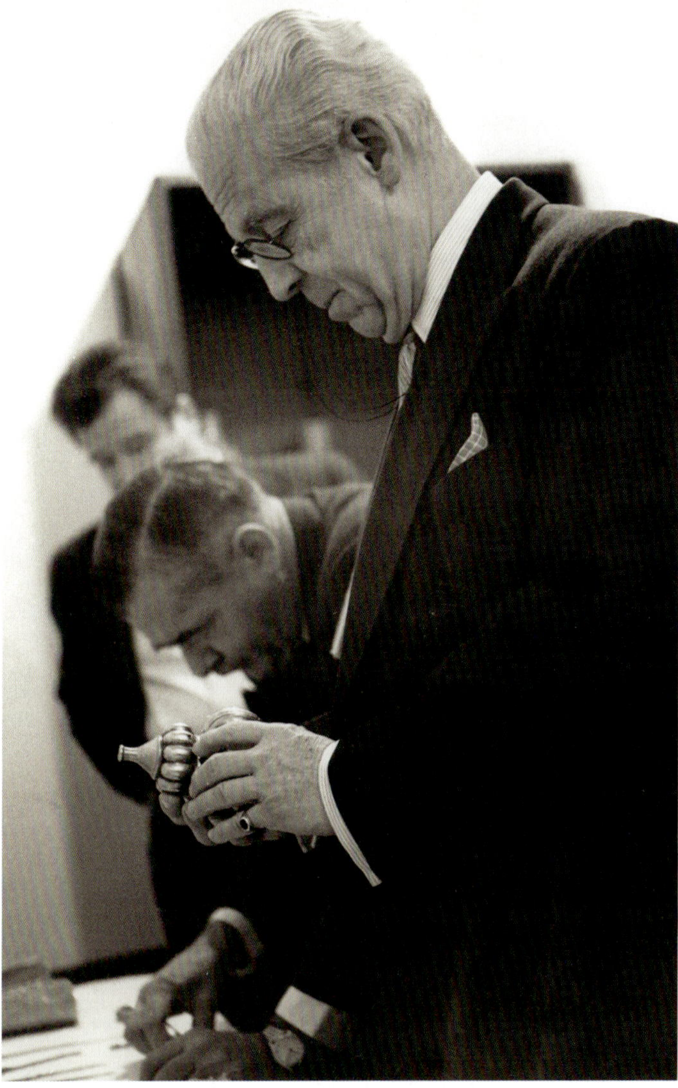

Figure 4. Robert Woods Bliss studying a pre-Columbian object, 1950s. Dumbarton Oaks Archive.

Paris thirty-five years ago were an antidote to the insidious charm of the XVIII Century and opened vistas I soon became eager to explore.[17]

Under Royall Tyler's tutelage, Mildred Bliss turned to Byzantine art, focusing, for example, more on Coptic than Gothic tapestries, which Tyler came not to favor.[18]

The Brummer Gallery that Robert Bliss and Royall Tyler visited on the fateful day supported both interests. Recently William D. Wixom, the former head of the medieval department of the Metropolitan Museum of Art, remarked that in the twentieth century the real tastemakers for medieval art had been the dealers, for "more often than not there are one or two dealers behind each of the major collectors."[19] Joseph Brummer (d. 1947) and his younger brothers Imre (d. 1928) and Ernest (d. 1964) were just such dealers for several fields of art.[20] Born in what once was Austria-Hungary, Joseph Brummer studied art in Budapest and Munich before moving to Paris to work with Auguste Rodin in the 1890s and Henri Matisse in the next decade. Penniless and doing odd jobs in Matisse's studio, Brummer began selling Japanese prints to support himself. In 1908 or 1909, he used his profits to open a small gallery on Boulevard Raspail. His brothers soon joined the business, and Ernest Brummer continued it after the deaths of the other two.

Part of a network of artists and sculptors in Paris, Joseph Brummer was the first dealer for Henri Rousseau, who painted his portrait in 1909.[21] Later, the Brummer Gallery exhibited many of the leading painters of the School of Paris. From the 1910s, the Brummers were trying to sell art in America. After World War I, they opened a successful branch in New York and soon became the trusted purveyors to American patricians and the museums they favored. They were known for supporting American collections of French medieval art and especially for their personal integrity as dealers.[22] By 1910 or so, Joseph Brummer began dealing in African art and played a crucial role in introducing it to the Parisian avant-garde. For pre-Columbian art, Brummer has been called "the pioneer dealer," the first to treat these objects as art.[23] His brother Ernest Brummer co-authored an important general book on the subject that appeared in 1928, the plates of which inspired Henry Moore to create modern versions of Mexican sculpture and further helped to make what had been ethnographic and remote seem artistic and contemporary.[24] As for classical, early Christian, and medieval art, Kurt Weitzmann remarked in his memoirs that Joseph Brummer had the finest collection "ever amassed by a single hand."[25]

Into this Parisian society, Royall Tyler introduced the newly arrived American diplomat from Argentina. One can only speculate what first took them to Brummer's shop—its reputation for displaying the latest artistic fashions, their shared interest in Hispanic countries, or perhaps Tyler's own collecting of pre-Columbian art.[26] Whatever the reason, the experience was formative, and Robert Bliss gained more than a few fine pre-Columbian pieces. As he wrote in the 1947 catalogue, he sought objects that gave him "pleasure—a sculpture boldly conceived; a gold object delicately wrought; a fabric of good design, and well-woven; ceramics with interesting iconography; metal work of quality:—a rhythm here a form there." These were precisely the formalist values of the Brummers and their Parisian milieu, and they would also be applied to the Byzantine art they collected.[27]

Joseph, in particular, had a strong effect on those he took seriously, and it was only these clients whom he wished to serve. William H. Forsyth, an earlier curator of medieval art at the Metropolitan Museum of Art, described how the chosen were taken into Brummer's inner sanctum to see an important work of art. There, Joseph Brummer "would sit brooding over the piece, fondling it as if he were the wizard who had created the treasure. The enthusiasm of this strong-willed, hypnotic little man was contagious, making one yearn to glimpse the other treasures he might have hidden."[28] The Blisses shared some of that intensity and applied it to their collecting of Byzantine art, as shown by their reactions to objects purchased during the 1920s.

But there is another important incident that took place at the Brummer Gallery in 1913.[29] A year after Robert Bliss's initial visit to the gallery, Royall Tyler too was smitten, for he saw something there that he could not easily afford, but also could not live without—a Byzantine silver chalice (fig. 5). On March 11, Tyler wrote in a letter to Mildred Bliss, while they both were in Paris, what today would be expressed simply in a telephone call:

Dear Mildred, I can't wait any longer to tell you that the chalice is here. I waited, sweating great drops of blood, in Brummer's back shop yesterday afternoon, while Stoclet made him an offer for the Egyptian relief, the chalice, and most of the other good things in the shop. Brummer said, I think quite truthfully, that the offer was much too low, considering that it cleared him out of pretty nearly everything fine in his shop. Stoclet made another offer, also rejected. Stoclet then said he was going back to Brussels, and would think the matter over and wire again. Brummer said he must decide at once or he would not undertake not to sell in the meantime.… Stoclet thought prudent to disregard this, and five minutes after he'd turned his back, I was running home, *toreando los automobiles por la calle* with *la santissima* under my arm. I have got to find 6,500 francs now, and selling in a hurry is a bore—however, the joy of having the thing leaves no room for care—I don't care what I sell.

Prichard, the only man alive who really knows and feels Byzantine art, and I spent most of last night over the chalice. He says it is a crown of glory, the finest thing out of S. Mark's etc. and tears came to his eyes when the inscription burst upon him. It runs + ΤΑ CΑ ЄΚ ΤѠΝ CѠΝ CΟΙ ΠΡΟC‑ΦЄΡΟΜЄΝ ΚЄ (abbrev, for ΚΥΡΙЄ) otherwise: "Those things that are thine, out of thy possessions, to thee we offer, Oh Lord!"

Prichard says it is the XI cent.—the greatest moment of Byzantine art. Not a word to a soul except Robert.[30]

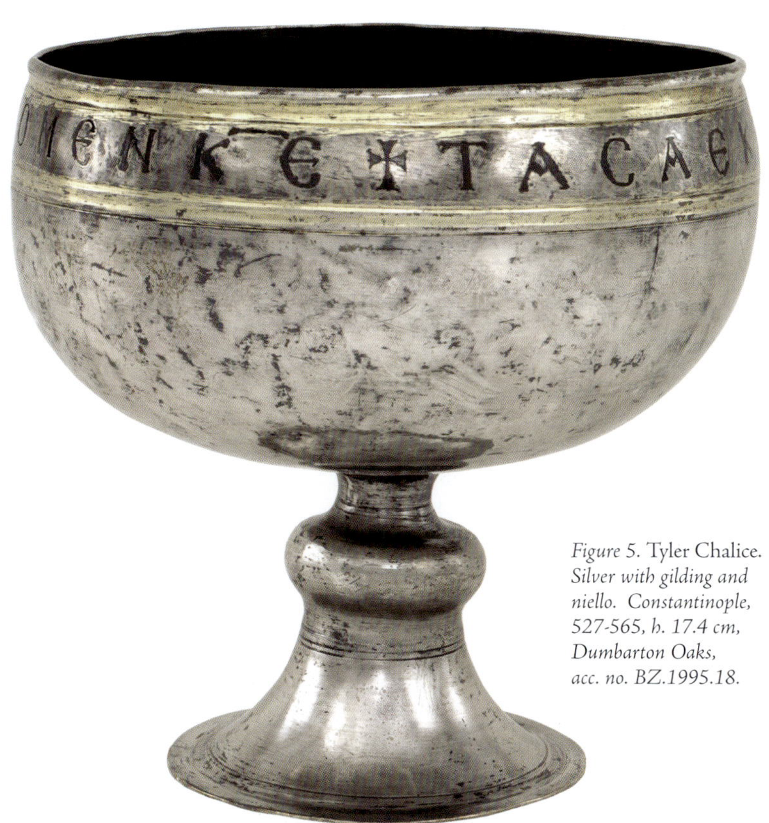

Figure 5. Tyler Chalice. Silver with gilding and niello. Constantinople, 527-565, h. 17.4 cm, Dumbarton Oaks, acc. no. BZ.1995.18.

On March 31, he writes again to Mildred Bliss that the chalice is theirs for 28,000 francs: "we are in the purée for years to come, but don't care ... please come and see it very soon."[31]

Certain details in this letter need glossing to be appreciated today. The collector Adolphe Stoclet, who also wanted the chalice, was indeed significant competition. Surely wealthier than Tyler, he and his wife, the daughter of the painter Alfred Stevens, whom the Blisses would later collect,[32] were steeped in the contemporary French aesthetics of art for art's sake regardless of period or culture. Two years earlier, the Stoclets had completed their mansion in Brussels designed by Joseph Hoffmann and decorated by Gustav Klimt and the Wiener Werkstätte. Their tastes in historical art were eclectic and wide-ranging and included Western medieval and Byzantine art, as well as Chinese, African, and pre-Columbian art.[33] Thus, they were perfect clients for the Brummer Gallery and hence Stoclet's proposal to buy most of its inventory.

The colleague with whom Royall Tyler initially shared the news of his chalice was Matthew Stewart Prichard, an English aesthete connected to artistic and intellectual circles in Boston, London, and Paris. The way that Tyler mentions Prichard indicates that he was already known to the Blisses. They were fortunate, for Prichard was a remarkable person. During these years in Paris, he was at the center of a vital network of artists, collectors, historians, and philosophers. Especially important was his friendship with Matisse, who made his portrait. An Oxford-educated barrister, Prichard had come to Boston in 1902 to accept a position at the Museum of Fine Arts. In 1907, Prichard left Boston but maintained strong ties to that community. A faithful, accurate, and evocative correspondent, he wrote hundreds of letters to Isabella Stewart Gardner until her death in 1924, and these are the principal sources about his life.[34]

Shortly after returning to Europe, Matthew Prichard visited Venice, where he too had an aesthetic epiphany. The Pala d'Oro at San Marco had the greatest attraction: "I suppose I shall not ever see a more glorious page in my life-time."[35] Later, he wrote Mrs. Gardner:

My study now is the Pala d'Oro and the byzantine treasures in the Marcian basilica. That will lead naturally to mosaics wh[ich] I shall see a little at Ravenna next week where I shall go expecting a blow in the face."[36]

"Sublimely romantical" Ravenna did not disappoint, and he found the ivory throne of Maximian to be "bone ... transformed into gates of heaven, all of this work ... sustained by the most exalted and permanent sentiment."[37]

Back in Paris, Matthew Prichard began visiting Matisse's studio in 1909, where Joseph Brummer was studying. During that time, Matisse was also becoming interested in Byzantine art, drawing the circle of associates even closer. Prichard's letters from 1908 mention meeting in Paris Mrs. J. Montgomery Sears, an artist, collector, member by marriage of a prominent and wealthy Boston family, and someone well known to Mrs. Gardner's artistic circles. Sears's godson was Royall Tyler, and he and Prichard had earlier met in Boston. After Prichard moved to Paris, his relationship with Tyler strengthened, secured by their mutual love of Byzantine art.

Entranced by Venice and Ravenna earlier than Matthew Prichard, Royall Tyler returned every few years. In 1905, he wrote Mildred Bliss about his regard for "Byzantine things," as he was about to revisit Ravenna. "I know no town in Italy that I like as well as Ravenna."[38] He and his wife, Elisina, toured to Venice and Ravenna in 1912 in the company of the British curator Eric Maclagan, whom Prichard knew.[39] Maclagan visited Paris periodically and was posted there during the war. In January 1913, Tyler wrote Robert Bliss to introduce Maclagan, the "head of Sculpture and Architecture at the S. Kensington," and to propose that he give them advice on their pictures.[40] The next month Tyler wrote that he took Maclagan along to see a tapestry of the Adoration of the Magi, and in April, Elisina Tyler proposed to bring Maclagan and "his bride-elect" to tea with the Blisses.[41] While serving in Paris during the Great War, Maclagan also became part of the circle of Edith Wharton that included the Tylers and the Blisses. After the war, he returned to the recently renamed Victoria and Albert Museum and became its director in 1924.

THIS SET OF COLLECTORS, CONNOISSEURS, AND curators took Western medieval and Byzantine art seriously. Elisina Tyler, for example, remembered how Matthew Prichard and Royall Tyler were earnestly discussing O. M. Dalton's *Byzantine Art and Archaeology*, then the finest general account of Byzantine art, shortly after it was published in 1911.[42] Two other people whom the Tylers knew during the 1910s were Louis Metman, the head of the Musée des Arts Décoratifs in Paris, and the aforementioned Hayford Peirce of Bangor, Maine. Metman would later agree to have the first international exhibition of Byzantine art at his museum, a show that was important to the Tylers and the Blisses.[43] Tyler met Hayford Peirce in 1918 through their common work in Army intelligence during the war, and he would become Tyler's close collaborator in the next two decades, fellow collector of Byzantine art, and someone who also helped the Blisses with acquisitions. After Peirce's death in 1946, Dumbarton Oaks acquired from his widow some of his art, as well as his extensive coin collection, formed during the 1920s and 1930s.[44] In sum, the friendships formed during the 1910s in Paris were for life.

Though seemingly soulmates when it came to Byzantine art, Matthew Prichard and Royall Tyler were otherwise quite different. Prichard was spiritual, ascetic, and otherworldly. Tyler enjoyed life. Lord Salter, who would later recommend him for positions at the League of Nations, remarked on the person whom his friends called Peter, noting that

[T]here was a curious affinity between Peter Tyler's unequalled subtlety of appreciation of a good wine or a good food—and of a work of art. In an exclusive French restaurant where all who served and all who supped did so with the devoutness of participants in a religious service, all looked to Peter Tyler as one of special authority. So too if his judgement were asked as to the dating of a picture he would seem to sniff at it just as he might have done at a wine of quality—and his verdict would be accepted as final by those professionally engaged in such identifications.[45]

Presumably that same taste led the Tylers in 1923 to purchase a Burgundian chateau, whose "chapel and the round tour," he noted proudly, "have been classé mounments [sic] historiques."[46] Today the property still remains in the Tyler family and may be rented for rather more than professors can afford.[47]

In Tyler's letters, religion is seldom mentioned, except for an odd note here and there about a certain high mass.[48] Popular piety did not interest him.[49] Mildred Bliss was yet more secular, as is shown by an exchange about whether she would agree to be the godmother of the Tylers' son. Owing to the circumstances of the relationship of father and mother, the baby's baptism was a concern for Royall Tyler. In agreeing to be the godmother, Mildred Bliss wrote Tyler on September 25, 1910:

It is only right however that you both understand the irregularity of my being sponsor. Although I was baptized by 3 protestant denominations (!), I have never been confirmed into any church. Several times I have been to the communion table in Episcopal churches, but it occasioned controversy. My other 6 godchildren were baptized in the Church of England, the Episcopal and Unitarian sects, and in each case the clergyman, when informed of my unorthodoxy, admitted me on the personal ground of Deism, right living and the hope of confirmation.[50]

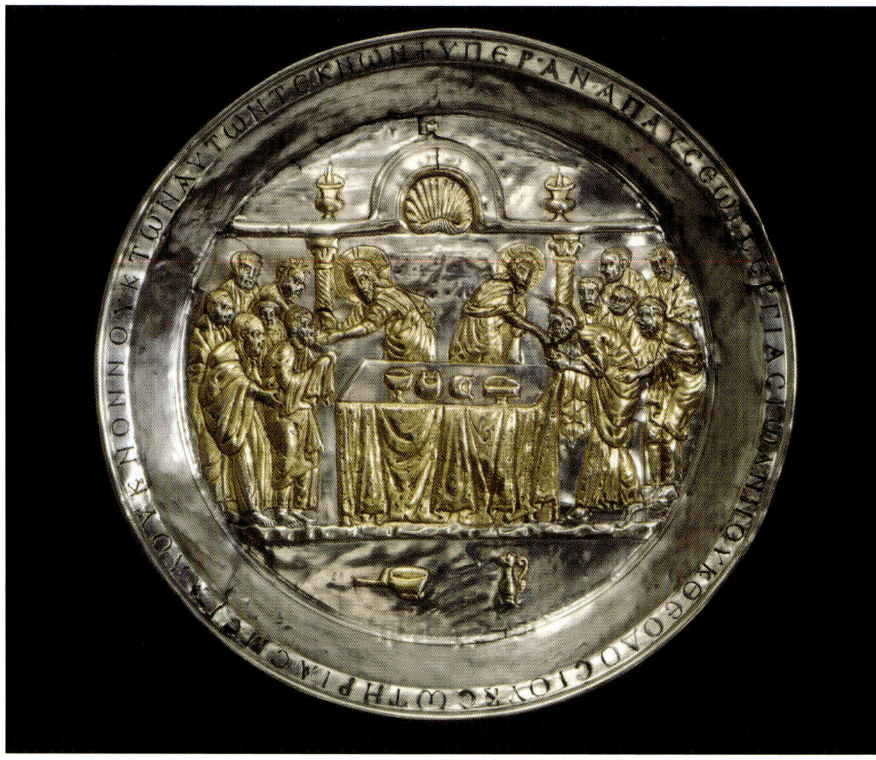

Figure 6. The Riha Paten (Bliss Paten). *Silver, with gilding and niello. Constantinople, 565-578, d. 35 cm. Dumbarton Oaks, acc. no. BZ.1924.5.*

Such a person, it must be emphasized, did not collect Byzantine art for its religious value, and in general, the Dumbarton collection, even after the Blisses gave it to Harvard, continued to emphasize the courtly, secular aspects of Byzantium.

FOR MANY YEARS, THE OBJECTS THAT THE BLISSES acquired owed much to the aesthetic acumen that Lord Salter described, for Mildred and Robert Bliss had complete trust in Tyler's judgments. Already in 1911, Mildred Bliss wrote Royall Tyler, inviting him to visit them in Buenos Aires, where Robert Bliss was posted, in order to advise them on their painting collection.[51] The Tyler-Bliss correspondence during the 1910s has few other references to Byzantine and related art, although the Blisses were buying during the period, if not always wisely. A silver bowl, bought in 1913 and later exhibited as post-Sassanian, is now attributed to sixteenth-century Ragusa.[52] The Blisses made few other significant purchases of Byzantine or early medieval material in the 1910s, perhaps because the war absorbed their full attention. Mildred Bliss was involved with the relief effort, and Robert Bliss with duties at the embassy. In 1919, he was reassigned to the U.S. State Department in Washington, D.C., and, while they still maintained an apartment in Paris, Robert Bliss began thinking of a permanent home in Washington.

In 1920, the Blisses bought what became known as Dumbarton Oaks and spent the rest of the decade renovating it from afar. The next year, they purchased from the Brummer Gallery five fragments from three crosses.[53] Their American sojourn lasted until Robert Bliss's appointment to be the American ambassador to Sweden in January 1923. That spring he and Mildred Bliss passed through Paris on the way to Stockholm and saw old friends.[54] On June 6, Royall Tyler wrote Mildred Bliss thanking her for an ivory that she had sent him and inviting her to see a church the next week.[55] In the same year, the Blisses purchased an ancient bronze ewer with silver incrustation and two Scythian ornaments. Their collecting had yet to find its eventual focus.

But 1924 was an auspicious year for most of those connoisseurs of Byzantine art, who had been together in Paris during the previous decade. The exception was Matthew Prichard, who had been imprisoned in Germany during the war. Afterward, he failed to settle into a regular profession but continued to see old friends and write about them to Mrs. Gardner until her death in July. In January, Prichard met Hayford Peirce and mentioned to Gardner that Peirce and Royall Tyler were preparing a book about Byzantine art; it appeared two years later.[56] In February, he wrote that Matisse's daughter had married one of his friends, Georges Duthuit, with whom Royall Tyler would collaborate for the Paris exhibition of Byzantine art in 1931.[57] In June, Mrs. Gardner learned that "Royall Tyler is second in command now in settling the finances of Hungary for the League of Nations; and there is to be a new head to the South Kensington Museum, a great friend of Tyler and a friend of mine, Eric Maclagan."[58] Mrs. Gardner knew of Tyler's new career and his book with Peirce before he wrote Mildred Bliss in September about both and asked to publish the sixth-century silver paten (fig. 6) that he had helped them buy the previous January.[59]

Because the Blisses were now ensconced in Stockholm, Royall Tyler's judgment about the paten, when it was on the Parisian art market, was most helpful:

It is unquestionably right, and has been given all the diplomas Paris can dis-
cern, having been dealt with (together with my chalice) in a communication to
the Institut by Diehl, and described and reproduced in a very important article
on Antiochene silver…. [T]he object … to me is perhaps the most moving
thing—possibly excepting my chalice—I've ever seen for sale….

If you get it, live with it for a good long time anyway. It will teach you
a great deal about the age when Santa Sophia and the great churches of
Ravenna were built, when the most perfect Byzantine enamels were made and
the throne of Maximian was carved. [60]

The Parisian dealer Kalebdjian Frères had offered the paten to
Tyler at the end of 1923. Shortly thereafter it passed to Georges
Demotte, another dealer, from whom Tyler bought it for the Blisses.
Thanks to the research of Marlia Mundell Mango, we now know
that the paten and Tyler's beloved chalice were from the same Syrian
hoard, an especially large one, unearthed in 1908.[61] Objects from it
continued to appear on the art market for a number of years.

Primed by these purchases, both Royall Tyler and the Blisses could
not help but be excited by the opportunity two years later to acquire
an entire silver cache that turned out to be—as they had begun to
suspect—the very treasure from which their chalice and paten derived. While Tyler labored in Budapest for the League of Nations,
returning occasionally to visit his family at Antigny, Elisina Tyler
made the rounds of Paris galleries and described what she saw to
Mildred Bliss. One day at Kalebdjian's, she and Hayford Peirce were
shown "photographs of a Byzantine silver treasure found in Syria. I
considered these objects so beautiful and interesting, that I told him
to send the photographs for you and Robert to see, and to tell you all
about it. You see the likeness to our two objects, don't you."[62] She was
referring to their liturgical silver. Among the photographs seen was
likely to be one photograph published by Marlia Mundell Mango.[63]

Her collecting instincts fully aroused, Mildred Bliss replied:

First I must tell you that the Kalebdjian photographs are most upsetting. Bless you
for having them sent. The likeness to your and our "family" features is so close that
we must surely wander up this alluring trail in the hope of increasing the family! [64]

She noted that Kalebdjian had wanted twelve thousand pounds
plus 20 percent and the expenses for someone to bring the objects
from Cairo or Aden. Four days later, Elisina Tyler responded that
the asking price is large indeed and offered to do what she could:
"If someone is needed to go to Cairo … either Royall, or I, or Peirce
would be very glad to go."[65] They too had become excited.

Next Robert Bliss wrote Royall Tyler at the League of Nations in
Geneva:

If the various pieces are as fine as they are represented in the photographs,
the collection is of great interest, particularly certain pieces resembling your
chalice…. When Kalebdjian's letter reached us, Mildred and I both said that
there was none we would rather have pass on the objects than you, with all
you have to do, whether it would interest you to go to Egypt to look at the
object…. Now what do you think? We are burning to know and a preliminary
wire would be a relief in our present state of excitement.[66]

On December 4, Tyler promised that either he or Hayford Peirce
would make the trip, to which Robert Bliss responded: "Great has

been the excitement caused by your letter and we hope and pray that
you may be able to arrange to go to Cairo."[67]

Further rapid exchanges resolved details. Robert Bliss would pay
the travel expenses of Royall Tyler and his son, Mildred Bliss's godson, William Royall, and wired one thousand dollars. In a final letter
from December 29, before sailing two days later, Tyler explained that
Elisina Tyler and Hayford Peirce had decided to come along (not at
the Blisses' expense), so great was the promise of an unknown cache
of Byzantine silver. A further paragraph shows how far they were
willing to go to secure it:

A point that I shall have to go into with some delicacy on arrival is: whether
the collection falls under the export-of-works-art-interdiction. I should be
glad if you would let me know whether or not you wish me, in case no other
way seems to be open, to appeal to the good offices of the U.S. Minister. A
wire "yes" or "no" would enlighten me on this point. You might consider the
possibility of depositing the things at the Legation, and letting them stay there
until an opportunity occurs for their removal by the bag. If I got from a wire
"deposit" that is what I'd try to do.[68]

In other words, what was contemplated was the clandestine export
of the silver by diplomatic pouch from one American embassy to another.

Given the degree of anticipation all shared, it should not be surprising, if surely disappointing even at this distance, that the great
adventure did not end successfully. The three connoisseurs were not
unanimous, but Royall Tyler, the most influential voice, was resolved
and cabled, "objects seen immediate decision inadvisable."[69] Peirce
agreed with his collaborator; Elisina Tyler held the minority opinion. Husband and wife wrote Robert Bliss on the same day:

I [Elisina] am told that my impression of the silver treasure may interest you. I
am giving it sous reserve expresse of the opinions of those wiser than I am.

When Royall came to call me to see the treasure he warned me that it had
all been washed with acids, and looked brand new. My eye was prepared, and
I was not shocked by the white look of the objects. I did not examine their
surface to discover the alterations produced by the acid. I saw traces of discol-
ouration on one of the chalices,—faint yellow marks supposed to be traces of
dissolved gilding. I did not mind these. It seems to me that the eye is carried
beyond the superficial accidents that have befallen the metal, and is held by the
intrinsic character of the objects.[70]

The letter is proof that in the years spent with Tyler she had developed her own eye and sense of value or "intrinsic character."

In his own letter, Royall Tyler, supported by his collaborator, focused on surface condition. Perhaps overly accustomed to the patina
of his chalice, Tyler thought that the color of the silver was wrong:

What first struck and rather shocked us was the colour of the objects. They
appear all to have been in the hands of the Bishop of Hama, who had them very
drastically cleaned with acid, so that the silver is quite white and the gilding has
almost all been removed with the patina—though here and there small blotches
of patina have defied all efforts, acid and scratching, to efface them. The quality
of the silver, as you may imagine, is not beautiful as a result of this treatment….
The collection is of very great interest archaeologically, and would make a very
valuable addition to any museum.[71]

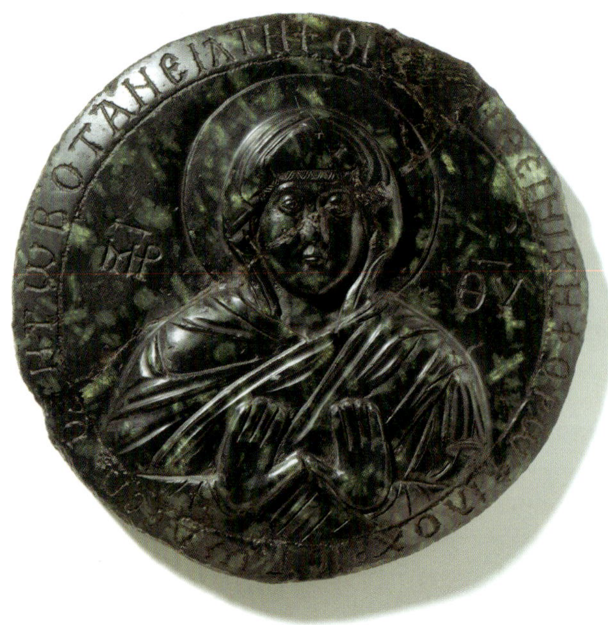

Figure 7. Medallion of Emperor Nikephoros Botaneiates (Roundel with the Virgin Orans). *Serpentine. Constantinople, 1078-1081, d. 17.5 cm. Victoria and Albert Museum, London, England, A.I-1927.*

T HE PRIORITIES OF THE THREE CONNOISSEURS differed from those of a museum. They preferred beauty to archaeological significance, but disagreed on the importance of surface condition. On the return voyage, Royall Tyler added that it would not have been difficult for the silver to leave Egypt because it did not originate in Egypt, and the owner had an official Egyptian declaration to this effect.[72] At the end of the month Robert Bliss wrote Tyler in Budapest and accepted his judgment.[73] There the matter ended. Sometime over the next two years, the ever astute Joseph Brummer obtained the silver and sold it to Henry Walters in 1929[74]; so ironically that which the Blisses rejected and thus never reached Dumbarton Oaks is today in nearby Baltimore at the Walters Art Museum.

While the Blisses were absorbed with the silver, they missed an important opportunity that Royall Tyler had introduced in the summer of 1926. The Austrian government, he had learned, was going to permit the abbey of Heiligenkreuz to sell a circular medallion decorated with an orant Virgin and inscribed with the prayer of Emperor Nikephoros Botaneiates (1078-1081) (fig. 7).[75] This medallion, which is of high quality and has a Constantinopolitan provenance, is comparable aesthetically to Robert Bliss's first purchase, a polished Olmec figure of similar color (fig. 3), although of a different stone. Yet, in spite of Tyler's enthusiasm ("It is one of the most beautiful objects of art I know"), the Blisses did not take the bait. In December, in the midst of the negotiations about the Egyptian expedition, Tyler informed Robert Bliss that not having heard from him about the serpentine relief, he negotiated for the Victoria and Albert Museum and bought it for eleven hundred pounds.[76] Eric Maclagan must have been pleased; the Blisses, on the other hand, ultimately were not. Four years later, Mildred was still thinking about the serpentine relief. It "stuck in

our crop, and the more I looked at the slide [provided by Royall] the worse I felt about it."[77]

In the spring of 1927, Robert and Mildred Bliss visited Paris on their way to Buenos Aires, where Robert Bliss was to be the new American ambassador. Afterward, Elisina Tyler sent Robert Bliss a small sculpture of a bird in basalt, now considered to be late Roman in date. She hoped that "it might grace your writing-table at Buenos Ayres. It was a great joy to see you both again and my most affectionate thoughts and good wishes linger round you both."[78] The small bird is now a part of the Dumbarton Oaks Collection.

But it was silver that still held the great attraction, as indicated by another flurry of letters the next year. In the beginning of January 1928, Royall Tyler enclosed a photo of a silver dish at a Parisian dealer:

[The] Stroganoff dish, well known to students, and a most marvelously beautiful object. This thing you certainly ought to buy, if it stirs you as I think it will…. Having it and the Riha paten, you would possess the two capital pieces of Christian plate of the early Byz. ages.[79]

The plate in question, at the State Hermitage Museum, in St. Petersburg, since 1911, represents two angels standing on either side of a large cross. It had recently been illustrated in Charles Diehl's *Manuel d'art byzantin* and there credited to the Stroganoff Collection, Rome.[80] Excitedly Mildred replied:

What have you done to us, dearest Royall? We are in a hyper-excited state over the Stroganoff dish. How came you not to cable us about that? I am familiar with it, and should have leapt at the chance, and am now terror-stricken lest, during the lapse of time required for the arrival of your letter, it should have escaped…. We dread what the price is almost certain to be, but an object of that kind is worth a sacrifice…. This Argentine chapter is simply ruinous, and we would rather barter our souls for such a majestic object as the Stroganoff dish than acquire four or five lesser pieces, however alluring they may be. Mind you get that Stroganoff dish! And when you do, won't you keep it with you and enjoy it for a bit?[81]

Robert Bliss's ambassadorship in Argentina was a difficult one,[82] and Byzantine art was a solace for both him and Mildred. To whet further their appetite for the Stroganoff plate, Royall Tyler reported on February 1 that Hayford Peirce had seen the plate and "says it is a most noble object…"[83] But the next letter brings the surprising and sad news that Hayford had decided that the plate was a fake, suspecting the original had been replaced by a copy.[84] Missing from the files is Mildred Bliss's reply, but it can be surmised from Tyler's empathetic response: "I ached when I got your letter of Jan. 31 and saw how you felt about the dish. But such accidents will happen."[85]

Three years later, the Blisses lost another purchase of an important work of art when they could not decide about an early Palaiologan miniature mosaic of the forty martyrs of Sebaste (fig. 8), even though Tyler had described it as "very beautiful…. infinitely varied and rich … marvelous technically."[86] Hayford Peirce bought it instead. Eventually the panel reached Dumbarton Oaks, when his widow donated it in his memory in 1947.[87] More satisfactory were the negotiations for two reliefs from Persepolis. In December 1930, Tyler sent Mildred Bliss a photograph of the first one (fig. 9)

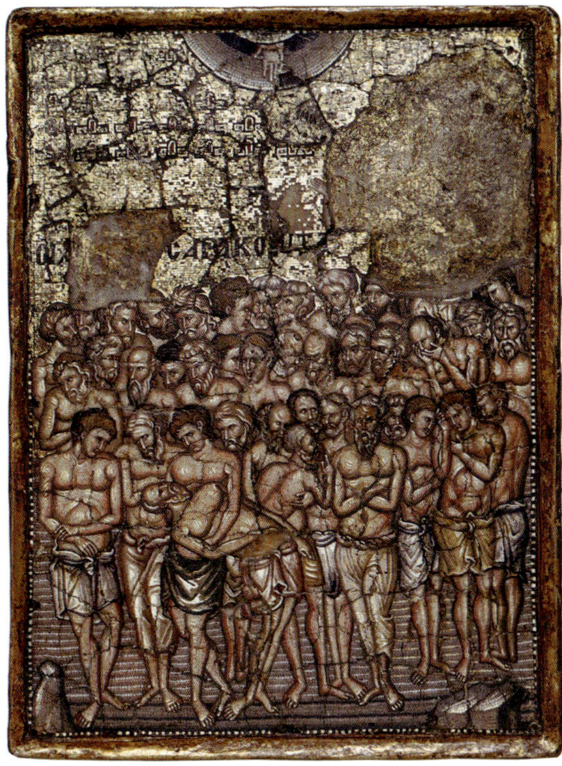

Figure 8. The Forty Martyrs of Sebaste. *Miniature mosaic. Constantinople, c. 1300, h. 22 cm. Dumbarton Oaks, acc. no. BZ.1947.24.*

for which the Parisian dealer Raphael Stora wanted $15,000.[88] This time, cables promptly secured the purchase, for Mildred described their initial response to the photograph as follows:

> You threw us into a flutter of excitement over the Persepolis relief. It was a crazy thing to do to take you up so promptly, but it hit Robert in the pit of the stomach luckily, for I saw the photograph first and it had done for me exactly the same. So when your answering cable came we were profoundly pleased, and long to touch the dark grey marble, whose patina you describe in a way that makes me thirsty.[89]

The letter attests to the Blisses' visceral reaction to the tactility of sculpture, a quality that Robert would continue to appreciate in pre-Columbian sculpture. For example, one curator reported that he liked to carry in his pocket a small piece of highly polished Olmec jade. "It was his 'lucky piece,' a fine object to be played with and caressed in the hand."[90] Because of his collecting habits, Robert Bliss was known to a pre-Columbian art dealer in Los Angeles as "a polished stone man."[91] Royall Tyler probably shared the same sensibility. On the first page of their book of 1926, Peirce and Tyler made a truth-in-materials argument, crediting the Byzantines with being "alive to the quality of the medium…. They treated hard stone with a sense of its texture, and Proconnesian marble in a new manner, produced an art of coinage based on a true appreciation of gold, [and] brought out the essential character of ivory."[92] This sensitivity to the surface of a work of art was the main reason that the silver treasure had been rejected a few years previously.

Among the highlights of the Tyler-Bliss correspondence in the period surveyed is Royall Tyler's letter to Mildred Bliss about the trip that he and Peirce took in 1927 through Bulgaria to Turkey. It reveals Tyler's reactions to the contemporary city of Istanbul and its Byzantine monuments, especially Hagia Sophia, and ends with the

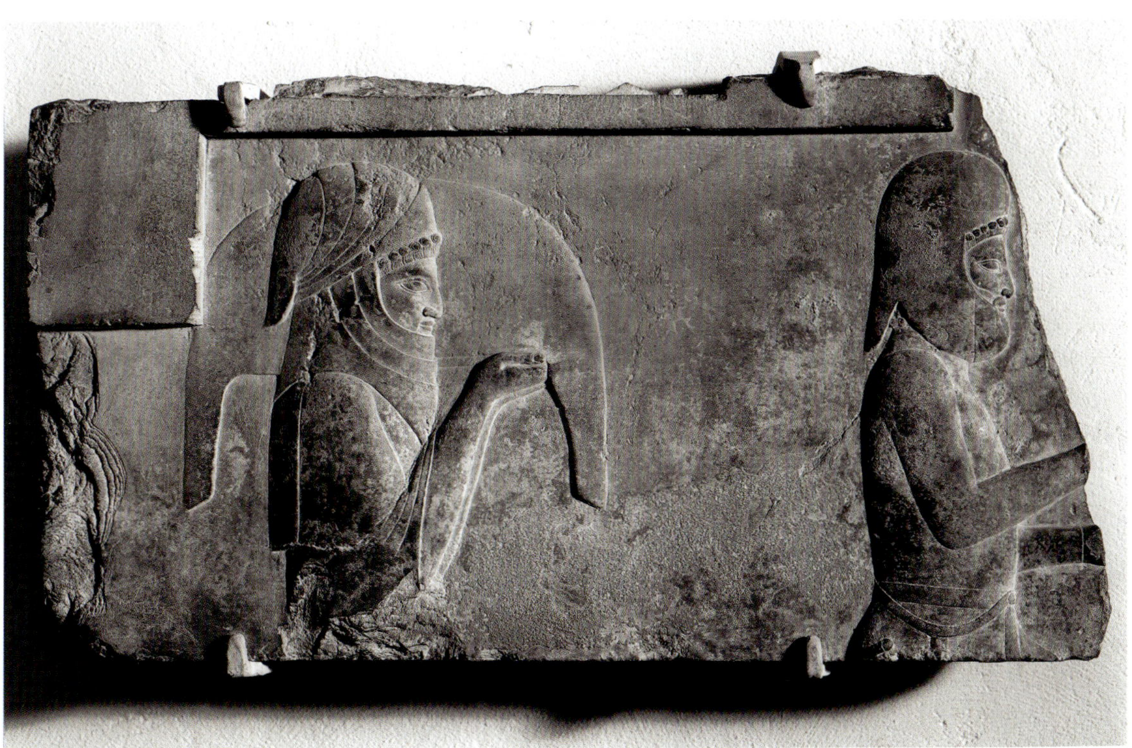

Figure 9. Relief of Two Attendants. *Limestone. Achaemenian; from the Palace of Darius or Xerxes at Persepolis, c. 500 BCE, h. 37.5 cm, w. 67.5 cm. Dumbarton Oaks, acc. no. BZ.1931.1.*

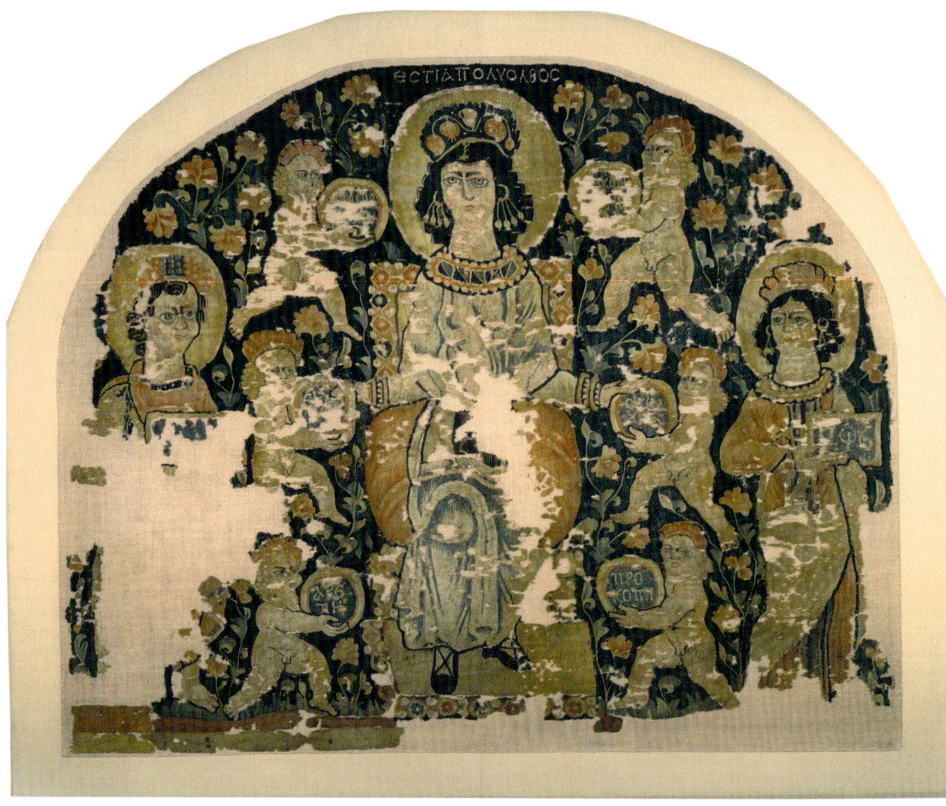

Figure 10.
Hestia Polyolbos
("Hestia— Goddess
of the Hearth—
rich in blessings").
Wool tapestry.
Egypt, 6th century,
113 x 137 cm.
Dumbarton Oaks,
acc. no. BZ.1929.1.

wish that he could show Mildred around the Great Church.[93] More relevant to the Blisses' collection are the letters about Tyler's preparations for the first international exhibition of Byzantine art held at the Musée des Arts Décoratifs, Palais du Louvre, from May 28 to July 9, 1931. The latter, according to Kurt Weitzmann, "was a spectacular event, which to a considerable extent reflected Tyler's taste: it was extraordinarily rich in the minor arts … while it neglected icons."[94] The exhibition was also the first major public display of the collection that the Blisses had been building, and it was the acme of Tyler's career as a Byzantine art historian/connoisseur. Two general books written with Peirce appeared in 1932 and 1934, and another was ready to be printed when World War II began. Peirce's death soon after the war's end turned Tyler to other projects, mainly the long-delayed editing of the State Papers for Spain and a biography of Emperor Charles V that appeared posthumously.

But in the early 1930s, Royall Tyler was thoroughly engaged with Byzantium. The Paris exhibition occupied the years between 1929 and 1931. Because Tyler had returned to Paris in 1928 to be the European representative for Hambro's Bank of London, he was available when, in October 1929, Georges Salles of the Louvre and Eustache de Lorey from Damascus sought his support for the exhibition.[95] Georges Duthuit and Hayford Peirce soon joined the group, and Duthuit became its secrétaire général. In November, Royall Tyler asked Mildred Bliss for loans from their collection, and "Milrob" telegraphed that they would participate.[96] Financing the exhibition was another issue discussed; the Blisses contributed $1,000.[97]

Royall Tyler particularly wanted their recently acquired Coptic textile of Hestia (fig. 10), and Mildred Bliss promised to bring it with them to Paris.[98] When it did arrive, without the Blisses unfortunately, Tyler examined it

…[with] Metman, Guérin, Alfassa, Salles and Duthuit. Their enthusiasm knew no bounds. Alfassa, who was inclined to be doubtful about our ability to get together a Byz. Exhibition of the first order, simply boiled over with delight, and proclaimed that it beat all the Gothic tapestries in the world into a cocked hat.

In his opinion, the Hestia tapestry "will be considered the finest thing in the Show."[99]

In the rush up to the opening—"working day and night at the Show, as well as my business … my nerves … ragged"—Tyler sent frank comments about different scholars and nationalities, including the Americans:

I'm sorry to say that the U.S. loan is, apart from your magnificent things, wretched. Mr. Morgan's things were refused at the last minute, and the stuff the American Ctee … selected, is such rubbish that we are hesitating about exposing it, which makes one feel rather sick considering the huge sums for which the muck is insured.[100]

But he remained most disappointed that Robert and Mildred Bliss were not able to see his exhibition. The Blisses were equally distraught:

Mildred and I can hardly bear missing that exhibition and if there were any way in which we could get away for a two-week visit to Paris, nothing would hold us back. But it cannot be done. Your letters are the bright spot in a monotonous, exacting life.[101]

The exhibition "opened its gates to a dense multitude," and Tyler reported that it

… is really being a huge success, and far more people are coming than we could have hoped for. Of course our expenses have been huge, and it's doubtful whether they'll be covered, but happily David Weill is immensely enthusiastic about it, tells people that it's the finest exhibition he's ever seen in his life, and has assured Metman that he'll look after any deficit.[102]

S WEPT UP IN THE EXCITEMENT, THANKS TO ROYALL Tyler's letters, Mildred Bliss asked him for photographs of the objects displayed in order to make slides for a lecture she was to give in French at the American Embassy. Robert Bliss was asked to speak on the exhibition in Spanish at the university in Buenos Aires.[103] Responding to a letter (not preserved), Tyler wrote, "Yes, I was delighted about the Byz. Show—from start to finish, though exhausting, it was the most enjoyable thing I've ever had anything to do with."[104] His enthusiasm was infectious. He and his friends had more objects exhibited than any other private collectors. Besides their Coptic tapestry (fig. 10), the Blisses loaned fourteen other pieces, including their paten (fig. 6). Hayford Peirce, surprisingly, sent the same number; Tyler loaned eighteen, a tribute to his collector's eye, but also perhaps to his role in the organization. And, of course, his chalice was there (fig. 5).

During the 1930s, these connoisseurs of Byzantine art, who once had learned from each other in Paris, began to go their separate ways. To attend to his family's business, Hayford Peirce returned to Bangor, Maine, in 1928, marrying in 1937. A son of the same name became a science-fiction writer. Matthew Prichard, ten to twenty years older than the rest, died in 1936. Royall Tyler returned to Hungary as a financial advisor to its government in 1932. The next year, Robert Bliss retired from the Foreign Service, moved back to Washington, and with Mildred Bliss devoted full attention to enlarging the library and art collection at Dumbarton Oaks.

During the spring of 1932, the Blisses told Royall Tyler of their ideas for the future of their collection and library. The subject could hardly have pleased Tyler more, and, on Whitsunday (May 15, 1932), he wrote with great enthusiasm about what the research center might become. During the 1930s, the pace of the Blisses' collecting increased, always keeping in mind the principles that Tyler had established. He had indeed set them and Dumbarton Oaks firmly *"dans la voie byzantine"* ("in the Byzantine path"), the last words of his introduction to the Paris catalogue.[105] Ultimately, the Research Library and Collection of Dumbarton Oaks would become the Blisses' most enduring achievement.

Soon after Royall Tyler's death in 1953, Mildred and Robert Bliss added an amethyst intaglio of Christ (fig. 11) to the collection in memory of Tyler (fig. 12).[106] In 1955 to 1956, his wife and son donated the silver chalice (fig. 5) that Prichard and Tyler had studied so intently that night in 1913.[107] Another important piece that once belonged to a friend—Hayford Peirce's miniature mosaic icon (fig. 8)—had been donated previously in 1947. These objects preserve the memory of their former owners and stand for the bonds of art, scholarship, and friendship that first brought them together in Paris long before. ◆

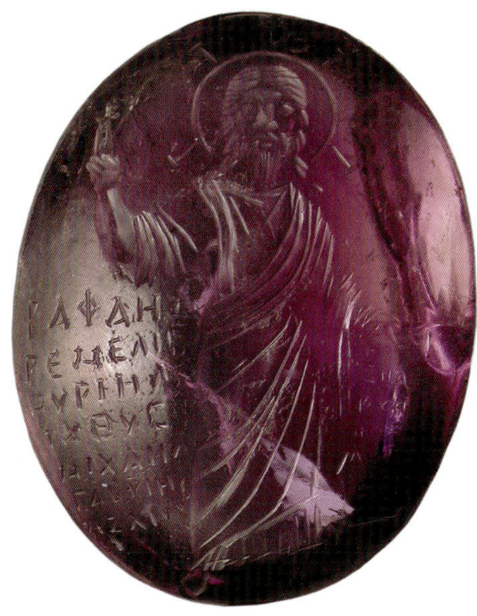

Figure 11. Intaglio of Christ. *Amethyst. Byzantine, 6th or 7th century, h. 3.4 cm, w. 2.9 cm [in the exhibition, cat. no. 1]. Dumbarton Oaks, acc. no. BZ.1953.7.*

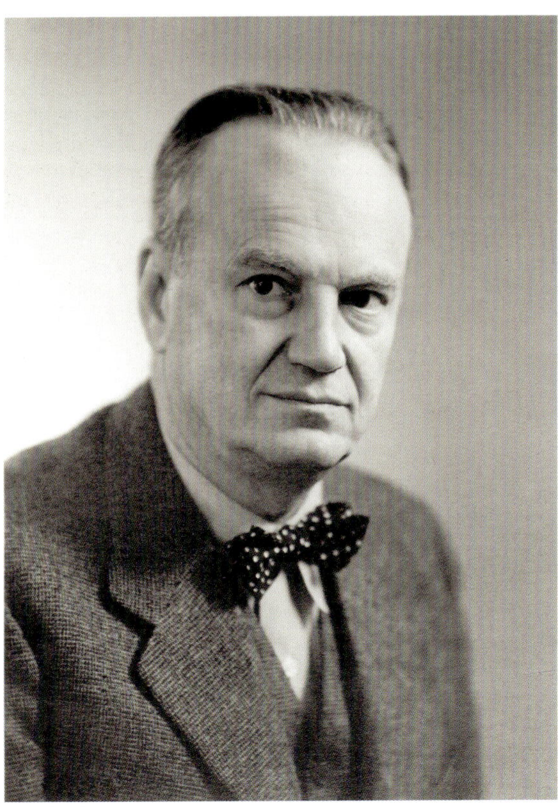

Figure 12. Royall William Tyler (1884-1953), photograph c. 1951.

1. BB to RWB, February 2, 1945. I Tatti, Bliss Letters.
2. Constable 1993, 144-145.
3. RWB to BB, March 30, 1945. I Tatti, Bliss Letters.
4. RWB to BB, January 10, 1946. I Tatti, Bliss Letters. Berenson knew the Tylers as early as 1913: Elisina Richards to MBB, December 1, 1913. HUA. A common friend was Edith Wharton.
5. On Royall Tyler, see Whitehill 1967, 60-61; and especially Whitehill n.d.
6. Whitehill n.d.
7. Peirce and Tyler 1932, 14.
8. Peirce and Tyler 1926, 1932.
9. Tamulevich 2001, 27, 30-32.
10. RT to MBB, April 12, 1910. HUA. By birth Mrs. Richards, soon-to-become Mrs. Royall Tyler, was a Florentine noblewoman, Contessa Elisina Palamidessi de Castelvecchio.
11. MBB to Elisina Richards, May 13, 1910. HUA.
12. RT to MBB, August 26, 1910; MBB to RT, September 25, 1910. HUA.
13. MBB to Elisina Richards, September 17, 1910; January 1, 1911. HUA.
14. ET to MBB, March 2, 1915; October 10, 1915. HUA.
15. RT to MBB, January 22, 1912, HUA.
16. Lothrop et al. 1957, 7.
17. Bliss 1947, 5.
18. Tyler corresponded with Mildred or Robert Bliss about Western tapestries early (March 20, 1909; January 29, 1913; February 7, 1913) and then at the beginning of the 1930s (January 26, 1930; February 19, 1930; February 23, 1930). In the early years, he seemed to share her enthusiasm. On March 20, 1909, Tyler wrote, "Thank you for the photograph of your tapestry, but I know the original! Unless I am very much mistaken indeed it was at a dealer's in Paris a year or two ago. It is a magnificent piece and I am delighted that you have it." This presumably was a tapestry of Christ and the Virgin that still belongs to Dumbarton Oaks, according to James Carder. On February 7, 1913, Tyler was interested enough in a tapestry of the Adoration of the Magi to show it to Eric Maclagan (about whom see below). But on July 20, 1931, Tyler wrote Mildred Bliss that while a particular millefleurs tapestry was indeed what she had been looking for, he would rather she spend her money on other things. HUA. The Blisses acquired their Hestia tapestry (fig. 10) in 1929 and other Coptic pieces in the 1930s.
19. Kaufman 1999, 10-11.
20. On the Brummers and their galleries in Paris and New York, see Barr 1951, 116-118; Leonard 1970, 36; Forsyth 1974; Paudrat 1984, 143-153; Coe 1993, 278-279; Bruzelius 1991; Johnston 1999, 213-214.
21. Paudrat 1984, 143.
22. Hayward and Cahn 1982, 39.
23. Coe 1993, 278-279.
24. Braun 1993, 98.
25. Weitzmann 1994, 114-115.
26. The Tylers loaned to the major exhibition in Paris in 1928: *Arts Anciens de l'Amérique*, nos. 478, 727, 730. The Blisses only loaned to the Byzantine exhibition that was held three years later at the Musée des Arts Décoratifs in 1931, as discussed later in this essay.
27. Cf. the descriptions of forms and media in Basler and Brummer 1928.
28. Forsyth 1974, 106.
29. Nelson 2004, 163-164; Carder's first essay in this volume.
30. RT to MBB, March 11, 1913. HUA. Cf. the translation of the inscription on the chalice as cited by Ross: "Thine own of Thine own we offer Thee, O Lord." As Ross points out "[t]hese words are found in almost all the Greek liturgies, and are alleged to have been used by Justinian for the inscription on the great altar of Hagia Sophia." *DOCat* 1, 10-11, no. 9.
31. RT to MBB, March 31, 1913. HUA.
32. MBB to ET, November 22, 1926. HUA.
33. Salles and Lion-Goldschmidt 1956.
34. Nelson 2004, 159-161.
35. MSP to ISG, August 4, 1907. ISGM.
36. MSP to ISG, September 29, 1907. ISGM.
37. MSP to ISG, October 27, 1907. ISGM.
38. RT to MBB, June 3, 1905. HUA.
39. ET to MBB, Venice, October 2, 1912. HUA.
40. RT to RWB, January 4, 1913. HUA.
41. RT to MBB, February 7, 1913; ET to MBB, April 13, 1913. HUA.
42. ET to H. R. Walker, March 8, 1938. ISGM.
43. ET to MBB, January 15, 1913. HUA.
44. Grierson 1999, 61; *DOCat* 1, 72.
45. Salter 1967, 93.
46. RT to MBB, September 5, 1923. HUA.
47. http://www.au-chateau.com/Antigny.htm
48. E.g., RT to MBB, received June 23, 1932. HUA.
49. E.g., RT to MBB, October 24, 1927, in which he worries that if H. Sophia were restored to Christian control, it would be overcome with modern Orthodox worshipers.
50. MBB to RT, September 25, 1910. HUA.
51. RT to MBB, June 26, 1911. HUA.
52. *DOCat* 1, 29-30.
53. Ibid., 25-28; communication from Marta Zlotnick, Dumbarton Oaks.
54. Tamulevich 2001, 88.
55. RT to MBB, June 6, 1923. HUA.
56. MSP to ISG, January 26, 1924, ISGM; Peirce and Tyler 1926.
57. MSP to ISG, February 25, 1924. ISGM.
58. MSP to ISG, June 30, 1924. ISGM.
59. RT to MBB, September 4, 1924. HUA.
60. RT to MBB, January 26, 1924. HUA. See also Carder's first essay in this volume and Nelson 2004, 163-164.
61. Mundell Mango 1986, 34.
62. ET to MBB, October 31, 1926. HUA.
63. Mundell Mango 1986, 26, fig. II.5. Of the two photographs that she published, only this one has a silver box. One is mentioned in the correspondence.
64. MBB to ET, November 22, 1926. HUA.
65. ET to MBB, November 26, 1926. HUA.
66. RWB to RT, November 30, 1926. HUA.
67. RWB to RT, December 8, 1926. HUA.
68. RT to RWB, December 29, 1926. HUA.
69. RT to "Milrob," January 7, 1927. HUA.
70. ET to RWB, January 7, 1927. HUA.
71. RT to RWB, January 7, 1927. HUA.
72. RT to RWB, January 13, 1927. HUA.
73. RWB to RT, January 31, 1927. HUA.
74. Mundell Mango 1986, 26; Johnston 1999, 214.
75. RT to MBB, July 21, 1926. HUA. On the medallion, see New York, *The Glory of Byzantium* 1997, 176-177, no. 130.
76. RT to RWB, December 12, 1926. HUA.
77. MBB to RT, November 11, 1931. HUA.
78. ET to RWB, May 4, 1927. HUA. In 1940, the Blisses gave the statue to Dumbarton Oaks. Vikan 1995, 18-19.
79. RT to MBB, January 8, 1928. HUA.
80. Diehl 1910, 297, fig. 156 (in the edition of 1925, fig. 160); Muñoz 1911, pl. 133; Bank 1977, 283-284, pl. 78.
81. MBB to RT, January 31, 1928. HUA.
82. Whitehill 1967, 67-68.
83. RT to MBB, February 1, 1928. HUA.
84. RT to MBB, February 17, 1928. HUA.
85. RT to MBB, March 13, 1928. HUA. Eventually, Dumbarton Oaks would acquire two major ivories once in the Stroganoff Collection, a plaque of Emperor Constantine VII and a pyxis of the Cantacuzene family that the Blisses obtained in 1936: *DOCat* 3, 58-60, no. 25; 77-82, no. 31.
86. RT to MBB, May 7, 1931. HUA.
87. *DOC* 1, 104.
88. RT to MBB, December 13, 1930. HUA; Richter 1956, 2-3.
89. MBB to RT, February 14, 1931. HUA.
90. Benson 1993, 23-24.
91. Coe 1993, 280.
92. Peirce and Tyler 1926, 5.
93. RT to MBB, October 24, 1927. HUA.
94. Weitzmann 1994, 144.
95. RT to MBB, October 23, 1929. HUA.
96. RT to MBB, November 13, 1929; Milrob to RT, December 14, 1929. HUA.
97. RT to MBB, November 3, 1930. HUA.
98. MBB to RT, March 1, 1930.

99. RT to MBB April 30, 1931. HUA.

100. RT to MBB, May 23, 1931. HUA.

101. RWB to RT, June 8, 1931. HUA.

102. RT to MBB, Paris, May 28, 1931; RT to MBB, June 10, 1931. HUA. David David-Weill was a major French collector of decorative arts and an important donor to the Louvre.

103. MBB to RT, November 11, 1931. HUA.

104. RT to MBB, August 12, 1931. HUA.

105. Paris, *Exposition d'art byzantin* 1931, 29.

106. *DOCat* 1, 96-97, no. 116. Also, cf. no. 1 in this catalogue.

107. Ibid., 11.

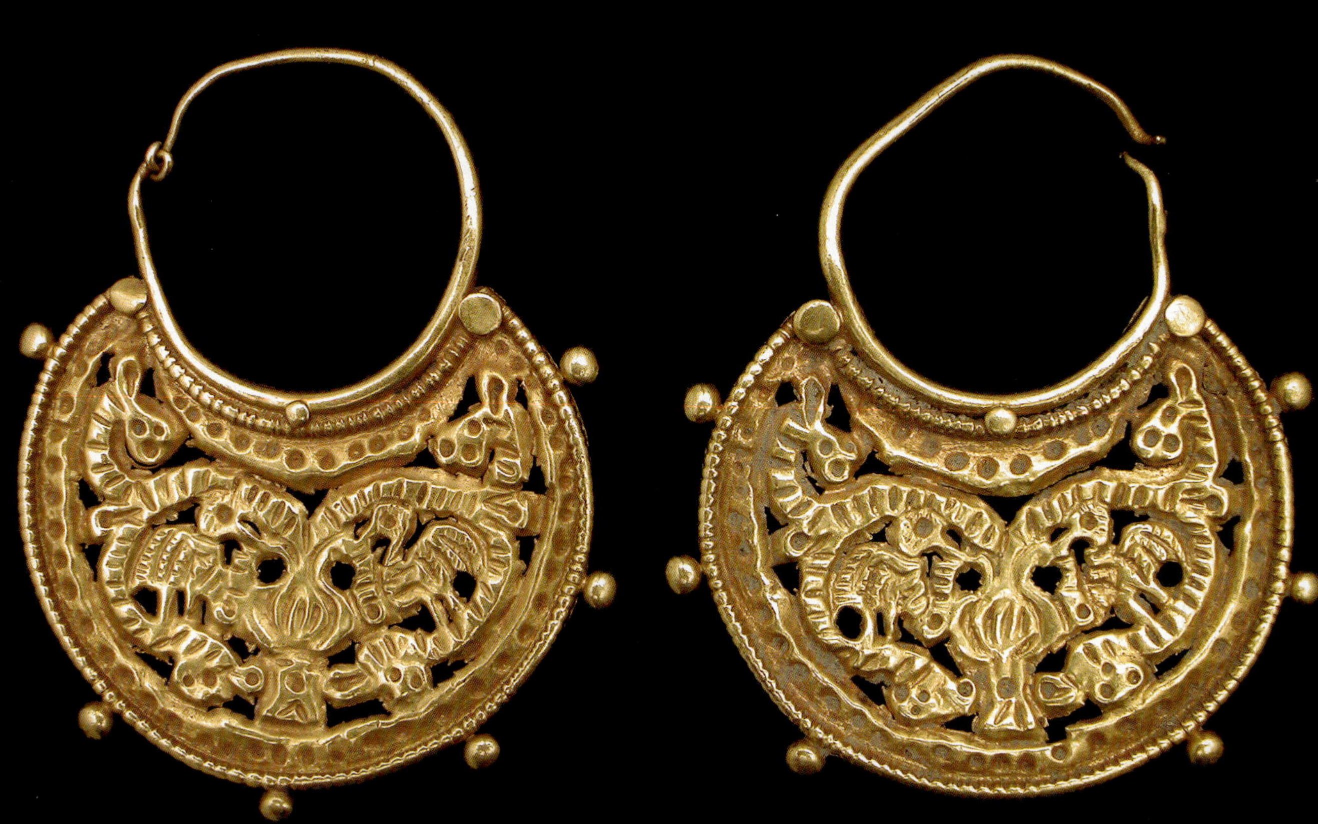

Objects of Art
from the
Byzantine Collection of Dumbarton Oaks

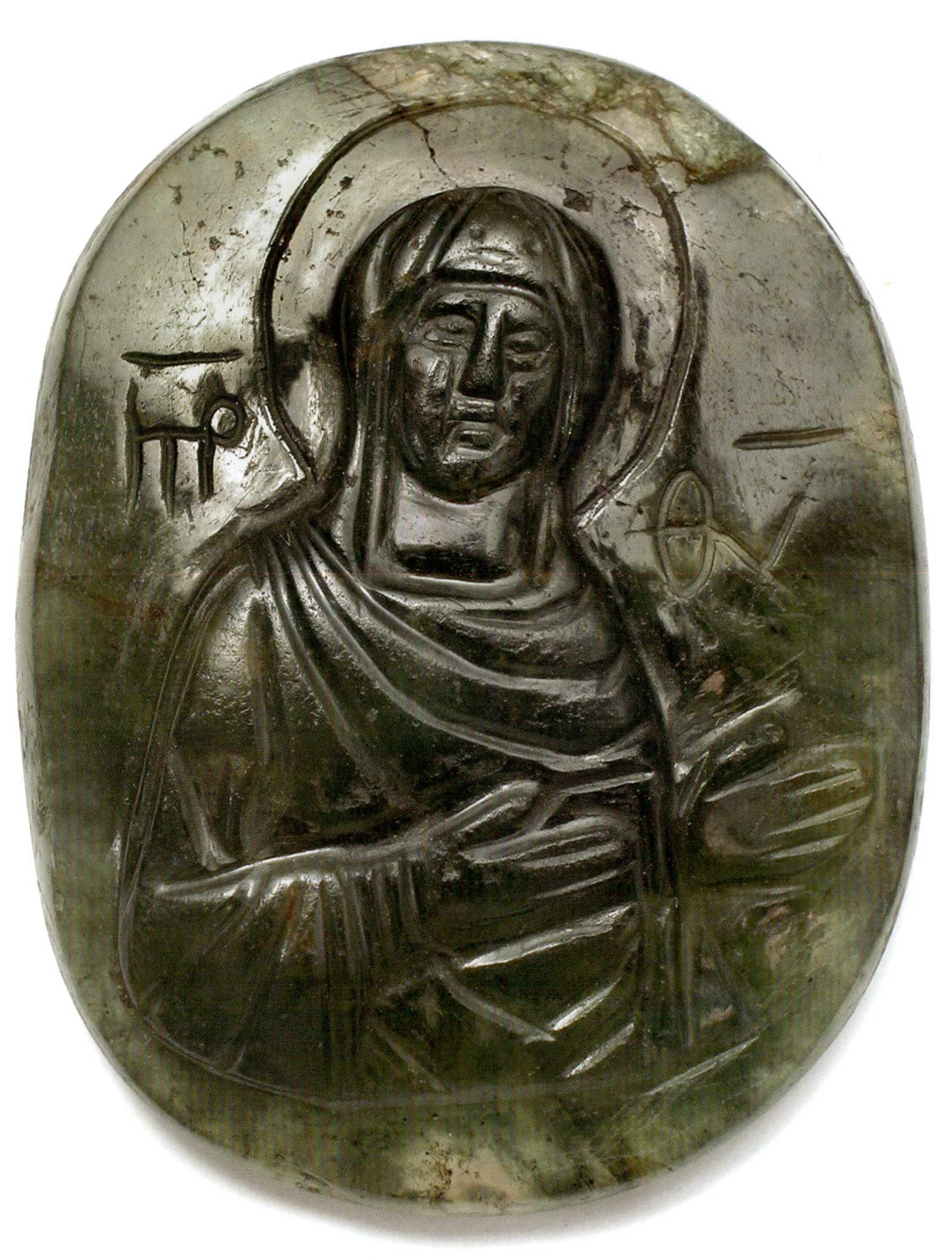

JEWELRY-GLYPTICS

Intaglios & Cameos

BY GENEVRA KORNBLUTH

BOTH INTAGLIOS AND CAMEOS WERE PRODUCED during the entire course of Byzantine history. Intaglios, with images sunken below the level of the background plane, have often been used as seal matrices. Apart from those mounted in rings, the intaglios pictured in this book appear not to have played that role. Their inscriptions are not retrograde and are, therefore, unsuitable for the production of legible imprints. The intaglios themselves, not their imprints, were meant to be viewed. Cameos, with images cut in relief above the level of the background plane, are almost always displayed as jewels. Engravers typically took advantage of the properties of layered stones (cat. nos. 11-13) by cutting some parts of the design in higher relief than others, giving garments colors different from flesh tones and background planes. When such translucent monochrome stones as sapphire are used for cameos (cat. no. 3), the greater thickness of parts in relief intensifies color in those areas.

All of these jewels are made from materials so hard that they can only be worked with rotating instruments and abrasive grit. Byzantine gem cutters normally used flat-sided engraving wheels, capable of cutting only straight lines in the stone. Apparent curves were produced by repeated applications of the engraving wheel, resulting in blocky engraving if the wheel was applied only a few times (e.g., cat. nos. 2, 7, 8, 10), or very fine curves if it was applied many times in a small area (e.g., cat. no. 1). Since a cameo is cut above the background plane, not sunken below it, the artist can avoid blocky cutting with little difficulty. But the traces left by the tools are much the same on intaglios and cameos.

Many Byzantine gems were used as medical or protective amulets. While some individuals may have disapproved, clearly most people saw no conflict between such practices and Christian belief. Numerous papyri attest to the harmony between what might now be seen as conflicting realms. One of the most succinct reads: "+Jesus Christ is victorious. Shivering, and fever with shivering, and fever, the Son of God pursues you. Holy, holy, holy is the Lord Sabaoth. Heal Gennadia, your maidservant. Jesus Christ is victorious.+"[1] Similar sentiments continued to be expressed on amulets used throughout Byzantine history: A tenth/eleventh-century cameo of Christ in St. Petersburg, for example, is inscribed "O Christ our Lord, he who puts his hope in thee will not fail."[2] Gemstone materials were generally thought to reinforce the power of images and words. Pliny the Elder (d. 79 CE) gives us a good sense of ideas popular before the founding of Constantinople. The Greek Orphic Lapidary (second century CE) records many additional practices, and a Byzantine version of it, the *Orphei Lithica Kerygmata*, reveals that they did not die out with Christianization.[3] Michael Psellus (1018-after 1081) provides evidence for the continuing popularity of such ideas into the Middle Byzantine period.[4]

---

1. Fifth century, Daniel and Maltomini 1990, 70-71, no. 25.
2. New York, *The Glory of Byzantium* 1997, 175-176, no. 128.
3. Halleux and Schamp date the text between the second and fourteenth centuries, emphasizing that it was compiled by "un chrétien byzantin, étranger à la complexe théurgie" of its source (Halleux and Schamp 1985, 138-139; date of original text, 51-57).
4. Cf. the entry on "Gems" in *ODB* 2, 828.

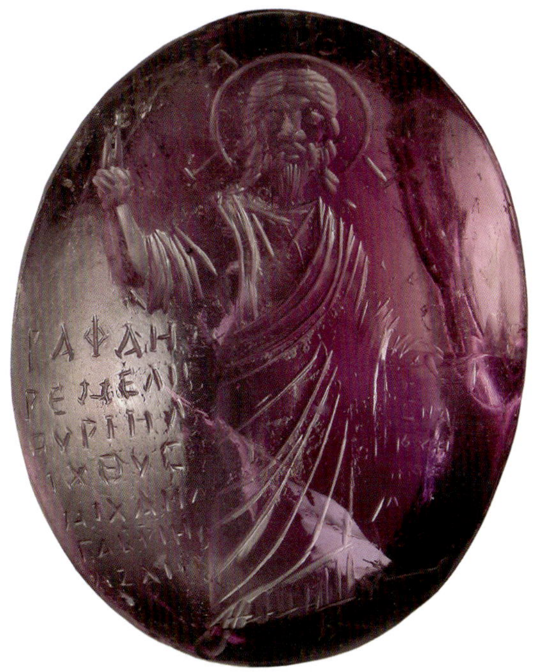

1. Obverse

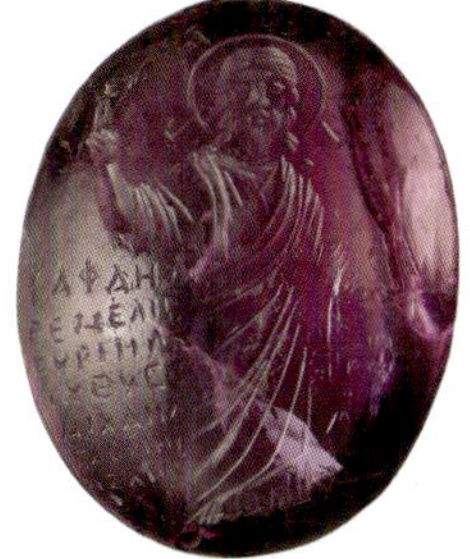
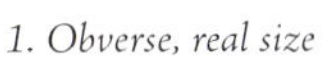

1. Obverse, real size

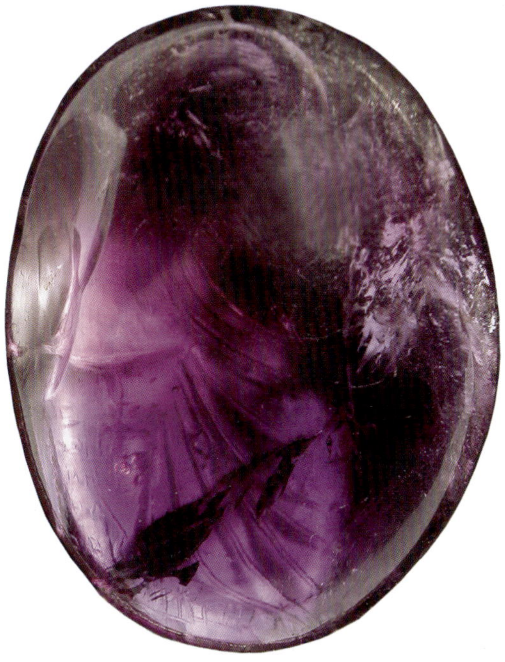

1. Reverse

1. Intaglio with Standing Christ

Byzantine, 6th to 7th century?
Amethyst (crystalline quartz), in a modern
gold setting
3.765 x 3 including mount x 1.455 cm

Inscribed: In field on Christ's right: ΡΑΦΑΗΛ
ΡΕΜΕΛΗ ΟΥΡΙΗΛ ΙΧΘΥС ΜΙΧΑΗΛ ΓΑΒΡΙΗΛ
ΑΖΑΗΛ (Raphael, Remiel [?], Uriel, Ichthys, Mi-
chael, Gabriel, Azael); on scroll: ЄΝ ΑΡΧΗ ΗΝ Ο
ΛΟΓΟС ("In the beginning was the Word," John 1:1).

Condition: The condition is unusually fine.
Apparent internal fractures are flaws (gas inclusions) formed during crystallization of the stone,
not later damage. Very small chips in the engraving
mark where those flaws have weakened the gem's
surface. Concavities on the reverse are probably
from a post-medieval owner's attempt to polish
away splintered stone.

Acquisition History: de Montigny Collection, Paris, in 1878; later purchased from Ratton,
Paris; gift of Mr. and Mrs. Bliss, April 14, 1953, in
memory of Royall Tyler.

Accession number: BZ.1953.7

Many features suggest that this object was
used as an amulet. Pliny reported the belief
that amethyst could prevent intoxication;[1]
Bishop Epiphanios of Salamis (c. 315-405)
noted that it might protect against storms;[2]
and the later Michael Psellus added that it
cured headaches.[3]

Christ holds the opening of the Gospel
of St. John, a text thought to have great
powers and often carried as an amulet,
as were the names of angels listed next
to Christ. A fifth/sixth-century papyrus
combined those names and a variation on
the incipit of John:

> In the name of the Father and the Son and the
> Holy Ghost—amen. In the beginning was God
> and God was light…. And you, heavenly doctor,
> in whose name and strength I write, I conjure
> you by the angel Michael and by the angel
> Gabriel and by the angel Raphael I conjure you,
> and by the angel Azaziel and by the angel Uriel I
> conjure you, and by the angel Ieremiel and by the
> angel Photuel.[4]

Powerful archangels were invoked for
healing and protection from all kinds of evil,
by image, name, or both.[5] While inclusion
of "Ichthys," possibly referring to Christ
as a messenger of God,[6] is unusual, there
are several gemstone amulets with angel
names, and one that includes "Emmanuel."[7]
Each being may have been invoked for a
specific reason. Isidore of Seville (d. 636)
attributed to Raphael the power of healing,
to Uriel domination over fire, to Michael
great strength, and to Gabriel the power of
prophecy.[8] A fourth-century amulet from
Beirut similarly divided up areas of responsibility between archangels.[9]

This particular amulet probably also
served as an ostentatious jewel. The stone
is itself very showy in its rare size and color
intensity. The engraving has been executed
so delicately that curves appear smooth
unless magnified. But most telling is the
placement of engraved details over the
stone's internal flaws. Christ's right arm
covers a major line of gas inclusions, and
the top of the scroll in his left hand is
positioned along a prominent horizontal
flaw. While cameo makers must always pay
attention to the peculiarities of individual
stones, Byzantine intaglio cutters rarely did.

A sixth- to seventh-century date is suggested by the unusual *Chi-Rho* monogram behind
the halo,[10] comparison with the Christ figure
in the Rabbula Gospels Ascension (586),
and the general style of the engraving, but
the amethyst is qualitatively so different from
other intaglios that this cannot be confirmed
by parallels within the gemstone corpus.

GK

References: Durand 1884, 767-772; Leclercq
1907, cols. 2088-2089; Leclercq 1924, col. 855;
Dölger 1928, vol. 1, 273-297; Pedrizet 1928, 256-
257; Barbel 1941, 208; *DOH* 1955, 98, no. 211;
Kitzinger 1956, 276; d'Alverny 1957, 292; Wentzel
1957, 55; Wentzel 1959, 20; *DOCat* 1, 96-97,

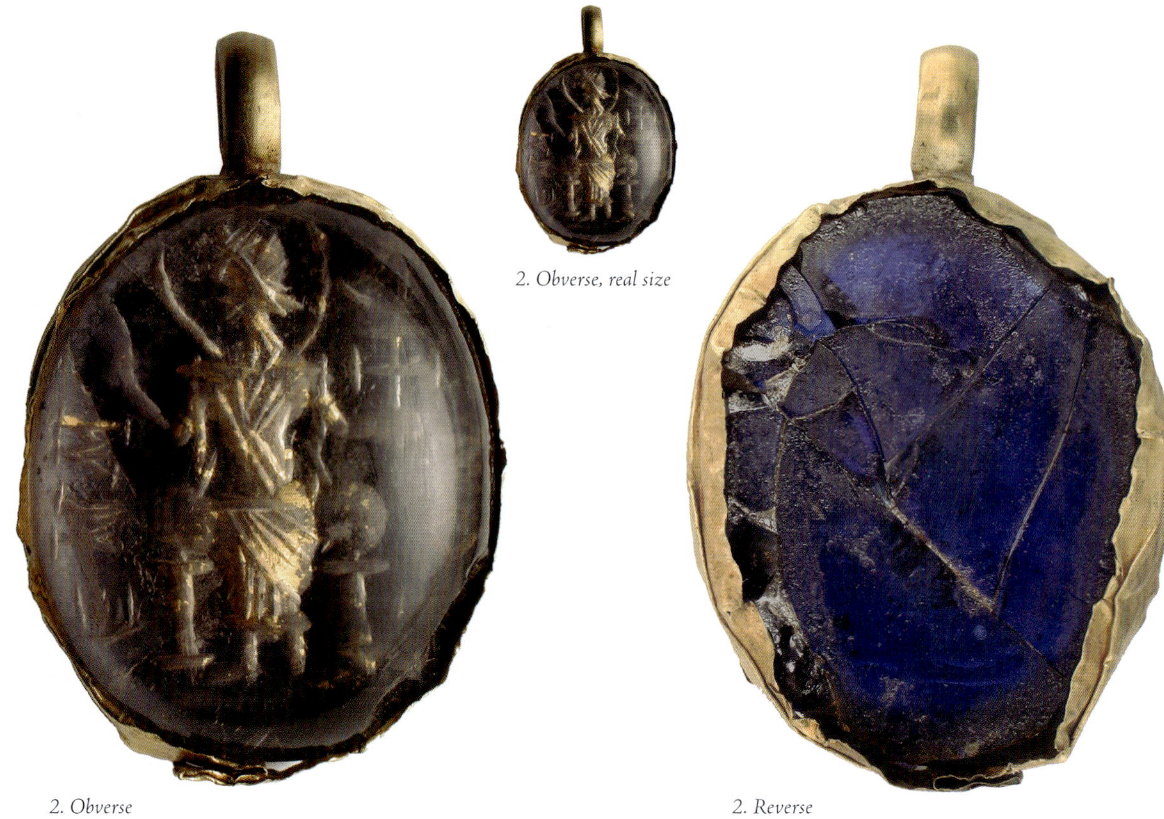

2. Obverse, real size

2. Obverse

2. Reverse

no. 116; *DOH* 1967, 98, no. 334; Wentzel 1968, note 12; Wentzel 1970, 370; Nees 1980, 140-142; Popovich 1983, fig. 2; Kornbluth 1994, 23; Spier forthcoming, no. 576.

1. Pliny, *Natural History*, book 37, 124: Eichholz 1962, 264-265.
2. On the twelve stones of the rational: Guenther 1898, 754-755.
3. Baldwin 1995, 398.
4. Daniel and Maltomini 1990, 104-112, no. 36. See also Kotansky 1994, 154-166, 270-300, nos. 33 and 52.
5. Bonner 1950, 170-171; Janowitz 2001, 27-35.
6. Dölger 1928.
7. E.g., Michel 2001, 315, nos. 521 and 522. "Emmanuel" among angel names: Leclercq 1907, col. 2088.
8. Flint 1991, 162.
9. Kotansky 1994, 270-300, no. 52.
10. Weigand 1929 and 1932.

2. Intaglio Christ Mounted in a Glass and Gold Pendant

Syria? 6th to 7th century?
Rock crystal (transparent crystalline quartz) with gilded engraving, mounted with blue glass in gold
3.295 (without suspension loop 2.69) x 2.12 x .89 cm

INSCRIBED: ЄMMANO(VHΛ) ("Emmanuel").

CONDITION: The pendant mount may be post-Byzantine. Its form is highly unusual, with a substantial ring attached to a setting of thin gold foil closed at the opposite end by rolling into a spiral. Breakage of the glass backing does not correspond to damage on the crystal. The original setting for the crystal may have held a second transparent stone rather than dark glass; compare cat. no. 8. Although patches have been lost, gilding survives on most details of the engraved image. The convex obverse of the intaglio is chipped on the lower right edge and near the suspension loop. The stone is not fractured internally, but rather allows the breaks in the blue glass to be seen through the crystal.

ACQUISITION HISTORY: Found in Antioch in 1947 (letter from Elie Bustros, October 15, 1950); purchased from Elie Bustros, Beirut; gift of Mr. and Mrs. Bliss, September 1950.

ACCESSION NUMBER: BZ.1950.35

The rock crystal is engraved on the flat back side, with the figure and inscription reversed so as to be correctly legible when viewed through the curved front surface. This stone belongs to a group of intaglios (including cat. nos. 7 and 8) that is generally dated to the sixth to seventh century by association with the "Abrasax gems," amulets whose obscure imagery is closely related to magical papyri from Egypt.[1] Many of those gems are now dated to the second to third century,[2] but production certainly continued later. It has been assumed that manufacture ceased with the triumph of Islam, though that break has not been documented. Most of the intaglios with Christian imagery can be dated to the sixth century or later because of their developed iconography.

The enthroned and nimbed Christ raises his enlarged right hand in blessing and holds in his equally large left hand a cross (not a "globe with a cross potent")[3]. The figure is very similar to those on two gold rings and to a jasper intaglio in Munich inscribed XPICTOC ("Christ") on the reverse. The inscribed "Emmanuel" is also found on a large sixth-century intaglio formerly in Vienna.[4]

This stone and related gems could have served as either amulets, private icons, or both. Rock crystal was credited with numerous powers. The Greek Orphic Lapidary describes how to kindle fire with crystal and sunlight, and notes, "This is what the Ancients called 'sacred fire.' You will not need to wait, I think, for flames of another sort to burn with greater effectiveness the thighs that offer such joy to the immortal gods. And also bound around the kidneys it relieves suffering."[5] Although the Byzantine *Orphei Lithica Kerygmata* drops the aphrodisiac reference, it reiterates the claim of help for the kidneys.[6] Michael Psellus notes that it "prevents shivering spells and fainting fits."[7]

GK

REFERENCES: *DOH* 1955, 99, no. 212; *DOCat* 1, 95-96, no. 115; *DOH* 1967, 96, no. 327; Leveto 1977, 44, no. 1b; Paris, *Byzance* 1992, 87;

Kornbluth 1994, 24, 29-30, no. 9; Spier
forthcoming, no. 689.

1.   Bonner 1950; Delatte and Derchain 1964.
2.   Michel 2001.
3.   *DOCat* 1, 96.
4.   Now Krakow, Wawel Collection; Zwierlein-Diehl
     1972, vol. 3, 147-148, no. 2173.
5.   Halleux and Schamp 1985, 91-92.
6.   Ibid., 146.
7.   Baldwin 1995, 398.

3. Sapphire Cameo with a Bust of Christ

Constantinople, 12th century?
Sapphire (corundum)
Including rim of modern setting: 3.445 x 2.6 x
1.49 cm; visible stone 3.27 x 2.37 x 1.49 cm

Inscribed: I(HCOV)C X(PICTO)C
("Jesus Christ").

Condition: The cameo is vertically pierced,
suggesting that it was cut from a large bead, probably flattened in back for mounting on a larger
object. Small chips are missing from the tip of the
nose and the right edge of the stone. A concavity on
the reverse was apparently ground down to remove
material associated with natural inclusions inside
the stone.

Acquisition History: Purchased from
Feuardent Frères, Paris, January 1936. Bliss Collection; acquired November 1940. The stone spent
four years in the Blisses' private collection before
coming to Dumbarton Oaks.

Accession number: BZ.1936.17

Christ, wearing a cross-nimbus, holds a
closed book in his covered left hand and
offers a blessing with his right.

Monochrome gemstone cameos were
common only in the post-Iconoclastic
period; the earliest datable one is a jasper
with an inscription naming Emperor Leo
VI (886-912).[1] Paul Williamson has placed
a group with elongated heads and sloping
shoulders in eleventh- or twelfth-century
Constantinople.[2] Several translucent Byzantine cameos have likewise been placed in
Constantinople during the twelfth century,
including a sapphirine St. Nicholas and a
sapphire John the Baptist in the Musée du
Louvre.[3] Our figure shares characteristics
with the later cameos. There is no evidence
of Middle Byzantine translucent gemstone
cameos before the tenth century. The Eastern fashion may well have been stimulated
by Western art: a sapphire cameo of
Christ blessing survives from the court of

Charlemagne (end of the eighth century).[4]

Both Solinus (third to fourth century) and
Bishop Epiphanios of Salamis (c. 315-405)
noted the cooling properties of sapphire
(then known as "hyacinth"[5]), the latter
adding that it could help in childbirth and
drive away evil spirits.[6] The eleventh-century
Michael Psellus claimed that the stone "cures
flatulence and fractures and if drunk with
vinegar arrests the onset of melancholy."[7]
Other exegetes, however, emphasized the
symbolic importance of the sky-blue gem:
Archbishop Andrew of Caesarea (563-614)
linked it with the apostle Simon, and was
echoed by his successor Arethas (d. after
932).[8] Middle Byzantine cameos with busts
of Christ blessing are sometimes inscribed
with apotropaic invocations: one pleads,
"Lord, help your servant John," and another
proclaims, "O Christ our Lord, he who puts
his hope in thee will not fail."[9] While this
sapphire lacks such explicit words, it too may
have served to protect its bearer. It could
equally well have served as a private icon.

GK

References: Paris, *Exposition d'art byzantin*
1931, 74, no. 84; Volbach, Duthuit, and Salles
1933, 56-57, pl. 49C; Bréhier 1936, 67, pl. 17;
Grabar 1938, no. 57; Boston, *Arts of the Middle
Ages* 1940, 60-61, no. 200; Wentzel 1941, 51; *Fogg
Bulletin* 1945, 116; *DOH* 1955, 99, no. 216;
Edinburgh-London 1958, p. 63, no. 184; Wentzel
1959, 20; Wentzel 1960, 90; Ross 1960, 45; *DOCat*
1, 99-100, no. 120; *DOH* 1967, 98, no. 336; Wentzel 1976, cols. 911-912; Bank 1978, chap. 6, pl. 110;
Brussels, *Splendeur de Byzance* 1982, 125; Popovich
1983, fig. 11; Paris, *Byzance* 1992, 287; Kornbluth
1997, 118, 126-129, 134-136, 146; Georgoula
1999, 349-350; Kornbluth 2001, 47, 50.

Exhibitions: *Exposition internationale d'art
byzantin, 28 mai–9 juillet, 1931,* Musée des Arts
Décoratifs, Palais du Louvre, Pavillon de Marsan,
Paris.

1.   London, Victoria and Albert Museum, inv. A.21-
     1932. New York, *The Glory of Byzantium* 1997, 174-
     175, no. 126. For Middle Byzantine glyptics see Paris,
     Byzance 1992, 275-288; New York, *The Glory of Byz-
     antium* 1997, 174-180, nos. 126-135; and Paderborn,
     Byzanz 2001, 241, 335-337.
2.   Williamson 1983.
3.   Paris, *Byzance* 1992, 287, nos. 201 and 202. Other
     translucent cameos: Bank 1985, 299, no. 160; Coche
     de la Ferté 1958, 62, no. 61; Dalton 1901, 17, no. 107;
     Dalton 1915, 2, no. 9; Eichler and Kris 1927, no. 130;
     Georgoula 1999, 349-350, no. 130; Ikonomaki-Pa-
     padopoulos, Pitarakis, and Loverdou-Tsigarida 2001,
     70-71, no. 20; New York, *Byzantium Faith and Power*
     2004, 240, no. 149; Paris, *Byzance* 1992, 278-279,
     nos. 185 and 186; Wentzel 1960, 90, figs. 82, 87.
4.   Kornbluth 1997; Kornbluth 2001. Cf. Buckton 1988.
5.   Freiss 1980, 26-27.
6.   Solinus: Mommsen 1958, 136. Epiphanios, On the
     twelve stones of the rational: Guenther 1898,
     753-754.
7.   Baldwin 1995, 399.
8.   Freiss 1980, 118-121.
9.   New York, *The Glory of Byzantium* 1997, 175-176,
     nos. 127 and 128.

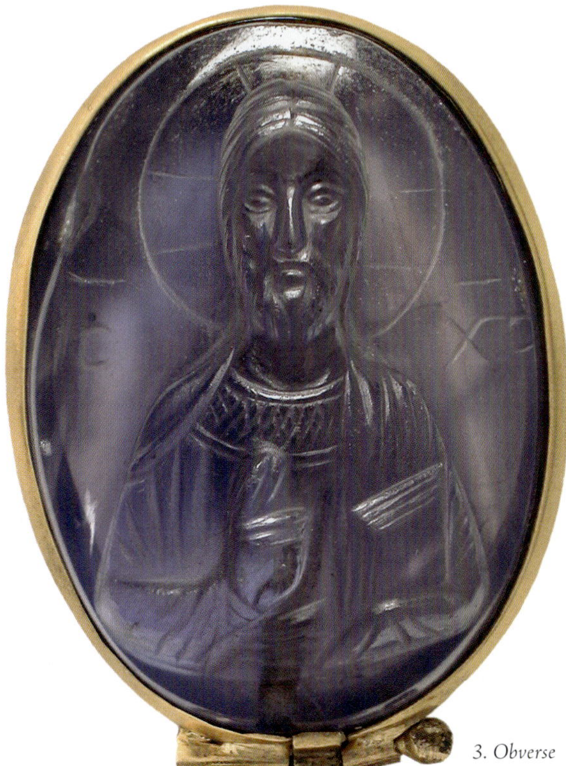

3. *Obverse*

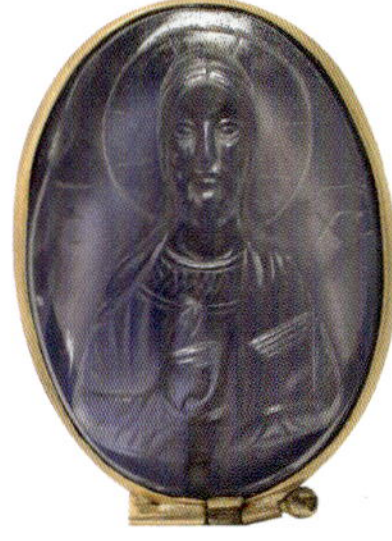

3. *Obverse, real size*

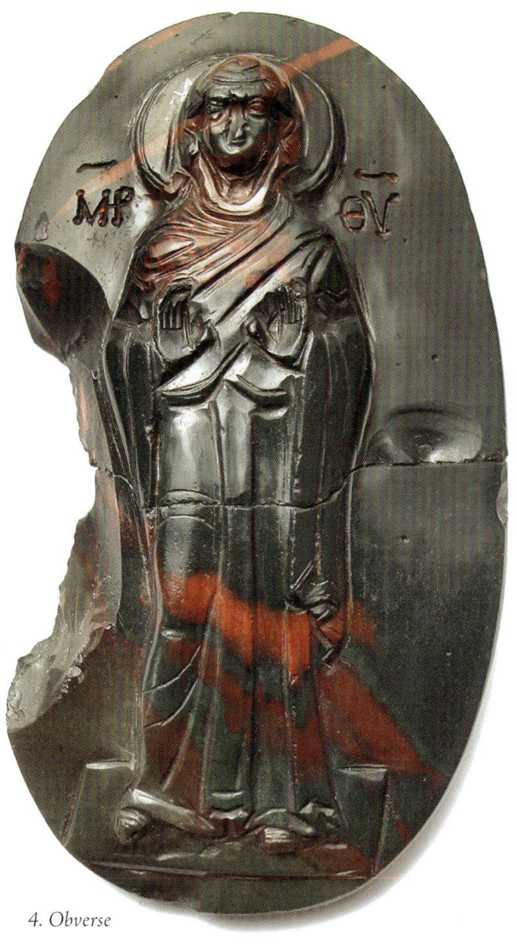

4. Obverse

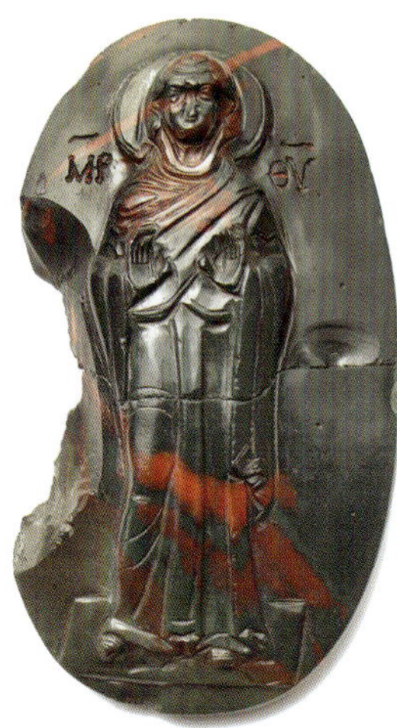

4. Obverse, real size

5. Cameo with the Virgin Hagiosoritissa

Constantinople, 12th century
Green quartz
3.1 x 2.4 cm

INSCRIBED: On the front on either side of the Virgin's head, M̅P̅ Θ̅V̅ (*Meter Theou*— "Mother of God").

CONDITION: Excellent.

ACQUISITION HISTORY: Acquired in 1946.

ACCESSION NUMBER: BZ.1946.6

This cameo depicting the Virgin Hagiosoritissa was meant to be worn as a pendant around the neck providing protection to the owner. It serves at the same time as an icon to which prayers can be addressed. It depicts in high relief the Virgin in bust length with both her hands extended toward the right. This gesture of prayer or entreaty commonly is associated with the composition of the Deesis in which the Virgin and St. John the Baptist, approaching respectively from left and right, pray on behalf of

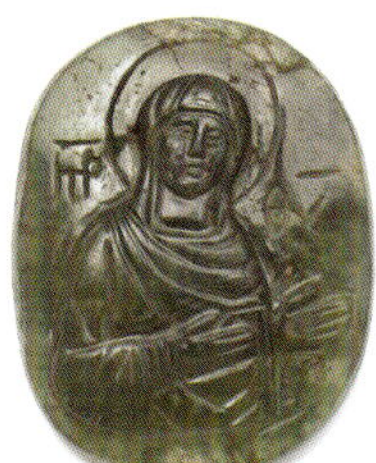

5. Obverse, real size

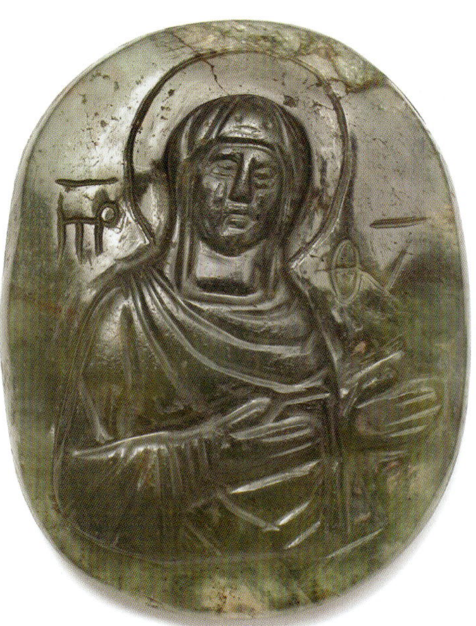

5. Obverse

4. Cameo with the Virgin Orant

Constantinople, early 11th century?
Bloodstone[1]
6.1 x 3.4 cm

INSCRIBED: M̅P̅ Θ̅V̅ (*Meter Theou*—"Mother of God") on either side of the Virgin, just above her shoulders.

CONDITION: The cameo is broken in two and has been mended. A large piece is missing on the left center. Several chips exist on its surface, including one chip that has taken the nose off.

ACQUISITION HISTORY: Mr. and Mrs. Bliss purchased this cameo in 1940.

ACCESSION NUMBER: BZ.1940.70

The oval cameo depicts in relief a full-length figure of the Virgin. She stands on a dais and holds her hands in an orant ("praying") position in front of her body.[2] This is one of the few iconographic types of the Virgin where she is depicted in her role as mediator without the Christ Child in her arms. She raises her palms in prayer to intercede for the wearer or owner of this cameo. The image of the praying Virgin is most appropriate for such objects, which

served as amulets. In the British Museum, a cameo of very similar dimensions and shape made of jasper can be compared with the Dumbarton Oaks piece.[3] Here, too, the Virgin is depicted in full length and is in an orant position, except that her hands are raised on either side of her body. It has been dated to the eleventh to twelfth century. Generally, it is very difficult to date these objects. For example, the difference in drapery style is often due to the pose of a figure and cannot be taken as a sure dating criterion. Nevertheless, an overall simplicity in the Dumbarton Oaks piece might be due to a slightly earlier stylistic phase in the eleventh century.[4]

IK

REFERENCES: *DOH* 1955, no. 217; *DOCat 1*, 100, no. 121; *DOH* 1967, no. 337; Popovich 1983, fig. 24.

1. See the discussion of bloodstone's symbolism in cat. no. 6.
2. On the terms *orant* and *orans* cf. *ODB* 3, 1531.
3. London, British Museum, M&LA 69, 7-12, 4; London, *Treasures of Byzantine Art* 1994, 158-159, no. 172.
4. For the dating see also *DOCat 1*, 100, no. 121.

mankind to Christ, rendered frontally.[1]

The type of the Virgin as portrayed on this cameo is known as the Hagiosoritissa ("The Virgin of the Holy Soros") and derives from a famous icon of the Virgin in Constantinople in the church of the Chalkoprateia. The same representation of the Virgin could bear different epithets, among them Parakleisis, "The Virgin Intercessor."[2]

Typically the Virgin Hagiosoritissa turns in three-quarter pose. Nevertheless, on this cameo, although the Virgin's body is shown turned slightly toward the right, her head remains frontal. This is most unusual for the representation of this type and shows a personal intervention in the iconography. Possibly the owner desired a more direct exchange with the Virgin, which the frontal position of her head made possible. He or she could look directly at her, addressing his or her prayer, and at the same time the Virgin as the Hagiosoritissa had her role as the intercessor clearly manifested through her raised hands.

IK

REFERENCES: *DOH* 1955, 219; *DOCat* 1, 102, no. 123; *DOH* 1967, no. 339.

1. Cf. *ODB* 1, 599-600; Cutler 1987; Walter 1968.
2. This epithet suggests that originally this icon type must have been in a church with a "holy soros," i.e., a reliquary chest. See *ODB* 3, 2171-2172, with older references.

6. Cameo with the Virgin Hagiosoritissa

Constantinople, 12th century
Bloodstone, set in a modern mount
3.5 x 3.0 cm

INSCRIBED: M̄H̄P̄ Θ̄V̄ (*Meter Theou*—"Mother of God") on either side of the Virgin, just above her shoulders.

CONDITION: Excellent.

ACQUISITION HISTORY: Mr. and Mrs. Bliss purchased this cameo in 1936.

ACCESSION NUMBER: BZ.1936.31

This cameo depicts in relief a bust of the Virgin with hands raised and facing right. She directs her gesture toward the hand of God emerging from a cloud at the top right above her head. The type, the Virgin Hagiosoritissa noted in cat. no. 5, seems to have been popular on Byzantine cameos, which were worn as protective amulets. Numerous examples can be found in the collections of other museums.[1] The subject matter of the Virgin as the intercessor is most appropriate, and the iconographic type of the Hagiosoritissa displays this special role well. In this particular example, the presence of God's hand above almost confirms the success of her intercession.

The heavenward direction of her prayers is especially emphasized on this cameo by the stone itself. The craftsman chose his piece very carefully; he turned it so the red veins of the stone run diagonally along with the Virgin's raised arms. One may even venture to suggest that the diagonal direction of the red veins determined the position of her entreating hands. They are shown in a much steeper angle than normal in this iconographic type (cf. cat. no. 5). The red color of the veins, the color of blood, not only is a visual aid to God's presence in heaven above, but the veins are also a reference to Christ's self-sacrifice and man's salvation through his death on the cross. Thus the hematite and its visual properties become an integral part of the function and message of this pendant. The blood veins are well suited as a reminder of his sacrifice, and most of these cameo amulets were carved with images of Christ Pantokrator (cf. cat. nos. 2 and 3) or the Virgin as the intercessor to him.[2]

Furthermore, bloodstone had additional properties. One unusual piece, now in the Metropolitan Museum of Art, makes very clear through its subject matter the reference to blood that the Byzantines associated with the red veins of this stone, as well as its medical properties.[3] It depicts on one side the miracle of Christ with the Woman with an Issue of Blood. Bloodstone was considered to halt the flow of blood, and it was the medium chosen by women as a protective amulet in matters of reproductive health, especially when they were afflicted with menstrual disorders. Possibly the depiction of the Virgin on this stone combined all these concerns, providing both intercession to Christ and physical well-being.

IK

REFERENCES: *DOH* 1955, no. 218; *DOCat* 1, 101, no. 122; *DOH* 1967, no. 338; Der Nersessian 1960, 77-78, fig. 2; Popovich 1983, fig. 21.

EXHIBITIONS: *Arts of the Middle Ages*, Museum of Fine Arts, February 17-March 24, 1940, Boston, MA; Fogg Museum of Art, Cambridge, MA, 1945.

1. For a number of examples see: *DOH* 1955, no. 218; *DOCat* 1, 101, no. 122. For the dating of these pieces to the late eleventh and twelfth centuries see *loc. cit.*, as well as the entries on the pieces referred to in the following footnote.
2. In the exhibition at the Metropolitan Museum of Art in 1997, there were at least five examples of hematite cameos. See New York, *The Glory of Byzantium* 1997, nos. 127, 128, 131, 134, and 135.
3. Cambridge, MA, *Byzantine Women* 2003, no. 165.

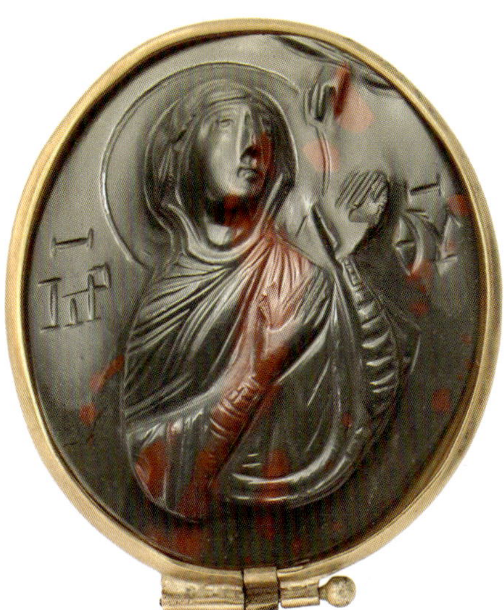

6. *Obverse*

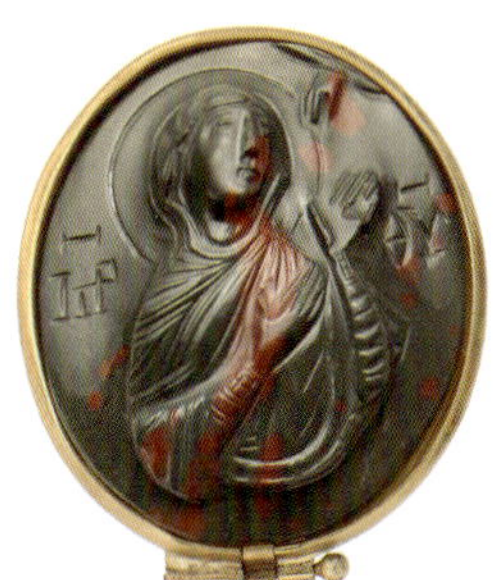

6. *Obverse, real size*

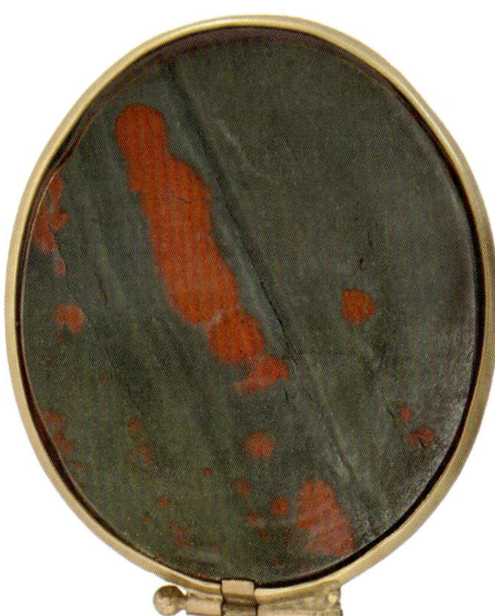

6. *Reverse*

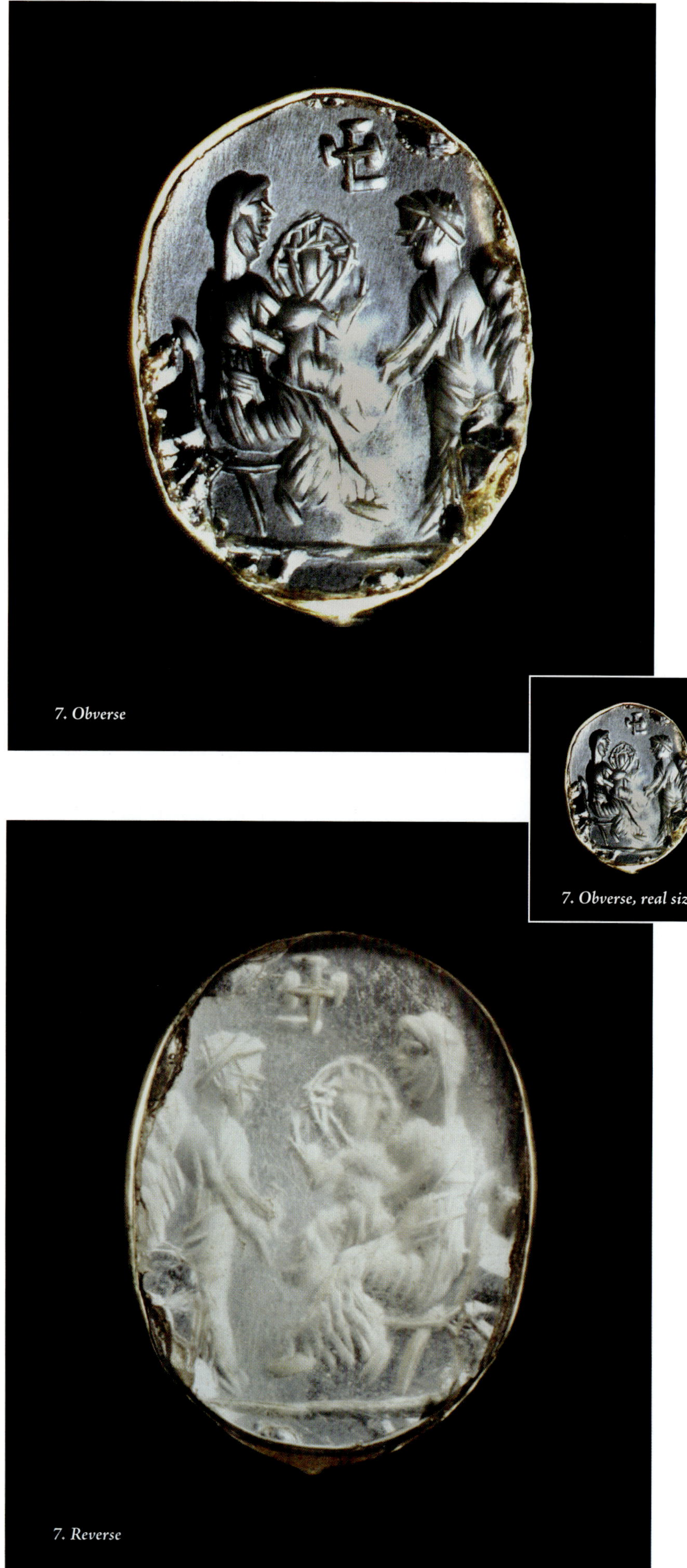

7. Obverse

7. Obverse, real size

7. Reverse

7. Rock Crystal Intaglio with Adoration

Syria? 6th century?
Rock crystal (transparent crystalline quartz)
Including rim of modern setting: 2.72 x 2.075 cm;
visible stone: 2.6 x 1.94 cm

CONDITION: Large chips are missing from the engraved reverse around almost the entire edge and from the convex obverse on one edge. The obverse is heavily abraded. The reverse may have been smoothed in postmedieval times. The original setting probably covered the image with another crystal of similar shape, unengraved, and bound the two stones together with a strip of gold around the edges and a suspension loop; compare cat. no. 8. Wear in a pendant would account for the heavy abrasion on the obverse.

ACQUISITION HISTORY: Said to have been found in Syria. Purchased from Elie Bustros, Beirut, December 1949; gift of Mr. and Mrs. Bliss, August 1950.

ACCESSION NUMBER: BZ.1950.18.1

This is not a conventional *Adoration of the Magi*, but rather depicts the Christ Child with cross-nimbus, hand raised in apparent blessing, seated on his mother's lap opposite a single winged profile figure (lower part of the wing chipped off). A cross floats above. This scene has been identified by Jeffrey Spier as an abbreviated *Adoration*, including the angel that sometimes leads the group of wise men but omitting the Magi themselves.[1] Three crystals are known with this composition: this stone, cat. no. 8, and one formerly in the Pangborn Collection, New York.[2] While the floating cross may represent the star of Bethlehem,[3] it is closely paralleled by detached crosses on several related Early Byzantine crystal intaglios[4] and by the cross held by Christ on cat. no. 2. It probably has a more generic Christian meaning not specifically linked to the *Adoration*.

On general dating, significance of the medium, and function, see cat. no. 2. The sixth-century date proposed by Ross is iconographically reasonable, though the stone could be later. Spier suggests production in north Syria.

GK

REFERENCES: *DOH* 1955, 99, no. 213; *DOCat*, 95, no. 114; *DOH* 1967, 97, no. 330; Volbach 1975, 202-203; Leveto 1977, 46, no. 3b; Kornbluth 1994, no. 8; Spier forthcoming, no. 671.

1. Compare a panel on the Cathedra of Maximian (missing the following panel with the Magi

themselves): Cecchelli 1936, pl. 26.

2.   Pangborn crystal: Osborne 1912, 385, no. 11.

3.   *DOCat* 1, 95.

4.   Kornbluth 1994, nos. 1 (rider and angel), 2 (Christ healing the woman with an issue of blood), 3 (Magi), 6 (cross with God the Father), 7 (Baptism), and 12 (Magi, here cat. no. 8).

8. Gold Pendant with Rock Crystal Intaglio of the Adoration

Constantinople? 6th century?
Gold mount and rock crystal (transparent crystalline quartz) intaglio with gilded engraving
3.4 x 2.405 x .76 cm

CONDITION: Parts of the gilding have been lost from the engraved crystal, notably on the lower part of the angel's wing. The gold of the mount has been crushed on one side of the obverse and all around on the reverse. The obverse is heavily abraded.

ACQUISITION HISTORY: Found as part of a treasure of gold with five necklaces, a small clasp with coins of Justinian I (reg. 527-565), a bracelet, two pendant crosses, a disk pendant, a hexagonal amulet case or reliquary, six rings, and another rock crystal pendant with the Holy Sepulcher. Said to have been found in Syria. Acquired in 1958.

ACCESSION NUMBER: BZ.1958.41

This is one of the few Early Byzantine crystals that has apparently retained its original setting. Two pieces of crystal—each flat on one side and slightly convex on the other—are held together by a gold strip decorated with a wavy gold ribbon and suspended from a grooved ring. One stone is cut in intaglio on the flat side, to be seen through the unengraved convex face (obverse) of the same stone.

On dating, significance of the medium, and function, see cat. no. 2. The intaglio is extremely similar to cat. no. 7, differing only in that Christ has no halo and the angel does not extend its hands toward the child. What Ross took to be an object held by Christ is probably the hand itself, enlarged as on cat. no. 2. This gem also situates the figures on a ground line, though that line is nearly hidden by the mount.

GK

REFERENCES: *DOCat* 2, 135-139, no. 179M; *DOH* 1967, 96, no. 329; Leveto 1977, 44, no. 1d; Kornbluth 1994, no. 12; Spier forthcoming, no. 672.

9. Intaglio with a Scene from The Seven Against Thebes

Italy, 1st century BCE
Rock crystal
1.4 x 1.1 cm

CONDITION: Several chips appear along the edges of the intaglio.

ACQUISITION HISTORY: Gift from Mrs. Benjamin Moore through Mrs. Bliss, August 1, 1950.

ACCESSION NUMBER: BZ.1950.10

The engraving on the flat surface of this gem's face depicts a group of three warriors flanking a bulbous vase with a slender base and neck. The vase is in the foreground slightly to the right of a column occupying the background and centering the composition. An incision in the central top area of the gem appears to be the scant rendition of a vessel surmounting the column. Left of the column stands a warrior wearing full armor, including a helmet and a spear, which rests on his shoulder, as well as a round shield, its blank face prominently displayed against the torso. This soldier turns toward the center and observes the action depicted in the composition's right-hand side. On that side in the foreground, a second warrior leans, half-kneeling, so he can reach into the vase at his feet. Although nude, he wears a helmet and holds a shield on his right arm. The shield appears behind the warrior's head as if it were a halo, which apparently encouraged the Christian reading of this composition.[1] The shields of the first and second warriors create a strong horizontal axis marking the center of the composition and complementing the strong verticals of the figures and the column. Behind the kneeling nude stands the third soldier seen, only from the waist up. His torso and his helmet-covered head rendered in profile mirror the pose of the first warrior, thus enhancing the sense of this scene's visual coherence.

Ross tentatively identified this scene as the *Denial of Peter* and dated it to the sixth century.[2] While accepting as possible this Early Byzantine date, Kornbluth referred to the subject of this gem as *The Seven Against Thebes*, basing her judgment on Zwierlein-Diehl who provided the attribution for the similar iconography of three carved stones located in Vienna.[3] With small variations the same iconography appears on a dozen gems, all likely to have been produced in the late second or the first century BCE in Italy.[4]

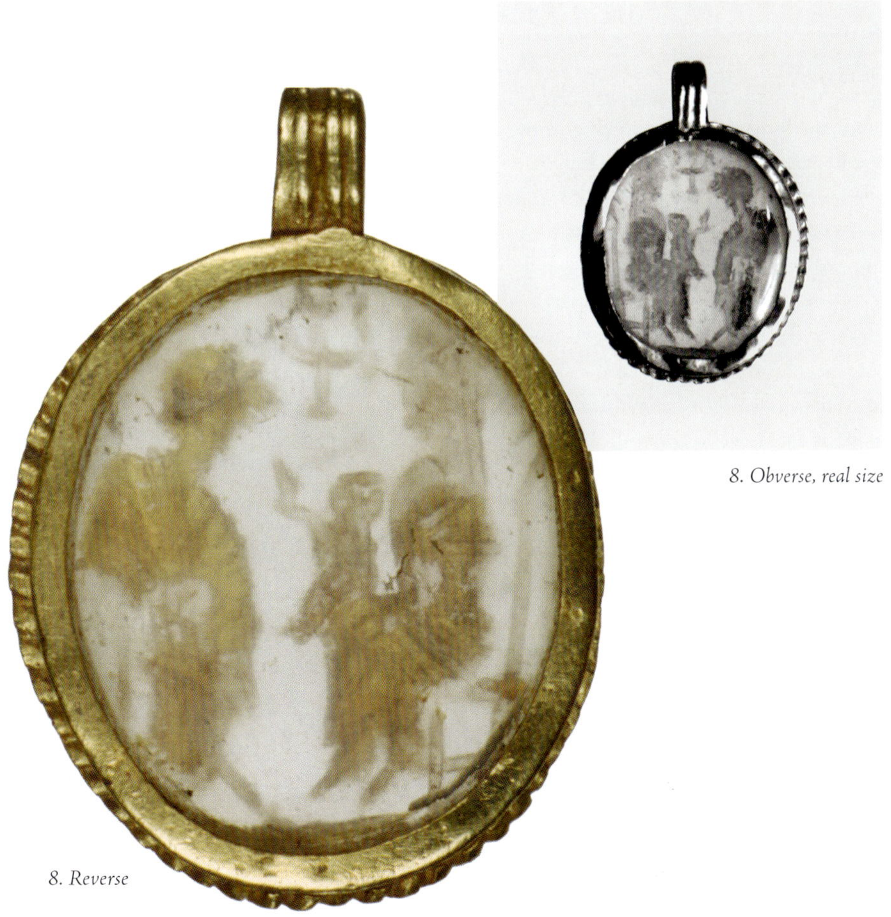

8. Obverse, real size

8. Reverse

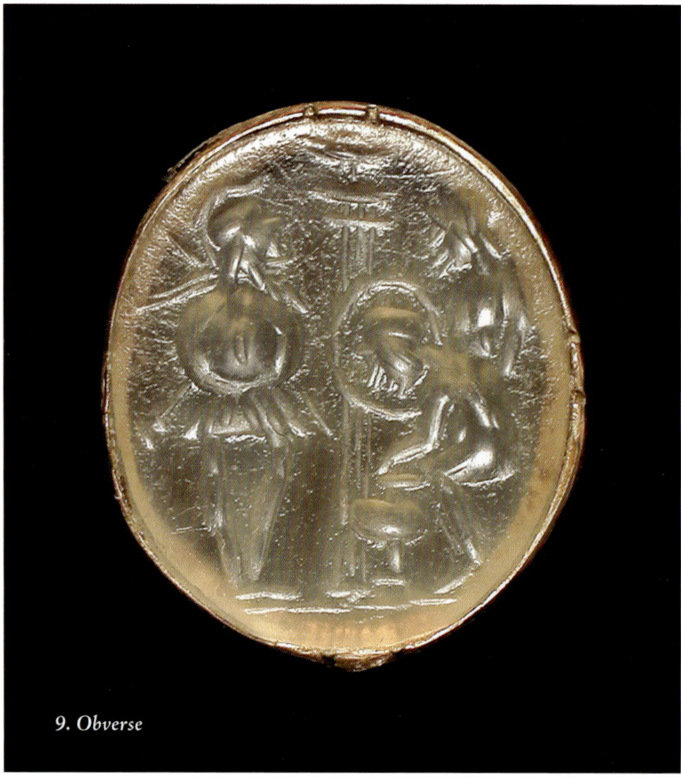

9. Obverse

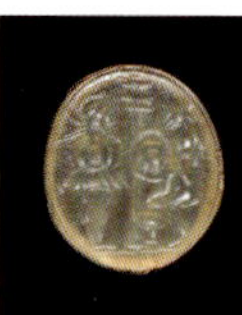

9. Obverse,
real size

Every one of these carved stones is small (approximately 1.5 x 1.0 cm), and thus they appear suitable for use on finger rings.

These gems depict the warriors drawing lots in order to determine which of Thebes's seven city gates each of them must attack.[5] In general, this subject reflects the tales of the Theban epic cycles—the *Oedipodea*, the *Thebaid*, and the *Epigoni*—only fragments of which have survived.[6] The most detailed surviving account of the episode rendered on the intaglio belongs to Aeschylus's tragedy *The Seven Against Thebes*, first staged in Athens in 467 BCE and interpreted visually in numerous works of art throughout the long period from the classical to the Late Antique era.[7] The unambiguous clue for solving this visual riddle is the blank face of the shield that one of these warriors holds. Aeschylus's text (lines 377-652) elaborates on the effigies displayed on the attackers' shields, since these visual devices foretell the destiny of their bearers. The only one of the seven Argives whose shield has a blank face is Amphiaraus—the seer who, although aware of the impending calamities, takes part in the assault because of his soldierly sense of duty.[8] During the combat and just before Amphiaraus's seemingly imminent demise, Zeus spares this virtuous Argive warrior and makes him immortal.[9] In fact, Amphiaraus was worshiped as a god and had an oracular shrine dedicated to him.[10]

This composition represents only the conclusion of the long episode involving drawing lots; hence, no more than three of the seven Argive chieftains appear in this scene: Parthenopaeus, the nude warrior reaching into the vessel; Amphiaraus, standing left of the column and emphatically displaying his shield; and Polynices, standing to the right of the column. The gems on which this scene appears might have functioned as talismans for those in the military.[11] On the whole, the popularity of this topic during the last century BCE in Italy may have been a reflection of the high regard for Attic drama in Magna Graecia, the place of perpetual theater revivals.[12] Also, it is possible that the stories about the fratricidal wars of the Greeks acquired new relevance at that time, when Romans were fighting against Romans in the civil wars that led to the establishment of the empire during the second half of the first century BCE.

AK

REFERENCES: *DOH* 1955, no. 214; *DOH* 1967, no. 326; *DOCat* 1, 94-95, no. 113; Kornbluth 1994, 24, 29, no. 10.

1. *DOCat* 1, 95.

2. *DOCat* 1, 94-95, no. 113, pl. LVIII. The reasons explaining Ross's identification have to do with the general similarity between the scene on this gem and a number of Late Antique depictions of the *Denial of Peter* featuring a column or a pier surmounted by a rooster and two or more figures in front of it. This iconography was well known during Late Antiquity as is apparent in the examples rendered in different media, for instance, popular ivory reliefs: Brescia, Museo Civico Cristiano—Volbach 1962, 328, pl. 89; Paris, Louvre—Volbach 1976, no. 121, pl. 65; and wall mosaics—Ricci 1905, pl. 73.

3. Kornbluth 1994, 24, 29, no. 10.

4. The following is a list of gems featuring iconography very close or virtually identical to the one discussed here: Aquileia, Sena Chiesa 1966, 300, pl. XLII, no. 829—carneol; Berlin, Furtwängler 1986, 54, pl. 10, nos. 739—carneol, 740—brown paste, 741—black paste; Cambridge, Middleton 1981, p. XXI, pl. II, no. 101—orange sard; Munich, *AGD*, 29, pl. 82, nos. 706—red carneol, 707—red carneol, 708—agate; St. Petersburg, Kagan and Neverov 2001, 65, no. 53/25—sard; Vienna, Zwierlein-Diehl 1972, 106-107, pl. 49, nos. 284—carneol, 285—brown sard, 286—brown sard; Bari, Tamma 1991, 31, no. 11—chalcedony.

   Zwierlein-Diehl cites all of these gems with the exception of the one in St. Petersburg. Notably, a seventeenth-century publication listing the gem currently at the Hermitage provides the correct identification of its subject; see L. Bergerus, *Thesaurus ex Thesauro Palatino Selectus* (Heidelberg, 1685), 14, tab. VIII; cited by Kagan and Neverov 2001, 65.

5. The vessel on the ground as an attribute of the act of lot drawing in late Roman art is discussed by Daszewski 1985, 29-33, pls. 2 and 8; Daszewski and Michaelides 1988, 63-64, figs. 26, 27, 30. I would like to thank Professor Hugo Meyer of Princeton University for providing me with these two references. For the imagery involving the drawing of lots and its significance, see Thalmann 1978, 63-79.

   The story of the expedition against Thebes revolves around the events leading to the ultimate fulfillment of the curse on Oedipus's sons Eteocles and Polynices—that they will divide their inheritance by means of war. The elder of the two, Eteocles, refuses to share the throne and banishes his brother from Thebes. While in exile at Argos, Polynices instigates the Argive leaders to assault Thebes in order to restore him to his father's throne. Although the attackers did suffer a defeat, the battle is not a triumph for the Thebans either. Their champion's decision to join the combat is dutiful and courageous, yet proves to be arrogant as well, because, by choosing to defend the seventh gate, he sets himself against his own brother. Ultimately, Eteocles and Polynices perish at each other's hands; see Gantz 1993, 502-522.

6. *Epicorum Graecorum Fragmenta*, 20-27, 141, 153. In my work on this catalogue entry, I benefited from Dr. Erica Hermanowitz's knowledge of the Homeric *Thebaid*.

7. *LIMC*, VII-2, pls. 539-546; Armantrout 1990.

8. Amphiaraus's shield is described as follows: "His shield is quiet—for all its bronze—with no surface device" (lines 590-592). For the shield scene in

Aeschylus's drama, see Thalmann 1978, 105-135, esp. 166-118. The visual interpretations of the shield devices are discussed by Small 2003, 26-27, esp. note 60 on 183.

One finds further evidence for the popularity of the motif involving the blank face of Amphiaraus's shield in Emperor Julian's *Letter to a Priest*: "For all others who were in the expedition against Thebes engraved a device on their shields before they had conquered the enemy, and erected trophies to celebrate the downfall of the Cadmians; but he, the associate of the gods, when he went to war had arms with no device; but gentleness he had, and moderation, as even the enemy bore witness." Julian 2, 303 C-D, 332-333.

9. The Thebans themselves appreciate the virtues of Amphiaraus; cf. the words of the scout: "Sixth I'll name a virtuous, valiant man, a prophet, mighty Amphiaraus" (lines 569-570), and Eteocles's judgment: "this seer, son of Oecles, a man both wise and just, devout and brave, a mighty prophet, linked with impious men" (lines 609-611). During the combat, one of the defenders of Thebes—Periclimenos— chases Amphiaraus and just before he can launch his spear Zeus throws his thunderbolt. It opens a chasm in the ground that then engulfs the Argive warrior along with his chariot and his charioteer; see lines 597-617, as well as Pindar, *Nemean* 9, 16-17. On making him immortal, see also Pausanias, 8.2.4 and Apollodorus, 3.6.8.

10. See references to the oracular shrine of Amphiaraus in Herodotus, 1.46, 49, 52, 92; 3.91; 8.134. Other literary sources that postdate the carved gem in question provide further details about the hero's oracular powers and the custom of revealing his prophecies to the visitors spending a night in the shrine; cf. Pausanias, 1.34.2-5; 2.13.7; 8.45.7; 10.10.3; Apollodorus, 3.6.1-8.

11. On the question about the potential of *The Seven Against Thebes* to inspire honorable warriors, see Thalmann 1978, 6 and 151, who cites Aristophanes, *Frogs* 1021-1022: "Every man watching it [the play *The Seven Against Thebes*] would have yearned to be a warrior." Also, see above, note 8, containing the comments of Emperor Julian.

12. Gigante 1970, 83-146; Trendall and Webster 1971, 11-13.

10. Hematite Intaglio with Archangel Michael

Byzantine, 5th to 7th century
Hematite (iron oxide)
1.95 x 1.51 x .4 cm

INSCRIBED: On reverse ΜΙ/ΧΑ/ΗΛ ("Michael").

CONDITION: Unlike most gemstones, hematite is subject to corrosion because of its high iron content. The figural obverse of this stone is covered with small granular deposits, probably corrosion by-products.

ACQUISITION HISTORY: Acquired from George Zacos in November 1957.

ACCESSION NUMBER: BZ.1957.68

Hematite's protective and curative powers are attested by Pliny, Galen, and the *Orphei Lithica Kerygmata*, which cites its efficacy against eye complaints and animal venom.[1] The stone was frequently used for amulets. An oval hematite in Munich depicts Michael holding a long cross as here, though he is nimbed and the cross rests on a globe; another in Marburg brings together a Michael very like this one with a similar Gabriel.[2] Yet another in Ann Arbor has a profile angel holding a cross (lacking the long staff here) and the name of St. Michael on the reverse.[3] The closest iconographic parallel is a sixth- to seventh-century rock crystal intaglio in Paris, inscribed "Saint Michael."[4]

Michael was popular on Christian amulets, reflecting his well-developed cult, though he and other archangels were more often named than depicted.[5] While his biblical fame, and presumably his reputation for great strength, rested on a few references to him as a great prince (Daniel 10 and 12), he was most frequently invoked as a healer. Sozomen (fifth century) reports that the archangel cured his colleague Aquiline of life-threatening fever, nausea, and jaundice.[6] A fifth-century inscription in the church of St. Michael in Hestiae-Anaplus proclaimed, "Here suffering mortals find divine remedies for the pains of their body or soul, for the evil quickly flees before your name, Michael, or your image or your shrine."[7] The intaglio in Munich cited above makes explicit the connection between the gem image and amuletic usage; it is inscribed "Michael, help Antiochus."

On this stone the name may have been hidden during use, since the evidence of corrosion is confined to the figural obverse. Images and inscriptions were often hidden in order to increase their secret power, though that practice is most commonly associated with objects meant to inflict harm.[8]

GK

REFERENCES: *DOCat* 1, 97-98, no. 117; Paris, *Byzance* 1992, 87.

1. Pliny, *Natural History*, bk. 36, lines 144-148: Eichholz 1962, 114-119; Galen, *De simplicium medicamentorum temperamentis ac facultatibus*, bk. 9, chap. 2, *De lapidibus*: Kühn 1965, vol. 12, 192-208; Halleux and Schamp 1985, 164.

2. Munich: Paderborn, *Byzanz* 2001, 333-334, no. IV.76. Marburg: Wiegandt 1998, 83-84, no. 111.

3. Kelsey Museum of Archaeology, no. 26128; Bonner 1950, 309, no. 336; Spier forthcoming, no. 600. Bonner 1950, nos. 334-337 are related hematites with Christian imagery; Bonner 1950, no. 334 is also Michel 2001, no. 470. On Byzantine Michael iconography, see Mango 1984.

4. Paris, *Byzance* 1992, 87, no. 36.

5. Schneider 1981, 13-57; Rohland 1977.

6. Sozomen, *Ecclesiastical History*, bk. 2, chap. 3: Festugière 1983, 242-245.

7. Waltz 1928, 24, no. 32.

8. Kotansky 1994.

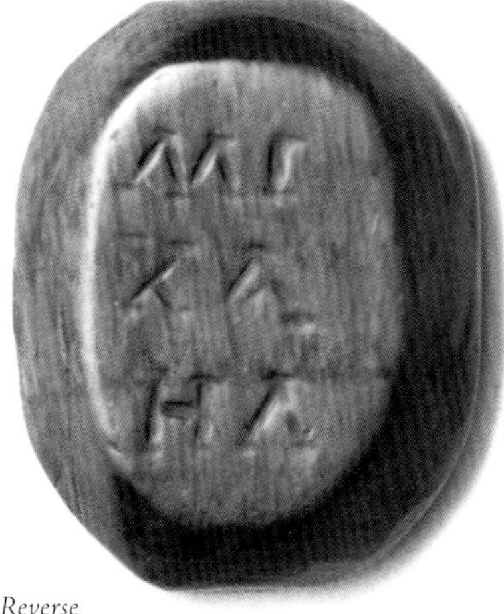

10. Reverse

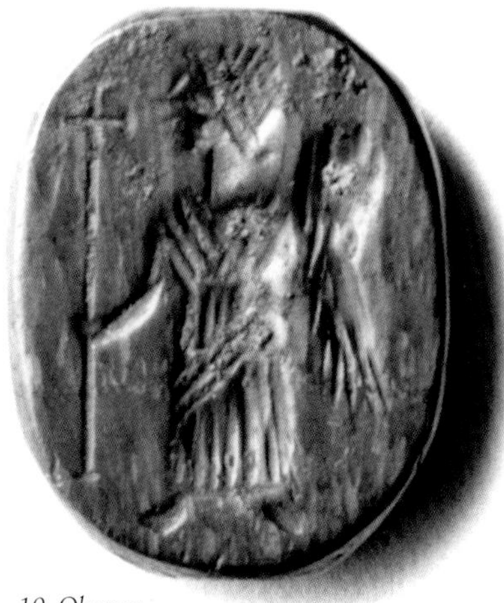

10. Obverse

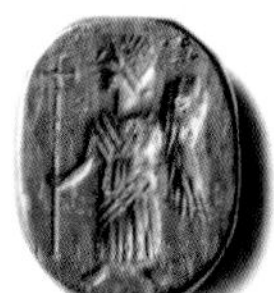

10. Obverse, real size

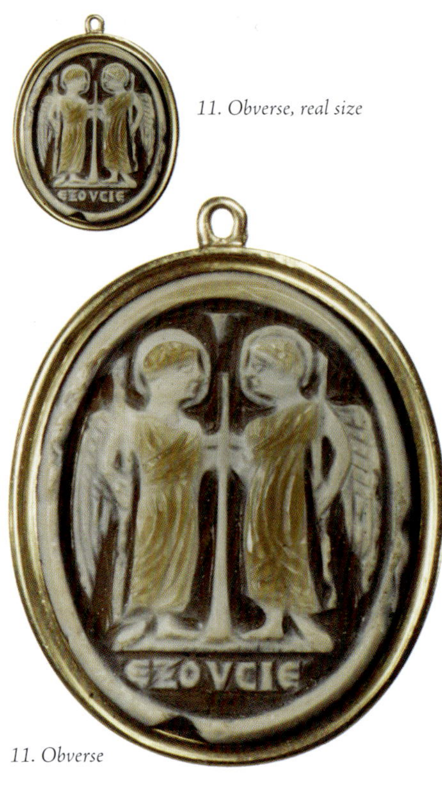

11. Obverse, real size

11. Obverse

11. Agate Cameo with Angels and a Cross (*Laus Crucis?*)

Constantinople, 6th or possibly 7th century
Banded agate (quartz) in a modern gold mount
Including rim of modern setting: 2.91 x 2.44 x
.5 cm; visible stone: 2.66 x 2.12 cm. The stone is
thicker on the right side, but regularized by its
mount.

Inscribed: ƐZOVCIE [*sic*] ("Powers").

Condition: The outer circle is chipped in
several places. The portion of the cross between the
angels' heads has been broken off, but the horizontal
bar remains just below the level of their shoulders.

Acquisition History: Wyndham Francis
Cook collection, London; William Randolph
Hearst collection, New York; acquired in 1947.

Accession number: BZ.1947.21

Two nimbed angels flank a tall cross, each
holding it with the nearer hand and a long
staff with the other. Unlike angels in the
standard *Laus Crucis* image, and perhaps
due to compositional compression, they do
not adore the cross but rather present it.

Two other cameos (Paris and formerly
Moscow) are extremely similar to this one.[1]
The closest dated parallel is a gold coin
of Justinian celebrating one of his consul-
ships (521, 528, 533, or 534).[2] The two
angels, rather than the more typical single
angel, may have commemorated Justinian's

nearly simultaneous coronation in late
527 and assumption of the consulship in
early 528.[3] A gold ring of the late sixth to
seventh century and a fifth- to sixth-century
hematite intaglio are compositionally close;[4]
on an eighth-century intaglio, two emperors
similarly grasp a cross with their nearer
hands;[5] and on a seventh-century ampulla,
two staff-bearing angels hold the horizontal
bar of a tall cross.[6]

The inscription "Powers" refers to a
specific type of messenger in the celestial hierarchy. The different types of beings mentioned in Ephesians 1:21 were discussed by
Pseudo-Dionysios the Areopagite (c. 500?)
and the Patriarch Nikephoros I (806-815),
among others, and formalized into a list
of seraphim, cherubim, thrones; virtues,
dominions, powers; principalities, archangels, and angels.[7] They were widely believed
to have both the capacity and inclination to
aid suppliants (see cat. nos. 1 and 10). The
similar cameo formerly in Moscow had an
explicitly apotropaic inscription ("protection
of Leontius"), and this cameo probably had
a similar function.

Agate may have been thought to reinforce
the power of the image. Pliny recorded its
use to heal spider and scorpion bites.[8] The
Orphei Lithica Kerygmata reiterates the pre-
scription against venom and recommends
its use against fevers (and as an aphrodisiac) as well.[9] Michael Psellus notes that
the stone "cures runny eyes and headaches,
reduces women's menstrual discharge, and is
a remedy for the dropsy."[10]

GK

References: Smith and Hutton 1908, 79, no.
345; Baltimore, *Early Christian and Byzantine Art*
1947, 113, no. 552; *Fogg Bulletin* 1947, 234; *DOH*
1955, 99, no. 215; Wentzel 1957, 55; *DOCat 1*,
98-99, no. 119; *DOH* 1967, 98, no. 335; Wentzel
1976, col. 910; Paris, *Byzance* 1992, 89; Spier
1993b, 50-51; Mango and Mundell Mango 1993,
63-65; Kornbluth 1997, 133-134; Spier forthcoming, no. 778.

1. Moscow: Leclercq 1924, col. 858, fig. 5145. Paris:
   Cabinet des Médailles; Paris, *Byzance* 1992, 88-89,
   no. 39.
2. Athens National Museum, Hahn 1973, 47, 108, pl.
   14, no. 4.
3. Caramessini-Oeconomides 1966.
4. Ring (angels without staffs): Paderborn, *Byzanz* 2001,
   324, no. IV.53. Intaglio (angels without nimbus or
   staffs): Wiegandt 1998, 83-84, no. 111.
5. Zwierlein-Diehl 1972, vol. 3, 149, no. 2176.
6. Paderborn, *Byzanz* 2001, 190-191, no. I.72.

7. Roques 1954, 143.
8. Pliny, *Natural History*, bk. 37, lines 139-142: Eichholz
   1962, 276-281.
9. Halleux and Schamp 1985, 163-164.
10. Baldwin 1995, 398.

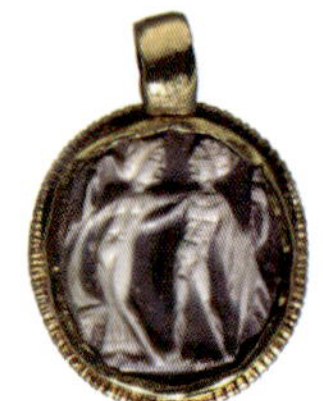

12. Obverse, real size

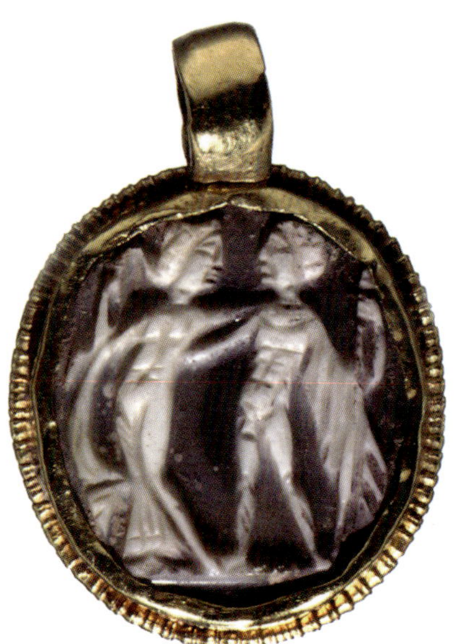

12. Obverse

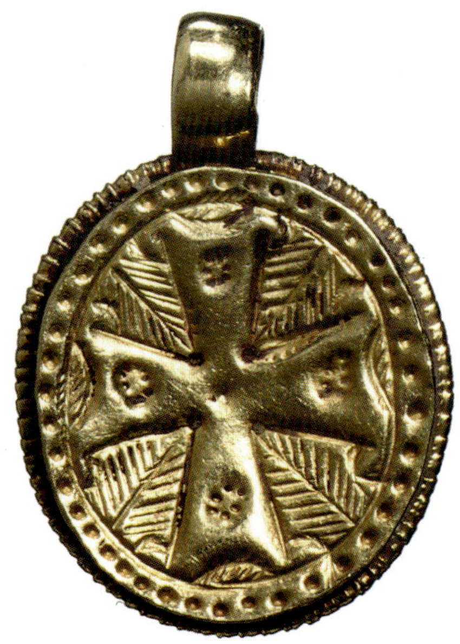

12. Reverse

12. Gold Pendant Enclosing a Cameo with Mythological Figures

Constantinople? pendant—6th or 7th century;
unknown location, cameo—3rd or 6th century?
Gold and agate
2.5 (without suspension loop 2.02) x 1.805 x
.48 cm

CONDITION: The stone is held by a plain strip of
gold on the obverse, crimped in around the figures.
It is very loose in its setting, suggesting that there
was formerly some filling material behind the cameo
that has washed away or decomposed. Both stone
and mount are otherwise in excellent condition.

ACQUISITION HISTORY: Said to have been
found in Sicily with two buckles. Purchased by
Mr. and Mrs. Bliss from P. & P. Santamaria, Rome,
in 1955. Acquired by the Byzantine Collection of
Dumbarton Oaks in 1969.

ACCESSION NUMBER: BZ.1969.15

This pendant has a wide suspension loop, a
beaded band around the edge, and on the reverse a cross formed in the interstices of four
inward-pointing leaves. One closely related
jewel includes a coin from the joint reign of
Justin I and Justinian in 527, and a similar
example was found with coins of Phokas
(602-610) and Herakleios (610-641).[1]

A nearly nude male figure holds a staff
with his left hand, the arm bent up. His
right arm extends around the waist of a female figure, also nude except for falling drapery. She places her left arm on his shoulder
and turns her head to face him. Her right
arm bends up, the hand touching the end of
her hair or veil. A short length of cloth falls
outside the elbow. A longer portion falls next
to her body, bows out around her hip, meets
her right knee, and billows out to create
folds on the edge of the cameo and a cone
of drapery over the lower leg. While nudity
links these figures to classical art, the previously accepted identification as Apollo and
Daphne is unlikely. Following Ross, Afuri
Soeda reads the woman's right leg as "a trunk
of a tree rooted in the earth."[2] That leg, however, terminates in a clearly delineated foot,
and the figures' mutual embrace contradicts
the story of flight and pursuit. The striations
on the woman's right thigh are analogous
to those on the man's lower legs, so they are
musculature rather than bark.

The closest parallel to this stone is a composite cameo in Vienna, identified as Bacchus and Ariadne.[3] Bacchus, with *kantharos*
or panther, often stands in this pose;[4] but

"Ariadne" is difficult to match. Alternatively,
Venus and Mars were frequently shown
standing together.[5] Our female figure is
related to the classical Venus reaching up to
her hair, her loose drapery blown out to her
side.[6] Mars is frequently represented nude
and holding a spear, though he normally
also has a *tropaion*;[7] the large head of our
figure could be understood as helmeted.
Above all, the embrace uncommon in other
contexts is a standard variant of this scene,
especially on love amulets.[8] The composition was also used for high-status couples
from the first century on.[9]

If this cameo indeed depicts (or was
understood to depict) Mars and Venus, it
could have retained the earlier association
with virtue and so been compatible with the
overtly Christian symbolism of the mount.
It could also have been used as an amulet,
as many Byzantine items were in the sixth
to seventh century, likewise in conjunction
with explicitly Christian symbols. On the
apotropaic use of agate, see cat. no. 11.

GK

REFERENCES: *DOCat* 2, 8-10, no. 5C; *DOH*
1967, 45-46, no. 158; Providence, *Survival of the
Gods* 1987, 194-195, no. 59; Spier 1987; Spier
1993b, 50; Zwierlein-Diehl 1972, vol. 3, 213; Spier
forthcoming, no. 765.

1. Spier 1987.
2. Providence, *Survival of the Gods* 1987, 194.
3. Zwierlein-Diehl 1972, vol. 3, 213, no. 2458.
4. e.g., Zazoff 1975, 173-174, nos. 857-859 (Hannover).
5. Zazoff 1975, 265-266, no. 1428 (Hannover); Delatte
    and Derchain 1964, 243, no. 335; Richter 1971, 37-
    38, no. 124.
6. Bieber 1977, 43-47; for drapery as here, see Bonner
    1950, 279, no. 158; and esp. Henig 1990, 68, no. 123.
7. e.g., Zwierlein-Diehl 1972, vol. 3, 1, 306-307, nos.
    2766-2773.
8. Delatte and Derchain 1964, 239-244, nos. 330-
    335bis; Zwierlein-Diehl 1972, vol. 3, 152, 305, nos.
    2181, 2757; Bonner 1950, 279, no. 159; Blanchet
    1923.
9. d'Ambra 1996.

13. Agate Cameo with Chalice and Doves

Unknown location, 4th to 8th century
Banded agate
1.42 x 1.65 x .46 cm

CONDITION: The bird on the right appears to
have been oddly cut during production, lacking a
normal head, rather than damaged later. Abrasion

on the reverse is confined to the center of the stone,
beginning about .15 cm from the edge, suggesting
that it was formerly set in a metalwork mount.

ACQUISITION HISTORY: Purchased by
Hayford Pierce from Kalebdjian in 1937; acquired
by the Byzantine Collection of Dumbarton Oaks in
October 1948.

ACCESSION NUMBER: BZ.1948.19

Two facing birds stand on the rim of a
chalice, a cross between them and palm
branches at the base of the footed vessel.
Birds drinking from a chalice are common in Early Christian and Byzantine art,
as most famously in the mosaics of the
mausoleum of Galla Placidia (c. 425-450),[1]
and signify Christians drinking the water
of life.[2] Doves also sometimes represent
apostles, and when two flank a cross they
may refer to Peter and Paul.[3] On the apotropaic use of agate, see cat. no. 11.

This cameo has been designated "Lan-
gobard (?), seventh century" by comparison
with another in the Dumbarton Oaks
Collection, an agate set into a *fibula* possibly
from seventh-century Italy.[4] There is, however, little reason to assume that the brooch
and gem have the same origins. That jewel,
therefore, cannot help to place this one.
Style and iconography allow our cameo to
be placed within the early medieval period,
but not in any specific century or place.

GK

REFERENCES: *DOH* 1955, 73, no. 157; *DOCat*
2, 124, no. 172; Zwierlein-Diehl 1997, 69; Spier
forthcoming, no. 728.

1. Romanini 1988, 117.
2. On the source of pure water, see Song of Songs 4:15;
    cited according to Zwierlein-Diehl 1997, 69.
3. Árnason 1938.
4. *DOCat* 2, 123-124, no. 171.

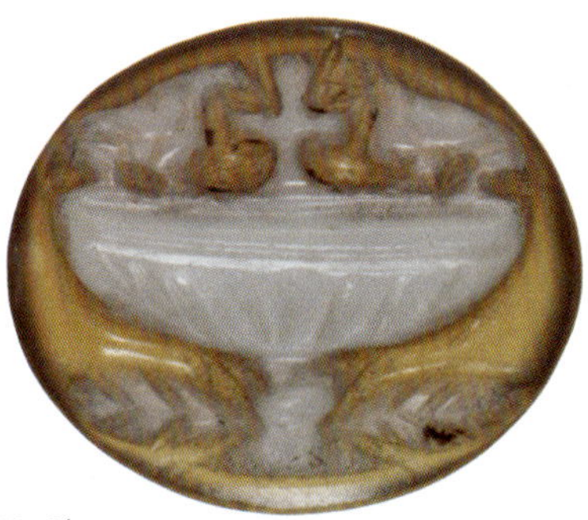

13. Obverse

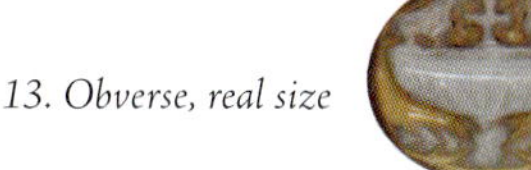

13. Obverse, real size

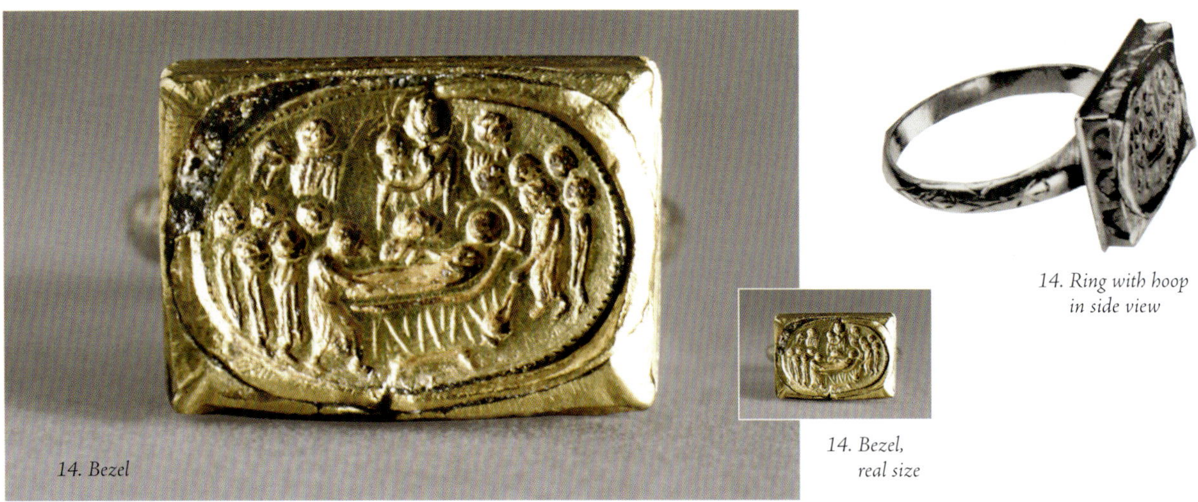

14. Bezel

*14. Ring with hoop
in side view*

*14. Bezel,
real size*

Finger Rings

14. *Gold Intaglio Ring with the Koimesis of the Virgin*

Intaglio—Constantinople, 11th century;
ring—16th century
Intaglio: 1.1 x 1.6 cm

Condition: Excellent.

Acquisition History: Originally in Sir Leigh Ashton's collection, London; acquired for the Byzantine Collection of Dumbarton Oaks in 1956.

Accession number: BZ.1956.15

The ring consists of a gold intaglio, probably of the eleventh century, now in a gold setting of the fifteenth or sixteenth century. The small gold plaque depicts the Koimesis or Dormition of the Virgin. The original Byzantine setting would have been oval and not rectangular as it is today. The small size of the intaglio does not allow for uses other than as a ring, and as an intaglio it was intended to function as a seal.

The scene depicts the Virgin lying on a draped bier with her head toward the right. When used as a seal, the scene would appear in reverse with the Virgin's head on the left. The twelve apostles, mourning her death, surround her. Five are standing at the head of the bier and six are at the foot, with Paul touching her legs. John, singled out behind the bier, is bending over her at the center of the scene. Christ, holding in his arms her soul in the form of a child, stands as the tallest figure directly behind John. Two angels have descended, one on either side of Christ, ready to accompany her soul to heaven.

Intaglios with narrative scenes are generally rare. By the eleventh century the Koimesis was a well-established and popular religious subject, but the rendition of this scene on or for a seal was quite unusual.

We know of only a few cases, such as a seal with the Koimesis belonging to a monastery and the seal of Theodora Komnene, the niece of Emperor Manuel Komnenos.[1] Another seal, known only from textual sources, is the wax seal of Anna Dalassena, the mother of Emperor Alexios I Komnenos, which depicted the Koimesis on one of its sides.[2] Although very few, the examples suggest that this seal ring most likely belonged to a woman of aristocratic status. Possibly, when retiring to a monastery—as it was common for such a lady to spend the later years of her life as a nun—she had it made for her personal use. The theme of the Koimesis is most appropriate for such circumstances. On the one hand it directly addresses death, while on the other it displays a hope for salvation through the image of the Virgin's soul held in Christ's hands, just before the awaiting angels take her to heaven.

IK

References: *DOCat* 2, 88, no. 123; *DOH* 1967, no. 229; Cambridge, MA, *Byzantine Women* 2003, 299, no. 182.

Exhibitions: *Byzantine Women and Their World*, Arthur M. Sackler Museum, Harvard University Art Museums, October 25, 2002-April 28, 2003, Cambridge, MA.

1. Schlumberger 1884, 25 and 644; *DOCat* 2, 88, no. 123.
2. Oikonomides 1985, 10.

15. *Gold and Niello Ring with Standing Virgin and Child*

Constantinople, 7th century
Diameter of hoop: 2.2 cm.; bezel: 1.4 x 1.2 cm

Condition: Niello missing from heads, body of Child, and Virgin's drapery under her left arm.

Acquisition History: Acquired from George Zacos, March 7, 1968.

Accession number: BZ.1968.8

The gold ring is made of an eight-sided hoop and a slightly oval bezel that depicts on its surface in niello a full-length Virgin and Child between two small crosses. The Virgin

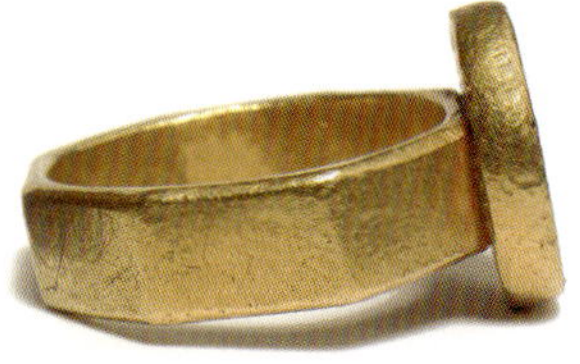

*15. Ring with hoop
in side view*

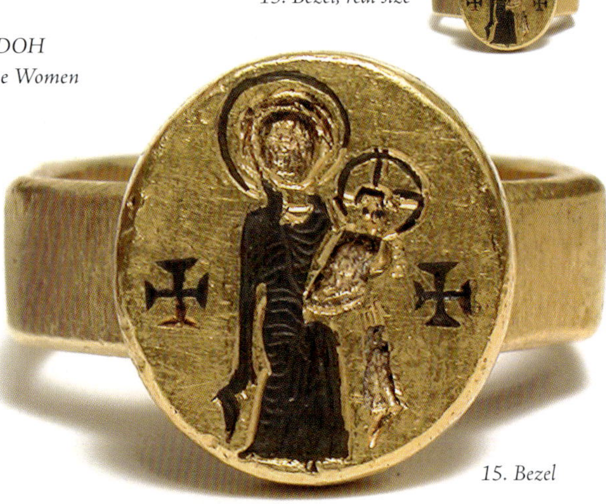

15. Bezel, real size

15. Bezel

is standing in contrapposto and is holding
the Child on her left arm in the manner that
would become famous as the Hodegetria.[1]
The Virgin and Child do not have any
inscriptions identifying them, an indication
of a pre-Iconoclastic date for the ring. After
Iconoclasm, the Virgin receives the title
M̄ (HTЄ)P̄ Θ̄(ЄO)V̄ (*Meter Theou*—
"Mother of God") inscribed in an abbreviated
form on either side of her head.[2] On the
ring we see an early pre-Iconoclastic version
of the Hodegetria type seen more often on
lead seals.[3] The two crosses on either side
are equal-armed and have flaring arms. This
type of cross is also found on jewelry of the
sixth to seventh century.[4] The iconographic
type of the standing Virgin and Child set
between two equal-armed crosses can be
seen on a very nice seal of Emperor Leo III,
now at Dumbarton Oaks, which is almost
identical and which places the ring more
precisely in the late seventh or even early
eighth century (fig. 15A).[5] The fact that this
is a golden ring of high quality and has an
imperial iconographic theme represented on
its bezel would suggest a possible imperial
ownership for the ring.

IK

References: unpublished.

1. The epithet Hodegetria (Ὁδηγήτρια) refers to an
    icon of the Virgin housed in the Hodegon Monastery
    in Constantinople. According to popular tradi-
    tion, this icon was painted by apostle Luke. Cf. N.
    Ševčenko's article on the Virgin Hodegetria in *ODB*
    3, 2172-2173, which contains further references.
2. Kalavrezou 1990, 170.
3. For examples featuring the standing figure of the Ho-
    degetria—*DOS* 1, nos. 8.1, 9.1. For post-Iconoclastic
    seals with similar iconography—op. cit., nos. 18.26,
    18.84, 59.7, 74.2.
4. New York, *Age of Spirituality* 1977, 328-329,
    no. 308.
5. D.O. acc. no.: BZ.1955.1.3431a in Zacos 1972,
    no. 33a; the same seal published in Penna 2000,
    213, fig. 151.

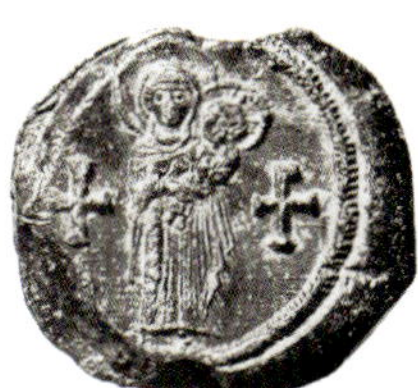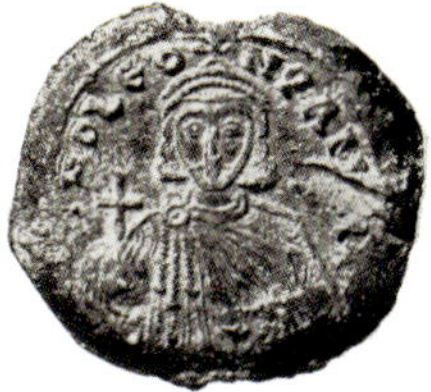

Figure. 15A. Seal of Emperor Leo III Isauros
(717-741), Dumbarton Oaks, BZ.1955.1.3431a.

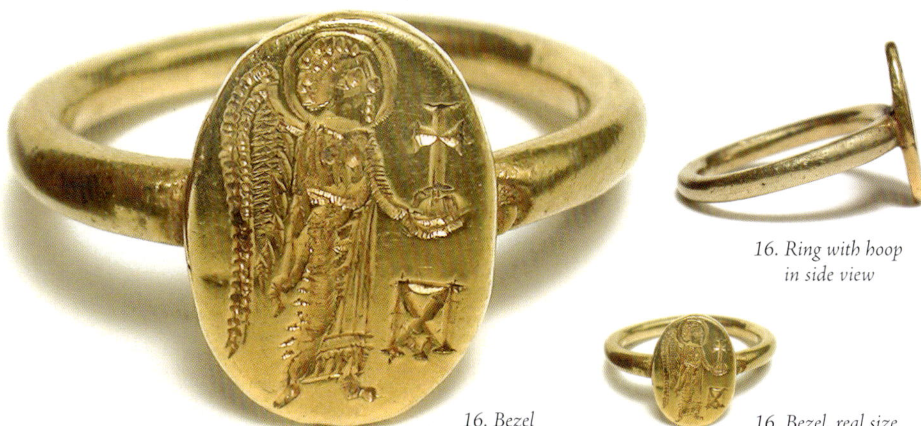

16. Ring with hoop
in side view

16. Bezel

16. Bezel, real size

16. Ring with Archangel and Monogram

Constantinople? late 5th to 6th century
Gold
Diameter: 2.3 cm

Inscribed: Box monogram.

Condition: Excellent.

Acquisition History: Said to have been
found in Constantinople. Acquired from
George Zacos.

Accession number: BZ.1953.12.6

This substantial gold ring is made of a
plain, thick wire hoop and a flat, oval
bezel. Engraved on the bezel is a standing
archangel, turned to the right and holding
a globus cruciger in his outstretched left
hand. Below the archangel's hand is a box,
or block, monogram that can be deciphered
as either ΠΑVΛΑ ("Paula") or ΠΑVΛΙΝΑ
("Paulina").[1] Particularly notable about the
archangel are the carefully rendered multi-
tiered wings, the elaborate drapery, and the
deep, sharp cutting of the intaglio.

The box monogram was the usual form
on lead seals from the late fourth to the
middle of the sixth century. Beginning in
the middle of the sixth century, the cross
monogram gradually replaced it. However,
the box type monogram was not eclipsed
until the seventh century (cf., cat. nos. 20,
23, 36).[2]

The image of an archangel appeared on
the reverses of gold coins for the first time
during the reign of Emperor Justin I (518-
527);[3] it continued to be the standard figure
on gold coinage throughout the rest of the
sixth century. This fact has been used as a
convenient *terminus post quem* for the use

of archangels in other media, but this is not
necessarily the case.

A gold ring in the Virginia Museum of
Fine Arts must be related to the Dumbarton Oaks ring.[4] Engraved on an oval bezel is
a personification of Constantinople seated
at the right and facing left. She holds a
globus cruciger in an outstretched arm with
a star above and a box monogram below,
which has been deciphered as ΒΑCΙΛЄΙΟV
(*Basileiou*—"belonging to Basil"). The strikingly similar configuration of elements—figure, *globus cruciger*, box monogram—on this
ring, though seen in reverse to those on the
Dumbarton Oaks ring, indicates a shared
taste in design. Although the engraving on
the Richmond ring is less accomplished, its
dating to the late fifth or early sixth century
places it within the same span of years as
the Dumbarton Oaks ring. Also, from the
obvious difference in the monograms it
appears that such rings could be worn by
either a man or a woman.

Ross suggested that the *globus cruciger* on
the Dumbarton Oaks ring implied a connection with the emperor. Although such
a connection cannot be substantiated, the
iconography is suggestive and the notably
high quality of the ring indicates production
in the best workshop in Constantinople of
the time. If the monogram is read as Paulina, then a connection may be suggested
with the mother of the usurper Emperor
Leontios (484-488). Mango argued that
she had an estate at Blachernae in the last
quarter of the fifth century.[5] If this connection is correct, then the dating of a rock
crystal intaglio of an archangel with *globus
cruciger* in Paris,[6] placed in the sixth or

seventh century, should be reassessed. Its date was based partly on the appearance of archangels on coinage. The possibility is raised that the image of an archangel with a *globus cruciger* was adapted for use on precious jewelry before its appearance on gold coinage.

SRZ

REFERENCES: *DOH* 1955, no. 168; *DOH* 1967, no.195; *DOCat* 2, no. 62.

1. John Nesbitt, research associate for Byzantine sigillography at Dumbarton Oaks, offered these readings.
2. Zacos 1972, 367, with earlier references.
3. *DOC* 1, 36, no. 2.
4. Gonosová and Kondoleon 1994, no. 6.
5. Mango 1994, 190-191.
6. Paris, *Byzance* 1992, no. 35.

17. Ring with the Ascent of Alexander the Great

Said to have been found in Constantinople, 11th to 12th century
Gold
Diameter: bezel, 1.3 cm; hoop, 1.5 cm

CONDITION: Excellent.

ACQUISITION HISTORY: Acquired from George Zacos.

ACCESSION NUMBER: BZ.1956.28

Cast in one piece, this ring has an intaglio representation of the ascent of Alexander the Great on its flat, circular bezel. He is crowned and dressed as a Byzantine emperor, standing in a chariot and holding a staff in each hand. Bait is skewered on each staff that griffins, yoked to the chariot, try to reach. Engraved on each side of the ring is a bird in profile with its head turned back, along with several branches.

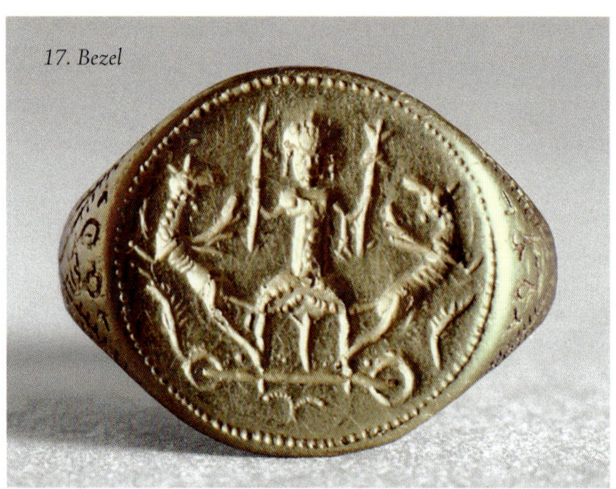

17. Bezel

The episode of the ascent of Alexander is derived from the ancient Greek novel known as the *Alexander Romance*. Although based on historical sources, much of it is fictional invention. Nonetheless, it was the foundation of knowledge about Alexander the Great throughout the Middle Ages.[1] Several versions and many translations exist, but there is only one extensively illustrated manuscript.[2] Excerpted from the literary tradition, Alexander's ascent became the most frequently reproduced scene of the epic. Twenty-three examples are extant from the Middle and Late Byzantine periods (843-1453),[3] and many more in Western medieval contexts.[4]

Alexander's ascent above the world was described in several versions of the *Alexander Romance*[5]: after conquering much of the known world, Alexander decides to extend his explorations into the heavens. He yokes two large white birds to a bag made of oxhide, and, while sitting in the bag, he suspends bait on the ends of two lances that he holds above the birds so that they fly upward. In this way, he rises into the sky and embarks on a heavenly journey. Eventually, he is admonished and sent back to earth by two winged creatures with human form. Before doing so, he looks down and views the world as a threshing floor encircled by a snake and is told that the snake is the sea and the threshing floor is the earth.[6] Although Alexander's descent to the depths of the ocean in a glass cage precedes the ascent, only his ascent became a popular image in the medieval world.

Through analyses of texts mentioning Alexander[7] and selected images of the ascent,[8] Trahoulia has determined that Alexander the Great and images of the ascent served as paradigms of rulership in Byzantium. Specifically, the ascent was a lens through which to see the Byzantine emperor's elevation and dominion over the known world. Although ideas relating to Alexander are documented from the fourth to the fourteenth century and beyond,

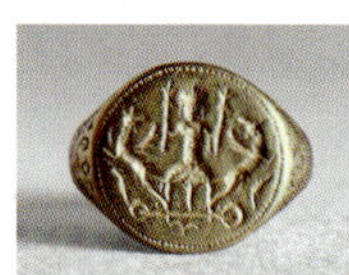

17. Bezel, real size

Trahoulia's analysis revealed that the high point of such analogies was the Komnenian era, the later eleventh and twelfth centuries.

The ascent of Alexander is found on objects that can be connected directly with rulership: for example, on the gold and enamel diadems from Preslav in modern Bulgaria,[9] and from Kiev in modern Ukraine.[10] These diadems could have been inspired by Byzantine works or sent as gifts from the court of Constantinople to the medieval rulers of Preslav and Kiev. Although it is not certain exactly whose heads they graced, the diadems clearly combine the ascension with ceremonial and courtly functions.

The interpretation of other objects is less certain, including the three gold rings with Alexander's ascent: a lozenge-shaped ring in Athens, Greece;[11] an oval ring in a private collection in Rome;[12] and the Dumbarton Oaks ring. Despite the differences in shape and details, the iconography, intaglio technique, and substantial amount of gold speak for a close relationship. Could they have served an apotropaic purpose, as Trahoulia states,[13] or might they have been a part of court regalia? Either suggestion is possible or both, but without knowing who wore the rings or on what occasion, their significance eludes us. The correlation between Alexander the Great and the Byzantine emperor suggests a link to the imperial court, but such a connection must remain speculative: determining if the ring was an aristocratic insignia, a courtly emblem, or a royal gift is beyond the facts at our disposal. Nonetheless, the Dumbarton Oaks ring is extremely well crafted, the image is crisply drawn, and the intaglio is handled with great finesse, indicating a work executed for a very discerning patron.

SRZ

REFERENCES: *DOCat* 2, no. 122; *DOH* 1967, no. 228.

1. Jouanno 2002.
2. Trahoulia 1997, passim.
3. Ibid., 227-235.
4. Settis Frugoni 1973, passim; Schmidt 1995, "Western tradition versus Byzantine tradition," 18-27 and passim.
5. Trahoulia 1997, 163-164.
6. One illustration of Alexander's vision of the earth and the sea exists. A cloisonné enamel roundel shows a tree, with peacocks and birds in it, surrounded by two snakes. The complementary enamel has Alexander's head in a central medallion flanked by griffons. The medallions are attached to the Pala d'Oro in

San Marco, Venice; Hahnloser 1965, nos. 151, 152
(W. F. Volbach).

7.   Trahoulia 1997, 9-52.

8.   Ibid., 162-215.

9.   Genova et al. 1980, no. 157; Totev n.d., figs. 6-12.

10. Khanenko Collection, vol. 5, pl. 33; Grabar 1968,
     vol. 3, 294, fig. 66c.

11. National Museum, formerly in the Stathatos collec-
     tion 1957, no. 21. Coche de la Ferté 1955, 72. It was
     found in the vicinity of Thessaloniki, with coins of
     Isaac II (1185-95, 1203-1204) and Alexios III
     (1195-1203).

12. Collection of Prof. G. Cellini; see Settis Frugoni
     1973, 201, fig. 69.

13. Trahoulia 1997, 163, note 4: "[O]bjects, such as rings
     and buckles … are not discussed [by her]…. These
     objects clearly had some sort of apotropaic function."
     See Grabar 1968, vol. 3, 295-296 (note 8) for remarks
     on the apotropaic nature of the image.

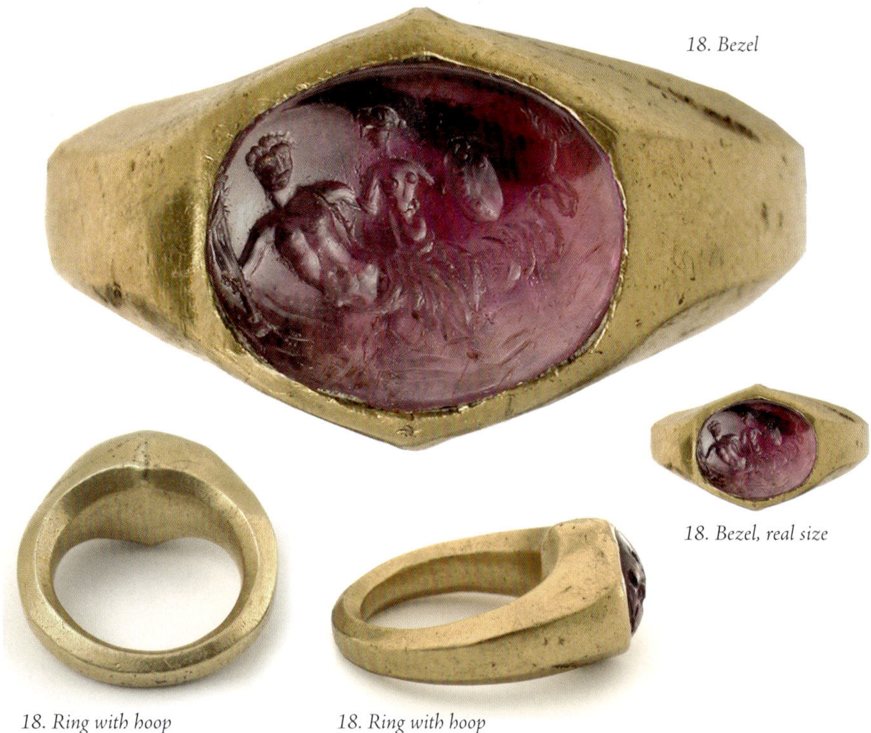

18. Bezel

18. Bezel, real size

18. Ring with hoop
in back view

18. Ring with hoop
in side view

18. Ring with Amethyst Intaglio

Said to have been found in Constantinople: intaglio,
1st century CE; ring, 9th to 10th century
Gold and amethyst
Diameter: 3.2 cm

CONDITION: Excellent, except for scratches on
the gold.

ACQUISITION HISTORY: Acquired from
George Zacos.

ACCESSION NUMBER: BZ.1953.12.1

This exceptionally large ring has a six-sided
hoop whose facets expand toward the bezel
to accommodate an impressive amethyst
intaglio. Above and below the gemstone, the
facets are formed into peaks. The convex
amethyst is engraved with a nereid facing
left, seated on a triton moving to the left.
He carries a staff in front of him, while
the nereid balances a shield upright on the
triton's tail behind her. The nereid's hair
forms a low crest over her forehead and
a bun at the nape of her neck, a hairstyle
worn by Roman women at the end of the
first century BCE and the beginning of the
first century CE.[1] The intaglio can be dated
to this period.

Ross attributed this ring to the ninth to
tenth century based on the shape of its gold
setting.[2] Several Roman rings have been
suggested as possible comparisons,[3] but
these have lozenge-shaped bezels or a lozenge-shaped gemstone. They have neither
the pointed frame and rounded setting nor
the faceted hoop that are distinguishing
features of the Dumbarton Oaks ring. A
Byzantine gold key-ring with a multifaceted
hoop, dated to the ninth century,[4] is related
to a key-ring at Dumbarton Oaks with a triangular profile.[5] The multifaceted key-ring,
though more slender than the present one,
reflects a similar design of the hoop and
belongs to the same period.

Situating the amethyst ring in the
post-Iconoclastic period places it in the
intellectual and aesthetic sphere of the
Macedonian Renaissance,[6] from the later
ninth century to the eleventh century.
During this time, there was an increase in
the copying of pre-Christian Greek texts
and the use of classical subjects and artistic
forms. One manifestation of this renewal
was using carved ivory and bone plaques
with classicizing subjects to cover small
wooden caskets.[7] Hunters, *erotes*, danc-
ers, and mythological scenes were all used,
sometimes without any narrative coherence. The classicizing nature of these scenes
might have contributed to the medieval
interpretation of the amethyst scene: first,
it may have been read as the Homeric
episode of Thetis bringing armor to her
son Achilles (*Iliad* bk. 18, 615ff.);[8] and, if
so, the representation should be recognized
as a conflation of the *Iliad*, where Thetis
carries the new armor down from Mount
Olympus where it was made by Hephaistos,
and a generic reference to Thetis, a nereid,
or denizen of the sea.

This intaglio with its "message from the
past" would have found a hospitable reception during the Macedonian Renaissance
because of its antique character, whether
identified at the time as Homeric or otherwise, and because of its inherent preciousness. The amethyst might have been set into
the large gold ring for purposeful, if not
ostentatious, display and as a counterpart to
the aforementioned ivory and bone caskets,
which, as has been suggested frequently,
may have served as jewelry boxes.[9]

SRZ

REFERENCES: *DOCat* 2, no. 112; *DOH* 1967, no.
226; Providence, *Survival of the Gods* 1987, no. 60.

EXHIBITION: *Survival of the Gods: Classical
Mythology in Medieval Art*, Bell Gallery, List Art
Center, Brown University, Providence, RI, February
28-March 29, 1987.

1.   Frel 1981, no. 18, perhaps Octavia the Younger, early
     first century CE.

2.   *DOCat* 2, 83; Ross 1954, 169-171, esp. p. 170f, figs.
     136-38b: a heavy, silver-gilt ring with points above
     and below an oval setting for a missing (gem) stone.

3.   Providence, *Survival of the Gods* 1987, 196, no. 60
     (Afuri Soeda).

4.   Chadour 1994, no. 500.

5.   *DOCat* 2, no. 109, dated ninth century.

6.   Weitzmann 1963.

7.   Weitzmann 1930, nos. 21-23, 25, 26, 28, and 40.

8.   Providence, *Survival of the Gods* 1987, 196, other
     ancient gemstones cited.

9.   See above, note 7.

Inscriptions as "Decoration" on Byzantine Jewelry

BY BRIGITTE PITARAKIS

THE MAJOR CHARACTERISTIC FEATURE OF Byzantine jewels is their decoration based on religious images. One notable exception is when the surface of a jewel is entirely devoted to inscriptions instead of any other decoration, the case with signet rings, the most prevalent object of adornment among the Byzantines in all segments of their society. Because of their practical function, signet rings were also the only type of jewelry tolerated by Early Christian writers, who were typically opposed to Christians wearing precious metal jewelry.[1] The use of a signet ring was allowed for women in their role as housewives for putting chests, food, and valuables under protection. Most of the extant signet rings provide the name of their owner in a monogrammatic form, usually with a genitive case ending, meaning "the property of/belonging to."

Compact monograms constructed around a square letter, known as box monograms, prevail in the sixth century, whereas cruciform ones dominate from the second half of the sixth to the early eighth century. From the ninth century onward, bezel devices of signet rings often take the form of a short invocation in which the wearer requests the help of the Lord or the Virgin. The most luxurious examples in precious metals include the owner's titles or official position, while inexpensive versions in bronze refer to a generic, anonymous wearer.[2] The circular flat disk of the signet rings was also appropriate for amuletic rings decorated with apotropaic images. Like the signet rings, this category also includes specimens with inscribed bezels without any figural or ornamental representation. The inscriptions are standard apotropaic formulae such as the *trisagion* (holy, holy, holy) and "Light-Life."[3]

Similar inscriptions of apotropaic intent also appear on pectoral crosses, especially on the reliquary crosses of the Middle Byzantine period. Like the signet rings, the plain surface of bronze reliquary crosses also was used for cruciform invocations, such as "Virgin help" on one side with the victorious acclamation "Jesus Christ conquers" on the other. In popular faith, inscribing the name of a powerful intercessor on the surface of a metal cross was meant to attract his or her benevolent power in the same manner as a figural representation. For example, on bronze pectoral reliquary crosses of the tenth to eleventh century, representations of saints and inscriptions of saints' names are interchangeable. Their decorative repertoire includes representations of saints in the conventional attitude of prayer, surmounted by an identifying inscription, next to plain surfaces enhanced by an inscription naming a powerful intercessor.[4] Later, in the Palaiologan period (1261-1453), crosses continue to display invocational prayers, which, as on the gold pectoral cross of the *sebastos* George Varangopoulos in the Benaki Museum in Athens, Greece, may provide the name and title of the owner.[5]

The bronze pectoral reliquaries, composed of two hollow sides, incorporated a compound of anonymous relics mixed with balm, incense, and other fragrant substances. Consequently the relics are not identified by any inscription. Such inscriptions are usually part of the decorative program of luxurious reliquaries, where they accompany figural representations of saints and vegetal ornaments. Nevertheless, jewelry mounts of private reliquaries, featuring a suspension loop, also may have a plain surface enhanced by an identification inscription without any further ornament. An example is the tenth- to eleventh-century gold reliquary pendant in the collection of the Cabinet des Médailles, Paris, decorated with the elegant letters of a nielloed inscription mentioning a relic of St. Stephen the Younger.[6]

1. See Finney 1987, 181-183.
2. See Vikan and Nesbitt 1980, 10, 16-20; Vikan 1987, 39-40. For a typology of the inscriptions on the bezels of rings, see the appendix in Hadzidakis 1944, 193-206.
3. See examples in Urbana-Champaign, *Art and Holy Powers* 1989, nos. 85-86.
4. Pitarakis, forthcoming.
5. Athens, *Byzantine and Post-Byzantine Art* 1985, no. 214.
6. Paris, *Byzance* 1992, no. 232.

19. Intaglio with a Monogram

6th century
Carnelian
1.3 x 1 x .4 cm

INSCRIBED: N Є O Փ Ѡ ("NEOFO").

CONDITION: Excellent.

ACQUISITION HISTORY: Acquired from
George Zacos, November 1957.

ACCESSION NUMBER: BZ.1957.65

This oval carnelian intaglio has a flat obverse
with a beveled edge and is engraved with an
N-shaped monogram containing the letters
N Є O Փ Ѡ. The monogram is topped by
a small star. The block or box monogram,
in which the letters of the owner's name
are organized around a central square letter
(here a *Nu*—N), is the characteristic feature
of monogrammatic intaglios in gemstone,
which, by the second half of the sixth century, are gradually superseded by incised metal
bezels. This shift in the medium of signet
rings follows the emergence of the cruciform
monogram, first found in Justinianic column
capitals of the 530s, and which becomes
the prevailing type by the end of the sixth
century.[1] The intaglio probably was mounted
on a gold signet ring.

BP

REFERENCES: *DOCat* 1, 98, no. 118.

1. Vikan and Nesbitt 1980, 17; Vikan 1987, 39. On rings
    with both block and cruciform monograms, see also
    Gonosová and Kondoleon 1994, nos. 6, 9, and 10.

20. Bezel from a Ring

Constantinople? 6th to 7th century
Gold
.9 x 1.3 cm

INSCRIBED: ΒΑСΙΛΙ ΘЄΟΔΟΡ ("Basil
Theodor").

CONDITION: The bezel is dislocated from its
hoop, which is now lost. The condition of the
bezel is excellent.

ACQUISITION HISTORY: Acquired in 1953.

ACCESSION NUMBER: BZ.1953.12.60

Early Byzantine marriage rings sometimes
incorporated the names of husband and
wife, often in association with additional
inscriptions relating to marriage, and always
in conjunction with pertinent iconography.[1]
In the Middle Byzantine period (late ninth

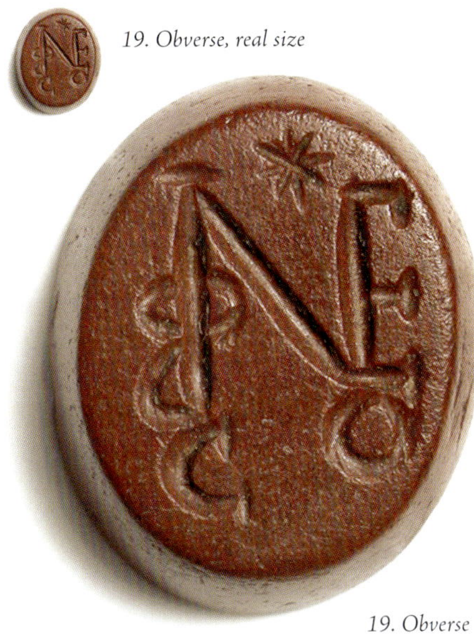

19. Obverse, real size

19. Obverse

to early thirteenth century), marriage rings
abandoned iconographic motifs in favor
of purely epigraphic designs.[2] It has been
argued that the inscription on this bezel may
record the names of a couple, Basil and Theodora, suggesting its use in a marriage ring.[3]

It must be noted, however, that the abbreviated second name lacks a final *Alpha*,
which would distinguish the name as
feminine (ΘЄΟΔΟΡΑ). It is possible, therefore, that the inscription was intended to
record the masculine version of this name,
Theodore (ΘЄΟΔΟΡΟС). The latter reading would argue against association of the
ring with marriage, suggesting instead that
both names belonged to one individual, or
that the object is a "friendship ring" for two
men.[4] Alternately, the ending of the second
name could be supplied as the genitive form
(ΘЄΟΔΟΡΟV; *Theodorou*—"of Theodore"),
in which case the ring should read "Basil,
son of Theodore."[5] The names are engraved,
but not in reverse, indicating that the ring
did not function as a seal.[6]

A Middle Byzantine date has been
proposed for the object, most likely because
of its identification as a marriage ring.[7] But
diagnostic features of its script find parallels
in Early Byzantine objects, especially lead
seals and papyri of the sixth to seventh
century.[8] In addition, the upward strokes of
the *Alpha*, *Iota*, *Lambda*, and *Delta*, which
end in three-pronged serifs, closely resemble
embellishments found in a sixth-century silver votive cross in the Walters Art Museum,
Baltimore.[9] Furthermore, the format of the
bezel—a two-line inscription separated by

a horizontal line—does not resemble the
multi-line inscriptions on Middle Byzantine
epigraphic marriage rings, but is strikingly
similar to a group of Roman bronze rings.[10]
These relatively early *comparanda* argue
against a Middle Byzantine attribution for
the ring, suggesting instead an Early Byzantine date, possibly in the sixth or seventh
century.

AW

REFERENCES: *DOCat* 2, 89, no. 126, pl. LXIII;
Vikan 1990, 147.

1. For example, see *DOCat* 2, nos. 50 and 69.
2. For example, an eleventh-century ring inscribed "I,
    Goudeles, give the betrothal ring to Maria" (Vikan
    1990, 145-146), and a tenth- to eleventh-century ring
    inscribed "Lord help Basil and Anna" (*DOCat* 2, 86,
    no. 119, pl. LXII and Vikan 1990, 147, note 20).
3. *DOCat* 2, 89.
4. The inscription on a tenth- to twelfth-century ring
    in the Cabinet des Médailles, Paris, poses a similar
    conundrum. It has been interpreted "Lord help
    Theophano and John," or "Lord help Theophanes and
    Jean," suggesting its use as a marriage ring (Bianchini
    1992, 321, no. 235). The inscription might, however,
    be read as recording the names of two men, "Lord
    help Theophanes and John," thereby eliminating the
    possibility that it served as a marriage ring. I thank
    John Nesbitt for this suggestion.
5. This reading is further supported by the lack of the
    conjunction *kai* ("and") in the inscription, which does
    appear in other rings engraved with the names of
    two individuals, for example, *DOCat* 2, no. 119 and
    Bianchini 1992, no. 235.
6. However, Byzantine stamping devices commonly
    neglected the retrograde format, resulting in backward
    impressions (Vikan 1984, 69, note 27).
7. *DOCat* 2, 89.
8. The initial *Beta* of Basil's name has an extended lower
    arm, similar to a Latin "R." This form is found in lead
    seals dating from the ninth to mid-thirteenth centuries
    (Oikonomides 1986a, 159). In lead seals, however, the

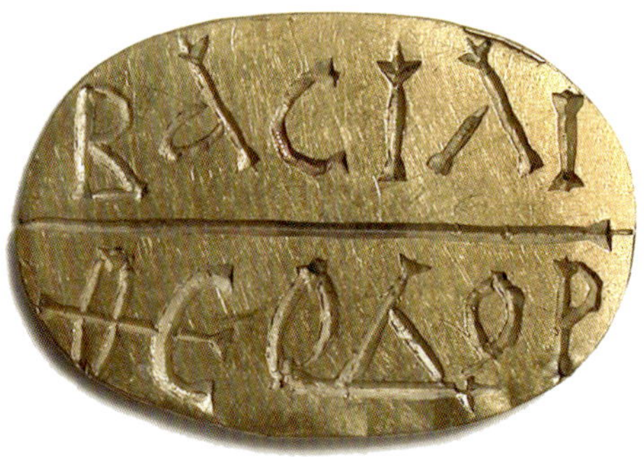

20. Obverse

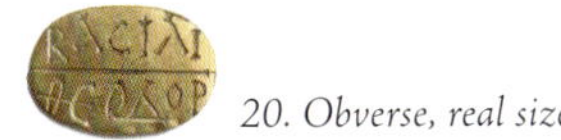

20. Obverse, real size

lower loop of the *Beta* is typically open; in the ring, the lower loop appears to be closed with a straight, horizontal line at the base. It corresponds more closely to the beta of a seventh-century seal, in which the lower loop has an angled, rather than rounded, form (Zacos 1972, no. 1372). The *Theta* and *Epsilon* of the second name share a continuous crossbar, a feature found in fourteenth-century glyptics (New York, *Byzantium. Faith and Power* 2004, no. 148). Nevertheless, this same letter combination is also attested in an Early Byzantine papyrus fragment tentatively dated to the seventh century (Cambridge, MA, *Byzantine Women* 2003, 292-293, no. 174). In addition, the document employs a lower-case *Alpha* comparable to that in cat. no. 20; a similar letter form is found in sixth- and seventh-century lead seals (Zacos 1972, nos. 963 and 1081). It must be noted, however, that lowercase *Alpha* letters are also found in inscriptions on Late Byzantine micro-mosaics dated from the thirteenth to fourteenth centuries (New York, *Byzantium. Faith and Power* 2004, figs. 7.1 and 7.3, nos. 129, 135 and 136) and in lead seals dating to the fourteenth century (Zacos 1972, no. 126).

9. Mango 1986, 94-95, no. 10.
10. Henkel 1913, nos. 819-873.

21. *Ring with Octagonal Bezel*

Said to have been found in Asia Minor,
7th to 9th century?
Gold and niello
Width: 2 cm

Inscribed: Cross monogram.

Condition: Excellent, except for a few gouges on the bezel's ring.

Acquisition History: Acquired in 1940 by Mr. and Mrs. Bliss; provenance unknown.

Accession number: BZ.1940.6

The bezel's octagonal shape is echoed in the ring's hoop, but only the bezel is decorated. It has a wreath formed by cut-ting away the background and filling it with niello, a silver alloy that becomes a lustrous black after being fired. The wreath frames a cruciform monogram with normal and retrograde letters that can be read as IAKⲰBȢ—*Iakovou*, genitive of Jacob, that is, "[belonging to] Jacob."

This ring is said to have been found in Asia Minor along with a steatite amulet and three coins. The small amulet with St. George carved in relief has been dated to the twelfth to thirteenth century;[1] the three coins date to the reign of Michael II (820-829).[2] Based on the coins, Ross considered the ring to be ninth-century and attributed it to Constantinople.[3]

Wreaths were used ubiquitously as decorative devices throughout antiquity and the early Middle Ages. Significantly, they appear on a variety of Late Antique objects, and niello wreaths specifically frame crosses on silver plates, for example, two in the Dumbarton Oaks collection (cf. cat. no. 37)[4] and another in the State Hermitage Museum.[5] These are dated by impressed stamps to the seventh century. Simple wreaths are also used on lead seals to surround a variety of words and formulae, including cruciform monograms. The wreaths appear over several centuries, of which the following are representative: Bonos, *magistros*, c. 550-650;[6] Sisinnios, metropolitan, seventh century;[7] and John, *apo hypaton* (former consul), son of Meze, late seventh century.[8]

These luxury items and personal signets form part of the background of this gold ring, with its cruciform monogram and niello wreath. However, the ring differs from them all by virtue of its octagonal shape.[9] The closest objects in both shape and decoration to the bezel of this ring are octagonal weights.[10] Made to weigh either commodities or coins, they were marked with Greek numbers, the same as Greek letters, which were framed by incised zigzags, cusps, or wreaths. In one case, a weight was marked with a box monogram, presumably of the owner or issuer.[11]

The similarity between the handsome gold and niello ring and the utilitarian bronze weights may be no more than the coincidence of shape and surface decoration. Whether the modest weights could have exerted any influence on the design of the gold ring must remain hypothetical until more information is retrieved about the manufacture of the ring and its owner, Jacob.[12]

SRZ

References: *DOH* 1955, no. 196; *DOCat 2*, no. 111; *DOH* 1967, no. 225.

1. *DOCat 3*, no. 38.
2. The coins are mentioned in *DOC 3.1*, 396, note 6.1: one miliaresion (silver coin) "[s]aid to have been found in a tomb in Asia Minor in company with two folles [bronze coins] of Michael II and Theophilos, as well as other objects."
3. *DOCat 2*, no. 111.
4. Cruikshank Dodd 1961, nos. 45 and 46; *DOCat 1*, nos. 16.1-2. Compare the distinctly thinner wreath with four medallions framing a cross monogram, dated to the reign of Justinian, c. 547-550 (Cruikshank Dodd 1961, no. 120), formerly in Berlin.
5. Effenberger et al. 1978, no. 25.
6. Zacos 1972, no. 295.
7. Ibid., no. 492.
8. Ibid., no. 363.
9. This ring also differs from those cited as comparisons by Ross, which have octagonal hoops but not

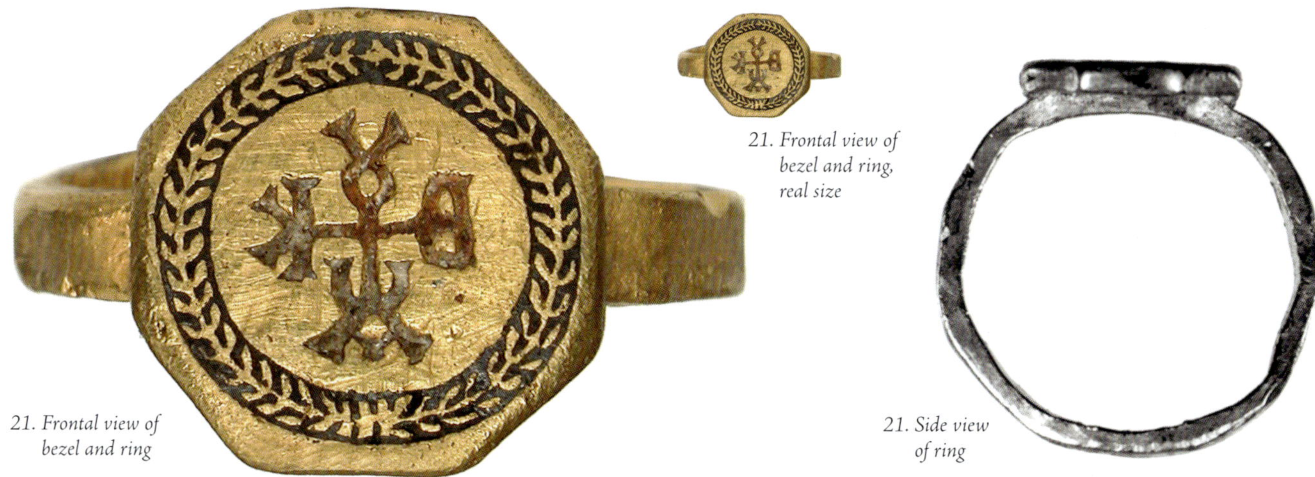

21. *Frontal view of bezel and ring*

21. *Frontal view of bezel and ring, real size*

21. *Side view of ring*

octagonal bezels; *DOCat* 2, no. 111.

10. Bendall 1996, 26-30.

11. Ibid., no. 37, with a monogram reading "Pappou":
      "[belonging to] Pappos."

12. Through chance preservation a square, three-pound
      bronze weight, found in Sidon in 1827, bears the
      name of Jacob (cf. Dumont 1870; Bendall 1996, no.
      46). The weight has the following inscription: letters
      in its corners (reading left to right, top to bottom)
      IAKⲰ; and, within the remains of a central wreath,
      a three-line inscription: the first reads: IAKⲰBOV;
      the second has the abbreviation: Θ(ΕΟΤΟΚ)Ε
      BO(HΘΕΙ) (*Theotoke boethei*—"Mother of God,
      help!"); the third has the sign for pounds and Γ
      (*Gamma*—the number three). The complete inscrip-
      tion reads: "Bearer of God (Virgin Mary), help Jacob;
      3 pounds." This weight affirms that it was owned
      by or officially issued in the name of a certain Jacob.
      Although the names on the weight and the ring are
      the same, this coincidence does not allow—in view of
      the uncertain dates of the two objects—any further
      deduction to be made.

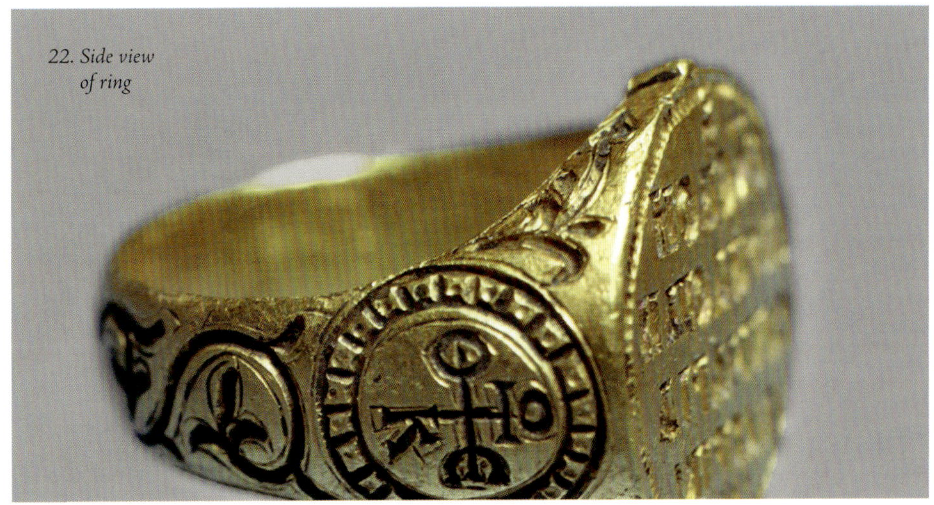

22. *Side view
of ring*

22. *Gold and Niello Ring of Maria Patrikia*

Constantinople, 9th or 10th century

Diameter: hoop, 2 cm; bezel, 1.8 cm

Inscribed: The two monograms, one on each
shoulder of the ring, are deciphered as ΘΕΟΤΟΚΕ
(*Theotoke*—"Mother of God" in vocative case) and
BOHΘΕΙ (*Boethei*—"Help") respectively; reversed
inscription on the bezel Θ(ΕΟΤΟ)ΚΕ ΒΟΗ/ΘΗ
ΤΗ ΔΟΥΛΗ / ϹΟΥ ΜΑΡΙΑ / ΠΑΤΡΙΚ(ΙΑ) (*Theotoke, boethei te doule sou Maria Patrikia*—"Mother
of God, help thy servant, Maria the Patrician").

Condition: Excellent, with some niello missing.

Acquisition History: Said to have been
found in Constantinople. Purchased by Dumbarton
Oaks in 1953.

Accession number: BZ.1953.12.2

The ring is made of solid gold, with the
bezel and hoop forming a continuous whole.
The hoop is decorated with a *rinceau* motif
in niello. Each of the shoulders is ornamented also in niello with a cruciform monogram and surrounded by a "beaded" border.
The monograms form a short prayer to the
Virgin Mary, and so does the inscription incised on the bezel. The fact that the latter is
reversed suggests that the ring was a signet
ring. The inscription also indicates that the
wearer was a woman named Maria who had
the title of patrician either in her own right
or as the wife of a patrician. Beyond that it
is not possible to identify this Maria since
the name was quite common.[1]

This ring belongs to a type that was worn
by members of the court. Most of these
rings are of solid gold, with niello decoration, and were meant to be signet rings.
They vary somewhat in date and in the
details of their decoration, and not all are
true seal rings since in some the inscription
is not in reverse and in others the incised
letters are in niello.[2] All of them are wrought
of a considerable quantity of gold, and their
impressive visual effect is very similar. Since
most of the wearers also had inscriptions
including their titles, Ross has suggested
that they were probably rings of investiture.
He also believes that they were produced in
Constantinople.[3] Maria's ring is said to have
been found in that city.

IK

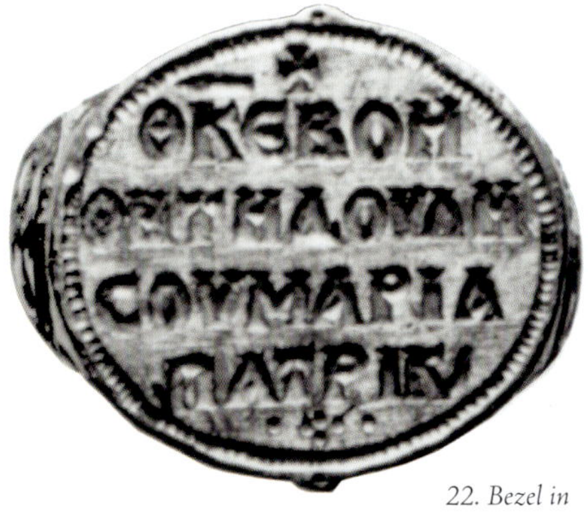

22. *Bezel in
reverse*

References: *DOH* 1955, no. 194; *DOCat* 2,
81-82, no. 110; *DOH* 1967, no. 224

1. *DOCat* 2, 82, no.110.

2. For two such examples and some further bibliogra-
     phy, see New York, *The Glory of Byzantium* 1997,
     247-248, nos. 172 and 173.

3. *DOCat* 2, 82.

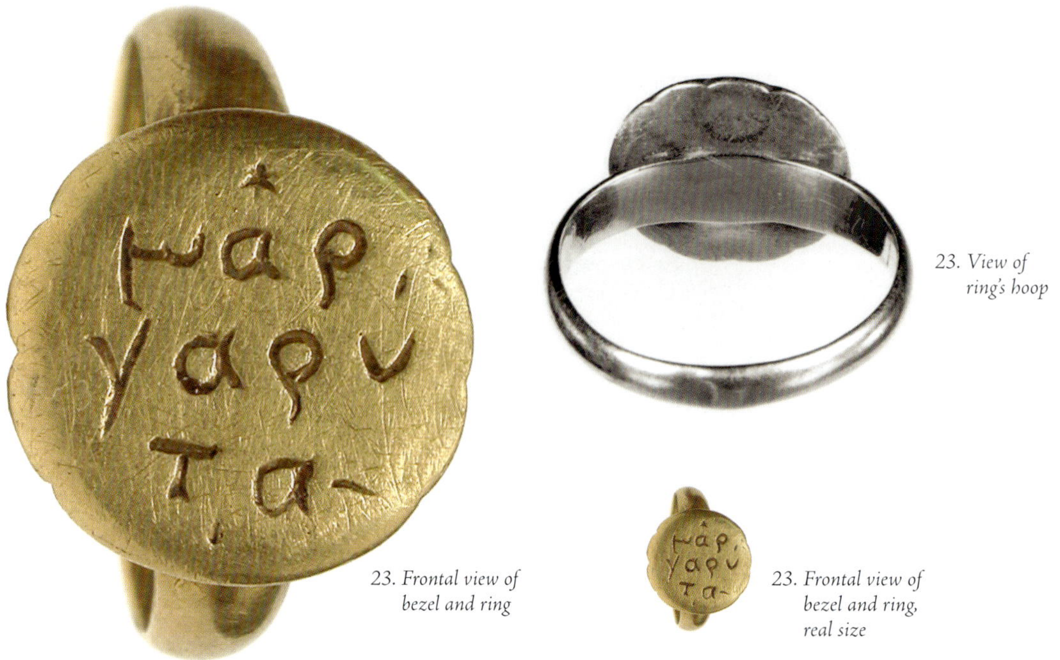

23. *View of ring's hoop*

23. *Frontal view of bezel and ring*

23. *Frontal view of bezel and ring, real size*

23. *Ring with Inscription*

Constantinople? 13th to 14th century?
Gold
Diameter: 1.8 cm

Inscribed: μαργαρύτα (*Margarita*—
"Margaret").

Condition: Very good.

Acquisition History: Said to have been
found in Constantinople. Acquired from George
Zacos in 1953.

Accession number: BZ.1953.12.18

This gold ring has a plain hoop and a bezel
in the form of a flat disk, engraved in Greek
with the name Margarita. A small star
appears on top of the elegant inscription
rendered in accentuated minuscule script.

The ring belongs to a standard type drawing on Early Byzantine models.[1] Such rings
were often used as signets, but this was also
a popular type for marriage and betrothal
rings, as well as for protective rings decorated with religious images. The inscription
of this ring is neither reversed nor in the
genitive form. Its recipient, a woman named
Margarita, used it as an adornment and not
as a signet. She may have received it as a
gift, perhaps as a betrothal ring.

In spite of the similarity of shape to
Early and Middle Byzantine rings, the
use of a minuscule script and the name
Margarita point to a later date also suggested by the slightly scalloped edges of the
bezel. Minuscule inscriptions have been
discovered in graffitis of the eleventh and

twelfth centuries,[2] but their occurence on
the works of Byzantine goldsmith works is
very rare. Such an example is the famous
silver reliquary of the hand of St. Marina,
which was brought to Venice in 1213.[3]
Margarita is also a rare name in Byzantine
society. It has been encountered only on a
set of three documents from the archives
of the monastery of Lavra, Mount Athos,
dated 1284.[4]

In light of the above considerations, a
thirteenth- to fourteenth-century date
seems appropriate for this ring, although
a later date is possible as well.

BP

References: *DOCat* 2, no. 121, pl. LXII.

1. See examples in Vikan 1987, 36-37.
2. See Kiourtzian 2000, nos. 87-89b.
3. New York, *The Glory of Byzantium* 1997, no. 332.
4. Lemerle et al. 1977, nos. 73, l. 63; 74, l. 45; 77, l. 70.

24. *Seal Ring*

Constantinople, 14th century
Gold
Diameter: hoop, 2.2 cm; bezel, 1.8 cm

Inscribed: + ΙѠ(ΑΝΝΗC) ΤΟΥ ΠΑ-
ΠΑΡΑΝΤΟΥ Ο ΥΙΟC (*Ioannes tou papa Rantou o
yios*—"John, son of the priest Rantos" or "John, son
of Paparantos").

Condition: The overall condition is fair, yet
there is considerable wear on the shoulders of
the hoop.

Acquisition History: Said to have been
found in Constantinople. Acquired from George
Zacos in 1957.

Accession number: BZ.1957.51

This heavy gold signet ring has a solid hoop
that widens toward a circular bezel. A lion
on a hatched background is surrounded
by a reversed inscription identifying the
owner: "John, son of the priest Rantos." On
each shoulder of the hoop is a scroll pattern
enclosing a medallion engraved with an
animal, now too worn to be identified but
probably a lion.

The compact shape of this finger ring, its
flat circular bezel, and its scroll pattern refer
back to earlier models of the ninth through
twelfth centuries.[1] However, by its decorative technique and motifs this piece relates
to thirteenth- to fourteenth-century examples. Two close parallels are to be found
among the crusader jewelry hoard from
the Castle of Chalcis, on Euboea, Greece,
and kept in the Ashmolean Museum of
Oxford.[2] The hoard, dispersed between
the Ashmolean and the British Museum,
includes some pieces imported from Gothic
Europe, but it has been suggested that the
bulk of its jewelry was probably manufactured in Greek lands either by Italian
goldsmiths settled there or by Greek goldsmiths imitating Western models.[3] Another
parallel, also from a crusader context, is the
gold ring found in the sea off the Monemva-
sia castle and kept at the Mystras Museum,

Peloponnesos, Greece. The bezel of this ring is decorated with a lion rampant set within a coat of arms, while the circular inscription refers to a *sebastos vestiariou*, a high-ranking official of the despotate of Morea.[4] Finally, a gold ring with a rectangular bezel carrying a stylized lion and vermiculated design on the shoulders, in the Canellopoulos Museum, Athens, has been attributed to fourteenth-century Italy, possibly Venice.[5]

The above-mentioned rings, together with the Dumbarton Oaks specimen, are members of a well-defined group sharing in common a particular decorative arrangement: a circular reversed inscription surrounding a central panel and providing the name, title, or office of the owner. Also, these rings' shoulders are usually enhanced with a scroll pattern that is sometimes enriched with heraldic animals, while the inner panel bears some characteristic motif from the Palaiologan repertoire, such as a coat of arms, a monogram, a double-headed eagle, or a heraldic lion. Usually, these decorative motifs are reserved on a hatched ground. This techique, called *guillochis*, emerged in

Gothic goldsmith works of the thirteenth century before being widely adopted in Byzantium throughout the fourteenth and fifteenth centuries.[6] The provenance of the Dumbarton Oaks ring suggests that it was manufactured in Constantinople, in a fertile artistic milieu combining the taste of Byzantium with that of Gothic Europe.

BP

REFERENCES: *DOCat* 2, no. 131, pl. LXIV.

1. See *DOCat* 2, no. 110; Paris, *Byzance* 1992, nos. 219-220; New York, *The Glory of Byzantium* 1997, nos. 172, 173.
2. Dalton 1911b, nos. 394-396.
3. Durand, in press.
4. Mystras, *The City of Mystras* 2001, no. 17.
5. Spieser 1972, no. 22.
6. See two rings from the Dumbarton Oaks Collection, decorated with a monogram and a bird respectively (*DOCat* 2, nos. 129, 130). Three examples from the Benaki Museum in Athens are respectively decorated with a Palaiologan monogram, a cross monogram, and an eagle attacking a smaller bird (Athens, *Byzantine and Post-Byzantine Art* 1985, nos. 213, 215, 216). A further example decorated with a cruciform monogram is in the Cabinet des Médailles, Paris (Paris, *Byzance* 1992, no. 252).

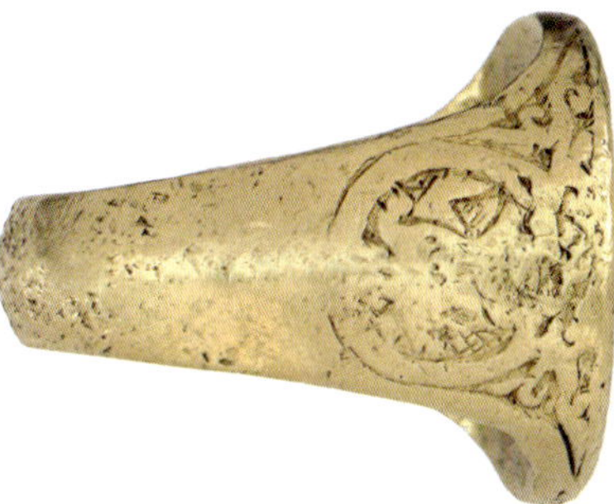

24. Side view of ring

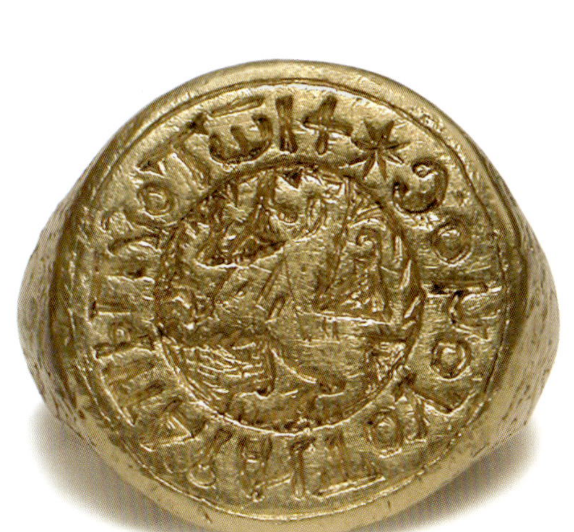

24. Frontal view of bezel and ring

24. Frontal view of bezel and ring, real size

Early Byzantine Marriage Rings

BY ALICIA WALKER

A GROUP OF EARLY BYZANTINE (FOURTH- TO eighth-century) rings indicates a clear association with marriage through their iconography and inscriptions. These objects no doubt served, much like modern wedding rings, to symbolize a couple's spiritual and legal bond. But Early Byzantine marriage rings may have provided an additional function: through a combination of apotropaic words and imagery, they protected the union of husband and wife from malevolent supernatural forces.[1]

The iconography of Byzantine marriage rings is essentially Roman in origin: full-length figures of a man and woman reach toward each other to grasp hands (cat. no. 26), or profile busts of husband and wife gaze toward each other, conveying their harmony of mind and soul (cat. no. 25). But while Roman images commonly depict pagan deities or personifications guarding over the couple, Byzantine marriage iconography replaces these figures with the cross (cat. nos. 25, 27) or Christ (cat. no. 26).[2] As such, Early Byzantine marriage rings attest to the close connections between Roman and Byzantine art and culture, while simultaneously recording the profound shift from pagan to Christian religion that the Byzantine era represents.[3]

The rings in this exhibition, like most Byzantine marriage rings, are fashioned from gold. Beyond its durability and value, gold was an appropriate medium because of its literary association with marriage and weddings. Early Byzantine *epithalamia* describe the bride as "wreathed in gold" and celebrate the couple in the phrases "gold has embraced gold" and "like gold you have found your golden bride."[4] This theme continued into the Middle Byzantine period, as attested in the *vita* of St. Thomaïs of Lesbos, whose parents were described as a "golden team."[5]

Judging from available evidence, it seems that rings did not figure prominently, if at all, in Early Byzantine marriage rituals.[6] Texts do, however, mention the exchange of rings in less formal circumstances.[7] For example, in the sixth-century *vita* of St. Alexios, the holy man recounts having presented his bride with jewelry, including a ring, in the intimate setting of their nuptial chamber.[8] Still, some rings do reflect aspects of Byzantine marriage rites. The climax of the marriage ceremony was the *dextrarum iunctio* (joining of the couple's right hands), which symbolized their spiritual union.[9] The frequent depiction of this action on marriage rings (cat. no. 26) may commemorate this key ritual moment. Another common motif in Byzantine marriage rings is a crown, typically rendered as schematic half-circles suspended over the couple's heads.[10] The crowning of husband and wife was a standard feature of Byzantine marriage rites at least as early as the eighth century.[11] Recording this moment on the ring would have served as a lasting commemoration of the ceremony that united husband and wife. Indeed, a seventh-century text describing the marriage of Emperor Maurice makes no mention of rings but does recount the crowning of the couple and the joining of their hands by a priest.[12] Early Byzantine marriage rings are perhaps best understood, therefore, as personal love tokens that sometimes referenced key moments of the wedding ceremony, but were not themselves integral parts of these rituals.

Although lacking a ceremonial function, Early Byzantine marriage rings may still have served as more than mere adornments. Clement of Alexandria (c. 150–before 215 CE), who criticized the wearing of jewelry by women as immodest, allowed for a housewife to wear a gold seal ring for the purpose of controlling access to domestic goods.[13] The ring would have been used to make an impression in the clay, wax, or pitch that sealed doors, cabinets, or containers. If the impression was disturbed, then the mistress of the house knew that the contents had been tampered with. Indeed, some Early Byzantine marriage rings include the couple's names inscribed in reverse, indicating the use of these objects as seals.[14] When decorated with the images of husband and wife, these rings further conveyed the couple's authority over the household and its provisions.

An additional and perhaps more essential function of Byzantine marriage rings may have been to guard over the marriage union itself. Inscriptions on marriage rings refer to "vow," "grace," and even "health" as concepts integral to marriage, but the most common inscription and the central concern that these rings addressed was "harmony" (cat. no. 27).[15] Byzantine magical texts refer specifically to demons and aggressive love spells dedicated to the ruin of marital harmony, and the Byzantines believed strongly in the destructive potential of supernatural forces.[16] For instance, a sixth-century Byzantine papyrus fragment records that a couple living in Antinoöpolis, Egypt, applied for a divorce because they were powerless against "a sinister and wicked demon" that had attacked their marriage and was determined to separate them.[17] In a world where malevolent powers were capable of destroying the bonds that united husbands and wives, Byzantine marriage rings may have repelled these ill-intentioned forces through potent Christian symbols. Rather than ritual objects, functioning in the limited context of religious ceremony, Byzantine marriage rings operated in perpetuity, guarding the bond between husband and wife against the potentially constant onslaught of demonic and magical forces.

1. For a general introduction to the material culture of Byzantine marriage, see Cambridge, MA, *Byzantine Women* 2003, 214-231.
2. Kantorowicz 1960, 4-6.
3. For further discussion of the intermixing of pagan and Christian traditions in Early Byzantine marriage jewelry, see Kantorowicz 1960, Vikan 1990, and Walker 2002.
4. MacCoull 1988, 89, 108.
5. Halsall 1996, 299.
6. For discussion of marriage rituals in Byzantium, see Ritzer 1970, 127-141, and 191-213 and Meyendorff 1990, 104-106.
7. Rings may have played a role in Byzantine rituals associated with betrothal (Ritzer 1970, 128 and Meyendorff 1990, 104).
8. Amiaud 1889, 12-13; Vikan 1990, 162.
9. Regarding the origins of the *dextrarum iunctio* and its appropriation within Byzantine marriage imagery, see Reeksman 1958 and Kantorowicz 1960.
10. For example, see *DOCat* 2, no. 67. Regarding Byzantine marriage crowns, see Walter 1979, Drossoyianni 1982, and Vikan 1990, 145, 152.
11. Ritzer 1970, 135-137; Meyendorff 1990, 106.
12. Whitby 1986, 33.
13. Finney 1987, 182; Vikan 1990, 147.
14. For example, see *DOCat* 2, no. 50.
15. Vikan 1990, 150-153 and 157, figs. 12, 14, 17, 24. Vikan suggested that the protective properties of marriage rings may be medicinal in nature, relating specifically to healthy conception and parturition (Vikan 1984, 83-84 and Vikan 1990, 153-157, and 160-163). For an alternate interpretation, which disassociates Early Byzantine marriage rings from a medical function and foregrounds their more general apotropaic properties, see Walker 2001 and Walker 2002.
16. Maguire 1996, 150; Walker 2002, 62-65.
17. Brown 1978, 10.

Marriage Rings

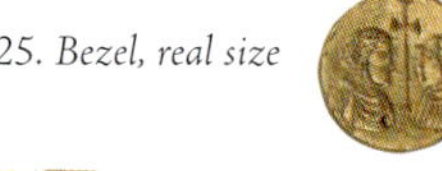

25. Bezel, real size

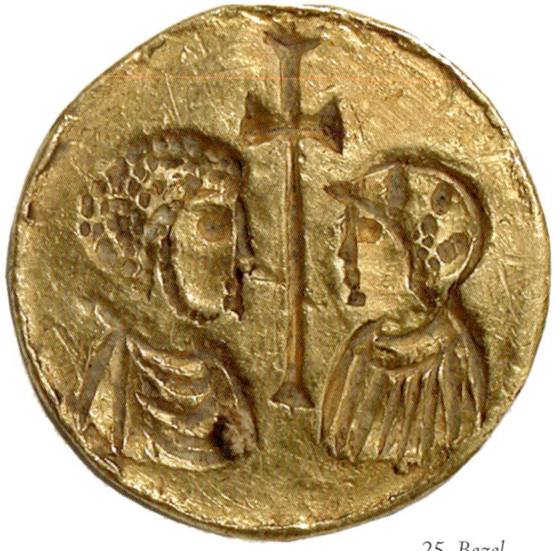

25. Bezel

25. Bezel from a Marriage Ring

Constantinople? 5th century
Gold
Diameter: 1.1 cm

Condition: The bezel is dislocated from its hoop, which is now lost. Otherwise, the bezel's condition is excellent.

Acquisition History: Acquired in 1953.

Accession number: BZ.1953.12.61

This ring depicts profile busts, representing a husband (left) and wife (right), on either side of a cross.[1] In Roman versions of this motif, the couple typically flanks a pagan deity or personification, such as Concordia, who blesses their union. In Byzantine rings, the pagan figure is replaced by a bust of Christ or, as here, the cross, which symbolically joins and guards over husband and wife. The even gaze of the couple, their absolute focus on each other, and their equal balance on either side of the cross recall the concept of harmonious union that was the ideal of Byzantine marriages.[2]

Considering the small size of the object, the figures' hair and clothing are rendered in great detail. The husband's *chlamys* (mantle) is gathered at his shoulder with a prominent *fibula* (pin); stippling conveys the texture of his beard and hair. A pattern of radiating lines, perhaps representing braids, embellishes the woman's head. The couple's costumes are carefully carved in parallel and concentric lines, indicating the graceful fall of the cloth. This refined craftsmanship attests to the high quality of the ring and suggests that its owner was affluent, a conclusion further supported by the object's valuable material. The meticulous representation does not, however, imply that the figures should be understood as portraits. Rather, they are generic types found in comparable examples.[3]

The fact that the figures and cross are incised into the metal indicates that this ring could have been used as a seal, recalling the potential function of marriage rings to secure containers of household goods.[4] The prominent cross articulates the ring's additional purpose, to guard over the union of husband and wife through the power of this most potent Christian sign.

AW

References: *DOH* 1967, 194; *DOCat* 2, 51, no. 52, pl. XXXIX; Vikan 1990, 148, fig. 5.

1. For discussion of this iconographic type and its likely fifth-century date, see Vikan 1990, 148-149.
2. Meyendorff 1990, 100; Vikan 1990, 148 and 153.
3. *DOCat* 2, 50, cat. no. 51, pl. XXXIX; Vikan 1990, 149.
4. It should be noted, however, that in depictions of married couples, the position of precedence, on the left, was typically occupied by the husband. Because an impression from this ring would render the husband on the right, it may be argued that it was not intended to be used as a seal; cf. Vikan 1990, 148.

26. Marriage Ring

Constantinople? 6th century
Gold
Diameter: 2.2 cm

Condition: Excellent.

Acquisition History: Acquired in 1953.

Accession number: BZ.1953.12.3

The iconography of this ring echoes Roman marriage imagery, which focused on the climactic moment of the *dextrarum iunctio* (joining of hands) during the marriage ceremony. In the Byzantine period, this iconography was Christianized.[1] Husband and wife stretch their right hands toward each other and Christ, identified by his cruciform halo, blesses them. Although no details of physiognomy are discernable, the couple's garments are carefully rendered. The husband (left) wears a short tunic and a *chlamys* (mantle) held at the shoulder with a *fibula* (pin). The wife (right) wears a full-length gown and a shawl draped horizontally across her shoulders. This composition appears also on a gold marriage belt from Constantinople, dating to the sixth or seventh century (see fig. 26A).

The depiction of full-length figures may derive in part from Early Byzantine numismatic imagery, particularly fourth- and fifth-century solidi, which commemorated imperial marriages.[2] Coins were often incorporated directly into items of adornment, but

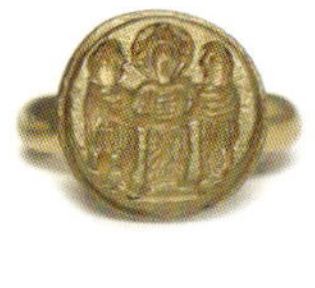

26. Frontal view of bezel and ring, real size

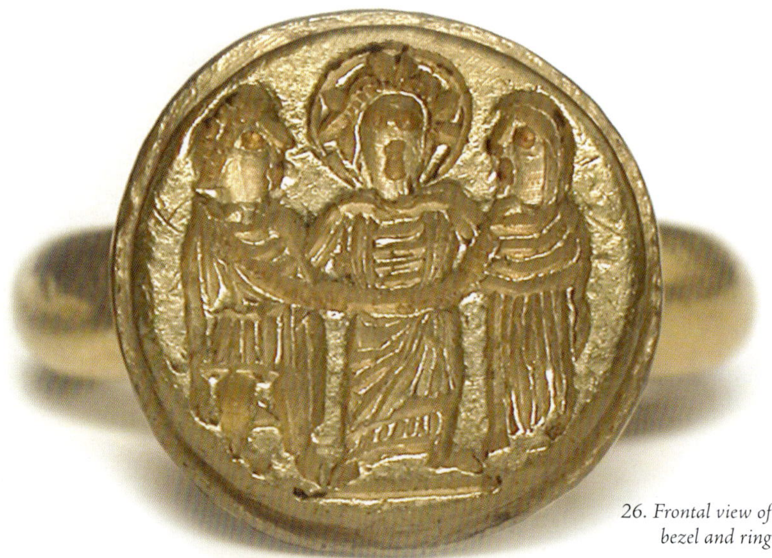

26. Frontal view of bezel and ring

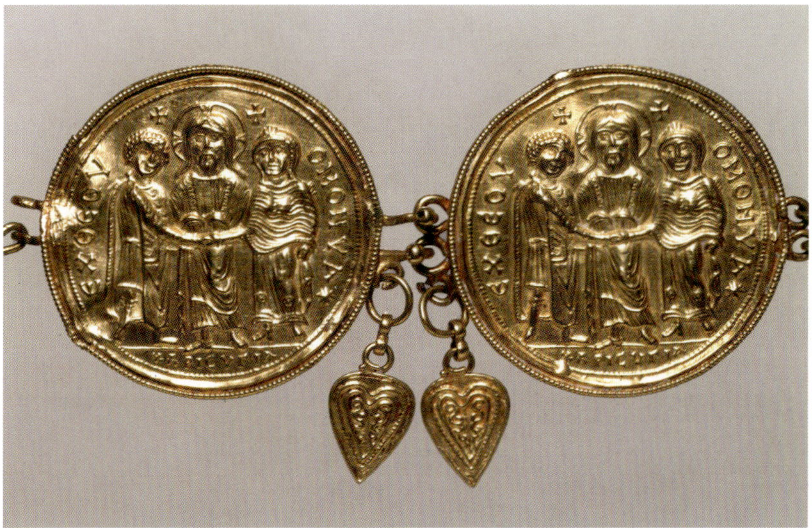

Figure 26A. Gold marriage belt representing *dextrarum iunctio. Constantinople, late 6th or 7th century, diameter of plaques 4.8 cm, Dumbarton Oaks, acc. no. BZ.1937.33.*

the pair above and below indicates that the "harmony" of their union is guarded by the "grace of God." These words literally spell out the protective intent of the object, which is simultaneously conveyed through the image of husband and wife guarded by a cross.[1]

The figures and their accoutrements are rendered in detail: the husband wears a *chlamys* (mantle) with a prominent *fibula* (pin) at his shoulder; the wife wears a gown, necklace, and earrings. Like other iconographic types (cat. no. 26), the frontal bust motif resembles imperial imagery of the period.[2]

AW

References: Kantorowicz 1960, 11, fig. 27b; *DOCat* 2, 7-8, cat. no. 4E, pl. IX; *DOH* 1967, 157E; Vikan 1990, 150-152 and 154, fig. 12; Walker 2001, 151-159, fig. 9.2; and Walker 2002, 60-64, fig. 4.2.

1. For discussion of this iconographic type and its date, see Vikan 1990, 150-154. Cat. no. 27 was found in a cache accompanied by a necklace, cross pendant, earrings, and belt buckle. The group is dated to the seventh century (*DOCat* 2, 7-8, no. 4E).
2. Vikan 1990, 151-152, figs. 15 and 16.

they also served as models for the format and design of Byzantine jewelry.[3] In some cases, coins seem to have been employed as amulets, protecting the wearer through the powers intrinsic to imperial portraits, Christian iconography, or both.[4] By imitating numismatic prototypes, Early Byzantine marriage rings may have emulated the imperial figures themselves, who served as models of marital harmony. In addition, these rings may have supplemented their amuletic powers by connoting the apotropaic properties inherent in imperial coins.[5]

AW

References: *DOH* 1955, no. 176; *DOCat* 2, 55, cat. no. 64, pl. XLII; *DOH* 1967, 201; Vikan 1990, 157 note 97.

1. Kantorowicz 1960, 4-11.
2. Kantorowicz 1960, 7-8, figs. 21, 22, 23a; Zacos 1960, 73-74.
3. Bruhn 1993; Maguire 1997, 1040-1041.
4. Maguire 1997, 1039-1041; Fulghum 2001.
5. Walker 2002, 72-73 note 16.

27. Marriage Ring

Constantinople? 7th century
Gold and niello
Diameter: ring, 2.5 cm; bezel, 1.5 cm

Inscribed: above ΘΕѴ ΧΑΡΙϹ (*Theou charis*—"Grace of God"), below ΟΜΟΝΟΙΑ (Omonoia—"Harmony").

Condition: There is some loss of niello.

Acquisition History: Acquired in 1959.

Accession number: BZ.1959.60

In this ring, husband (left) and wife (right) are depicted *en buste* and facing forward. Like the couple in cat. no. 25, they flank a prominent cross. The inscription framing

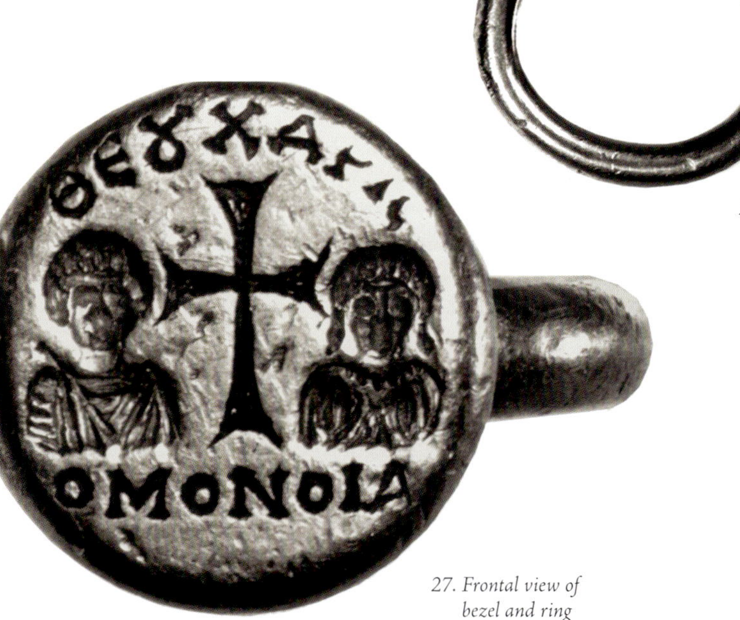

27. *Frontal view of bezel and ring*

27. *Side view of ring*

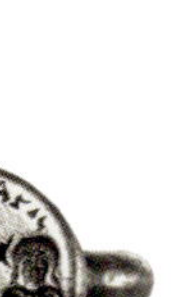

27. *Frontal view of bezel and ring, real size*

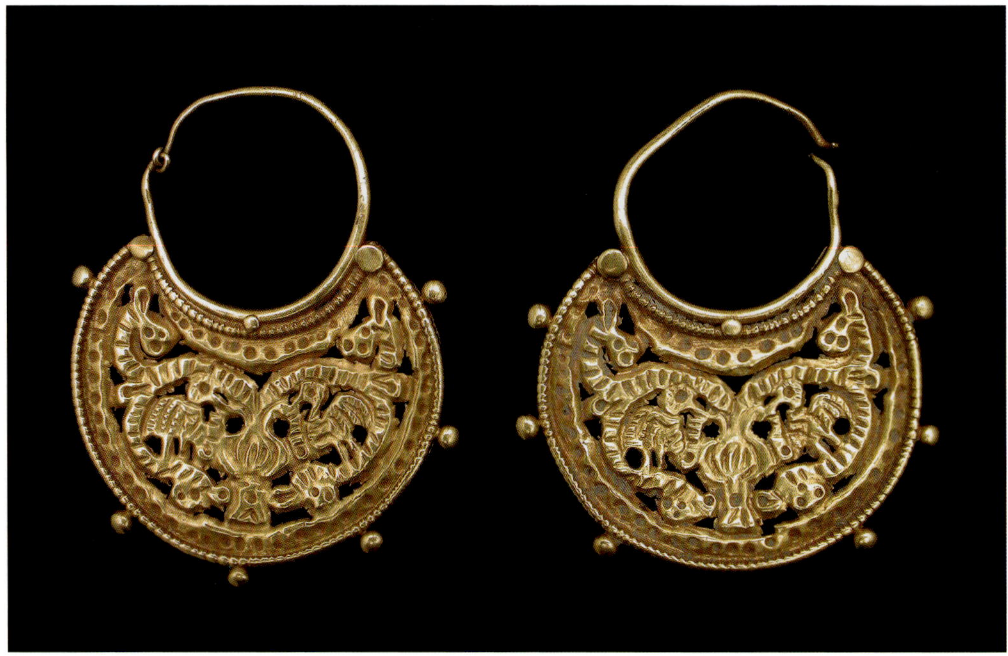

28-29.

Earrings

28-29. Pair of Openwork Earrings with Confronted Birds

Constantinople? late 6th to 7th century
Gold
(28) 4.6 x 3.3 cm; (29) 4.5 x 3.5 cm

Condition: Some bending, loss of spheres and suspension wire ends.

Acquisition History: (28) Said to have been found in Constantinople; acquired from George Zacos. (29) Anonymous gift.

Accession numbers: (28) BZ.1953.12.96; (29) BZ.1965.15

These crescent-shaped earrings are executed in openwork technique, where the background is cut away with a fine chisel leaving the desired forms in silhouette. From a tall vase in the center, ribbons emerge and surround a pair of birds placed symmetrically on either side. All the surfaces are tamped, which creates an irregular texture and enhances the luster of the gold. Each earring is further embellished with beaded wires around the edges, spheres along the bottom, and pellets anchoring the thick, smooth suspension wire. Overall, the earrings are a combination of contrasting forms and scintillating surfaces.

One of these earrings acquired in 1953 was published in 1965 and dated to the twelfth century.[1] Over the subsequent twenty-five years, as more examples of this type became known, it was possible to place the series in the late sixth and the seventh century through datable finds.[2] Examples have been found throughout the Mediterranean area and some even as far north as Germany.[3]

Although the second earring entered Dumbarton Oaks in 1965, enough evidence exists to deem the two a pair. First, one is said to have been found in Constantinople, and the other, by virtue of its donation source, suggests a find spot in the capital city as well; second, the effective identity between the techniques, execution, design, and details argues strongly for a close relationship; and third, analyses of their alloy compositions show them to be made from the same metal,[4] indicating that they are an intentional pair.

Birds flanking vases are found on other earrings, as are a number of variations of the symmetrical composition: palm leaves or crosses in the center, among other elements; and with peacocks—by far the most frequently represented birds—at the sides (cf. cat. nos. 13, 57).[5] Such imagery was not limited to earrings of the period, but was also found on bracelets, necklaces, buckles, and pendants. This jewelry attests that the imagery was worn on other parts of the body, revealing that the iconography was not only popular[6] but also had protective (apotropaic) connotations for the wearer. In terms of their interpretation, doves, peacocks, vases, palmettes, and crosses were symbols of long life, protection against evil, and the wish for abundance in this life and in the one to come.[7]

These earrings were specifically auspicious and especially protective amulets for the woman who wore them. It is noteworthy that such crescent earrings were most popular at the time from which most marriage jewelry survives.[8] Whereas the marriage rings and belts are associated specifically with the marriage ceremony, these earrings cannot be; nevertheless, they may be understood in a broader social framework as gifts to the young betrothed or newly married woman. In such cases, the earrings would have expressed generic but eminently suitable wishes through their auspicious connotations for protection and abundance. These qualities were certainly enhanced by the intrinsic, material value of the earrings.[9] Because gold never lost its monetary value, they may have represented a part of either the bride's dowry or the husband's donation, transformed into personal adornment and given, perhaps, for both short-term enjoyment and as a long-term asset.[10]

SRZ

References: (28) *DOCat* 2, no.137; (29) *DOCat* 2, 2nd ed., no. 185.

1. *DOCat* 2, no. 137.
2. Baldini 1991; further references in *DOCat* 2, 2nd ed., no. 185 (S. R. Zwirn).
3. Sage 1976.
4. *DOCat* 2, 2nd ed., no. 185.
5. Baldini Lippolis 1999, 81ff., 104-108, Type 7b (*traforato*).
6. The general role of jewelry in women's lives is discussed by Walker 2003; for a related pair of gold earrings with peacocks, see Cambridge, MA, *Byzantine Women* 2003, no. 138 (A. D. Gossen).
7. Cf. cat. no. 57; further for peacocks, see Reimbold 1983, 37-43; Urbana-Champaign, *Art and Holy Powers* 1989, 11. The crescent of the earring might have been associated with health, taking on this meaning from the crescent-shaped stamps that bore the word ΥΓΙΑ ("health") as their imprint; ibid., 14, 18, no. 40.
8. Marriage jewelry—rings and belts—is distinguished by its iconography of the bridal couple and inscriptions; Kantorowicz 1960; Walker 2001; Cambridge, MA, *Byzantine Women* 2003, 215-231.
9. Urbana-Champaign, *Art and Holy Powers* 1989, 160.
10. Arjava 1996, 56.

30. Crescent Earring with Globules

Said to have been found in Constantinople,
11 to 12th century
Gold
2.8 x 1.9 cm

Condition: Both sides are dented and have slight cracks and tears.

Acquisition History: Acquired from George Zacos.

Accession number: BZ.1953.12.26

The convex sides of this crescent earring are soldered together along their lower edge. The join is reinforced by two rows of twisted wire, topped by a strip of flat wire, and capped off by a beaded wire. Along the edges, the elliptical opening at the top is twisted wire. The suspension rings are soldered on short strips, which are in turn soldered across the tips of the opening. The present suspension wire is modern.

The sides of the earring seem to be covered by a random distribution of gold globules. In fact, the globules are placed in a pattern that can be traced at the widest section of the earring: a triangle (three globules) is set against the upper edge and moving downward are a diamond (four globules), a circle (six globules surrounding one in the middle), another diamond, another circle, a diamond and a triangle at the lower edge. The crescent shape of the earring limits the

extent of the pattern, with fewer elements toward the narrower ends. In addition, a few single globules are scattered over the surface.

The crescent earring is related to several other types of jewelry of the same basic shape. Among these are Islamic earrings of the eleventh and twelfth centuries. With many variations, they use filigree, pearls, and stones and elaborate combinations of wire, strips, and openwork.[1] At the other end of the spectrum is the "garlic-clove" type, a style with undecorated sides.[2] A pair of such earrings was found in the Tiberias Hoard, dated to the early eleventh century.[3]

This crescent shape also echoes the larger pendants known as *kólti* (sing. *kól't*), associated with Kievan Rus'. Made during the eleventh through the early thirteenth century,[4] they are embellished with cloisonné enamel or niello and thought to have been filled with perfumed cloth.[5] The Dumbarton Oaks earring might be a reflection, in both form and function, of the larger *kólti* of the period.

Very few examples of jewelry decorated only with globules and wire like the Dumbarton Oaks earring are known. One is a lunate pendant, whose crescent is oriented downward, found at the ancient city of Vyshgorod, near Kiev.[6] It is edged with a double row of twisted wire and its smooth background is filled with triangles of different sizes made of globules. It is dated to the tenth to eleventh century.

Although the Dumbarton Oaks earring

is related typologically to Islamic jewelry and examples from Kievan Rus', it has not been possible to identify another Middle Byzantine earring or piece of jewelry whose decoration was restricted to the same degree. This earring is best understood as part of a broad, cosmopolitan taste shared across political borders during the eleventh and twelfth centuries expressed in distinct ways in each cultural milieu.

SRZ

References: *DOCat* 2, no. 135; New York, *The Glory of Byzantium* 1997, no. 171 (O. Z. Pevny).

Exhibition: *The Glory of Byzantium*, Metropolitan Museum of Art, New York, March-July 1997.

1. Jenkins and Keene 1982, nos. 41, 43, 48, 50a, 50b, 51a.
2. New York, *The Glory of Byzantium* 1997, no. 275A (M. Jenkins-Madina). The earrings have three small loops along the lower edge to support a wire with small pearls or beads.
3. Ibid., for the Hoard, also see cat. no. 31.
4. Cf. Makarova 1986. This period begins with the establishment of Orthodoxy as the official religion in 988, and thus directed Byzantine influence, and ends with the Mongol invasions of the 1230s. For individual examples, see *DOCat* 2, no. 161; *DOCat*, 2nd ed., no. 201; New York, *The Glory of Byzantium* 1997, no. 212A-G. Recently, a *kól't* has been attributed to Constantinople: ibid., no. 170.
5. *Kólti* are not earrings, but were suspended on chains attached to a head band, hair knot, or similar support. They are sometimes referred to as temple pendants. One interpretation is illustrated in Seipel 1993, 52.
6. Milan, *Ori e argenti russi* 1991, no. 1.

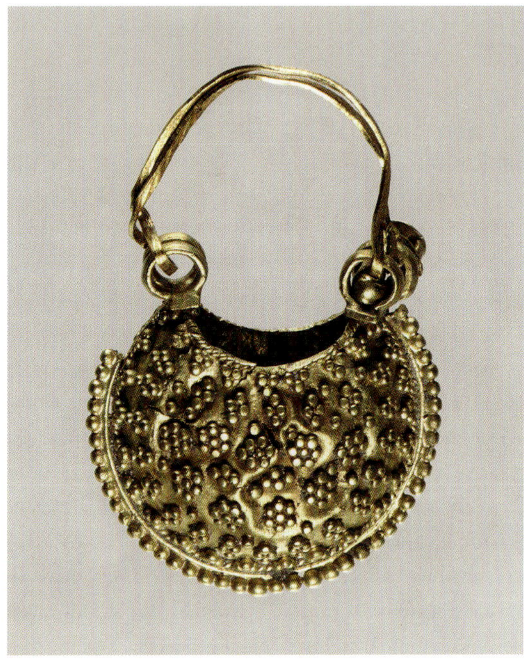

30.

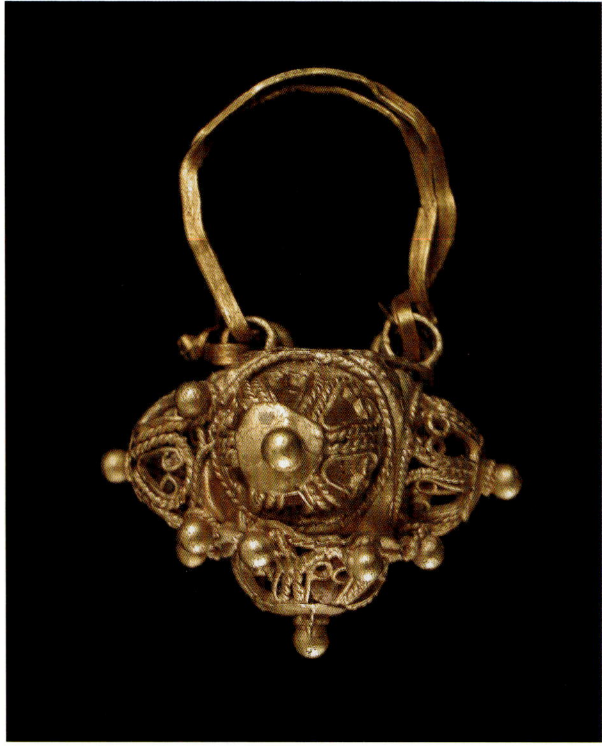

31.

31. Earring with Five Hemispheres

Said to have been found in Constantinople,
11th century
Gold
2.2 x 1.7 cm

Condition: Some hemispheres are slightly crushed, but overall the condition is very good.

Acquisition History: Acquired from George Zacos.

Accession number: BZ.1953.12.99

The earring is formed of five hemispheres, each made of twisted wire, flat strips, and globules, projecting from the sides and bottom of a small, hollow cube. A smooth disk, open at the center, rests over the open cube, and provides the surface for the suspension rings. The present wire loop is modern.

This type of earring, also called a basket earring, was known in the eastern Mediterranean basin since the sixth century.[1] There is a wide variety of construction methods among this type, ranging from closed hemispheres, like one in Richmond,[2] to the delicate, lattice-like openwork of the present example. Other variations include additional, small hemispheres between the large ones,[3] round "windows" pierced through the base of the hemispheres,[4] gold granule triangles between hemispheres,[5] and

"disks" made of openwork wire circles edged with twisted wire.[6] The attraction of these earrings lies, it would seem, in the contrast between the volume of the "baskets" and the refined tracery and contrasting textures out of which they are composed.

The relatively large number of basket earrings attests to the long-lived and widespread popularity of the type, though the exact source of any particular example is difficult to pinpoint. This situation is illustrated by a pair of earrings that has been identified as Islamic, from within the Abbasid sphere of influence and dated to the eleventh to thirteenth century,[7] and as Byzantine of the tenth to eleventh century.[8] An exception within this debate are the basket earrings found in 1973 buried in Tiberias, Israel.[9] In the same earthenware vessel was another pair of earrings, several finger rings, and sixteen Islamic coins dated as late as 1036. These allow the burial to be dated to the second quarter of the eleventh century and places the exceptionally well-preserved earrings in the same period or within a generation or two of that date. The collection of objects buried together also supports an Islamic origin for the earrings.

The location of the Tiberias find puts the earrings at the crossroads of extensive commercial exchange and raises questions

of manufacturing localization and trade, sources of style, and directions of influence. Similar questions exist for another, slightly earlier, earring type that was made by both Byzantine and Islamic artists: the flat arc earring with cloisonné enamel on both sides and with projections of pearls and gold globule triangles along the lower edge.[10] The evidence suggests that they were made contemporaneously during the late ninth and the first half of the tenth century, but it is not clear in which direction the stylistic influence was traveling.

Essential to evaluating the similarities between Byzantine and Islamic basket earrings throughout the medieval centuries are the official embassies between royal courts that brought representatives of foreign rulers face to face. The role of such embassies extended well beyond political contact because they provided opportunities for lavish exchanges of gifts.[11] Against this background, basket earrings may be considered one of the self-consciously complex and fashionable styles of jewelry that were demonstrably shared across cultural borders.[12]

SRZ

References: *DOCat* 2, no. 134.

1. Gonosová and Kondoleon 1994, no. 22, with other references.
2. Ibid.
3. New York, *The Glory of Byzantium* 1997, no. 275B: a pair in the Israel Museum, Jerusalem (IAA74-2139).
4. Ibid., no. 168: a pair in the Metropolitan Museum of Art (along with additional, small hemispheres).
5. Gonosová and Kondoleon 1994, no. 29; New York, *The Glory of Byzantium* 1997, no. 169.
6. A pair in the National Museum, Athens; Stathatos Collection 1963, vol. 3, 287, no. 220 bis, fig. 178, said to have been found in Ephesos.
7. Jenkins and Keene 1982, no. 39b.
8. See note 4 above.
9. See note 3 above, and Lester 1987, 21-29.
10. (1) Stathatos Collection 1957, nos. 4A-B, 5A-B, pls. II-IIbis (E. Coche de la Ferté), Islamic earrings from Crete. (2) London, *Treasures of Byzantine Art* 1994, no. 142, a Byzantine earring close to material in the Preslav Treasure.
11. Qaddumi 1990; Cutler 1996; Grabar 1997 (I thank Henry Maguire for bringing my attention to this reference).
12. For a different kind of cross-cultural awareness, see *DOCat* 2, 2nd ed., no. 200, *Ornament in the Form of a Composite Figure* (S. R. Zwirn): the blend of Byzantine technique and imagery with Islamic iconography. Also, see Zwirn 2003.

Enamel

32. Plaque with a Bust of St. Demetrios

Said to have been found in Smyrna, 11th century
Gold and cloisonné enamel
.8 x .85 cm

Inscribed: Ο΄ (ΑΓΙΟΣ) ΔΗΜΙΤΡΙΟΣ ("Saint Demetrios").

Condition: Despite some missing areas of enamel, the condition is very good.

Acquisition History: Acquired from George Zacos.

Accession number: BZ.1957.9

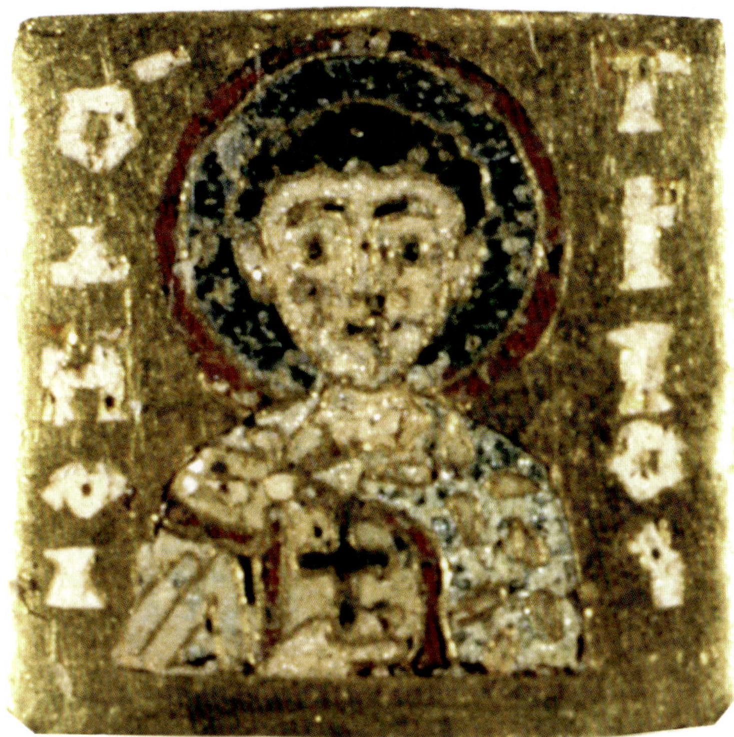

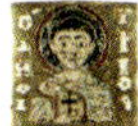

32. 32. *Real size*

This small, gold plaque presents a frontal, bust-length image of St. Demetrios. In his right hand, he holds a cross in front of his chest—the sign of martyrdom—while his name is written in vertical lines along the sides of the plaque. The dominant colors are green, blue, black, red, and white; in a few places, the enamel has deteriorated to a chalky white, especially the green of the tunic.

The extremely small size of this plaque indicates that it was made as a component of a larger ensemble. Although the exact nature of this plaque's origin cannot be determined, other small cloisonné enamel plaques are known: e.g., a roundel with St. John the Prodromos (or Baptist) is 1 cm in diameter,[1] and a quatrefoil with a blessing Christ measures 1.7 x 1.7 cm.[2] Similarly, there are five medallions—each less than one centimeter in diameter—on the back of "Dagmar's" Cross, a cloisonné enamel cross reliquary discovered in Denmark.[3] Although these medallions are integral to the cross rather than separate, they attest to the extremely small scale on which the individual components were conceived and made. The recent attribution of the cross to c. 1000,[4] rather than the previous date of c. 1200, is supported by comparison to the cloisonné enamel double-hinged medallion in Dumbarton Oaks from the late tenth to early eleventh century.[5] The treatment of the figures of Christ Pantokrator and, in particular, the elongated vertical lines at the corners of the mouths are characteristic of enamels at this time.[6] The approximate date would be appropriate for the St. Demetrios plaque.

St. Demetrios, the patron of Thessaloniki, was a popular saint throughout the Byzantine Empire. For several centuries after his martyrdom in the early fourth century, he was characterized as a protector saint,[7] but, beginning in the tenth century, he was transformed into a military saint. The representation of St. Demetrios as martyr rather than soldier argues for a date in the tenth or eleventh century, rather than any later. It is as a soldier that he appears on a miniature cloisonné enamel locket at Dumbarton Oaks. Its size and fineness make it one of the most exceptional creations of the thirteenth to fourteenth century.[8] St. Demetrios is shown half-length holding spear and sword, while full-length figures of St. Sergios and St. Bakchos hold up crosses in front of their chests on the back.[9] Inside the locket, behind shutter-like doors, lies a golden figure of St. Demetrios in a shrine, presumably like the one in his church in Thessaloniki. The miniaturism of the locket, of the square plaque, and of all religious images executed on so small a scale require close viewing and contemplation to see and appreciate fully. I suggest that the connections established through this visual intimacy reflected the union sought between the worshiper and the world of the holy, the goal of every pious person in Byzantium.

SRZ

References: *DOCat* 2, no. 152; *DOH* 1967, no. 253.

1. Volbach 1930, no. 6647, bought in 1911 in Constantinople.
2. Makarova 1975, cat. no. 133, pl. 13, no. 8; Milan, *Ori e argenti russi* 1991, no. 12.
3. Fleischer, Hjort, and Rasmussen 1996, no. 96 (Ø. Hjort); New York, *The Glory of Byzantium* 1997, no. 335 (H. C. Evans).
4. See Fleischer, Hjort, and Rasmussen 1996, no. 96.
5. *DOCat* 2, 2nd ed., no. 199 (S. R. Zwirn).
6. Hahnloser 1965, vol. 2, Chalice of Romanos I or II (920-944 or 959-963); no. 92, Crown of Leo VI (886-912); and nos. 101 (Christ), 103 (St. Cosmas), and 105 (St. Probus), which are dated c. 1050 by A. Grabar.
7. Skedros 1999; Cormack 1985, 50-94.
8. Diameter of locket: 2.8 cm; Grabar 1954; *DOCat* 2, no. 160; New York, *The Glory of Byzantium* 1997, no. 117 (D. Katsarelias); Thessaloniki, *Everyday Life in Byzantium* 2002, no. 202 (S. Boyd).
9. Like St. Demetrios, Sts. Sergios and Bakchos were martyred under Emperor Maximian (286-305).

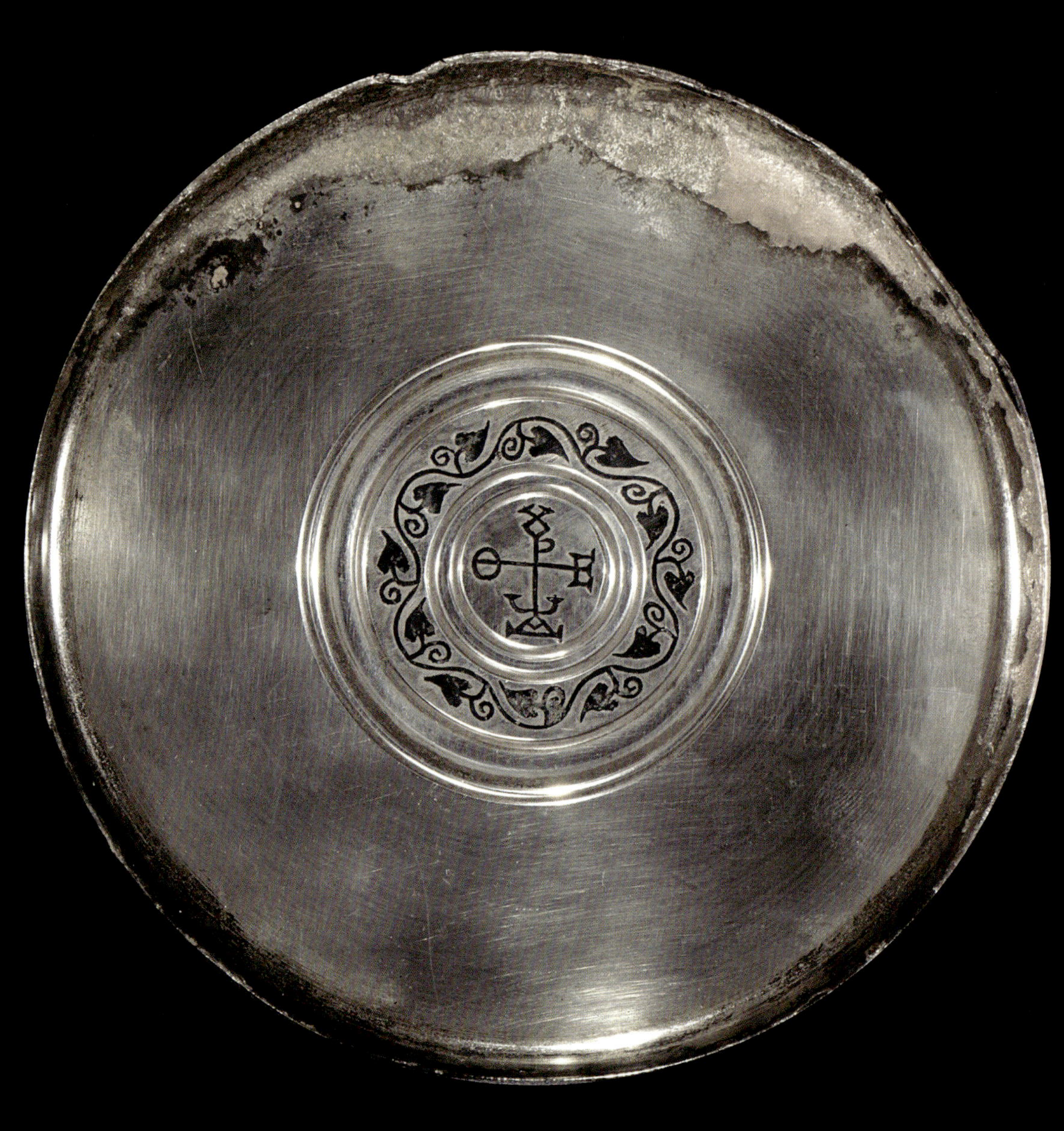

SILVER

Silver Plate

BY MARIA G. PARANI

BYZANTINE DOMESTIC SILVER PLATE COMPRISED a dazzling array of objects, ranging from complete table services to a variety of toilet articles and from furniture fittings and lighting devices to horse trappings and display pieces, such as statuettes. Whether bought, inherited, or received as a private gift or as an official donative, silver plate came to constitute a significant portion of wealth held by affluent households; it also was the preferred means by which the established upper classes, and even parvenus, could advertise their material prosperity and social status.

We are fairly well informed concerning domestic silver plate in Late Antiquity (fourth to seventh centuries). Our knowledge largely derives from a number of important silver treasures dating to that period, such as the magnificent Esquiline, Kaiseraugst, and Sevso treasures, as well as from numerous isolated finds that have come to light from different parts of the empire and from areas beyond its frontiers but within its sphere of political and cultural influence.[1] In their majority, the domestic silver objects that have come down to us belong to the category of luxury tableware, as do the five silver pieces included in this exhibition.

In the context of Late Antique upper-class dining, where the consumption of food and drink could become transformed into an ostentatious ritual taking place in especially appointed dining rooms (*triclinia*), silver vessels were given a central role. During meals involving the entertainment of guests, such luxurious objects, beyond fulfilling their primary utilitarian purpose as receptacles of food and drink, served as manifestations of the host's wealth and as an index of the cultural values he espoused and of his artistic tastes. The vessels' figural decoration or the sayings and witticisms sometimes inscribed on them would serve as the subject of discussion and interpretation, providing the table-companions with the opportunity to demonstrate their erudition, refinement, and appreciation of art,[2] while certain items not used for the meal could be displayed on tables at the entrance of the dining room or on stands along its side walls, further impressing the guests with the owner's affluence and good taste.[3]

A variety of decorative techniques was employed to adorn the surfaces of the silver vessels used at the table, including *repoussé*, engraving, and chasing, with details often highlighted with gilding (cat. no. 33) and niello (cat. no. 37). In some cases, the decoration was very simple, almost austere, consisting of incised concentric circles or the monogram of the owner enclosed within a central wreath or medallion (cat. no. 37). In other instances, a vessel's function would be articulated in its decorative scheme, as was the case of the fish plate from Kaiseraugst, which bears the engraved image of a fish eating a worm. More elaborate examples were adorned with intricate geometric, vegetal, or figural decoration. The latter could comprise mythological representations, such as Dionysiac processions or episodes from the lives of the great heroic figures of epic poetry and classical drama, or it might render genre scenes, inspired by the favorite pastimes of the upper classes, such as the hunt, thereby celebrating visually the elite's life of leisure and luxury.

Christian symbols, such as the cross and the Christogram or Chrismon (Christ's monogram made up of the first two letters of his name in Greek, *Chi-Rho*), make their appearance on silver tableware during the fourth century, at a time when they also can be seen on tableware made of glass and clay.[4] Christian symbols could be integrated into the larger scheme of an object's decoration that was not necessarily Christian in content, as was the case of the great hunting plate of the Sevso treasure, or they could constitute the main element of the decoration, as in the case of three spoons from the Mildenhall treasure. The presence of Christ's symbols invoked his blessing both on the owner's household and on the particular meal

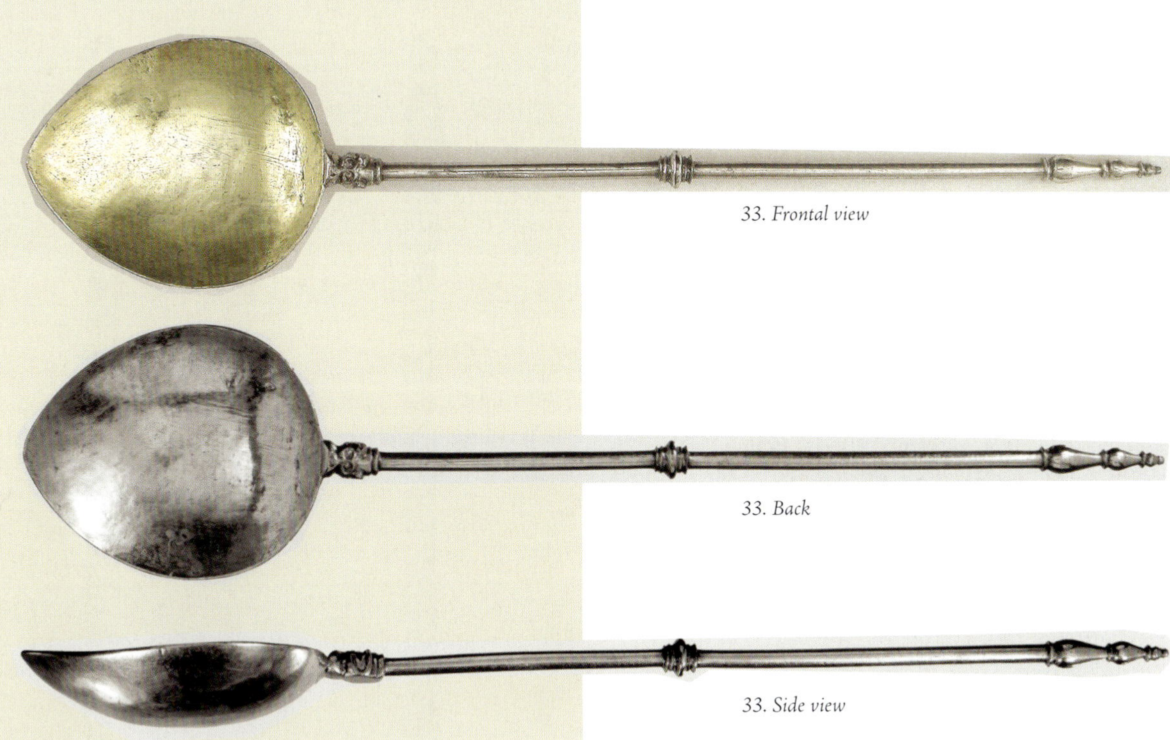

33. *Frontal view*

33. *Back*

33. *Side view*

and the individual users of the objects concerned. It is interesting to point out that, despite the ideal of Christian poverty and the invectives of the church fathers against an extravagant way of life,[5] the Christian members of the empire's elite, in their use of silver tableware, adopted traditional Roman customs to display their social and financial status. Still, Christian signs on silver may have been perceived as a kind of visual acknowledgment of God as the source of all wealth—something that may have helped justify its possession in Christian eyes.

By introducing Christian imagery into the decorative schemes of domestic silver, Christians could advertise with confidence their religious affiliation; notably, the empire was no longer hostile to their faith. Furthermore, they could assert their Christian identity within a social class where the ties of a common classical education and a shared style of life left little to distinguish them from their pagan counterparts.[6] Even so, by the sixth and seventh centuries, Christianity had become the dominant religion, and the continuous occurrence of its symbols and imagery on contemporary domestic silver plate could, by this time, be construed as an indication of the growing impact of Christianity on all aspects of everyday life, including those with no direct relevance to the Church.

1. Shelton 1981; Cahn and Kaufmann-Heinimann 1984; Kaufmann-Heinimann 1999; Mundell Mango and Bennett 1994; Kent and Painter 1977; *DOCat* 1, nos. 1, 4, 6-8, 13, 15. Finds of medieval Byzantine domestic silver plate are comparatively rare: Ballian and Drandaki 2003.
2. Cf. Baratte 1992; Leader-Newby 2004, 123-171.
3. Cf. Ellis 1997; the contributions of Bradley and Dunbabin in Nielsen 1998, 36-55, 81-101; Dunbabin 2003, esp. 141-202.
4. Engemann 1972.
5. Mondésert and Marrou 1965, vol. 2, 35.1-3.
6. Cf. Markus 1990, 27-43; Leader-Newby 2004, 173-216.

33. *Spoon*

Eastern Mediterranean (Syria?), 4th century
Silver with gilding
Length, 22 cm; weight, 39.3 grams

CONDITION: Very good.

ACQUISITION HISTORY: Acquired in the Near East. Gift of Mr. and Mrs. Robert Woods Bliss, 1960.

ACCESSION NUMBER: BZ.1960.126

This spoon consists of a rounded bowl with a slightly pointed tip and a cylindrical handle with a baluster molding halfway down the shaft, which terminates in a double-baluster finial. The opposite end of the handle, at the point of its juncture with the bowl, is shaped into an animal head. The bowl was rounded by hammering and has no rim. Traces of gilding are preserved on the inner surface of the bowl and the animal head. The baluster molding of the handle and its finial were also possibly gilded. The presence of the molding on the handle had a practical purpose as well as a decorative one: it ensured a firm grip on the otherwise smooth and, consequently, slippery handle when the spoon was used for eating.[1]

Animal heads—lion, boar, or griffin—can be seen at the juncture of the handle with the bowl of spoons in the late third century and continue to appear up to the sixth and early seventh centuries. In most cases, however, the animal head either forms part of an openwork scroll offset joining the handle to the bowl or, in later examples, rests on a vertical disk at the juncture between the two parts of the spoon.[2] The only other known example where the animal head is joined directly onto the bowl is a silver spoon forming part of a fourth-century treasure from Syria, now in the Cleveland Museum of Art.[3] The Cleveland example also has a smooth shaft with a molding in the middle, though its handle terminates in a knob instead of a baluster and its bowl is oval rather than rounded. Despite these differences, Ross considered the two sufficiently alike to attribute the same date and place of origin to the Dumbarton Oaks spoon.[4]

If one is to judge by the relatively large numbers in which they have survived, silver spoons, often made in sets of twelve,[5] constituted a standard component of domestic silver plate in Late Antiquity. Their exact shape and size varied according to the use for which they were intended. They were employed for eating eggs, liquid foods, desserts, and even berries. Examples with a handle terminating in a point could also be used for extracting and eating shellfish.[6] Given the relatively small size of Late Antique dining tables,[7] it seems rather improbable that spoons, which could be quite bulky, were set out on the table from the beginning of the meal. More likely, they were brought out and distributed to the guests when a course was served that required their use, then removed once they had fulfilled their function.[8]

MGP

REFERENCES: *DOCat* 1, 1-2, no. 2; *DOH* 1967, no. 54.

1. Cf. two later spoons of unknown provenance with two baluster moldings down their smooth handle-shaft: Hauser 1992, nos. 222-223.
2. Strong 1966, 178, 206; Johns and Potter,1983, 38-39; Mundell Mango 1986, no. 49; Hauser 1992, 23-24, 43-45.
3. Milliken 1958, 39, illustrated on 46.
4. *DOCat* 1, 2.
5. Cf. Adhémar 1934, 52, for references to three such sets.
6. Strong 1966, 129; Urbana-Champaign, *Art and Holy Powers* 1989, 112-113, fig. 39.
7. Ellis 1997, 49-50.
8. Cf. Petronius, *Satyricon*, xxxi.3-xxxiv.4, trans. in N. Lewis and M. Reinhold, eds., *Roman Civilization. Selected Readings. II. The Empire* (New York, 1990), 159.

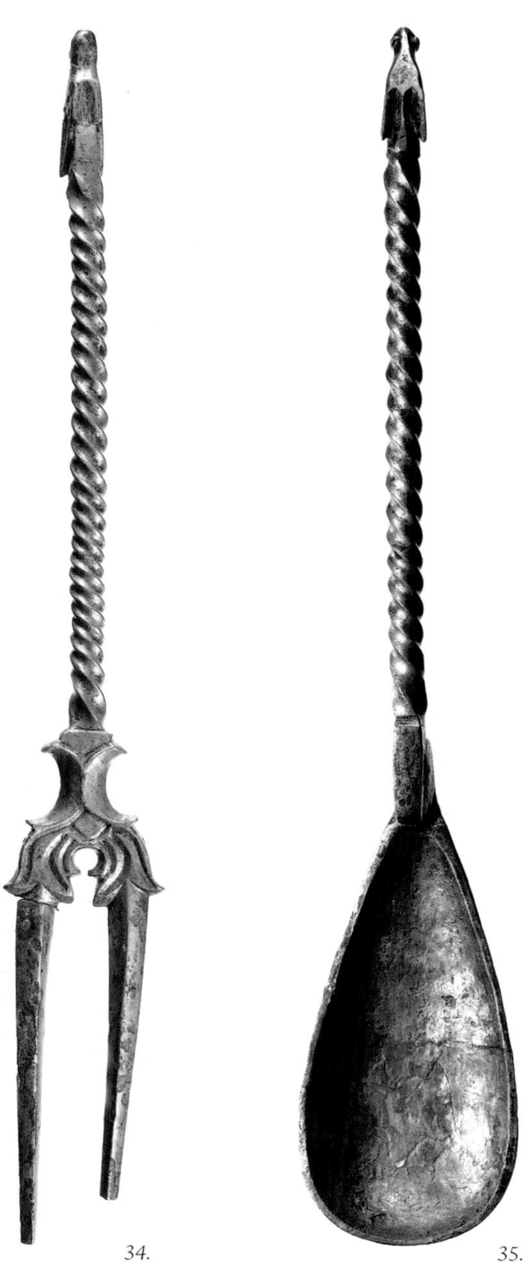

34.

35.

34-35. Fork and Spoon

Sassanian (Iraq?), 6th to 7th century
Silver, cast and engraved
Fork: length, 24 cm; weight: 99 grams. Spoon: length, 24.3 cm; weight 85 grams

CONDITION: One of the tines of the fork was broken off in the past and reattached by means of a dowel and lead solder. The other tine is missing its tip. The surface of the fork is somewhat pitted. The bowl of the spoon was heavily damaged, with a small hole at the center that was later repaired with a piece of modern silver. The surface of the spoon is quite pitted.

ACQUISITION HISTORY: Said to have been found at the ancient site of Nineveh (Iraq) in 1938; Bliss Collection, 1940.

ACCESSION NUMBER: (34) BZ.1940.53, (35) BZ.1940.54

Both the fork and spoon have spirally fluted handles terminating in equine animal heads. Pairs of depressions at the top of the heads indicate the animals' eyes. The handle of the fork is joined to a stylized vegetal element from which extend the two tapering tines, which are rhomboidal in section. The handle of the spoon, on the other hand, is attached to the bowl by means of a solid vertical undecorated disk. The bowl is pear shaped and has a flattened rim. The implements' matching handles and comparable sizes suggest that the fork and spoon were made as a set.

A practically identical fork, made of bronze, with the same spirally fluted handle terminating in an equine head and stylized

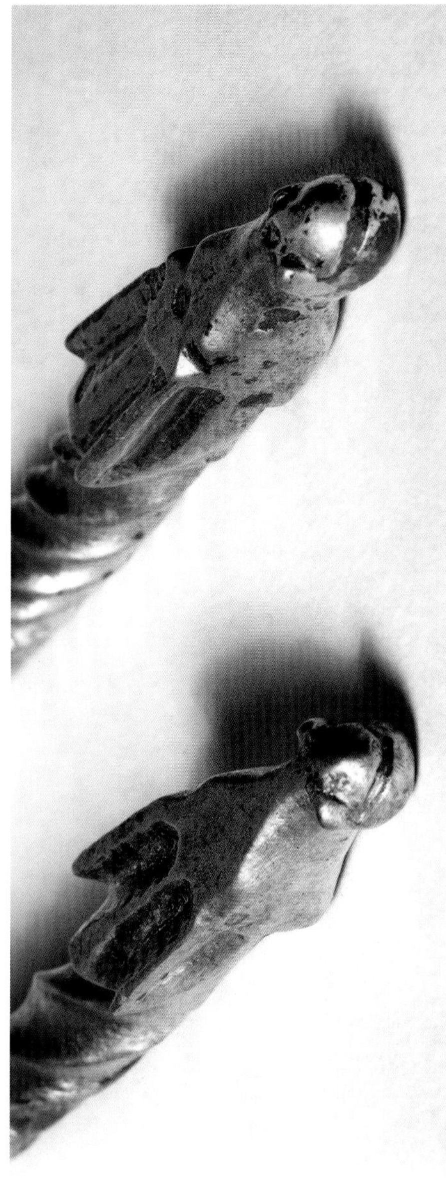

34-35. Finials, detail

vegetal element at the springing of the tines, was discovered during the excavations of the Sassanian fortress of Qasr-i Abu Nasr in Iran, dating from the sixth to the seventh century.[1] Other Sassanian examples, dating from the fifth to the seventh century, evidence the same long tines, handles terminating in animal heads—equine, in most cases—and a curving, looplike element from which the tines spring, reminiscent of the vegetal element of the Dumbarton Oaks and the Qasr-i Abu Nasr forks.[2] The Dumbarton Oaks fork is comparable to Sassanian examples also in terms of its great size: examples in Persian collections range from 18 to 24.7 cm in length. By contrast, Roman and Late Antique silver and bronze

two-pronged forks are relatively smaller, ranging from 10 to 14.5 cm in length, have shorter tines, and their handles often have an animal hoof finial.[3] Even so, reference should be made to an unpublished two-pronged silver fork said to be from Italy and dating to the late fourth or early fifth century, now in the Cleveland Museum of Art. Though much simpler, it is evocative of Sassanian examples both in terms of form, with its long tines and smooth handle terminating in an equine head, and size (length 20.4 cm).

The similarities in appearance between the Cleveland fork and the Sassanian examples intimate the existence of mutual influences between Sassanian and Byzantine silverwork in Late Antiquity. These are even more apparent in the case of the spoon that forms a set with the Dumbarton Oaks fork. Spirally fluted handles are encountered on Byzantine spoons as early as the fourth century and as late as the seventh.[4] The pear-shaped bowl has a long tradition in Roman silversmithing, going back to the first century, and would become widely used again after the fifth, while the solid disk at the juncture between the bowl and the handle becomes common in the sixth century, gradually replacing the openwork scroll seen on earlier examples.[5] The occurrence of such a disk on the Dumbarton Oaks example would argue in favor of a dating in the sixth century or later, rather than the late fourth or the early fifth century as originally proposed by Ross.[6]

As has become apparent, table forks, though rare, were not unknown in Roman and Late Antique times.[7] Forks with three tines formed part of two Roman folding traveler's sets of eating utensils, one from Italy and the second of unknown provenance.[8] Individual examples, made of silver or bronze, have either two or three tines. One may mention, by way of illustration, the elegant silver three-tined fork with traces of gilding from the treasure of Late Antique domestic silver plate discovered at Vienne in France (length 16.4 cm); its handle terminates in a point, which could also have been used for eating.[9] Late Antique artistic representations of forks as eating, rather than cooking or serving, implements are nonexistent, while written references to them are extremely rare. A reference to a fork (*fuscina*) adorned with a lion's head

is in the Auxerre inventory of domestic silver plate,[10] but one cannot be certain of its precise usage. However, in one of his homilies, St. Gregory of Nyssa seems to be alluding to the use of silver forks (*argyrai peronai*) at the table for eating in the fourth century.[11] The straight tines of Late Antique and Sassanian forks indicate that they were used for spearing the food and bringing it to the mouth, not for scooping it up like present-day forks. In other words, they simply replaced the fingers with which one usually picked up morsels of food from the common serving plates. Still, given the small numbers in which forks have survived, when compared to spoons, their use for eating at the table must have been the exception rather than the norm, limited perhaps to the most distinguished participants at a meal, as a sign of distinction, or to dainty, fashionable individuals who wished to avoid soiling their fingers.

MGP

References: Swarzenski 1941, 79; *DOCat* 1, no. 3; *DOH* 1967, no. 50; Hauser 1992, no. 228, pl. 51b.

1. Hauser and Upton 1934, 22, fig. 32; Whitcomb 1985, 169, fig. 65j. That the Dumbarton Oaks fork was Sassanian rather than Byzantine was first suggested by Dr. P. O. Harper, in a personal communication to Miss S. Boyd, emerita curator of the Byzantine Collection at Dumbarton Oaks. I thank Miss Boyd for sharing this information with me.
2. Washington, D.C., *Iranian Art*, 1964, nos. 488, 503-505; Sotheby's, *Antiquities, including Western Asiatic Cylinder Seals and Antiquities from the Erlenmeyer Collection*. Part II, 12 June 1997 (London, 1997), no. 320. Cf. Bonhams and Brooks, Knightsbridge, *Antiquities*, Auction of April 26, 2001 (London, 2001), no. 426.
3. See, for example, Castellani 1874, 116-125; Milliken 1957, 184-187; Mitten 1975, no. 50.
4. See, for example, Kent and Painter 1977, no. 72; Johns and Potter 1983, nos. 73, 74, 81; Cruikshank Dodd 1961, no. 97.
5. Mundell Mango 1986, no. 18 (with more references).
6. *DOCat* 1, 2-3, no. 3.
7. On the use of spoons at the Late Antique table, see previous catalogue entry.
8. Sherlock 1988, 310-311; Baratte 1990, 81, fig. 56.
9. Baratte 1990, no. 20, with an informative discussion on the question of the use of forks in Late Antiquity and detailed bibliographical references.
10. Adhémar 1934, 50.
11. *PG* 44, col. 752.

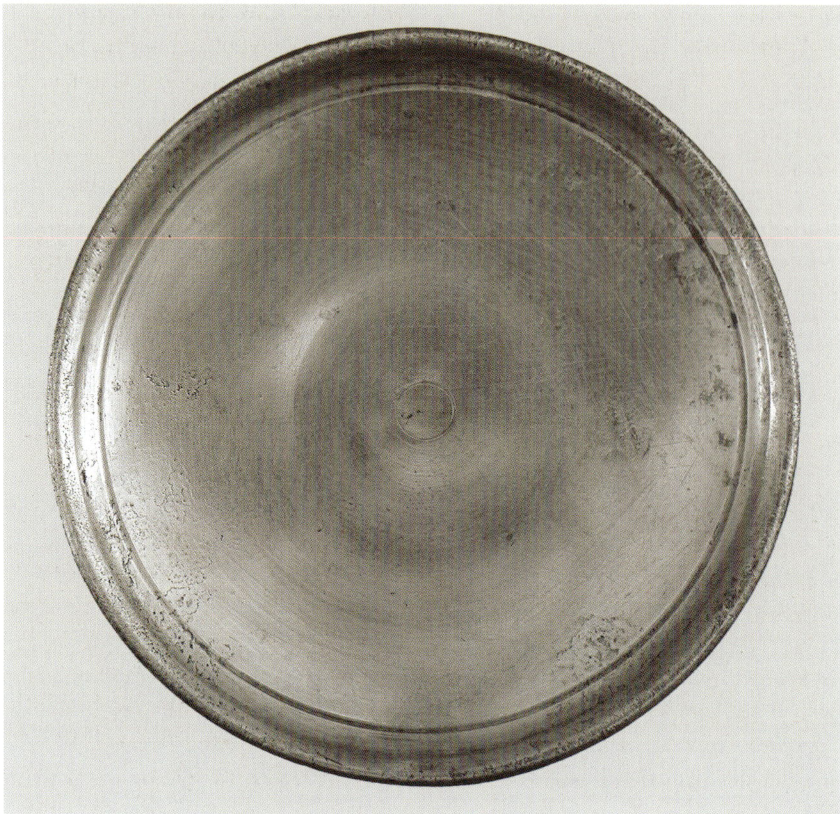

36. Obverse

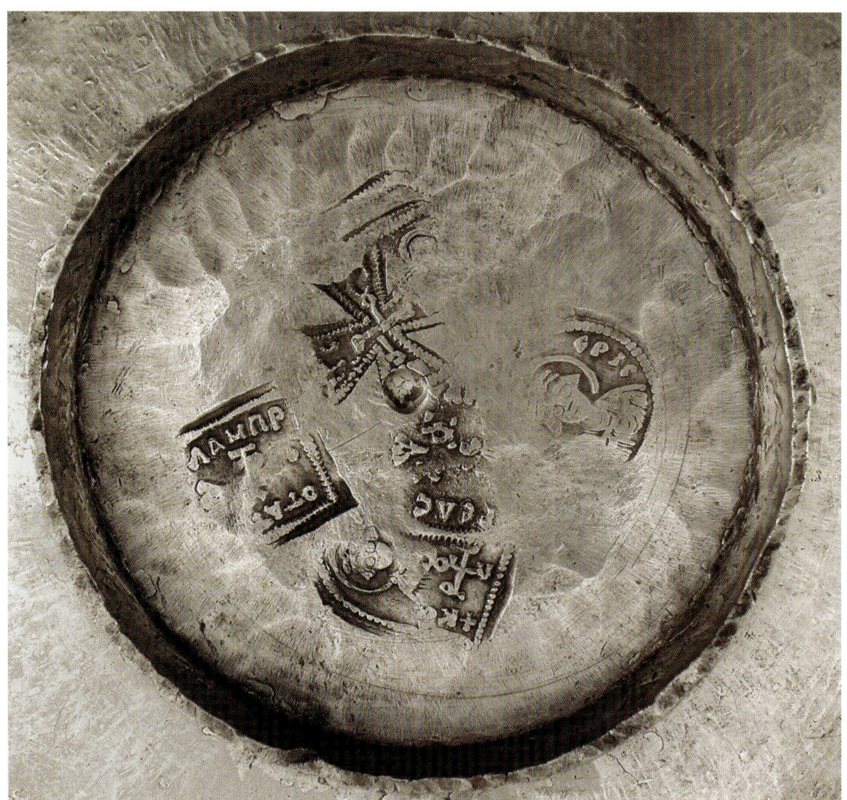

36. Reverse

36. Small dish

Constantinople, 613-629/30
Silver, cast, finished with hammering and turning
on a lathe
Diameter: 13.3 cm; diameter of foot-ring: 6 cm;
height: 1.9 cm; weight: 194.2 grams
Five control stamps of the reign of Herakleios (610-
641) on the reverse, inside the foot-ring.

CONDITION: Certain areas are pitted from corrosion; there is a small hole in the rim.

ACQUISITION HISTORY: Acquired in 1951 in
Constantinople, along with silver dish BZ.1951.23.
Both were said to have been found in or near
Smyrna (modern Izmir, Turkey). A third dish
(BZ.1951.31), believed to have been discovered
with the first two, was obtained shortly afterward
(gift of Mrs. Gilbert L. Steward, 1951).

ACCESSION NUMBER: BZ.1951.24

This small shallow silver dish has a raised
rim adorned with a concave molding and a
concentric, engraved line. The plain obverse
features only a small engraved circle at the
center. Hammering marks are clearly visible
on the reverse of the plate, indicating that
the back of the dish was left unpolished.[1] At
the center of the reverse, there is a circular
depression left by the lathe on which the
dish was turned for finishing.

On the back, within the circular area
delineated by the foot-ring, there are five
control stamps of Emperor Herakleios
(610-641): one round, one hexagonal, one
square, one long, and one cruciform. Busts
of the emperor, who is portrayed beardless, are included in the round and the long
stamps. In addition to the imperial busts,
the five stamps contain monograms of the
emperor as well as secondary monograms
and names of state officials. On the basis
of the type of the imperial bust seen on the
stamps, Cruikshank Dodd dates this series
and, consequently, the manufacture of the
dish, to the early years of Herakleios's reign
(613-629/30). The five-stamp system for
silver objects was introduced under Anastasios (491-518) and continued in use down
to the reign of Constans II (641-668). It
appears on different categories of objects
intended for usage in secular as well as
in ecclesiastical contexts. Comparisons
between stamped objects of the same type
(e.g., plates, candlesticks, lamps) point
toward a high degree of standardization
in their manufacture, in terms of shape,
size, weight, and metallic composition.
Stamped plates of the sixth and seventh

centuries, which are of particular interest to us here, apparently came in standard sizes of approximately 50, 35, 26, and 15 cm. Considering that the metallic composition of comparable unstamped silver objects does not differ significantly from that of stamped silver plate, it has been suggested that the imperial stamps did not serve merely as a guarantee of metallic purity but as an indication that the objects bearing them were manufactured (or, at least, shaped) in and distributed by state-controlled workshops. These would have been located in Constantinople and, probably, in certain other cities of the empire such as Antioch (Syria), Carthage (North Africa), and Tarsus (south Asia Minor).[2] The imperial portraits and monograms indicated the ultimate source of the authority that lay behind the manufacture and circulation of stamped silver objects.[3]

The manufacture of small plain dishes, probably in sets of four, as part of Late Antique silver table services is evidenced by the inclusion of such a set in the famous Kaiseraugst treasure of the middle of the fourth century (diameter of dishes, approximately 15 cm).[4] It continued in the centuries that followed as well, as indicated by one small plain dish of the fifth century now in the Ashmolean Museum, Oxford, and another in the State Historical Museum of Moscow, dating between 629/30 and 641; both these examples bear control stamps.[5] A third example, this one without control stamps, is located in a private collection in Germany and is dated to the sixth to seventh century (diameter 12.8 cm).[6] Apparently, the Dumbarton Oaks dish also belonged to a set of four dishes; two of the remaining three are also at Dumbarton Oaks (BZ.1951.23, BZ.1951.31). They, however, are decorated in niello, with a cross enclosed in a wreath and inscriptions between the arms of the cross honoring God and invoking his protection on the Christian household of the owner.[7] Such small dishes may have served as individual plates in the modern sense, as dessert plates, or as side dishes containing various delicacies and choice tidbits that would have been placed in whatever space was left by the large serving platters and trays on the small Late Antique dining tables.

MGP

REFERENCES: Gettens and Waring 1957, no. 21; Cruikshank Dodd 1961, no. 44; *DOCat* 1, 21-22, no. 16.3; Bruce-Mitford 1983, fig. 128; Mundell Mango 1986, no. 106.

1. Cf. Bruce-Mitford 1983, 170, fig. 127.a (silver dish with the reverse left unpolished from Cyprus, dated by control stamps to the same period as the Dumbarton Oaks example, 613-629/30 CE).
2. Mundell Mango 1993, 203-216; Cruikshank Dodd 1993, 217-223.
3. Cf. Oikonomides 1986b, 36-37.
4. Kaufmann-Heinimann 1999, nos. 103-106, fig. 4.
5. London, *Treasures of Byzantine Art* 1994, no. 51; Cruikshank Dodd 1961, no. 74.
6. Wamser and Zahlhauss 1998, no. 48.
7. The inscriptions read "Hope of God" and "Honor of God" respectively; see Cruikshank Dodd 1961, nos. 45, 46; *DOCat* 1, no. 16.1-2. A similar plate in the George Ortiz collection, Switzerland, probably formed the fourth member of the group (unpublished). It too is decorated and inscribed with the phrase "Glory of God."

37. Small dish

Constantinople, 610-613
Silver, cast, finished with hammering and turning on a lathe; decorated with niello inlay
Diameter: 13.5 cm; diameter of foot-ring: 6 cm; height: 2.4 cm; weight: 313 grams

INSCRIBED: Greek cross-monogram, undecipherable. Five control stamps of the reign of Herakleios (610-641), on the reverse, inside the foot ring.

CONDITION: Corroded on the reverse and along the top edge on the obverse.

ACQUISITION HISTORY: Probably from Cyprus; gift of Mrs. Paul I. Fagan, San Francisco, 1960.

ACCESSION NUMBER: BZ.1960.60

This small flat silver dish with the vertical rim is adorned with a central medallion comprising a cross monogram encircled by an ivy scroll, both executed in niello inlay. The scroll is framed on either side by alternating concave and raised, concentric moldings. The central medallion was burnished separately, after the application of the niello, with parallel diagonal strokes. The reverse of the dish was also polished. Within the circular area delineated by the foot-ring, there are five control stamps of Emperor Herakleios (610-641), one round, one hexagonal, one square, one long, and one cruciform. According to Cruikshank Dodd, this type of imperial bust and the form of the imperial monogram indicate a date in the first years of Herakleios's reign, 610-613.[1]

An identical silver dish in terms of size, decoration, and control stamps can be found in the collections of the Metropolitan Museum of Art. It probably formed part of a set of four similar dishes, which also included the Dumbarton Oaks example.[2] The exact same monogram and control stamps can also be seen on a larger dish (diameter 25.5 cm), also said to be from Cyprus, today at the Walters Art Museum.[3] If it is indeed true that all three pieces were found in Cyprus and formed part of the same original find, one may envisage them as belonging to a single table service, which would have comprised a set of four small side dishes and, possibly, a second set of four, larger serving plates, all sharing the same decoration and acquired at the same time from the same source.

The letters of the monogram are arranged in the shape of a cross, as was the case with monograms from the reign of Justinian I onward (527-565). Our example consists of the Greek letters often used in monograms to render the name "Theodore" in the genitive case (ΘΕΟΔΩΡΟΥ meaning "of Theodore") and an *Alpha*. It is the presence of this last letter that introduces complications in deciphering the monogram. On the basis of the occurrence of the name "Theodore" on one silver spoon from the so-called first Cyprus treasure and of the peculiar legend "AUAL" on a set of others from the same find, Mundell Mango has suggested that the monogram on the plates, of probable Cypriot provenance, may be a combination of these two elements, alluding to the name of the individual who owned the table service of which the dishes (and the spoons?) formed a part.[4] The name of the owner rendered in the form of a monogram occurs on a number of silver objects belonging to Late Antique table services. The monograms are prominently displayed and, in most cases, constitute the only decoration of the object concerned. The fourth-century Esquiline treasure, for example, comprises, among others, eight objects (a set of four circular dishes and a set of four rectangular dishes) all bearing the same Latin block monogram, with the owner's first and family names, enclosed in a wreath of laurel leaves.[5] A mid-sixth-century silver plate from Asia Minor, now in Berlin, is adorned with a Greek cross monogram within a wreath, which gives not only the name but also the

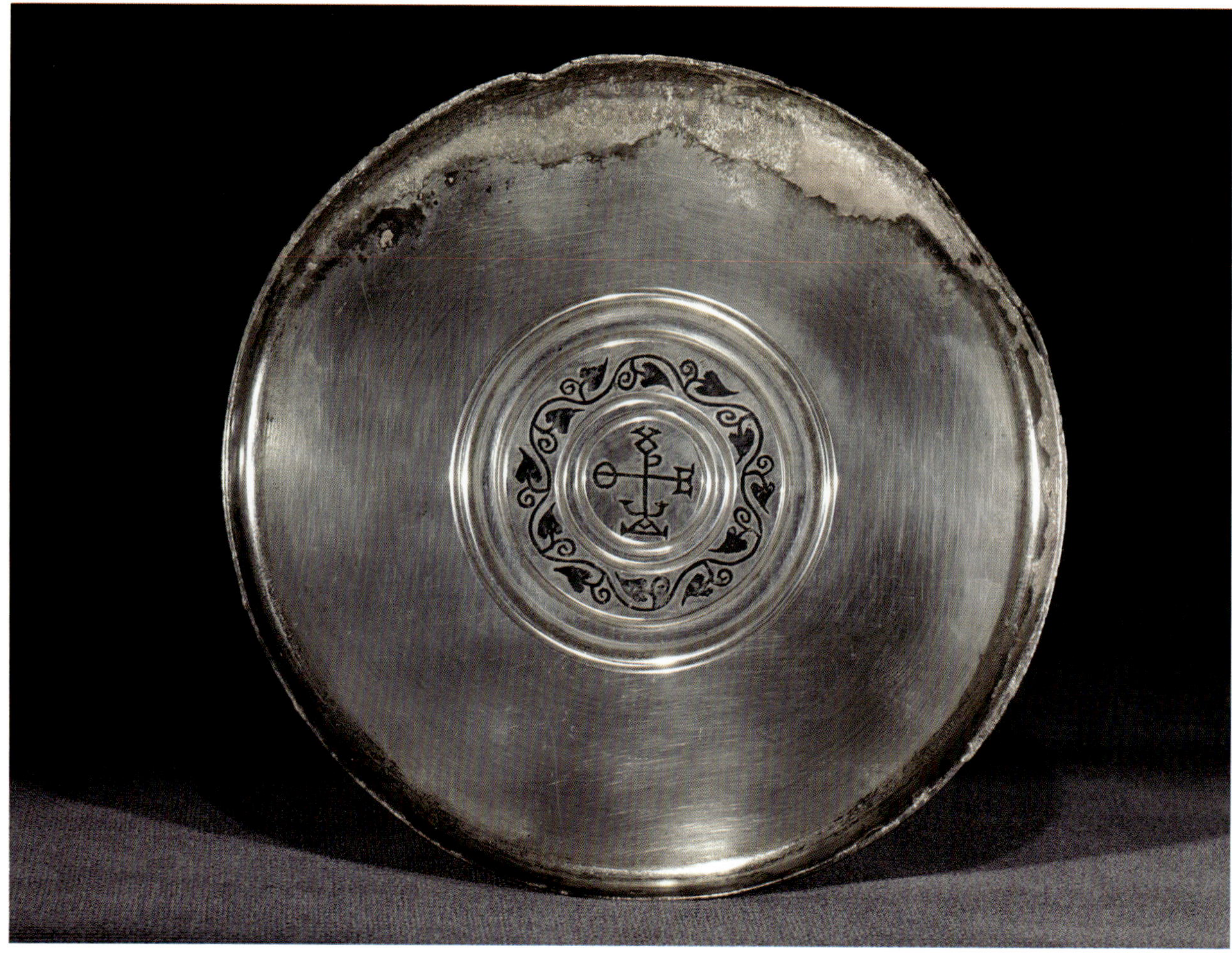

37. Obverse

official title of the owner.[6] Finally, a cross monogram with the owner's name can be seen on a silver dish of the first decade of the seventh century from the second Cyprus treasure, now in the Cyprus Archaeological Museum.[7]

However, there might be another way to read the mysterious monogram on the Dumbarton Oaks and associated dishes. The problematic *Alpha* could be an abbreviation of the Greek word for "saint" and, consequently, the monogram's solution would be Α(ΓΙΟΥ) ΘΕΟΔΩΡΟΥ, meaning "of Saint Theodore."[8] Given that there is no indication that these objects ever belonged to a church—their typology also argues against an ecclesiastical context for their usage—one could perceive the monogram as an invocation of the blessing "of Saint Theodore," rather than a statement of ownership (plate "of Saint Theodore").[9] Perhaps the owner of the dishes was named Theodore (or Theodora) and chose this way to invoke the protection of his or her patron saint. It would be interesting if this were

indeed the case, as it would intimate that at that time there was a certain degree of experimentation in the way people chose to express their personal piety in the decoration of their personal effects. Apart from the use of monograms and inscriptions, the other approach involves the use of the visual likeness of a saint, beautifully illustrated by a silver bowl of the mid-seventh century, from the first Cyprus treasure, now in the British Museum, which is adorned with the half-figure of a military saint (St. Sergius), enclosed in a medallion in the bowl's base.[10]

MGP

REFERENCES: Dalton 1906, 615-617; Cruikshank Dodd 1961, no. 39; *DOCat* 1, 22-23, no. 17; *DOH* 1967, no. 76; Mundell Mango 1986, no. 105.

1. On the significance of control stamps on silver objects, see cat. no. 36.
2. Cruikshank Dodd 1961, no. 37; Mundell Mango 1986, no. 104.
3. Baltimore, *Early Christian and Byzantine Art* 1947, no. 378; Cruikshank Dodd 1961, no. 38; Mundell Mango 1986, no. 103.
4. Mundell Mango 1986, no. 103.
5. Shelton 1981, 80-81; Effenberger and Severin 1992, no. 55.
6. Cruikshank Dodd 1961, no. 12; Wamser 2004, no. 360.
7. Cruikshank Dodd 1961, no. 33; New York, *Age of Spirituality* 1977, no. 548 (identified as a paten).
8. I wish to thank Dr. Michael Grünbart for this suggestion.
9. The actual formula "blessing of..." followed by the name of an apostle occurs on the set of eight late sixth- to early seventh-century spoons in the Dumbarton Oaks Collection; see *DOCat* 1, 17-18, no. 13; Mundell Mango 1986, no. 149.
10. Kent and Painter 1977, no. 175; Leader-Newby 2004, 207, fig. 4.22.

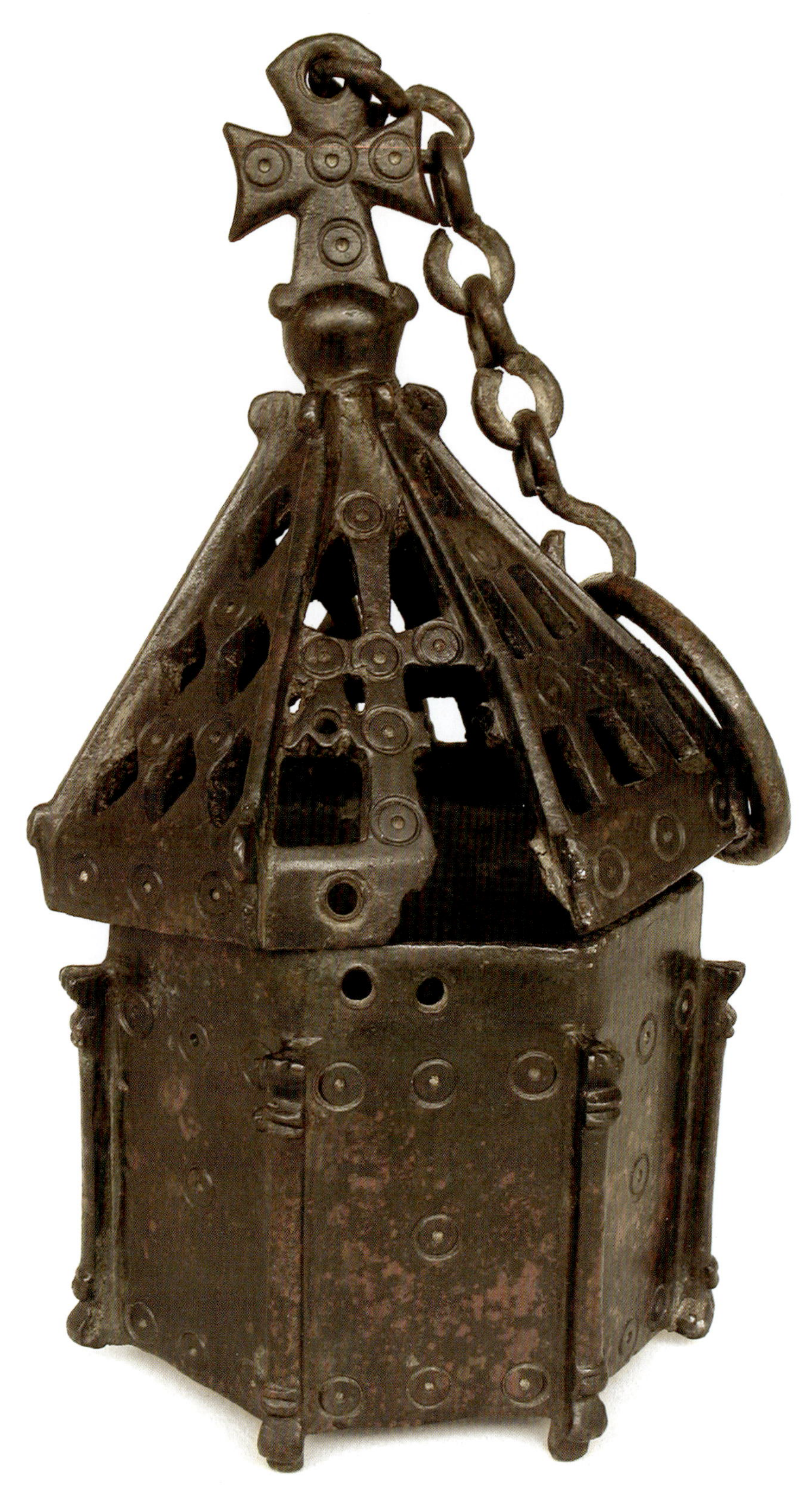

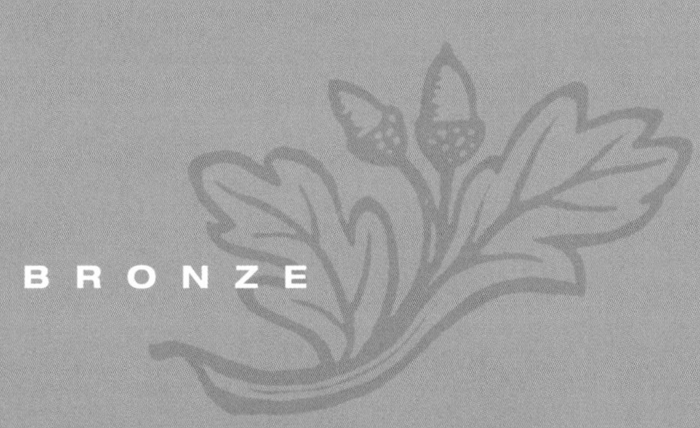

BRONZE

Bronze Jewelry

BY BRIGITTE PITARAKIS

W HILE THE PREDILECTION OF THE Byzantines for gold and precious stones is a well-known fact, the most popular jewelry types and shapes were always reproduced in the cheaper metal of bronze and often enhanced with gilding or tinning. Close affinities between some categories of gold and bronze earrings, finger rings, and belt buckles may even indicate that they were cast in similar molds. Signet rings, the prevalent type of jewelry, both for their functional and ornamental roles, also allow interesting comparisons between luxurious examples in gold and cheaper, mass-produced variants in bronze. On the other hand, the constant fear of evil forces, considered as the main cause of sickness, generated significant demand for a wide range of bronze amuletic jewelry, including medallions (cat. no. 39), finger rings, and armbands. These all shared a common repertoire of apotropaic images, signs, and inscriptions often combined with Christological scenes and representations of the Virgin and saints.[1]

The anonymous Holy Rider, predecessor of the Christian military saints, stands out as one of the most popular figures in amuletic imagery. Very early, the use of bronze amulets was fused with that of the pectoral cross, considered the most powerful weapon against demons. Bronze pectoral crosses of various shapes, imitating precious examples in gold and silver, were mass-produced throughout the history of the Byzantine Empire. The most widespread type has a plain surface often enhanced with rows of punched circles forming cruciform patterns.[2] Circular cavities of un-iconic crosses may also be inlaid with glasspaste cabochons imitating precious stones. However, very early the cross also became an ideal vehicle for religious imagery.

A popular type, which marked the period of iconoclastic controversy before reaching its widest distribution in the eleventh century, is the pectoral reliquary cross made up of two hollow sides hinged together to hold relics. The earliest group, dated to the ninth and tenth centuries, bears a standard molded decoration combining the representation of the Crucifixion on one side with the Virgin and Child or the Virgin Orans on the other.

During the eleventh century, pectoral reliquary crosses are invaded by engraved images of saints in the attitude of prayer with both hands uplifted on either side of the torso.[3] Similar representations of Christ, the Virgin, and saints with schematic features are also introduced on the bezel of cone seals or bivalve seals in copper alloy, the production of which also developed in the Middle Byzantine period. Endowed with a suspension hoop, these sealing implements could be worn around the neck on one's chest as protective jewelry.[4] The increasing interest in the intercessory role of saints in the eleventh and twelfth centuries is also reflected in the production of small plaquettes of the period decorated with cast bust representations of the Virgin and saints (cat. no. 38). Like icons, such plaquettes may have served as devotional objects and as *phylacteria*, but silversmiths may also have used them as dies for impressing *repoussé* figures on metal sheets intended for icon frames, crosses, and reliquaries.

1. See Vikan 1991, 33-44.
2. On the ornament consisting of concentric circles; see Urbana-Champaign, *Art and Holy Powers* 1989, 5-7.
3. Pitarakis, forthcoming.
4. Vikan and Nesbitt 1980, 20-25.

Bronze Jewelry

38. Bronze Plaquette of St. John the Baptist

Constantinople, 11th to 12th century
Bronze
Diameter: 3.49 cm

Inscribed: O (AΓIOC) IO(ANNHC) (O) ΠΡΟ–ΔΡΟΜΟC (*O agios Ioannis o Prodromos*—"Saint John the Precursor").

Condition: The lower edge of the plaquette is chipped.

Acquisition History: Acquired from George Zacos, November 1957.

Accession number: BZ.1957.54

This small bronze medallion with a raised border displays the half-length figure of St. John the Baptist dressed in a cloak with ample draperies and identified by an engraved inscription placed on both sides of the torso. The prophet of salvation is depicted nearly in profile with both his hands extended in prayer, the very pose that he assumes in Deesis compositions of the eleventh and twelfth centuries (cf. cat. nos. 5 and 6).

Two close parallels of similar shape, dimension, and thickness, respectively in the collection of the Princeton University Art Museum[1] and the Paul and Alexandra Canellopoulos Museum,[2] Athens, bear representations of St. Peter and the Virgin in profile, both of whom are rendered in the same attitude of prayer. All of these cast medallion, none of which features a suspension loop, may be considered as inexpensive versions of hard-stone cameos after which they may have been modeled. Like the cameos, it is possible that they were worn as *phylacteria*, that is, providing supernatural protection for their owners. Nevertheless, in one case the unusual thickness of the medallion and the metal that has run out of the mold in several places around the edge have led to the assumption that the Canellopoulos example may have served as a die for impressing *repoussé* silver medallions for icon frames or processional crosses. Indeed, bronze matrices of various dimensions and shapes featuring representations of the Virgin and saints were discovered within Middle Byzantine archaeological contexts in Bulgaria.[3] The group of medallions in Dumbarton Oaks, Princeton, and Athens might then be considered as members of a standard set of dies used by silversmiths for

making impressions on sheets of metal.

The medallions of St. John the Baptist produced in this manner could have been attached to icon frames or circular *enkolpia*, such as a twelfth-century example carrying the bust-length figure of the Baptist in the Vatopedi monastery, Mount Athos.[4] A further example, which may have been fashioned by impressing a metal sheet on a die of a similar type, is the gold medallion in Dumbarton Oaks representing the Prophet Daniel, attributed to the early Palaiologan period.[5]

BP

References: *DOCat 1*, 54-55, no. 62, pl. XXXCIII.

1. Princeton, *Byzantium* 1986, no. 62.
2. Athens, *Byzantine and Post-Byzantine Art* 1985, no. 206.
3. Vasiliev 1982, 90-96.
4. Ikonomaki-Papadopoulos, Pitarakis, and Loverdou-Tsigarida 2001, no. 17.
5. *DOCat 2*, 78-79, no. 106, pl. LVI; Majeska 1974, 361-366.

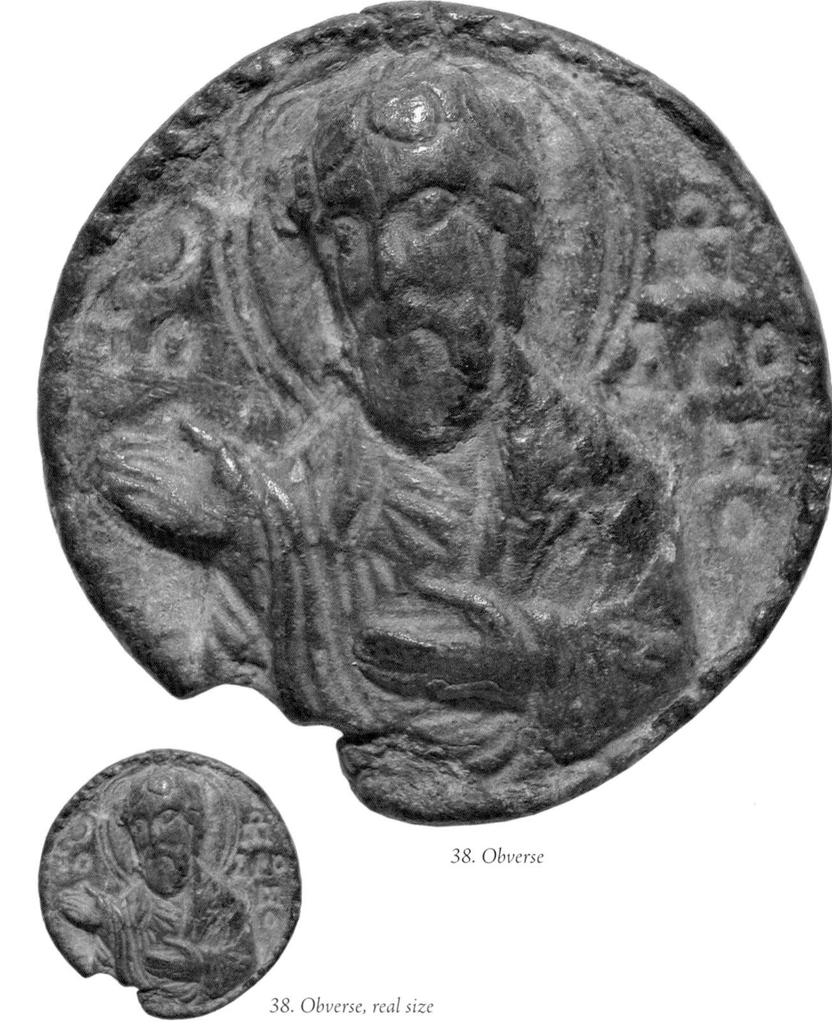

38. Obverse

38. Obverse, real size

39. Bronze Amulet

Syria or Palestine, 6th century
Bronze
Diameter: 5.3 cm

Inscribed: Obverse: On the rim: Ὁκατοικὸν ἐν βοηθία τοῦ ὑψίστου ἐ(ν) σκέπη τοῦ θεοῦ τοῦ οὐρανοῦ αὐλισθέσεται εκ [*sic*] [Psalm 91 (90): 1], ("He that dwelleth in the secret place of the most High shall abide under the shadow of the Almighty"). On the left in the background: Εἷς θ(εὸ)ς ὁ νικὸν τὸν πονερόν [*sic*] ("One God who conquers evil"). Reverse: On the rim: Σφραγὶς θ(εο)ῦ ζόντος φύλαξον ἀπὸ παντὸς κακοῦ τὸν φοροῦντα τὸ φυλακτήριον τοῦτο ("Seal of the living God, protect from all evil the wearer of this amulet"). In the center: ἅγιος, ἅγιος, ἅγιος κ(ύριο)ς σαβαώθ ("Holy, holy, holy Lord Sabaoth").

Condition: Substantial wearing on the surface of the reverse.

Acquisition History: Elie Bustros, Beirut (according to Bustros, found in Djéblé, Iskilon, south of Latakia). Purchased through Royall Tyler from Bustros, December 1949, for Mr. and Mrs. Bliss. Brought to Dumbarton Oaks by R. Tyler, May 19, 1950. Gift of Mr. and Mrs. Bliss, August 1950.

Accession number: BZ.1950.15

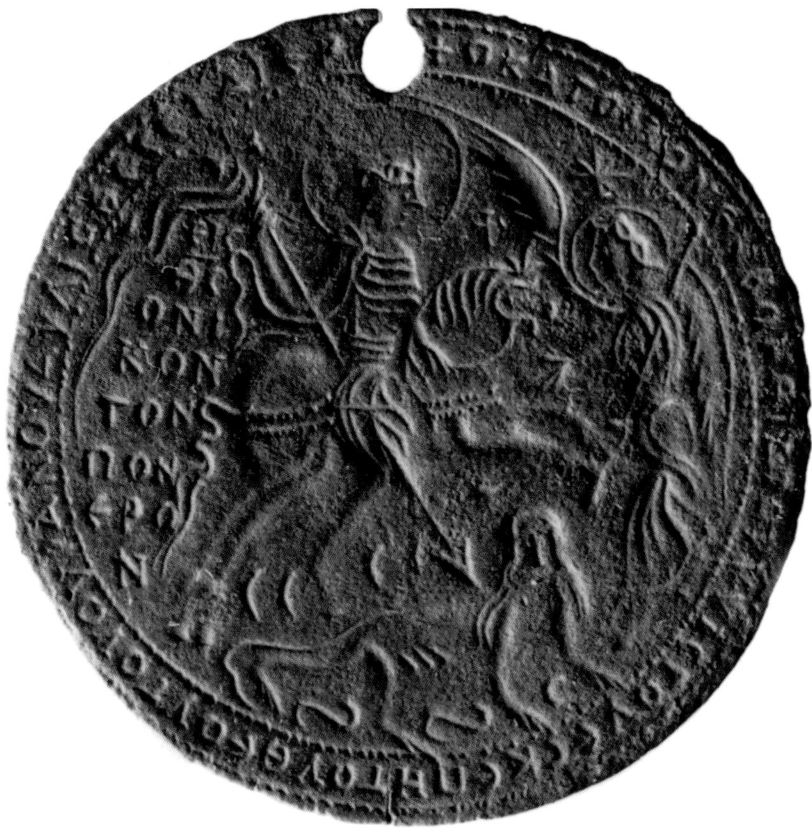

39. Obverse

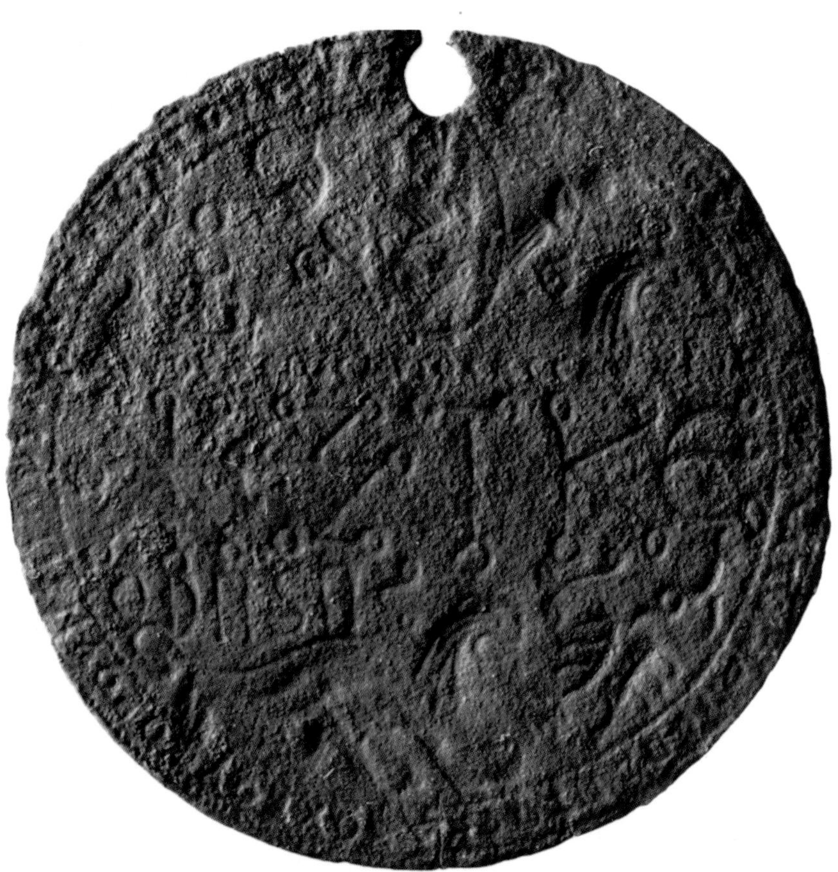

39. Reverse

The bronze medallion is thinly cast and bears a small suspension hole in the top. Each side displays an engraved decoration with shallow outlines. The front depicts the anonymous Holy Rider, one of the most popular figures in amuletic imagery, spearing a demonic creature, half-human and half-animal. The spear is topped with a cross and a pennant waving to the left. The crawling demon is a lion with a long-haired woman's head. The mounted warrior faces a standing nimbed angel, seen in profile, who points his spear to the same foe. A star is placed above the head of the angel. An inscription of the initial verses of Psalm 91 (90) encircles this composition, while the popular acclamation "One God who conquers evil" is to the left of the warrior. Both inscriptions are recurrent formulae in amuletic jewelry. The iconography and inscriptions of the obverse are recurrent elements on a group of amulets, believed to be particularly efficient at protecting women in childbirth.[1]

The surface of the reverse is considerably worn from contact with the chest area of its wearers, but its decoration can be reconstructed with precision from an almost identical example kept in the Kelsey Museum of Archaeology, University of Michigan.[2] The decoration features three registers. Christ in Majesty on the top, cross-nimbed, is shown holding a book in his left hand while raising his right hand. His figure is set within a mandorla surrounded by the Four Beasts of the Apocalypse. Below this composition is the text of the *trisagion*, a prayer for the dismissal of evil spirits, chanted to God by the six-winged seraphim surrounding his throne. Beneath the *trisagion* are magical letterlike symbols with ring-shaped terminals. Appearing under these symbols are a roaring lion turning to the right, a snake beneath the lion, and a scorpion in front of it. The ring patterns generally seem to have been valued for their putative healing powers, especially for the abdominal area.[3] The inscription placed on the rim refers to the "seal" that, according to the Testament of Solomon, the king of Israel had received from God in order to give him power over demons.[4]

In earlier literature, the Dumbarton Oaks amulet and the group to which it belongs were attributed to the fourth or fifth century. Since that time, a careful consideration of the associated finds from graves that yielded such medallions in Palestine confirmed a sixth- to seventh-century date, which is also substantiated by their style and iconography.[5] One finds further corroboration of this dating in a steatite mold intended for the casting of both a Holy Rider medallion and a medallion bearing the image of the enthroned Virgin and Child in profile with an angel opposite them.[6] The Dumbarton Oaks medallion and affiliated pieces were produced, most likely, in Syria or Palestine. Nevertheless, the discovery of similar objects on sites along the western coast of Asia Minor suggests the existence of multiple centers of production.

BP

References: *DOH* 1955, no. 77; *DOCat* 1, 53-54, no. 60, pl. XXXVIII.

Exhibitions: Cambridge, MA, Sackler Museum, informal exhibition, March 11-July 12, 1993.

1. For a thorough survey on the amulets with the Holy Rider, see Matantseva 1994, 110-121. See also Walter 1989, 33-42; Vikan 1984, 79-81. The amuletic use of psalm texts is studied in Pillinger 2001, 75-80; see also Vikan 1991, 35. The use of these medallions, especially in childbirth, is discussed in Sorlin 1991, 411-436.
2. Urbana-Champaign, *Art and Holy Powers* 1989, 214-215, no. 134.
3. See the entry "Ring Signs" in *ODB* 3, 1797.
4. Vikan 1984, 79-80.
5. See discussion, Spier 1993a, 60-62.
6. Collection Shlomo Moussaief, Herzliya, Israel, and London. See Jerusalem, *Cradle of Christianity* 2000, 158.

Bronze Objects

40. *Hanging Lamp*

Constantinople, 4th to 5th century[1]
Bronze
19.7 x 22.5 cm

Condition: Excellent.

Acquisition History: It has been reported, though unconfirmed, that the lamp was discovered in the area of the Dardanelles near Istanbul, Turkey. In 1956, Mr. and Mrs. Bliss purchased this lamp from George Zacos and donated it to Dumbarton Oaks.

Accession number: BZ.1956.20

Although common throughout the Roman world for centuries, this type of lamp rarely features decoration involving Christian symbols.[2] Ross has pointed out that lamps of this design became increasingly rare during the Late Antiquity.[3]

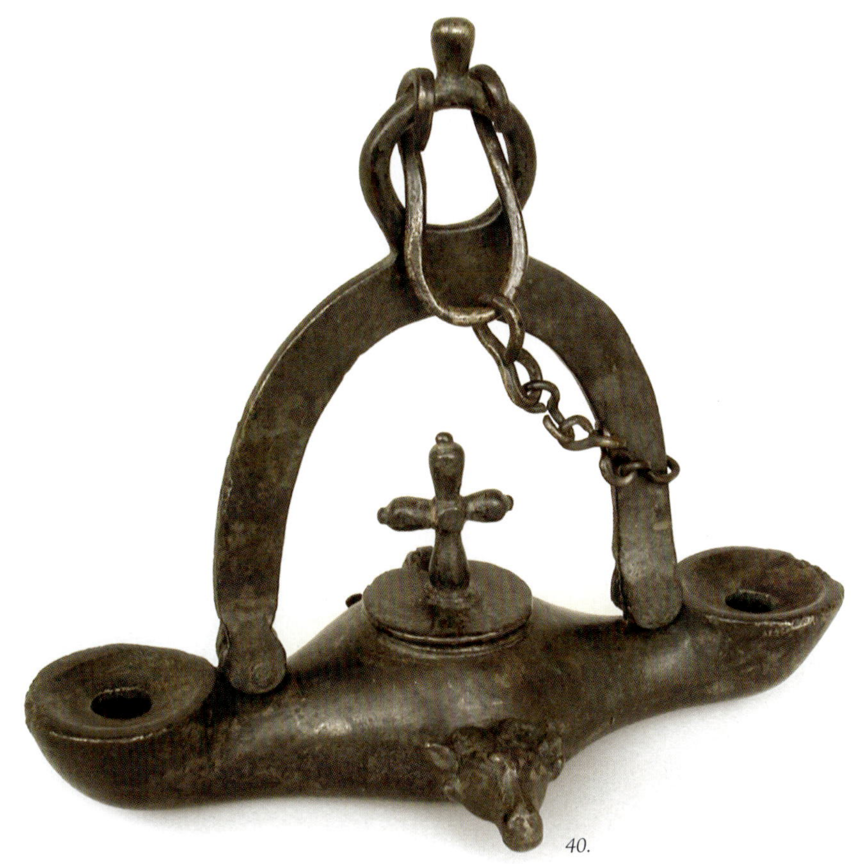

40.

The main body of the lamp is an elongated vessel with three axially arranged apertures facing up. In the middle is the filling hole equipped with a hinged lid. A cross surmounts this flat lid and fulfills the pragmatic function of a finial facilitating the opening and closing of the reservoir. The cross's rounded arms taper toward the center and display small globules at the three unattached tips. Two nozzles flank the central section of the lamp. A raised ridge surrounds the two small openings for wicks. Apart from the cross, the only other decoration consists of two rams' heads symmetrically attached to the central section of the lamp along an axis perpendicular to the main body's alignment.

Cast in several different pieces, the lamp is suspended by a series of interconnecting arches, rings, and links, diminishing in scale as they progress upward. Distinctly flat, the main structure that stems from the lamp's body arcs high over the cross finial, seeming both substantial and light. At the apex of this arch, a thick ring rises up crowned by a solid knob. To this ring there is an elongated arch fastened in a manner allowing for the lamp to swing freely back and forth. It is from this arcing loop that the suspension chain emanates, of which only four interlocking links survive.

Most similar two-nozzle lamps have flat tops with pronounced edges, as well as decoration that often is distinctly two-dimensional. Instead, this lamp appears to be carefully modeled. The design creates the impression that three gracefully bulbous receptacles have become organically fused together and unified by the continuous smooth surface. The central section of this appealingly curvaceous form is larger and rises modestly above the two flanking parts. Thus, its added breadth can visually sustain the two rams' heads, and its greater height lends the appropriate prominence to the cross perched atop it. The flattened suspension arch above appears as an outline of a halo of light for the cross, a connection reiterated by the two flanking flames. In this manner, by physically associating the cross with light, the overall design alludes to an enlightenment of a spiritual nature (cf. cat. no. 55).[4]

AK

References: *DOH* 1967, no. 106; *DOCat* 1, no. 31, pl. XXVI; Xanthopoulou 1997, no. LA 2.230, pl. 81.

Exhibitions: Cambridge, MA, Sackler Museum, March 11- July 12, 1993.

1. A later dating to the fifth to sixth century was suggested by Xanthopoulou 1997, vol. 2, 109.
2. See examples of older Roman bronze hanging lamps in Walters 1914, nos. 55, 57 and pls. III, XXXVIII-2;

De Spagnolis and De Carolis 1988, nos. 21, 22, 56-59, 82.

In general, the same design appears on four ceramic lamps dating to the second century and belonging to the Schloessinger collection. For discussion of this type, *dilychni*, see Rosenthal and Sivan 1978, 90-91, nos. 373-376. The decorative motives of the examples cited above are volutes, dolphins forming the suspension arch, and masks appearing below the nozzles, possibly representing Osiris.

3. *DOCat* 1, no. 32.
4. Symbolic meanings could transcend the utilitarian function of lamps; see Urbana-Champaign, *Art and Holy Powers* 1989, 58-59; Thessaloniki, *Everyday Life in Byzantium* 2002, 282.

41. Seven-Sided Incense Burner

Egypt, late 6th or early 7th century
Bronze
16.6 x 7 cm

Condition: The censer does not close properly; its top does not fit well the upper rim of the main body. The pyramidal lid's front panel is missing its bottom right section to which a hinge must have been fixed. Originally, two hinges connected the lid to the censer's main body. The lost front one must have featured a small peg allowing for opening and fastening the lid. The permanently fixed back hinge is still intact and functional and so is the suspension chain. The main body is in a good state of preservation.

Acquisition History: Mr. and Mrs. Bliss purchased this incense burner from Joseph Brummer on March 26, 1940.

Accession number: BZ.1940.16

Cast in several pieces, the incense burner consists of a seven-sided main body, pyramidal lid, and a suspension chain. Seven colonnettes mark the corners on the main body. The lid has the shape of a pyramid of seven triangular panels separated by ribs corresponding to the colonnettes. Each rib emanates from a globular projection at the lid's bottom, while at the top it curves outward. At the summit stands a finial composed of a globule supporting a cross. The lid features openwork of three different patterns: a cross at the front, with rhombs and rectangles alternating on the remaining six sides. Originally, the front panel also featured the letters *Alpha* and *Omega* suspended from the cross's horizontal bar (cf. cat. no. 55). While the former is still preserved, the latter must have been lost when the low right section of the panel broke off.[1] On all sides of the main body, one finds the same

41.

punched-in decoration of seven circles, each of them with a central dot. Set in different configurations, the same simple ornament appears across the lid and the finial as well.[2]

Architectural elements do appear on Egyptian bronze censers from this period.[3] Nevertheless, the overall design of this seven-sided incense burner stands out because of its resemblance to the *Aedicule*, which Emperor Constantine the Great (305-337) built above the Tomb of Christ in Jerusalem. All the uncertainty concerning the exact architectural articulation of the *Aedicule* notwithstanding, current knowledge does support such an association (figs. 41A and B; cf. cat. no. 56).[4]

The strong Christian message that the *Aedicule* design conveys does not necessarily mean this incense burner was intended exclusively for ecclesiastical use. It might well be that originally the censer was used in a Christian home.[5] This object is a fairly early example of a tradition that was to gain great popularity for centuries to come. It involved the use of small objects whose designs, resembling *ciboria*, made a statement about the sanctity of the substance that they held;

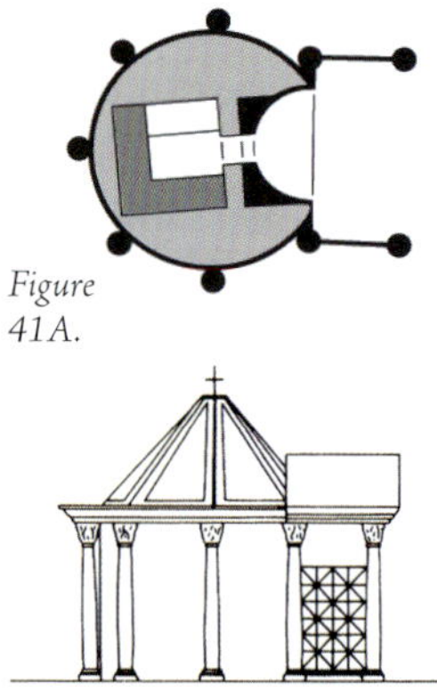

Figure 41A.

Figure 41B.

Ground plan and side elevation of the original Aedicule Christi, hypothetical reconstruction of the structure erected around the rock-cut tomb by Emperor Constantine the Great (305-337). Redrawn by Meredith S. Boyter, after Biddle 2002, 82, figs. 66A.

those objects included censers, reliquaries, and Holy Host containers.[6]

AK

References: *DOH* 1955, no. 85; *DOCat* 1, no. 48; Badawy 1978, 329, fig. 5.17.

1. Apparently, the damage to the lid occurred because its front panel was less stable since in addition to the openwork forming a cross with *Alpha* and *Omega*, it featured additional punctures for fastening the hinge.
2. The same ornament appears on other bronze censers from Egypt; see *DOCat* 1, no. 49. Cf. the discussion of a similar design, described as "concentric circles," in Urbana-Champaign, *Art and Holy Powers*, 1989, 5-6.
3. Badawy 1978, 329; Bénazeth 1988, 298-299, fig. 15; Caseau 1994, 26-27.
4. As Biddle points out, the analysis of both textual and visual sources has demonstrated that the *Aedicule* consisted of two parts, a portico and a tomb chamber. The chamber was carved out from the rock that enveloped the tomb originally. Whether circular or polygonal, this chamber's exterior displayed five engaged columns. The portico featured a pediment and pitched roof rising above four colonnettes, two of which were freestanding and the other two abutted the chamber's exterior wall. Such an arrangement would have given the *Aedicule* an appearance resembling a seven-sided polygon. On the reconstruction of the Constantinian *Aedicule* see Biddle 1999, 65-88, esp. 69, figs. 64B, 64C, 66A, and 66B; Wilkinson

1972, 83-97, esp. figs. 12-14. Cf. also Nitowski 1979 and Brooks 1921.

5. Caseau 1994, 1-11. As Caseau (ibid., 27) wrote: "We cannot assert simply from the shape of a censer that it was used either only at home or only in the church."

6. Underwood 1950; Grabar 1957a; Saunders 1982; Sterligova 1994; Beliaev 2000.

42. Bronze Situla with Monogram of Christ

Italy, 4th century
Bronze with inlay
Height: 16.2 cm; diameter at top: 16.6 cm; at base: 9.9 cm; depth: 16.2 cm

CONDITION: The situla is in an excellent state of preservation. Even so, the four *Chi-Rho* monograms have lost their original black inlay.[1] The pink substance currently filling the engraved monograms must be of a later date since it appears on top of the remnants of the older black inlay. Initially, the black monograms must have stood out against the yellowish-brown newly cast situla, whose surface must have changed color over time, becoming progressively darker due to the naturally occurring patina. As a result, at a certain point the four monograms must have become virtually indistinguishable. Therefore, the later pink inlay might have been introduced with the explicit intention of making the monograms legible once more, now on a vessel that had become nearly black in color.

ACQUISITION HISTORY: Mr. and Mrs. Bliss purchased it on October 3, 1940, from the antiquities dealer Joseph Brummer, whose notation indicates that the situla was discovered in Italy. Before 1940 it belonged to the collection of Marchese Ridolfo Peruzzi dei Medici. Although the original context in which this vessel was found remains unknown, one must bear in mind that the great majority of bronze situlae come from burial sites.

ACCESSION NUMBER: BZ.1940.50

The bowl of the situla rises above a low, flaring foot. The handle, cast separately, curves into a semicircle that lines up with the arc of the rim when the handle rests down on the bowl. At both ends the handle has an identical hook featuring five parallel incised rings, terminating in a knob-like tip. Each of these two hooks passes through a hole; the holes puncture two symmetrically positioned triangular projections, rounded and rising above the situla's upper rim. The walls of the bowl are vertical; yet, the vessel tapers at the bottom in order to connect with the foot. The overall design of the situla finds parallels among Roman vessels cast in silver and bronze, ranging in date from the first to the fourth century and manufactured in Italy and in some of the provinces. In terms of both design and material, the vessel's closest matches come from locations in Gaul and in the area of the lower Rhine.[2]

On the exterior of the bowl is a narrow frieze defined by two parallel bands of turnery work—one around the middle, the other just below its rim. This frieze contains four *Chi-Rho* symbols, set in two pairs. The design of the *Chi-Rho* symbol, with the characteristically pronounced loop of the *Rho*, is very similar to a series of monograms rendered on different objects, most of which appear to have been produced in Italy during the fourth century.[3] Christian symbols are rarely found on situlae, which typically have hunting scenes, mythological subjects, aquatic creatures, or floral ornaments.[4] In fact, the situla from the Byzantine Collection of Dumbarton Oaks aside, there is only one other well-known example of such a vessel displaying Christian symbols: a fifth-century bronze situla discovered in Turkish Mesopotamia featuring a row of crosses set below arches, yet having an overall design different from the Dumbarton Oaks vessel.[5]

Because of the four *Chi-Rho* monograms, Ross asserted that the situla must have fulfilled a liturgical function, possibly related to the ritualistic sprinkling of holy water.[6] Nevertheless, during Late Antiquity, crosses and *Chi-Rho* monograms frequently appeared on objects intended for domestic use.[7] Most likely, the original function of the situla had to do with bathing and washing.[8] Still, such vessels could have been used in many different ways within the domestic sphere and beyond it.[9] This may be particularly pertinent to these objects' apparent usage in the military, since situlae seemed to have been part of the soldier and/or officer kits used in the Roman army.[10]

AK

REFERENCES: *DOH* 1955, no. 74; *DOH* 1967, no.136; *DOCat* 1, no. 50.

EXHIBITIONS: *A Selection of Ivories, Bronzes, Metalwork and Other Objects from the Dumbarton Oaks Collection,* Cambridge, MA, Fogg Museum of Art, November 15-December 31, 1945; Cambridge, MA, Fogg Museum of Art, August 1972-December 1976.

1. The report of Mr. Gettens, chief of technical research, Fogg Museum of Art, of November 8, 1950, contains the following paragraph: "The inlay occurs in the four incised monograms of *Chi-Rho.* The principal inlay is a dull pinkish substance, which is set into the monogram flush with the smooth sides of the bucket. There is, however, a narrow border of black inlay

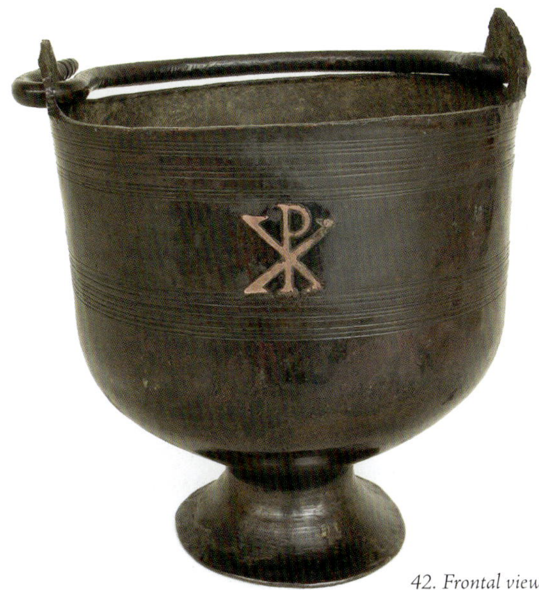

42. Frontal view

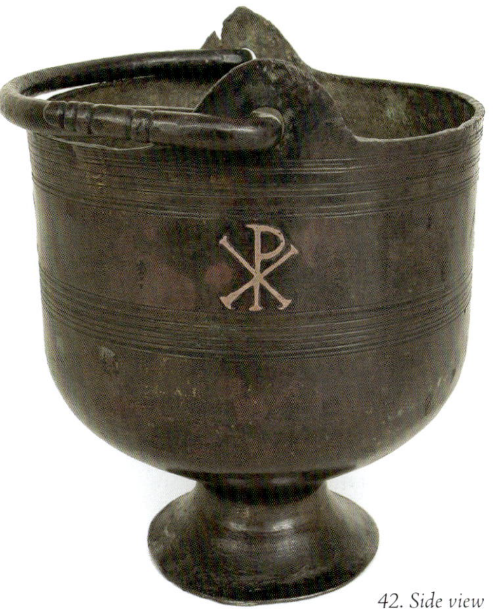

42. Side view

entirely surrounding the pink and which serves as a sort of lining between the pink and the metal.... It has been first suspected that the thin marginal layer of black might be a reaction product between the molten sulphur of the pink inlay and the bronze support, but careful examination seems to indicate that the black layer is deliberate, not accidental. The pink inlay, because of its high sulphur content, might be considered a very special kind of niello." Cf. the original letter filed with the object's dossier at the Byzantine Collection of Dumbarton Oaks.

2. Willers 1901, 50-71, pl. I-6 and 7, II, III; Déchelette 1902, figs. 4 and 5; Willers 1907, pl. III-3. For early examples of this type, cf. the second-century silver situlae from the Chaource Treasure, Walters 1921, XIX-form 6, nos. 148, 149. See the discussion of the issues of import from Italy versus local production: Gaul and the region of the lower Rhine—Willers 1901, 79 and Willers 1907, 182; Moesia and Thracia—Nenova-Merdjanova 1997, 34-35.

3. The closest parallels for the rendition of the *Chi-Rho* come from fourth-century Italy. See Henkel 1913, no. 992, pl. XXXIX, nos. 74, 75, pl. LXXIV, no. 1864, pl. LXX; Morey 1959, no. 36, pl. VI, no. 76, pl. XII, no. 112, pl. XIX, no. 126, pl. XX, no. 455, pl. XXX-VI; New York, *Age of Spirituality* 1977, nos. 506, 508; Gonosová and Kondoleon 1994, 98-99, no. 32.

4. See examples of (a) hunting scenes: Willers 1901; Bellido 1936; Mundell Mango et al. 1989; London, *Treasures of Byzantine Art* 1994, no. 77; Thessaloniki, *Everyday Life in Byzantium* 2002, no. 148; (b) mythological themes: Carandini 1964, New York; *Age of Spirituality* 1977, no. 196, Mundell Mango and Bennett 1994, 319-363; (c) aquatic creatures: Willers 1901, 54-55, fig. 26; (d) floral ornaments: Walters 1921, no. 148.

5. The situla from Kale e-Zerzevan at the Archaeological Museum in Istanbul, Bellido 1936, 71-73, figs. 4 and 5; Carandini 1964, 28-30, pl. XXIX, figs. 39 and 40; Herrmann 2002, 211-212, fig. 7.

6. *DOCat* 1, 45-46.

7. For instance, the *Chi-Rho* symbol appears—in the context of dining—on the hunting plate from the Sevso Treasure. In this case the monogram fulfills the function of a symbolic invocation of Christ since it is a part of an inscription; Mundell Mango and Bennett 1994, 55-97, esp. 77. Cf. the general discussion of use of the cross and other Christian symbols on household objects in Urbana-Champaign, *Art and Holy Powers* 1989, 18-22; also Elsner 1995, 255-261. See Parani "Silver Plate" above in this catalogue.

8. Nenova-Merdjanova 1997, 31-34, figs. 2-11; Nenova-Merdjanova 2002, figs. 1-13. Cf. also the much more elaborate Sevso Treasure silver situlae that were part of a bath service: Mundell Mango and Bennett 1994, 319-363, esp. 363, figs. 8.1-79. As further proof of this suggested function one might consider the inscriptions on situlae referring to health and washing: Mundell Mango et al. 1989, esp. 297-298; London, *Treasures of Byzantine Art* 1994, 85, no. 77; Thessaloniki, *Everyday Life in Byzantium* 2002, 137, no. 148.

9. Cf. the rendition of a situla filled with fruit on a stone relief; Willers 1907, 41-43, figs. 23, 24. Also, cauldrons were used as incense burners since Etruscan times; see Caseau 1994, 27.

10. London, *Treasures of Byzantine Art* 1994, 85-86; Nenova-Merdjanova 1997, 36.

Steelyards & Weights

BY JOHN NESBITT

Honest weights and measures were at the core of the orderly collection of taxes or the exchange of coin for commodities in the marketplace. To ensure the maintenance of pacific conditions among the general public, the Byzantine government regularly issued edicts regarding the integrity of weights, scales, and weighing procedures. Thus, Emperor Constantine the Great (305-337), for example, warns that there should be no trickery with fingers when coin was weighed with a balance scale and expresses his concern in the following words: "Now, when gold is paid, it shall be received with level pans and equal weights, in such a fashion, that the end of the cord [i.e., the cord from which the balance was suspended] is held with two fingers … so as to permit the level and equal movement of the balance."[1] One will find a contemporary illustration of the correct way of holding a scale on a round money weight of the fifth century (see cat. no. 50). No less a figure than a personification of the imperial monetary system, Moneta is shown holding a balanced scale by a cord between fingers of her right hand. An equation between fair weighing practices and prosperity is implied by the fact that Moneta (who is a cross between Justice and Abundance) holds a horn-of-plenty in her left hand. So that disputes might be settled impartially concerning the quality and weight of gold coins, Emperor Julian (361-363) ordered that an official weigher (*zygostates*) should be installed in each municipality.[2] After this time, bronze money weights (*exagia*) began to appear. Some are round and bear the inscription "weight of one gold coin," while others are square or spheroid and are engraved with simple marks of value, such as NIЄ (i.e., fifteen nomismata or gold coins; see cat. no. 53). From inscriptions, we know that weights were issued under the authority of the eparchs of Constantinople, the *comites sacrarum largitionum* (see cat. no. 50), and the praetorian prefects.[3] Constantine the Great created the solidus (Greek nomisma), the standard gold coin. It weighed 1/72 of a Roman pound. To give an idea of the value of the solidus, we note that in the early Byzantine period a good copy of the New Testament on parchment cost three nomismata, the same price as a donkey.[4]

In a Byzantine market, one would have encountered two types of scales and two types of weights. A balance scale and small bronze weights were used for weighing high-value commodities of relatively light weight or restricted dimensions. If the buyer tendered gold coinage in payment, the seller would have weighed the coins with his balance scale in order to verify that the coins were genuine or that a pair of metal cutters had not been used to clip the coins. A steelyard and weights of substantial mass and size were employed by butchers and greengrocers for ascertaining the weight of large or bulky foodstuffs, such as meat or vegetables. A steelyard in the collection of the Arthur M. Sackler Museum, Harvard University, would be used to weigh objects up to eighty-five pounds.[5] In the Early Byzantine period, heavy weights were commonly cast in the shape of imperial figures, an emperor or empress. The idea behind such representations may have been to inspire faith in the accuracy of weighing equipment. In the period with which we are dealing, the following weight system was employed[6]:

Divisions of the pound:

1 pound (libra)	=12 unciae	= 327.45 grams
1/2 pound (semis)	= 6 unciae	= 163.73 grams
1/12 pound (uncia)	= 1 uncia	= 27.29 grams

Divisions of the ounce (uncia):

1/2 ounce	= 12 scruples	= 13.65 grams

The nomisma and its fractions:

1 nomisma	= 4.55 grams
2 nomismata	= 9.10 grams
3 nomismata	= 13.65 grams
6 nomismata	= 27.29 grams

The weights given are theoretical. Actual weights may vary due to loss of weight from cleaning, corrosion, imperfections of manufacture, or deliberate cheating.[7]

1. The translation is that of Hendy 1985, 329.
2. Grierson and Mays 1992, 30.
3. In Paris, *Byzance* 1992, no. 71, there is published a spheroid weight of one pound, weighing 323.5 grams, issued in 532 by the praetorian prefect Phokas. A round weight of 18 solidi, issued in the name of the City Prefect Zemarchos in 562 or 565, is illustrated in Feissel 2001, 35.
4. See Ostrogorsky 1932, 326, 330-331.
5. Cambridge, MA, *Byzantine Women* 2003, 52.
6. We use here, in abbreviated form, the chart appearing in Walbaum 1983, 85.
7. See Waldbaum's remarks regarding weights found at Sardis, ibid.

43. Steelyard Beam

Eastern Mediterranean, 5th to 6th century
Copper alloy
Length: 47 cm

CONDITION: Excellent.

ACQUISITION HISTORY: Provenance unknown; Bliss Collection 1940.

ACCESSION NUMBER: BZ.1940.17.1

The beam or rod consists of two sections of unequal length. The shorter one has two holes for suspension hooks (now missing), while the longer part is engraved and punched with graduated markings on two sides. One side was used for weighing lighter loads and the other for weighing heavier ones. When weighing, a person suspended the beam from a hook, selected based upon a desired set of calibrations. Next to the finial of rosebud shape at the short end is a groove into which a collar would have been fitted. From the collar, there usually hung one chain with figure-eight-shaped links ending with a hook on which was placed the object to be weighed. In the present instance, three parts comprise the steelyard: a beam, a collar with a weighing pan (cat. no. 44), and a sliding weight (cat. no. 45). Originally three of the chains ended in long metal tabs, which were attached to the bottom of the weighing pan and supported it along with any object set on it. The hook at the end of the fourth chain probably served to steady an object placed on the weighing pan. Once an object was placed on the pan and was secured by the hook, a weight was slid along the beam until the scale was in balance.

JN

REFERENCES: *DOCat* 1, no. 74. For further reading, see Vikan and Nesbitt 1980, 32-33; and London, *Treasures of Byzantine Art* 1994, 100.

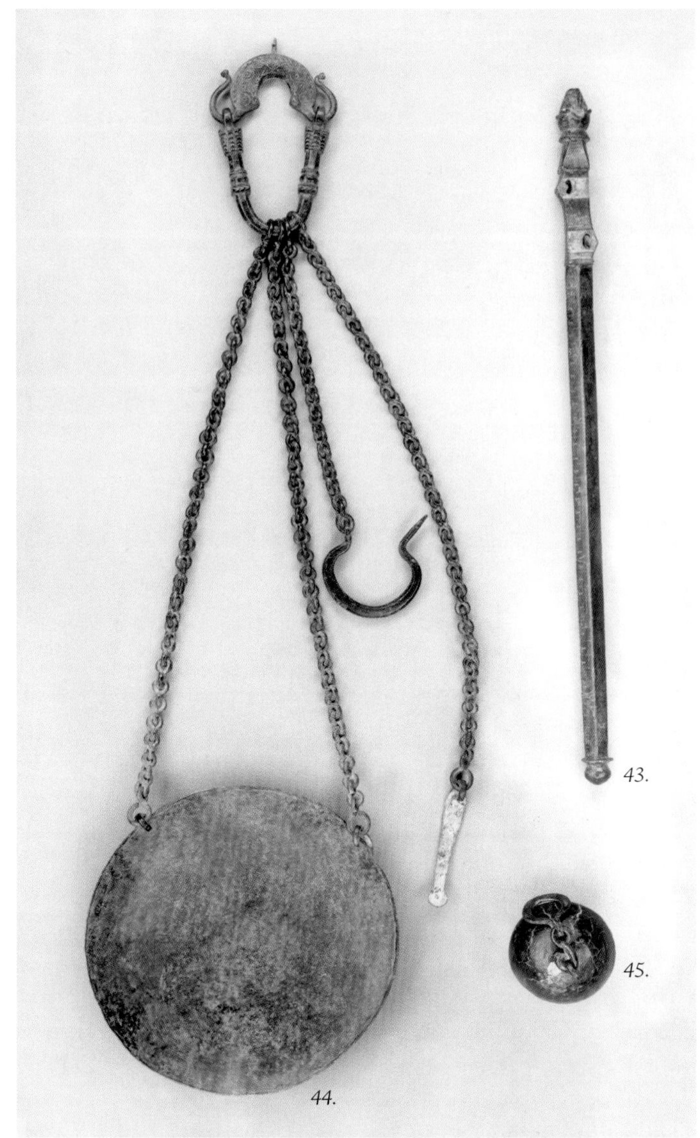

44. Balance Pan and Collar

Eastern Mediterranean, 5th to 6th century
Copper alloy
Diameter: 20.3 cm

CONDITION: The surface retains incrustation due to burial.

ACQUISITION HISTORY: Provenance unknown; Bliss Collection 1940.

ACCESSION NUMBER: BZ.1940.17.2

Four chains hang from the collar. At the end of one chain is a hook. Originally the other three chains ended in metal tabs, which were attached to the bottom of the pan. The collar was suspended from the short end of the steelyard beam. The object to be weighed was pierced by the hook and then placed on the balance pan.

JN

REFERENCES: *DOCat* 1, no. 74.

45. Weight of Globular Form

Eastern Mediterranean, 5th to 6th century
Composition undetermined
Height: 7.3 cm; weight: 1375 grams

CONDITION: The overall condition is good.

ACQUISITION HISTORY: Provenance unknown; Bliss Collection 1940.

ACCESSION NUMBER: BZ.1940.17.3

The weight is equipped with a hoop, which allows it to slide along a steelyard beam. At 1375 grams, its weight is close to the weight of cat. no. 48, a statuette counterpoise weight of 1405 grams.

JN

REFERENCES: *DOCat* 1, no. 74.

46. Steelyard Beam

Constantinople, 5th century
Copper alloy
Length: 60 cm
INSCRIBED: +ΠΑΝΔΩΛΕΩΝΤΩC+ ("of Pandoleon").
CONDITION: The overall condition is excellent.
ACQUISITION HISTORY: Reportedly from Constantinople; Bliss Collection 1940.
ACCESSION NUMBER: BZ.1940.18.1

The complete ensemble of weighing equipment consists of a steelyard beam, a collar with two chains, and two sliding statuette weights (cat. nos. 48 and 49). There are two sections of the beam, a longer one and a shorter one. The shorter one is outfitted with two hooks, which serve as fulcra, and terminates with a finial of budlike shape. The longer portion is marked on two of its four faces with punched and engraved scale marks and bears on the third side an inscription reading "of Pandoleon." The inscription identifies the owner of the beam, a merchant named Pandoleon. Merchants' names are commonly found on steelyard rods. For example, another rod at Dumbarton Oaks bears the inscription "of Edesios."[1]

JN

REFERENCES: *DOH* 1955, no. 101; *DOCat* 1, 61-62, no. 71; *DOH* 1967, no. 133.

1. *DOCat* 1, no. 73.

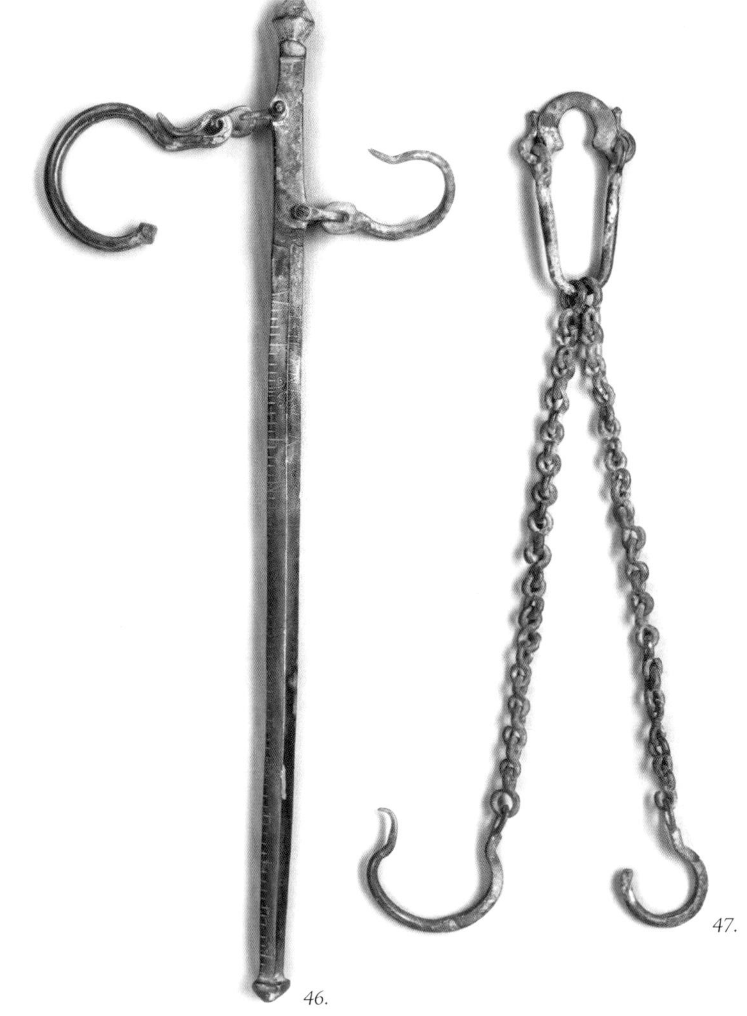

46.

47.

47. Semicircular Collar for Use with a Steelyard Beam

Constantinople, 5th century
Copper alloy
Length of chain: 52 cm
CONDITION: The object exhibits some encrustation from burial.
ACQUISITION HISTORY: Reportedly from Constantinople; Bliss Collection 1940.
ACCESSION NUMBER: BZ.1940.18.2

Two chains are attached to the collar. The chains comprise figure-eight links from which hang two hooks used for supporting the object to be weighed by the steelyard beam. One hook appears to have lost its tip.

JN

REFERENCES: *DOH* 1955, no. 101; *DOCat* 1, no. 71; *DOH* 1967, no. 133.

48. Weight in the Form of a Bust of an Empress

Constantinople, 5th century
Copper alloy
Height: 13.3 cm; weight: 1405 grams
CONDITION: The overall condition is good, but the casting is of indifferent quality.
ACQUISITION HISTORY: Reportedly from Constantinople; Bliss Collection 1940.
ACCESSION NUMBER: BZ.1940.18.3

The weight has been cast in the form of a bust of an empress wearing a diadem set with large stones, pearl earrings, a cloak, a tunic, and a necklace. With her right hand, she holds one edge of her cloak; in her left, she may be holding a scroll (no longer visible) against the outer garment. Above an intricate coiffure appears a ring for suspending the weight from a steelyard beam by means of a chain and hook.

Steelyard weights first appeared in the Late Hellenistic period. For example, the Museum of Fine Arts, Boston, had in their collection a weight dating from c. 100 BC to 50 CE, which is cast in the form of the goddess Artemis. Representations of gods, goddesses, and personifications were popular in Roman times. The same museum possesses a steelyard weight (dating from 150 to 275 CE) cast in the form of a bust of Victory and another (dating from 280 to 310 CE) cast in the form of a bust of the demigod Herakles.[1]

Statuette weights cast in the form of an imperial bust began to appear in the fifth century. Among the latest examples is a steelyard weight cast in the form of Emperor Phokas (602-610).[2]

JN

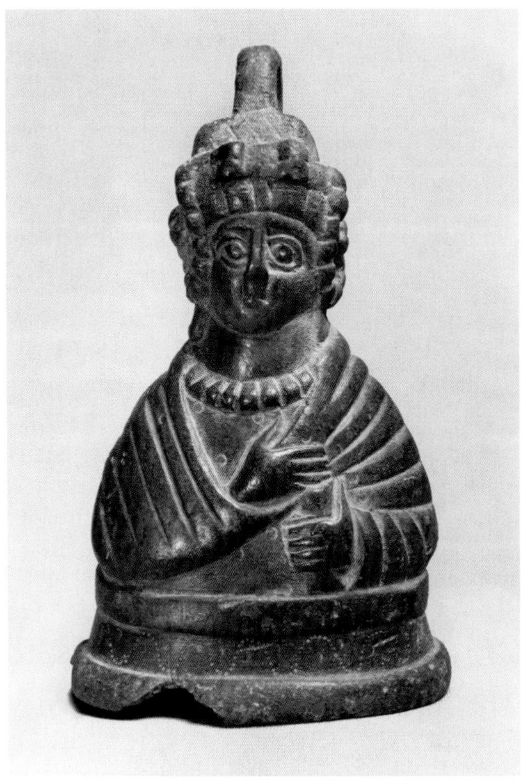

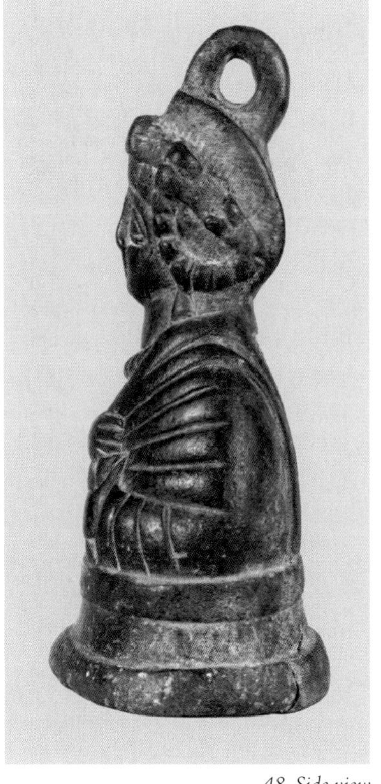

48. Frontal view

48. Side view

References: *DOH* 1955, no. 101; *DOCat* 1, no. 71, Weight A; *DOH* 1967, no. 133.

1. Comstock and Vermeule 1971, nos. 641-643.
2. London, *Treasures of Byzantine Art* 1994, no. 110.

49. Weight in the Form of a Bust of an Empress

Constantinople, 5th century
Copper alloy
Height: 14.5 cm; weight: 2627 grams

Condition: Except for chipping along the base, the condition is excellent.

Acquisition History: Reportedly from Constantinople; Bliss Collection 1940.

Accession number: BZ.1940.18.4

The weight has been cast in the form of a bust of an empress wearing a diadem set with large stones, pearl earrings, a cloak, a tunic, and a necklace. With her right hand she touches one edge of her cloak; in her left hand, she holds a scroll against the outer garment. Round punch marks are suggestive of a decorative pattern woven into her tunic. Above the high-piled hair appears a suspension ring.

Although the Byzantines were fond of steelyard weights cast in the form of emperors or empresses, statuette weights cast in the form of Athena were also popular. We note that excavations at Ostrakine in Lower Egypt have recovered a weight (unpublished; no. 94.182.8) cast with a suspension ring in the shape of a stylized animal—a baboon or bear—resting on its hindquarters. Not all weights, however, were figural. Merchants also used weights of globular (cat. no. 45) or pear shape.

JN

References: *DOH* 1955, no. 101; *DOCat* 1, no. 71, Weight B; *DOH* 1967, no. 133. For comparative specimens, see Comstock and Vermeule 1971, no. 644; Cambridge, MA, *Byzantine Women* 2003, nos. 10-13; and Munich, *Rom und Byzanz* 1998, nos. 219, 225, 226.

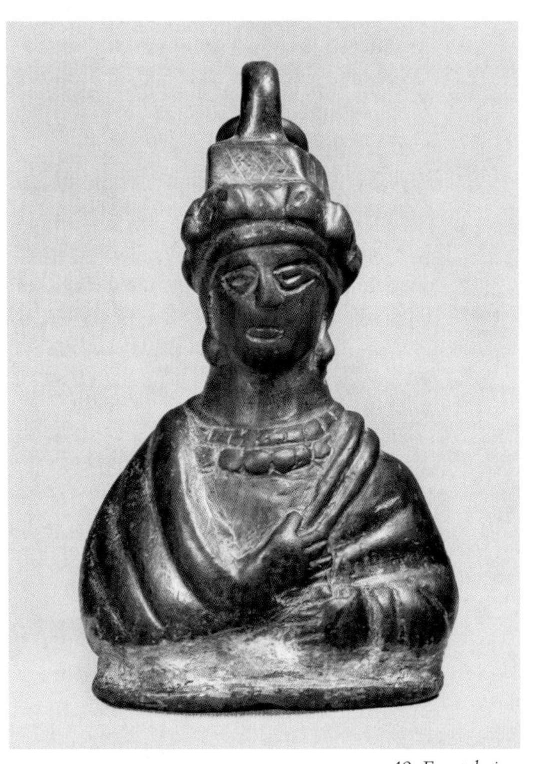

49. Frontal view

49. Side view

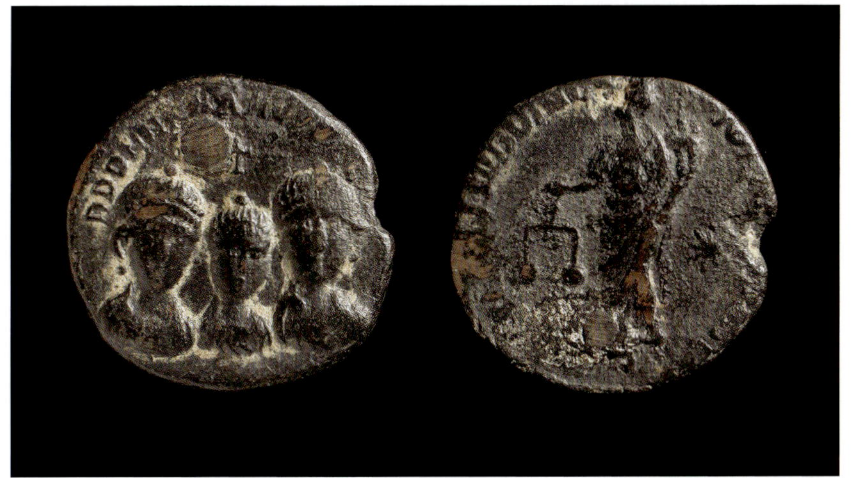

50. Obverse and Reverse

51. Weight with Depiction of Two Emperors

Eastern Mediterranean, 5th century
Copper alloy with silver inlay
Height: 2.3 cm; width: 2.1 cm; weight: 23.3 grams
ACQUISITION HISTORY: Unknown provenance; acquired in 1950.
ACCESSION NUMBER: BZ.1950.14

The surface is decorated with two engraved imperial busts, filled with silver, of two beardless and unidentified emperors. Each wears a diadem and a heavy cloak fastened with a *fibula* on the right shoulder. The letters Γ A, signifying "one ounce," are engraved below the busts.

JN

REFERENCES: *DOCat* 1, 64-65, no. 76. For more weights with imperial representations, see London, *Treasures of Byzantine Art* 1994, nos. 29, 31-33.

50. Round Money Weight with Three Busts

Constantinople, c. 403-408
Copper alloy
Weight: 3.78 grams
CONDITION: The object is worn on both sides, is chipped along the rim, and has suffered corrosion on the reverse. It was at one time pierced; in modern times the hole was plugged.
ACQUISITION HISTORY: Provenance unknown; ex-Bertelè collection 1960.
ACCESSION NUMBER: BZ.1960.88.5608

The obverse is decorated with a row of three imperial busts in frontal view. Theodosios II (402-450) appears in the middle, flanked by Emperors Arkadios (395-408) and Honorius (393-423). Each of them wears a pearl diadem. Above the busts is found a cross and a circular inscription that, based upon a better-preserved example at the Arthur M. Sackler Art Museum, Harvard University, may be reconstructed as follows: DDDNNNAAAV[VVCCC]: "Our Lords [the Three] Augusti."[1]

The reverse is ornamented with a representation of Moneta facing front and holding a balance scale in her right hand and a horn-of-plenty on her left arm. She is flanked by an eight-rayed star at right. The figure is encircled by an inscription that can be partially read: SOLSVBVI.-IOHAN....MSL. Based again upon the Sackler specimen, the legend may be completed as follows: [EXAC(IVM)] SOL(IDI) SVB V(IRO) I[L(LVSTRI)] IOHAN[NE CO]M(ITE) S(ACRARUM) L(ARGITIONVM):

"Weight of a solidus [issued] during the administration of the *vir illustris* John, *comites sacrarum largitionum*." Moneta stands above a legend reading [CO]N[S], an abbreviated form of Cons(antinopolis).[2]

JN

REFERENCES: Unpublished.

1. The Sackler weight is published in Cambridge, MA, *Byzantine Women* 2003, no. 9. See also the coin weight with three imperial busts published in London, *Treasures of Byzantine Art* 1994, no. 28.
2. The *comites sacrarum largitionum* was the director of mines and was in charge of mint activities at Constantinople.

51. Obverse

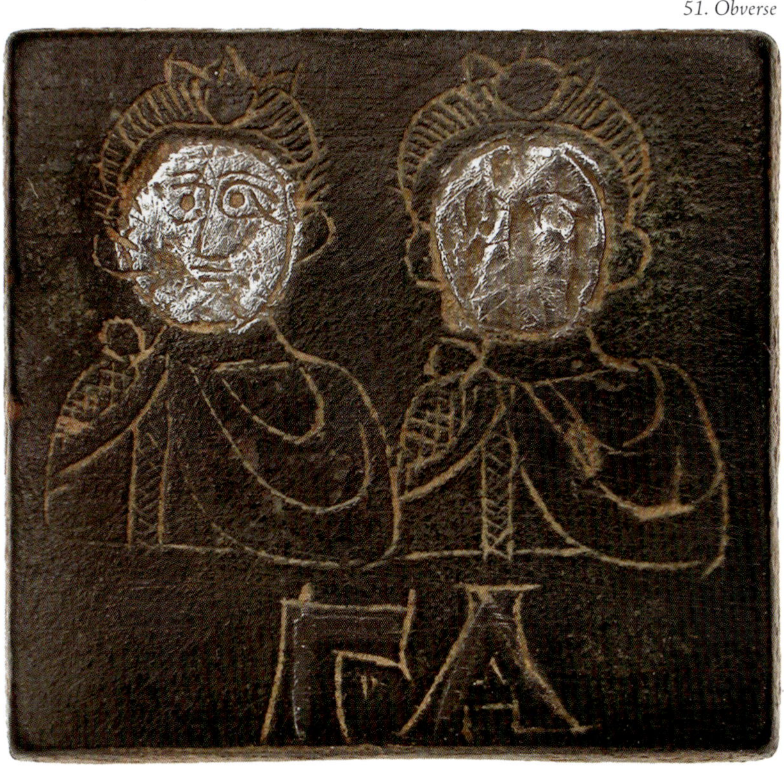

52. Spheroid Weight

Eastern Mediterranean, 5th century
Copper alloy with silver inlay
Diameter: 8 cm; height: 1.9 cm;
weight: 26.96 grams

CONDITION: There is some evidence of
corrosion.

ACQUISITION HISTORY: Provenance
unknown; ex-Bertelè collection 1960.

ACCESSION NUMBER: BZ.1960.88.5612

The weight is of spheroidal shape and bears
an engraved weight designation filled with
silver of "one ounce" (૪A).

JN

REFERENCES: Unpublished.

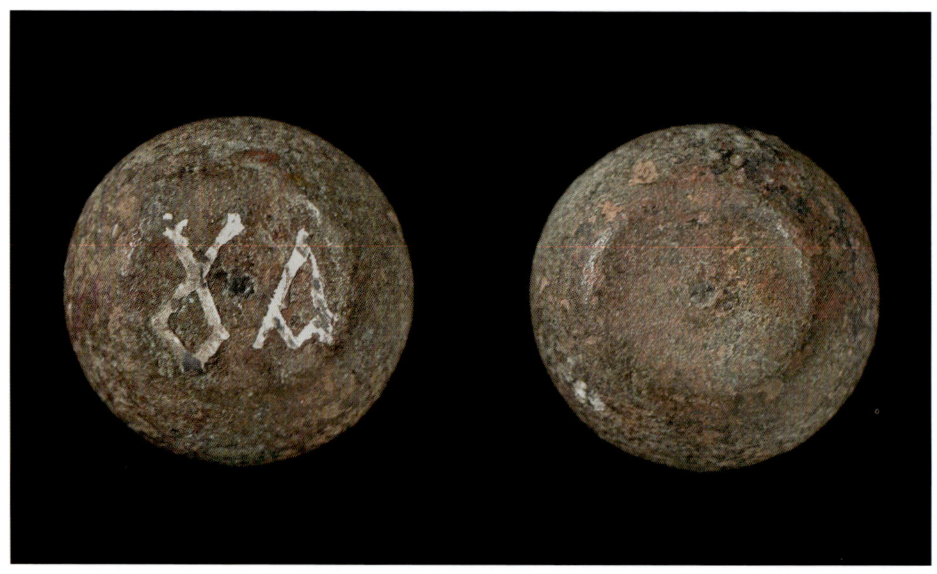

52. Obverse and Reverse

53. Flat Weight

Eastern Mediterranean, 5th century
Copper alloy with silver inlay
3.3 cm square; weight: 64 grams

CONDITION: Excellent.

ACQUISITION HISTORY: Provenance
unknown; Bliss Collection 1938, ex-W. de
Grüneisen collection.

ACCESSION NUMBER: BZ.1938.18

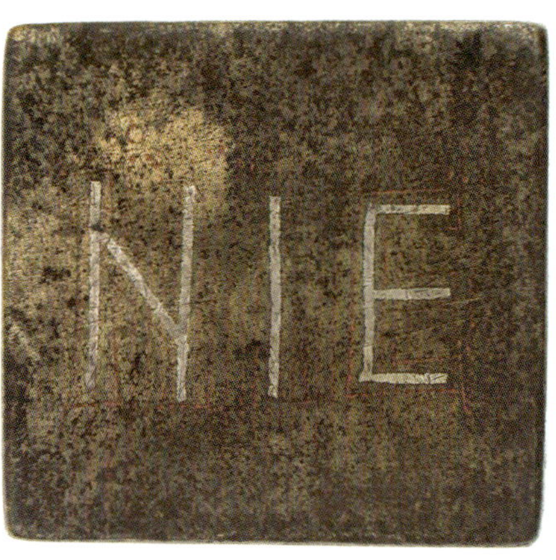

53. Obverse

This weight was used specifically for
weighing coins, as indicated by the inscription NIE, which has been engraved in the
center of the field and decorated with
silver inlay. The letter N is an abbreviated
form of the word n[omismata], a term
for gold coins. In Greek, letters of the
alphabet stand for numbers, as is the case
also with Roman numerals. The letter I
is the tenth letter of the Greek alphabet
and hence has a numerical value of ten.
The letter E is the fifth letter and has a numerical value of five. Combined, the letters
stand for the number "15."

JN

REFERENCES: *DOCat* 1, 67-68, no. 82.

54. Flat Weight

Eastern Mediterranean, 5th to 6th century
Copper alloy with silver inlay
4.4 cm square; weight: 157.2 grams

CONDITION: Excellent.

ACQUISITION HISTORY: Provenance
unknown; Bliss Collection 1938, ex-W. de
Grüneisen collection.

ACCESSION NUMBER: BZ.1938.17

In the center of the field appear the letters
Γ and S. The letter Γ is an abbreviation for
the word "ounces"; the letter S is the sixth
letter of the Greek alphabet and has the
numerical value 6.

JN

REFERENCES: *DOCat* 1, 68, no. 83.

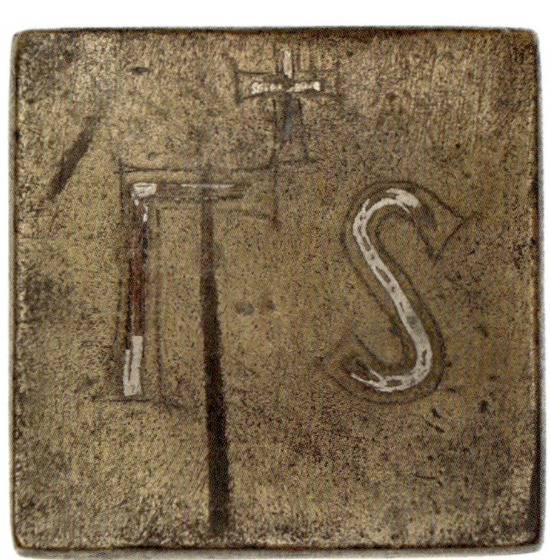

54. Obverse

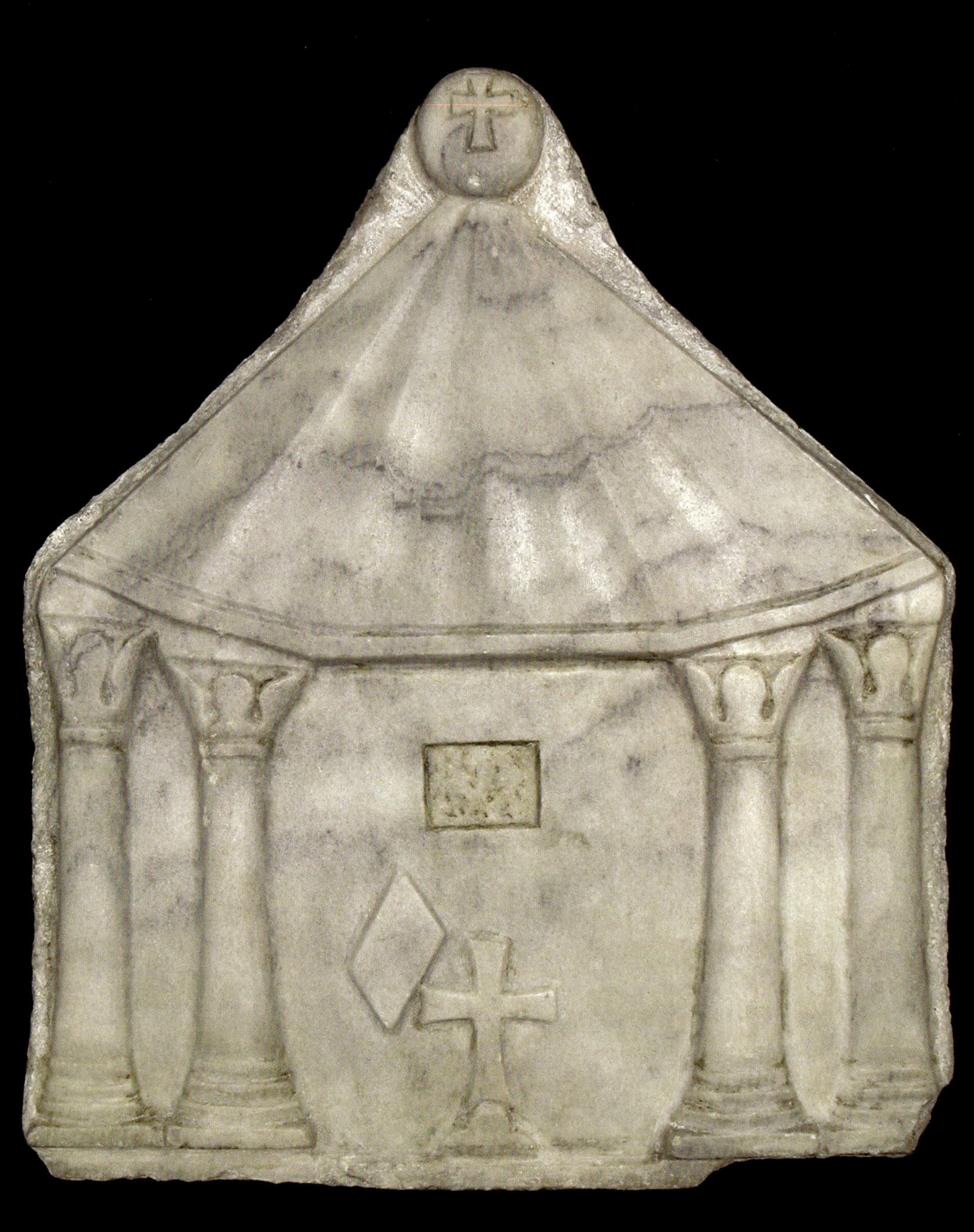

SCULPTURE

Northern Syria, late 5th to early 6th century
Yellow limestone
Diameter: 36.6 cm; depth: 6.7 cm; thickness: c. 6.5
cm; depth of relief: 1.5 cm

CONDITION: Limited weathering and negligible
scratches.

ACQUISITION HISTORY: Acquired from
Beirut in 1946.

ACCESSION NUMBER: BZ.1945.7

The main feature on this stone medallion
is the Chrismon, the monogram of Christ
consisting of the "X" or *Chi*, and the "P"
or *Rho*. The roundel must have been set
above the door of a private residence, most
likely a rubble-stone masonry house located
in northern Syria. Similar sculpted disks
appear on the lintels of houses, churches,
and fortifications around this region.[1] The
apotropaic function of these medallions
manifested itself in their location on thresh-
olds and found further substantiation in the
content of the inscriptions—invocations for
protection—that appear in similar contexts
(see figs. 55A and 55B).

The Chrismon developed from a solar
symbol, ✳, a six-pointed star.[2] It retained its
original symbolism that involved celestial radiance, even though it had become
Christianized and most certainly reflected
Christ's saying, "I am the light of the world,"
(John 8:12). Accordingly, the theme of light
underlies the individual elements of the
Chrismon medallion. The two concentric
circles forming the outer rim of the roundel
represent a double halo of heavenly glow.[3]
Furthermore, the carver rendered each of
the three shafts of the letters *Chi* and *Rho* as
pairs of slender elongated triangles joined at
their upper points; ultimately, they appear
as six beams of light radiating from the
roundel's center.

In addition to the Chrismon, the medallion features two more Greek letters, *Alpha*
and *Omega*, the first and last letters of the
Greek alphabet, a reference to Revelations
21:6: "I am *Alpha* and *Omega*, the beginning
and the end." The carver rendered these two
letters as if they were suspended from the
upper tips of the *Chi*. As Vikan observed,
the notion that the *Alpha* and *Omega* hang
in the air must have been enhanced by the
application of different colors of paint to the
surface of the relief.[4] Certainly, the color

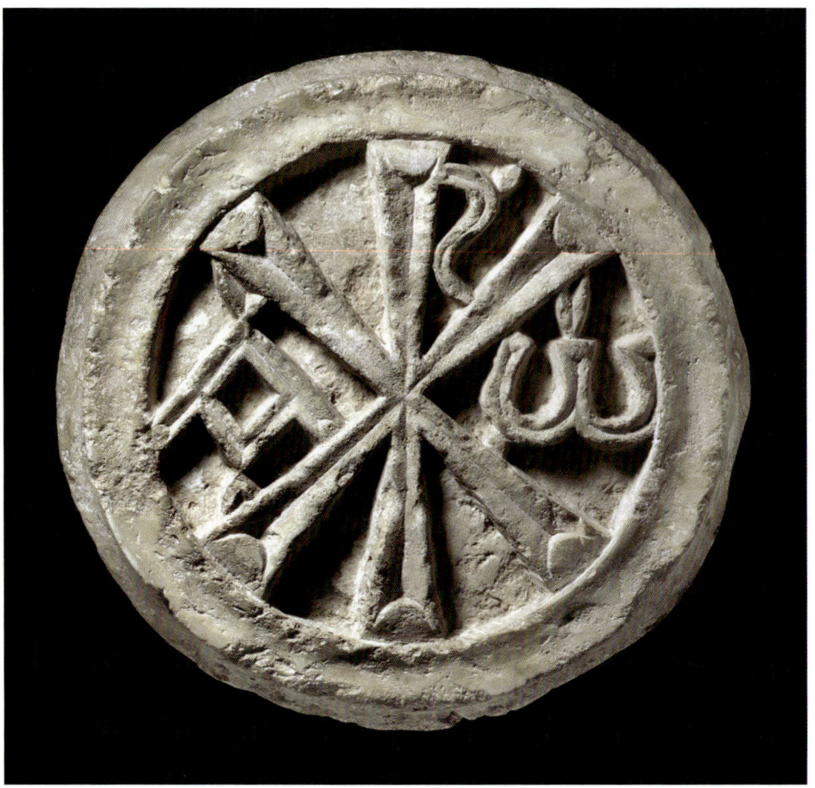

55. Front

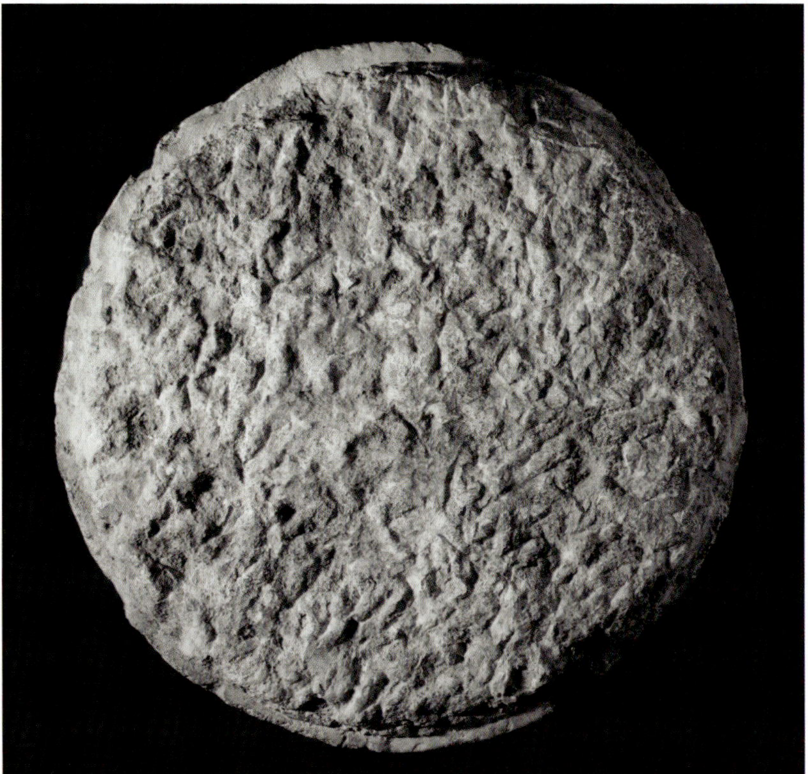

55. Back

of the *Alpha* and the *Omega* could have expressed also the notion of divine light.[5]

Still, the Dumbarton Oaks medallion seems to convey another layer of meaning generated by the specific way it depicts the *Alpha* and *Omega*. By virtue of suspending them in the air, the designer objectified the two letters and, in this manner, evoked associations with hanging lamps. In fact, lamps—not letters—hang from the horizontal bar of the cross that is inscribed into a roundel found in the region from which the Dumbarton Oaks relief originates (fig. 55C).[6] This reference seems to be to the common Late Antique practice of adorning bronze and ceramic lamps with the sign of the cross, the Chrismon, and the *Alpha* and *Omega*.[7] The symbol on the lamp stands for the lamp itself. This visual trope pulls together into a single focal point the godly radiance of heaven and the humble light of oil lamps. Ultimately, the design of the medallion expresses the union of the divine and the earthly worlds through the light of Christ, that is, by means of faith.[8] Awareness of the widespread presence of the Chrismon in ecclesiastical and imperial contexts must have bestowed an aura of prestige on the use of this symbol in the domestic sphere (cf. cat. no. 42).[9]

AK

References: *DOH* 1946, no. 40; *DOH* 1955, no. 46; *DOH* 1967, no. 25; Vikan 1995, no. 32, pl. 32A, B; Worcester, *Antioch* 2000, no. 113.

Exhibitions: *Antioch: The Lost Ancient City*, Worcester, MA, Worcester Art Museum, October 7, 2000-February 4, 2001; Cleveland Museum of Art, March 18-June 3, 2001; and Baltimore Museum of Art, September 16-December 30, 2001.

1. Vikan 1995, 78.
2. Weiss has argued convincingly that Constantine's vision involved observing a real atmospheric phenomenon that occurs when ice crystals in the high levels of the atmosphere refract the sunlight. Ancient authors refer to this occurrence as a "halo" or a "corona." Both terms—the first, Greek, and the second, Latin—designate a circle of light around the sun or the moon. See Weiss 2003, 237-259, esp. 240-245.
3. The elaborate rendition of the ring encircling the monogram attracted the attention of Vikan (1995, 77), who stated while describing its profile that "the frontal band is slightly concave and the side bulges towards the back."
4. Vikan 1995, 77. Surviving evidence proves that ornaments shaped as letters were used during Late Antiquity. Cf. a sixth-century lead ornament shaped as an *Alpha* within a medallion, which must have been suspended from a ciborium or a lintel along with another lost piece in the form of an *Omega*. At present, this *Alpha* ornament is in the collection of the University of Oslo, originally from the Ustinow collection. See Fleischer, Hjort, and Rasmussen 1996, no. 71. For the discussion of metal crosses with suspended letter ornaments, see Paderborn, *Byzanz* 2001, 147-150, no. I.50; Cuscito 2002, fig. 1. Cuscito's article discusses the associations of this arrangement with suspended lamps and votive crowns. As is well known, suspended letter ornaments appear in the votive crown of Recceswinth, Fuente de Guarrazar, from the seventh century, now in the National Archaeological Museum, Madrid; see Stokstad 1988, 84-85, fig. 7. Written sources document the popularity of votive crowns in early Byzantium; see Mango 1986, 100, 156-157.
5. Such was the case in the sixth-century apse mosaic of San Apollinare in Classe where the *Alpha* and *Omega* are among the stars surrounding the vision of the cross. The mosaicist portrayed the cross, the stars, and the two letters in gold tesserae against a dark blue background.
6. From il-Odjeh, an H.C. Butler drawing kept at Research Photographs, Department of Art and Archaeology, Princeton University.
7. See examples in Urbana-Champaign, *Art and Holy Powers* 1989, 18-19, no. 12; Fleischer, Hjort, and Rasmussen 1996, nos. 56, 57.
8. In addition to their apparent utilitarian significance, oil lamps conveyed symbolic meanings. See a brief discussion of this issue in Urbana-Champaign, *Art and Holy Powers* 1989, 58-59.
9. On the rendition of the Chrismon on the ceiling of a chamber in Emperor Constantine's palace itself, see Eusebius, *Vita Constantini*, 3.49, cited by Weiss 2003, 256.

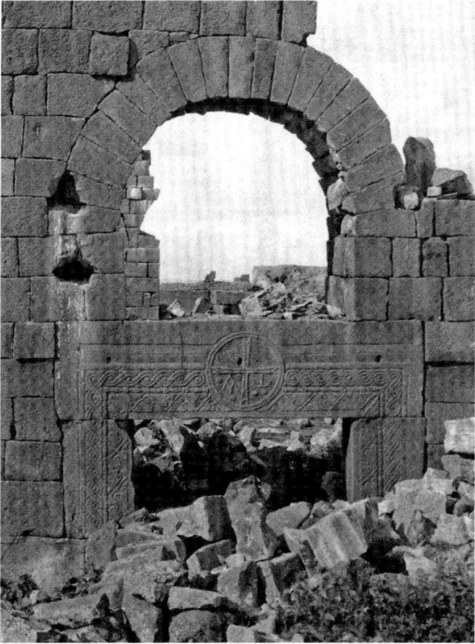

Figure 55A. il-Anderin, South Church, portal and window in the south wall, before 528 CE, Research Photographs, neg. no. 977, Department of Art and Archaeology, Princeton University. (cf. Butler 1929, ill. 86)

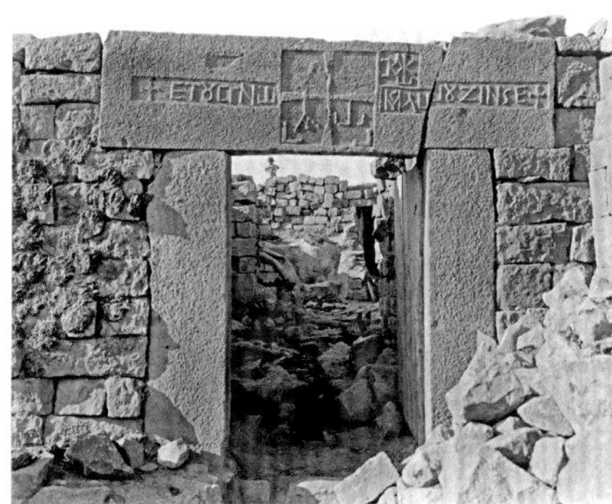

Figure 55B. il-Anz, Incribed lintel, 442 CE, Research Photographs, neg. no. 958, Department of Art and Archaeology, Princeton University. (cf. Princeton University Archaeological Expeditions to Syria, Division 2, ill. 21; Division 3, 35)

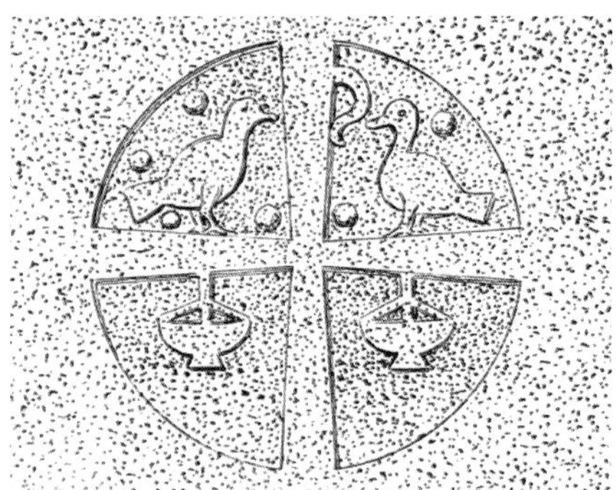

Figure 55C. il-Odjeh, Medallion with a cross, two birds and suspended lamps, no neg. no.—from an H.C. Butler drawing, Research Photographs, Department of Art and Archaeology, Princeton University. (cf. Princeton University Archaeological Expeditions to Syria, Division 2, ill. 71)

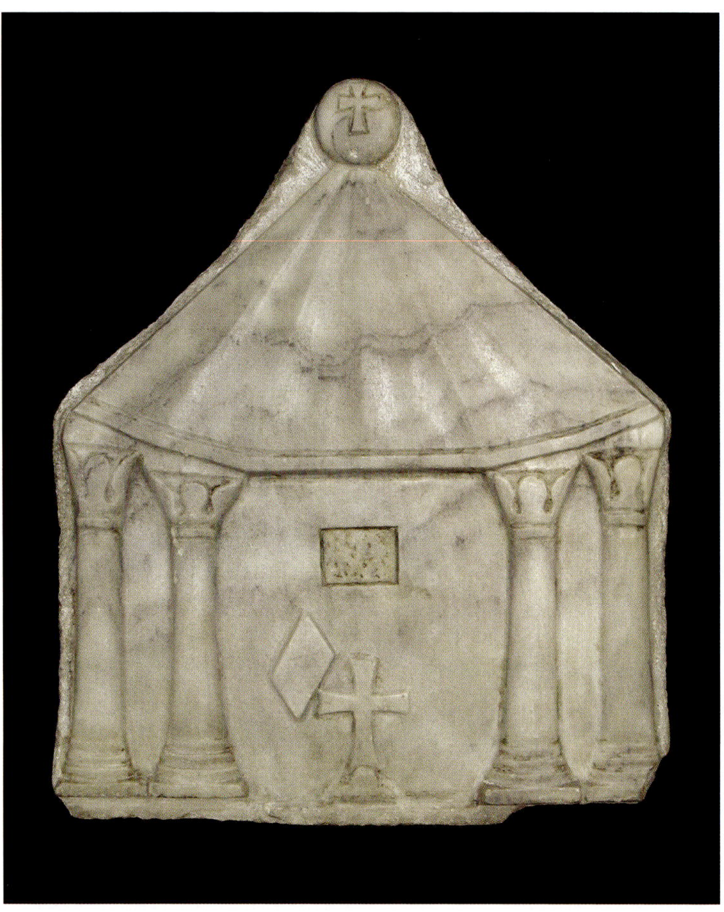

56. Obverse

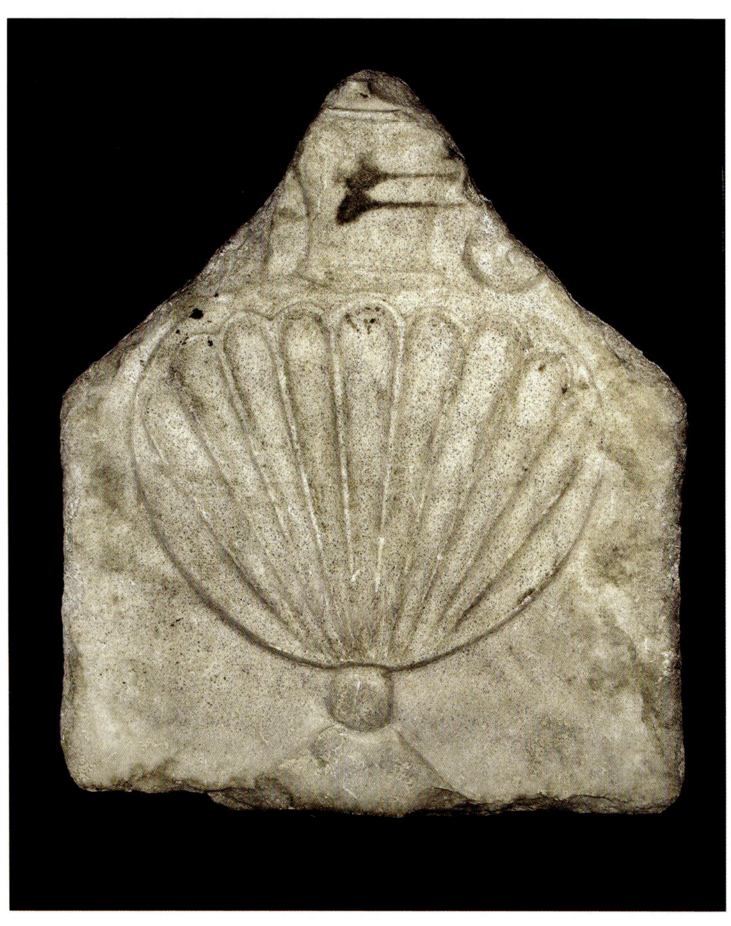

56. Reverse

56. Fragment of a Chancel Barrier with Double-Sided Relief Depicting the Holy Sepulcher and a Vase

Northern Palestine, late 6th or early 7th century
Marble
68.5 x 57 x 2.5 cm; depth of the relief: 2 cm

CONDITION: Both sides of this marble slab display a small degree of weathering. On the reverse, Vikan observed relatively fresh scuffing along the ridges of the vase's scalloped face.[1] The slab was trimmed substantially to the point of making it difficult to establish the dimensions of the original relief. The trimming followed the outline of the Holy Sepulcher on the obverse, thereby cutting off the vase's upper rim and handles on the reverse. In modern times, the plaque was set in a wall displaying the obverse, which acquired thick layers of paint in intense colors—blue, red, and green—setting off the individual elements of the relief. In 1982, the paint was removed mechanically from the surface of the plaque. The reverse bears only faint traces of polychromy.

ACQUISITION HISTORY: Acquired in 1938, possibly of Syrian provenance.

ACCESSION NUMBER: BZ.1938.56

On the obverse, the carving represents a canopy whose pyramidal roof is surmounted by a globe displaying an engraved cross. This canopy is a stripped-down rendition of the *Aedicule Christi*, the baldachin above the tomb of Christ (see cat. no. 41). The relief features four stocky columns with unfluted shafts and simply rendered Corinthian capitals. These four columns support a pyramidal roof consisting of six triangular segments, an unambiguous reference to the polygonal design of the original *Aedicule*.[2]

Within the space framed by the inner pair of columns, one finds along the central vertical axis a recessed rectangle at the top, a raised rhomb in the middle, and a cross rising above a tri-lobe base at the bottom. The first two represent Christ's vacant sepulcher, gaping open, as a symbol of the Resurrection: the rectangle stands for the empty tomb, while the rhomb signifies the lid placed aside, as described in all four gospels (Matthew 28:1-7, Mark 16:1-7, Luke 24:1-7, John 20:1-11). The tri-lobe shape with the cross rising above it is a representation of Golgotha, located not within the *Aedicule*, but in proximity to it.[3] Images representing these two sites appear on lead *ampullae* that pilgrims brought from the Holy Land as keepsakes (fig. 56A).[4]

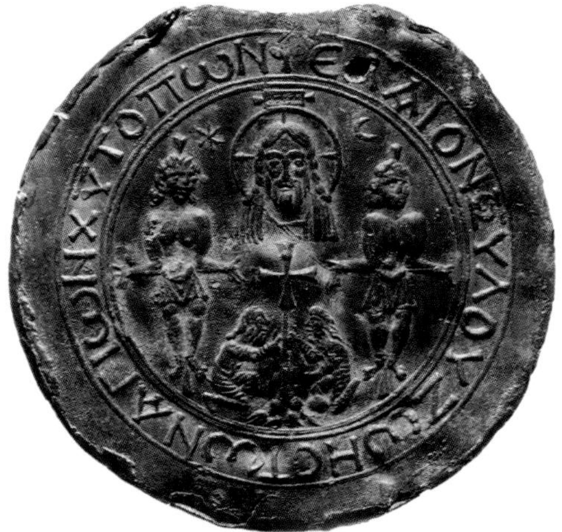

Obverse: Symbolic representation of the Crucifixion,
surrounding the scene is an inscription: +ЄΛΑΙΟΝ
ΖΥΛΟΥ ΖΩΗϹ ΤΩΝ ΑΓΙΩΝ Χ(ΡΙϹΤΟ)Υ ΤΟΓⳆΝ
("Oil of the wood of life from the holy sites of Christ")

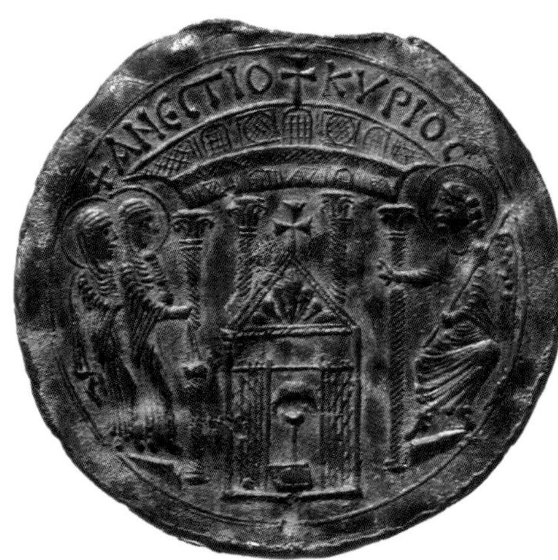

Reverse: Holy Women at the Tomb, Above the Tomb
of Christ inscription: +ΑΝΕϹΤΙ Ο +ΚΥΡΙΟϹ [sic]
("The Lord is Risen")

Figure 56A.
Lead Ampulla,
6th or 7th century,
diameter: 4.6 cm,
Dumbarton Oaks,
acc. no. BZ.1948.18.

On the marble relief, the rendition of these holy sites in Jerusalem is scant and unrestrained by obsessions with topographic precision because this is a symbolic composition. Its purpose is not to document the actual layout of the Holy Sepulcher complex but, instead, to make a powerful statement about the Redemption achieved through Christ's passion and his ensuing triumph over death. It is the *Aedicule's* contents that convey this message: the arrangement of the images along the main vertical axis expresses the notion that the Holy Tomb is a receptacle holding nothing less than the Salvation of mankind.

On the reverse, the relief features one very large vessel, a *kantharos*. It has a rounded body rising above a base consisting of a conical foot topped by a sphere. As if emanating from this sphere, eleven radial ribs fan out and upward, creating a form with a distinctive wavy edge. This arrangement emphatically elaborates on the common decorative motif of fluting, turning it into a shell design. By means of exaggerating a simple decorative motif, the carver bestowed on the *kantharos* an aura of distinction, if not sanctity. This pronounced pattern calls to mind scallop-headed niches whose shape was meant to exalt what they contained—the figures of holy persons or the sign of the cross.[5]

Commonly a *kantharos* would occupy the center of a composition with flanking deer or birds, a well-known visual formula representing the Fountain of Life in Paradise (cf. cat. nos. 13, 28-29, 57).[6] Evidently both compositions on this double-sided relief represent the spring emanating eternal life because they both depict a receptacle from which spiritual salvation flows.[7] As Vikan has argued, this slab could have been a chancel screen or a partition enclosing a baptismal font.[8] Either way, the connection between iconography and function would have been apparent to the medieval beholder.

Acknowledging this arrangement does not prevent one from appreciating its complexity. Most notably, there is a relevant distinction between these two images in the manner in which they convey their related messages. On the obverse, one encounters a direct rendition of an earthly manifestation of the divine—a specific structure at a particular holy site. In contrast, the reverse displays a composition that is at once allegorical and elliptical. The omission of the flanking animals or birds would have steered the viewer's attention to the deliberate and essential correlation between the two compositions on this double-sided relief. The explicit depiction on the obverse informs with meaning the less overt image on the back, as does this relief's position with its reverse facing a sacred space, whether an altar table or a baptismal font. To understand this intricate arrangement would have meant to immerse oneself in this sanctified space that brings with it the promise of a spiritual advancement and ultimate redemption.

AK

REFERENCES: *DOH* 1946, no. 14; *DOH* 1955, no. 47; Underwood 1950, 91-93, figs. 39-40; Ringbom 1958, 277-281, figs. 147, 153-154; Elbern 1964, 120, figs. 109, 110; Frolow 1965, 43, no. 2; Elbern 1975, 895, pl. XXX; Kötzsche 1991, 275, pl. 28d; Vikan 1995, no. 34; Biddle 1999, 26, fig. 24.

EXHIBITIONS: *Selection of Sculpture from the Early Byzantine Period*, Dumbarton Oaks, November 1995-August 1996.

1. Vikan 1995, 82.
2. As Vikan (1995, 83) pointed out, this relief's iconography offers no details that help resolve the debatable issue of the actual architectural articulation of the shrine above the Tomb of Christ. Cf. the discussion of the *Aedicule Christi's* shape in Biddle 1999, 65-88, esp. 69, figs. 64B, C, 66A, B; Wilkinson 1972, 83-97. Also, see Nitowski 1979 and Brooks 1921.
3. Cf. Wilkinson 1977, 83-95; Vikan 1995, 83, esp. note 4.
4. *DOCat* 1, 71-72, no. 87; Vikan 1995, 83, 34.1 a-b.
5. Urbana-Champaign, *Art and Holy Powers* 1989, 6-7.
6. The composition with the harts relates to the first verse of Psalm 42: "As the hart panteth after the water brooks, so panteth my soul after thee, O God." Vikan 1995, 84, 88-89, 90 note 7; Elbern 1964, 120; Ringbom 1958, 277-281; Underwood 1950, 51-53.
7. St. John of Damascus (c. 675-749) applied the epithet "life-giving" to the Holy Sepulcher, while Patriarch Photius of Constantinople (858-867, 877-886) referred to it as "the sepulcher, fountain of immortality," cited according to Underwood 1950, 96.
8. Vikan 1995, 84-85.

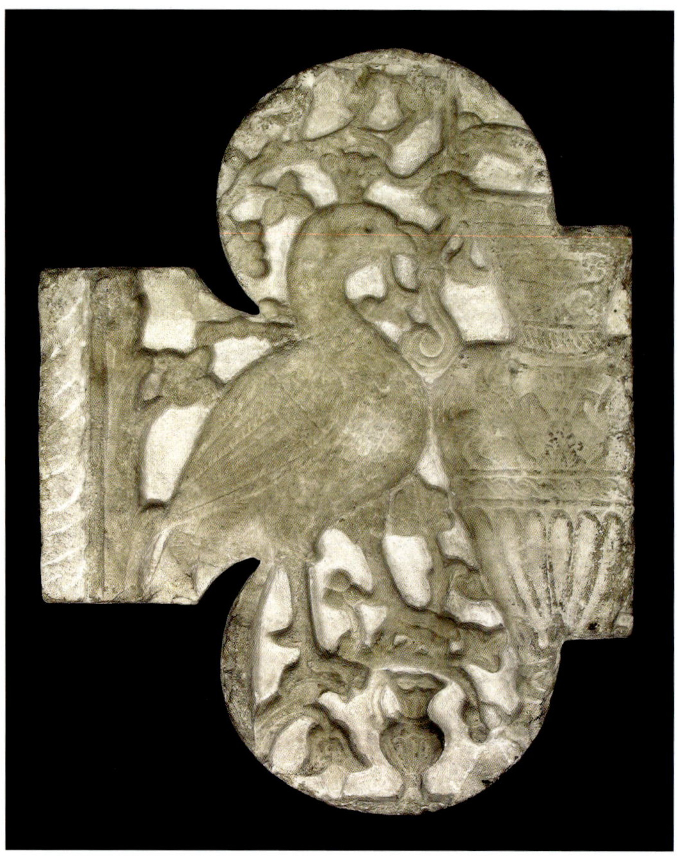

57. Obverse

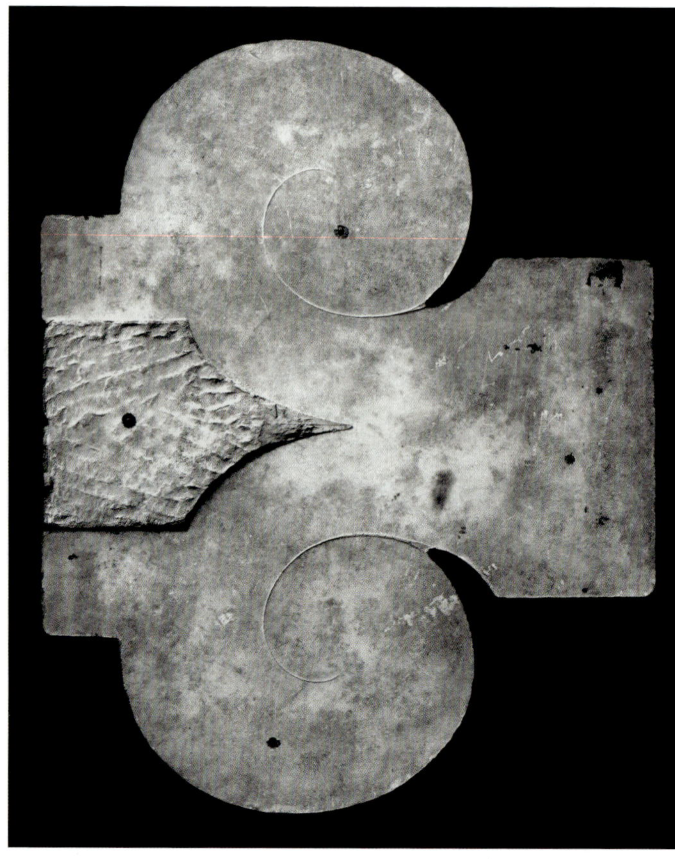

57. Reverse

57. *Fragment of a Chancel Panel (?) with Peacock*

Southern Italy, Salerno? 8th to 9th century
Marble
63 x 48.5 x 2.5 cm; depth of the relief: 1.5 cm

Condition: This plaque's obverse has acquired a grainy texture, most likely through weathering. Also, sometime in the past, it was imbedded face down into a wall or a floor.[1] This is a fragment from a larger rectangular relief, which measured approximately 75 x 93 cm.[2] Sections of the relief's original border survived to the left and at the bottom of the fragment. The original plaque was cut into two parts, each of them further trimmed in a nearly identical manner.

Acquisition History: Acquired in 1936 from Paris. The sellers, M. and R. Stora, alleged that the piece dated to the twelfth century and came from the cathedral on the island of Torcello, located in the Venetian lagoon.[3] The cathedral contains similar choir screen panels, as well as eleventh-century Byzantine-style wall mosaics. Given the Blisses' interest in Byzantium, the attribution to Torcello, erroneous as it has proven to be, might have been a factor determining the decision to purchase this relief.

Vikan established the origin of the relief by studying its counterpart cut from the same original marble plaque. The other slightly smaller piece—63.5 x 43.5 cm—belongs to the collection of Mr. and Mrs. Louis Jones. The relief is built into a wall in the collectors' house in Yorkshire, England. Vikan examined both

this fragment and the notes taken by the antiquities dealer, Dr. Kurt Cassirer, who had sold the relief to the Joneses. Cassirer's records revealed that in the early 1930s he purchased both the Dumbarton Oaks and the Yorkshire pieces from a Salerno stonemason who collected rejected fragments from churches undergoing reconstruction. Most likely, until as late as the 1920s, both fragments remained built into the cathedral of Salerno, which underwent reconstruction in the early 1930s.[4]

Accession number: BZ.1936.19

On the obverse, the carving represents a peacock flanking a large vessel that occupies the fragment's right section (cf. cat. nos. 13, 28-29). From this vessel emanate the curving tendrils of a vine sprouting leaves, buds, and small clusters of grapes. Amidst this dense foliage, the peacock stands on a thicker stem and holds a small budding tendril in its beak.[5] The bird's closed tail fits into what once must have been the relief's lower left corner, a section of the plaque that was cut off. The tendrils above the peacock shelter a much smaller bird also facing right, while in the lower part of the relief one sees a little vessel with a single handle.

The carving on the Dumbarton Oaks relief finds its mirror reflection in the Yorkshire fragment (fig. 57A). Here, too, a large bird is rendered in profile while curving tendrils surround a little bird and a diminutive vessel. For all the obvious symmetry, there are notable differences—only the two small birds have an identical appearance, while the large birds flanking the vase and the little vessels are all different. Instead of the common juxtaposition of two peacocks, on the right side of the original relief was a decidedly different bird, referred to as a cock, slightly bigger than its counterpart, sporting erect pointed ears and a tail emphatically curving upward.[6]

The focal point of the original relief was the large vase. The shallow carving on the vase's middle section includes two griffins flanking a vessel, in this case not a vase but a goblet. The design on the bowl of this smaller vessel reflects the banded register above and suggestively blends upward with it. Atop this register rise highly stylized vines, echoing the relief's overall foliage. In fact, the same hierarchical formula appears in three renditions across the relief: starting with the griffins, goblet, and its vines; expanding to the two large birds, central vase, and the surrounding tendrils; and, finally, encompassing the small birds and the diminutive vessels at the extreme edges of the foliage.

This arrangement certainly contributes to the relief's visual cohesiveness. Yet, even more, the composition with the griffins infuses with order and meaning the realm that spreads out and around the depicted object on which they appear. As a result, the design of the entire piece generates the notion that the relief itself expands beyond its borders into the realm of the beholders in order to draw them into the symbolically charged space of swirling vine tendrils. These observations lead one to consider the correlation between this relief's iconography and function. If indeed the carved plaque was originally a part of a chancel screen, then its design not only marked an important threshold but made a statement about this boundary's potential for permeability in both physical and spiritual terms.

AK

References: *DOH* 1946, no. 48; *DOH* 1955, no. 54; *DOH* 1967, no. 41; Glass 1970, no. 2; Vikan 1995, no. 35.

1. When examing the relief in order to prepare its publication, Vikan observed traces of plaster in the crevices of the obverse and remnants of colored clay in the recessed areas on the reverse; Vikan 1995, 87.
2. Ibid., 88.
3. R. Stora's description of the relief from January 20, 1936, reads: "Bas relief en marbre, représentant un oiseau dans des feuillages, stylisés, devant un vase décoré de deux animaux ailés et affrontés. Bas relief provenant de l'Eglise de Torcello, Italie." Cf. the object's dossier at the Byzantine Collection of Dumbarton Oaks.
4. Vikan 1995, 88 and 90.
5. Cf. the detailed discussion of this relief's iconography in Vikan 1995, 97-89.
6. Several elements of this relief, including the heraldic composition with griffins and the exotic cock with pointed ears, bear a resemblance to works of Sassanian art. On the Sassanian motifs in works of art created in medieval Italy, see the comments of Vikan and the older publications he cites. When addressing the general question concerning the role of Sassanian and Early Islamic luxury art in the proliferations of these motifs in Italy, Vikan emphasizes the strong possibility of a Constantinopolitan intermediary. The most likely context of origin for this relief appears to be the building program carried out in Salerno and Benevento by the Langobardic ruler Arechis II (758-788), who maintained close ties with Byzantium. Cf. Vikan 1995, 89, as well as 91-93, no. 36; Glass 1991, 3-4 with older references.

58. Fragment of a Frieze Sarcophagus with Christ Blessing the Loaves and Fishes

Rome, second to third decade of 4th century
Marble (Carrara according to the analysis of Norman Herz in 1991)
30.5 x 25 to 26 x 3 to 9.5 cm

Condition: Broken on three sides, backside rough-picked; abrasions and chips over entire surface and broken-off noses of figures carved in high relief.

Acquisition History: Acquired in 1959. Formerly in the Collection of Robert E. Hecht, New York.

Accession number: BZ.1959.3

Only the upper edge of this marble fragment is intact and shows the original frame of the figural relief. A notable feature of this piece is the space left between the heads of the figures and the upper edge of the frieze.

Although only parts of three figures are preserved, one can identify them through specific details of their representation, as well as reconstruct the original context within which they appear. It is also possible to determine the approximate date when the marble relief was carved and the place where it was produced.

The frontally standing figure at the right represents the youthful Christ. His right hand rests on a small cylindrical container carried by a figure approaching from the left. The man turned toward Christ, with the long bearded face and bald forehead, may be identified as St. Paul. To the left, carved in low relief, is the head of a man who turns away from Christ. This detail clearly indicates a scene from the frieze that preceded the one involving Christ and St. Paul.

The comparison of the fragment to a series of similar reliefs on Roman sarcophagi—for instance, the famous Sabinus sarcophagus in the Vatican (cf. fig. 58A)—proves that it represents the most popular scene found in Early Christian sculpture, namely, the Blessing of the Loaves and Fishes. The complete scene shows a third figure on the other side of Christ, offering a second basket. At the feet of the group, we usually find a row of baskets filled with bread and fishes.

A second piece from the same sarcophagus was offered for sale with the Dumbarton Oaks fragment, but its location is now

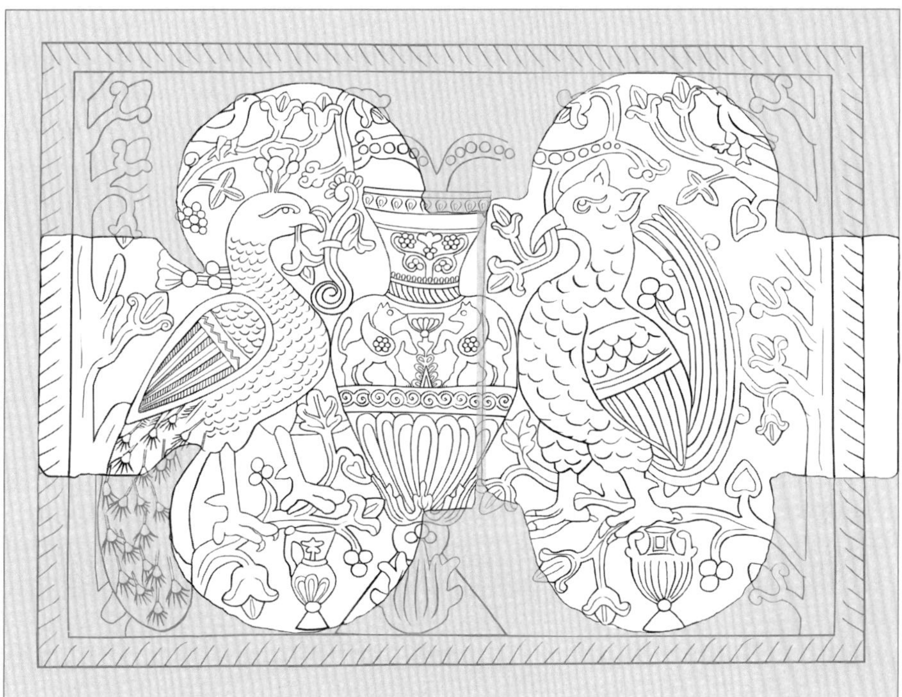

Figure 57A. Reconstruction including the Yorkshire panel. Drawing by Meredith S. Boyter, after Vikan 1995, pls. 35A, 35.1a, 35.2.

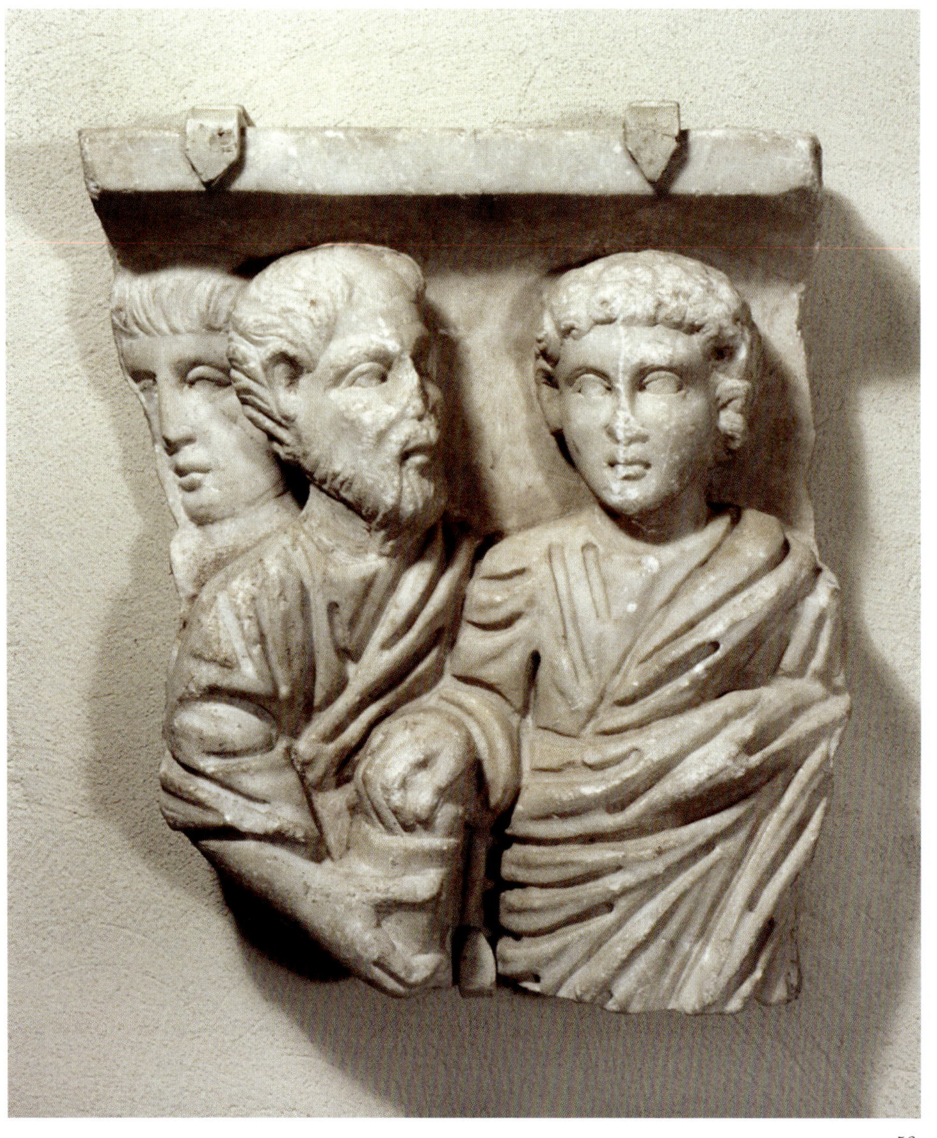

58.

unknown (see fig. 58B).[1] This fragment shows only two figures: Christ turned in profile, presumably healing the blind man, and a witnessing apostle.

The Blessing of the Loaves and Fishes is the most popularly depicted scene in early Christian art, represented even more often than the Raising of Lazarus.[2] The complete frieze sarcophagus may have shown several scenes depicting the miracles of Christ, which would have been flanking a central figure of an orant, a female figure in the gesture of praying.

Typical features of these relief sarcophagi are figures that are arranged in a dense row with all of their heads carved at the very same equal height (i.e., isocephalic). These would be usually in groupings of three persons—Christ flanked by two apostles—along with the witnessing figures in the background, often only shown as shallow heads or faces. Instead of creating the illusion of an open space in which figures move freely, the carver repeated nearly identical units.

These sarcophagi must have been produced in Rome during the early decades of the fourth century. The evidence for this date is not so much the serially produced scheme or composition; rather, it is the specific way in which the figures are carved—the method of production or style—that might reflect the practice of an individual workshop.[3] Instead of modeling the drapery in a manner expressing the movement of the figures, the carver drilled a dense series of holes and channels in several lines across the roughly shaped figures all dressed in tunics and pallia. Nevertheless, looking at the delicate faces of Christ and the apostle to his right, it becomes

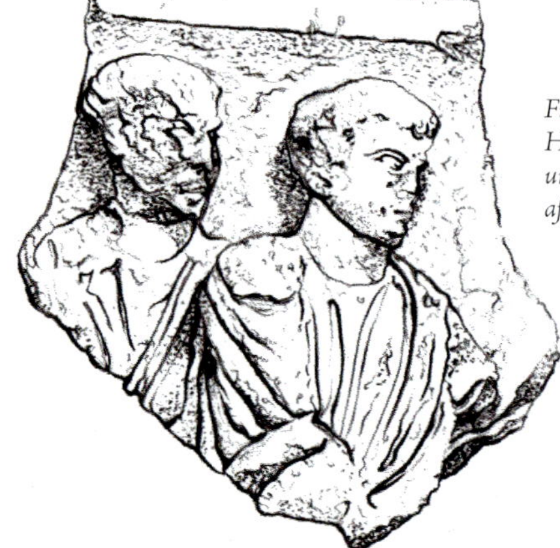

Figure 58B. Fragment of a frieze sarcophagus: Healing of the Blind Man (?), Location unknown. Drawing by Meredith S. Boyter, after Vikan 1995, pl. 12.2.

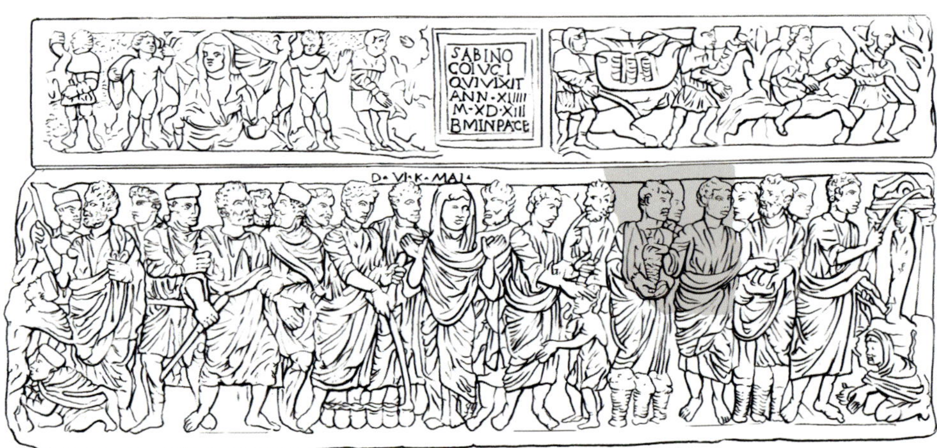

Figure 58A. Frieze sarcophagus with biblical scenes, Vatican City, Museo Pio Cristiano, no. 161. Drawing by Meredith S. Boyter, after Vikan 1995, pl. 12.1.

evident that this specific way of carving is
not due to a decline in craftsmanship, but
is a reflection of a particular current in the
style of fourth-century relief carving. The
landmark for that most important stylistic
development of Early Christian sculpture
is the Arch of Constantine, dedicated to
the emperor by the Roman Senate in 315.
The manner in which the carvers worked
the friezes of the triumphal arch is quite
the same as here, and both result in figures
that seem to be packed between two imagi-
nary planes.

Also, two fragments of Roman sarcophagi in particular are closely related
to the stylistic features of the Dumbarton
Oaks fragment, one in a private collection in
Heidelberg, Germany, and the other in the
Museo Archeologico Nazionale, Arezzo.[4]
The figures of both fragments not only
share the same proportions and an identical
way of carving drapery, but also they have
in common a very similar and distinctly
delicate treatment of faces.

GB

REFERENCES: *DOH* 1967, no. 18; Vikan 1995,
25-27, no. 12, pl. 12; Dresken-Weiland 1998, no. 27a.
EXHIBITIONS: Dumbarton Oaks, *Selections of
Sculpture from the Early Byzantine Period*, November
1995-August 1996.

1. Vikan 1995, 25, fig. 12.2.
2. Lange 1996, 122-123.
3. Eichner 1977, passim.
4. Dresken-Weiland 1998, 12, nos. 27-29, pl. 12, 3-6.

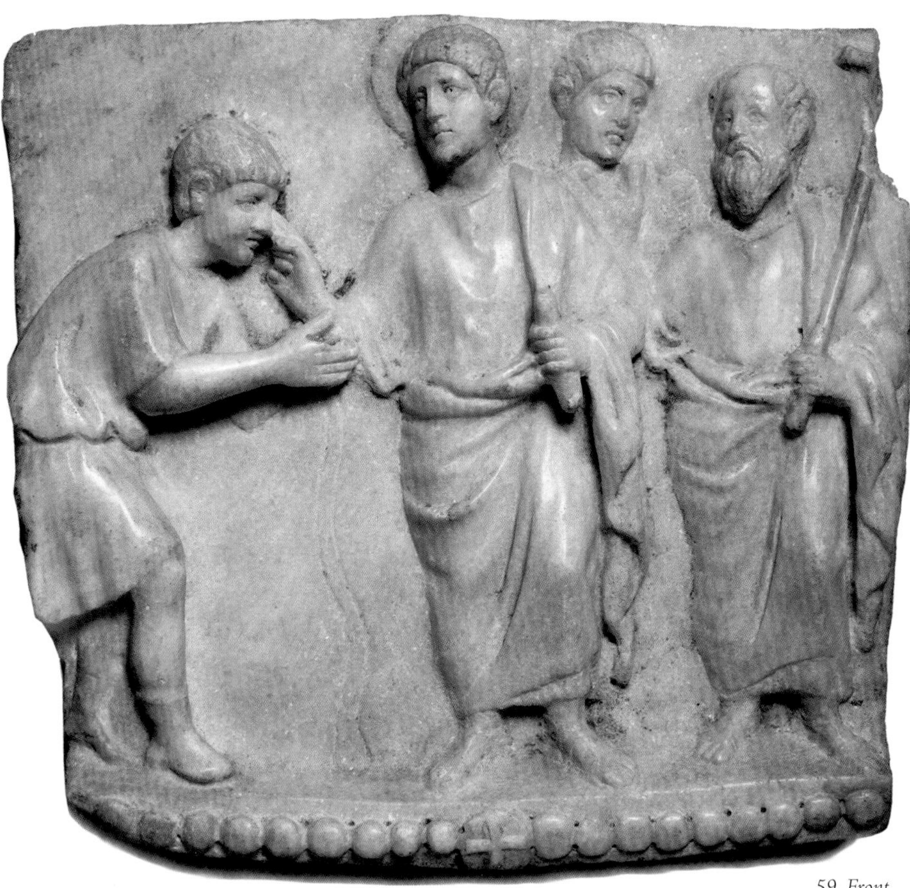

59. Front

59. Relief with the Healing of the Blind Man

Constantinopolitan style of the late 4th century
Fine grain white marble, most likely from Carrara[1]
26.5 x 27.5 x 27.5 to 25.5 cm

CONDITION: The marble slab's edges—top, left,
and right—are uneven. The bottom rim is curved
slightly, and it preserves ornaments rendered in a
manner suggesting that it could have been the edge
of an originally larger object.

ACQUISITION HISTORY: It was acquired
supposedly in Egypt for the collection of Levi de
Benzion, Paris. Nevertheless, the sale of the de Benzion collection did not include this piece. Mr. and
Mrs. Bliss purchased the relief from R. Stora and
donated it to Dumbarton Oaks on April 14, 1952.

ACCESSION NUMBER: BZ.1952.8

Approaching from the left, the blind man
supports himself with a walking stick while
bowing and extending his right arm toward
Christ. In the center of the composition,
Christ enacts the cure by placing his finger
on the young man's sightless eyes (Mark
8:22-25). Two apostles standing to the right
witness the miracle: St. Paul, who is next
to Christ, and a second beardless disciple
behind them.

Ernst Kitzinger argued that this relief is
representative of the visual culture during
the time of Emperor Theodosios I (379-
395), who made Christianity the official
religion of the Roman state. The so-called
Theodosian renaissance often combined
Christian subjects with the formal qualities
that previously distinguished refined pagan
art. Kitzinger asserted that the relief was a
fragment of a very large circular tabletop,
approximately 2 m in diameter, thereby
explaining the curving bottom edge. The
shallow carving appears consistent with
other examples of relief decoration on
tabletops.[2] Nevertheless, a rarely mentioned
feature of this panel, the undercutting that
appears below the right forearm of the blind
man, speaks against such association. Detached from its background, this part of the
relief would have been precariously fragile,
especially if it formed part of a tabletop.[3]

Several factors contribute to the visual
appeal of this relief. First of all, the scene's
accomplished composition fits perfectly
within the rectangular space. Even though
the top of St. Paul's cross is missing, all
other elements essential for the work's
aesthetic impact remain fully intact. It
would be difficult to believe that accidental

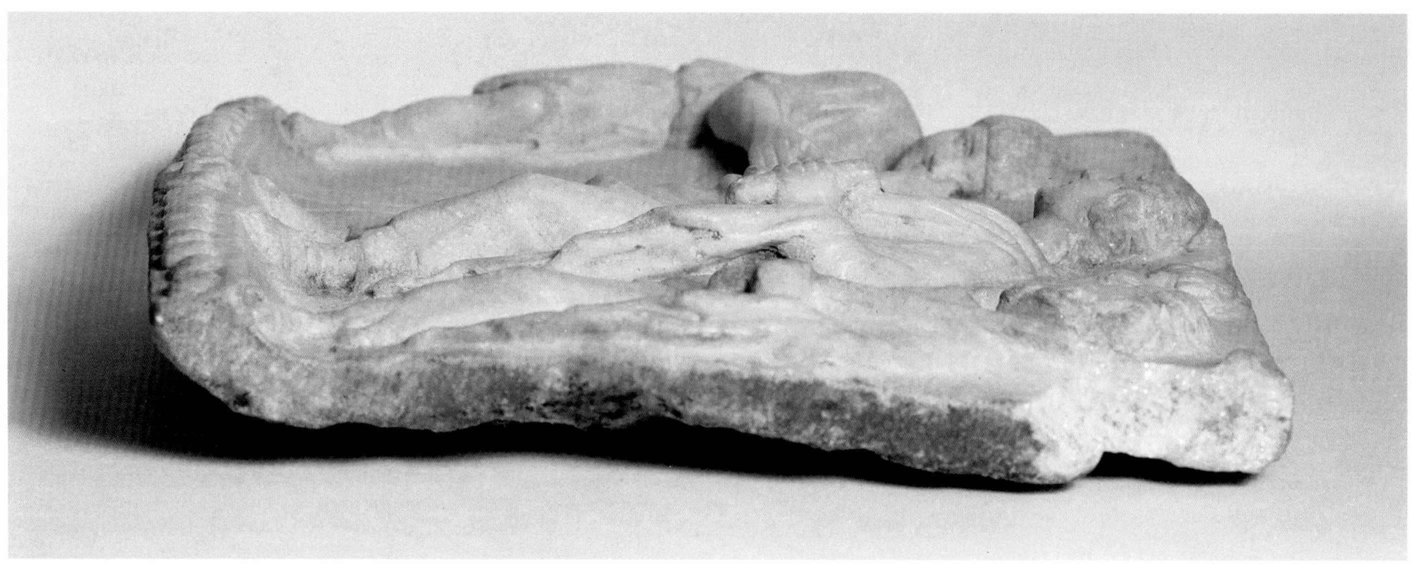

59. Side view showing the undercutting below the right forearm of the blind man

breakage could have produced such a fault-less piece.[4] Except for the odd treatment of the blind man's right forearm, one finds no elements of undercutting, commonly seen in Late Antique marble reliefs. Instead, this relief's surface displays smooth transitions between the polished raised forms and the flat background. The carver enhanced the relief's three-dimensional quality by using a whole set of devices to manipulate the sense of depth. The elements of the composition that are set deeper into the space of the relief—the blind man's left arm and leg, as well as the young apostle's right hand hold-ing a scroll—barely emerge from the flat surface. Contributing to the uniform texture of the relief is the rendition of the blind man's walking stick, which is engraved on the surface. One curving incised line renders the twisted tree limb being used as a cane. Although one might find some of these individual devices in different Late Antique works, their combination in a single relief is virtually unknown in the art of the late fourth century. Curiously, it is precisely this treatment of relief surface that is common in Italian quattrocento sculpture.[5]

The widespread admiration for this relief notwithstanding, experts have become increasingly concerned with its enigmatic character. The relief has no documented history before the year 1952 and, more to the point, it does not conform readily to the firmly authenticated examples of Early Byzantine stone carving. The verdict came in 1981, when the piece was included in an exhibition displaying forgeries of Byzantine art. In the exhibition catalogue, Boyd and Vikan presented the arguments asserting that this relief dated to c. 1951. The authors identified the actual Theodosian renaissance models that the modern carver emulated.[6]

The *Healing of the Blind Man* is the creation of an able carver who must have been well versed in matters of art history. The carver seemed to have been aware of the qualities that would make an Early Byzantine relief desirable to connoisseurs.[7] Aside from the excellence of its subtle modeling, there is the carefully arranged composition itself, expressing the restrained exchange of figures that are at once dignified and humble, serene yet poignant. In general, these are some of the qualities that were most admired in Late Byzantine painting and in early Italian Renaissance art. One cannot help but think of the *Healing of the Blind Man* as an artistic commentary on mid-twentieth-century perceptions of Byzantine art and its pivotal role as a mediator between the classical tradition and

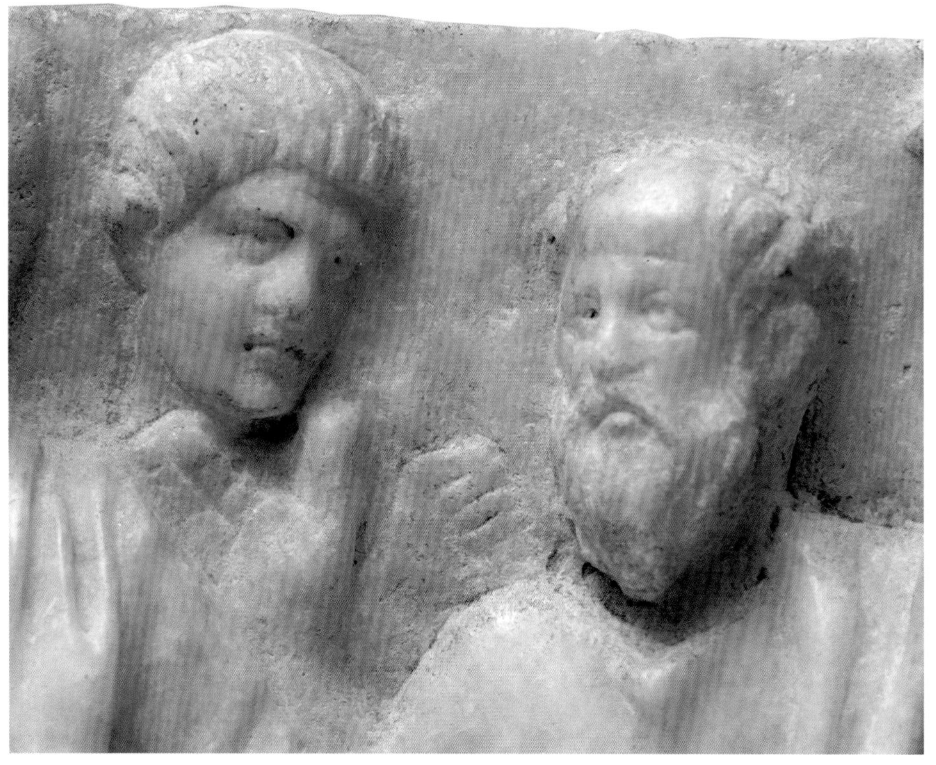

59. Heads of apostles (detail)

the early Italian Renaissance.[8] In effect, by demonstrating that the *Healing of the Blind Man* relief was a modern forgery, Boyd and Vikan brought to light a genuine piece of visual evidence embodying a particular view of Byzantine art and its place in the history of Western visual culture.

AK

References: *DOH* 1955, no. 41; Kitzinger 1960, 19-42; Testini 1964, 129, fig. 22; *DOH* 1967, no. 19; Severin 1970, 227-228, fig. 14; Kitzinger 1977, 38-38, fig. 72; New York, *Age of Spirituality* 1977, no. 399; Dumbarton Oaks, *Questions of Authenticity* 1981, 5-6, no. 1, figs. a, b, c; Kitzinger 1984, 78-79, fig. 72, esp. note 43 on 256; Kiilerich and Torp 1990, 102 and 115, fig. 9; Downing 1998, 269-270, note 34, fig. 18; Knipp 1998, 30-32, 40-41; Avalos 1999, book cover.

Exhibitions: *Age of Spirituality. Late Antique and Early Christian Art, 3rd-7th Century*, Metropolitan Museum of Art, New York, November 1977-February 1978; *Questions of Authenticity Among the Arts of Byzantium*, Dumbarton Oaks, January 7-May 11, 1981.

1. In a letter from February 27, 1991, kept in the object's dossier, Professor Norman Herz, director of the Center for Archaeological Sciences at the University of Georgia, writes: "the isotopic values for sample No. 52.8 do overlap into the fields of Carrara marble…. if No. 52.8 is relatively fine grained, it may well be from Carrara." Cf. the dossier of the object at Dumbarton Oaks.
2. Kitzinger 1960, 22-23, figs, 8, 12; Mauroeidi 1999, nos. 8-10.
3. Kitzinger 1960, fig. 9.
4. Indeed, recarving could have enhanced the aesthetic appeal of an older sculptural fragment by introducing certain relevant details. Nevertheless, ultraviolet examination has revealed no traces of such recarving, thus indicating that this relief was made with the intention of looking like a fragment; see Dumbarton Oaks, *Questions of Authenticity* 1981, 5.
5. Although until now left unmentioned, the similarities between the *Healing of the Blind* and Italian quattrocento sculpture do help explain why this relief was liked so much. Notably, the apparent parallels for our relief can be found in famous quattrocento sculptures reproduced in most twentieth-century studies of Italian art; see the works cited later in this note. The connection is relevant whether or not one considers this relief to be an authentic Theodosian renaissance work. Those who believe in its authenticity might view the parallels as evidence for the common sources of Late Antique and quattrocento art. Nevertheless, from a different perspective these similarities emerge as references to the models that a modern carver might have sought to emulate.

   Set within an imperfect square, the succinct and cohesive composition on the marble relief with its strong vertical axis calls to mind Luca della Robbia's panels for the bronze doors of the Florence Duomo, 1464-1469. Further similarities involve the shallow relief and the neutral background. See Freeman 1901, 91-97; Marquand 1914, 183-188, the individual panels on pp. 188-195, figs. 120-131; for more recent discussion, cf. Pope-Hennessy 1980, 67-72, 258-261, cat. no. 47, figs. 112-121; Poeschke 1990, 129-130, figs. 172, 173.

   The carver of the *Healing of the Blind Man* modeled the young apostle's figure in such a manner that the face is in deeper relief, while the shoulders are much shallower. A textbook example of this device can be seen in the back-row musicians in della Robbia's Cantoria reliefs of the *Cithara Players* and *Drummers*; see Marquand 1914, 12-13, fig. 11; Pope-Hennessy 1980, 19-21, 225-231, cat. no. 1, pls. 1, 7, 10; Poeschke 1990, 125-126, fig. 45.

   Finally, the incised walking stick of the blind man finds a parallel in Mino da Fiesole's panel *St. Jerome in the Wilderness and in His Study*, 1429-1484, where in the wilderness background behind the saint the snakes are engraved as negative forms. Cf. Athens, *Palazzo Venezia* 1996, 40-41, no. 1.

   I would like to express my gratitude to Shelley Zuraw, who generously shared with me her knowledge of Italian Renaissance sculpture.
6. For example, St. Paul's portrait combines the face of the same apostle on the so-called Prince's Sarcophagus from Constantinople with the figure of St. Peter as it appears on a marble relief in Berlin. The Berlin relief provided the model for the figure of the blind man as well. Furthermore, Christ's face replicates the marble portrait head of Emperor Arkadios (395-408), excavated in 1949 and published in 1951. It was only fourteen months later that the *Healing of the Blind Man* relief was offered for sale to Dumbarton Oaks; see Dumbarton Oaks, *Questions of Authenticity* 1981, 5-6.
7. See Nelson's essay in this volume.
8. See Dalton 1911a, 2-3 and the discussion of "La question Byzantine" in Diehl 1910, 668-702. Cf. also Mullett and Scott 1981, as well as some recent brief comments in Cormack 1997, 2-5.

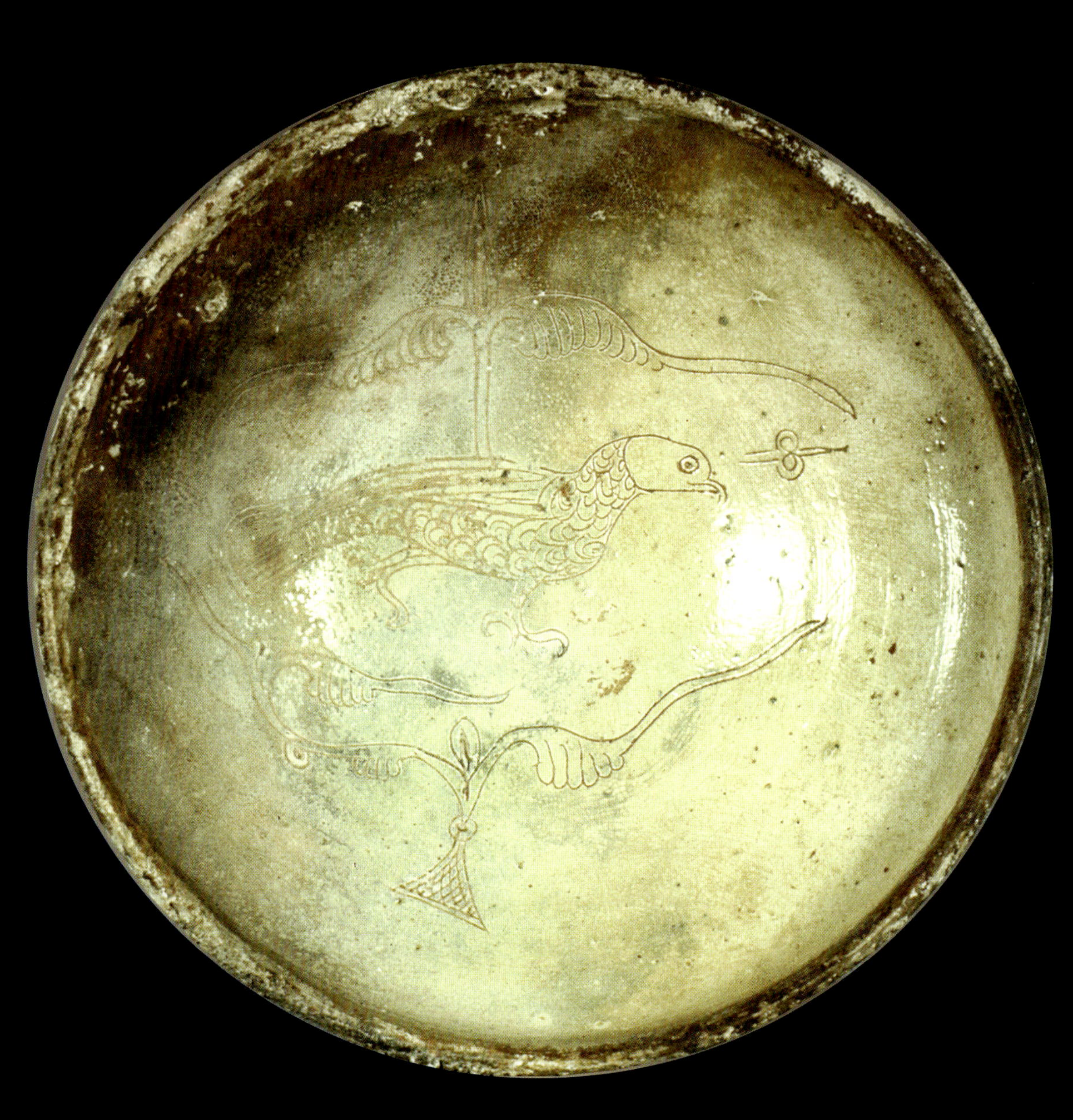

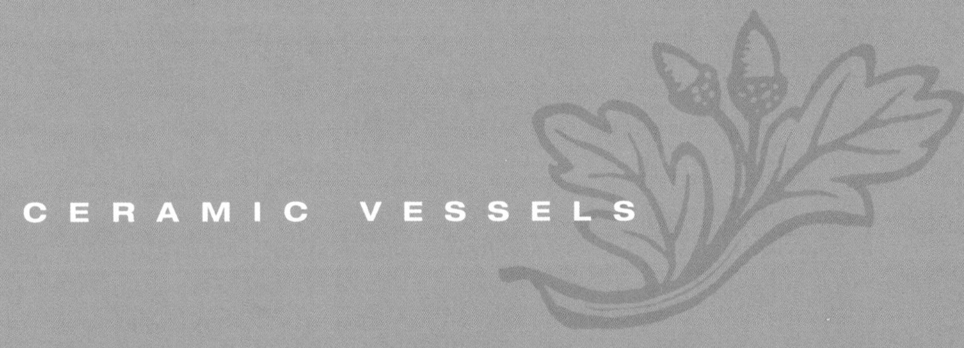

CERAMIC VESSELS

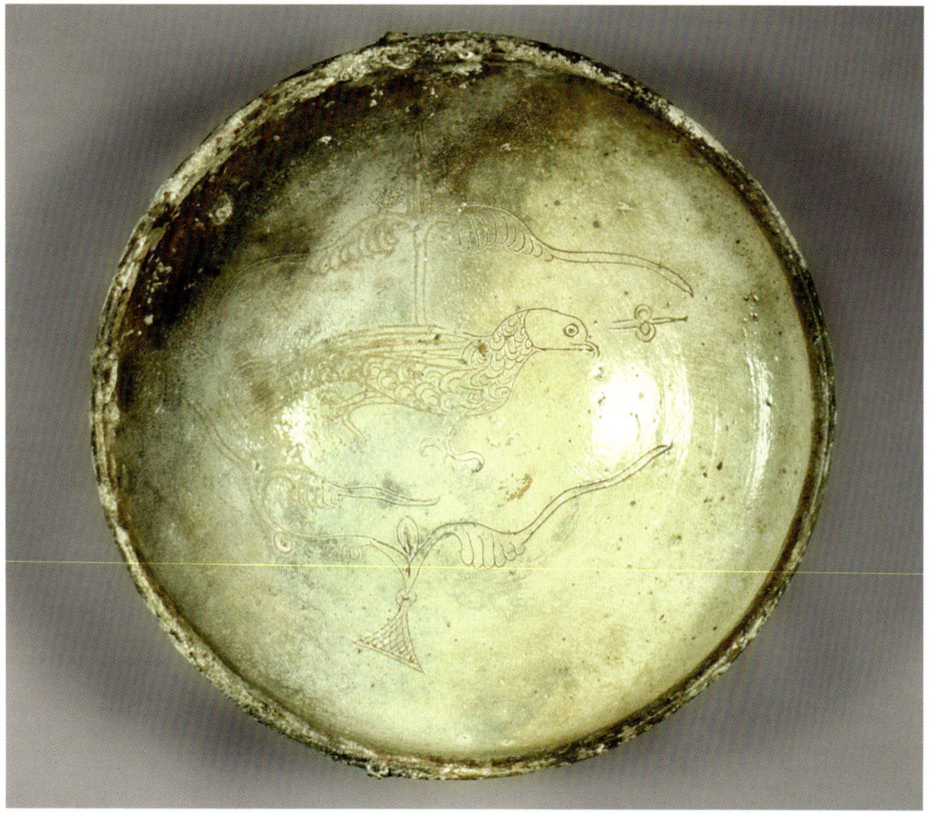

60. Interior

in a kind of artisanal mass production.[3]

The process of making this bowl began by throwing local clay on the wheel; there, a shallow segment of a sphere would soon emerge under the potter's hands until downward pressing altered the direction on the exterior to finish the rim with a slight inward roll that strengthens the lip, visually and structurally. A subtly splayed ring-foot was formed separately and attached to the base. This spherical shaping, along with a similar rim and foot, characterizes several of the bowls from the Pelagonnesos-Alonnysos shipwreck.[4]

The clay was left to dry until it could be slip-coated, usually by dipping. The slip, a suspension of whitish clay in water, covered and lightened the surface, especially on the inside where it had to be thick enough when dry to engrave. A sharp tool cut through to the dark surface underneath, making the engraved lines appear in strong contrast under the clear shine of the glaze.[5]

The engraved bird striding across the center, bracketed by leafy stems, is one of many variations of a favorite central motif. The work requires an experienced freehand technique, since the engraved line permits no corrections. To create the long sweep of these dancing branches and leaf-tips looping in curved extensions within the bowl's contours, the potter may have used the wheel for support, rotating and stopping it at will as the tool drew whimsical departures from strict symmetry.

Given the deftness of this irregularity, the bird presents several anomalies. Like a falcon or eagle on an imperial silk, it has the unpatterned head above the plumage in a double-outlined scale-pattern, huge talons,

60. Shallow Bowl of Glazed Pottery Engraved with a Striding Bird

Byzantine, 12th century
Red earthenware covered on the interior with engraved white slip and transparent lead glaze (*sgraffito* ware)
Height: 8 cm; diameter: 24 cm

CONDITION: Marine encrustations, almost entirely removed from the interior, still cling to the bowl's exterior and rim. The unevenly yellowed glaze shows some eruption of limestone grit through the surface in firing, as well as some pitting from abrasion; above and behind the bird it appears partly devitrified and mottled with dark blue-gray staining.

ACQUISITION HISTORY: Acquired by purchase from an unspecified source, September 1958, and said by the dealer to come from Mytilene.

ACCESSION NUMBER: BZ.1958.101

This shiny, engraved ceramic tableware imitates models in silver or other metals.[1] Examples found in museum collections come either from known excavations in Greece or Turkey or else, like this bowl, through the art market as undocumented finds from shipwrecks. Cargoes shipped from their places of manufacture supplied a popular demand.[2] The making of vessels decorated with engraved slip under glaze was a major occupation for potters from the Komnenian (1081-1185) through the Palaiologan (1261-1453) periods. They could complete a number of similar bowls

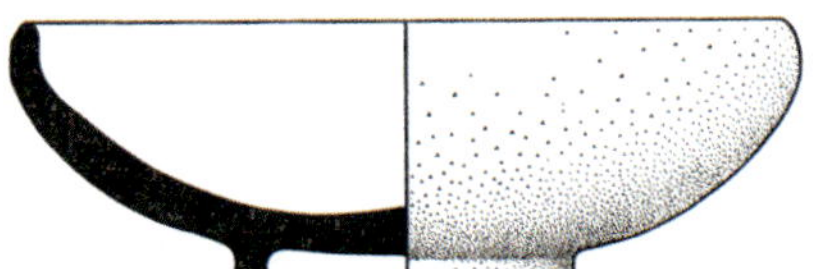

60. Cross section. Redrawn by Meredith S. Boyter, after Talbot Rice 1966, no. 4, text fig. D.

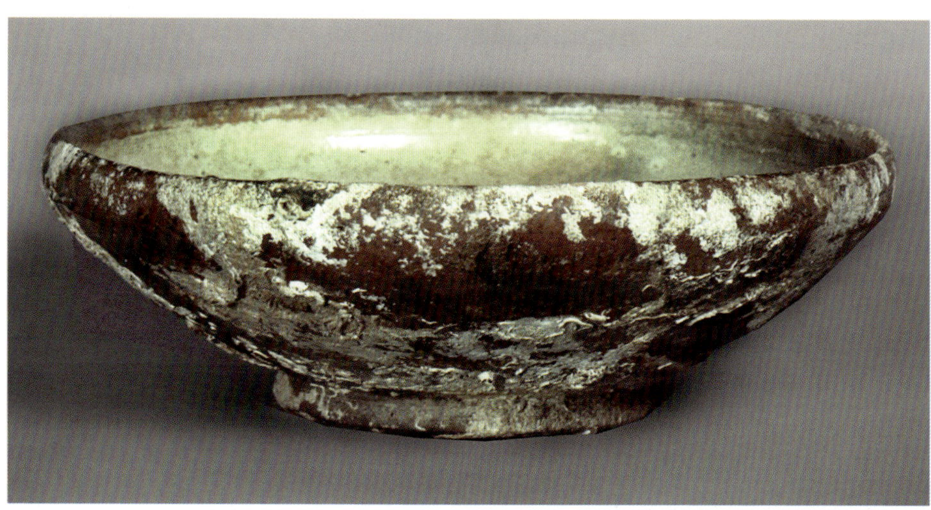

60. Profile

and a meat-tearing hooked beak.[6] The popular formula, varied here, brackets the bird between two plants; in this bowl, the spearlike sprig above the bird's back, with winglike branches, would have served well as a falconer's lure.[7] Yet, instead of keeping the traditional upright pose of an alert and noble raptor, this bird thrusts its flattened head forward, bobbing and strutting with the insouciance of a pigeon while the end of its body drags along a raptor's long tail and wing as if they were a fish's fin and tail.[8] If these departures from the usual imagery are no accidents, then they must be a purposeful joke, a mixture of fish and fowl, of raptor and prey.

EDM

REFERENCES: Talbot Rice 1966, no. 4, fig. 7 and text fig. D; *DOH* 1967, 88, no. 304.

1. The existence and appearance of engraved metal vessels in Byzantium has had to be inferred mostly from a very few extant Byzantine copper-alloy vessels, from their Islamic counterparts, and from patterns apparently copied in other media. For an important new publication, see Ballian and Drandaki 2003.

2. See Papanikola-Bakirtzi 1999, 118-157, for a good summary of the shipwreck evidence for the trade in these ceramics. The dark, bluish stains and the apparent devitrification seen on the Dumbarton Oaks bowl occur frequently in glazed slipware vessels rescued from shipwrecks after centuries undersea. Cleaning with acid or abrasives to remove marine encrustations frequently takes its toll on the glaze. Laboratory examination and cleaning by Pete Dandridge of a bowl in the collection of the Metropolitan Museum of Art to determine what had caused the bluish stains proved inconclusive.

3. See Papanikola-Bakirtzi 1999, 17-20, on the various glazed wares current in this period; p. 158 on workshops for this pottery, and for the statistics on production at Corinth, Guy Sanders, ibid., 159-164. For interpretation of the pottery as a popular art reflecting or mocking aristocratic taste, see Dauterman Maguire 1997.

4. Papanikola-Bakirtzi 1999, nos. 134-142 illustrate a variety of shapes in this cargo.

5. The sources of the pale slips have yet to be identified with the known white clay beds outside Constantinople or Nicaea, or with any other locality. Mary K. Seyfarth has demonstrated the stages of manufacture for this pottery by making a bowl to represent every step of the process, for two exhibitions, as illustrated in the frontmatter of Papanikola-Bakirtzi 1999.

6. Papanikola-Bakirtzi 1999, nos. 134-142; nos. 138 and 139, both from the Pelagonnesos-Alonnysos shipwreck, depict birds with this kind of body plumage.

7. See New York, *The Glory of Byzantium* 1997, no. 184 (E. D. Maguire); Kypraniou 1995, nos. 18, 19, and 27 depict an alternative type of falconer's lure—a skewer with a tempting tidbit at its tip—that was not new

in the fourteenth century when these scenes were engraved.

8. For plant-bracketed falcons from the Pelagonnesos-Alonnysos shipwreck, see Papanikola-Bakirtzi 1999, as follows. Nos. 138, 139, and 140, one in a nearly horizontal posture, the others upright, look back over their shoulders toward a branch-shaped tree or scrolling stem; these birds have descended on their quarries. Two of the birds are hybrids or composites: no. 141, exceptionally, is centered and seen from behind with its wings spread, and with a griffin's ears added to its head; and no. 144, a fan-tailed bird with a raptor's legs and beak. A bowl from the Kastellorizou shipwreck, no. 181, dwarfs the raptor between large bracketing branches. For another variation, see Armstrong 1991, fig. 12, a possible hybrid (or a knowing slip of the engraver's hand) since the beak disappears into a muzzle as the bird, in a transgenic gesture like a ruminant mammal, bites the end of the stem. An unambiguous raptor takes the same pose in New York, *The Glory of Byzantium* 1997, no. 187 (E. D. Maguire). Further variations on pottery in U.S. collections may be seen in photographs assembled at Dumbarton Oaks in the *Census of Early Christian and Byzantine Objects in North American Collections* and the *Census of Byzantine Textiles in North American Collections*. These two very useful tools were initiated by Ernst Kitzinger. For hybrids in Byzantine art and culture, see Maguire 1999, 192-197.

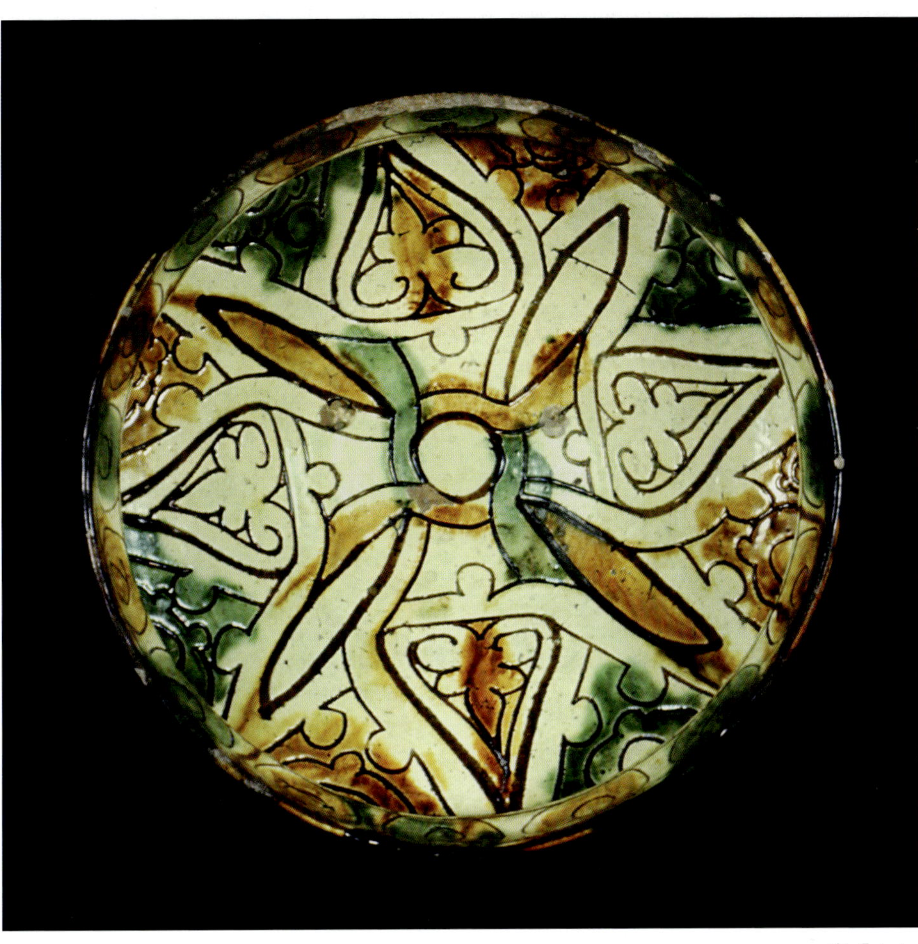

61. Interior

61. Carinated Bowl

Eastern Mediterranean, 13th to 14th century
Pink (7.5 YR 7/4) fabric with green (copper oxide) and brown (iron oxide) pigment over a cream-colored slip; clear overglaze
Diameter of rim: 22.5 cm; diameter of base: 8.4 cm; height: 12 cm

CONDITION: Complete bowl. Tripod marks on interior; slight damage to glaze on exterior due to adhesion to other vessels in kiln; traces of burning on exterior.

ACQUISITION HISTORY: Purchased from George Zacos in September 1958.

ACCESSION NUMBER: BZ.1958.95

Supported on a high ring base, this deep bowl is elegantly shaped. Its flaring sides and carinated shoulder rise to a tall, vertical rim with a rounded lip. The subtle transitions in the vessel's shape lend plasticity to the floral and geometric motifs that are deeply gouged into the interior and exterior surfaces. The carinated shoulder of the vessel also facilitated handling.

A four-petaled flower centered on a medallion marks the interior of the vessel. Ornate leaves fill the spaces between the

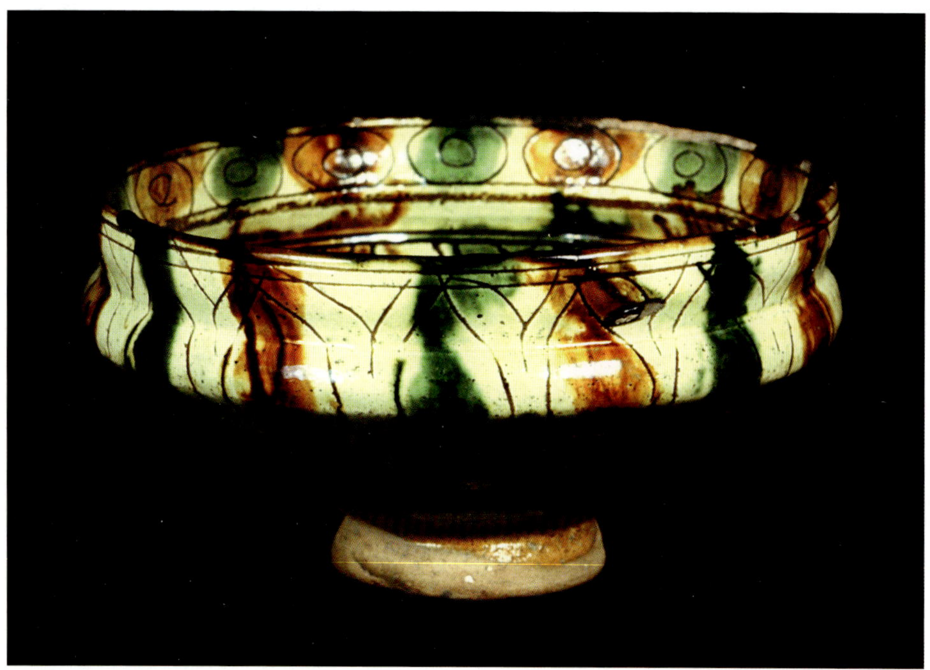

62. Hemispherical Bowl

Eastern Mediterranean, 13th to 14th century
Reddish-yellow (7.5YR 6/6) fabric; green (copper
oxide) and brown (iron oxide) pigment over a
cream-colored slip; clear overglaze
Diameter of rim: 22.5 cm; diameter of base: 8.1 cm;
height: 12.5 cm

CONDITION: Complete bowl. Tripod marks on
interior; some losses to glaze on interior and exterior.

ACQUISITION HISTORY: Purchased from
George Zacos in September 1958.

ACCESSION NUMBER: BZ.1958.98

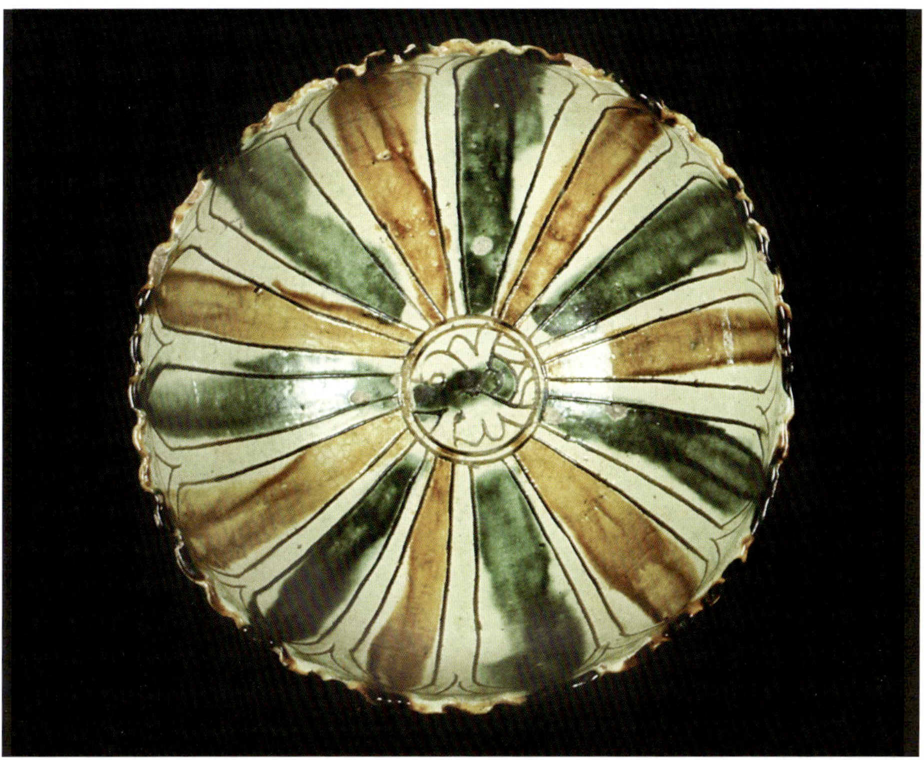

62. Interior

This thick-walled, deep bowl is supported
by a high ring base and terminates in a
crimped or notched rim.[1] Such rims are
frequently found on Port St. Symeon ware
or its imitations. The rim design provides a
lively decorative aspect to the vessel shape.

On the interior of the bowl, fourteen
incised radiating petals stem from a central medallion enclosing a split leaf. Such
radiating elements are frequently found on
Islamic pottery, including lustre-painted
bowls from Egypt and Syria. Vessels from
Port St. Symeon and neighboring areas often
combined features from Byzantine, Egyptian,
and Syrian artistic traditions, and the use of a
radiating design witnesses the lively exchange
in decorative motifs in the eastern Mediterranean. The petals are highlighted alternately
in brown and deep green pigment, giving the
interior of the vessel a colorful appearance.

A similar petal design on the vessel's
exterior extends nearly to the ring base.[2] Alternating glaze colors are used to enliven the
repeating pattern. The lower part of the base,
however, is left undecorated and is simply
covered with a transparent glaze. The repetition of designs on the exterior and interior of
the bowl is an interesting decorative feature
and, viewed from an angle, this unusual
duplication of radiating arches seemingly
negates the opacity of the vessel's walls. Such
a decorative feature—dividing the surface by
means of vertical elements—may derive from
metalwork, which was often fluted to emphasize the height of the vessel. The use of alternating brown and green pigments on this
and other bowls may also refer to the practice
of gilding or using inlay on portions of silver
vessels or ones executed in baser metals such
as brass. Although few Byzantine metal
vessels survive from this period, certain elements, such as the articulation of the rim, can
be seen in silver vessels of the twelfth century,
and may suggest that affinities between the
shape and decoration of metal and ceramic
bowls continued in the later period.[3]

SEJG

REFERENCES: Talbot Rice 1966, 218 no. 6, fig. 8
and text fig. F; *DOH* 1967, no. 311.

1. Among others, see Djobadze 1986, figs. LX, LXI
   (termed fluted); Riis and Poulsen, 1957, 235, no. 813;
   Kubiak 1970, 120, fig. 2 (termed crinkled).
2. Radiating petals commonly decorated the exterior of
   Islamic vessels of the period.
3. On similarities in the shape and decoration of metal and
   ceramic vessels, see Vickers 1986; Vickers et al. 1986
   (for Islamic vessels). A discussion of such relationships
   in the Middle Byzantine period, based on silver vessels
   currently displayed in the Benaki Museum, Athens, can
   be found in Ballian and Drandaki 2003, 47-80.

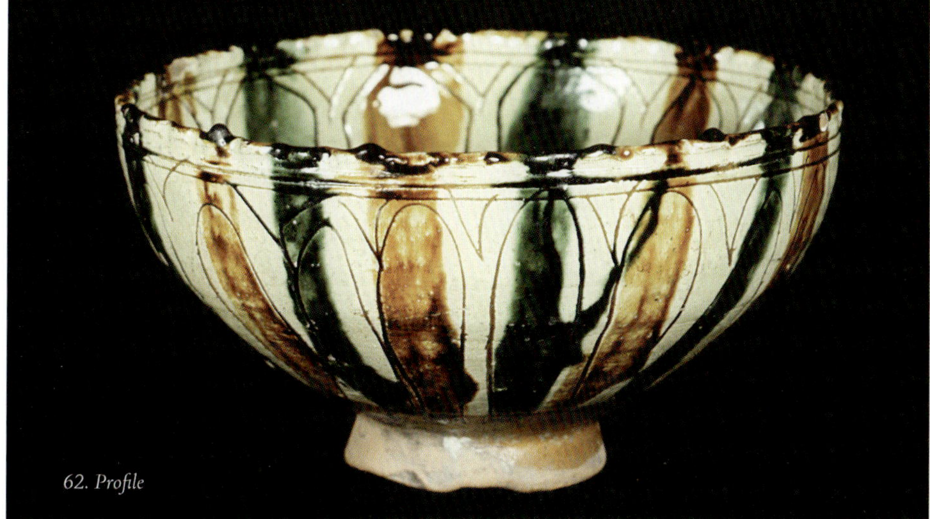

62. Profile

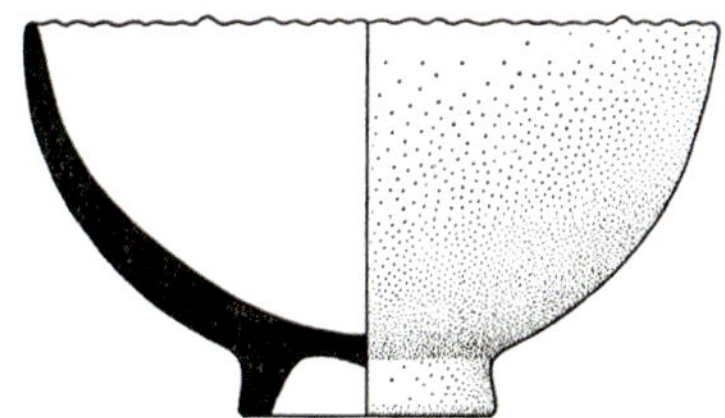

*62. Cross section. Redrawn by Meredith S. Boyter,
after Talbot Rice 1966, no. 6, text fig. F.*

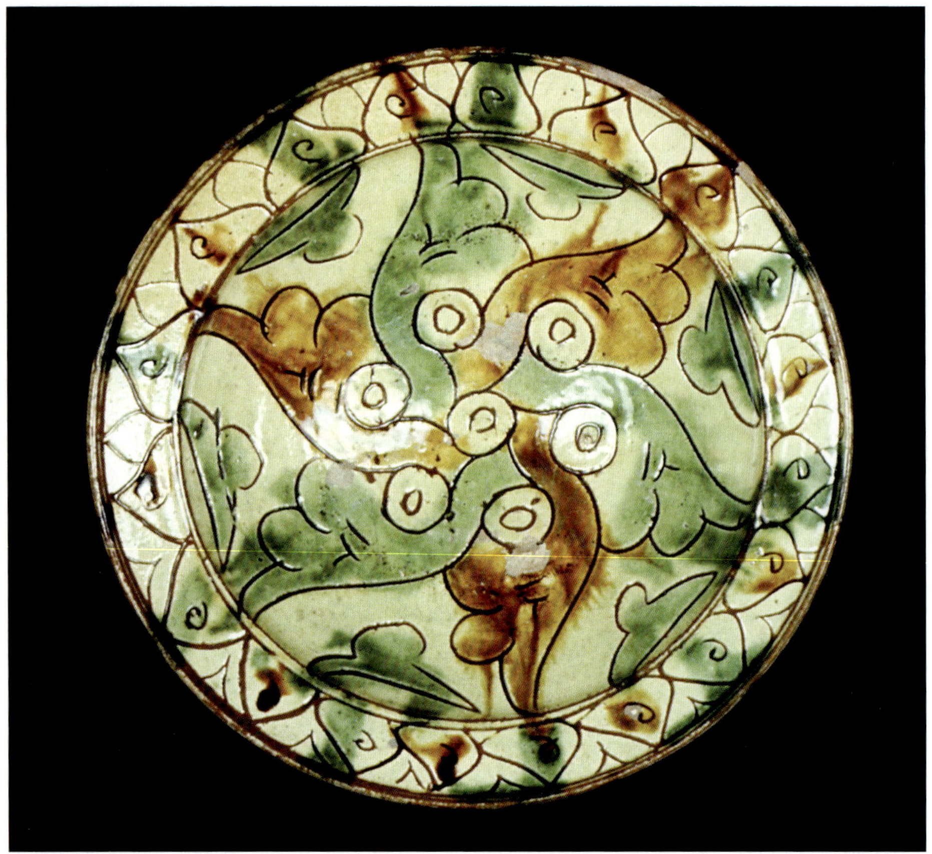

63. Interior

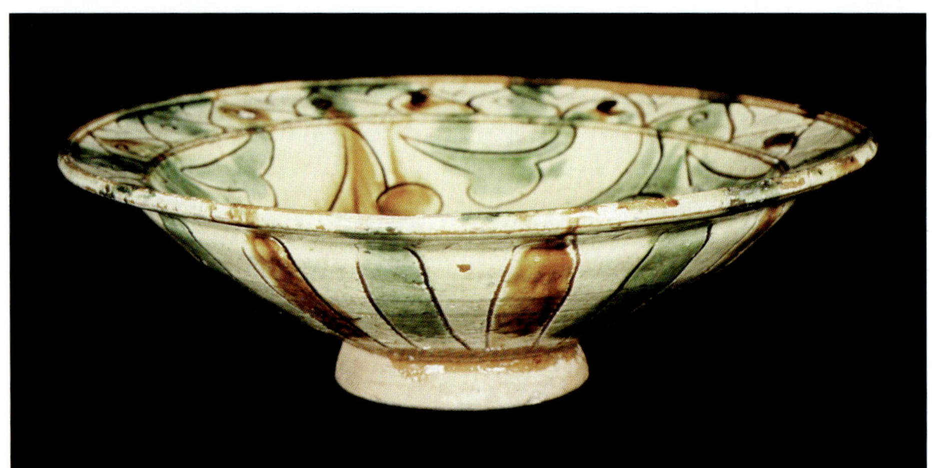

63. Profile

be ascribed to the same potter.

The bowl's interior is decorated with a six-frond spiral alternating in pale green and yellow glaze around concentric circles. The flaring rim of the vessel is covered with a band of leaves oriented toward the exterior of the vessel. Lines incised around the well and rim of the vessel both isolate the physical components of the pot and enclose the decorative motifs within discrete zones. Radiating bands, alternately glazed green and brown, encircle the vessel's exterior above the raised ring base.

While the decoration on the vessel's interior appears to have a purely foliate character, similar patterns of spiraling fronds recently have been associated with astrological symbols, such as Cancer.[2] Such associations remind us that ornamental motifs in the medieval Mediterranean could have held numerous meanings, depending on the viewer, and derived their inspiration from a variety of religious, social, and cultural contexts.

SEJG

REFERENCES: Talbot Rice 1966, 219 no. 8, fig. 10 and text fig. H; *DOH* 1967, no. 311.

1. Vessels of this shape have been found at al-Mina' (Lane 1938, 48, pls. XXIV.1, XXVI.2, 3); Antioch (Waagé 1948, 96); Hama (Riis and Poulsen 1957, nos. 805, 806, 809, 810, 811, 813); Caesarea (Pringle 1985, 193, fig. 13), and elsewhere.
2. Redford 2004, 298, fig. 12.14.

63. Shallow Bowl with Everted Rim

Eastern Mediterranean, 13th to 14th century
Diameter of rim: 24.5 cm; diameter of base: 7.8 cm; height: 7.8 cm
Light brown (7.5YR 6/4) fabric with green (copper oxide) and brown (iron oxide) pigment over white slip; thick, clear overglaze

CONDITION: Complete bowl. Tripod marks on interior; some loss to glaze on surface; pooling of glaze on rim due to upside-down firing.

ACQUISITION HISTORY: Purchased from George Zacos in September 1958.

ACCESSION NUMBER: BZ.1958.99

This shallow bowl presents a common shape for polychrome tableware from Syria and other locations in the eastern Mediterranean.[1] Set on a ring base, the walls of the vessel gently curve outward to support a broad, flaring rim. The well of the bowl and the rim receive different decorative treatments but are nonetheless unified through the application of brown and green pigments. A second bowl in the Dumbarton Oaks Collection (BZ.1958.97), purchased from George Zacos in the same lot, is nearly identical in size and decoration and should

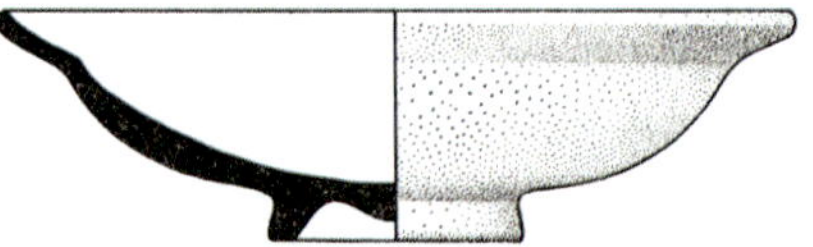

63. Cross section. Redrawn by Meredith S. Boyter, after Talbot Rice 1966, no. 8, text fig. H.

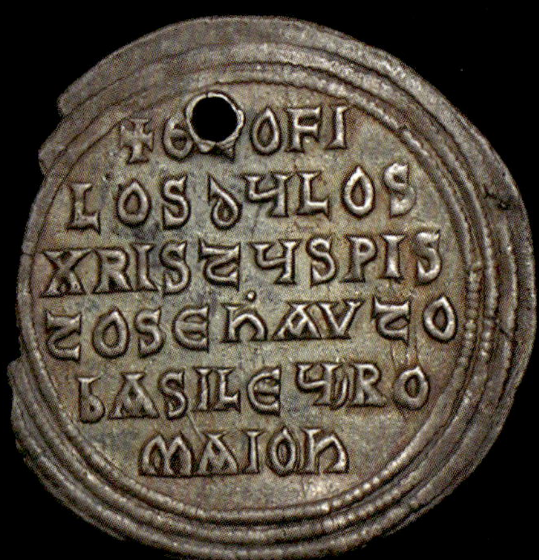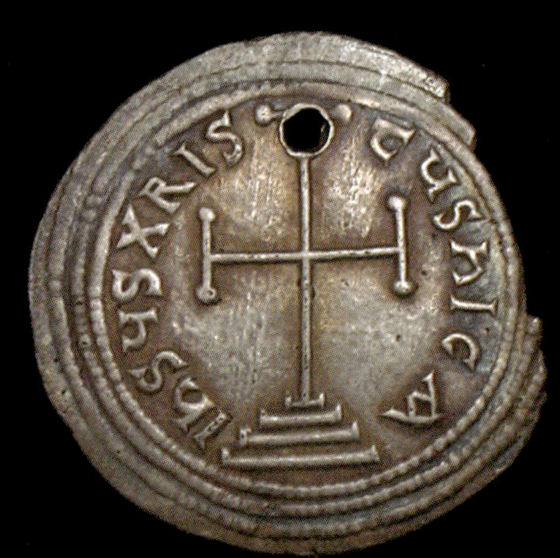

COINS

Sacred Art on Coins
and Their Secular Context

BY CÉCILE MORRISSON

I N THE WORDS OF ST. JOHN CHRYSOSTOM, BISHOP OF Constantinople (398-404), "[t]he use of coins welds together our whole life and is the basis of all our transactions. Whenever anything is to be bought or sold, we do it all through coins."[1] The coins in this exhibition are a limited selection of the thousands of types, and the millions of specimens thereof, struck in the Byzantine Empire over the course of one millennium.[2] Nevertheless, these coins are representative of the evolution of Byzantine monetary art and iconography from the Late Roman tradition to the various forms of Christian expression in the late fifth and early sixth centuries, extending to the late 1200s.

Throughout this long period of time, the ruling emperor's portrait was a consistent feature of coin iconography. Over the centuries, however, sacred art permeated the field of coin design. In the early examples (cat. nos. 64, 65), the personifications of Victory displayed small signs of the Chrismon. Subsequently, the Christian theme took over the entire field of the reverse side where one would see a larger rendition of the cross (cat. no. 67). By the middle of the ninth century, after the end of Iconoclasm, icons of Christ and other saintly figures replaced the images of the Chrismon and the cross (cat. nos. 68-71).

In all these examples, the emperor presents himself as a ruler respecting and defending Christian values, proclaiming himself *pistos* ("faithful," as in cat. no. 69) or *eusebes* ("pious"). Beginning in the tenth century the majority of coin types show either the emperor together with Christ or with other religious figures who are crowning or blessing him. The representation of the emperor kneeling, or even in the pose of full *proskynesis*, is the ultimate manifestation of this evolution, rendering the emperor as a subordinate of Christ (cat. no. 71). The godlike emperor of the Late Roman period had finally evolved into the god-blessed and "faithful-in-Christ" ruler of the Byzantine era. Coin imagery served as an expression of the emperor's position as an intermediary between heaven and his terrestrial subjects. According to Cyril Mango, "[w]hat the emperor was for his subjects, God was to the emperor."[3] Therefore, the two liturgies of divine adoration and prostration, or veneration, of the emperor, both formed in the fourth century, display a remarkable interrelation.

When considering the coins' secular context, it is worth remembering their ubiquitous presence in the Byzantine world. Coins were one of the most widely distributed media of the imperial portrait, reproducing in thousands or millions of copies the official images of the current ruler. These standardized images were sent to the provinces on the accession of a new emperor, and they would serve as models for a multitude of objects displaying the ruler's likeness, from colossal statues to ivory portraits crowning consular scepters, from silk embroideries to stamps certifying quality silverware (cat. nos. 36, 37).[4]

As might be found in any pre-industrial economy, currency and its circulation differed throughout the empire. It was high in the capital and along the main sea and land routes and low in the provincial cities and in remote areas or the countryside where coins changed hands less frequently. Monetization also varied over time, being highest during two periods, from the fourth to the sixth and from the eleventh to the twelfth century. Whatever the degree, the circulation of coins was divided into three different categories: gold solidi or nomismata for the wealthier officials or merchants; gold fractions or silver coins for the intermediary transactions; and copper coins for the minor expenses of everyday life and for almsgiving.

Moneychangers provided the means for currency to pass from one level to another. The difference in value between the gold coin and its smallest division in the sixth to the twelfth century was on the order

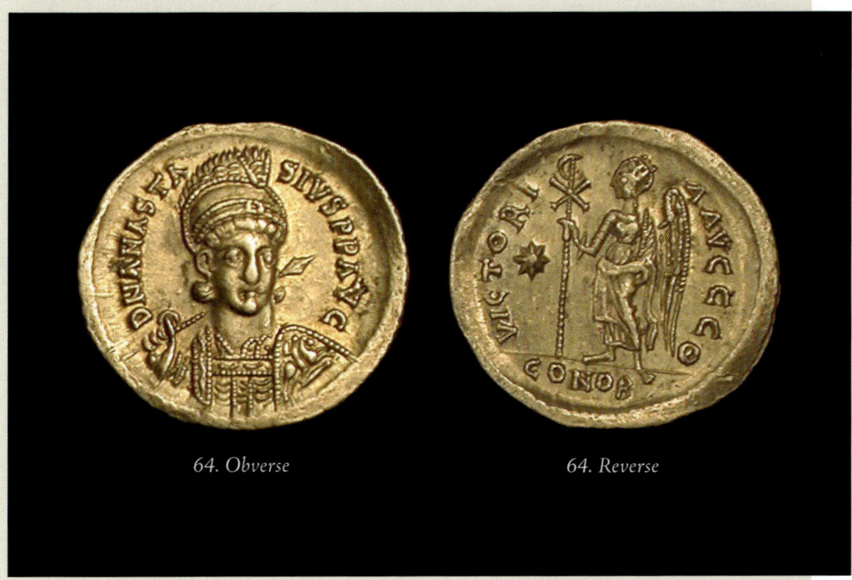

64. Obverse   64. Reverse

of one to one thousand. An unqualified worker or mason would earn about a third of a solidus a month, assuming he was employed each day; however, a notary would receive more than two solidi. In 535, a physician on the staff of the Prefect of Africa collected slightly less that twelve solidi a month, while the prefect himself would receive one hundred pounds of gold, that is 7,200 solidi weighing approximately 32.5 kilos, every year (600 solidi a month).[5]

The presence of religious imagery on coins resulted in their frequent transformation into amulets or medals, as evidenced by the many specimens that have been pierced in order to be used as pendants (cat. no. 69). Even an imperial figure on a coin would be a reason for similar usage, as shown by a large follis of Justinian I pierced on top of the emperor's helmet and crudely incised with the inscription +XE ΒΟ-ΗΘΕΙ ΤΟΝ ΦΟΡΙΝΤΑ ("Christ protect the wearer [of this medal]"). In this respect too, coins welded together the lives of the Byzantines.

1. Harl 1996, 250; cf. the Greek original, *In Principium Actorum Hom.* 1-4, PG 51.99 (line 37). The editor owes gratitude to Dr. Jaclyn Maxwell, who identified the source of this citation.
2. Besides the Dumbarton Oaks catalogues series—*DOC*—quoted in the following coin catalogue entries, for a general comprehensive introduction, see Grierson 1982, a lavishly illustrated book containing a clear outline of Byzantine coin issues from 491 to 1453, as well as the brochure Grierson 1999, the digitized text of which is now available at http://www.doaks.org. Also, online one can visit the Dumbarton Oaks coin exhibition mounted in 1999 in conjunction with a colloquium that marked the completion of the Dumbarton Oaks coin catalogues. This exhibition displays and comments on 118 coins in three vitrines. Each of the coins can be viewed and enlarged. It has seven wall panels with substantial written texts and comparative images: http://www.doaks.org/CoinExhibition/First/First1Main3.html.
3. Mango 1980, 219-220.
4. Grabar 1936, 4-30.
5. Morrisson and Cheynet 2002.

64. Solidus of Anastasios I (491-518)

Constantinople, 507-518
Gold
21 mm, 4.46 grams

OBVERSE: DNANASTASIVSPPAVC (*Dominus Noster Anastasius Perpetuus Augustus*—"Our Lord Anastasios Forever Augustus")
Bust of Anastasios, three-quarter right, wearing tunic, cuirass, diadem, and helmet with plume trefoil ornament. The emperor holds spear behind head in right hand; on left shoulder, shield with device of horseman spearing fallen foe.

REVERSE: VICTORIA AVCCC Θ (*Victoria Augusti thèta*—"Victory of the emperor. 9th [officina]"). Victory standing left, holding a long staff with Chrismon at top.

ACQUISITION HISTORY: Ex-Grierson collection from Seaby, London, 14.xi.1950.

ACCESSION NUMBER: BZC.1956.6.56

Following the death of Emperor Zeno (474-491), his widow, Empress Ariadne, married Anastasios I, a financial officer in the Roman Empire who thus became emperor. The armed bust depicting Anastasios I on the obverse of the solidus is presented at a three-quarter position. Constantius II (337-361) first introduced this three-quarter position, subsequently used by the Eastern emperor Arkadios (383-408) on his solidus. The reverse shows a standing Victory holding a long cross. This representation was a compromise between the pagan personifications of Victory, favored by all Romans, and the Christian symbol of the cross. It is believed that Theodosios II (402-450) introduced this combination around 422 on the occasion of his tenth consulship and following a recent victory over the Persians. Anastasios I's solidi show Victory holding various types of crosses: first a bejeweled cross, then the cross with the Christogram—as it is here—and finally a cross with ☧. These variants were designed to indicate different succesive issues of coins.

CM

REFERENCES: *DOC* 1, 7, no. 6b; *MIB* 1, 83, no. 5; Paris, *Byzance* 1992, 166, no. 111.

Constantinople, 537-565
Silver
24 mm, 4.1 grams
OBVERSE: DNIVSTINI ANVSPPAVC (*Dominus Noster Iustinianus Perpetuus Augustus*—"Our Lord Justinian Forever Emperor")
Bust right wearing helmet with plume and diadem, cuirass, and paludamentum.
REVERSE: CLORIARO HANORVH (*sic* for *Gloria Romanorum*—"Glory of the Romans"); Emperor diademed, nimbate in military garb, standing left, holding in right hand long spear, in left globus cruciger. In field right star. In exergue, COB.
ACQUISITION HISTORY: Ex-Grierson collection.
ACCESSION NUMBER: BZC.1956.13.174

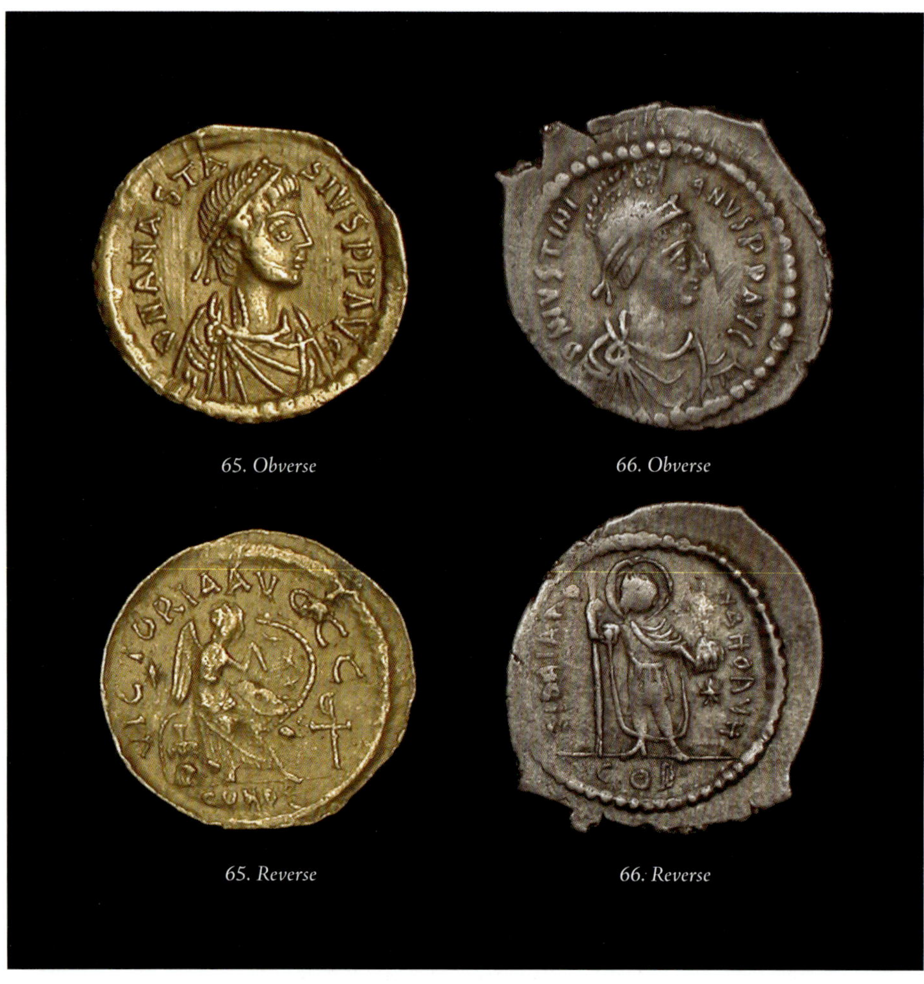

65. Obverse   66. Obverse

65. Reverse   66. Reverse

65. *Semissis of Anastasios I (491-518)*

Constantinople, 492(?)-507
Gold
18 mm, 2.13 grams
OBVERSE: DNANASTASIVSPPAVC (*Dominus Noster Anastasius Perpetuus Augustus*—"Our Lord Anastasios Forever Augustus")
Bust of Anastasios right with diadem, cuirass, and paludamentum.
REVERSE: VICTORIA AVCCC (*Victoria Augusti*—"Victory of the emperor") Victory, nude to the waist, seated right on shield and cuirass inscribing XXXX on shield, which she holds on her knee. In left field there is a star, to the right a reversed Christogram. In exergue, CONOB.
ACQUISITION HISTORY: Ex-Peirce collection from the Istanbul dealer Andronikos.
ACCESSION NUMBER: BZC.1948.17.1281

Probably intended for distribution on ceremonial occasions, the semissis was one-half of the value of the solidus, the standard Byzantine gold coin. The tremissis, the more common of the two smaller coins, was worth one-third of the amount of a solidus. The image of the seated Victory was retained on coins for Eastern emperors well into the sixth century, down to the rule of Maurice (582-602). Victory is writing the roman numeral X, which stands for imperial decennalia, the tenth anniversary of accession to the throne. This coin features XXXX, which would refer to the last *vota* of a forty-year reign. Anastasios I ruled for seventeen years only, which suggests that by that time the XXXX have lost their meaning. Originally, their use on Byzantine coins must have referred to the exceptionally long reign of Theodosios II (408-450).

CM

REFERENCES: *DOC* 1, 8, no. 8.1, pl. I; *MIB* 1, 83, no. 9.

Silver was the most important coined metal in the Roman Republic and in the early Roman Empire. Yet, surprisingly, it played a secondary role in the monetary system revamped by the reforms of Diocletian (284-305) and Constantine I (305-337). The most plausible explanations for the steady depreciation of silver coins during the third century CE were the constant fluctuations in the relative value of silver to gold and the consequent defiance of the public. This situation lasted into the sixth century when the silver coins of Constantinople were struck mainly for ceremonial distribution, as was the case with the semisses.

During the sixth century in the Eastern Roman Empire, silver coins were extremely rare or simply nonexistent, which is in sharp contrast to the number of vessels made of silver that were produced during the same period (see cat. nos. 33-37). One explanation may be the higher prices at which mints had to buy silver, which—if acquired for other purposes—was more affordable on the market.[1] Silver export might have been an additional factor; the Sassanian kings struck their coins almost exclusively in silver and were willing to pay the highest price for this metal.[2]

The obverse type of a left-facing bust and the reverse type of standing emperor raising his right hand and holding a globe goes back to the fifth century and was struck down to Justin II (565-574). Later in his reign, Justin is shown holding a globe with cross and not a plain orb as on the previous types.[3]

CM

REFERENCES: *DOC* 1, 77, no. 24.1, pl. XIII;
MIB 1, 121, no. 49.

1. Grierson 1993, 137-146.
2. *MIB* 1, 13.
3. The globe with cross was introduced by Justinian I on most of his coins at the beginning of a new indiction (fifteen-year fiscal cycle) in 537.

67. *Hexagram of Herakleios (610-641)*

Constantinople, 625(?)-629
Silver
25 mm, 6.77 grams

OBVERSE: ƆNҺЄRACILIЧIЄᴢҺЄPACON (*Domini Nostri Heraclius et Heraclius Constantinus*—"Our Lords Herakleios and Herakleios Constantine") To left Herakleios with short beard; to right Herakleios Constantine beardless, but same size. They are seated together on double throne. Each wears chlamys and crown with cross, and holds globus cruciger in right hand. Between heads, cross. In field right Κ.

REVERSE: ƆЄЧSАӘIЧᴢAROMANIS (*Deus adiuta Romanis*—"God, help the Romans"). Cross potent on globe and three steps.

ACQUISITION HISTORY: Ex-Shaw collection.

ACCESSION NUMBER: BZC.1947.2.40

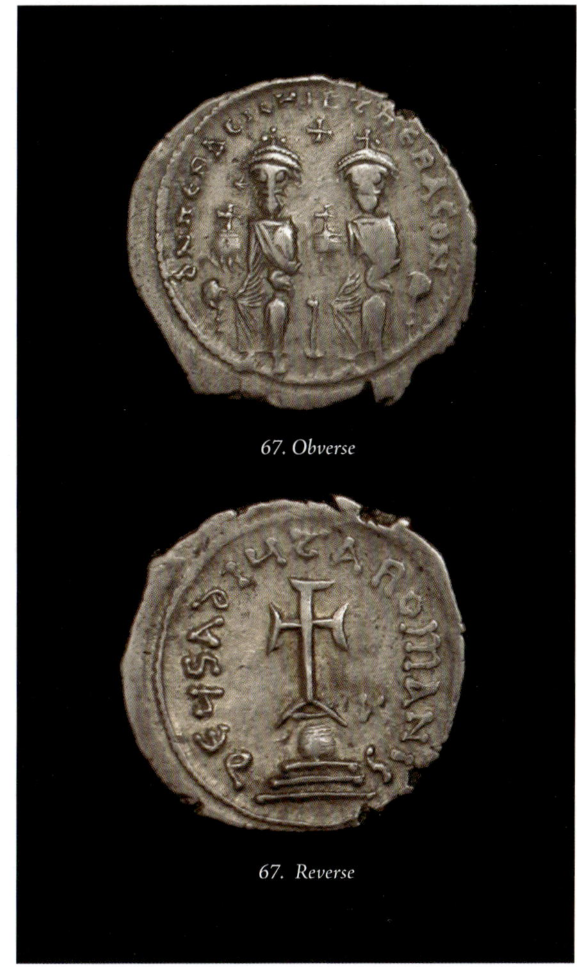

67. *Obverse*

67. *Reverse*

The hexagram coin, created in 616, marks a return to silver for common coinage, such a turnabout that it is reported in the *Chronicon Paschale*, which, like all Byzantine documents, contains only the most brief of numismatic references.[1] The name was derived from its weight, six grammata (scruples) (6.82 g), and it was the cash exchange used to pay the imperial rogai—salaries of members of the armed forces and civil servants—at half the old rate. Hence, this reduction in pay resulted in the creation of the hexagram. The dire straits of the economy occurred because of the Empire's struggle against the Persians who had invaded in 613 a large section of Asia Minor. In 621, being short of funds, "he [Herakleios] took on loan the moneys of religious establishments and he also took the candleabra and other vessels of the holy ministry from the Great Church [Saint Sophia], which he minted into a great quantity of gold and silver coins."[2] Such confiscation accounts for the abundant issue of hexagrams of this type. Many specimens have been found in Caucasian lands where the emperor campaigned and recruited allies.

The circumstances of this issue also led to the choice of the reverse legend, "God help the Romans," as an invocation reminiscent of the battle cry of charging soldiers, according to Emperor Maurice's (582-602) *Strategikon*.[3] The type of the "Cross on Steps" had already been introduced on gold coinage by Tiberios II (574-578). Scholars have referred to this rendition of the cross as either the one erected on Golgotha in 420, or as the monumental one set on the Forum of Constantine in Constantinople.[4] In any event, the invocation was all the more necessary since the relic of the True Cross had been taken by Chosroes from Jerusalem to his palace in Ctesiphon on the Tigris.

If the hexagram's value was indeed one-half of the solidus, as is commonly believed, the gold to silver ratio would have been 1:18; the nominal value would have come close to the metallic value. Hence, resuming the abundant issues of coins can be ascribed to a more realistic value being assigned to money. However, the quantities struck declined swiftly at the end of Constantine IV's reign (668-685), and the hexagram became a "ceremonial" coin that was struck to the solidus type, using solidus dies.

CM

REFERENCES: *DOC* 2.1, 273, no. 64.16, pl. XI; *MIB*, 3, 223, no. 140, pl. 9; Paris, *Byzance* 1992, 171, no. 117.

1. Dindorf 1832, 1, 706 and Whitby 1989, 158, 164, 169, 201-202.
2. De Boor 1883, 1, 302-303; cf. the English translation Mango and Greatrex 1997, 435.
3. The actual battle cry was *Nobiscum Deus* ("God is with us"), cf. Dennis 1984, chap. 2.18, 33-34.
4. Frolow 1948; Grabar 1957b, 34 and no. 22.

68. *Solidus of Constans II (642-668)*

Constantinople, 651-654
Gold
20 mm, 4.24 grams

OBVERSE: ƆNCONSƷAN ƧINYSPPAV
(*Dominus Noster Constantinus Perpetuus Augustus*—
"Our Lord Constantine Forever Augustus")
Bust facing, with long beard and moustache, wearing chlamys and crown with cross on circlet. In right hand globus cruciger.

REVERSE: VICTORIA AVƧY (*Victoria Augusti*—"Victory of the emperor")
In exergue, CONOB+
Cross potent on base and three steps.

ACQUISITION HISTORY: Acquired from Santamaria Sale (Rome) 4.v.1961, no. 275.

ACCESSION NUMBER: BZC.1961.8

Constans II was the grandson of Emperor Herakleios (610-641) and child of his first son, Herakleios Constantine, who was proclaimed co-emperor in 613, only a few months after his birth. The reign of Constans's father lasted a few months, from January to April 641. A progeny of emperors, the grandson Constans II was baptized as Herakleios and given the official name of Constantine, which appears on this gold coin.

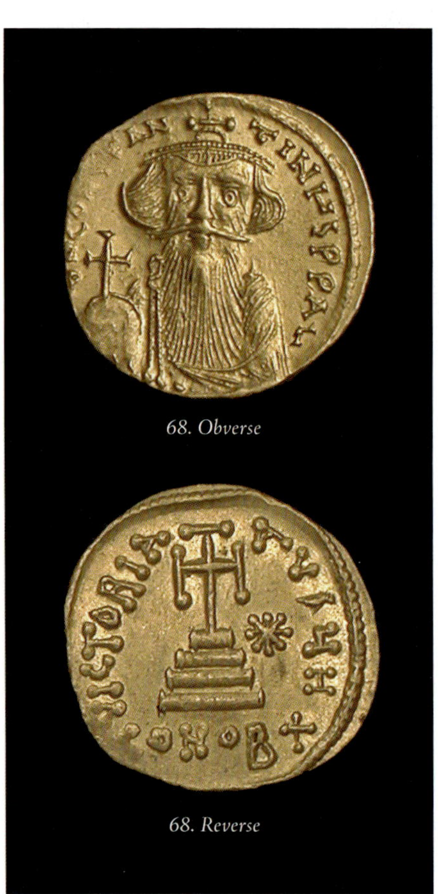

68. *Obverse*

68. *Reverse*

Later, his name was abbreviated in popular speech to Constans, a name historians have kept for clarity. Constans assumed power at an early age, beginning his reign as emperor when only eleven years old.[1]

Constans II's solidi are quite common during this period of abundant issues designed to meet the military needs of the battered empire, assailed by the Arabs who had already conquered a great part of Syria, Palestine, and Egypt and who were then launching raids on North Africa. The solidi form seven classes distinguished by the changes in the representation of the emperor himself and the number of sons associated with him. This coin depicts the emperor with a long beard and dates to 651-654, when he was in his twenties. The spectacular long beard earned him the nickname Pogonatos ("The bearded one").

This coin belongs to one of the two varieties of lightweight solidi only known in this class with the long-beard effigy. In contrast with the standard solidus whose weight had been fixed since Constantine the Great at 1/72nd of a Roman pound or 24 carats (4.45 grams), this solidus weighs only 23 carats (4.24 grams). The weight of 23 carats is indicated by the exergue inscription of another variety, BOΓK, where BO stands for Obryzum (fine gold) and ΓK (in Greek numeral letters—3 and 20). The function of these lightweight coins, which were issued irregularly from the mid-sixth to the late seventh century, is still a matter of discussion. The fact that they are typologically distinct from the full-weight coins shows they were not intended to deceive the public. They are more frequently found outside the Byzantine Empire, as far away as Germany, which has led to some speculation that they were special issues intended for the barbarians. Nevertheless, the simplest possible answer is that their inferior value may have prevented the Byzantines from hoarding them.

CM

REFERENCES: *DOC* 2.2, 426, no. 23b, pl. XXIV; *MIB* 3, 241, no. 47, pl. 21.

1.   See Foss forthcoming.

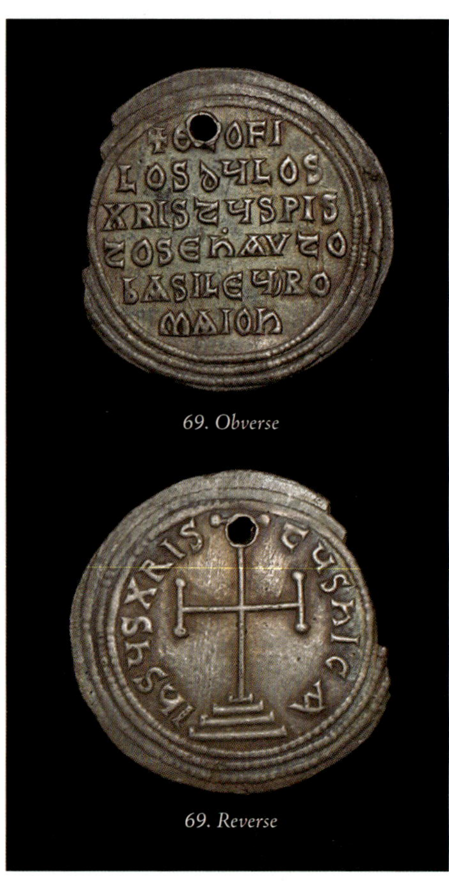

69. *Obverse*

69. *Reverse*

69. *Miliaresion of Theophilos (829-842)*

Constantinople, 830-c. 838
Silver
28 mm, 3.12 grams

OBVERSE: +ΘEOFI|LOSƌYLOS|XRISƷYSPIS|ƌ OSEΠAVƷO|bASILEYRO|ΜAIOΠ within triple circle of dots (*Theophilos, Doulos Khristou Pistosen Auto Basileus Romaion*—"Theophilos servant of Christ and faithful in Him, Emperor of the Romans")

REVERSE: IhSYSXPIS ƷYSΠICA (*Iesus Christus Nika*—"Jesus Christ Conquers")
Cross potent on base and three steps within triple circle of dots.

CONDITION: Pierced above the cross on reverse.

ACQUISITION HISTORY: Schindler collection from Grabow (Rostock), November 1941.

ACCESSION NUMBER: BZC.1960.125.1308

This coin is an excellent specimen of the miliaresion, considered the preeminent Iconoclastic coin.[1] This silver denomination was introduced in 720 by Leo III (717-741), the first Iconoclastic emperor and founder of the Isaurian dynasty. The coin's broad, thin fabric, triple border of dots, and use of an epigraphic instead of a figured type with an inscription that covers the whole of one face of the coin may have been copied from the Arab *dirhem*.[2] It could also have been inspired by the inscriptions on earlier seals. Whatever the source may be, this iconography is typical of the Iconoclasts' exclusive insistence on the cross. The inscription around the cross is the invocation of Constantine.[3] The emperor's titulature is more developed on this second and main issue of the reign than on the first, which had retained the usual ЄC ΘЄ4 bASILE4S ROΠAIOΠ, "through God, emperor of the Romans," of previous reigns.

This formula (instead of the simple ЄC ΘЄ4 bASILE4S—"through God, emperor") had been expanded by Michael I (802-811) to underline the superiority of the Byzantine ruler over Charlemagne to whom the title of emperor (not emperor of the Romans) had to be conceded in 812.

The coin has been pierced above the cross design in order to be worn as a pendant, turning its economic function into a religious, apotropaic one. This coin was bought in Rostock, a German port on the Baltic Sea, by Captain Leo Schindler (1885-1957), an Austrian collector.[4] It could be a local find considering the evidence of various other silver or copper coins, as well as lead seals of Theophilos, unearthed around the Baltic region in southern Sweden, northern Germany, and Russia. These discoveries have been linked to embassies exchanged between Byzantium, the Carolingian court at Ingelheim, and Kievan Rus'.[5]

CM

REFERENCES: *DOC* 3.1, 431, no. 10.3.

1. Iconoclasm is an eighth- and early ninth-century movement. The iconoclasts ("image-destroyers") rejected the sanctity of icons and their veneration as idolatry. Iconoclasts prohibited the depiction of holy personages while allowing only nonfigural religious images. Cf. Kirin's essay earlier in this volume, as well as *ODB* 2, 975-977.
2. On which it is often found overstruck. See Paris, *Byzance* 1992, 204, no. 139, fig. 1.
3. See Walter 1997.
4. Whose collection was acquired *en bloc* by Dumbarton Oaks from his widow in 1960. See his obituary notice and bibliography by T. Bertelè in *Rivista italiana di numismatica* 59 (1957): 120-122.
5. For this "northern connection," see Shepard 1995 and McCormick 2001, 226-276, where the emphasis is on the Byzantine activity in recruiting Viking mercenaries.

70. Nomisma of Michael III (842-867)

Constantinople, 843-856
Gold
20 mm, 4.45 grams
OBVERSE: IhS4SX RIS⊆OS✶ (*Iesus Christos*—"Jesus Christ")
Bust of Christ facing, bearded with cross behind head, wearing tunic and himation; right hand raised in blessing in front of the body, book held from beneath in left.
REVERSE: +ΠIXAHLSΘEOΔORA (*Michael kai Theodora*—"Michael and Theodora")
Busts of Michael on left, beardless, wearing *chlamys* and crown with cross; and Theodora on right, larger, wearing loros and crown with pendilia, two pinnacles, and cross. Above, cross.
CONDITION: Plugged above Christ's bust.
ACQUISITION HISTORY: Ex-Peirce collection.
ACCESSION NUMBER: BZC.1948.17.2685

In 843, the Restoration of the Holy Images and their worship, known as the Triumph of Orthodoxy, ended the era of Iconoclasm by allowing figural images to be used in religious art. No longer was religious imagery restricted to the use of symbols such as the cross or the Chrismon, and this change was immediately reflected in the coins and seals of that time. It was easier and faster to modify the instructions sent to the engravers in the imperial workshop of the *archon tes kharages* ("master of the mint")[1] than to execute a new mosaic in the imperial palace. Human figures that appeared on both faces of the gold coins of Iconoclastic emperors were not representations of Christ, the Virgin, or the saints, for any representation of these holy images during this period meant persecution. Instead, the figures were typically depictions of the ruling emperor fulfilling the functions of dynastic propaganda.

The nomisma of Michael III, on the contrary, leaves the obverse to the image of Christ with a cross behind his head, instead of the more usual nimbus, thus replicating the coins of Justinian II (685-695), which at that time were already 150 years older. Christ's image on Michael III's coin is a somewhat clumsy version of the fine seventh-century model, but the quality of the solidi's engraving and fabric improved over the following decades. In 843, after the long period of Iconoclasm, the dies' engraver was not skilled enough to reproduce the full obverse titulature

of Christ; hence, the short, half-Latin, half-Greek inscription IhS4S XRIS⊆OS instead of the full legend IhS4S XRIS⊆OS REX RE⊆NANTI4M (Iesus Christos Rex Regnantium—"Jesus Christ King of Kings").

CM

REFERENCES: *DOC* 3.1, 463, no. 2.6, pl. XXVIII.

1. This official, according to the *kletorologion* of Philotheos (899 CE), belonged to the staff of the *vestiarion*, the imperial wardrobe and treasury.

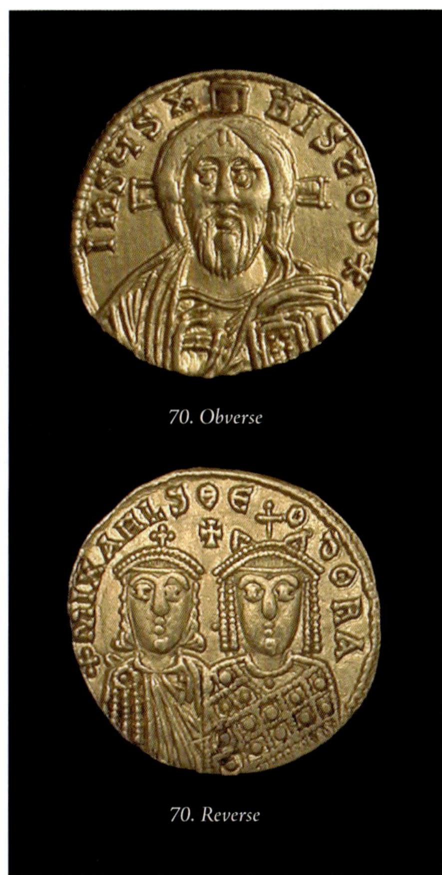

70. Obverse

70. Reverse

71. Hyperpyron of Michael VIII Palaiologos (1259-1282)

Constantinople, 1261-1282
Gold
24 mm, 4.13 grams
Obverse: In upper field M̅P̅ Θ̅V̅ (*Meter Theou*—"Mother of God")
In field below left P right M
Half-figure of Virgin Orans within walls of Constantinople furnished with six towers.[1]
Reverse: to left X|M|Δ∈|CΠ|T in center I̅C̅ ("Jesus") to right X̅C̅ ("Christ")
Archangel Michael presents the kneeling emperor to Christ, who holds a codex while seated on a low throne.
Acquisition History: Ex-Peirce collection from the Istanbul dealer Andronikos.
Accession number: BZC.1948.17.3591

After 1204, when the knights of the Fourth Crusade conquered Constantinople, most of the territory of the Byzantine Empire fell under the control of several competing Greek, Slav, and Latin successor states. Consequently, throughout the following one and a half centuries, coins in the Byzantine tradition became increasingly varied. This hyperpyron represents one of the best-known iconographic innovations of that era.[2] The design celebrates the events of 1261, the Byzantine reconquest of the "God-guarded City" of Constantinople by Michael VIII Palaiologos, the first in a long succession of emperors of the Palaiologan dynasty, rulers of Byzantium until its demise in 1453.[3] On the obverse, the Virgin appears within the confines of the city's fortification walls. This coin's size and format do not allow a correct depiction of the city's fortifications. The basic composition, however, conveys a message of documentary relevance by referring to the famous icon of the Virgin, located in the church of Blachernai, positioned in immediate proximity to the fortification walls in the northwestern corner of the city. The Holy Virgin of Blachernai was venerated as guardian of Constantinople. According to Anthony Cutler, as rendered on this coin, the Virgin "is evidently neither circumscribed nor confined by the *enceinte*. Only in the most profane sense could she be said to be 'within' or 'amongst' these bulwarks. Rising above them from the interior of the city, her station defies precise prepositional qualification. For this and other reasons … we describe her as the Virgin on the Walls."[4]

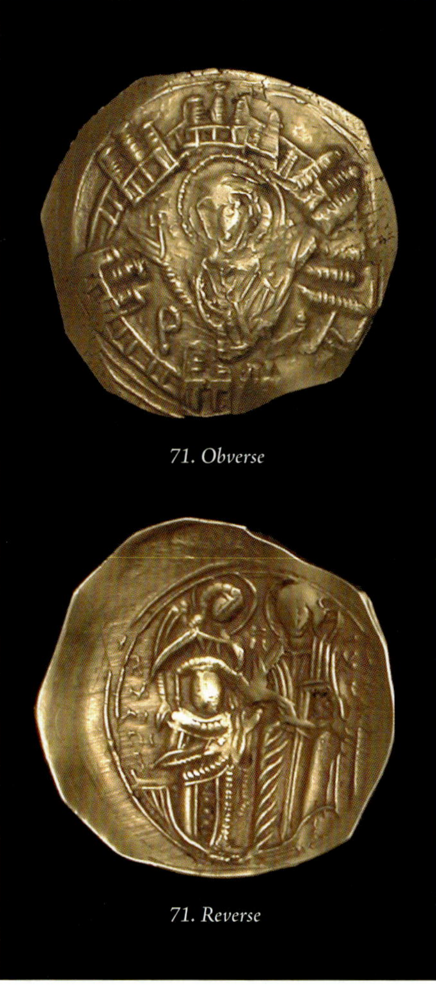

71. Obverse

71. Reverse

On the concave reverse, the composition includes the emperor, his patron saint, Archangel Michael—Archistrategos, that is, the commander of the celestial armies—and Christ enthroned. For the first time in Byzantine numismatics, the emperor is shown kneeling in *proskynesis*, a gesture of adoration generally demanded of people granted an imperial audience.[5] The iconography of the coin is an expression of the general notion that "[w]hat the emperor was for his subjects, God was to the emperor"[6] and, in addition, an assertion of the special favors that God bestowed on Michael VIII Palaiologos. A passage from this emperor's autobiography clearly states his conviction that he was chosen by God:

> "Who shall tell the mighty acts of the Lord? who shall cause all his praises to be heard?" (*Ps. 105:2*) I am lifted by you onto the empire of your people … It was neither the orderly multitude of my soldier's arms, nor their fearful weapons that placed me above the heads of the Romans…. Instead, it is your will, Lord, that performed a miracle; it is your will that elevated me and made me master over all things.[7]

CM

References: *DOC* 5.2, no. 20, pl. 2.

1. Obverse, according to numismatists' usage, although the contemporary historian George Pachymeres (1242-c. 1310) when describing this composition referred to "the City [of Constantinople] being imprinted on the back" of the coin; see Bekker 1835, vol. 2, 494 and Failler 1984, 541.
2. The term designating this type of coin—*hyperpyron*—means *hyper-pyron*, refined "above fire," but not "hyper-pure" as sometimes wrongly stated.
3. The present type with the Virgin within the walls was preceded by a short-lived one with the same reverse but showing the Virgin enthroned, *DOC* 5.2, no. 1.
4. Cutler 1975, 114.
5. Michael VIII was represented in the same posture offering a model of the city of Constantinople to St. Michael on a bronze statue kept in front of the church of the Holy Apostles in Constantinople. This kneeling clearly conveyed the idea of offering and consecrating the imperial city to divine protection, as stated by George Pachymeres; cf. Bekker 1835, vol. 2, 234 and Failler 1984, 259-261.
6. Mango 1980, 219-220; cf. Morrisson's essay preceding cat. nos. 64-71.
7. *Imperatoris Michaelis Palaeologi de vita sua*, 6:533-534; translation of the editor according to Grégoire 1966, 453-456. English text of Psalm verse after *The Septuagint with Apocrypha: Greek and English*, ed. L. C. L. Brenton (London, 1851), 4th printing, 1992.

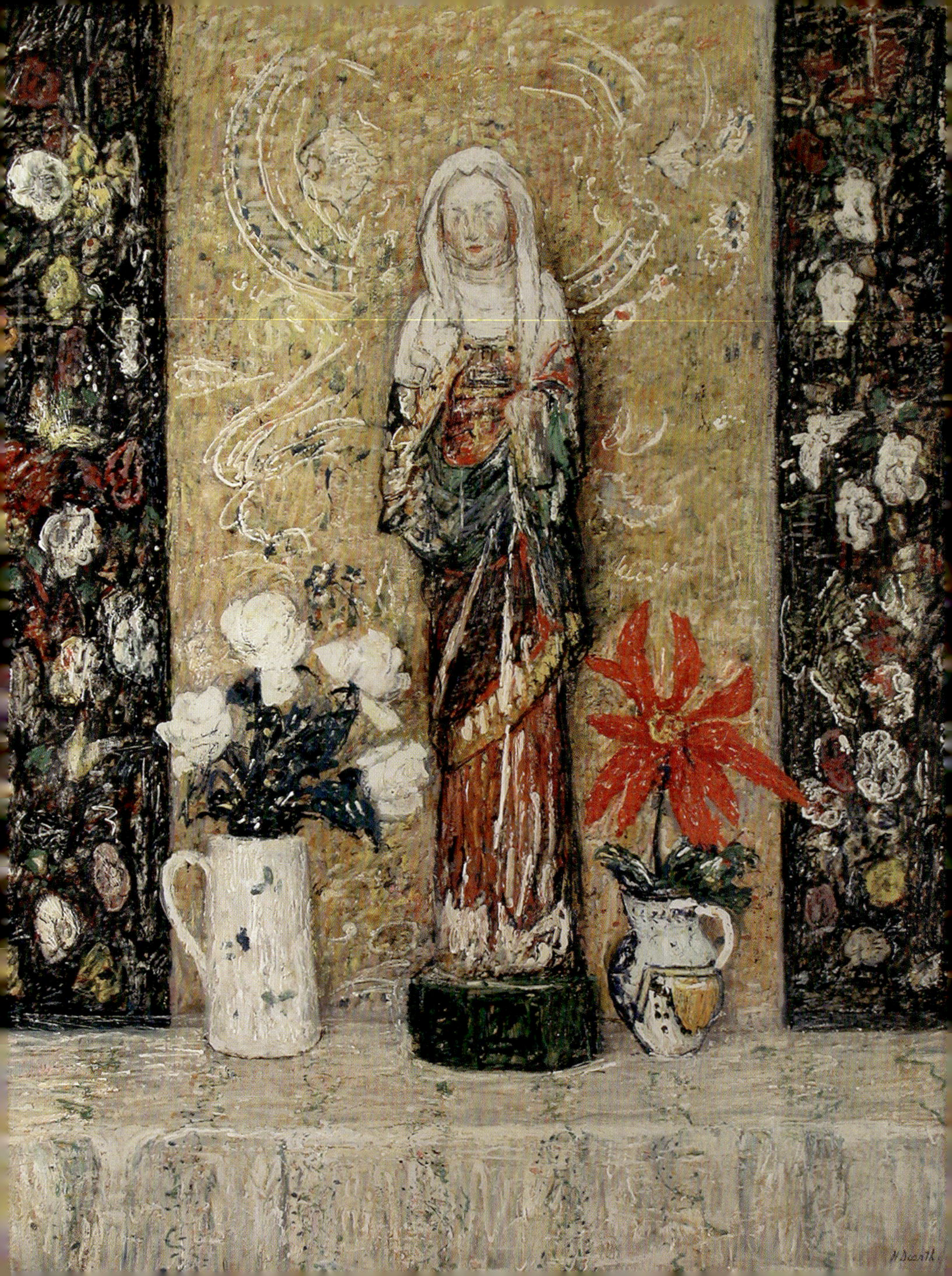

American Paintings

FROM THE
Bliss Collection

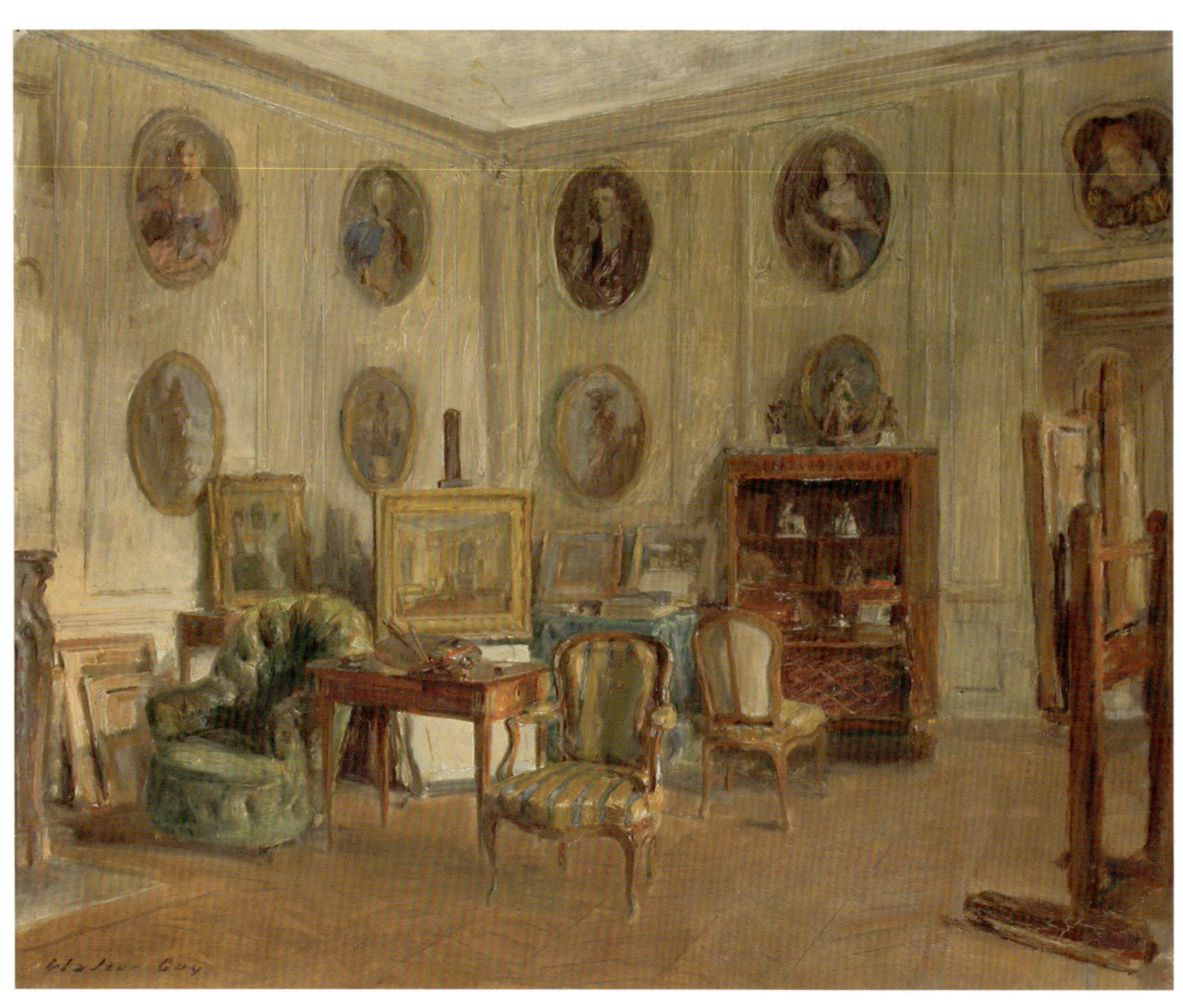

Mildred and Robert Woods Bliss & American Art

BY JAMES N. CARDER

MILDRED AND ROBERT WOODS Bliss were not, per se, collectors of American art in much the same way that they were not, per se, collectors of modern art. Nevertheless, as collectors, the Blisses acquired interesting and, at times, important examples of both American and European modern paintings and sculptures. Such acquisitions were but a part of an overall collection that comprised ancient Chinese, Byzantine, pre-Columbian, ancient Greek and Roman, and European Old Master works of art, as well as rare books, literary manuscripts and holographs, important furnishings, unusual bibelots, and concert-quality instruments—including a Stradivarius viola. In combination with gracious interiors and formal gardens, these acquisitions were a part of a "home of the Humanities," as Mildred Bliss termed Dumbarton Oaks in the preamble to her last will and testament.[1] This ensemble was never meant to be "a mere aggregation of books and objects of art," as she also explained in that same document, but rather a collection of objects of either great rarity and importance or great artistic appeal and often those possessing both qualities. This broad-palette approach to collecting coupled with the Blisses' great wealth would bring Mildred Bliss to serve on the board of trustees of the Museum of Modern Art and Robert Bliss to serve as president of the American Federation of Arts, as vice-chairman of the Smithsonian Art Commission, as vice-chairman of the board of the National Trust for Historic Preservation, and as a trustee of the Santa Barbara Museum of Art.

Mildred Bliss's mother, Anna Dorinda Blakesley Barnes Bliss (1851-1935), and Robert Bliss's father, William Henry Bliss (1844-1932), who married in 1894, were both collectors of American art and, especially, patrons of living American artists. And it is undoubtedly from their "parents" that the younger Blisses first developed their interests in collecting, as well as their taste in American art. Both Anna and Mildred Bliss were great admirers of the work of James Abbott McNeill Whistler, and the teenaged Mildred Barnes acquired a considerable number of Whistler's etchings. She was meticulously concerned about the artistic merits of each etching's state and its condition, rarity, and provenance.[2] Dealer correspondence shows that Anna Bliss occasionally purchased for her own collection prints that her daughter had considered for acquisition but ultimately had declined. Anna Bliss also acquired in 1914 from M. Knoedler & Company, New York, an important Whistler painting, *Nocturne in Blue and Silver, The Lagoon, Venice*. Mildred Bliss inherited it in 1935, and the Blisses later sold the painting in 1942 to the Museum of Fine Arts, Boston, to increase the endowment at Dumbarton Oaks.[3]

It is also from the senior Blisses that their children acquired an appreciation for the American Impressionist artists known as The Ten, especially Childe Hassam and John Twachtman, with both of whom all four Blisses were friendly. William Bliss acquired at least five Twachtman canvases, including *Freshet*, which he purchased in 1903 from the American Art Association's sale of the artist's estate paintings and which he and his wife gave to their children in 1922. In 1905, Mildred Bliss also had purchased a Twachtman, *Snow*.[4] The Blisses hung this painting in their apartment in Paris and then at Dumbarton Oaks. In 1953, Duncan Phillips personally requested *Freshet* and *Snow*, which he knew well, for an exhibition of works by Twachtman, Julian Alden Weir, and Ernest Lawson at the Phillips Gallery, Washington, D.C.[5] When Ira Spanierman, the New York gallery owner, wrote the seriously ailing Mildred Bliss in late 1967, her secretary responded for her on January 5, 1968: "It interested and pleased her [Mildred Bliss] to learn that you have a number of clients anxious to acquire paintings by John Henry Twachtman…. Both [of Mrs. Bliss's Twachtman paintings] rank highly on the list of her favorites among her collection, and she therefore asks me to inform you that, regretting the possible disappointment her decision could be to you, she does not care to offer either of the works for sale."[6] William Tyler, director of Dumbarton Oaks (1969-1977), later sold both Twachtman paintings in the mid-1970s—in keeping with the past practice and general wishes of the Blisses—in order to increase the acquisition endowment and secure funding for the purchase of an important Byzantine gold treasure.

ALSO IN THE BLISSES' PARISIAN APARTMENT UNTIL 1933 and then at Dumbarton Oaks were canvases by William Morris Hunt (*Fontainbleau Forest*), William Keith (*Landscape under Trees*), and Henry Golden Dearth (*Maine Coast*).[7] The exact provenance of the five works by Childe Hassam known to have been in the collection of Mildred and Robert Woods Bliss is less clear, although the senior Blisses purchased at least one of them. *Gloucester Harbor* (cat. no. 73) and Dearth's *Maine Coast* were housewarming gifts to the Blisses from their parents in 1920; it is likely that the Hassam was a painting that the younger Blisses either directly requested or had greatly admired, as was often the case with important gifts from the senior Blisses to their children. In several of Robert Bliss's letters, he mentions having known Childe Hassam well, as in a letter of March 10, 1947, to the Milch Galleries, New York, in which he discusses owning three Hassams.[8] One of these must be *Gloucester Harbor*; another is likely to be *L'Épicerie* of 1889 (cat. no. 72); and the third may be *Hollyhocks*, an early 1890s oil painted in the garden of Hassam's friend Celia Thaxter on the Isles of Shoals, Appledore. The exact provenance of these last two paintings, however, is unrecorded. The remaining two Hassam works from the Bliss collection are a pastel, *Isles of Shoals, Appledore* (cat. no. 74), which was discovered in a drawer of prints and drawings in the Garden Library at Dumbarton Oaks after Mildred Bliss's death in 1969, and a watercolor, *View of Venice*, which Dumbarton Oaks sold in 1975. Mildred and Robert Bliss acquired a second painting by Henry Golden Dearth, *Madonna (Still Life)* (cat. no. 81), when it passed to Mildred Bliss upon the death of her mother in 1935.

It is possible that Mildred and Robert Woods Bliss acquired on their own few American works of art, relatively speaking, knowing that they would inherit their parents' collections. In 1935—in addition to the Dearth, the Whistler *Nocturne*, and, presumably, a Hassam—Mildred Bliss also inherited paintings by Thomas W. Dewing, Thomas Hill, William Morris Hunt, William Keith, John La Farge, Willard LeRoy Metcalf, Robert Reid, and John Singer Sargent, among others.[9] As Mildred Bliss's inheritance coincided with the beginning stages of the Blisses' planning for the institutional phase of Dumbarton Oaks, it is noteworthy that they seriously considered amplifying their newly enlarged American painting collection through additional acquisitions. They sent photographs and, later, the paintings themselves to be appraised by Edward Forbes and Paul Sachs—directors of the Fogg Museum of Art at Harvard University—inquiring whether these works warranted being the nucleus of

an additional collection at Dumbarton Oaks.

Forbes's response on November 8, 1935, although equivocal, probably cast the die against maintaining or improving the American painting collection. As a result of this decision, Dumbarton Oaks later sold the majority of the Blisses' American paintings to increase the acquisition endowment. Forbes wrote:

As to the modern paintings, there again I should say it depends on the quality of the paintings. The Corcoran Gallery has a fairly representative collection of American art, and Whistler, of course, is very well represented in Washington in the Freer Gallery. I think in the long run American art is bound to be well represented in Washington, so I should think that having a large and representative collection of American paintings which take a great deal of room, would be a mistake unless at some time you feel like building a small, separate museum of one or two rooms somewhere on the place, which is for modern art; also again, as I have said, it depends largely on the quality. You ask me to withhold my more definite decision until I have seen the pictures from California when they arrive at Samuels' gallery…. The ones that I should be inclined to think are the more important to keep are the Whistlers, Twachtman, La Farge, Jacques, Childe Hassam, and the Keith of Mrs. Bliss. In these cases, I am judging partly from the photographs and partly from what you say of them, as well as the importance of the man. I happen to like the picture by Douglas Parshall. I know practically nothing about him, but his work seems to me to have a certain beauty. Remington's work has a certain interest for me, and I think he is an interesting figure in American art as is Metcalf. The picture of the statuette of the Virgin looks as if it had charm and beauty.[10]

Forbes was more receptive to maintaining and increasing the Blisses' collection of prints, stating in the same letter: "As for the prints, I should say definitely 'yes.' I think a print department is a valuable asset to any museum." For this reason, Mildred Bliss had her mother's print collection sent to FitzRoy Carrington at M. Knoedler & Company to be stored there with her own print collection. She requested that Carrington send her a checklist of quality prints from Knoedler's print room that would augment and strengthen the Bliss collection. On June 19, 1935, Carrington wrote back: "As directed by you, we have made out a check list of Engravings by Albrecht Dürer, and of Etchings by Rembrandt and by Whistler, now in our stock, the quality and condition of which, 'to the best of our knowledge & belief,' is of such nature as to justify their inclusion in a Collection which aims to have the best—and only the best."[11] This part of the Dumbarton Oaks Collection, however, was not to advance further, in large part due to Paul Sachs's negative reception of the idea. In 1948, the Blisses sold a large part of the print collection—thirty-two Whistlers, two Dürers, three Rembrandts, two Meryons, one Behan, twelve Hadens, and six Zorns—to M. Knoedler & Company, leaving a residual collection of fifteen Whistlers, twelve Dürers, thirteen Rembrandts, and a color lithograph, *The Letter*, by Mary Cassatt, most of which the Blisses gave away or Dumbarton Oaks sold at a later date for the acquisition endowment.

Any appraisal of the Blisses' collection needs to be tempered with the recognition that, like their friend Royall Tyler, the Blisses enjoyed and sought out art that was, with certain exceptions, either outside the mainstream of popular collecting or conceived in an expressive, primitive, or exotic style.[12] In a sense, the Blisses also appreciated "yet-to-be discovered" art or art that was intimately associated with archaeology—having come to light then for the first time. Despite this recognition, it is still surprising, but instructive, to read a lecture on American painting that Mildred Bliss delivered in 1930, in Buenos Aires, on the occasion of an exhibition of American paintings there, which may well have included or even primarily comprised paintings from her own and her mother's collections. In this lecture, her appraisal of the birth of the modern school of American art takes a not-surprising Francocentric point of departure. Also, her dismissal of the traditional early American canon of artists, including the Hudson River Valley painters, is reminiscent of her friend Royall Tyler's similar rejection of the then-accepted European canon. Nevertheless, as delivered in a public forum and by the wife of an ambassador of the United States, Mildred Bliss's remarks ventured far beyond the confines of the private epistolary observations of her friend. The draft of her remarks, which was translated into Spanish for the lecture, is as follows:

> Since colonial times there have been not only artists but a school of Art in North America. The dignified but somewhat feckless Copleys and Stuarts, the aftermath of England's Eighteenth-Century portraitists, were followed by the landscapists, a body wholly lacking in originality and freedom. It failed to develop a romantic movement and merged into the wooden school of realistic nature-painters, with all the stiff mediocrity implied by the term Early Victorian. In the Seventies the Harts and Wyants gave way to a new impulse brought from Paris ateliers and largely under the influence of W. Chase, the modern school of North American Art was born. The original impetus was undoubtedly French, and of recent years most of the younger men have studied, if not abroad, at least with French masters transplanted to schools in the United States. Owing this much to France, it is the more significant of their inherent gift that the painters of North America should have developed such striking individualities as units and as a school. They are fearless interpreters and colourists and unconventional in the choice of material. With the vitality that delights in light and wind, they have a special instinct for the poetry of power, be it of muscle, machinery or architecture. And unlike most young movements it is without caprice or pose. Often its work is exaggerated, but rather from exuberant spirits than from excess of self-esteem. The presence is to be regretted of an element careless and superficial in the handling of paint, which seeks to convey visual impressions with naïf spontaneity and without proper attention to workmanship. On the other hand there is undeniably a disproportionate respect for technique much to be deplored. But these extremes are gradually modifying into an established standard of excellence, and recent exhibitions show an unmistakeable [sic] gain in tone quality. Then too there has been a Secession, without which no modern movement in Art would seem to be complete. Without in the least wishing to imply a limit in either number of artists or types of work, one may say, broadly speaking, that it is from among these men, known as The Ten that the best in North American landscape painting is to be found. They are sincere in their search for Truth which they see through a temperamental similarity, but express in wholly individual manners. The action and wind of Benson, the poetic and mystic quality of Twachtman and the whites and blues of Metcalf are as distinct manifestations of personal vision as Tarbell's crispness, Hassam's haze and Alden Weir's modeling. The work of The Ten is unquestionably significant of the innate sense of Art in the North American people. No sketch of the development of painting in the United States would be complete without mention of the subject or philosophic work of William Hunt, who painted and modeled portraits and allegories 30 years ago, with a largeness and tonal beauty not yet surpassed; nor of John La Farge, who stands high in the three fields of poetic landscape, philosophical and decorative painting…. Of the three greatest portrait painters produced in the United States, Miss Bey Emmet, James McNeill Whistler and John Sargent, the last two have unfortunately preferred to become associated with countries other than their own…. In him [Sargent], despite the faults which come of prolific output, may be found the justification of North America's claim to be a lineal descendant of the great Dutch traditions in the art of painting.[13]

THE ONE CONTEMPORARY AMERICAN PAINTER, albeit an expatriate artist living in France, with whom the Blisses enjoyed a close personal friendship was Walter Gay. The Blisses and the Gays had been introduced by Edith Wharton in 1913, when Robert Bliss was posted to Paris as secretary to the United States Embassy. Their friendship was easily cemented through mutual interests in art and culture and, more immediately, by their shared position as expatriates in a beloved foreign country that was at war. They also had mutual friends who lived in or regularly visited France, including Wharton, Margaret "Daisy" Chanler, Walter Berry, Royall Tyler, and Geoffrey Dodge, whom the Blisses often met at the Gays' country property, the Château du Bréau.

As an aspiring artist, Walter Gay had moved to Paris in 1876, and married an American, Matilda Travers, in 1889.[14] After discovering the eighteenth-century château Le Bréau near the Fontainebleau Forest in 1904, the Gays first leased the property and then, in 1907, purchased it completely furnished in period antiques. The interiors at Le Bréau quickly became the principal subjects of Gay's paintings and solidified his reputation as a painter of quiet, uninhabited rooms possessing only their elegant but casually arranged furnishings, a genre he had first begun to explore in the later 1890s. The Gays' friend Margaret "Daisy" Chanler's reminiscence about the château on December 21, 1905, might equally apply to a Walter Gay painting of one of its interiors: "The memory of Le Bréau haunts and soothes me—as of something very lovely and calm and complete."[15]

Before they left Paris in 1919 to go to Washington, the Blisses had acquired two of Gay's paintings, *The Open Window, Le Bréau* (cat. no. 79), a watercolor, and *Le Bréau sous la neige* (cat. no. 80), an oil. Mildred Bliss greatly admired the Château du Bréau. Notably, this brick-and-stone residence flanked by projecting wings, and surrounded by formal parterre gardens at the side and back, curiously presaged the appearance of Dumbarton Oaks—the property that the Blisses would purchase and begin to renovate extensively in 1920 (see Carder, "Mildred and Robert Woods Bliss and Dumbarton Oaks," fig. 2).[16] Although Mildred Bliss would come to have a fondness for Walter Gay's renderings of Le Bréau's interiors, the Blisses' first purchases of Gay's paintings were not of this signature style but, tellingly, of the architecture and gardens at Le Bréau. *The Open Window* depicts the mullioned glass panes of a casement window seen at close range from inside the house and against a background of the implied textures and colors of the brick and stone of the château's central block beyond. *Le Bréau sous la neige* is a more traditional impressionist rendering of one of the Bréau parterres adrift in snow.

In 1933, the Blisses were offered, at a special price of $2,700, a painting of the sitting room at Le Bréau, in which, according to a letter from Geoffrey Dodge dated December 12, 1933, the Blisses had expressed interest. At the bottom of the letter, in a handwritten draft

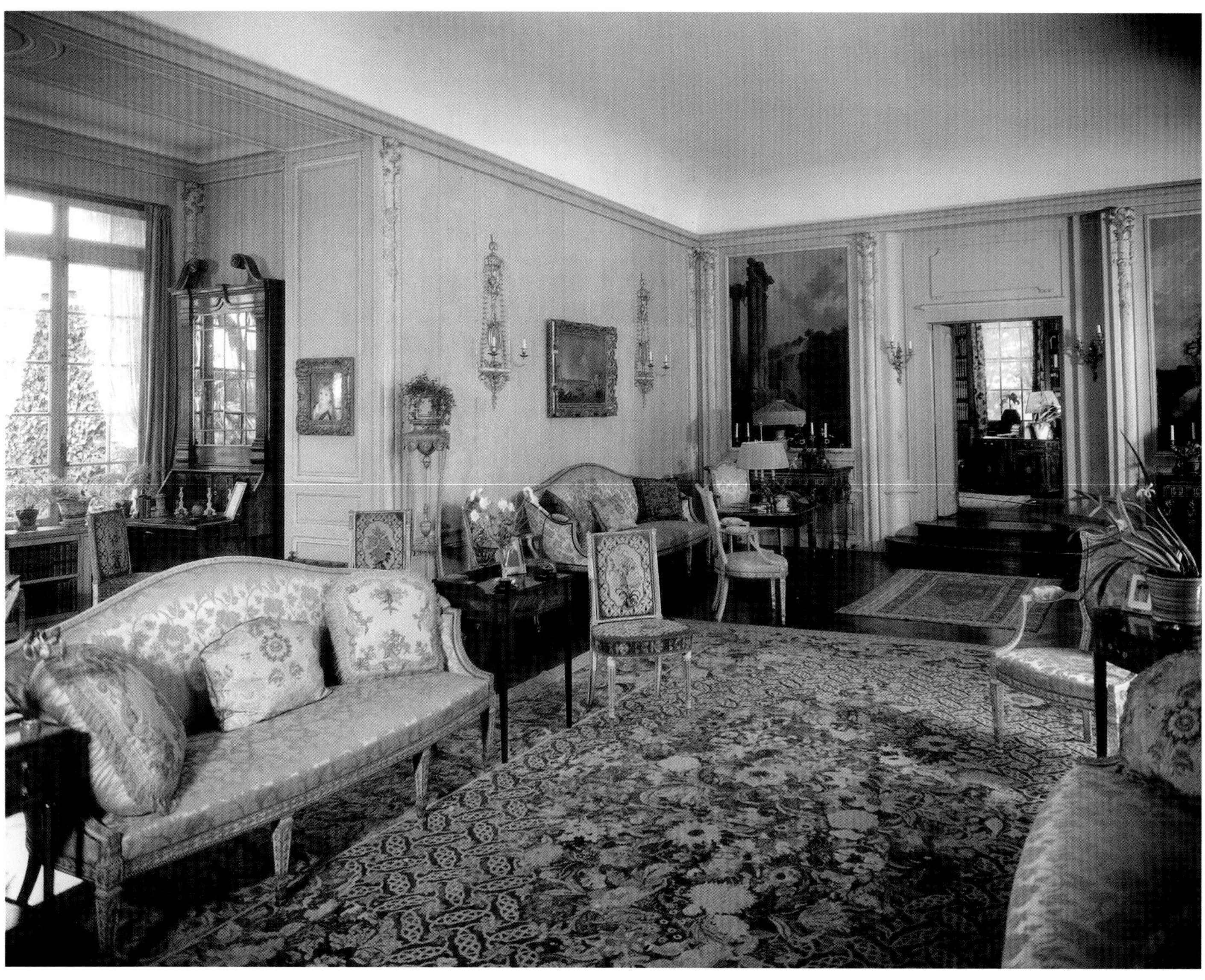

Figure 1. Founders' Room (Living Room), Dumbarton Oaks, December 15, 1940, as designed by Armand Albert Rateau.

for a cabled response, Robert Bliss wrote: "most sorry Gay picture now impossible." In a belated return letter to Dodge dated May 25, 1934, Bliss gave a fuller explanation: "I was sorry about the Walter Gay picture, but we did not feel that we could go in for that extravagance at this time, especially as we already have three of his works, though I should, of course, have been delighted to have had another by him."[17] In 1936, however, as the Blisses prepared Dumbarton Oaks for its transfer to Harvard University and as they embarked on an accelerated period of acquisition activity, they purchased three works directly from the artist, receiving a fourth as a gift. The purchased works, *The Green Bed*, *The Blue Bed*, and *Les Tableaux* (cat. nos. 77, 76, and 78), were all signature Gay works of quiet interiors. *Les Tableaux* is a depiction of the small salon that Walter Gay used as a studio, and the painting records his series of oval views of sculptures in the gardens at Le Bréau as well as an unfinished canvas of Edith Wharton's drawing room at the Pavillon Colombe, her country house in Saint-Brice-sous-Forêt. The green bedroom interior may possibly be the room that the Bliss-

es themselves had occupied when visiting the Gays and therefore of particular sentimental interest.

The Blisses' growing admiration for Walter Gay's paintings of interiors mirrors a significant change in Mildred Bliss's interior design orientation at Dumbarton Oaks. During the early renovation of the house by Frederick Brooke between 1921 and 1923, it is clear that the Blisses desired to create a Georgian-style country property with interiors of an essentially Anglo-American aesthetic. This aesthetic was in keeping with the majority of furnishings that the Blisses had acquired since their marriage in 1908 and was equally appropriate to the origins of the house, the core of which dated to 1801 and the American Federal period. An inventory of their furniture at Dumbarton Oaks prepared in 1924 by the antiques dealer Arthur Vernay, who also had supplied and installed the period Jacobean oak paneling in their library, shows a preponderance of English pieces, mostly of walnut or mahogany, japanned, or painted in the English Neo-classical fashion.[18] A similar, although more extensive, inventory by Arthur P. Thompson in 1938 shows the increased presence of French pieces and a near absence in the principal rooms of the heavier and darker pieces of the English or American schools.[19]

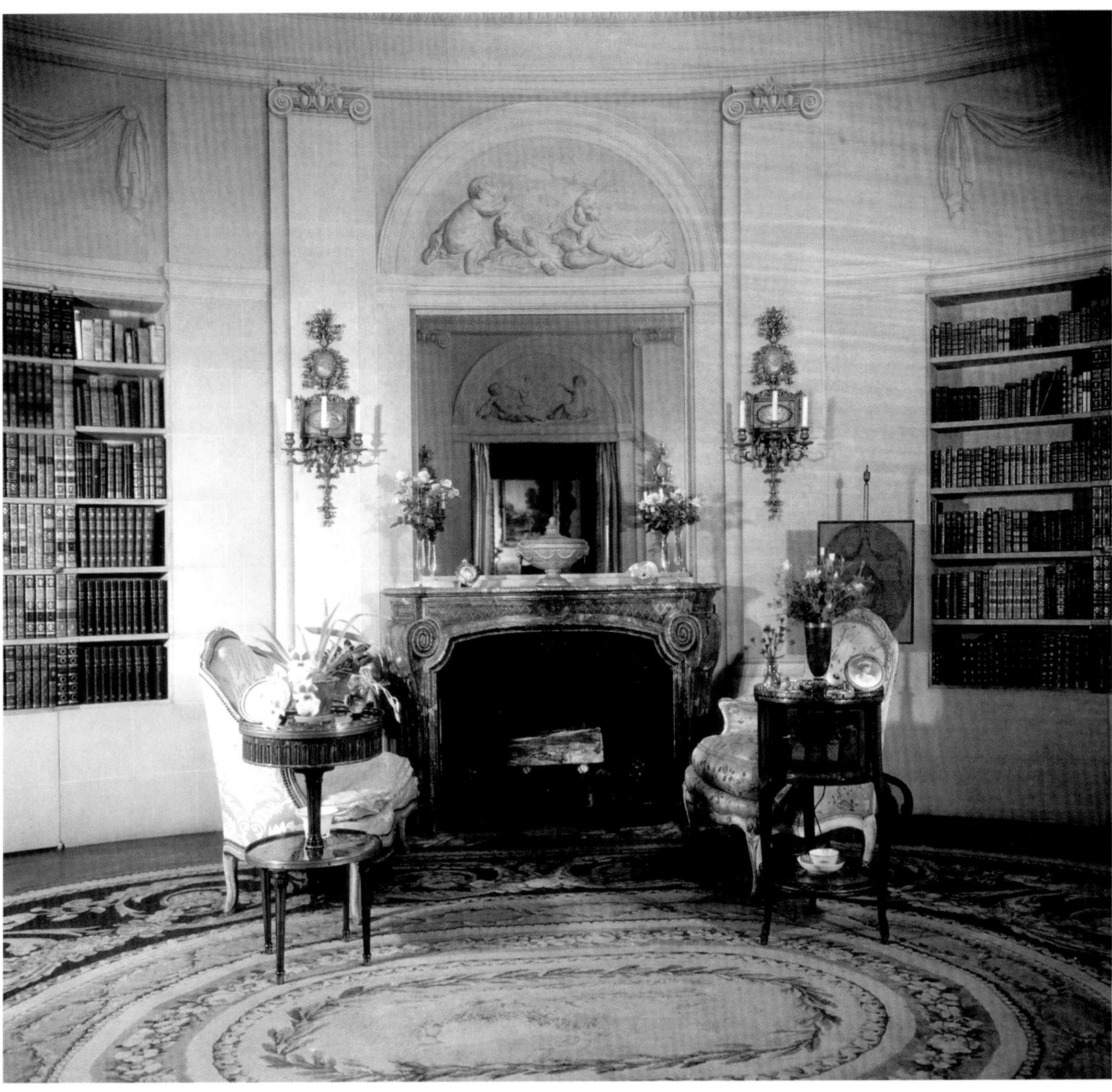

Figure 2. Oval Room (Oval Salon), Dumbarton Oaks, December 15, 1940, as designed by Armand Albert Rateau.

The Blisses' friend, the interior designer Geoffrey Dodge, appears early on to have been aware of what would become a growing dichotomy between the Blisses' expressed interests for Dumbarton Oaks and Mildred Bliss's inherent Francophile aesthetics, especially her love of Le Bréau and its interiors. Being close friends of both the Blisses and the Gays, Dodge well understood the attraction that the French eighteenth-century interior and Walter Gay's taste in furnishings had for Mildred Bliss. He realized that even at Dumbarton Oaks she would want her private chambers to be in the French style despite an otherwise Anglo-American design orientation in the house. On November 30, 1921, he wrote recommending a French antique desk and daybed that "should be perfect in any 'boudoir' that you should have in Washington, if it is going to be a French one. The '*lit de repos*' and this desk I feel so sure of that I wish you would give me 'carte blanche' to buy them with Walter Gay's approval as your 'boudoir' must be absolutely perfect as it is going to be the only French room in the house."[20] Similarly, he tellingly wrote Mildred Bliss on March 9, 1922, recommending the purchase of an English Neo-classical period rug for the Dumbarton Oaks living room, stating: "Of course it is not your period in rugs, but as your room is to be an Adam one, and this is an historical document, it might be worthwhile and would be a good investment."[21]

At the same time that the Blisses were endeavoring to renovate Dumbarton Oaks as a Georgian-style residence, they commissioned Dodge to renovate their Parisian apartment in a French eighteenth-century manner, approving purchases for the apartment of French period paneling and appropriate antique furnishings. Again, the "Walter Gay aesthetic" is frequently alluded to in the transatlantic exchange of correspondence regarding this renovation. Dodge frequently solicited Gay's opinion, and, for example, he reported to Mildred Bliss on March 23, 1922: "I will get Gay to come over and give suggestions as soon as I have the colour schemes worked out."[22] His progress report to Mildred Bliss on May 11, 1922, although unctuous in tone, could serve as a description of a Walter Gay painting of a French interior:

The "salon" especially is turning out very well. I changed a bit as I found a lovely stuff for the curtains which went in well with the other colours in the room and they look delightful, and I am sure will give the same effect as the curtains in my rooms as they are of the apricot colour you like with blues and

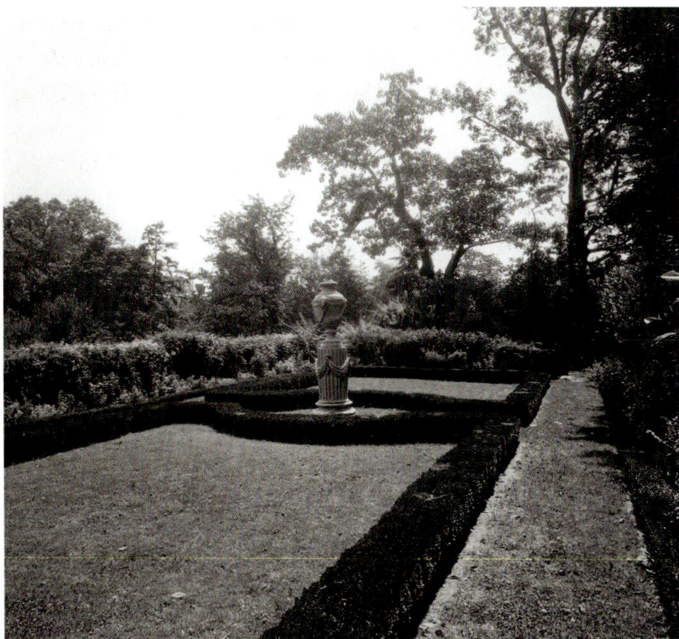

Figure 3. Urn Terrace (Box Terrace), Dumbarton Oaks, summer 1930, as designed by Beatrix Farrand.

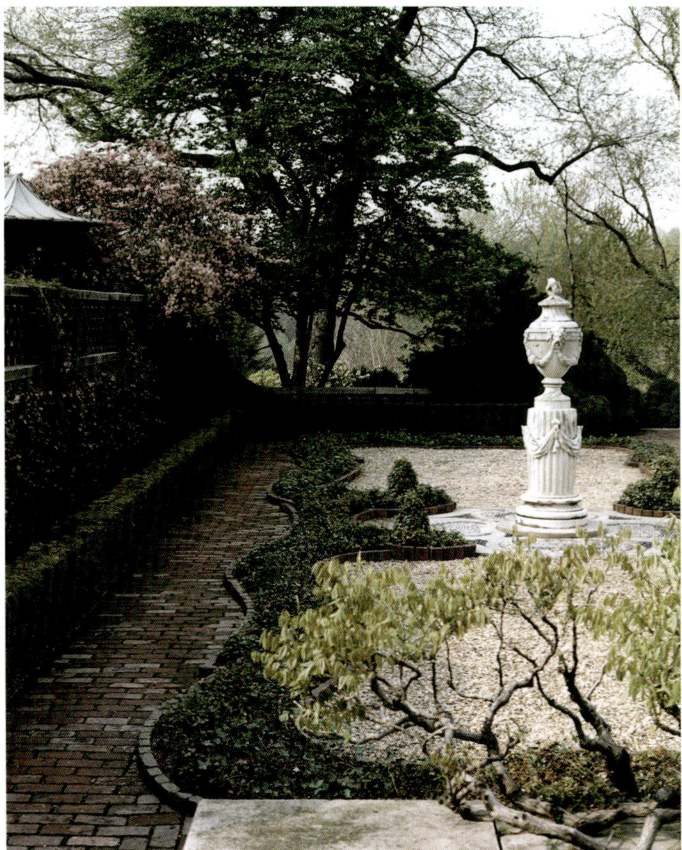

Figure 4. Urn Terrace, Dumbarton Oaks, 1963, as redesigned by Ruth Havey.

greens in them. The green *"lit de repos"* from Buvelot is covered in the loveliest pinky apricot gold Spanish material you have ever seen, and I think the small *"bergère"* with the upholstered back, is the most attractive thing I have ever seen covered in a heavenly Louis XV material with apricot and gold flowers on a *"crème fond"* and goes next to the *"lit de repos."* One can almost say that the two together make a beautiful picture.[23]

IT WAS PERHAPS THE DESIGN OF THE MUSIC ROOM addition at Dumbarton Oaks between 1926 and 1929, and especially the commissioning of the Parisian designer Armand Albert Rateau to provide a reproduction French Renaissance ceiling and a reproduction French eighteenth-century parquet floor, that first signaled a change in the Blisses' aesthetic orientation at Dumbarton Oaks.[24] As quoted elsewhere in this catalogue, Robert Bliss himself acknowledged this change by accurately describing the Music Room as "a delightful medley of Italian renaissance, French eighteenth century, Georgian and American!" The unexpected opportunity of Rateau's coming to America to visit Dumbarton Oaks on December 14 and 15, 1928, to view his work installed in the Music Room, apparently gave Mildred Bliss the impetus to rethink the Georgian decoration of two principal rooms, the living room and the oval salon, as well as some of the landscape designs in the gardens. Her anticipation of Rateau's potential help in changing these features at Dumbarton Oaks may be cryptically recorded in her personal appointment calendar where, for November 21, 1928 (when both she and Rateau were still in Paris), an appointment with Rateau is annotated with the word "attack!"[25] Shortly after Rateau's meeting at Dumbarton Oaks and his return to France, Mildred Bliss commissioned him to design new French-style Neo-classical interiors for the living room and oval salon, for which he was provided measured drawings and photographs. After meeting again with Rateau in Paris, Mildred Bliss reported to the architect Lawrence White on January 29, 1929: Rateau "certainly does understand better than any one I have ever come across, how to reproduce old ébinistrie [*sic*]. [The New York interior designer] Powell might do it equally well, but I rather doubt it. Perhaps his workshops are better equipped than those of Vernay who made the library, but that room I think would have been more successful, both to ceiling and as to wood finish, had Rateau undertaken it…. This man is a treasure, isn't he?" And again on February 5, 1929, Mildred Bliss wrote White: "I await with great eagerness the sketch and suggestions, etc., to be submitted by the omniscient Rateau…. He is an expensive but, I feel, indispensable luxury."[26]

The Rateau rooms were delivered to Dumbarton Oaks in late 1930 and installed soon after (figs. 1 and 2). Although recognizably French Neo-classical in inspiration, the rooms also betray a contemporary *style moderne* quality masquerading as classical. This is especially true of the living room *boiserie* whose carved palm trunks are reminiscent of the plaster designs of Serge Roche, an early twentieth-century French designer. This updated Old World aesthetic was Rateau's specialty, and Mildred Bliss was delighted with the result. The new rooms allowed her to replace the heavier pieces of English antique furniture with French antique pieces, and to achieve an overall aesthetic similar to that found in the rooms at Le Bréau and in the artistic "rooms" of Walter Gay's paintings.

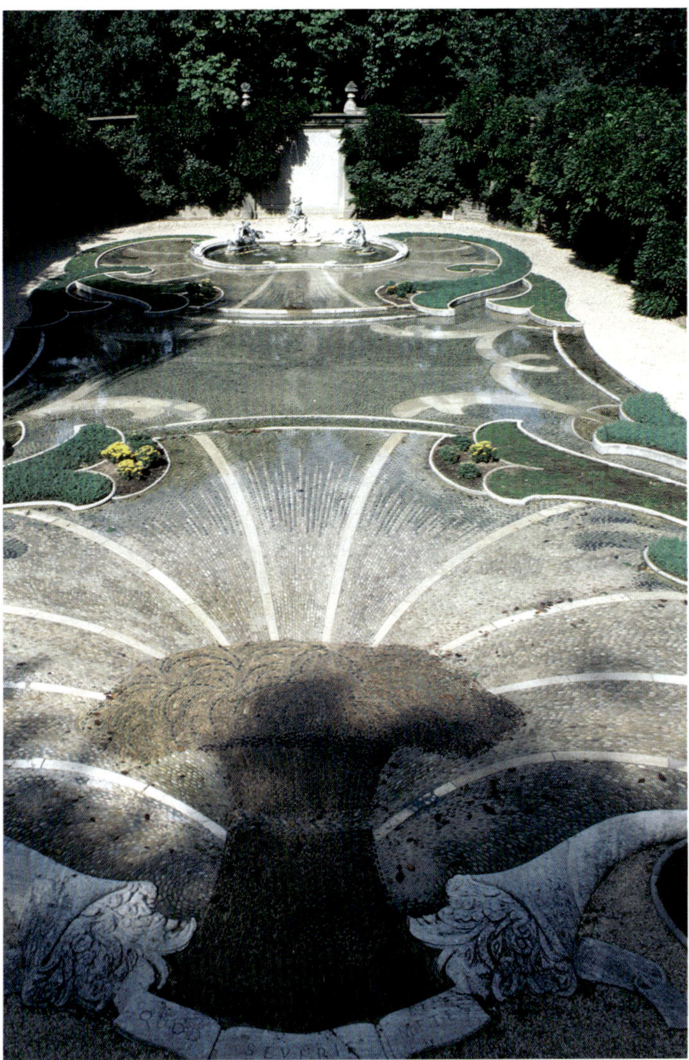

Figure 5. Pebble Garden, Dumbarton Oaks, 1981, designed by Ruth Havey.

SIMILAR CHANGES FROM AN ENGLISH TO A FRENCH aesthetic would appear subsequently in the Dumbarton Oaks gardens under Mildred Bliss's direction. Notable are the changes to the Urn Terrace (Box Terrace), which was originally designed in the 1920s by Beatrix Farrand in collaboration with Mildred Bliss as "an introduction to the Rose Garden, rather than a garden of importance on its own account…. The center of the terrace should always be kept in plain sward, outlined by a simple Box design kept in rather small sizes."[27] In the mid-1950s, the architect Ruth Havey redesigned this and other spaces in a predominantly Rococo style, dramatically changing the Farrand scheme "with the addition of colored pebbles in intricate design at the base of the pedestal, and with the replacement of the straight lines of box with a curved line of ivy, thereby changing the focus of interest from the walls to the ground plane and introducing an altogether more ambitious scheme" (figs. 3 and 4).[28] An even greater transformation occurred in the redesign of the Farrand-era Tennis Court. Again under Mildred Bliss's direction and in order to create "a bang-up finale" as she put it, Ruth Havey designed a Parc de Versailles-like, Rococo-style fountain parterre, the Pebble Garden, best viewed from the vantage point of the terrace above (fig. 5).

As collectors of American art, the Blisses also acquired or commissioned a small number of American sculptures: for example, an Egyptian black granite *Bust of a Polynesian Woman* by Boris Lovet-Lorski; a relief of a female head by Elihu Vedder; two works of sculpture each by Malvina Hoffman and Gutzon Borglum;[29] and a lead garden sculpture, *Virgin and Unicorn*, by the Washington, D.C., sculptor Dan Olney. This last work, which the Blisses commissioned at the height of the Great Depression in 1935 and at a time when many artists were unemployed, may have been motivated more by philanthropy than by a passion to collect. Indeed, throughout the Depression years, the Blisses purchased a fair sampling of both contemporary Argentinian works of art—during their residency in Buenos Aires between 1929 and 1933—and contemporary American works in New York and Washington, D.C. They acquired watercolors, for example, from the Washington, D.C., artists Robert Franklin Gates, Richard Sargent, Aaron Sopher, and Malcolm Hackett, although there is no record that these works were ever displayed at Dumbarton Oaks or elsewhere, and those watercolors that entered the Dumbarton Oaks House Collection came unframed and without mats. Nevertheless, these acquisitions continued both the larger tradition of the Blisses' and their parents' patronage of living artists, as well as their general and long-established tradition of philanthropy. Indeed, Anna Bliss had similarly supported the cause of southwestern American artists until her death in 1935, and, in at least one case, Mildred Bliss concluded her mother's unfinished business when she wrote the artist Kenneth Gordon Grant of Santa Barbara on September 4, 1935: "Meantime, I send you the enclosed cheque for the picture, of which I send a tracing of the photograph, not knowing how else to identify it, there being two paintings with buffalo heads and no number…. I hope you will find the enclosed cheque satisfactory. It seems to me just to us both; I want to help you both immediately with the money and subsequently by showing the picture."[30] In 1942 Mildred Bliss offered this gouache, *San Ildefonso Buffalo Dance*, along with a watercolor by Robert Gates, *The Storm*, an oil landscape by Olin Dows, and other works of art to the Museum of Modern Art to be sold at a fair to benefit the war effort.

In appraising the Bliss collection of American art, a summary of the Blisses' acquisitions of works by contemporary European and American artists not only unmistakably demonstrates a collecting success rate skewed in favor of the Europeans, but it also underscores equally the Blisses' strong interest in acquiring contemporary art while simultaneously building important collections of ancient Chinese, Byzantine, pre-Columbian, and Old Master art and antique furnishings. Although the modern European works that they collected by Degas, Daumier, Seurat, Cézanne, Vuillard, Stevens, Rouault, Matisse, and Picasso perhaps are more familiar than their American images by Twachtman, Dewey, Hunt, Keith, Dearth, Hassam, and Gay, the fact that the Blisses collected any of these modern artists illustrates well the breadth of their interests and their commitment to an art world where collectors were often polarized between the Old Masters (e.g., Andrew Mellon) and the *avant-garde* (e.g., Duncan Philips). Moreover, the Blisses commissioned other contemporary creative talents—Igor Stravinsky, for two important musical compositions, including the famous *Dumbarton Oaks Concerto*; Aaron Copland, for the *Nonet for Strings* to commemorate their fiftieth wedding anniversary; Philip Johnson, to design the Pre-Columbian Collection Wing

at Dumbarton Oaks; and Armand Albert Rateau, to design interiors
for important rooms in their house and sculptures for their gardens,
further demonstrating their interest in and commitment to the world
of their time. The Blisses and Dumbarton Oaks ultimately may have
come to the realization that the Bliss collections of Byzantine and
pre-Columbian art, rare books on landscape architecture, and their
"home of the Humanities" were what should and could be maintained for posterity, but the Blisses' vision and interests were clearly
much broader. The small number of American works of art from the
collection of Mildred and Robert Woods Bliss that remain at
Dumbarton Oaks offer an important insight into this remarkable
breadth of vision. ◆

1. See the epigraph in this volume.

2. Dumbarton Oaks Archives (DOA), Washington, D.C., House Collection, M. Knoedler
    & Co. and H. Wunderlich & Co. correspondence.

3. Museum of Fine Arts, Boston, inv. no. 42.302.

4. DOA, House Collection, Twachtman files.

5. Ibid.

6. Ibid.

7. These paintings, including Twachtman's *Snow*, were hung in the principal reception sa-
    lon of the Parisian apartment along with Alfred Stevens's *Femme Assise à la Japonaise*,
    Bernhard Strigel's *Portrait of Marie of Burgundy*, Walter Gay's *The Open Window, Le
    Bréau*, a fifteenth-century *desco da parto* from the Ferrara School, Jacques Daret's (at-
    tributed) *Portrait of a Lady*, Auguste Renoir's study for *Madame Charpentier and Her
    Children*, Edgar Degas's *The Song Rehearsal*, as well as a Gothic Madonna, two small
    carved and polychromed Spanish figures, a Chinese polychromed wooden figure, a
    Byzantine ivory *pyx*, and a Chinese carved jade drinking horn (packing list sent by
    Mildred Bliss to her secretary, March 25, 1933, DOA, House Collection, M corre-
    spondence).

8. DOA, House Collection, M correspondence.

9. Cf. the "Appendix of American Paintings and Drawings Known To Have Been in the
    Collection of Mildred and Robert Woods Bliss" that follows.

10. DOA, Dumbarton Oaks History, Forbes correspondence. On March 15, 1937, the
    Blisses gave the Fogg Art Museum their John La Farge, *Virgin and His Muse*.

11. DOA, House Collection, M. Knoedler & Co. correspondence.

12. See further Carder's first essay and Nelson's essay in this catalogue.

13. DOA, Blissiana, MBB Lectures.

14. Cf. Rieder 2000a.

15. Margaret "Daisy" Chanler to Matilda Gay (Walter Gay papers, Archives of American
    Art, Smithsonian Institution, Washington, D.C.) as quoted by Rieder 2000b, 861.

16. Carder's first essay in this volume.

17. DOA, House Collection, Dodge correspondence. The third painting that Bliss refers
    to is *Intérieur, Galerie, Le Bréau*, which Gay gave to Robert Bliss as a birthday gift in
    August 1917; the Blisses gave this painting to Matilda Gay's nephew, James W. Wad-
    sworth, in 1949.

18. Arthur S. Vernay, *Robert Woods Bliss, "The Oaks," Washington, D.C., Appraised Inven-
    tory* (May 16, 1924).

19. Arthur P. Thompson, *Inventory and Appraisal of the Personal Property owned by the
    Hon. Mr. and Mrs. Robert Woods Bliss* (July 29, 1938).

20. DOA, House Collection, Dodge correspondence.

21. Ibid.

22. Ibid.

23. Ibid.

24. Cf. Carder's first essay in this volume.

25. Harvard University Archives (HUA), Pusey Library, Cambridge, MA, call no. HUG-
    FP 76.xx, MBB Diaries.

26. DOA, House Collection, McKim, Mead & White correspondence.

27. McGuire 1980, 59-60.

28. Ibid.

29. The Blisses gave a sculpture by Borglum to the Fogg Art Museum on December 19,
    1940, the month after they gave Dumbarton Oaks to Harvard.

30. DOA, House Collection, G Correspondence.

*American Paintings and Drawings Known
to Have Been in the Collection of Mildred
and Robert Woods Bliss*

COMPILED BY JAMES N. CARDER

- Baer, William Jacob, *Miniature Portrait of Mildred
  Barnes*; oil on ivory; commissioned from the art-
  ist, 1897 [Dumbarton Oaks House Collection
  HC.P.1897.03.(O)].

- Beckwith, Carroll, *Nude*; oil; acquired 1935 from ABB
  estate; disposition unknown.

- Boyhan, William, *Study of a Nude*; charcoal; acquisition date unknown; given away, c. 1961.

- Breck, John, *Venetian Marine*; oil; acquired 1904;
  disposition unknown.

- Coleman, Charles Caryl, *Nocturne*; unknown medium;
  acquired 1935 from ABB estate; disposition unknown.

- Cox, Allyn, *Diana and Acteon*; oil; commissioned from
  the artist 1949 [Dumbarton Oaks House Collection
  HC.P.1949.02.(O)].

- Cross, Bernice, *Negro Children*; oil; means and date of
  acquisition unknown [Dumbarton Oaks House Collection HC.P.xxxx.08.(O)].

- Dearth, Henry Golden, *Maine Coast*; oil; acquired
  1920, gift of ABB/WHB; sold through Parke Bernet
  84, NYC, 1975.

- Dearth, Henry Golden, *Still Life with Madonna*; oil;
  acquired 1935 from ABB estate [Dumbarton Oaks
  House Collection HC.P.1935.17.(O)].

- Dewey, Charles Melville, *Setting Sun*; oil; acquired
  1935 from ABB estate; given to the Santa Barbara
  Museum of Art, c. 1942.

- Dewing, Thomas W., *An Interior with Seated Woman*;
  oil; acquired 1935 from ABB estate (purchased by
  ABB from Knoedler & Co., NYC, 3/23/1915, for
  $7,500); disposition unknown.

- Dows, Olin, *Women with Baskets on Their Heads*;
  watercolor; acquisition date unknown; disposition
  unknown.

- Dows, Olin, *Washerwoman*; watercolor; acquisition
  date unknown [Dumbarton Oaks House Collection
  HC.P.xxxx.50.(WC)].

- Gates, Robert Franklin, *Charleston, SC*; watercolor;
  acquired 1934 from Public Works Project, Corcoran
  Gallery of Art, Washington, D.C., for $50; disposition
  unknown.

- Gates, Robert Franklin, *The Storm*; watercolor;
  acquired 1934 from Public Works Project, Corcoran
  Gallery of Art, Washington, D.C., for $50; given to
  the Museum of Modern Art, NYC, to be sold for
  charity.

- Gates, Robert Franklin, *Haines Point*; watercolor;
  acquired 1934 from Public Works Project, Corcoran
  Gallery of Art, Washington, D.C., for $50 [Dumbar-
  ton Oaks House Collection HC.P.1934.20.(WC)].

- Gates, Robert Franklin, *Dust Storm, Langley,
  Virginia*; watercolor; acquired 1934 from Public
  Works Project, Corcoran Gallery of Art, Washington,
  D.C., for $50 [Dumbarton Oaks House Collection
  HC.P.1934.19.(WC)].

- Gates, Robert Franklin, *Autumn Hills*; watercolor;
  acquired 1934 from Public Works Project, Corcoran
  Gallery of Art, Washington, D.C., for $50 [Dumbar-
  ton Oaks House Collection HC.P.1934.24.(WC)].

- Gay, Walter, *Le Bréau sous la neige*; oil; acquired 1916 from the artist [Dumbarton Oaks House Collection HC.P.1916.82.(O)].

- Gay, Walter, *The Open Window, Le Bréau*; watercolor; acquired 9/9/1919 from the artist for 6,000 francs ($400) [Dumbarton Oaks House Collection HC.P.1919.02.(WC)].

- Gay, Walter, *The Blue Bed*; pastel; acquired 1936 from the artist for 10,000 francs ($662) [Dumbarton Oaks House Collection HC.D.1936.034.(P)].

- Gay, Walter, *The Green Bed, Le Bréau*; oil; acquired 1936 from the artist for 5,000 francs ($331) [Dumbarton Oaks House Collection HC.P.1936.35.(O)].

- Gay, Walter, *Les Tableaux, Le Bréau*; oil; acquired 1936 from the artist for 30,000 francs ($1,986) [Dumbarton Oaks House Collection HC.P.1936.36.(O)].

- Gay, Walter, *Nude Figure of a Boy*; oil; acquired 1/29/1936, gift of the artist [Dumbarton Oaks House Collection HC.P.1936.37.(O)].

- Gay, Walter, *Intérieur, Galerie, Le Bréau*; oil; 1917 gift from the artist; given to Matilda Gay's nephew, James W. Wadsworth, 1949.

- Grant, Kenneth Gordon, *San Ildefonso Buffalo Dance*; oil; acquired 9/4/1935 from the artist; given to the Museum of Modern Art, NYC, to be sold for charity.

- Greeley, Russell, *Winter Landscape, Le Bréau*; oil; acquired 1917 (?), gift from the artist; sold through Parke Bernet 84, NYC, 1975.

- Hackett, Malcolm, *Front and Back*; watercolor; acquired 4/15/1938 from the Federal Art Project, Museum of Modern Art Gallery of Washington, D.C.; disposition unknown.

- Hall, C. M., *La Cuna*; oil; acquired 1935 from ABB estate; disposition unknown.

- Hart, William, *Landscape with Cattle*; oil; acquired 1935 from ABB estate; disposition unknown.

- Hart, William, *Landscape with Haywagon*; oil; acquired 1935 from ABB estate (purchased by WHB from American Art Association, NYC, 3/19/1900, for $185); disposition unknown.

- Hassam, Childe, *Gloucester Harbor*; oil; acquired 1920, gift of ABB/WHB (probably purchased by WHB from American Art Association, NYC, 2/1896) [Dumbarton Oaks House Collection HC.P.1920.02.(O)].

- Hassam, Childe, *L'Épicerie*; oil; acquisition date unknown [Dumbarton Oaks House Collection HC.P.xxxx.83.(O)].

- Hassam, Childe, *View of Venice*; watercolor; acquired 1935 from ABB estate; sold to Hirschl & Adler, NYC, 1975.

- Hassam, Childe, *Hollyhocks*; oil; acquisition date unknown; disposition unknown.

- Hassam, Childe, *Isles of Shoals, Appledore*; pastel; acquisition date unknown [Dumbarton Oaks House Collection HC.D.xxxx.008.(P)].

- Hill, Thomas, *Bow River Gap*; oil; acquired 1935 from ABB estate; sold through Sotheby's-Parke Bernet, NYC, auction 3823, lot 41, 12/12/1975.

- Hunt, William Morris, *Fontainbleau Forest*; oil; acquired 1912, gift of ABB/WHB; sold through Sotheby's-Parke Bernet, NYC, auction 3823, lot 25, 12/12/1975.

- Hunt, William Morris, *Sketch for* The Bathers; crayon; acquired 1932; given to the Worcester Art Museum, 1942.

- Keith, William, *Landscape with Mountains*; oil; acquisition date unknown; disposition unknown.

- Keith, William, *Landscape under Trees*; oil; acquisition date unknown, purchased from the artist; sold through Parke Bernet 84, NYC, 1975.

- Kellogg, Jean, *The Green Wave*; oil; acquisition date unknown; disposition unknown.

- Korzybska, Mira Edgerly, *Portrait of William Henry Bliss*; oil on ivory; commissioned 1912 by WHB from the artist; acquired 1932 or 1935 from WHN or ABB estate [Dumbarton Oaks House Collection HC.P.xxxx.10.(O)].

- La Farge, John, *Virgil and His Muse*; oil; acquired 1935 from ABB estate; given to the Fogg Art Museum, Cambridge, 1937.

- Lebrun, Rico, *Nude Rider on Horse*; ink; acquisition date unknown (1940 or after) [Dumbarton Oaks House Collection HC.D.xxxx.038.(I)].

- Lebrun, Rico, *Guitarrero*; ink; acquisition date unknown (1940 or after) [Dumbarton Oaks House Collection HC.D.xxxx.039.(I)].

- Metcalf, Willard LeRoy, *Winter Mantel*; oil; acquired 1935 from ABB estate (purchased by ABB from N. E. Montross, Works of Art, NYC, 4/18/1907, for $1,500); sold to Hirschl & Adler, NYC, 1975.

- Metcalf, Willard LeRoy, *The Pool*; medium unknown; acquisition date unknown; owned by Mildred Bliss in 1921; disposition unknown.

- Minor, Robert, *Landscape with Deer*; oil; acquisition date unknown; disposition unknown.

- Moran, Peter, *Santa Fe*; oil; acquired 1935 from ABB estate (gift to ABB from artist, 1880); given to Mrs. Charles Warren, Washington, D.C., c. 1936.

- Parshall, Douglas, *Eucalyptus*; oil; acquired 1935 from ABB estate; disposition unknown.

- Parshall, Douglas, *Eucalyptus Trees*; oil; acquired 1935 from ABB estate; disposition unknown.

- Reid, Robert, *Forest Brook*; oil; acquired 1935 from ABB estate; sold through Sotheby's-Parke Bernet, NYC, 12/12/1975, auction 3823, lot 82 to John W. Graves, Wichita, KS.

- Remington, Frederic, *Tail Wind*; oil; acquired 1935 from ABB estate; sold through Stendahl Galleries, Los Angeles, to Buell Hammett.

- Sargent, John S., *Corner of the Church St. Mark's, Venice*; unknown medium; acquired 1935 from ABB estate (purchased by ABB from Knoedler & Co., NYC, 2/23/1915, for $6,000); disposition unknown.

- Sargent, Richard, *Still Life*; watercolor; acquired 1934 from Public Works Project, Corcoran Gallery of Art, Washington, D.C., for $25 [Dumbarton Oaks House Collection HC.P.1934.25.(WC)].

- Smith, F. Hopkinson, *Sailboats in Venetian Lagoon*; watercolor; acquired 1908, gift from the artist; disposition unknown.

- Smith, F. Hopkinson, *A Shady Path*; watercolor; acquisition date unknown; given to the Santa Barbara Museum of Art, c. 1942.

- Sopher, Aaron, *Provincetown, No. 1*; wash; acquired 1934 from Public Works Project, Corcoran Gallery of Art, Washington, D.C.; disposition unknown.

- Sopher, Aaron, *The Windows, 1934*; wash; acquired 1934 from Public Works Project, Corcoran Gallery of Art, Washington, D.C.; disposition unknown.

- Sopher, Aaron, *Negro Head*; wash; acquired 1937 from Studio House, Washington, D.C.; disposition unknown.

- Sopher, Aaron, *Diamond Studs*; ink; acquired 1937 from Studio House, Washington, D.C.; disposition unknown.

- Sopher, Aaron, *John L. Lewis*; ink; acquired 1937 from Studio House, Washington, D.C.; disposition unknown.

- Sterner, Albert, *Portrait of Mrs. Arthur Aldis*; pastel; acquired 1908 (gift of Mrs. Arthur Aldis); disposition unknown.

- Sterner, Albert, *Portrait of Mrs. Robert Woods Bliss*; crayon; commissioned 1908 from the artist [Dumbarton Oaks House Collection HC.D.1908.003.(Cr)].

- Sterner, Albert, *Portrait of Lady Kitty*; charcoal; acquired by Mildred Barnes from Frederick Keppel & Co, NYC, 7/3/1907, for $300 [Dumbarton Oaks House Collection HC.D.1907.030.(Ch)].

- Story, Julian Russell, *Portrait of Mildred Barnes*; oil; commissioned by ABB from the artist, 1899; collection of MBB and RWB, Washington, D.C., [?]-1969; collection of Mrs. Gilbert L. Steward, Topsfield, MA, 1/17/1969-11/7/1980; gift of Victoria T. Steward to House Collection, Dumbarton Oaks, Washington, D.C., 11/7/1980 [HC.P.1980.07.(O)].

- Truex, Van Day, *View of Piazza at Urbino*; ink; acquired from the artist, 12/22/1958, for $400 [Dumbarton Oaks House Collection HC.D.1958.001.(I)].

- Tuckerman, Lilia McCauley, *Mountain Scene*; oil on board; acquisition date unknown [Dumbarton Oaks House Collection HC.P.xxxx.14.(O)].

- Tuckerman, Lilia McCauley, *Mountains and Trees*; oil on board; acquisition date unknown [Dumbarton Oaks House Collection HC.P.xxxx.13.(O)].

- Twachtman, John, *Freshet*; oil; acquired 1922, gift of ABB/WHB (purchased by WHB from American Art Association, NYC, 3/24/1903, for $400); sold to Hirschl & Adler, NYC, 1976.

- Twachtman, John, *Snow*; oil; acquired 1/16/1905 by MBB from Silasa S. Dustin for $1,200; sold to Hirschl & Adler, NYC, 1975.

- Vedder, Elihu, *Birth of the Pearl*; crayon; acquisition date unknown, gift of WHB; disposition unknown.

- Vedder, Elihu, *The Pleiades*; crayon; acquisition date unknown [HC.D.xxxx.55.(Cr)].

- Watson, Nan, *Head of a Girl*; unknown; acquisition date unknown; disposition unknown.

- Whistler, James Abbot McNeill, *Nocturne, Blue and Silver—The Lagoon, Venice*; oil; acquired 1935 from ABB estate (purchase by ABB from M. Knoedler & Co., NYC, 3/21/1914, for $25,000); sold to the Boston Museum of Fine Arts, Boston, 1948.

- Whistler, James Abbot McNeill, *Venetian Scene*; pastel; acquired 1935 from ABB estate; sold to William Rolfe, Jr., Marblehead, MA, 1961.

- Whistler, James Abbot McNeill, *Venetian Sunset*; pastel; acquired 1935 from ABB estate; sold to William Rolfe, Jr., Marblehead, MA, 1961.

- Winder, W. Smallwood, *Landscape*; oil; acquired 1935 from ABB estate; disposition unknown.

- Wright, James Couper, *Landscape*; wash; acquisition date unknown; disposition unknown.

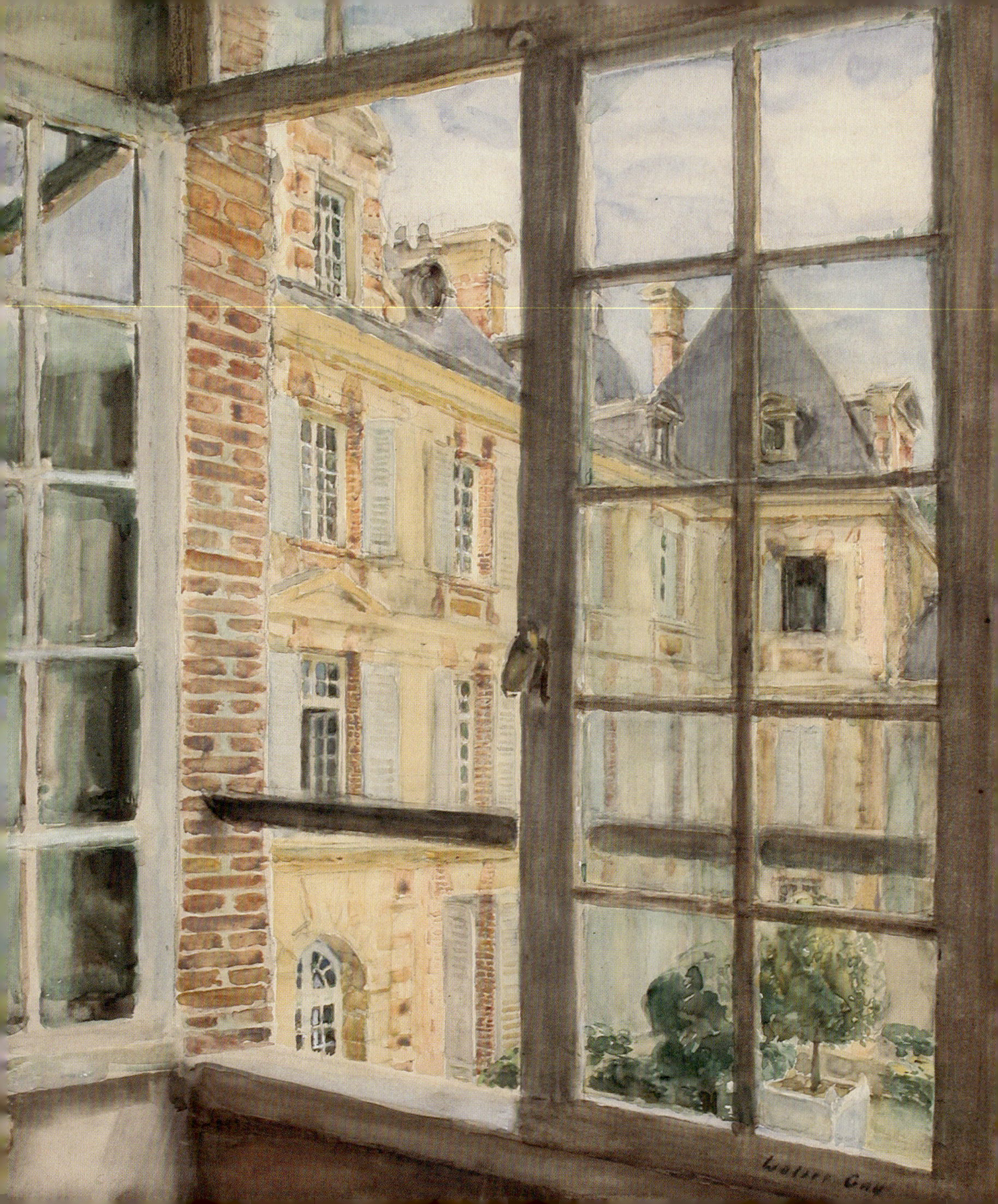
Walter Gay

PAINTINGS

72. CHILDE HASSAM (American, 1859-1935)
L'Épicerie, 1889

Oil on panel
21.59 x 31.75 cm

INSCRIBED: Signed and dated, lower left: Childe Hassam Paris 1889.

CONDITION: Cleaned at the National Gallery of Art, Washington, D.C., 1969.

ACQUISITION HISTORY: Acquired at an unrecorded date and from an unrecorded source by Mildred and Robert Woods Bliss, Washington, D.C.; House Collection, Dumbarton Oaks, Washington, D.C., January 17, 1969-present.

ACCESSION NUMBER: HC.P.xxxx.83.(O)

IN 1886, CHILDE HASSAM MADE HIS SECOND trip to Europe, returning to Paris with his wife for a three-year stay intended to complete his artistic training. Like many Americans, he enrolled at the Académie Julian and studied with Gustave-Rodolphe Boulanger and Jules-Joseph Lefebvre. He soon grew weary of the French academic methods and returned to painting on his own. Hassam also worked to achieve critical notice and submitted images to the Paris Salon in 1887, 1888, and 1889.

In *L'Épicerie*, Hassam presents an intimate view of the facades of two buildings along a sloping French street. This tiny horizontal panel portrays a mundane scene of French urban life and suggests that he found aesthetic potential in everyday places. At the left of the image, a woman in a long, blue skirt stands in a doorway to one of the buildings and looks at the viewer. Flowerpots with blooming plants decorate the windows along the street. At the right, Hassam shows a storefront with a sign inscribed "15 ÉPICERIE." The red-earth-faced marketplace, where groceries are sold, has a large, open-shuttered window with more blooming plants in flowerpots. Utilizing quick brushstrokes intermingled with occasional solid blocks of color, the image creates the impression of a gradual downhill slope, moving from left to right, and a rhythm of rectangles broken by greenery. This composition, featuring a line of shop fronts running parallel to the picture plane, is similar to the contemporary experiments in form and color by James McNeill Whistler, such as the Georgia Museum of Art's *Rose and Red: The Barber's Shop, Lyme Regis* of 1895.

After 1900, Hassam would return to the theme of simple images of little shops lining a town's street. He had visited Charles Lang Freer's collection of Whistler's works in Detroit and later recalled how much he had admired Whistler's "small street things," which Hassam associated with his own "little shop windows."[1]

PM

REFERENCES: Curry 1990, 164, pl. 83.

EXHIBITIONS: *Childe Hassam: 1859-1935*, Guild Hall Museum, East Hampton, New York, March 21-May 10, 1981, no. 3.

1. Hassam interview by DeWitt M. Lockman, February 2, 1927, New-York Historical Society, DeWitt Lockman Papers, quoted in Atlanta, *After Whistler* 2003, 196.

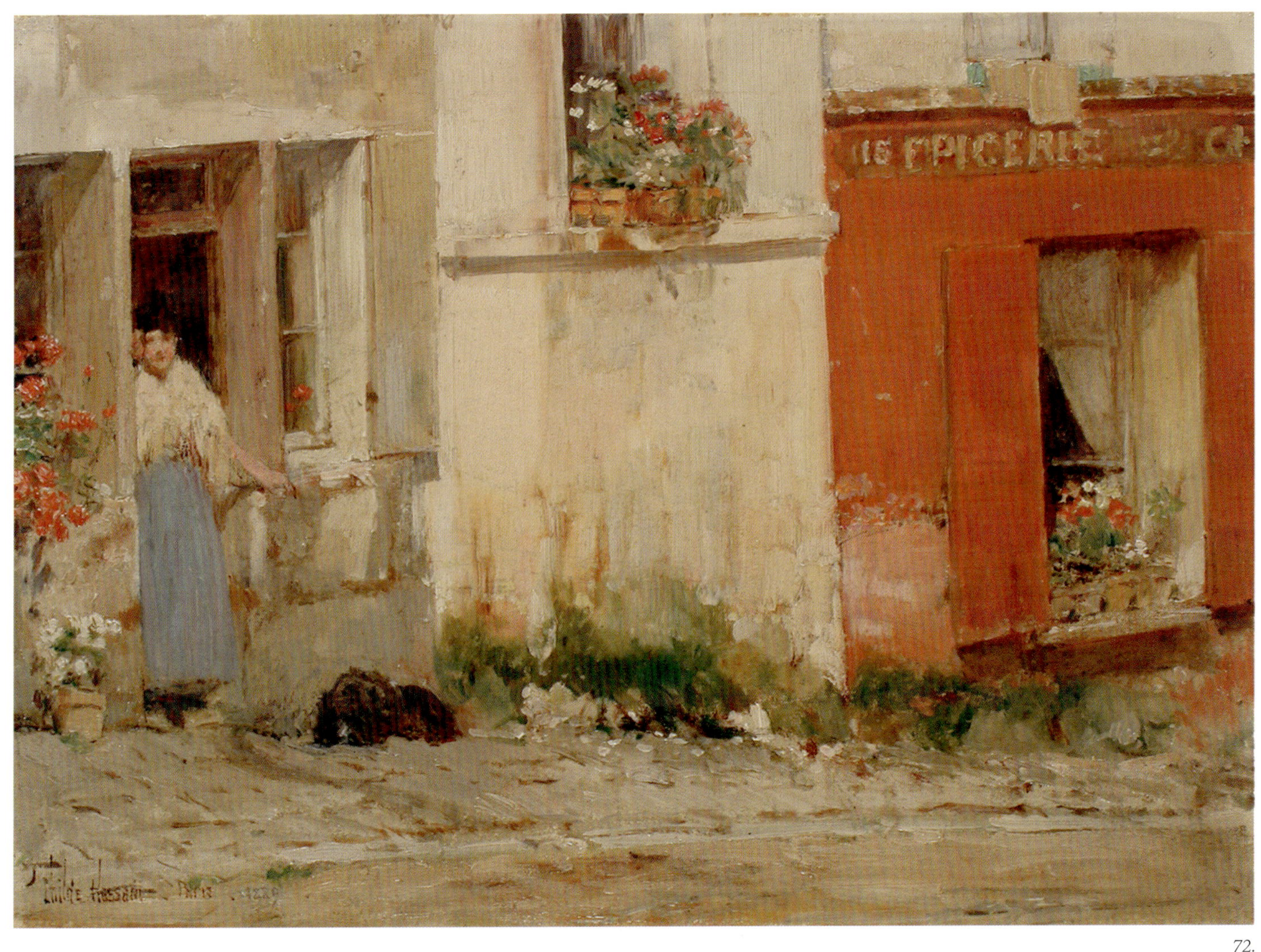

72.

73. CHILDE HASSAM (American, 1859-1935)
Gloucester Harbor (View of Gloucester Harbor), c. 1889

Oil on canvas
60.96 x 50.8 cm

INSCRIBED: Signed, lower left: Childe Hassam.

CONDITION: Relined and remounted, cleaned, varnish removed, retouched,
and refinished (where necessary) by F. Sullivan, Washington, D.C., after February 12, 1969;
cleaned at the National Gallery of Art, Washington, D.C., December 11-28, 1969.

ACQUISITION HISTORY: Probable gift of William H. Bliss to
Mildred and Robert Woods Bliss, Washington, D.C., in 1920; House Collection,
Dumbarton Oaks, Washington, D.C., November 1, 1940-present.

ACCESSION NUMBER: HC.P.1920.02.(O)

CHILDE HASSAM WAS A GREAT AND convivial traveler. In addition to numerous visits to Europe, over the years he lived at most of the east coast's art colonies in the United States. Among the other American Impressionists who spent summers in Gloucester, Massachusetts, were Willard Metcalf, John H. Twachtman, and J. Alden Weir. Like Hassam, they were drawn to Gloucester, by the town's extraordinary seaside light, by the intermingling of older industry and recent tourist activity, and by the area's embodiment of American, specifically New England, culture. During the 1890s, Hassam painted in Gloucester often, stopping there on the way to other tourist locales of the northeast, or spending entire summers in town. His Gloucester works—oils, watercolors, and a series of lithographs produced in 1918—include scenes of the harbor and figure studies of Gloucester citizens.[1]

Hassam's *Gloucester Harbor*, likely painted in the summer of 1889, situates the viewer at the edge of the water, peering across pilings, the harbor, and its boats to the town's houses and churches. The majority of the boats and pilings dominate the right side of the canvas and thereby create an asymmetrical composition. Using an impressionist pastel palette, Hassam fills the Gloucester sky with luminous clouds.

PM

REFERENCES: Hiesinger 1994, 122, fig. 131.

EXHIBITIONS: *American Impressionism [Impressionnistes Américains]*, Smithsonian Institution Traveling Exhibition Service, Washington, D.C., cat. no. 28: Musée du Petit Palais, Paris, France, March 30-May 30, 1982; National Galerie, East Berlin, German Democratic Republic, June 15-July 25, 1982; Museum Moderner Kunst/Museum des 20 Jahrhunderts, Vienna, Austria, August 12-September 25, 1982; Art Museum of the Socialist Republic of Romania, Bucharest, Romania, October 24-December 4, 1982; National Art Gallery, Sofia, Bulgaria, December 15, 1982-January 31,1983; *New Horizons: American Painting 1840-1910*, Smithsonian Institution Traveling Exhibition Service, Washington, D.C.: State Tretiakov Gallery, Moscow, November 16, 1987-January 6, 1988; State Russian Museum, Leningrad, January 22-March 13, 1988; State Museum of Belorussia, Minsk, March 30-May 13, 1988.

1. The scholarly literature on Childe Hassam is vast. For some of the more recent work on Hassam and other artists at Gloucester, see Weinberg 1994, 89-133, and Truettner and Stein 1999.

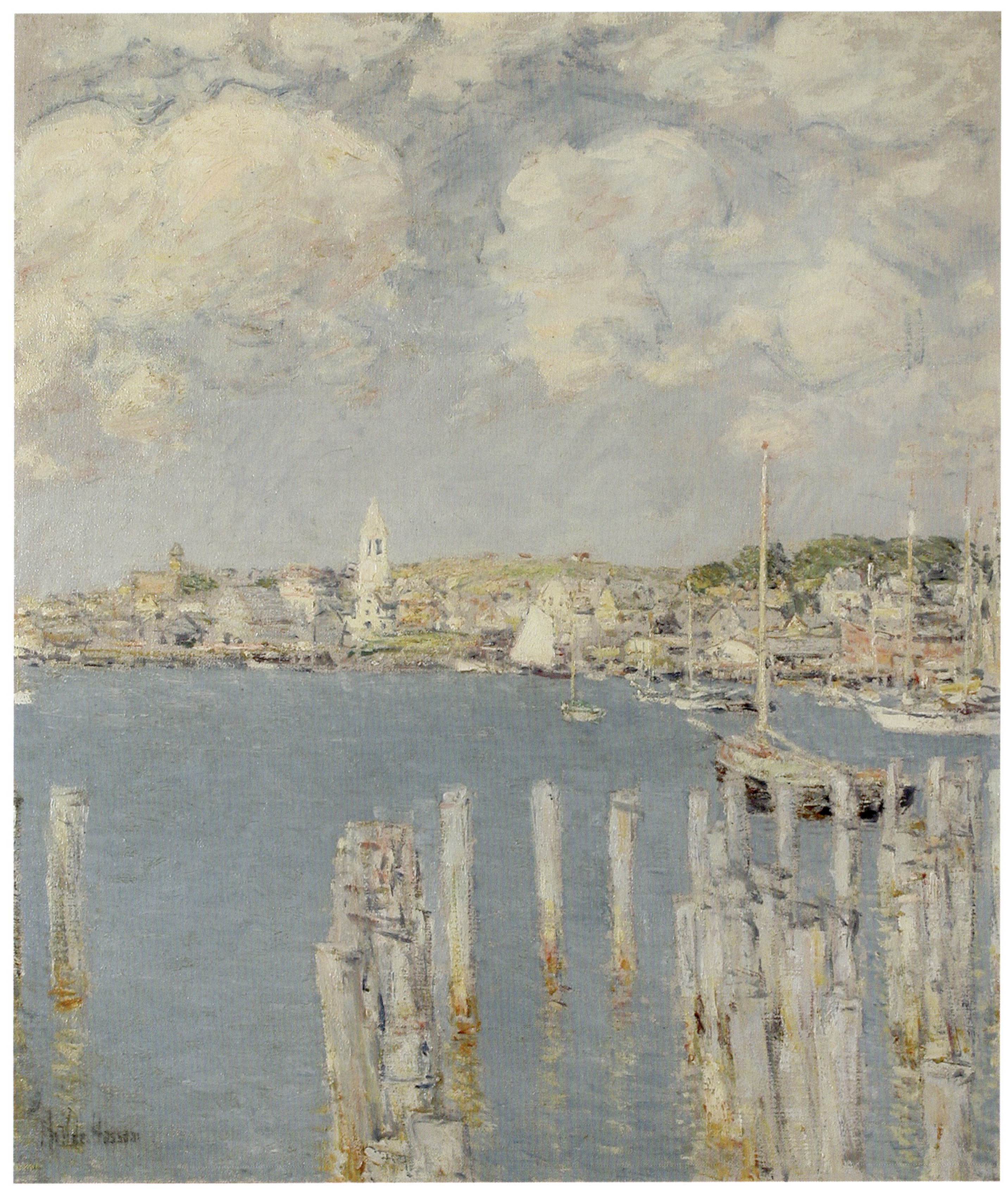

73.

74. Childe Hassam (American, 1859-1935)
Isles of Shoals, Appledore, 1901

Pastel on paper on artist board
26.67 x 29.21 cm

Inscribed: Signed and dated, lower left: Childe Hassam 1901.

Condition: Fair; medium is smooth rather than rich, and
paper support is brittle due to its being glued to an artist board
support; moisture has caused mold spots and some of the medium
to solidify as paint.

Acquisition History: Acquired at an unrecorded date
and from an unrecorded source by Mildred and Robert Woods Bliss,
Washington, D.C.; House Collection, Dumbarton Oaks,
Washington, D.C., January 17, 1969-present.

Accession number: HC.D.xxxx.008.(P)

After Childe Hassam returned to New York from Paris in 1889, he began to take many summer trips to Appledore, one of the islands that make up the rocky Isles of Shoals off coastal Maine and New Hampshire. There, he visited his friend the poet Celia Thaxter, whose summer home served as something of an artists' colony and whose crescent-moon hairpiece Hassam would adopt as an insignia preceding his signature on paintings. The dramatic immediacy of the island's rocky shoreline captured the artist's imagination, and he treated this subject a considerable number of times. The layers of ancient bedrock inundated by the sea fascinated Thaxter as well, and she wrote of its "rifts and chasms, and roughly piled gorges, and square quarries of stone, and stairways cut as if by human hands."[1]

In this pastel, Hassam contrasts vigorous strokes of dark olive green, yellow ochre, and brown to depict the shore's outcroppings of rocks with lighter, more blended tones of blue green, turquoise, and cobalt blue with white highlights for the sea's foam and aqua green and white for the misty atmosphere above. Hassam depicted the coastline from a similar vantage point but on a sunnier, calmer day in the Minneapolis Institute of Arts' canvas, *Isles of Shoals* (14.115).

JNC

Exhibitions: This exhibition marks the first time this pastel
has been published and seen outside Dumbarton Oaks.

1. Curry 1990, 156.

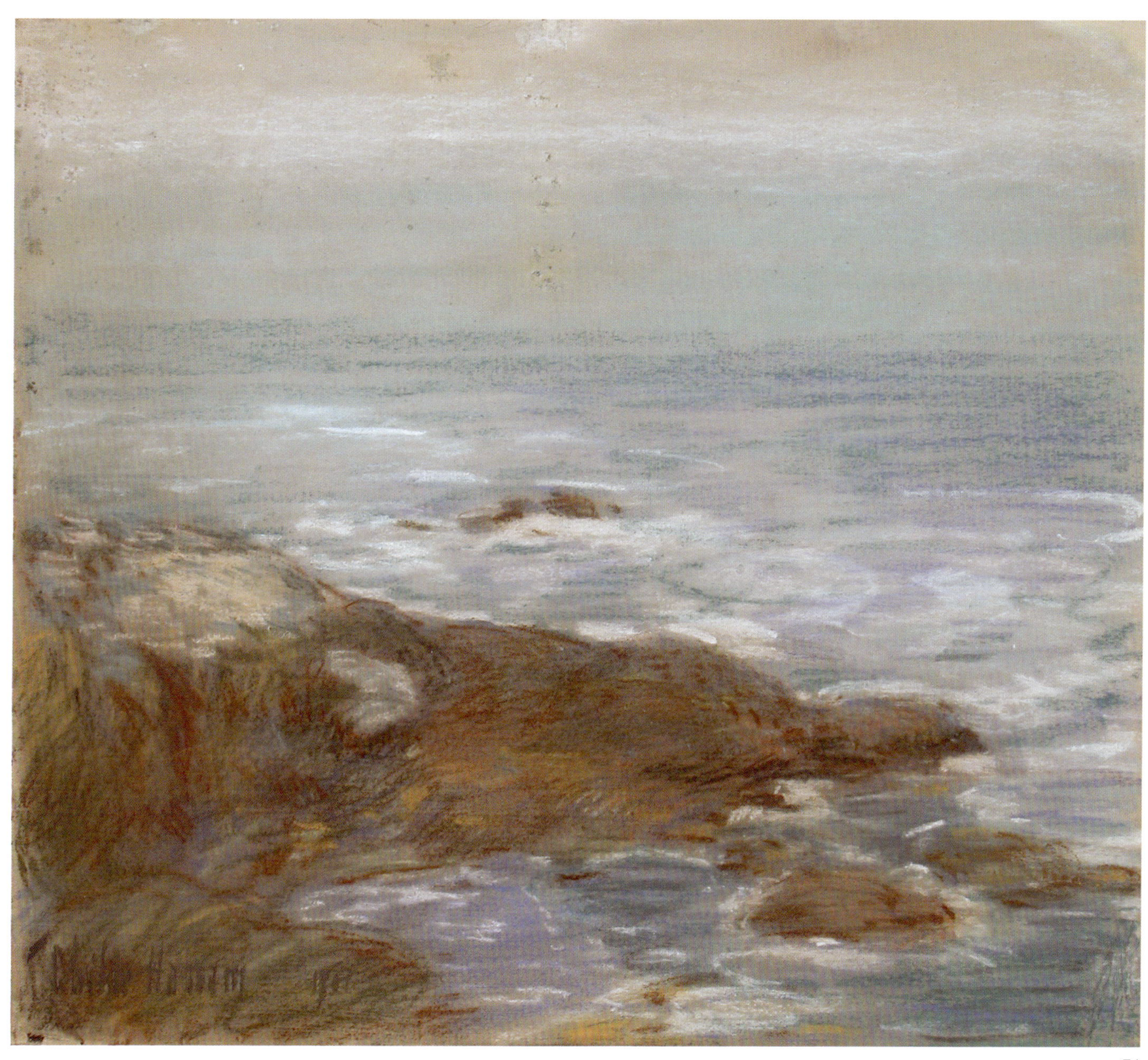

74.

75. **WALTER GAY** (American, 1856-1937)
Nude Figure of a Boy, c. 1876-1879

Oil on canvas
52.07 x 38.42 cm
INSCRIBED: Signed and inscribed, lower left:
To / Mildred Bliss / her affectionate friend / Walter Gay.
CONDITION: Good.
ACQUISITION HISTORY: Gift of the artist to Mildred Bliss,
Washington, D.C., January 29, 1936; House Collection,
Dumbarton Oaks, Washington, D.C., January 17, 1969–present.
ACCESSION NUMBER: HC.P.1936.37.(O)

IN 1876, WALTER GAY WENT TO PARIS to study for three years with the portrait painter Léon Bonnat and, in 1879, made a trip to Spain to study the work of Velázquez. This painting of a young nude boy viewed from the back and standing in closed *contrapposto* is likely a student work from this period. In many respects—the nude subject, linear emphasis, and the tonal clarity of the paint—the painting relates directly to the French Academic tradition of Jean-Auguste-Dominique Ingres. Gay made his professional debut in the Salon of 1879 with *The Fencing Lesson*, which received favorable criticism from both the French and the Americans.

After Gay gave *Nude Figure of a Boy* to Mildred Bliss, she prepared an undated, typed notice on its acquisition for her dossier files:

This picture was found by me in Walter Gay's studio at his Paris home, 11, rue de l'Université, on Wednesday, January 29th, 1936. It was covered with dirt and unframed, and lay behind some canvases and easels in a corner. Bringing it forth, I placed it on a chair, where Walter could see it, saying: "I like that—what is it?"

"I painted that nearly fifty years ago in Bonnat's studio. It isn't bad, is it?" On leaving I told him I was going to steal it from him, and he asked me to accept it. Mildred Bliss.

JNC

EXHIBITIONS: This exhibition marks the first time this painting has been published and seen outside Dumbarton Oaks.

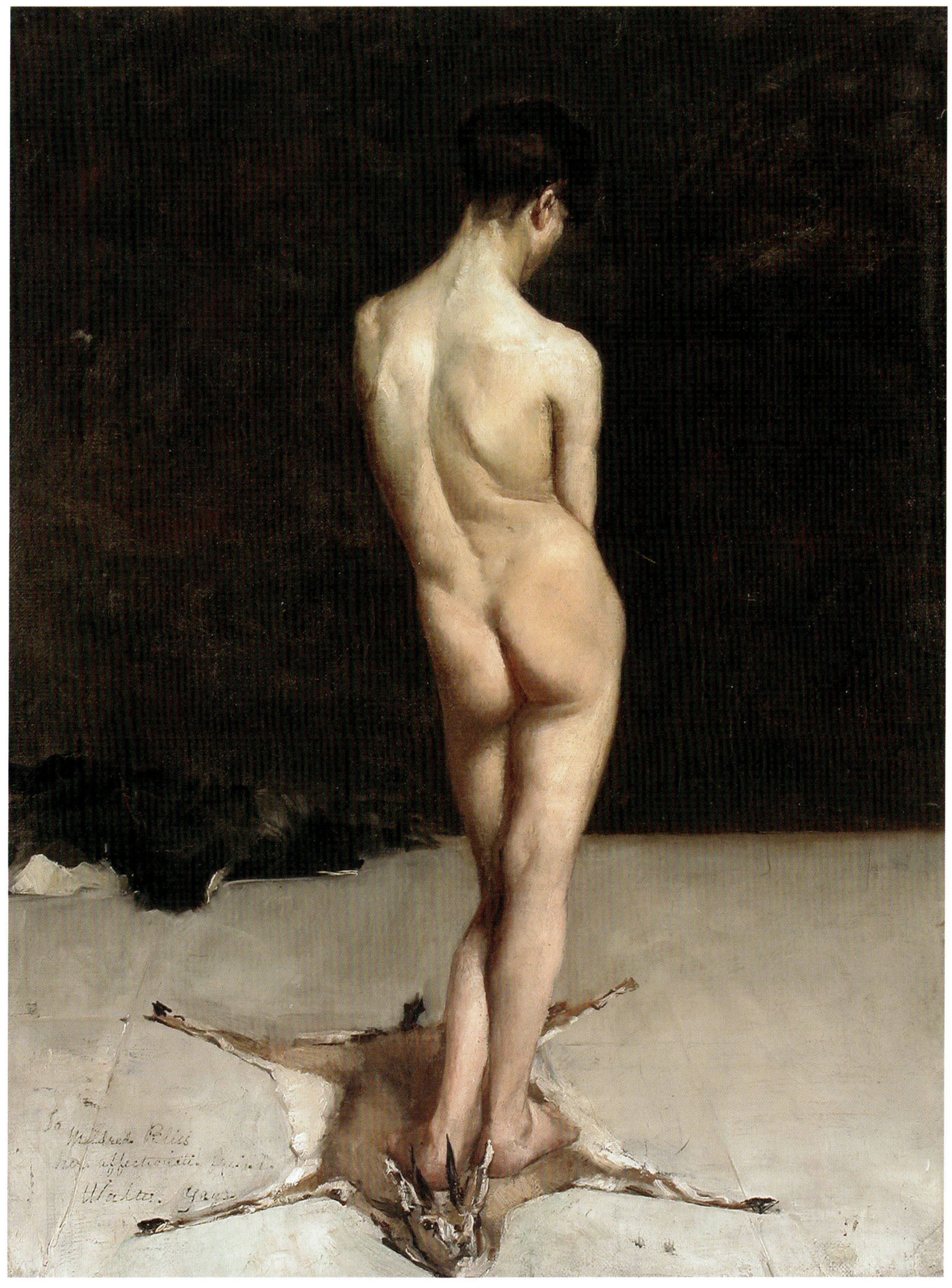

75.

76. **WALTER GAY** (American, 1856-1937)
The Blue Bed, c. 1900-1908

Pastel on paper on artist board
53.98 x 43.18 cm

INSCRIBED: Signed, lower left, Walter Gay.

CONDITION: Good.

ACQUISITION HISTORY: Purchased for 10,000 francs ($662)
from the artist by Mildred and Robert Woods Bliss, Washington, D.C.,
1936; House Collection, Dumbarton Oaks, Washington, D.C.,
November 29, 1940-present.

ACCESSION NUMBER: HC.D.1936.34.(P)

THE RESIDENCE OF THE DOMESTIC bedroom interior depicted in this drawing remains unidentified; possibly it is a bedroom in the Gays' Parisian apartment on the rue de l'Université. According to William Rieder, Walter Gay was known to have appointed this apartment with French Empire furnishings before his marriage to Matilda Travers in 1889.[1] The mahogany Empire bed of Roman banqueting couch design is simply fitted with white linens and draped from a valence with hangings of a Neo-classical-style fabric of alternating blue stripes and stripes of red flowers on a cream ground. The same fabric is used for the draperies and valence of the casement windows to the left, and the colors of the fabric complement those of the rug, which appears to be of European design. The crucifix on the fabricated wall behind the bed and the Empire pedestal nightstand supporting possibly an open book are the only other furnishings seen in the room. The somewhat spare, seemingly more masculine quality of this bedroom contrasts with the more decorated, perhaps feminine decor of the *The Green Bed, Le Bréau* (cat. no. 77).

The inclusion in this drawing of a pair of men's shoes carefully placed beside the nightstand, as well as the open book on top of the nightstand, allows Gay to create an uninhabited yet lived-in interior. As Barbara Scott has written, "the originality of Gay's paintings lies in the absence of human beings, since he wanted to avoid the anecdotal quality of Alfred Stevens's interiors. The two interiors have the feeling of rooms, which are lived in and enjoyed, and the presence of their occupants is often suggested by a vase or spring flowers or an open book."[2] This pastel was in the 1908 exhibition at the Galeries Georges Petit, Paris, and is seen in an installation photograph from this exhibition.[3] Matilda Gay cited this drawing as No. 6. *Le Lit* (pastel) 10.000 frs in her list of paintings sent to Robert Bliss (see cat. no. 77).

JNC

EXHIBITIONS: Galeries Georges Petit, Paris, *Exposition Walter Gay*, April 1, 1908, as no. 20. *Le Lit* (pastel); (possibly) the house of Jean Charpentier, Paris, *Exposition de Peintures, Aquarelles et Gouaches de Walter Gay*, February 8-22, 1923, as no. 22. *Le Lit.*

1. I am grateful to William Rieder, curator of European sculpture and decorative arts, Metropolitan Museum of Art, New York, for providing this information.
2. Scott 1995, 83.
3. Smithsonian Institution, Washington, D.C, Archives of American Art, "Walter Gay Papers," microfilm 2138.

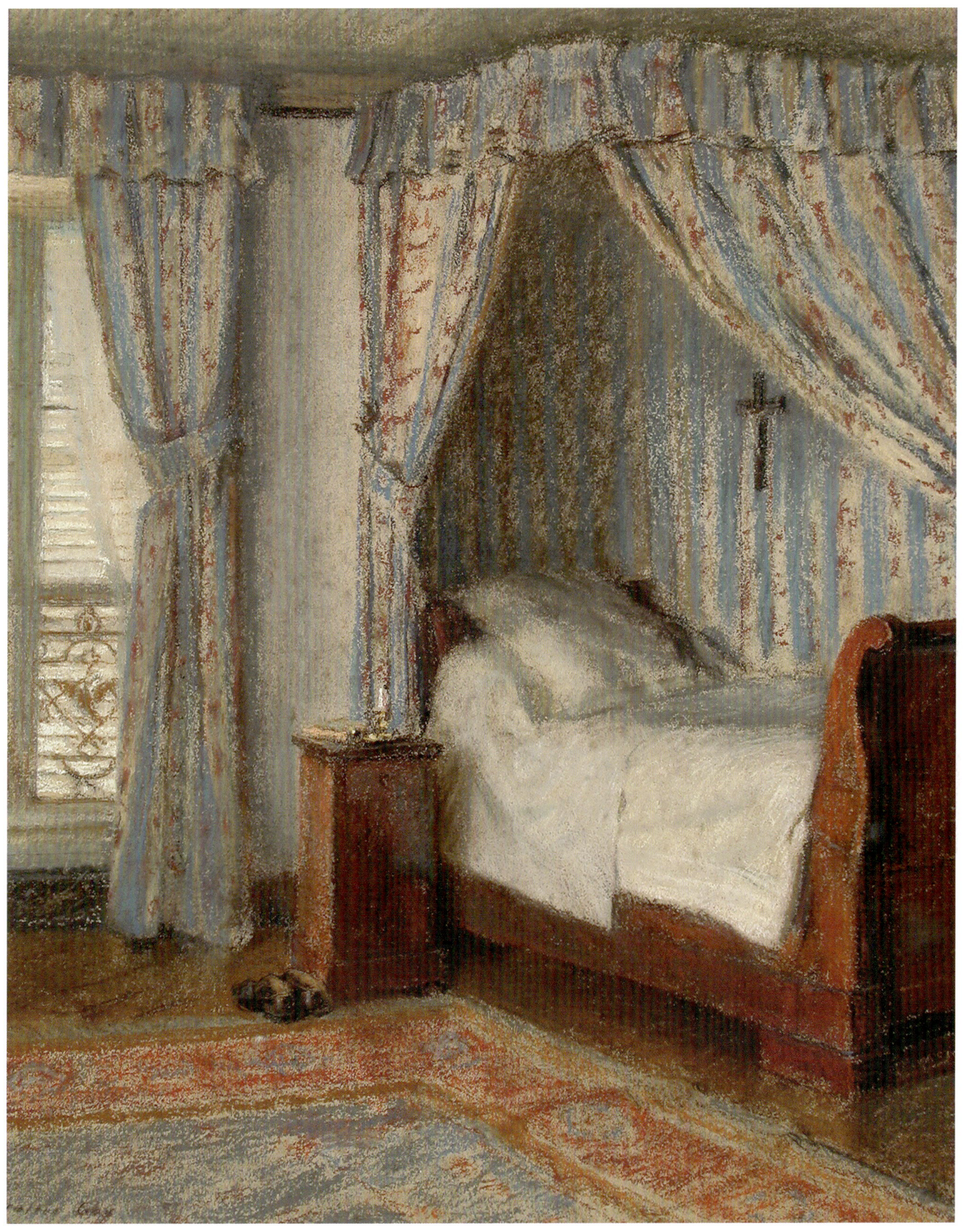

76.

77. **WALTER GAY** (American, 1856-1937)
The Green Bed, Le Bréau, c. 1908

Oil on panel
39.37 x 30.48 cm

INSCRIBED: Signed, lower left: Walter Gay.

CONDITION: Good condition; surface cleaned and small amount of in-fill paint added on August 26, 1980, by H. Stewart Treviranus.

ACQUISITION HISTORY: Purchased for 5,000 francs ($331) from the artist by Mildred and Robert Woods Bliss, Washington, D.C., 1936; House Collection, Dumbarton Oaks, Washington, D.C., November 29, 1940-present.

ACCESSION NUMBER: HC.P.1936.35.(O)

THIS PAINTING SHOWS PART OF A bedroom at the Château du Bréau, near Fontainebleau, which Walter Gay and his wife, Matilda, purchased fully furnished in 1907 from the Comtesse de Gramont d'Aster. The prominent element of the painting is a bed and canopy, each having swags trimmed with fringe and tassels and fashioned in the style known as a *lit à la Polonaise*. In front of the bed is a small Middle Eastern prayer rug that partly covers parquet flooring laid in the *point de Versailles* pattern. Two framed works of art and a crucifix hang on the paneled walls, which are painted a dull green-gold. A Rococo *table de nuit*, supporting a vase of flowers, and two Neo-classical side chairs complete the furnishings.

Other renderings of the green bed are known: a version given by Walter Gay to the Comtesse de Gramont d'Aster and now in a private collection,[1] and a version auctioned by Samuel T. Freedman & Company on June 4, 2000, lot 85, and again by William Doyle Galleries on December 5, 2000, lot 48. The bed and canopy, the chair casually placed at the edge of the rug, and the *table de nuit* are all found in each of the three versions; however, the other furnishings, works of art, and accessories differ. As Rieder has observed, "few of these pictures show the same furnishings because furniture, pictures, sculptures, and porcelain were added and moved about at Le Bréau at a rate that belied the 'calm and complete' effect so admired by their friends."[2] This and Matilda

Gay's antipathy toward the stuffy formality of French houses where there was "never a cosy [sic] confusion"[3] accounts for the informal and seeming asymmetrical compositional arrangement seen in all three versions.

In 1936, the Blisses purchased from the artist three paintings, including *The Green Bed, Le Bréau*. They apparently had considered six paintings and inquired after the prices, and, in an undated correspondence, Matilda Gay wrote Robert Bliss: "Here is a list of prices of the pictures. Walter added another of the green bed. Hoping that you and Mildred will not wrinkle your brows over the decision." The list comprised: No. 13. *Le canapé vert* 5.000 frs; No. 5. *Les portraits* 30.000 frs; No. 3. *Le Cartel* 12.000 frs; No. 7. *Pavillon Colombe* 10.000 frs; No. 6. *Le lit* (pastel) 10.000 frs; No. 27. *Le Boudoir* 6.000 frs; and *Le lit vert–Le Bréau* 5.000 frs. It is the last painting, possibly the one added by Walter Gay, that the Blisses purchased and accessioned as *The Green Bed, Le Bréau*.

JNC

REFERENCES: Rieder 2000b, 862, pl. IX.

EXHIBITIONS: (possibly) Galeries Georges Petit, Paris, *Exposition Walter Gay*, April 1, 1908, as no. 19. *Le lit vert, château de* [sic] *Bréau*; M. Knoedler and Co., New York, *Loan Exhibition of Interiors and Paintings of Interiors*, June 19-July 19, 1934, no. 19.

1. Rieder 2000a, 70, ill. 48.
2. Ibid., 58.
3. Ibid., 62.

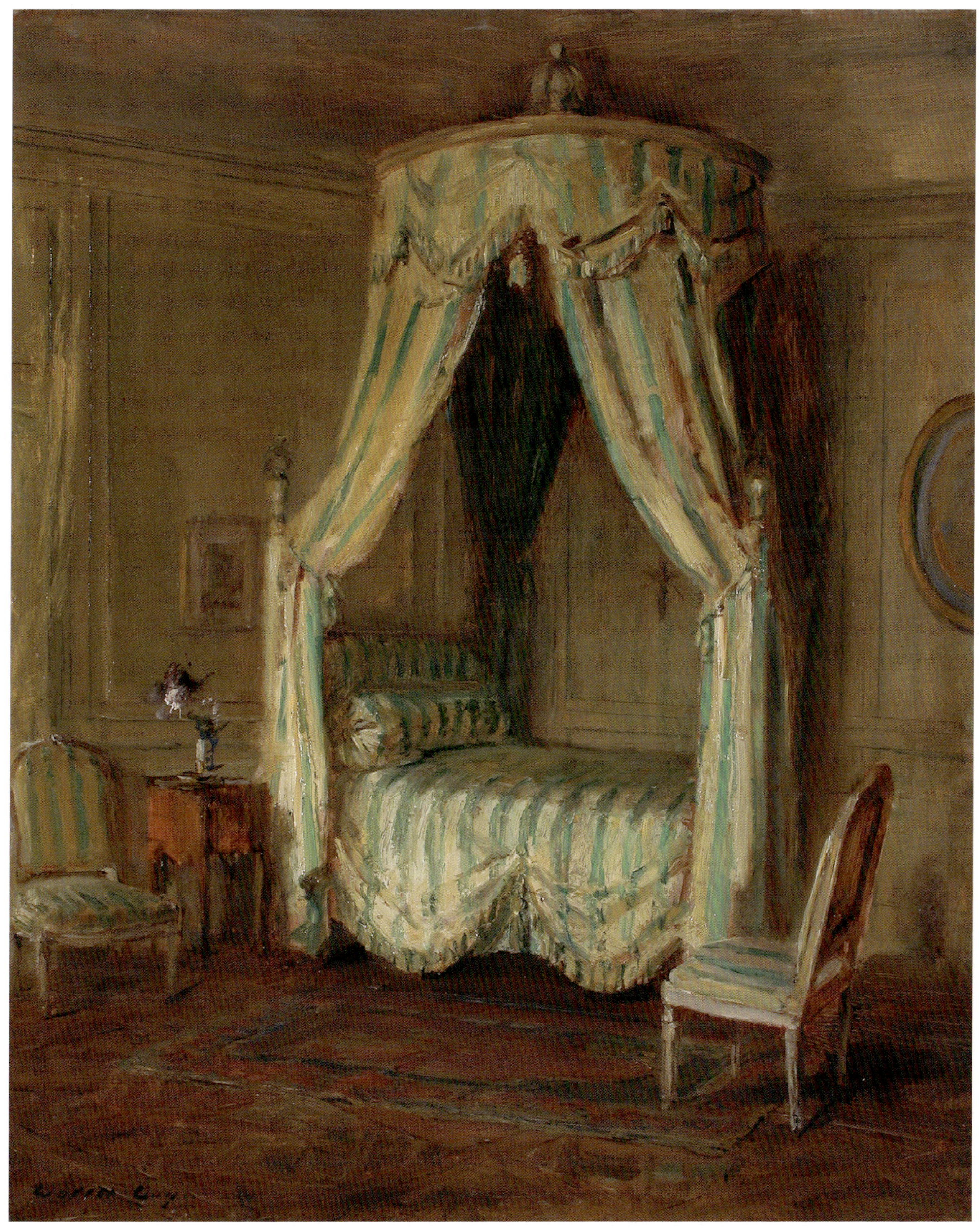

77.

78. **WALTER GAY** (American, 1856-1937)
Les Tableaux, Le Bréau, c. 1908

Oil on canvas
44.45 x 53.34 cm
INSCRIBED: Signed, lower left: Walter Gay.
CONDITION: Good.
ACQUISITION HISTORY: Purchased for 30,000 francs ($1,986)
from the artist by Mildred and Robert Woods Bliss, Washington, D.C.,
1936; House Collection, Dumbarton Oaks, Washington, D.C.,
November 29, 1940-present.
ACCESSION NUMBER: HC.P.1936.36.(O)

THIS PAINTING SHOWS PART OF THE *petit salon* used as a studio at the country home of Walter and Matilda Gay, the Château du Bréau, near Fontainebleau. The depicted corner is situated to the right of a mantel located on the longer wall and to the left of a typical *enfilade* doorway at the edge of the shorter wall. Furniture, paintings, sculptures, and other bibelots fill the corner in a casual, if not crowded, arrangement evocative of Matilda Gay's desire that interiors have a "cosy [*sic*] confusion" instead of the usual "icy" formality of French houses.[1] Flanking the mantel, Gay pairs a Victorian tuxedoed easy chair with a French Rococo *fauteuil*. These are separated by a small French Neo-classical writing desk on which the artist's palette and brushes rest casually. At the far right, he depicts an easel supporting a stretched canvas seen from the back.

Prominent in the depiction are the two rows of oval paintings hung within the rectangular *boisseries*. The paintings in the top row are portraits of Gramont family members; these and other furnishings were conveyed with the house when the Gays purchased Le Bréau fully furnished in 1907 from the Comtesse de Gramont d'Aster. Beneath the Gramont paintings are depictions by Walter Gay of statuary in the gardens at Le Bréau.[2] Gay had painted two related views of this salon, presumably in 1907, before he began to use it as his studio and before the lower row of oval paintings were installed, c. 1908. One view is a watercolor now at the Metropolitan Museum of Art (52.110), and the other

an oil belonging to the Musée d'Orsay (R.F. 1977-441) and presently on loan to the Musée de la Coopération Franco-Américaine, Blérancourt.[3] The painting on the easel seen behind the small writing table is of Edith Wharton's drawing room at the Pavillon Colombe.[4] The other painting nearby is Gay's *The Grandfather's Clock, Longfellow House, Cambridge, Mass.*

Matilda Gay cited this painting as "No. 5. *Les Portraits* 30.000 frs" in her list of paintings sent to Robert Bliss (see cat. no. 77). *Les Tableaux* appears to be a pendant to another painting, *Les Médaillons*, in the Musée du Louvre, Paris.

JNC

REFERENCES: Scott 1995, 85, fig. 6; Rieder 2000a, 60, pl. 38; Rieder 2000b, 862, pl. V.

EXHIBITIONS: (probably) Galeries Georges Petit, Paris, *Exposition Walter Gay*, April 1, 1908, as no. 48. *Les Portraits, château du Bréau*; Metropolitan Museum of Art, New York, *Memorial Exhibition of Paintings by Walter Gay (1856-1937)*, February 9-May 30, 1938, no. 7; Grey Art Gallery, New York University, New York, *Walter Gay*, September 15-November 1, 1980, catalogue p. 110, no. 86.

1. Rieder 2000a, 62.
2. These paintings were exhibited at the Galeries Georges Petit, Paris, *Exposition Walter Gay*, April 1, 1908, as "nos. 52-57. Série de décorations ovales, 6 panneaux."
3. For the Musée d'Orsay painting, see Rieder 2000a, ill. 14; for the Metropolitan watercolor, see Grey Art Gallery, New York University, New York, *Walter Gay*, September 15-November 1, 1980, catalogue p. 110, no. 87.
4. Rieder 2000a, 60.

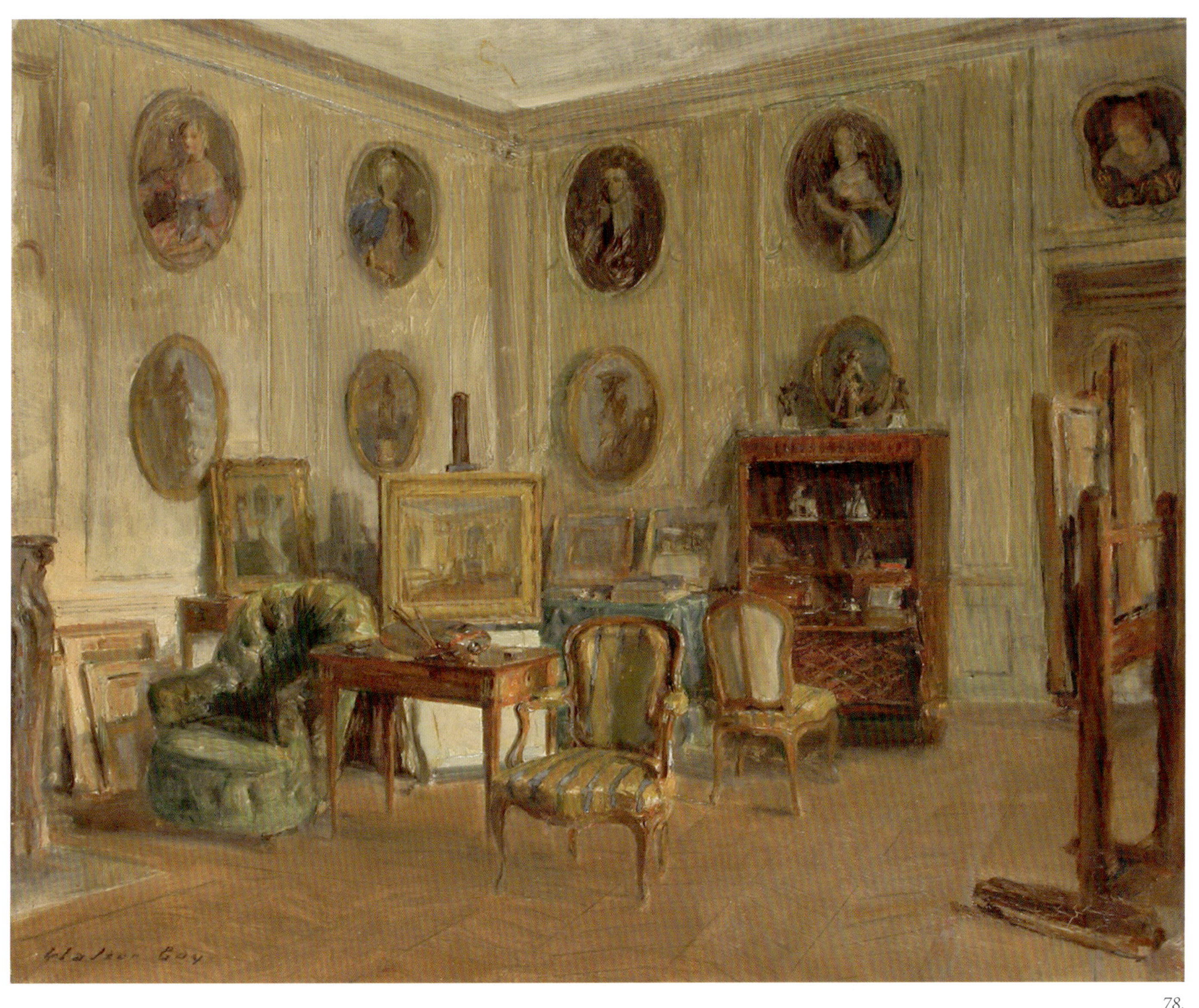

78.

79. **WALTER GAY** (American, 1856-1937)
The Open Window, Le Bréau, c. 1915

Watercolor on artist board
54.61 x 44.45 cm

INSCRIBED: Signed, lower right: Walter Gay.

CONDITION: Good.

ACQUISITION HISTORY: Purchased for 6,000 francs ($400)
from the artist by Mildred and Robert Woods Bliss, Washington, D.C.,
September 19, 1919; House Collection, Dumbarton Oaks,
Washington, D.C., January 17, 1969-present.

ACCESSION NUMBER: HC.P.1919.02.(WC)

THE CHÂTEAU DU BRÉAU, PURCHASED by Walter and Matilda Gay in 1907, was built in 1705. The three-and-a-half-story house, built of stone quoined in brick, featured a mansard roof and end pavilions with pyramidal roofing. Flanking the main block, and attached to the end pavilions, were two-and-a-half-story projecting wings that defined an entrance forecourt. The artist's viewpoint is from the second floor of the left wing. In the forecourt below is a wooden tub planted with a hothouse tree. The close vantage point through the casement window, with one side opened into the room, creates contrasts in pattern between the grid of the window mullions and the wall of windows beyond.

Other paintings by Walter Gay depict exteriors seen through windows or doors, notably an undated gouache-on-paper, *Suffolk Street London* (in the trade with Brown Corbin Fine Art, Boston, 2004). It depicts a winter cityscape scene viewed through the irregular and slightly frosted glass of the lower six panes of a sash window. In the undated *Yellow Curtains, Château du Bréau* (sold Christie's East, New York, May 21, 1991, lot 576), the exterior of Le Bréau is viewed through the open French doors of a salon. A work related to the Dumbarton Oaks watercolor, and possibly painted in the same room, is *La Fenêtre, Bréau* (1915).[1] This canvas shows more of the room, including an octagonal Empire table with a shelf haphazardly covered with books, papers, a glass bowl of water, and a paintbrush. The casement window is closed and only a small part of the château's brickwork is viewed beyond. Traces of the artist's signature, which has been partially erased, can be seen in the lower left corner of the Dumbarton Oaks watercolor.

JNC

REFERENCES: Gallatin 1920, no. 16; Gillet 1921, 42; Scott 1995, 85, fig. 1; Rieder 2000a, 53-54, pl. 30; Rieder 2000b, 861, pl. II.

EXHIBITIONS: Gimpel and Wildenstein Galleries, New York, *An Exhibition of Paintings and Water Colors by Walter Gay*, February 17-March 6, 1920, as "no. 23. *The Open Window* (Water Color);" Knoedler & Co., New York, *American Institute of Decorators, Loan Exhibition*, 1934; Metropolitan Museum of Art, New York, *Memorial Exhibition of Paintings by Walter Gay (1856-1937)*, April 9-30, 1938, no. 30; Grey Art Gallery, New York University, New York, *Walter Gay*, September 15-November 1, 1980, catalogue p. 111, no. 88.

1. Caldwell 2003, no. 8, private collection, New York.

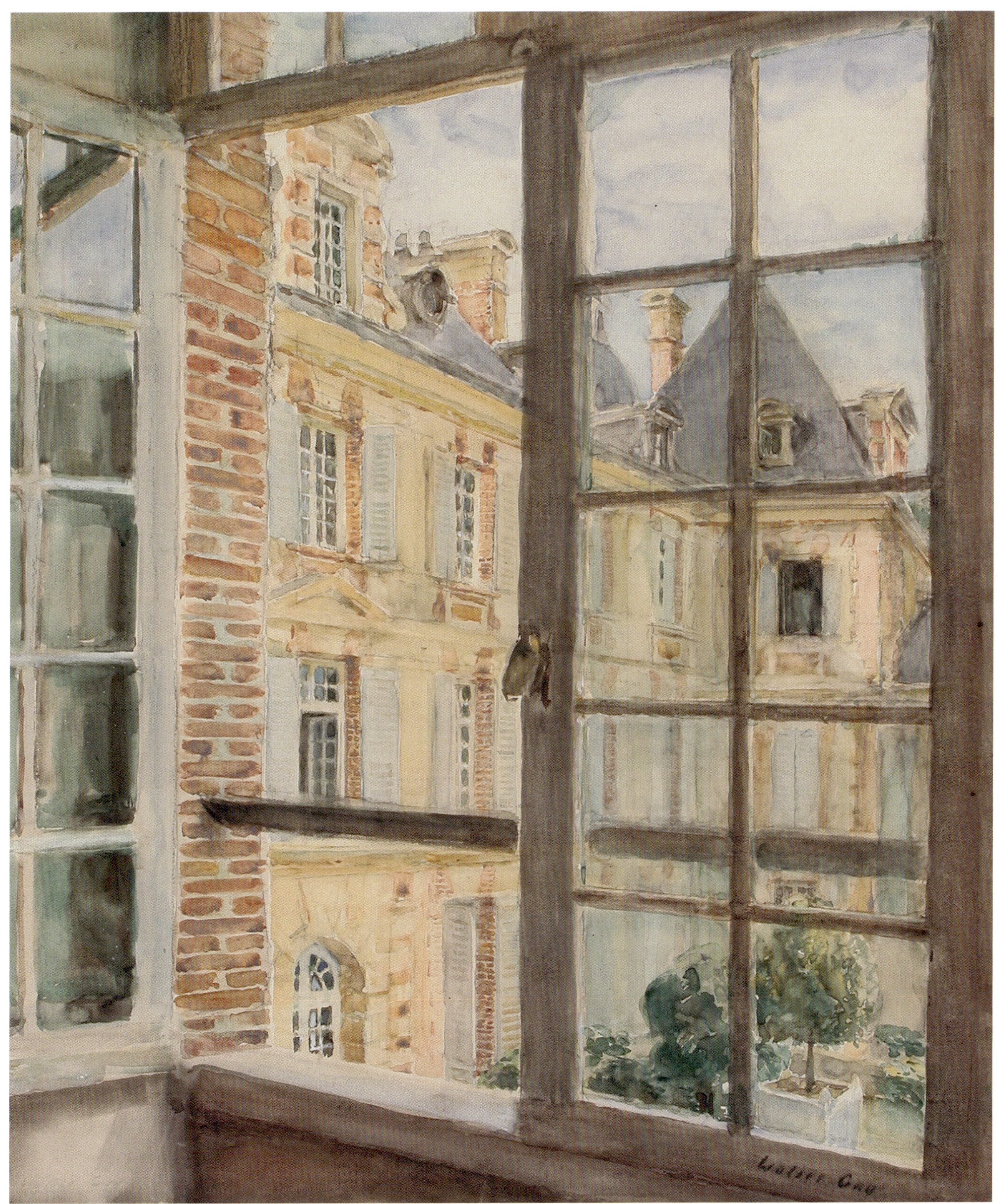

79.

I N *L E B RÉAU SOUS LA NEIGE* G AY PRESENTS the grounds of his château during the winter. In the foreground, he shows a terrace where a large decorative urn marks the corner of the railing wall or balustrade, overgrown by an evergreen vine and covered with snow. In front of this wall is a green park bench on top of which several inches of snow have piled. The terrace rises above the moat surrounding the building and seen in the middle ground. The formal gardens, which include a pavilion and a small stone fountain, feature prominently in the distance. Beyond these are the woods by which Le Bréau was surrounded, a three-hundred-acre walled park bordering the Forest of Fontainebleau.[1]

Although Gay painted almost every corner of the château's interior, with the single exception of the chapel, he made very few exterior views of his country residence. Three of them include the moat—one of the most distinct features of the Gays' eighteenth-century estate.[2] A similar view toward the formal garden rooms including the terrace and the moat, shown in the autumn, exists in two renditions, which clearly demonstrates that these parts of the grounds captured Gay's attention.[3] Notably, while the lookout point in the snowscape is the terrace, in the autumn landscape the view is toward the terrace from the garden and across the moat (see fig. 80A).

Gay uses broad brushstrokes of blues, greens, grays, and browns in rendering the *effets de neige*—the visual effects of the light-reflecting snow cover.[4] *Le Bréau sous la neige* is intimate, quiet, and contemplative without being brooding and melancholic. Certainly familiar with French Impressionist snowscapes, Gay echoes their mood of serenity and peaceful solitude.[5]

The exterior views of Le Bréau share key characteristics with many of Gay's paintings of interiors. Indeed, the painter composed *Le Bréau sous la neige* like some of his signature interior views, which focus on a corner of a room and look toward spaces seen though an open window, an *enfilade*, or reflected in a mirror (cf. cat. nos. 76-79).[6] More than the distant vista, it is a lookout that generates the mood in this landscape. Gay enhances the sense of wintertime by choosing as a vantage point the terrace, reminiscent of an interior not only because of its railing wall, but also for the reason of being elevated above the ground and removed from the forest by two clearly defined spaces—the garden and the moat.

A reference to *Le Bréau sous la neige* appears in an unpublished manuscript of William Royall Tyler (1910-2003), the second director of Dumbarton Oaks and the son of Elisina and Royall Tyler, close friends of both the Gays and the Blisses. During World War I, the Tylers remained in Paris in their residence on Île Saint-Louis. William Tyler remembered his early childhood in Paris—then under the bombardment of German artillery—and his subsequent escape to the safety of the Gays' country estate:

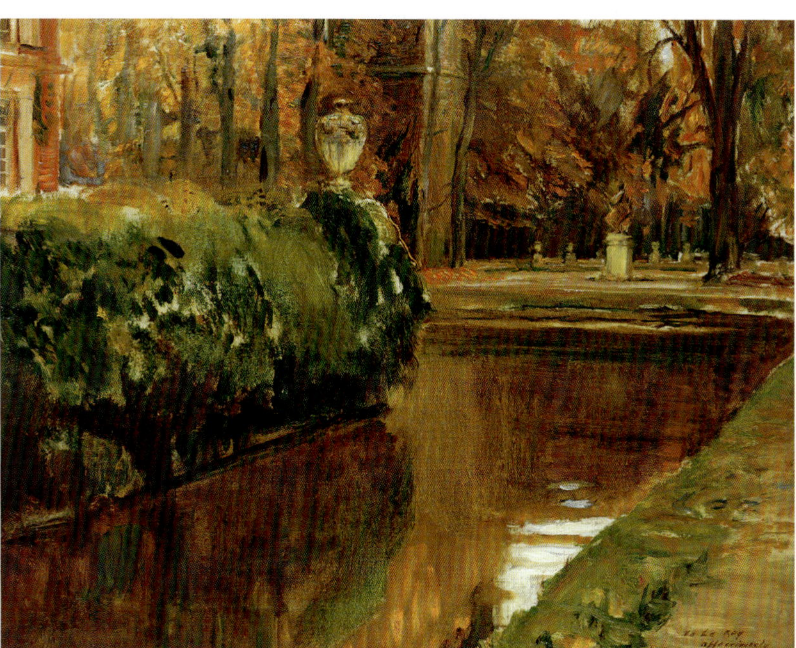

Figure 80A. Walter Gay, *The Moat, Le Bréau, 1921,* Oil on canvas, 54 x 44 cm, Signed lower right: *Le Bréau, 1921, To Le Roy affectionately Walter Gay. Private Collection.*

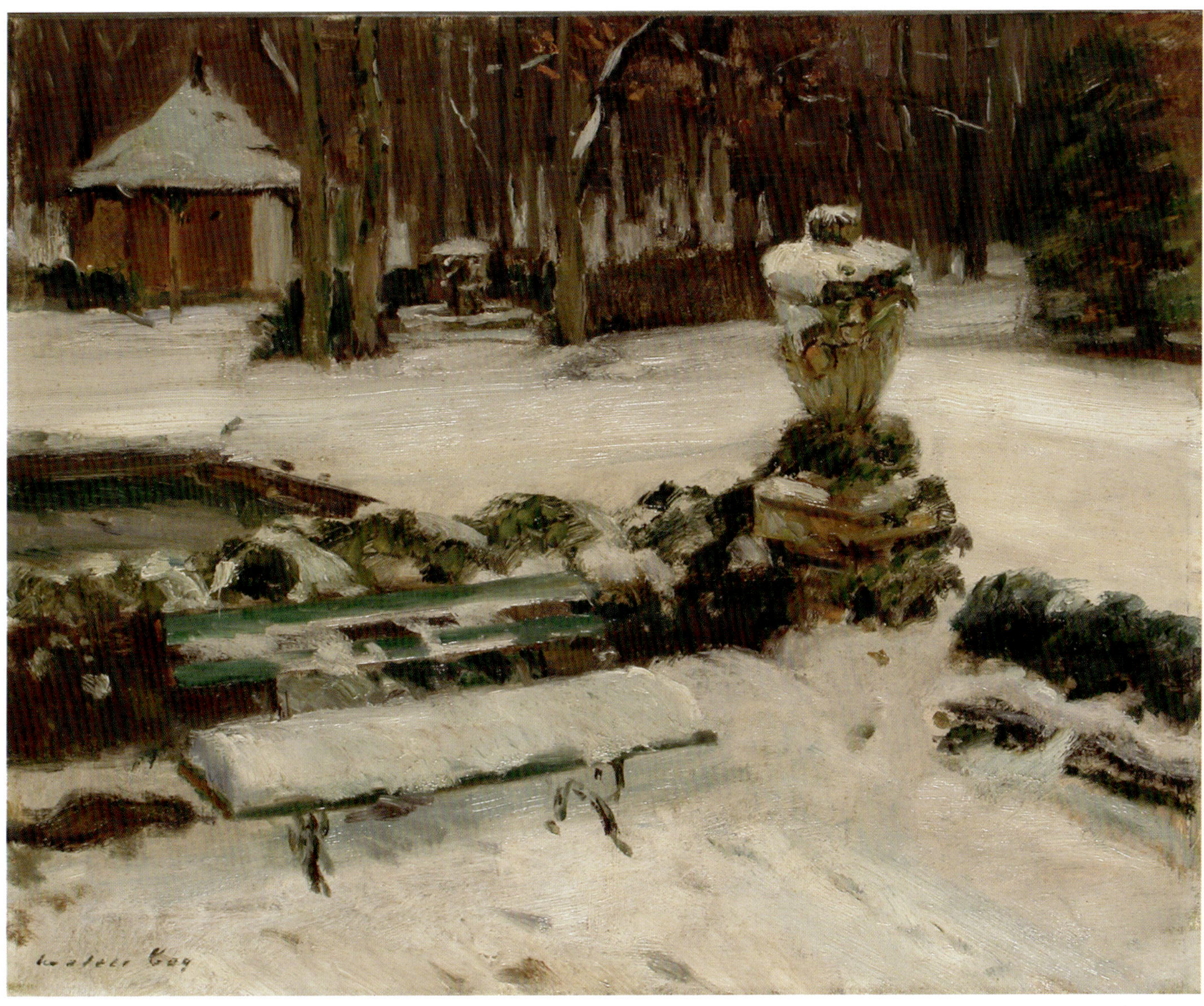

80.

[A] shell from the other Bertha had struck a flying buttress of the Cathedral [of Notre Dame] before falling into the river where it exploded. There was no panic and the congregation filed out.... It may have been this narrow shave which prompted my parents to accept the proposal by Mr. and Mrs. Walter Gay that little William be evacuated with his nurse to Le Bréau, their large château near Fontainebleau.... My special friend at "Le Bréau" was a black dachshund called "Poilu," the French equivalent in World War I of "G.I." In the atmosphere of the war it was just as well that he had been given a French patriotic name.

In the Garden Library wing of Dumbarton Oaks is a painting by Walter Gay of the corner of the terrace at "Le Bréau," with a snow-covered bench, where I used to play with "Poilu," while my nurse sat sewing. Across the waters of the moat is seen the little summer pavilion with a thatched roof, under the trees, in which we often took shelter.[7]

AK and PM

1. Rieder 2000a, 54.

2. Showing the moat are Rieder 2000a, figs. 29 and 31; Caldwell 2003, no. 17. Caldwell 2003, no. 5 depicts Le Bréau's chapel viewed from the southeast.

3. Rieder 2000a, no. 31—watercolor, private collection; Caldwell 2003, no. 17—oil on canvas, private collection, Athens, Georgia.

4. Washington, D.C., *Impressionists in Winter* 1998, 13-23.

5. Some well-known snowscapes by Paul Cézanne and Alfred Sisley were painted on the outskirts of Fontainebleau; cf. ibid., 20, fig. 8, 167, 188, no. 57.

6. To list only a few: Rieder 2000a, figs. 17, 20, 42; Caldwell 2003, nos. 7, 10, 11, 14, 21.

7. The quoted passages come from a text that William Royall Tyler composed during his tenure as the director of Dumbarton Oaks between 1969 and 1977. He planned to include the essay in a volume containing the correspondence between Royall Tyler and the Blisses. Unfortunately, this selection of 236 letters has remained unpublished.

    In the early 1920s, Matilda Gay, saddened by Poilu's death, received a letter from Edith Wharton who comforted her childhood friend with the empathy of " [t]hose who love and understand the little four-foots." Cited according to Rieder 2000a, 126.

References: Unpublished.

Exhibitions: Not shown previously.

81. HENRY GOLDEN DEARTH (American, 1864-1918)
Madonna (Still Life), (The Shrine), early 20th century

Oil on canvas
115.57 x 83.82 cm

INSCRIBED: Signed, lower right: H Dearth.

CONDITION: Excellent.

ACQUISITION HISTORY: Purchased for $2,500 on April 15, 1912,
by Anna Dorinda Blakesley Barnes Bliss, Santa Barbara, California, from M. Knoedler
& Co., Inc., New York; acquired by Mildred and Robert Woods Bliss, Washington, D.C.,
in 1935; House Collection, Dumbarton Oaks, Washington, D.C., January 17, 1969-present.

ACCESSION NUMBER: HC.P.1935.17.(O)

ORN IN BRISTOL, RHODE ISLAND, during the Civil War, Henry Golden Dearth studied art at the Ecole des Beaux-Arts in France. The aesthetic and techniques of the French landscape painters of the Barbizon school had a formative influence on Dearth. Upon returning to America in the 1890s, he painted landscapes showing views of Long Island. Subsequently, while a member of several artist associations in New York during the early part of the twentieth century, Dearth became known for his landscape paintings of the French countryside, created during summers spent in Normandy. During his lifetime, he won medals for painting at international exhibitions, including the 1900 Paris Exposition, the 1901 Pan-American Exposition, and the 1902 Charleston Exposition. Late in his career, the artist enjoyed considerable popularity among both art collectors and the general public. After Dearth's death in 1918 in New York, an exhibition of his works traveled across the country to nineteen different venues.[1]

A connoisseur with an affinity for Asian and medieval European art, Dearth sometimes incorporated objects from his own collection into his still lifes. *Madonna (Still Life)* centers on a statuette of the Virgin Mary that, most likely, belonged to the artist himself. Four white roses to the left and a red poinsettia blossom to the right, casually placed in simple pitchers, flank the figure of the Virgin. Dearth sets this arrangement on top of a long and narrow ledge, reminiscent of a mantelpiece, against a wall cover featuring a rose pattern. In this still life, he creates a highly textured surface with prominent brushwork and the use of vibrant, solid colors.

Unassuming as it might appear, the environment in which Dearth places the Virgin figurine is full of Christian symbols. To state the obvious, the rose is one of the most popular emblems of the Virgin, while the two flanking flower arrangements evoke the Immaculate Conception, the Birth of Christ, and the Passion, among other things. What makes this painting particularly poignant is that both arms of the figurine are broken. Her left shoulder is raised somewhat awkwardly, perhaps because originally this arm was supporting the Christ Child. The physical damage not only alludes to the tragedy of the Passion, but also it literally transforms the statuette of the Virgin and Child into the

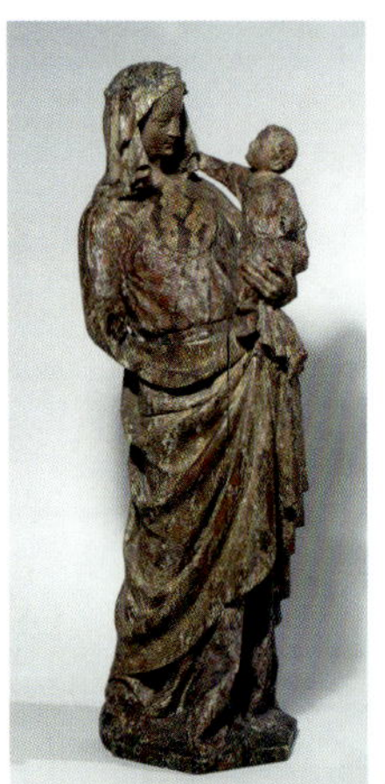

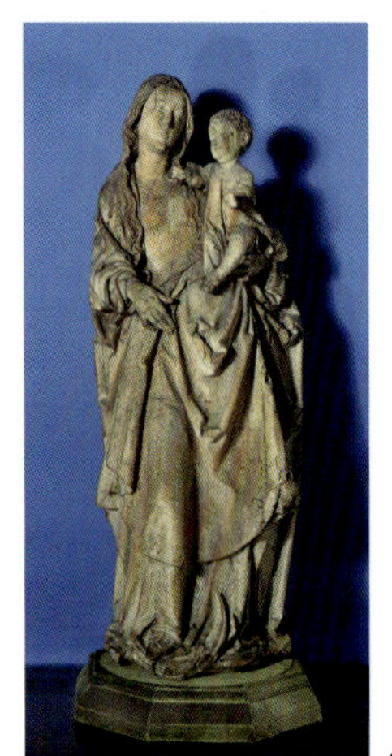

81A   81B   81C

Figure 81A. Virgin and Child, *Oak with polychromy and gilding, late 13th century, Île-de-France, Height: 57 cm, Dumbarton Oaks, acc. no. BZ.1912.2*

Figure 81B. Mourning Virgin from a Calvary Group, *Wood, end of the 13th beginning of the 14th century, said to be from León, Height: 136.5 cm, Dumbarton Oaks, acc. no. 1936.25*

Figure 81C. Tilmann Riemenschneider (1460-1531), Virgin and Child, ("Queen of Heaven"), *Wood, 1521, Würzburg, Germany, Height: 95.2 cm, Dumbarton Oaks, acc. no. HC.1937.6*

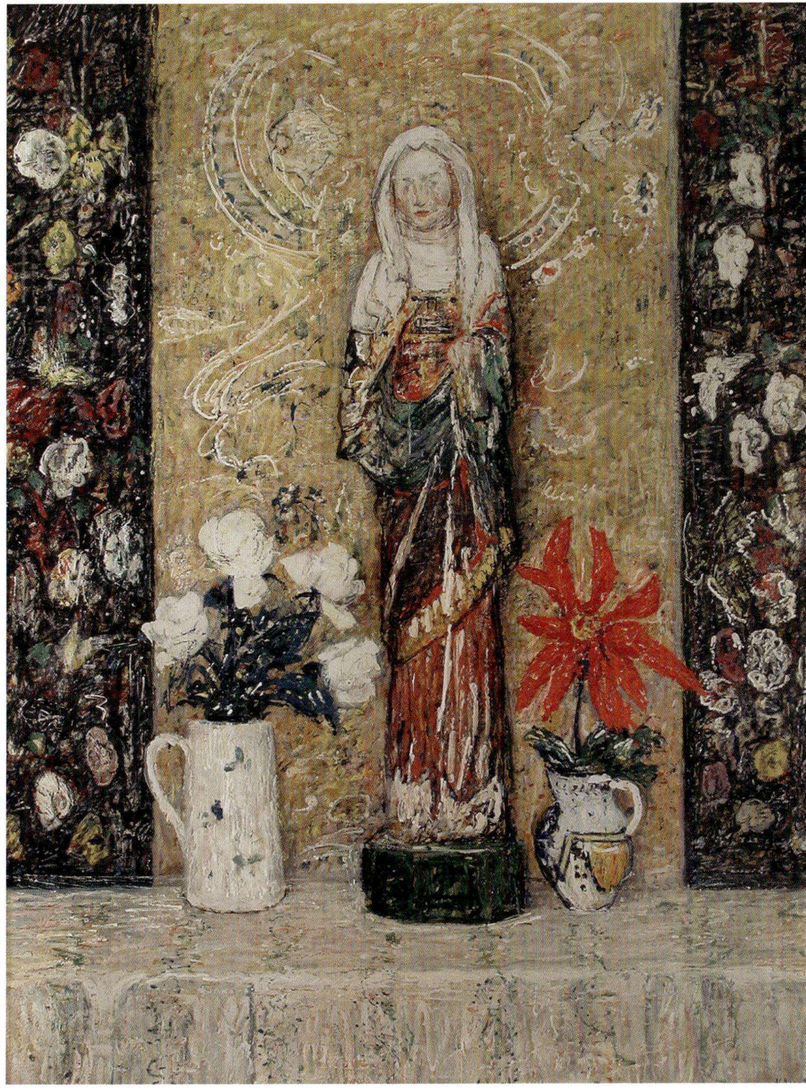

81.

mourning Virgin, as commonly represented standing to the right of her crucified son (see fig. 81B).

Remarkably, the Blisses owned four statuettes of the Virgin—one represents the mourning Virgin, another a *Pietà*, while the remaining two feature the Virgin and Christ Child. In 1912, when Anna Dorinda Blakesley Barnes Bliss bought Dearth's still life, Robert and Mildred Bliss purchased a late-thirteenth-century oak figurine with polychromy and gilding said to be from Île-de-France (fig. 81A).[2] This is one of the acquisitions they made in France during the first year of Mr. Bliss's appointment to the American embassy in Paris. In 1915, they acquired the *Pietà*, which dates to the last quarter of the fifteenth century.[3] After inheriting Dearth's still life from their mother's estate in 1935, the Blisses bought the remaining two works in 1936 and 1937, dating respectively to the late thirteenth or early fourteenth century and 1521 (figs. 81B and 81C).[4]

While showing sacred art in a secular context, this American modernist's still life, featuring a devotional statuette, brings into focus certain themes essential for understanding the attitudes of the Blisses as collectors. Among them are modernity's appreciation of medieval art, an interest in painting techniques, and the fascination with the appearance of a work of art's surface. Furthermore, the fact that this painting came from the collection of their parents must have been quite important for the Blisses, who deemed relevant the preservation of the circumstances surrounding individual acquisitions (cf. cat. no. 75). Throughout their lives, strong personal affections and attachments were an essential component of the process of collecting.[5]

AK and PM

References: Unpublished.

Exhibitions: Not shown before.

1. For more on Dearth, see Bermingham 1975 and New York, *Tonalism* 1982.
2. Vikan 1995, 123-126, no. 45.
3. Ibid., 129-132, no. 47.
4. Ibid., 126-128, no. 46 and 133-135, no. 48
5. See in this volume the essays by Carder, Nelson, and Kirin.

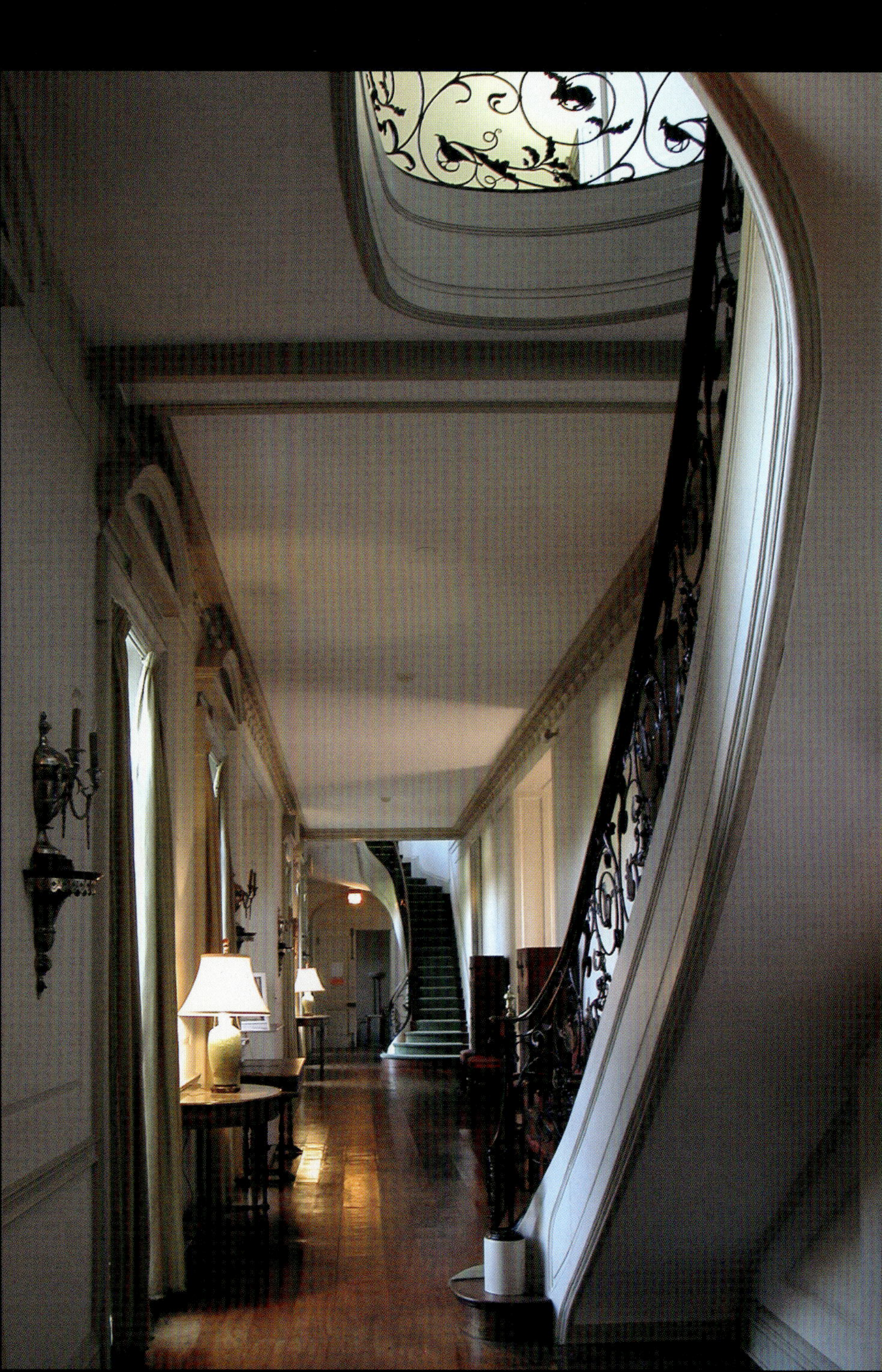

Bibliography

ABBREVIATIONS

ABB Anna Dorinda Blakesley Barnes Bliss

AGD Antike Gemmen in deutschen Sammlungen; Berlin, Braunschweig, Göttingen, Hamburg, Hannover, Kassel, München, vol. 2: *Italische Gemmen etruskisch bis römisch-republikanisch* (Munich, 1968).

ArtB Art Bulletin

BB Bernard Berenson

BF Byzantinische Forschungen

BZ Byzantinische Zeitschrift

CahArch Cahiers archéologiques

DOA Dumbarton Oaks Archives, Washington, D.C., House Collection

DOC A. R. Bellinger and P. Grierson, *Catalogue of the Byzantine Coins in the Dumbarton Oaks Collection and in the Whittemore Collection,* 5 vols. (Washington, D.C., 1966-1999). Vol. 1: A. R. Bellinger, *Anastasius to Maurice, 491-602;* vol. 2, pt. 1: P. Grierson, *Phocas and Heraclius, 602-641;* vol. 2, pt. 2: P. Grierson, *Heraclius Constantine to Theodosius III, 641-717;* vol. 3, pt. 1: P. Grierson, *Leo III to Michael III, 717-867;* vol. 3, pt. 2: P. Grierson, *Basil I to Nicephoros III, 867-1081;* vol. 4, pt. 1: M. F. Hendy, *Alexius I to Alexius V, 1081-1204;* vol. 4, pt. 2: M. F. Hendy, *The Emperors of Nicaea and Their Contemporaries, 1204-1261;* vol. 5, pt. 1: P. Grierson, *Introduction, Appendices and Bibliography;* vol. 5, pt. 2: P. Grierson, *Catalogue, Concordances and Indexes.*

DOCat Catalogue of the Byzantine and Early Mediaeval Antiquities in the Dumbarton Oaks Collection, vol. 1: M. C. Ross, *Metalwork, Ceramics, Glass, Glyptics, Painting* (Washington, D.C., 1962); vol. 2: M. C. Ross, *Jewelry, Enamels, and Art of the Migration Period* (Washington, D.C., 1965), 2nd edition 2005; vol. 3: Kurt Weitzmann, *Ivories and Steatites* (Washington, D.C., 1972).

DOH 1946. Dumbarton Oaks Research Library and Collection, *Handbook of the Collection* (Washington, D.C., 1946).

DOH 1955. Dumbarton Oaks Research Library and Collection, *Handbook of the Dumbarton Oaks Collection* (Washington, D.C., 1955).

DOH 1967. Dumbarton Oaks Research Library and Collection, *Handbook of the Byzantine Collection* (Washington, D.C., 1967).

DOP Dumbarton Oaks Papers

DOS N. Oikonomides, ed., *Catalogue of Byzantine Seals at Dumbarton Oaks and in the Fogg Museum of Art,* vols. 1-4 (Washington, D.C., 1991-2001). Vol. 1: J. Nesbitt and N. Oikonomides, *Italy, North of the Balkans, North of the Black Sea* (Washington, D.C., 1991); vol. 2: J. Nesbitt and N. Oikonomides, *South of the Balkans, the Islands, South of East Asia Minor* (Washington, D.C., 1994); vol. 3: J. Nesbitt and N. Oikonomides, *West, Northwest, and Central Asia Minor and the Orient* (Washington, D.C., 1996); vol. 4: E. McGeer, J. Nesbitt, and N. Oikonomides, *The East* (Washington, D.C., 2001).

ET Elisina Tyler

HUA Harvard University Archives

ISG Isabella Stewart Gardner

ISGM Archives of the Isabella Stewart Gardner Museum

JbAC Jahrbuch für Antike und Christentum

JRA Journal of Roman Archaeology

LIMC Lexicon iconographicum mythologiae classicae, 8 vols. in 16 pts. (Munich, 1981-1999)

MBB Mildred Barnes Bliss

MIB W. Hahn, *Moneta Imperii Byzantini,* vol. 1: *Von Anastasius I. bis Justinianus I. (491-565);* vol. 2: *Von Justinus II. bis Phocas (565-610);* vol. 3: *Von Heraclius bis Leo III. Alleinregierung (610-720)* (Vienna, 1973-1981).

MSP Matthew Stewart Prichard

ODB Oxford Dictionary of Byzantium, ed. A. Kazhdan et al. (New York and Oxford, 1991).

PG Patrologiae cursus completus, Series graeca, ed. J.-P. Migne, 161 vols. in 166 pts. (Paris, 1977).

RA Révue archéologique

REB Revue des études byzantines

RT Royall Tyler

RWB Robert Woods Bliss

WRT William Royall Tyler

BIBLIOGRAPHY

Adelson 1957. H. L. Adelson, *Light-Weight Solidi and Byzantine Trade during the Sixth and Seventh Centuries* (New York, 1957).

Adhémar 1934. J. Adhémar, "Le trésor d'argenterie donné par Saint Didier aux églises d'Auxerre (VIIe siècle)," *RA* 4 (1934): 44-54.

Aeschylus Septem. Aeschylus, *The Seven Against Thebes,* ed. C. M. Dawson (London, Sydney, Toronto, New Delhi, Tokyo, 1970).

Amiaud 1889. A. Amiaud, *La légende syriaque de Saint Alexis, l'homme de Dieu* (Paris, 1889).

Anderson 2000. D. Anderson, ed., *On the Divine Images; Three Apologies Against Those Who Attack the Divine Images,* St. John of Damascus (Crestwood, NY, 2000).

Apollodorus. Apollodorus, *The Library.* Loeb Classical Library, 2 vols. (Cambridge, 1921).

Arjava 1996. A. Arjava, *Women and Law in Late Antiquity* (Oxford, 1996).

Armantrout 1990. G. L. Armantrout, *The Seven Against Thebes in Greek Art* (Ph.D. dissertation, University of Michigan, 1990).

Armstrong 1991. P. Armstrong, "A Group of Byzantine Bowls from Skopelos," *Oxford Journal of Archaeology* 10, no. 3 (1991): 335-347.

Armstrong 1997. P. Armstrong, "Byzantine Glazed Ceramic Tableware in the Collection of the Detroit Institute of Arts," *Bulletin of the Detroit Institute of Arts* vol. 71, no. 1/2 (1997): 4-15.

Árnason 1938. H. H. Árnason, "Early Christian Silver of North Italy and Gaul," *ArtB* 20 (1938): 193-226.

Athens, *Byzantine and Post-Byzantine Art* 1985. *Byzantine and Post-Byzantine Art*. Exh. cat., Old University (Athens, Greece 1985).

Athens GA, *Palazzo Venezia* 1996. *Masterpieces of Renaissance and Baroque Sculpture from the Palazzo Venezia, Rome*. Exh. cat., ed. S. Zuraw, Georgia Museum of Art (Athens, GA, 1996).

Atlanta, *After Whistler* 2003. L. Merill et al., *After Whistler: The Artist and His Influence on American Painting*. Exh. cat., High Museum of Art (Atlanta, GA, 2003).

Avalos 1999. H. Avalos, *Health Care and the Rise of Christianity* (Peabody, MA, 1999).

Badawy 1978. A. Badawy, *Coptic Art and Archaeology. The Art of the Christian Egyptians from the Late Antique to the Middle Ages* (Cambridge, MA, and London, 1978).

Bailey 1975. D. M. Bailey, *A Catalogue of the Lamps in the British Museum*. Vol. 1: *Greek, Hellenistic, and Early Roman Pottery Lamps* (London, 1975).

Bailey 1980. D. M. Bailey, *A Catalogue of the Lamps in the British Museum*. Vol. 2: *Roman Lamps Made in Italy* (London, 1980).

Baldini 1991. I. Baldini, "Gli orecchini a corpo semilunato: Classificazione tipologica (Nota preliminare)," *Corso di cultura sull'arte ravennate e bizantina* 38 (1991): 67-101.

Baldini Lippolis 1999. I. Baldini Lippolis, *L'Oreficeria nell'Impero di Costantinopoli tra IV e VII secolo* (Bari, 1999).

Baldwin 1995. B. Baldwin, "Michael Psellus on the Properties of Stones," *Byzantinoslavica* 56 (1995): 397-405.

Ballian and Drandaki 2003. A. Ballian and A. Drandaki, "A Middle Byzantine Silver Treasure," *Mouseio Benake* 3 (2003): 47-80.

Baltimore, *Early Christian and Byzantine Art* 1947. The Walters Art Gallery, *Early Christian and Byzantine Art, an Exhibition Held at the Baltimore Museum of Art, April 25- June 22* [1947]. Organized by the Walters Art Gallery, in collaboration with the Department of Art and Archaeology of Princeton University and Dumbarton Oaks Research Library and Collection of Harvard University, and forming part of Princeton's bicentennial celebration (Baltimore, MD, 1947).

Bank 1977. A. Bank, *Byzantine Art in the Collections of Soviet Museums* (Leningrad, 1977); 2nd ed. Leningrad, 1985.

Bank 1978. A. Bank, *Prikladnoe iskusstvo Vizantii IX-XII vv.* (Moscow, 1978).

Baratte 1990. F. Baratte et al., *Le trésor de la place Camille-Jouffray à Vienne (Isère). Un dépôt d'argenterie et son contexte archéologique* (Paris, 1990).

Baratte 1992. F. Baratte, "Vaisselle d'argent, souvenirs littéraires et manières de table: L'exemple des cuillers de Lampsaque," *CahArch* 40 (1992): 5-20.

Barbel 1941. J. Barbel, *Christos Angelos* (Bonn, 1941).

Barber 2002. C. Barber, *Figure and Likeness: On the Limits of Representation in Byzantine Iconoclasm* (Princeton and Oxford, 2002).

Barbera and Petriaggi 1993. M. Barbera and R. Petriaggi, *Le lucerne tardo-antiche di produzione africana* (Rome, 1993).

Barr 1951. A. H. Barr, Jr., *Matisse: His Art and His Public* (New York, 1951).

Basler and Brummer 1928. A. Basler and E. Brummer, *L'art précolombien* (Paris, 1928).

Batalov and Lidov 1994. A. Batalov and A. Lidov, eds., *Ierusalim v russkoi kul'ture* (Moscow, 1994).

Bekker 1835. I. Bekker, ed., *Georgii Pachymeris De Michaele et Andronico Palaeologis*, 2 vols. (Bonn, 1835).

Beliaev 2000. L. Beliaev, "The Holy Sepulchre and Relics of the Holy Land," **Lidov 2000**, 94-110.

Bellido 1936. A. García y Bellido, "La sítula romana de Bueña (Teruel)," *Archivo español de arte y arqueología* 34 (1936): 63-73.

Belting 1994. H. Belting, *Likeness and Presence: A History of the Image before the Era of Art* (Chicago and London, 1994).

Bénazeth 1988. D. Bénazeth, "Les encensoirs de la collection copte du Louvre," *La revue du Louvre et des Musées de France* 4 (1988): 294-300.

Bendall 1996. S. Bendall, *Byzantine Weights: An Introduction* (London, 1996).

Benson 1993. E. P. Benson, "The Robert Woods Bliss Collection of Pre-Columbian Art: A Memoir," **Boone 1993**, 15-34.

Bermingham 1975. P. Bermingham, *American Art in the Barbizon Mood* (Washington, D.C.: Published for the National Collection of Fine Arts by the Smithsonian Institution Press, 1975).

Bezançon 2000. A. Bezançon, *The Forbidden Image: An Intellectual History of Iconoclasm* (Chicago, 2000).

Bianchini 1992. M. C. Bianchini, *Byzance. L'art byzantin dans les collections publiques françaises* (Paris, 1992).

Biddle 1999. M. Biddle, *The Tomb of Christ* (Gloucestershire, UK, 1999).

Bieber 1977. M. Bieber, *Ancient Copies* (New York, 1977).

Blanchet 1923. A. Blanchet, "Vénus et Mars sur des intailles magiques et autres," *Comptes rendus des séances de l'Académie des Inscriptions et Belles-Lettres* (1923): 220-234.

Bliss 1947. R. W. Bliss, *Indigenous Art of the Americas, Collection of Robert Woods Bliss* (Washington, D.C., 1947).

Bonner 1950. C. Bonner, *Studies in Magical Amulets, Chiefly Graeco-Egyptian*, University of Michigan Studies, Humanistic Series, vol. 49 (Ann Arbor, 1950).

Boone 1993. *Collecting the Pre-Columbian Past: A Symposium at Dumbarton Oaks, 6th and 7th October 1990*, ed. E. H. Boone (Washington, D.C., 1993).

Boston, *Arts of the Middle Ages* 1940. *Arts of the Middle Ages*. Exh. cat., Boston, Museum of Fine Arts, February 17-March 24, 1940 (Boston, 1940).

Boyd 1979. S. Boyd, *Dumbarton Oaks Collections: Byzantine Art* (Chicago and London, 1979).

Boyd and Mundell Mango 1993. S. Boyd and M. Mundell Mango, eds., *Ecclesiastical Silver Plate in Sixth-Century Byzantium*. Papers of the symposium held May 16-18, 1986, at the Walters Art Gallery, Baltimore, and Dumbarton Oaks, Washington, D.C. (Washington, D.C., 1993).

Braun 1993. B. Braun, *Pre-Columbian Art and the Post-Columbian World: Ancient American Sources of Modern Art* (New York, 1993).

Bréhier 1936. L. Bréhier, *La sculpture et les arts mineurs byzantins* (Paris, 1936).

Brooks 1921. N. C. Brooks, *The Sepulchre of Christ in Art and Liturgy; With Special Reference to Liturgical Drama* (Urbana, IL, 1921).

Brown 1978. P. Brown, *The Making of Late Antiquity* (Cambridge, MA, 1978).

Brubaker and Haldon 2001. L. Brubaker and J. Haldon, eds., *Byzantium in the Iconoclastic Era (ca 680-850): The Sources. An Annotated Survey* (Aldershot, UK, and Burlington, VT, 2001).

Bruce-Mitford 1983. R. Bruce-Mitford, *The Sutton Hoo Ship-Burial*, 3/1 (London, 1983).

Bruhn 1993. J.-A. Bruhn, *Coins and Costume in Late Antiquity* (Washington D.C., 1993).

Brussels, *Splendeur de Byzance* 1982. *Splendeur de Byzance: Europalia 82, Hellas-Grèce, 2 octobre- 2 décembre 1982*. Exh. cat., ed. J. Lafontaine-Dosogne (Brussels, 1982).

Bruzelius 1991. C. Bruzelius, Introduction to *The Brummer Collection of Medieval Art: The Duke University Museum of Art* (Durham, NC, 1991), 1-11.

Buckton 1988. D. Buckton. "Byzantine Enamel and the West," *Byzantium and the West, c. 850-c.1200; Proceedings of the XVIII Spring Symposium of Byzantine Studies 1984*, ed. J. D. Howard-Johnston, *BF*13 (1988): 235-244 and pls. 1-23.

Bullen 1999. J. B. Bullen, "Byzantinism and Modernism 1900-14," *Burlington Magazine*, November (1999): 665-675.

Butler 1929. H. C. Butler, *Early Churches in Syria, Fourth to Seventh Centuries*. Princeton Monographs in Art and Archaeology (Princeton, 1929).

Cahn and Kaufmann-Heinimann 1984. A. Cahn and A. Kaufmann-Heinimann, eds., *Der spätrömische Silberschatz von Kaiseraugst*, 2 vols. (Derendingen, 1984).

Caldwell 2003. P. V. Caldwell, *Walter Gay. Poèmes d'Intérieurs* (New York, 2003).

Cambridge, MA, *Byzantine Women* 2003. *Byzantine Women and Their World*. Exh. cat., ed. I. Kalavrezou, Arthur M. Sackler Museum, Harvard University Art Museums, October 25, 2002-April 28, 2003 (New Haven and London, 2003).

Cameron 1971. H. D. Cameron, *Studies on the Seven Against Thebes of Aeschylus* (The Hague, 1971).

Cantor 1991. N. F. Cantor, *Inventing the Middle Ages: The Lives, Works, and Ideas of the Great Medievalists of the Twentieth Century* (New York, 1991).

Caramessini-Oeconomides 1966. M. Caramessini-Oeconomides, "An Unpublished Consular Solidus of Justinian I," *American Numismatic Society Museum Notes* 12 (1966): 75-77.

Carandini 1964. A. Carandini, "La secchia doria: Una 'Storia di Achille' tardo-antica. Contributo al problema dell'industria artistica di tradizione ellenistica in Egitto," *Studi Miscellanei* [Seminario di archeolgia e storia dell'arte greca e romana dell'Università di Roma] 9 (1963-1964): 5-45.

Carder 2000. J. Carder, "Giulia Bellelli, Study for 'The Bellelli Family,'" A. Dumas and D. A. Brenneman, *Degas and America, The Early Collectors* (New York, 2000), 101, no. 9.

Caseau 1994. B. A. Caseau, *Euodia: The Use and Meaning of Fragrances in the Ancient World and Their Christianization (100-900 A.D.)* (Ph.D. dissertation, Princeton University, 1994).

Castellani 1874. A. Castellani, "Due antiche forchete di argento," *Bollettino della Commissione Archeologica Municipale* 2 (1874): 116-125.

Cecchelli 1936. C. Cecchelli, *La Cattedra di Massimiano ed altri avori Romano-orientali* (Rome, 1936).

Chadour 1994. A. B. Chadour, *Ringe: Die Alice und Louis Koch Sammlung*, 2 vols. (Leeds, 1994).

Coche de la Ferté 1955. E. Coche de la Ferté, "Sur quelques bagues byzantines de la collection Stathatos," *Comptes rendus de l'Académie des Inscriptions et Belles-Lettres* 1955 (1956): 72-81.

Coche de la Ferté 1958. E. Coche de la Ferté, *L'antiquité chrétienne au Musée du Louvre* (Paris, 1958).

Coe 1993. M. D. Coe, "From Huaquero to Connoisseur: The Early Market in Pre-Columbian Art," **Boone 1993**, 271-290.

Comstock and Vermeule 1971. M. Comstock and C. Vermeule, *Greek, Etruscan and Roman Bronzes in the Museum of Fine Arts, Boston* (Boston, 1971).

Conn 1998. S. Conn, *Museums and American Intellectual Life, 1876-1926* (Chicago and London, 1998).

Constable 1993. G. Constable, ed., *The Letters Between Bernard Berenson and Charles Henry Coster* (Florence, 1993).

Cormack 1985. R. Cormack, *Writing in Gold* (New York, 1985).

Cormack 1997. R. Cormack, *Painting the Soul; Icons, Death Masks, and Shrouds* (London, 1997).

Cormack 2000. R. Cormack, *Byzantine Art* (Oxford and New York, 2000).

Cruikshank Dodd 1961. E. Cruikshank Dodd, *Byzantine Silver Stamps. With an Excursus on the Comes Sacrarum Largitionum by J. P. C. Kent, Dumbarton Oaks Studies 7* (Washington, D.C., 1961).

Cruikshank Dodd 1993. E. Cruikshank Dodd, "The Location of Silver Stamping: Evidence from Newly Discovered Stamps," **Boyd and Mundell Mango 1993**, 217-223.

Curry 1990. D. Park Curry, *Childe Hassam: An Island Garden Revisited* (New York, 1990).

Cuscito 2002. G. Cuscito, "Bronzi paleocristiani di Aquileia," *Bronzi di età romana in Cisalpina. Novità e riletture* (Trieste, 2002), 379-410.

Cutler 1975. A. Cutler, *Transfigurations: Studies in the Dynamics of Byzantine Iconography* (University Park, PA, and London, 1975).

Cutler 1987. A. Cutler, "Under the Sign of the Deesis: On the Question of Representativeness in Medieval Art and Literature," *DOP* 41 (1987): 145-154; reprinted in **Cutler 2000**, 46-64.

Cutler 1992. A. Cutler, *Imagery and Ideology in Byzantine Art* (Hampshire, UK, and Brookfield, VT, 1992).

Cutler 1996. A. Cutler, "Les échanges de dons entre Byzance et l'Islam (IXe-XIe siècles)," *Journal des Savants* 1 (1996): 51-66.

Cutler 2000. A. Cutler, *Byzantium, Italy and the North. Papers on Cultural Relations* (London, 2000).

Dalton 1901. O. M. Dalton, *Catalogue of Early Christian Antiquities and Objects from the Christian East in the Department of British and Mediaeval Antiquities and Ethnography of the British Museum* (London, 1901).

Dalton 1906. O. M. Dalton, "Byzantine Silversmith's Work from Cyprus," *BZ* 15 (1906): 615-617.

Dalton 1911a. O. M. Dalton, *Byzantine Art and Archaeology* (Oxford, 1911).

Dalton 1911b. O. M. Dalton, "Mediaeval Personal Ornaments from Chalcis in the British and Ashmolean Museums," *Archaeologia* 62 (1911): 391-404.

Dalton 1915. O. M. Dalton, *Catalogue of the Engraved Gems of the Post-Classical Periods in the Department of British and Mediaeval Antiquities and Ethnography of the British Museum* (London, 1915).

d'Alverny 1957. M. T. d'Alverny, "Les anges et les jours," *CahArch* 9 (1957): 271-300.

d'Ambra 1996. E. d'Ambra, "The Calculus of Venus: Nude Portraits of Roman Matrons," *Sexuality in Ancient Art*, ed. N. Boymel Kampen (Cambridge, 1996), 219-232.

Daniel and Maltomini 1990. R. W. Daniel and F. Maltomini, eds. and trans., *Supplementum Magicum 1, Papyrologica Coloniensia 17.1, Abhandlungen der Rheinisch-westfälischen Akademie der Wissenschaften* (Cologne, 1990).

Daszewski 1985. W. A. Daszewski, *Dionysos der Erlöser. Griechische Mythen im spätantiken Cypern* (Mainz am Rhein, 1985).

Daszewski and Michaelides 1988. W. A. Daszewski and D. Michaelides, *Mosaic Floors in Cyprus* (Ravenna, 1988).

Dauterman Maguire 1997. E. Dauterman Maguire, "Ceramic Arts of Everyday Life," **New York, The Glory of Byzantium, 1997**, 254-271.

Day 1939. F. E. Day, review of **Lane 1938**, *Ars Islamica* 6.2 (1939): 186-197.

De Boor 1883. C. de Boor, ed., *Chronographia*, 2 vols. (Leipzig, 1883-1885).

Déchelette 1902. J. Déchelette, "Les seaux de bronze de Hemmoor, d'après une récente publication de M. Willers," *RA* 2 (1902): 281-292.

Delatte and Derchain 1964. A. Delatte and P. Derchain, *Les intailles magiques Greco-Égyptiennes. Bibliothèque Nationale, Cabinet des Médailles et Antiques* (Paris, 1964).

Delivorrias 2000. A. Delivorrias, *A Guide to the Benaki Museum* (Athens, 2000).

Demus 1947. O. Demus, *Byzantine Mosaic Decoration: Aspects of Monumental Art in Byzantium* (London, 1947).

Dennis 1984. G. T. Dennis, ed., *Maurice's Strategikon: Handbook of Byzantine Military Strategy* (Philadelphia, 1984).

Der Nersessian 1960. S. der Nersessian, "Two Images of the Virgin at the Dumbarton Oaks Collection," *DOP* 14 (1960): 71-86.

De Spagnolis and De Carolis 1988. M. Conticello De Spagnolis and E. De Carolis, *Le lucerne di bronzo di Ercolano e Pompei* (Rome, 1988).

Diehl 1910. C. Diehl, *Manuel d'art byzantin* (Paris, 1910); 2nd ed. 2 vols. (Paris, 1925).

Dindorf 1832. L. Dindorf, ed., *Chronicon Paschale*, 2 vols. (Bonn, 1832).

Djobadze 1976. W. Djobadze. *Materials for the Study of Georgian Monasteries in the Western Environs of Antioch on-the-Orontes, Corpus Scriptorum Christianorum orientalium, 372, Subsidia, 48* (Louvain, 1976).

Djobadze 1986. W. Djobadze, *Archeological Investigations in the Region West of Antioch on-the-Orontes* (Stuttgart, 1986).

Dölger 1928. F. J. Dölger, *Das Fisch-Symbol in frühchristlicher Zeit*, 2nd ed. (Münster in Westf., 1928).

Downing 1998. C. Downing, "Wall Paintings from the Baptistery at Stobi, Macedonia, and Early Depictions of Christ and the Evangelists," *DOP* 52 (1998): 269-280.

Dresken-Weiland 1998. J. Dresken-Weiland, *Repertorium der christlich-antiken Sarkophage, II, Italien mit einem Nachtrag Rom und Ostia, Dalmatien, Museen der Welt* (Mainz, 1998).

Drossoyianni 1982. P. A. Drossoyianni, "A Pair of Byzantine Crowns." *XVI. Internationaler Byzantinistenkongress*, II, 3 (Vienna, 1982), 529-538.

Dumbarton Oaks Bulletin 1950. *The Dumbarton Oaks Research Library and Collection, Harvard University, Bulletin Number One, 1940-1950* (Washington, D.C., 1950).

Dumbarton Oaks, Questions of Authenticity 1981. *Questions of Authenticity Among the Arts of Byzantium.* Exh. cat., ed. S. Boyd and G. Vikan, Dumbarton Oaks, January 7-May 11, 1981 (Washington, D.C., 1981).

Dumont 1870. A. Dumont, "Un poids byzantin du cabinet de M. Verdot, à Paris," *RA* (1870): 236-248.

Dunbabin 2003. K. Dunbabin, *The Roman Banquet: Images of Conviviality* (Cambridge, 2003).

Dupont 1989. F. Dupont, *Daily Life in Ancient Rome* (Oxford and Cambridge, MA, 1989).

Durand 1884. Julien Durand, "Les Sept Anges," *Bulletin monumental* ser. 5, 12 (1884): 767-772.

Durand in press. Jannic Durand, "Innovations gothiques dans l'orfèvrerie byzantine sous les Paléologues," *DOP* 58, in press.

Duthuit 1926. G. Duthuit, *Byzance et l'art du XIIe siècle* (Paris, 1926).

Duthuit and Volbach 1933. G. Duthuit and F. Volbach, *Art byzantin. Cent planches reproduisant un grand nombre de pièces choisies parmi les plus représentatives des diverses tendances* (Paris, 1933).

Dvornik 1969. F. Dvornik, *Les légendes de Constantin et de Méthode vues de Byzance*, 2nd ed. (Hattiesburg, MS, 1969).

Dvornik 1970. F. Dvornik, *Byzantine Missions Among the Slavs; SS. Constantine-Cyril and Methodius* (New Brunswick, NJ, 1970).

Eastmond and James 2003. *Icon and Word: The Power of Images in Byzantium. Studies Presented to Robin Cormack*, eds. A. Eastmond and L. James (Hants, UK, and Burlington, VT, 2003).

Edinburgh-London 1958. *Masterpieces of Byzantine Art.* Exh. cat by D. Talbot Rice, Edinburgh International Festival, August 23-September 13, 1958; London, Victoria and Albert Museum, October 1-November 9, 1958 (Edinburgh, 1958).

Effenberger et al. 1978. A. Effenberger et al., *Spätantike und frühbyzantinische Silbergefässe aus der Staatlichen Ermitage Leningrad* (Berlin, 1978).

Effenberger and Severin 1992. A. Effenberger and H. G. Severin. *Das Museum für Spätantike und Byzantinische Kunst. Staatliche Museen ze Berlin* (Mainz, 1992).

Eichholz 1962. D. E. Eichholz, ed. and trans., *Pliny: Natural History* (Cambridge, MA, and London, 1962).

Eichler and Kris 1927. F. Eichler and E. Kris, *Die Kameen im Kunsthistorischen Museum* (Vienna, 1927).

Eichner 1977. K. Eichner, *Die Werkstatt des sogenannten dogmatischen Sarkophags: Untersuchungen zur Technik der konstantinischen Sarkophag-Plastik in Rom* (Heidelberg, 1977).

Elbern 1964. V. H. Elbern, *Der Eucharistiche Kelch im Frühen Mittlater* (Berlin, 1964).

Elbern 1975. V. H. Elbern, "Frühmittelalterliche Zierkunst im Lichte der'"Renevatio,'" *La cultura antica nell'occidente latino dal VII all'XI secolo, settimane di studio del Centro Italiano di Studi sull'Alto Medioevo 22/2* (Spoleto, 1975), 799-807.

Ellis 1997. S. P. Ellis, "Late-Antique Dining: Architecture, Furnishings and Behavior," in *Domestic Space in the Roman World: Pompeii and Beyond*, eds. R. Laurence and A. Wallace-Hardill, *JRA Supplementary Series 22* (Portsmouth, RI, 1997), 41-51.

Elsner 1995. J. Elsner, *Art and the Roman Viewer: The Transformation of Art from the Pagan World to Christianity* (Cambridge and New York, 1995).

Engemann 1972. J. Engemann, "Anmerkungen zu spätantiken Geräten des Alltagslebens mit christlichen Bildern, Symbolen und Inschriften," *JbAC* 15 (1972): 154-173.

Epicorum Graecorum Fragmenta. *Epicorum Graecorum Fragmenta*, ed. M. Davies (Göttingen, 1988).

Failler 1984. A. Failler, ed., *Pachymérès. Relations historiques*, Books 1-6, vol. 1-2, with French translation by V. Laurent (Paris, 1984).

Feissel 2001. D. Feissel et al., eds., *Trois donations byzantines au Cabinet des Médailles* (Paris, 2001).

Festugière 1983. A.-J. Festugière, ed. and trans., *Sozomène Histoire Ecclésiastique livres I-II*, Sources Chrétiennes 306 (Paris, 1983).

Finney 1987. P. C. Finney, "Images on Finger Rings and Early Christian Art," *DOP* 41 (1987): 181-186.

Fleischer, Hjort, and Rasmussen 1996. J. Fleischer, Ø. Hjort, and M. B. Rasmussen, eds., *Byzantium: Late Antique and Byzantine Art in Scandinavian Collections* (Copenhagen, 1996).

Flint 1991. V. I. J. Flint. *The Rise of Magic in Early Medieval Europe* (Princeton, 1991).

Fogg Bulletin 1941. *The Bulletin of the Fogg Museum of Art, A Special Number Devoted to the Dumbarton Oaks Research Library and Collection, Harvard University* vol. 9/4 (March 1941).

Fogg Bulletin 1945. "Dumbarton Oaks Research Library and Collection: Exhibition," *Bulletin of the Fogg Museum of Art* 10/4 (December 1945): 108-123.

Fogg Bulletin 1947. "Dumbarton Oaks Research Library and Collection: Acquisitions, December 1, 1946-November 1, 1947," *Bulletin of the Fogg Museum of Art* 10 (1947): 219-239.

Forsyth 1974. W. H. Forsyth, "The Brummer Brothers: An Instinct for the Beautiful," *Art News* (October 1974): 106-107.

Foss forthcoming. C. Foss, "Emperors named Constantine," forthcoming.

Freedberg 1989. D. Freedberg, *The Power of Images: Studies in the History and the Theory of Response* (Chicago and London, 1989).

Freeman 1901. L. J. Freeman, *Italian Sculpture of the Renaissance* (London, 1901).

Freiss 1980. G. Freiss, *Edelsteine im Mittelalter: Wandel und Kontinuität in ihrer Bedeutung durch zwölf Jahrhunderte (in Aberglauben, Medizin, Theologie und Goldschmiedekunst)* (Hildesheim, 1980).

Frel 1981. J. Frel, *Roman Portraits in the Getty Museum* (Malibu, 1981).

Frolow 1948. A. Frolow, "Numismatique byzantine et archéologie des lieux saints," *Archives de l'Orient chrétien* 1 (1948): 78-94.

Frolow 1965. A. Frolow, "Les reliquaires de la Vraie Croix," *Archives de l'Orient chrétien* 8 (Paris, 1965).

Fulghum 2001. M. M. Fulghum, "Coins Used as Amulets in Late Antiquity," *Between Magic and Religion*, eds. S. R. Asirvatham, C. O. Pache, and J. Watrous (Lanham, MD, 2001), 139-147.

Furtwängler 1986. A. Furtwängler, *Beschreibung der geschnittenen Steine im Antiquarium* (Berlin, 1986).

Gallatin 1920. A. E. Gallatin, *Walter Gay. Paintings of French Interiors* (New York, 1920).

Gantz 1993. T. Gantz, *Early Greek Myth: A Guide to Literary and Artistic Sources* (Baltimore and London, 1993).

Genova et al. 1980. I. Genova, V. Dimova, G. Germanova, and T. Matakieva, eds., *La Bulgarie médiévale. Art et Civilisation.* Exh. cat., Grand Palais (Paris, 1980).

Georgoula 1999. E. Georgoula, ed., *Greek Jewellery from the Benaki Museum Collections* (Athens, 1999).

Gettens and Waring 1957. R. J. Gettens and C. L. Waring, "The Composition of Some Ancient Persian and Other Near Eastern Silver Objects," *Ars Orientalis* 2 (1957): 83-90.

Gigante 1970. M. Gigante, "Teatro greco in Magna Grecia," *Atti del VI Convegno di Studi sulla Magna Grecia, 1967* (1970), 83-146.

Gillet 1921. L. Gillet, "Walter Gay," *Revue de l'art ancien et moderne* 39 (January 1921).

Glass 1970. D. F. Glass, "Romanesque Sculpture in American Collections. V: Washington and Baltimore," *Gesta* 1 (1970): 46-59.

Glass 1991. D. F. Glass, *Romanesque Sculpture in Campania: Patrons, Programs, and Style* (University Park, PA, 1991).

Gleason 1917. A. H. Gleason, *Our Part in the Great War* (New York, 1917).

Gonosová and Kondoleon 1994. A. Gonosová and C. Kondoleon, with L. Becker. *Art of Late Rome and Byzantium in the Virginia Museum of Fine Arts* (Richmond, 1994).

Grabar 1936. A. Grabar, *L'empereur dans l'art byzantin: Recherches sur l'art officiel de l'empire d'Orient* (Paris, 1936).

Grabar 1938. A. Grabar, *L'art byzantin* (Paris, 1938)

Grabar 1954. A. Grabar, "Un nouveau reliquaire de Saint Démétrios," *DOP* 8 (1954): 307-313.

Grabar 1957a. A. Grabar, "Le reliquaire byzantin de la cathédrale d'Aix-la-chapelle," *Karolingische und ottonische Kunst. Werden. Wesen. Wirkung* (Wiesbaden, 1957): 282-297.

Grabar 1957b. A. Grabar, *L'iconoclasme byzantin; dossier archéologique* (Paris, 1957); 2nd ed.,1984.

Grabar 1968. A. Grabar, *L'art de la fin de l'Antiquité et du Moyen Âge*, 3 vols. (Paris, 1968).

Grabar 1997. O. Grabar, "The Shared Culture of Objects," *Byzantine Court Culture from 829 to 1204*, ed. H. Maguire (Washington, D.C., 1997), 115-129.

Grégoire 1966. H. Grégoire, ed., "Imperatoris Michaelis Palaeologi de vita sua," *Byzantion* 29-30 (1966): 447-476, with French translation.

Grierson 1982. P. Grierson, *Byzantine Coins* (London and Berkeley, CA, 1982).

Grierson 1993. P. Grierson, "The Role of Silver in the Early Byzantine Economy," **Boyd and Mundell Mango 1993**, 137-146.

Grierson 1999. P. Grierson, *Byzantine Coinage* (Washington, D.C., 1999).

Grierson and Mays 1992. P. Grierson and M. Mays, *Catalogue of Late Roman Coins in the Dumbarton Oaks Collection and in the Whittemore Collection* (Washington, D.C., 1992).

Guenther 1898. O. Guenther, ed., *Epistulae Imperatorum Pontificum Aliorum, Corpus Scriptorum Ecclesiasticorum Latinorum* 35 (Vienna, 1898).

Hadzidakis 1944. M. Hadzidakis, "Un anneau byzantin. En appendice: Catalogue de bagues byzantines à inscriptions," *Byzantinisch-Neugriechische Jahrbücher* 18 (1944): 174-206.

Hahn 1973. W. Hahn, *Moneta Imperii Byzantini*, vol. 1: *Von Anastasius I. bis Justinianus I. (491-565)* (Vienna, 1973).

Hahnloser 1965. H. R. Hahnloser, ed., *Il Tesoro di San Marco* vols. 1-2 (Florence, 1965-1971).

Halleux and Schamp 1985. R. Halleux and J. Schamp, eds. and trans., *Les Lapidaires grecs*, Collection des Universités de France (Paris, 1985).

Halsall 1996. P. Halsall, trans., "Life of St. Thomaïs of Lesbos," *Holy Women of Byzantium. Ten Saints' Lives in English Translation*, ed. A.-M. Talbot (Washington, DC, 1996), 291-322.

Harl 1996. K. W. Harl, *Coinage in the Roman Economy, 300 B.C. to A.D. 700* (Baltimore, 1996).

Hauser 1992. S. Hauser, *Spätantike und frühbyzantinische Silberlöffel. Bemerkungen zur Produktion von Luxusgütern im 5. bis 7. Jahrhundert* (Münster, 1992).

Hauser and Upton 1934. W. Hauser and J. M. Upton, "The Persian Expedition, 1933-1934," *Bulletin of the Metropolitan Museum of Art* 29 (1934): 3-22.

Hayward and Cahn 1982. J. Hayward and W. Cahn, *Radiance and Reflection: Medieval Art from the Raymond Pitcairn Collection* (New York, 1982).

Hefford 1980. W. Hefford, *Victoria and Albert Museum, The Tapestry Collection: Medieval and Renaissance* (London, 1980).

Hendy 1985. M. Hendy, *Studies in the Byzantine Monetary Economy, c. 300-1450* (Cambridge, 1985).

Henig 1990. M. Henig, *The Content Family Collection of Ancient Cameos* (Oxford, 1990).

Henkel 1913. F. Henkel, *Die römischen Fingerringe der Rheinlande und der benachbarten Gebiete. Mit Unterstützung der Römisch-Germanischen Kommission des Kaiserl. Archäologischen Instituts*, vols. 1-2 (Berlin, 1913).

Herodotus. Herodotus, *The Histories*, ed. A. D. Godley, 4 vols. (Cambridge, MA, 1920).

Herrmann 2002. J. J. Herrmann, Jr., "A Bacchic Bucket of Rhenish Origin in the J. Paul Getty Museum," *From the Parts to the Whole. Vol. 2. Acta of the 13th International Bronze Congress, held at Cambridge, Massachusetts, May 28-June 1, 1996*, eds. C. C. Mattusch, A. Brauer, and S. E. Knudsen (Portsmouth, RI, 2002), 205-212.

Hiesinger 1994. U. W. Hiesinger, *Childe Hassam: American Impressionist* (Munich and New York, 1994).

Ikonomaki-Papadopoulos, Pitarakis, and Loverdou-Tsigarida 2001. Y. Ikonomaki-Papadopoulos, B. Pitarakis, and K. Loverdou-Tsigarida, *Enkolpia: The Holy and Great Monastery of Vatopaidi* (Mount Athos, 2001).

Janowitz 2001. N. Janowitz, *Magic in the Roman World: Pagans, Jews, and Christians* (London and New York, 2001).

Jenkins and Keene 1982. M. Jenkins and M. Keene, *Islamic Jewelry in the Metropolitan Museum of Art* (New York, 1982).

Jerusalem, Cradle of Christianity 2000. *Cradle of Christianity.* Exh. cat., eds. Y. Israeli and D. Mevorah, The Israel Museum (Jerusalem, 2000).

Johns and Potter 1983. C. Johns and T. Potter, *The Thetford Treasure: Roman Jewelry and Silver* (London, 1983).

Johnston 1999. W. R. Johnston, *William and Henry Walters: The Reticent Collectors* (Baltimore, MD, 1999).

Joseph, Fanning, and Davison 2000. M. De Lay Joseph, K. Fanning, and M. Davison, *Cultural Landscape Report: Dumbarton Oaks Park, Rock Creek Park, Part 1: Site History, Existing Conditions, and Analysis and Evaluation* (Washington, D.C., 2000).

Jouanno 2002. C. Jouanno, *Naissance et métamorphoses du Roman d'Alexandre: domaine grec* (Paris, 2002).

Julian. *The Works of the Emperor Julian*, Loeb Classical Library, 3 vols. (Cambridge, MA, 1949).

Kagan and Neverov 2001. J. Kagan and O. Neverov, *Splendeurs des collections de Catherine II de Russie. Le Cabinet de pierres gravées du Duc d'Orléans* (Paris, 2001).

Kalavrezou 1990. I. Kalavrezou, "Images of the Mother: When the Virgin Mary Became *Meter Theou*," *DOP* 44 (1990): 165-172.

Kammen 1991. M. Kammen, *Mystic Chords of Memory: The Transformation of Tradition in American Culture* (New York, 1991).

Kantorowicz 1960. E. Kantorowicz, "On the Golden Marriage Belt and the Marriage Rings of the Dumbarton Oaks Collection," *DOP* 14 (1960): 3-16.

Kaufman 1999. J. E. Kaufman, "Bill Wixom, Grand Acquisitor of Medieval Art" (Interview), *The Art Newspaper* (April 1999): 10-11.

Kaufmann-Heinimann 1999. A. Kaufmann-Heinimann, "Eighteen New Pieces from the Late Roman Silver Treasure of Kaiseraugst: First Notice," *JRA* 12 (1999): 333-341.

Kent and Painter 1977. J. P. C. Kent and K. S. Painter, *The Wealth of the Roman World: Gold and Silver AD 300-700* (London, 1977).

Khanenko Collection. *Drevnosti Pridneproviia. Kamennyi i bronzovui veka. Sobranie B. N. i V. I. Khanenko. Antiquités de la région du Dniepre. Ages de la pierre et du bronze*. Collection B. Khanenko, 5 vols. (Kiev, 1899).

Kidson 1967. P. Kidson, *The Medieval World* (New York and Toronto, 1967).

Kiilerich and Torp 1990. B. Kiilerich and H. Torp, "A Christ and the Apostles Relief in Search of a Date," *Arte medievale* 1 (1990): 99-113.

Kiourtzian 2000. G. Kiourtzian. *Recueil des inscriptions grecques chrétiennes des Cyclades de la fin du IIIe au VIIe siècle après J.-C.*, Travaux et Mémoires du Centre de Recherche d'Histoire et Civilisation de Byzance, Collège de France, Monographies 12 (Paris, 2000).

Kirin 1989. A. Kirin, "The Ktitors' Inscription from 1492 in the Monastery of Kremikovtsi," *Paleobulgarica* (Sofia) 13 (1989): 87-99 (in Bulgarian).

Kisyov 1997. K. Kisyov, "Late Iron Grave Finds from the Archaeological Museum in Plovdiv," *Archaeologia Bulgarica* 2 (1997): 1-7.

Kitzinger 1956. E. Kitzinger, "The Coffin-Reliquary," *The Relics of Saint Cuthbert*, ed. C. F. Battiscombe (Oxford, 1956), 202-304.

Kitzinger 1960. E. Kitzinger, "A Marble Relief of the Theodosian Period," *DOP* 14 (1960): 19-42.

Kitzinger 1965. E. Kitzinger, "The Dumbarton Oaks Center for Byzantine Studies," *Sonderdruck aus Jahrbücher für Geschichte Osteuropas* 10/3 (1965): 485-491.

Kitzinger 1977. E. Kitzinger, *Byzantine Art in the Making: Main Lines of Stylistic Development in Mediterranean Art, 3rd-7th Century* (Cambridge, MA, 1977).

Kitzinger 1984. E. Kitzinger, *Byzantinische Kunst im Werden* (Cologne, 1984).

Knipp 1998. D. Knipp, *Christus Medicus in der frühchristlichen Sarkophagskulptur* (London, 1998).

Kollwitz 1941. J. Kollwitz, *Oströmische Plastik der theodosianischen Zeit* (Berlin, 1941).

Kornbluth 1994. G. Kornbluth, "'Early Byzantine Crystals: An Assessment," *Journal of the Walters Art Gallery* 53/54 (1994/95): 23-30.

Kornbluth 1997. G. Kornbluth, "Ein karolingischer Kameo am Dreikönigenschrein im Kölner Dom," *Kölner Domblatt* 62 (1997): 111-150.

Kornbluth 2001. G. Kornbluth, "The Heavenly Jerusalem and the Lords: A Sapphire Christ at the Court of Charlemagne and on the Shrine of the Magi," *CahArch* 49 (2001): 47-60.

Kotansky 1994. R. Kotansky, *Greek Magical Amulets: The Inscribed Gold, Silver, Copper, and Bronze "Lamellae,"* 1: *Published Texts of Known Provenance*, Papyrologica Coloniensia 22/1 (Opladen, 1994).

Kötzsche 1991. L. Kötzsche, "Das Heilige Grab in Jerusalem und seine Nachfolge," *Akten des XII. Internationalen Kongresses für christliche Archäologie, Bonn, 22-28 September 1991*, Part I (Vatican City, 1995), 272-290.

Kubiak 1970. W. B. Kubiak, "Crusaders' Pottery of Al-Mina' Found at Fustat," *Folia Orientalia* 12 (1970): 113-123.

Kühn 1965. C. G. Kühn, ed., *Claudii Galeni opera omnia*, 20 vols. (Leipzig 1821-1835; reprinted Hildesheim, 1965).

Kypraniou 1995. E. Kypraniou, ed., *Sylloge Demetriou Oikonomopoulou* (Athens, 1995).

Laiou 2002. A. E. Laiou, ed., *The Economic History of Byzantium: From the Seventh through the Fifteenth Century*, 3 vols. (Washington, D.C., 2002).

Lamb 1929. W. Lamb, *Greek and Roman Bronzes* (London, 1929).

Lane 1938. A. Lane, "Medieval Finds at Al-Mina' in North Syria," *Archaeologia* 87 (1938): 19-78.

Lange 1996. U. Lange, ed., *Ikonographisches Register für das Repertorium der christlich-antiken Sarkophage*, 1 (Rom und Ostia), (Dettelbach, 1996).

Leader-Newby 2004. R. E. Leader-Newby, *Silver and Society in Late Antiquity: Functions and Meanings of Silver Plate in the Fourth to Seventh Centuries* (Aldershot, Hants, and Burlington, VT, 2004).

Leclercq 1907. H. Leclercq, "Anges," *Dictionnaire d'archéologie chrétienne et de liturgie*, ed. F. Cabrol, vol. 1.2 (Paris, 1907), cols. 2080-2161.

Leclercq 1924. H. Leclercq, "Gemmes," *Dictionnaire d'archéologie chrétienne et de liturgie*, ed. F. Cabrol, vol. 6.1 (Paris, 1924), cols. 794-864.

Lemerle et al. 1977. P. Lemerle, A. Guillou, N. Svoronos, and D. Papachryssanthou, *Actes de Lavra II : De 1204 à 1328*, Archives de l'Athos 8 (Paris, 1977).

Leonard 1970. E. Leonard, *Henri Rousseau and Max Weber* (New York, 1970).

Lester 1987. A. Lester, "A Fatimid Hoard from Tiberias," *Jewellery and Goldsmithing in the Islamic World, International Symposium at the Israel Museum, Jerusalem*, ed. N. Brosh (Jerusalem, 1987).

Leveto 1977. P. Leveto, "A Byzantine Gold and Rock Crystal Pendant," *Indiana University Art Museum Bulletin* 1 (1977-1978): 44-57.

Lidov 2000. A. M. Lidov, *Christian Relics in the Moscow Kremlin* (Moscow, 2000).

London, Treasures of Byzantine Art 1994. *Byzantium: Treasures of Byzantine Art and Culture from British Collections*, ed. D. Buckton, The British Museum (London, 1994).

Lothrop et al. 1957. S. K. Lothrop, W. F. Foshag, and J. Mahler, *Pre-Columbian Art* (New York, 1957).

MacCoull 1988. L. S. B. MacCoull, *Dioscorus of Aphrodito: His Work and His World* (Berkeley, 1988).

Maguire 1996. H. Maguire, *The Icons of Their Bodies: Saints and Their Images in Byzantium* (Princeton, 1996).

Maguire 1997. H. Maguire, "Magic and Money in the Early Middle Ages," *Speculum* 71 (1997): 1037-1054.

Maguire 1999. H. Maguire, "The Profane Aesthetic in Byzantine Art and Literature," *DOP* 53 (1999): 189-205.

Majeska 1974. G. P. Majeska, "A Medallion of the Prophet Daniel in the Dumbarton Oaks Collection," *DOP* 28 (1974): 361-366.

Makarova 1975. T. I. Makarova, *Peregorodchatye emaili Drevnei Rusi* [Cloisonné Enamels of Medieval Russia] (Moscow, 1975).

Makarova 1986. T. Makarova, *Chernevoe delo Drevnei Rusi* [Niellos of Medieval Russia] (Moscow, 1986).

Mango 1980. C. Mango, *Byzantium: The Empire of New Rome* (London, 1980).

Mango 1984. C. Mango, "St. Michael and Attis," *Deltion tes Christianikes Archaiologikes Hetaireias*, ser. 4, 12 (1984): 39-62.

Mango 1986. C. Mango, *The Art of the Byzantine Empire 312-1453: Sources and Documents* (Toronto, 1986).

Mango 1994. C. Mango, "On the Cult of Saints Cosmas and Damian at Constantinople," *Thymiama ste mneme tes Laskarinas Bouras* (Athens, 1994), 189-192.

Mango 2001. C. Mango, "Taking a Negative View of the Picture," *The Times Literary Supplement*, June 15 (2001): 29.

Mango and Greatrex 1997. C. Mango and G. Greatrex, *The Chronicle of Theophanes Confessor: Byzantine and Near Eastern History*, AD 284-813 (Oxford and New York, 1997).

Mango and Mundell Mango 1993. C. Mango and M. Mundell Mango, "Cameos in Byzantium," *Cameos in Context: The Benjamin Zucker Lectures, 1990*, eds. M. Henig and M. Vickers (Oxford, 1993), 56-76.

Markus 1990. R. A. Markus, *The End of Ancient Christianity* (Cambridge, 1990).

Marquand 1914. A. Marquand, *Luca della Robbia* (Princeton and London, 1914); 2nd ed., New York, 1972.

Matantseva 1994. T. Matantseva, "Les amulettes byzantines contre le mauvais oeil du Cabinet des Médailles," *JbAC* 37 (1994): 110-121.

Mauroeidi 1999. M. S. Mauroeidi, *Glypta tou Byzantinou Mouseiou Athinon* (Athens, 1999).

McCormick 2001. M. McCormick, *Origins of the European Economy: Communications and Commerce* A.D. 300-900 (Cambridge, 2001).

McGuire 1980. D. K. McGuire, ed., *Beatrix Farrand's Plant Book for Dumbarton Oaks* (Washington, D.C., 1980).

Meyendorff 1990. J. Meyendorff, "Christian Marriage in Byzantium: The Canonical and Liturgical Tradition," *DOP* 44 (1990): 99-107.

Michel 2001. S. Michel, *Die Magischen Gemmen im Britischen Museum*, eds. P. and H. Zazoff (London, 2001).

Middleton 1981. J. H. Middleton, *The Engraved Gems of Classical Times with a Catalogue of the Gems in the Fitzwilliam Museum* (Cambridge, 1981).

Milan, Ori e argenti russi 1991. *Ori e argenti russi: Mille anni di storia dal Museo Storico Statale di Mosca*, Fiera di Milano, 11 guigno-28 luglio 1991 (Milan, 1991).

Miles 1960. G. C. Miles, "Byzantine Miliaresion and Arab Dirhem: Some Notes on Their Relationship," *American Numismatic Society, Museum Notes* 11 (1960): 189-218.

Milliken 1957. W. M. Milliken, "Early Christian Fork and Spoon," *Bulletin of the Cleveland Museum of Art* 44 (1957): 184-187.

Milliken 1958. W. M. Milliken, "Early Byzantine Silver," *Bulletin of the Cleveland Museum of Art* 45/3 (1958): 35-41.

Mitten 1975. D. G. Mitten, *Classical Bronzes; Museum of Art, Rhode Island School of Design* (Providence, 1975).

Mommsen 1958. T. Mommsen, ed., *C. Iulii Solini Collectanea rerum memorabilium* (Berlin, 1958).

Mondésert and Marrou 1965. C. Mondésert and H. I. Marrou, *Clément d'Alexandrie, Le Pédagogue*, 2 vols. (Paris, 1965).

Morey 1959. C. R. Morey, *The Gold-Glass Collection of the Vatican Library: With Additional Catalogues of Other Gold-Glass Collections* (Vatican City, 1959).

Morrisson and Cheynet 2002. C. Morrisson and J.-C. Cheynet, "Prices and Wages in the Byzantine World," **Laiou 2002**, 815-876.

Mullett and Scott 1981. *Byzantium and the Classical Tradition*, eds. M. Mullett and R. Scott (Birmingham, UK, 1981).

Mundell Mango 1986. M. Mundell Mango, *Silver from Early Byzantium: The Kaper Koraon and Related Treasures* (Baltimore, MD, 1986).

Mundell Mango et al. 1989. M. Mundell Mango, C. Mango, A. C. Evans, and M. Hughes, "A 6th-Century Mediterranean Bucket from Bromeswell Parish, Suffolk," *Antiquity* 63 (1989): 295-309.

Mundell Mango 1990. M. Mundell Mango, *The Sevso Treasure: A Collection from Late Antiquity* (London and New York, 1990).

Mundell Mango 1993. M. Mundell Mango, "The Purpose and Places of Byzantine Silver Stamping," **Boyd and Mundell Mango 1993,** 203-216.

Mundell Mango and Bennett 1994. M. Mundell Mango and A. Bennett, *The Sevso Treasure*. Part One (Ann Arbor, MI, 1994).

Munich, *Rom und Byzanz* 1998. *Archäologische Kostbarkeiten aus Bayern*. Exh. cat., eds. L. Wamser and G. Zahlhaas, Prähistorische Staatssammlung München, October 20, 1998-February 14, 1999 (Munich, 1998).

Muñoz 1911. A. Muñoz, *Pièces de choix de la collection du comte Grégoire Stroganoff à Rome*, pt. 2, *Moyen-Âge, Renaissance, Époque moderne* (Rome, 1911-1912).

Mystras, *The City of Mystras* 2001. *The City of Mystras*. Exh. cat., Mystras Museum (Athens, 2001).

Nees 1980. L. Nees, "Two Illuminated Syriac Manuscripts in the Harvard College Library," *CahArch* 29 (1980-1981): 123-142.

Nelson 2004. R. S. Nelson, *Hagia Sophia, 1850-1950: Holy Wisdom, Modern Monument* (Chicago, 2004).

Nenova-Merdjanova 1997. R. Nenova-Merdjanova, "Roman Precious Bronze Vessels from Moesia and Thracia," *Archaeologia Bulgarica* 1 (1997): 30-37.

Nenova-Merdjanova 2002. R. Nenova-Merdjanova, "Bronze Vessels and the Toilette in Roman Times," *From the Parts to the Whole*. Vol. 2. Acta of the 13th International Bronze Congress, held at Cambridge, Massachusetts, May 28-June 1, 1996, eds. C. C. Mattusch, A. Brauer, and S. E. Knudsen (Portsmouth, RI, 2002), 200-204.

New York, *Age of Spirituality* 1977. *Age of Spirituality. Late Antique and Early Christian Art, Third to Seventh Century*. Exh. cat., ed. K. Weitzmann, The Metropolitan Museum of Art, November 19, 1977-February 12, 1978 (New York and Princeton, 1978).

New York, *Byzantium Faith and Power* 2004. *Byzantium: Faith and Power (1261-1557)*. Exh. cat., ed. H. C. Evans, Metropolitan Museum of Art (New York, 2004).

New York, *The Glory of Byzantium* 1997. *The Glory of Byzantium: Art and Culture of the Middle Byzantine Era, A.D. 843-1261*. Exh. cat., eds. H. C. Evans and W. D. Wixom, The Metropolitan Museum of Art, March 9-July 6, 1997 (New York, 1997).

New York, *Tonalism* 1982. W. H. Gerdts et al., *Tonalism: An American Experience* (New York, 1982).

Nielsen 1998. I. Nielsen and H.S. Nielsen, eds. *Meals in a Social Context: Aspects of the Communal Meal in the Hellenistic and Roman Worlds* (Aarhus, 1998).

Nitowski 1979. E. L. Nitowski, *Reconstructing the Tomb of Christ from Archaeological and Literary Sources* (Ph.D. dissertation, University of Notre Dame, 1979).

Oikonomides 1985. N. Oikonomides, *Byzantine Lead Seals* (Washington, D.C., 1985).

Oikonomides 1986a. N. Oikonomides, *A Collection of Dated Byzantine Lead Seals* (Washington, D.C., 1986).

Oikonomides 1986b. N. Oikonomides, "Silk Trade and Production in Byzantium from the Sixth to the Ninth Century: The Seals of the Kommerkiarioi," *DOP* 40 (1986): 33-53.

Osborne 1912. D. Osborne, *Engraved Gems, Signets, Talismans and Ornamental Intaglios, Ancient and Modern* (New York, 1912).

Ostrogorsky 1932. G. Ostrogorsky, "Löhne und Preise in Byzanz," *BZ* 32 (1932): 293-333.

Paderborn, *Byzanz* 2001. *Byzanz. Das Licht aus dem Osten. Kult und Alltag im Byzantinischen Reich vom 4. bis 15. Jahrhundert*, ed. C. Stiegemann (Mainz, 2001).

Pannuti 1994. U. Pannuti, *Catalogo della collezione glittica. Museo Archeologico Nazionale di Napoli*, vol. 2 (Rome, 1994).

Panofsky 1953. E. Panofsky, *Early Netherlandish Painting, Its Origins and Character* (Cambridge, MA, 1953).

Papanikola-Bakirtzi 1999. D. Papanikola-Bakirtzi, *Byzantine Glazed Ceramics* (Athens, 1999).

Paris, *Arts Anciens de l'Amérique* 1928. *Les Arts Anciens de l'Amérique*. Exposition organisée au Musée des Arts Décoratifs. Palais du Louvre. Pavillon de Marsan, mai-juin 1928 (Paris, 1928).

Paris, *Byzance* 1992. *Byzance: L'art byzantin dans les collections publiques françaises*. Exh. cat., ed. J. Durand, Musée du Louvre (Paris, 1992).

Paris, *Exposition d'art byzantin* 1931. *Exposition internationale d'art byzantin, 28 mai-9 juillet, 1931*, Musée des Arts Décoratifs, Palais du Louvre, Pavillon de Marsan (Paris, 1931).

Paudrat 1984. J.-L. Paudrat, "From Africa," *"Primitivism" in 20th Century Art: Affinity of the Tribal and the Modern*, ed. W. Rubin, vol. 1 (New York, 1984), 125-175.

Pausanias. Pausanias, *Description of Greece*, eds. W. H. S. Jones and H. A. Ormerod, 4 vols. (Cambridge and London, 1918).

Pedrizet 1928. P. Pedrizet, "L'archange Ouriel," *Seminarium Kondakovianum* 2 (1928): 241-276.

Peirce and Tyler 1926. H. Peirce and R. Tyler, *Byzantine Art* (London, 1926).

Peirce and Tyler 1927. H. Peirce and R. Tyler, "Deux mouvements dans l'art byzantin du Xe siècle," *Arethuse* 16 (1927): 3-8.

Peirce and Tyler 1932. H. Peirce and R. Tyler, *L'art byzantin*, vols. 1-2 (Paris, 1932-1934).

Penna 2000. V. Penna, "The Mother of God on Coins and Lead Seals," **Vassilaki 2000,** 209-217.

Pillinger 2001. R. Pillinger, "Drei Amulettarmbänder mit Psalmzitaten," *Realia Coptica: Als Festgabe zum 60. Geburtstag von Hermann Harrauer*, ed. U. Horak (Vienna, 2001), 75-80.

Pitarakis forthcoming. B. Pitarakis. *Les croix-reliquaires pectorales byzantines en bronze*, Bibliothèque des Cahiers archéologiques (Paris, in press).

Pliny, *Natural History*. Pliny the Elder, *Natural History*, with an English translation by H. Rackham, Loeb Classical Library (Cambridge, MA, 1938-1963).

Poeschke 1990. J. Poeschke, *Die Skulptur der Renaissance in Italien*, Band 1, *Donatello und seine Zeit* (Munich, 1990). English edition: *Donatello and His World: Sculpture of the Italian Renaissance* (New York, 1993).

Pollini 2002. J. Pollini, *The Cobannus Hoard: Gallo-Roman Bronzes and the Process of Romanization* (Leiden, 2002).

Pope-Hennessy 1980. J. W. Pope-Hennessy, *Luca della Robbia* (Ithaca, NY, 1980).

Popovich 1983. L. Popovich, "An Examination of Chilandar Cameos," *Hilandarski Zbornik* 5 (1983): 7-45.

Princeton, *Byzantium* 1986. *Byzantium at Princeton: Byzantine Art and Archaeology at Princeton University*. Exh. cat., eds. S. Ćurčić and A. St. Clair, Firestone Library, Princeton University (Princeton, 1986).

Princeton University Archaeological Expeditions to Syria. *Syria: Publications of the Princeton University Archaeological Expeditions to Syria in 1904-1905 and 1909*, vols. 1-4; Division 1: H. C. Butler, F. A. Norris and E. R. Stoever, *Geography and Itinerary*; Division 2: H. C. Butler, *Architecture*; Division 3: E. Littman et al., *Greek and Latin Inscriptions*; Division 4: E. Littman, *Semitic Inscriptions* (Leiden, 1907-1949).

Pringle 1985. D. Pringle, "Medieval Pottery from Caesarea: The Crusader Period," *Levant* 17 (1985): 171-202.

Pringle 1986. D. Pringle, "Pottery as Evidence for Trade in the Crusader States," *I Comuni italiani nel regno crociato di Gerusalemme*, eds. G. Airaldi and B. Kedar (Genoa, 1986), 451-475.

Providence, *Survival of the Gods* 1987. *Survival of the Gods: Classical Mythology in Medieval Art*. Exh. cat., ed. S. Bonde, Brown University, February 28-March 29, 1987 (Providence, RI, 1987).

Qaddumi 1990. G. H. Qaddumi, *A Medieval Islamic Book of Gifts and Treasures: Translation, Annotation, and Commentary on the "Kitab al-Hadaya wa al-Tuhaf"* (Ph.D. dissertation, Harvard University, 1990).

Ravenna, *Scultura bizantina* 2000. *Scultura bizantina. Konstantinopel. Scultura bizantina dai Musei di Berlino*. Exh. cat., Museo Nazionale di Ravenna, Complesso Benedettino di S.Vitale, Ravenna, aprile 15-settembre 17, 2000 (Ravenna, 2000).

Redford 2004. S. Redford, "On *Saqis* and Ceramics: Systems of Representation in the Northeast Mediterranean," *France and the Holy Land: Frankish Culture at the End of the Crusades*, ed. D. Weiss (Baltimore, MD, 2004), 282-312.

Reed 1996. C. Reed, ed., *A Roger Fry Reader* (Chicago and London, 1996).

Reeksman 1958. L. Reeksman, "La 'dextrarum iunctio' dans l'iconographie romaine et paléochrétienne," *Bulletin de l'Institut Historique Belge de Rome* 31 (1958): 23-95.

Reimbold 1983. E. T. Reimbold, *Der Pfau: Mythologie und Symbolik* (Munich, 1983).

Ricci 1905. C. Ricci, *Ravenna* (Bergamo, 1905).

Richter 1915. G. M. A. Richter, *Greek, Etruscan and Roman Bronzes. The Metropolitan Museum of Art* (New York, 1915).

Richter 1956. G. M. A. Richter, *Catalogue of Greek and Roman Antiquities in the Dumbarton Oaks Collection* (Cambridge, MA, 1956).

Richter 1971. G. M. A. Richter, *Engraved Gems of the Romans* (London, 1971).

Rieder 2000a. W. Rieder, *A Charmed Couple: The Art and Life of Walter and Matilda Gay* (New York, 2000).

Rieder 2000b. W. Rieder, "Walter and Matilda Gay in Paris and the Country," *The Magazine Antiques* 157, no. 6 (December 2000): 857-863.

Riis and Poulsen 1957. P. J. Riis and V. Poulsen, *Hama: fouilles et recherches, 1931-1938, 4.2, Les verreries et poteries médiévales* (Copenhagen, 1957).

Ringbom 1958. L.-I. Ringbom, *Paradisus terrestis: Myt, Bild och Verklighet*, Acta Societatis Scientiarum Fenniacae, nova series (Helsingfors, 1958).

Ritzer 1970. K. Ritzer, *Le mariage dans les églises chrétiennes du Ier au XIe siècle* (Paris, 1970).

Rohland 1977. J. P. Rohland, *Der Erzengel Michael, Arzt und Feldherr, Beihefte der Zeitschrift für Religions- und Geistesgeschichte* 19 (Leiden, 1977).

Romanini 1988. A. M. Romanini, *L'arte medievale in Italia*, Storia dell'arte Sansoni (Florence, 1988).

Roques 1954. R. Roques, *L'Univers Dionysien* (Aubier, 1954).

Rosenthal and Sivan 1978. R. Rosenthal and R. Sivan, *Ancient Lamps in the Schloessinger Collection* (Jerusalem, 1978).

Ross 1942. M. C. Ross, "A Group of Coptic Incense Burners," *American Journal of Archaeology* 1 (1942): 10-12.

Ross 1954. M. C. Ross, "Two Byzantine Nielloed Rings," *Studies in Art and Literature for Belle da Costa Greene* (Princeton, 1954), 169-171.

Ross 1960. M. C. Ross, "Three Byzantine Cameos," *Greek, Roman, and Byzantine Studies* 3 (1960): 43-45.

Roth 1981. C. P. Roth, ed., *On the Holy Icons, St. Theodore Studies* (759-826) (Crestwood, NY, 1981).

Sage 1976. W. Sage, "Ein bemerkenswerter Fund aus dem Reihengräberfeld von Steinhöring, Lkr. Ebersberg (Oberbayern)," *Archäologisches Korrespondenzblatt* 6 (1976): 247-251.

Salles and Lion-Goldschmidt 1956. G. A. Salles and D. Lion-Goldschmidt, *Adolphe Stoclet Collection*, pt. 1 (Brussels, 1956).

Salter 1967. A. Salter, *Slave of the Lamp: A Public Servant's Notebook* (London, 1967).

Saunders 1982. W. B. R. Saunders, "The Aachen Reliquary of Eustathius Maleinus, 969-970," *DOP* 36 (1982): 211-219.

Schlumberger 1884. G. Schlumberger, *Sigillographie de l'Empire byzantin* (Paris, 1884).

Schmidt 1995. V. M. Schmidt, *A Legend and Its Image: The Aerial Flight of Alexander the Great in Medieval Art* (Groningen, 1995).

Schneider 1981. J. W. Schneider, *Michael und seine Verehrung im Abendland* (Goetheanum, 1981).

Scott 1995. B. Scott, "Dancing Sunbeam," *Country Life* (April 20, 1995): 82-85.

Seipel 1993. W. Seipel, ed., *Gold aus Kiew*. Exh. cat., Kunsthistorisches Museum (Vienna, 1993).

Sena Chiesa 1966. G. Sena Chiesa, *Gemme del Museo Nazionale di Aquileia* (Aquileia, 1966).

Settis Frugoni 1973. C. Settis Frugoni, *Historia Alexandri elevate per griphos ad aerem* (Rome, 1973).

Severin 1970. H.-G. Severin, "Oströmische Plastik unter Valens und Theodosius I," *Jahrbuch der Berliner Museen* 2 (1970): 211-251.

Shelton 1981. K. J. Shelton, *The Esquiline Treasure* (London, 1981).

Shepard 1995. J. Shepard, "The Rhos Guest of Louis the Pious: Whence and Wherefore?" *Early Medieval Europe* 4 (1995): 41-60.

Skedros 1999. J. C. Skedros, *St. Demetrios of Thessaloniki, Civic Patron and Divine Protector, 4th-7th Centuries* CE (Harrisburg, PA, 1999).

Sherlock 1988. D. Sherlock, "A Roman Combination Eating Implement," *Antiquaries Journal* 68 (1988): 310-311.

Small 2003. J. P. Small, *The Parallel Worlds of Classical Art and Text* (Cambridge, 2003).

Smith and Hutton 1908. C. H. Smith and C. A. Hutton, *Catalogue of the Antiquities (Greek, Etruscan and Roman) in the Collection of the Late Wyndham Francis Cook, Esqre., Catalogue of the Art Collection*, vol. 2 (London, 1908).

Snyder 1988. J. Snyder, *Medieval Art: Painting, Sculpture, Architecture, 4th-14th Century* (New York, 1988).

Sorlin 1991. I. Sorlin, "Striges et géloudes. Histoire d'une croyance et d'une tradition," *Travaux et Mémoires* 11 (1991): 411-436.

Sozomen. *The Ecclesiastical History of Sozomen*, trans. C. D. Hartlanft (New York, 1980); reprinted Grand Rapids, MI, 1952.

Spier 1987. J. Spier, "A Byzantine Pendant in the J. Paul Getty Museum," *The J. Paul Getty Museum Journal* 15 (1987): 5-14.

Spier 1993a. J. Spier, "Medieval Byzantine Magical Amulets and Their Tradition," *Journal of the Warburg and Courtauld Institutes* 56 (1993): 25-62.

Spier 1993b. J. Spier, "Late Antique Cameos c. A.D. 250-600," *Cameos in Context: The Benjamin Zucker Lectures,*

1990, ed. M. Henig and M. Vickers (Oxford, 1993), 43-54.

Spier 1997. J. Spier, "Early Christian Gems and Their Rediscovery," *Engraved Gems: Survivals and Revivals*, ed. C. M. Brown (Washington, D.C., 1997), 33-39.

Spier forthcoming. J. Spier, *Late Antique and Early Christian Gems* (Wiesbaden, in press).

Spieser 1972. J. M. Spieser. "Collection Paul Canellopoulos (II). Bagues romaines et médiévales," *Bulletin de correspondance hellénique* 96 (1972): 117-135.

Stathatos Collection 1957. *Collection Hélène Stathatos, les objets byzantins et post-byzantins* (Limoges, 1957).

Stathatos Collection 1963. *Collection Hélène Stathatos*, 3 vols. (Strasbourg, 1963).

Sterligova 1994. I. A. Sterligova, "Ierusalimy kak liturgicheskie sosudy v Drevnei Rusi," **Batalov and Lidov 1994**, 46-55.

Stocking 1985. G. Stocking. Jr., "Philanthropoids and Vanishing Cultures: Rockefeller Funding and the End of the Museum Era in Anglo-American Anthropology," *Objects and Others: Essays on Museums and Material Culture* (Madison, WI, 1985).

Stokstad 1988. M. Stokstad, *Medieval Art* (New York, 1988).

Strong 1966. D. E. Strong, *Greek and Roman Gold and Silver Plate* (London, 1966).

Sutton 1984. D. Sutton et al., "Dumbarton Oaks, Washington, D.C.," *Apollo* 119, no. 266 (April 1984): 1-44.

Swarzenski 1941. H. Swarzenski, "The Dumbarton Oaks Collection," *ArtB* 23 (1941): 77-79.

Talbot Rice 1966. D. Talbot Rice, "Late Byzantine Pottery at Dumbarton Oaks," *DOP* 20 (1966): 209-219; reprinted in D. Talbot Rice, *Byzantine Art and Its Influences: Collected Studies* (London, 1973), no. 13.

Tamma 1991. G. Tamma, *Le gemme del Museo Archeologico di Bari* (Bari, 1991).

Tamulevich 2001. S. Tamulevich, *Dumbarton Oaks: Garden into Art* (New York, 2001).

Tanghini 1998. C. Tanghini, *Qal'at Ja'Bar Pottery: A Study of a Syrian Fortified Site of the Late 11th-14th Centuries* (Oxford, 1998).

Testini 1964. P. Testini, "Un rilievo cristiano poco noto del Museo di Barletta," *Vetera Christianorum* 1 (1964): 129ff.

Thalmann 1978. W. G. Thalmann, *Dramatic Art in Aeschylus's 'Seven Against Thebes'* (New Haven and London, 1978).

Thessaloniki, *Everyday Life in Byzantium* 2002. *Everyday Life in Byzantium*. Exh. cat., ed. D. Papanikola-Bakirtzi, Thessaloniki, White Tower, October 2001-January 2002 (Athens, 2002).

Totev n.d. T. Totev, *The Preslav Treasure* (Shoumen, n.d.).

Trahoulia 1997. N. S. Trahoulia, *The Venice Alexander Romance, Hellenic Institute Codex Gr. 5: A Study of Alexander the Great as an Imperial Paradigm in Byzantine Art and Literature* (Ph.D. dissertation, Harvard University, 1997).

Trendall and Webster 1971. A. D. Trendall and T. B. L. Webster, *Illustrations of Greek Drama* (London, 1971).

Truettner and Stein 1999. W. H. Truettner and R. B. Stein, *Picturing Old New England: Image and Memory* (New Haven and London, 1999).

Underwood 1950. P. Underwood, "The Fountain of Life in Manuscripts of the Gospels," *DOP* 5 (1950): 41-138.

Urbana-Champaign, *Art and Holy Powers* 1989. E. Dauterman Maguire, H. Maguire, and M. J. Duncan-Flowers, *Art and Holy Powers in the Early Christian House* (Urbana-Champaign, 1989).

Vasiliev 1982. V. P. Vasiliev, "Matrizenmodelle in der byzantinischen Toreutik," *Metallkunst von der Spätantike bis zum ausgehenden Mittelalter*, ed. A. Effenberger (Berlin, 1982), 90-96.

Vassilaki 2000. M. Vassilaki, ed., *The Mother of God: Representations of the Virgin in Byzantine Art* (Milan, London, and New York, 2000).

Vickers 1986. M. Vickers, ed., *Pots and Pans: A Colloquium on Precious Metals and Ceramics in the Muslim, Chinese and Graeco-Roman Worlds, Oxford 1985* (Oxford, 1986).

Vickers et al. 1986. M. Vickers, O. Impey, and J. Allen, *From Silver to Ceramic: The Potter's Debt to Metalwork in the Graeco-Roman, Oriental and Islamic Worlds* (Oxford, 1986).

Vikan 1984. G. Vikan, "Art, Medicine, and Magic in Early Byzantium," *DOP* 38 (1984): 65-86; reprinted in *Sacred Images and Sacred Power in Byzantium*, Variorum Collected Studies Series, Aldershot, 2003, no. 9.

Vikan 1987. G. Vikan, "Early Christian and Byzantine Rings in the Zucker Family Collection," *Journal of the Walters Art Gallery* 45 (1987): 32-43; reprinted in *Sacred Images and Sacred Power in Byzantium*, Variorum Collected Studies Series, Aldershot, 2003, no. 13.

Vikan 1990. G. Vikan, "Art and Marriage in Early Byzantium," *DOP* 44 (1990): 145-163.

Vikan 1991. G. Vikan, "Two Byzantine Amuletic Armbands and the Group to Which They Belong," *Journal of the Walters Art Gallery* 49/50 (1991/1992): 33-44; reprinted in *Sacred Images and Sacred Power in Byzantium*, Variorum Collected Studies Series, Aldershot, 2003, no. 11.

Vikan 1995. G. Vikan, *Catalogue of the Sculpture in the Dumbarton Oaks Collection from the Ptolemaic Period to the Renaissance* (Washington, D.C., 1995).

Vikan and Nesbitt 1980. G. Vikan and J. Nesbitt, *Security in Byzantium: Locking, Sealing and Weighing*, Dumbarton Oaks Byzantine Collection, 2 (Washington, D.C., 1980).

Volbach 1930. W. F. Volbach, *Mittelalterliche Bildwerke aus Italien und Byzanz*, Staatliche Museen zu Berlin, Bildwerke des Kaiser Friedrich-Museums (Berlin, 1930).

Volbach 1962. W. F. Volbach, *Early Christian Art* (New York, 1962).

Volbach 1975. W. F. Volbach. "Geschnittene Gläser und Gemmen des frühen Mittelalters," *Beiträge zur Kunst des Mittelalters: Festschrift für Hans Wentzel zum 60. Geburtstag*, eds. R. Becksmann, U.-D. Korn, and J. Zahlten (Berlin, 1975), 199-204.

Volbach 1976. W. F. Volbach, *Elfenbeinarbeiten der Spätantike und des frühen Mittelalters* (Mainz, 1976).

Volbach, Duthuit, and Salles 1933. W. F. Volbach, G. Duthuit, and G. Salles, *Art byzantin; cent planches reproduisant un grand nombre de pièces choisies parmi les plus représentatives des diverses tendances* (Paris, 1933).

Waagé 1948. F. O. Waagé, *Antioch on-the-Orontes*, vol. 4.1, *Ceramics and Islamic Coins* (Princeton, 1948).

Walbaum 1983. J. Walbaum, *Metalwork from Sardis: The Finds through 1974* (Cambridge, 1983).

Walker 2001. A. Walker, "A Reconsideration of Early Byzantine Marriage Rings," *Between Magic and Religion*, eds. S. R. Asirvatham, C. O. Pache, and J. Watrous (Lanham, MD, 2001), 149-164.

Walker 2002. A. Walker, "Myth and Magic in Early Byzantine Marriage Jewelry: The Persistence of Pre-Christian Traditions," *The Material Culture of Sex Procreation and Marriage in Pre-modern Europe*, eds. A. L. McClanan and K. Rosoff Encarnación (New York, 2002), 59-78.

Walker 2003. A. Walker, "Adornment," **Cambridge, MA, Byzantine Women 2003**, 233-239.

Walter 1968. C. Walter, "Two Notes on the Deesis," *REB* 26 (1968): 311-336.

Walter 1979. C. Walter, "Marriage Crowns in Byzantine Iconography," *Zograf* 10 (1979): 83-91.

Walter 1989. C. Walter, "The Intaglio of Solomon in the Benaki Museum and the Origins of the Iconography of the Warrior Saints," *Deltion tes Christianikes Archaiologikes Hetaireias* 15 (1989-1990): 33-42; reprinted in *Pictures as Language, How the Byzantines Exploited Them*, 23, London, 2000, 397-414.

Walter 1997. C. Walter, "IC XC NI KA. The Apotropaic Function of the Victorious Cross," *REB* 55 (1997): 193-220.

Walters 1914. H. B. Walters, *Catalogue of the Greek and Roman Lamps in the British Museum* (London, 1914).

Walters 1921. H. B. Walters, *Catalogue of the Silver Plate (Greek, Etruscan and Roman) in the British Museum* (London, 1921).

Waltz 1928. P. Waltz, ed. and trans., *Anthologie Grecque 1: Anthologie Palatine 1* (Paris, 1928).

Wamser and Zahlhauss 1998. L. Wamser and G. Zahlhauss, eds. *Rom und Byzanz. Archäologische Kostbarkeiten aus Bayern* (Munich, 1998).

Wamser 2004. L. Wamser, ed., *Die Welt von Byzanz— Europas östliches Erbe. Glanz, Krisen und Fortleben einer tausendjährigen Kultur* (Munich, 2004).

Washington, D.C., *Impressionists in Winter 1998*. C. S. Moffett, E. E. Rathbone, K. Rothkopf, and J. Isaacson, *Impressionists in Winter. Effets de Neige*. Exh. cat., Phillips Collection, September 19, 1998-January 3, 1999 (Washington, D.C., 1998).

Washington, D.C., *Iranian Art 1964*. *7000 Years of Iranian Art*. Exh. cat., Smithsonian Institution, 1964-1965 (Washington, D.C., 1964).

Watson 1941. F. Watson, "The Benefits of Great Art," *Magazine of Art* 3 (1941): 113-114.

Weigand 1929. E. Weigand, "Der Monogrammnimbus auf der Tür von S. Sabina in Rom," *BZ* 30 (1929/30): 587-595.

Weigand 1932. E. Weigand, "Zum Denkmälerkreis des Christogrammnimbus," *BZ* 32 (1932): 63-81.

Weinberg 1994. H. B. Weinberg, et al., *American Impressionism and Realism: The Painting of Modern Life, 1885-1915* (New York, 1994).

Weiss 2003. P. Weiss, "The Vision of Constantine," *JRA* 16 (2003): 237-259.

Weitzmann 1930. K. Weitzmann, *Die byzantinischen Elfenbeinskulpturen des X.–XIII. Jahrhunderts* (Berlin, 1930); reprinted Berlin, 1979.

Weitzmann 1963. K. Weitzmann, *Geistige Grundlagen und Wesen der makedonischen Renaissance, Arbeitsgemeinschaft für Forschungen des Landes Nordrhein-Westfalen, Geisteswissenschaften* 107 (Cologne and Opladen, 1963); Eng. trans., "The Character and Intellectual Origins of the Macedonian Renaissance," in K. Weitzmann, *Studies in Classical and Byzantine Manuscript Illumination*, ed. H. Kessler (Chicago, 1971).

Weitzmann 1994. K. Weitzmann, *Sailing with Byzantium from Europe to America: The Memoirs of an Art Historian* (Munich, 1994).

Wentzel 1941. H. Wentzel, "Mittelalterliche Gemmen: Versuch einer Grundlegung," *Zeitschrift des deutschen Vereins für Kunstwissenschaft* 8 (1941): 45-98.

Wentzel 1957. H. Wentzel, "Die Mittelalterlichen Gemmen in der staatlichen Münzsammlung zu München," *Münchner Jahrbuch der bildenden Kunst* 8 (1957): 37-56.

Wentzel 1959. H. Wentzel, "Datierte und datierbare byzantinische Kameen," *Festschrift Friedrich Winkler*, ed. H. Möhle (Berlin, 1959), 9-12.

Wentzel 1960. H. Wentzel, "Die byzantinischen Kameen in Kassel. Zur Problematik der Datierung byzantinischer Gemmen," *Mouseion. Studien aus Kunst und Geschichte für Otto H. Förster*, eds. H. Ledendorf and H. Vey (Cologne, 1960), 88-96.

Wentzel 1968. H. Wentzel, "Die Kamee der Kaiserin Anna. Zur Datierung byzantinisierender Intaglien," *Festschrift Ulrich Middledorf*, eds. A. Kosegarten and P. Tigler (Berlin, 1968), 1-11.

Wentzel 1970. H. Wentzel, "Der Bergkristall mit der Geschichte der Susanna," *Pantheon* 28 (1970): 365-372.

Wentzel 1976. H. Wentzel, "Kameen," *Reallexikon zur byzantinischen Kunst*, vol. 3 (Stuttgart, 1976), cols. 903-927.

Whitby 1986. M. Whitby and M. Whitby, eds., *The "History" of Theophylact of Simocatta* (Oxford, 1986).

Whitby 1989. M. Whitby and M. Whitby, eds. *Chronicon Paschale 284-628 A.D.* (Liverpool, 1989).

Whitcomb 1985. D. S. Whitcomb, *Before the Roses and Nightingales: Excavations at Qasr-i Abu Nasr, Old Shiraz* (New York, 1985).

Whitehill 1967. W. M. Whitehill, *Dumbarton Oaks: The History of a Georgetown House and Garden, 1800-1966* (Cambridge, MA, 1967).

Whitehill, n.d. W. M. Whitehill, introduction to the unpublished edition of the Royall Tyler letters, HUA.

Wiegandt 1998. H. Wiegandt, *Charms of the Past* (Marburg, 1998).

Wilkinson 1972. J. Wilkinson, "The Tomb of Christ: An Outline of Its Structural History," *Levant* 4 (1972): 83-97.

Wilkinson 1977. J. Wilkinson, *Jerusalem Pilgrims Before the Crusades* (Warminster, 1977).

Willers 1901. H. Willers, *Die römischen Bronzeeimer von Hemmoor. Nebst einem Anhange über die römischen Silberbarren aus Dierstorf* (Hannover and Leipzig, 1901).

Willers 1907. H. Willers, *Neue Untersuchungen über die römische Bronzeindustrie von Capua und von Niederergermanien* (Hannover and Leipzig, 1907).

Williamson 1983. P. Williamson, "Daniel Between the Lions: A New Sardonyx Cameo for the British Museum," *Jewellery Studies* 1 (1983-1984): 37-39.

Woolley 1937. L. Woolley, "Excavations near Antioch in 1936," *Antiquaries Journal* 17 (1937): 1-15.

Woolley 1938. L. Woolley, "Excavations at Al Mina, Sueidia, I-II," *Journal of Hellenic Studies* 58 (1938): 1-30.

Worcester, *Antioch* 2000. *Antioch: Lost Ancient City*. Exh. cat., ed. C. Kondoleon, Worcester Art Museum, Cleveland Museum of Art, and Baltimore Museum of Art (Princeton, 2000).

Wright 2002. D. H. Wright, "Wilhelm Koehler and the Original Plan for Research at Dumbarton Oaks," J. W. Barker, ed., *Pioneers of Byzantine Studies in America, BF* 26 (2002): 150-151.

Xanthopoulou 1997. M. Xanthopoulou, *Les luminaires en bronze et fer aux époques paléochrétienne et byzantine. Typologie, technologie, utilisation* (Ph.D. dissertation, Université de la Sorbonne, Paris, 1997).

Zacos 1960. G. Zacos and A. Veglery, "Marriage Solidi of the Fifth Century," *Numismatic Circular* 68/4 (1960): 73-74.

Zacos 1972. G. Zacos and A. Veglery, *Byzantine Lead Seals*, 2 vols. (Basel, 1972-1985).

Zazoff 1968. P. Zazoff, *Etruskische Skarabäen* (Mainz am Rhein, 1968).

Zazoff 1975. P. Zazoff, ed., *Antike Gemmen in Deutschen Sammlungen*, vol. 4, *Hannover, Kestner-Museum; Hamburg, Museum für Kunst und Gewerbe* (Wiesbaden, 1975).

Zovatto 1968. P. L. Zovatto, *Il Mausoleo di Galla Placidia* (Ravenna, 1968).

Zwierlein-Diehl 1972. E. Zwierlein-Diehl, *Die antiken Gemmen des Kunsthistorischen Museums in Wien*, 3 vols. (Munich, 1972-1991).

Zwierlein-Diehl 1997. E. Zwierlein-Diehl, "'Interpretatio christiana': Gems on the Shrine of the Three Kings in Cologne," *Engraved Gems: Survivals and Revivals*, ed. C. M. Brown (Washington, D.C., 1997), 63-75.

Zwirn 2003. S. R. Zwirn, "A Silhouette Enamel at Dumbarton Oaks," *Deltion tes Christianikes Archaiologikes Hetaireias* 24 (2003): 393-401.

Glossary

COMPILED BY: *Bojana Bjeličić-Miletkov, Micheal A. Karczewski, Maria Lundin, Michael J. Melen, and Jessica Cole Rubinski*

aedicule (Lat., "small building"), **Aedicule Christi:** the polygonal structure on top of Christ's tomb, the exterior of which featured columns, a pediment, and a pyramidal roof. The original *aedicule* on the site of the Holy Sepulcher was built by Emperor Constantine the Great (305-337).

Alpha and Omega: the first and last letters of the Greek alphabet; cf. Revelations 8:1, "I am *Alpha* and *Omega*, the beginning and the end, said the Lord."

ampulla (Lat.): A vessel of lead, clay, or other material used to transport oil, water, earth, etc.

amulet: a small artifact, such as a pendant, ring, or token, worn on the body to protect one from evil forces.

apotropaic (from Gr., "to turn away, to avert"): intended to ward off evil or ill luck.

baldachin: see **ciborium.**

baluster: a short pillar or post of circular section, slender above and swelling below, that supports a rail or coping, thus forming part of a balustrade.

bezel: the face of a finger ring attached to the hoop.

bloodstone: a semiprecious mineral consisting of green chalcedony sprinkled with red spots resembling blood.

cameo: a precious or semiprecious stone decorated with raised carving, usually with two or more layers of different colors.

chancel screen: also called an altar screen, rood screen, or templon. This screen separates the nave from the sanctuary of a church.

Chi-Rho: the first two letters of Christ's name in Greek (XP).

chlamys (Gr., "mantle"): a short cloak fastened at the right shoulder by a **fibula** so as to leave the right arm free. By the sixth century it became a standard garment worn by the Byzantine court.

Chrismon (also Christogram): Christ's monogram; see also **Chi-Rho.**

ciborium (Lat., "canopy"): an awning with a domed or pyramidal roof resting on columns, or a container for the Eucharist bread.

cloisonné (Fr., "partitioned"): decorative work of enamel sections in various colors separated by strips of flattened wire.

cross potent (from Lat., "power"): having a straight bar across the end of each extremity of a cross.

cuirass (Lat.): a piece of armor consisting of breastplate and backplate fastened together.

dais: a raised platform.

Deesis (Gr., "entreaty"): a representation of Christ flanked by the figures of the Virgin and John the Baptist with their hands extended in the gesture of supplication.

dextrarum iunctio (Lat., "joining of the right hands"): the joining of the bride and groom's right hands, which takes place during the climactic segment of the Byzantine marriage ceremony.

diadem: an ornamental jeweled headdress or crown worn to signify sovereignty.

dihrem (Arabic; also formerly in Italian: **diremo**): an Arabian measure of weight, originally two-thirds of an Attic (Greek) drachma

(44.4 grains troy), used with varying weight from Morocco to Abyssinia, Turkey, and Persia; in Egypt (1895) = 47.661 troy grains. Various spellings include: **dirhem, di'rhem, dirham,** and **derham.**

Dormition of the Virgin (also Gr., **Koimeisis,** "falling asleep"): the ecclesiastical feast commemorating the death of the Virgin, celebrated on August 15.

enceinte (Fr.): an enclosure, chiefly in fortification.

exergue (Fr.): a small space—usually on the reverse of a coin or medal and below the principal device—for any minor inscription such as the date, engraver's initials, etc.; also, the inscription there inserted.

fibula: a pin made of bronze, gilt bronze, silver, or gold used to fasten a **chlamys.**

filigree: delicate and intricate ornamentation, usually in gold, silver, or other precious metal wire.

finial: a terminal ornament surmounting an object or a structure.

follis (Lat., original meaning "purse"): a word used to describe bags of coins made from any metal of determined value. This remained the principal meaning until the end of the fourth century CE. The bishop-metrologist Epiphanios of Salamis defined follis as a bag of 125 silver pieces. With the reintroduction of heavy copper denominations at the end of the fifth century, the term follis came to describe the heaviest of these coins. This new meaning lasted until the end of the eleventh century, the notional value of a follis being $\frac{1}{24}$ of a miliaresion, and $\frac{1}{288}$ of a solidus, though it is unlikely that these ratios were sustained during the seventh to eighth centuries, when the weight of a follis fell from approximately 16 grams to approximately 4 grams; see also **hyperpyron** and **dihrem.**

globus cruciger: globe surmounted by a cross; also used as an imperial symbol of power from the time of Emperor Theodosios II (402-450) onward.

Greek cross: a cross with arms of equal length.

griffin: a mythological creature with the head and wings of an eagle and the body of a lion.

guilloche (Fr.): also called **interlace,** a regular pattern formed of two or more interwoven or plaited bands, usually as a filler or border ornament. Most Byzantine examples of guilloches or interlace, especially manuscripts, seemed to have been composed freehand, as opposed to Latin examples that used a compass and ruler. They also differ from the arabesque, an overall decorative pattern based on stylized leaf and scrollwork developed by the Arabs that appears in Byzantine art by the tenth century.

Hagiosoritissa (Gr.): "The Virgin of the Holy Soros" reflects an original image gracing a holy soros, i.e., a reliquary chest; depicted in a three-quarter view, the Virgin raises her hands in a gesture of prayer or intercession as in the **Deesis.**

hematite: a red, reddish-brown, or black mineral consisting of sesquioxide of iron.

himation (Gr., "outer garment"): a long mantle common in antiquity and in medieval representations of Christ, the apostles, and the prophets; made of wool or linen, it was worn over a tunic and draped over the left shoulder and body so as to leave the right shoulder free.

Hodegetria (Gr.): image of the Virgin holding the Christ Child on her left arm derived from an icon at the Hodegon monastery in Constantinople.

hyperpyron (Gr., "highly refined"): the gold coin of standard weight (4.55 grams), but only 20.5 carats fine, introduced by Alexios I in 1092 and continued by his successors. The term continued in use until the end of the Byzantine Empire; see also **dirhem, follis, miliaresion,** and **solidus.**

Iconoclasm (Gr., "breaking of images"): a religious movement of the eighth and ninth centuries in Byzantium that denied the holiness of icons and rejected icon veneration.

iconoclast (Gr., "image-destroyer"): a supporter of Iconoclasm.

iconophile or iconodule (Gr., "image lover" or "image servant"): a defender of icons and icon veneration.

indiktion, also **indiction** (Lat.): initially an extraordinary tax on produce imposed by the emperor to meet specific needs. It was regularized on a yearly basis by Diocletian (five-year cycle) and finally under Constantine I became a fifteen-year cycle (starting in September 312) during which the amount of the indiction was to remain unchanged. In spite of this, extra indictions were imposed; because the fiscal and calendar years coincided (September 1 through August 31 of the following year), the word indiction acquired its chronological meaning after losing the fiscal meaning: it indicated one year within the fifteen-year cycle.

intaglio: a negative relief incised on a precious or semiprecious stone; cf. **cameo.**

interlace: see **guilloche.**

investiture: the ceremonial conferral of symbols of office or honor.

kantharos: an ancient Greek drinking vessel with two handles and a wide, footed bowl.

loros, plural **loroi** (Gr., "a strip of leather"): a long scarf, especially the heavy stole about five meters long and studded with precious stones worn by both emperor and empress on festive occasions. A vestige of the Roman toga of consuls, the *loros* was arranged in an X over the upper body. One section then fell straight down the front, while the other came from behind the right shoulder to cross the chest and drape over the left arm (as on the coins of Justinian II). In the tenth to eleventh centuries the garment had a hole for the head to go through. The *loros* symbolized the cross as a sign of Christ's victory; archangels attending Christ are often shown wearing *loroi.*

miliaresion (Lat.): a name applied in the fourth century CE to silver coins struck 72 to a pound; Byzantine sources of the seventh to eleventh centuries use it for the basic Byzantine silver coin reckoned 12 to the solidus; see also **dirhem, follis,** and **hyperpyron.**

Nereids: in Greek mythology, female spirits of the sea that are the daughters of the sea god Nereus.

niello (Lat., *nigellus*, "blackish"): black metal alloy filled into incisions in metal for decorative purposes; the black color contrasts effectively with gold, bronze, or silver to create salient effects and inscriptions.

nimbus (Lat., "cloud"): a halo; in art, a nimbus is rendered as a colored disk encircling the head of a prominent or saintly figure indicating the presence of light and grace.

nomisma, pl. **nomismata** (Gr., "coin"): the standard gold coin created by Constantine the Great, which weighed 4.55 grams and formed the basis of the Byzantine monetary system.

numismatics: the study of coins and coin-like objects such as coin weights.

orans or orant (Lat., "praying"): the name given to the Early Christian posture of prayer, the body upright and frontal, and the open hands lifted to shoulder height on either side.

Palaiologos dynasty and **Palaiologan** period in Byzantine history: the dynasty founded by Michael VIII, who ruled as emperor from 1259 to 1282. This dynastic name also refers to the final period of Byzantine art that began with the recapturing of Constantinople by the Byzantines in 1261 and continued until the fall of the empire in 1453.

paludamentum: military cloak fastened over one shoulder with a **fibula**, worn by Roman generals.

pendilia: hanging ornaments, sets of pearls and gems suspended from a crown.

phylacteria (from Gr., "to guard"): amulet, lucky jewelry, or object thought to provide protection against evil, injury, disease, or bad luck.

proskynesis (Gr., "prostration"): a gesture of supplication or reverence, the physical act of full prostration.

repoussé (Fr.): relief decoration on metal achieved by hammering and punching mainly from behind so the decoration projects. It was one of the first metalworking techniques to be developed and is found in many early civilizations.

sgraffito (It.): scratched decoration on pottery, first used in China, which spread to Europe via Persia. To complete this technique, a vessel is dipped in slip and given a preliminary firing. Designs are then scratched through the slip to reveal the darker body underneath. An overlaying glaze is applied to the bowl and is fired one final time.

situla (Lat.): bucket.

slip: clay mixed with water to form a smooth, creamy liquid. It was used to decorate earthenware by trailing lines or dots in a contrasting color, usually cream on brown, or by combing and feathering.

solidus (Lat.): a gold coin, the Latin equivalent of **nomisma**; also used to refer to the standard gold coin of the Byzantine Empire.

Theotokos (Gr.): "God-bearer," the Mother of God.

triclinium (Gr., "a dining room with three couches"): in antiquity, dining rooms with couches on which to recline during meals.

Triton: proper name of a Greek mythological sea demigod who is the son of Neptune as well as his trumpeter. He is usually depicted as having the upper body of a human and a lower body like that of a fish.

tropaion: a trophy or memorial of victory.

Photography Credits

List of Illustrations

MAP OF MEDITERRANEAN REGION

*Map by Tibor G. Toth,
after DOH 1967.*

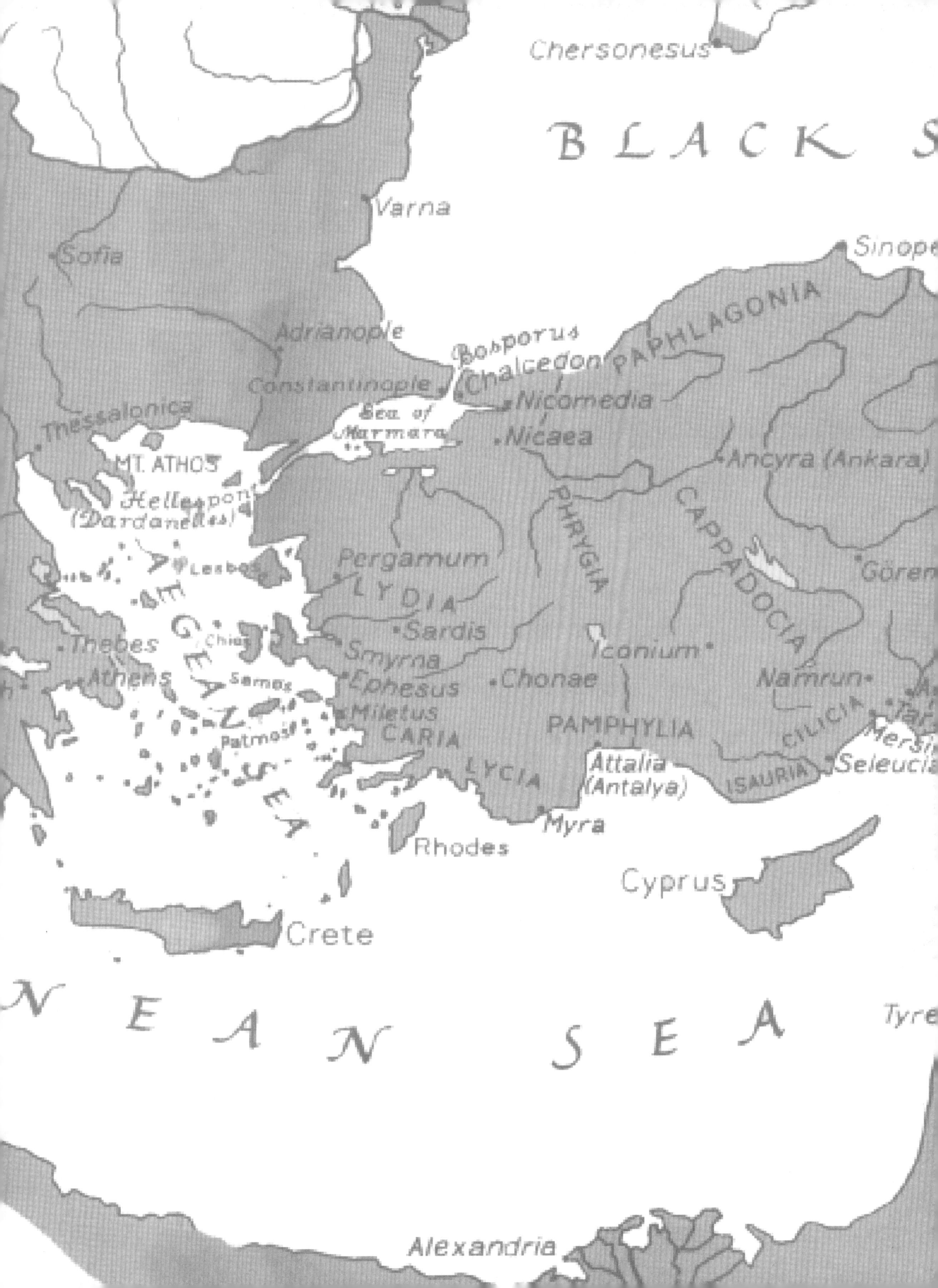

Chersonesus
BLACK S
Varna
Sofia
Sinope
PAPHLAGONIA
Adrianople
Bosporus
Chalcedon
Constantinople
Nicomedia
Thessalonica
Sea of
Marmara
Nicaea
Ancyra (Ankara)
MT. ATHOS
PHRYGIA
CAPPADOCIA
Hellespont
(Dardanelles)
Pergamum
Gören
Lesbos
LYDIA
Thebes
Chios
Sardis
Iconium
Athens
Smyrna
Chonae
Namrun
Samos
Ephesus
Miletus
Patmos
CARIA
PAMPHYLIA
CILICIA
Mersi
LYCIA
Attalia
(Antalya)
ISAURIA
Seleucia
AEGEAN SEA
Myra
Rhodes
Cyprus
Crete
NEAN
SEA
Tyre
Alexandria

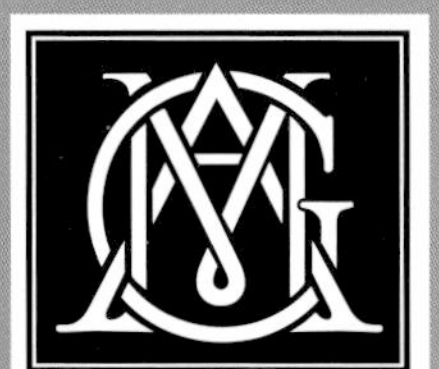